Living Hinduisms

An Explorer's Guide

NANCY AUER FALK

Western Michigan University

THOMSON

™

WADSWORTH

Australia • Canada • Mexico • Singapore • Spain
United Kingdom • United States

Publisher: Holly J. Allen
Acquisitions Editor: Steve Wainwright
Assistant Editor: Lee McCracken and Barbara Hillaker
Editorial Assistant: John Gahbauer
Technology Project Manager: Julie Aguilar
Marketing Manager: Worth Hawes
Marketing Assistant: Andrew Keay
Advertising Project Manager: Bryan Vann
Project Manager, Editorial Production:
    Megan E. Hansen
Art Director: Maria Epes

Print/Media Buyer: Lisa Claudeanos
Permissions Editor: Chelsea Junget
Production Service: Aaron Downey,
    Matrix Productions, Inc.
Copy Editor: Ann Whetstone
Cover Designer: Yvo Riezebos
Cover Image: Lindsay Hebberd/CORBIS
Compositor: International Typesetting
    and Composition
Printer: Webcom Limited

Printed in Canada
1 2 3 4 5 6 7 09 08 07 06 05

Library of Congress Control Number: 2004115707

ISBN 0-534-52011-1

Thomson Higher Education
10 Davis Drive
Belmont, CA 94002-3098
USA

Asia (including India)
Thomson Learning
5 Shenton Way
#01-01 UIC Building
Singapore 068808

Australia/New Zealand
Thomson Learning Australia
102 Dodds Street
Southbank, Victoria 3006
Australia

Canada
Thomson Nelson
1120 Birchmount Road
Toronto, Ontario M1K 5G4
Canada

UK/Europe/Middle East/Africa
Thomson Learning
High Holborn House
50–51 Bedford Road
London WC1R 4LR
United Kingdom

Latin America
Thomson Learning
Seneca, 53
Colonia Polanco
11560 Mexico
D.F. Mexico

Spain (including Portugal)
Thomson Paraninfo
Calle Magallanes, 25
28015 Madrid, Spain

Dedication

To the many friends in India and of Indian descent who have helped to make this volume a reality.

Contents

II Hinduisms in Space: Home, Temple, and the Pilgrim Road **113**

Preface

Globalization, the increasingly free flow of goods, information, and services across international borders, is now a popular subject for study among intellectuals. One aspect of globalization sometimes overlooked is the accompanying increase in border crossing by people. Americans find themselves on jets heading for job assignments in Beijing, Bangalore, or Dubai. My own suburban neighborhood includes residents from India, Korea, Japan, the Philippines, Iran, Egypt, and several locales in Latin America. In such a world of dissolving boundaries and people of different cultures living side by side, it becomes increasingly urgent that humans seek better understanding of values and viewpoints beyond those of the regions and social groups into which they were born.

For thirty-eight years, I have studied and taught in a discipline that works to promote such understanding by means of the cross-cultural study of religion. Some of its most influential textbooks have been published in Thomson\Wadsworth's Religious Life in History series. I am deeply pleased and flattered to see my own work now listed beside them. At the same time, I have come to wonder if their largely historical approach to religious studies is the most effective way for us religionists to achieve our stated aim. Our students, after all, live in the present, and it is other present-day humans whose values and practice they seek to understand. Might there be some way of introducing the study of religious traditions that accounts more fully for the here and now, without losing access to the historical dimension that remains important to our work?

The following volume is an experiment in shaping such an introduction. Approaching the cluster of traditions known today as Hinduism, it works through a combination of typology and history, introducing teachers, practices, and movements that are encountered today and then exploring the premises, aims, and histories that lie behind them. It offers tools in the forms of categories and examples that will help readers recognize sights and activities they see if they travel or live among Hindus or visit Hindu groups or foundations in their own countries. Among the topics it takes up are domestic and temple practice, pilgrimage, low-caste protest movements, and several kinds of movements working for reform and revival of traditional Hinduism. Extensive attention is paid to the roles of women in such practice and movements. The volume ends with an analysis of the special problems faced by and the institutions created by Hindus living outside of India, the Hindu homeland and holy land. It shows a varied and rich heritage, one that, contrary to stereotypes, is changing swiftly and creatively even as it reaffirms continuity with its often quite ancient past.

Optimal benefit will be gained from this book if the reader works through it from beginning to end. Nonetheless, chapters are also designed to be sufficiently self-contained that instructors can excerpt and use them independently of one another. To aid readers, the volume includes a glossary of central and frequently used Hindu terms. It also features an index of cited names, texts, and movements. Each chapter is followed by an annotated bibliography for use by readers who would like to pursue its subjects further.

Acknowledgments

Dozens of unseen contributors have helped make this volume a reality. They have taught me, encouraged me, sent me leads, or read chapters and early versions as the manuscript evolved through many drafts. I shall undoubtedly miss some in this too-short list of those owed my thanks. To those unnamed people, I also express my very deep gratitude.

I must thank first of all many friends in India. My wonderful Defence Colony neighbors invited me into their homes, answered unending questions, and took me along to many events and places important to them. Extra special thanks goes to Umi Singh, who not only hosted me, but also traveled through much of India with me as my companion and research assistant. Similarly generous have been the family and disciples of the late Yogi Raushan Nath, especially the generous Manorama Nath and Drs. Usha and Jagdish Shourie. Dr. Balbir Singh and Lili Bhardwaj introduced me to many aspects of Hindu religious life that I would never have encountered otherwise. Janet Chawla helped me make many of the connections so indispensable to any kind of inquiry in India. I am also deeply grateful to University of Delhi professors K. M. Shrimali and J. P. S. Uberoi, who served as my faculty sponsors during my 1984–85 and 1991–92 visits, respectively.

Farther afield in India, I am grateful to the Women's Studies Centre at S.N.D.T. Women's University for housing and helping me during a crucial stage of my work, especially its then-director Meera Kosambi, who has sent me much of her own research on woman reformers of Maharashtra. Swami Bodhananda's friends and disciples of New Delhi, Mumbai, Bangalore, and Trivandrum have been overwhelmingly generous with time and hospitality; I thank especially the gracious Radhika of Bangalore, the Nayyars of Trivandrum, and Sangita Menon of both locations. Thanks are due also to my husband's generous friends from the Philosophy Department of Kolkata's Jadavpur University.

Five religious leaders have been of special aid at various stages of my inquiry. Yogi Raushan Nath was a friend and mentor from the time of his first Kalamazoo visit until his much regretted death in 1990. Pravrajika Atmaprana of Sharada Math and Mission and Sister Shanti of the Brahma Kumaris were generous both with interviews and with access to their organizations. Swami Bhashyananda of the Chicago Vedanta Society and his disciples issued many invitations that led me to know their organization better. My deepest debt is owed to Swami Bodhananda, who not only opened all doors of his community to me, but also answered many questions about pesky details and read much of my manuscript—without ever trying to dictate what I would say or how I should say it.

In my own city of Kalamazoo, I am grateful to leaders of the Indo-American community who granted me interviews and reviewed portions of my manuscript, especially Gopal Singh, Sunder Hattangadi, Pradip Sagdeo, Kailash Bafna, and Vijay Mehta. Ruth Harring taught me much about Kalamazoo's Hindu-derived groups and reviewed much of my manuscript. I thank also members of the Kalamazoo Meditation Group who aided the research of my student Scott Ballinger. Thanks are due as well to Scott himself, and to students Jason Messana and Emily Vermilya for sharing findings of their research.

My debt to Western Michigan's circle of South Asianists is endless. Carol Anderson read several versions of the manuscript. Cybelle Shattuck and my former colleague Susanne Mrozik reviewed many chapters. Selva Raj has been a treasured source of support and commentary. Another much-prized reader is my daughter, Indira Falk-Gesink of Baldwin-Wallace College. I also wish to thank the following reviewers who went through my penultimate draft and made many fine suggestions: Aditya Behl, University of Pennsylvania; Raymond Brady Williams, Wabash College; Ariel Glucklich, Georgetown University; and Laurie Patton, Emory University. I wish I could have incorporated all their excellent advice.

Finally, I must thank the several sources who put up funds at critical times to support my travels in India: the U.S. Fulbright program, which sponsored my first and second trips; the American Institute of Indian Studies, which funded the third; and the Western Michigan University Research and Creative Activities Support Fund, which partially sponsored my fourth. Last but never least comes my thanks to my husband Arthur and younger daughter Amelia, who put up with much neglect and testiness, especially during my final push toward completion.

Introduction

For many years, I have taught "Religion in the Indian Tradition," a course that introduces students to religious traditions originating in India. Most of its students are Americans of European descent who have had little or no previous experience of India; but it also usually draws at least a few enrollees who were born and raised in India or are the American-born offspring of Indian-born parents. Sometimes, too, it fires a student enough so that he or she travels to India to study under one of the several programs now available.

Some years ago, a student with India-born parents came to me at the end of the course with a cautious complaint. "Dr. Falk, I really liked this class. But one thing about it bothers me. My parents say they are Hindus, and we do Hindu rituals at home. We talked a lot about Hinduism in this course. But I can't locate my family or the things we do within it." Then, I started hearing similar comments from American students who had studied in India. They had a hard time matching what they had seen of religion in India with what they had learned about it in my course. I understood all too well what they were talking about. When I first traveled to India to study, I experienced the same disjuncture between the learning gained through my classes and the scenes I was viewing. Connections were there, of course. But they were oblique, not obvious.

It took me a while to figure out why this disjuncture existed. The students encountering India firsthand were approaching Indian religion from a different direction than that taken in my class. They were coming in contact with people and practice—meeting Indian religion where it is most concrete. I was teaching about it in the abstract, talking about the beliefs and values that motivated those people and their practice. Furthermore, even when I talked about practice, I was describing mostly prescriptions for practice laid out in India's rich heritage of sacred books. My students were viewing performance, the things people actually do, which can depart significantly from guidelines given for doing them. To make the problem more complex, because I was dealing with texts, I was spending much of our time on religion in India's past, at the times when those texts had been composed. My students were encountering the religion of India's present. As is true of many religious traditions, much change has occurred in Indian religion during the last two centuries.

In the past, when students reported these problems of disjuncture in their encounters with India, I contented myself with explaining causes. I even warned students who were heading off to India: "Now don't expect to see everything there as you've learned about it. . . ." But still the problem gnawed at me. I wasn't giving my students the introduction to Indian religions that they most needed.

Why not? My problem resided in the fact that I am a product of my own discipline. I am an American-born student of religion, trained during the early 1960s in the History of Religions graduate program at the University of Chicago. In those days, much of the material we studied concerning Indian religions came out of an academic tradition called Indology. Indologists were the first European students of Indian religion. When they began to investigate religious traditions of India, they took crucial premises from their own culture with them. One such premise was the assumption that belief is prior to practice, that is, people do certain things because they hold certain beliefs. Therefore one must always look to beliefs first to figure out why people act in the way they do. The Indologists got this assumption straight out of Europe's Christian heritage, where declarations of belief hold a central role and where people tend to say that they follow Christian practice because they accept Christian belief.

This assumption sometimes caused Indologists to gloss over a central assertion of the Indian teachings that they were studying: that practice of religion comes first. It does not even matter whether people understand why they follow a given practice, so long as they do it correctly. Moreover, the assumption that belief comes first was based on a simplistic understanding of the relationship between practice and belief that religionists only now are beginning to correct. Although it is true that belief often gives rise to practice when a religion is founded, as that religion develops the relationship reverses. People acquire beliefs through practice. Most Christians, for example, learn about their central tenets by going to church. If one wants to learn what motivates Christians to do what they do in everyday life, one must look at the values and ideals they absorb during Sunday services.

Because of their prior acquaintance with Western religions and Islam, the one "Eastern religion" with which they had contact, Indologists also assumed that everything really important to a religion was laid out in its sacred books, the Bible for Protestant Christians, the Torah for Jews, or the Qur'an for those who practice Islam. Although sacred books are indeed quite important among certain religious communities of India, they are less focal for others, who incorporate in their practice a great deal of lore carried through oral traditions. Until recently, India has not been a highly literate society. Even when sacred books are highly honored and important guidelines for practice, these are mediated through teachers who study them and explain their contents to others. Finally, it is important to realize that many early Indologists shared a premise that the India of their day was in a state of decline. It had to be put into better working order if it was to enter into full exchange with other nations. The Indologists had in their own past history a fine example of how a stumbling culture could be rejuvenated by tapping riches developed during an earlier era. The European Enlightenment of the seventeenth century had been set in motion through the study of philosophy and art from the so-called Golden Age of ancient Greece. Many Indologists thought that India's own past might hold resources that could help to awaken and restore her. They were correct in this belief, although with unintended consequences. Their strategy, plus Indian pride in the past recovered by Indologists' scholarship, eventually helped Indians push the British out of India.

When my own discipline of History of Religions was founded, its scholars continued the work that Indologists had started, following the precedents they had established.

Then its graduates went out to teach in universities, where students needed answers to questions different from the ones that were being asked. My students had been telling me, in effect, that they needed to understand not the India of long ago, but the new India the Indologists had helped to make.

For a long time, I put my discomfort with my course aside. It was popular as it was; its sections always filled up quickly. I myself was busy and had a young family to raise. And I really had no way to resolve the problems I was seeing. The resources did not exist to teach in a different way. All textbooks of that time were products of my discipline and its Indological heritage. They presupposed that courses would be structured much as my own was.

Two developments since then recalled me to that old problem. The first was an experience I had on Halloween Day in 1984. My husband and I were both Fulbright Scholars that year, and we had taken our two daughters with us to India. My girls and I were in New Delhi when all hell broke loose around us. Mobs, mostly Hindu, turned on the Delhi region's sizable Sikh community and began beating up and murdering Sikh males *en masse*. Like the rest of the world, I knew superficially what had set this off. Two Sikh bodyguards had shot Prime Minister Indira Gandhi to retaliate for an attack she ordered earlier on Sikh separatists encamped in the Golden Temple, the shrine most sacred to the Sikh community. But other than this, I hadn't a clue about what was in back of this. Why were the mobs holding *all* Sikhs accountable for the actions of just two men? Many who were murdered did not support the separatists. And why were separatists in that temple? What might religion have to do with all of this? There I was, supposedly an expert on Indian religions, and I knew more about what had happened in the first millennium B.C.E. than I did about what was happening under my nose. Yet I would have to explain this horror to my students and colleagues when I arrived home—and to my own children, who stood on the roof of our home each day, watching fires going up around them and asking "Why, Mom? Why would these nice people do such a thing to each other?" I decided that I needed to learn more about today's India, including the roots of her all-too-frequent explosions into interreligious violence.

The second factor was that new data is now available in my discipline. I am not the only scholar of Indian religion who thinks that we need to know more about Indian religion as it exists today and in performance. Increasingly, scholars of Indian religion have been turning to field research to supplement textual knowledge. This trend was started by cultural anthropologists, whose research tradition differed from that of religion scholars. At first, few anthropologists studying India were interested in religion, but trends changed. Some quite talented people began to study religious practice. Once they blazed a trail, religion scholars followed. Some even sought dual training in cultural anthropology and religion. Their findings produced rich new insights into the organization and workings of Indian religion—as it was actually practiced, not just in theory.

As these studies came out, I realized that it was now possible to introduce students to Indian religion as a lived tradition. Such an introduction would have to meet three criteria. It would have to be anchored in sights that students would see if they visited India or came to know Indians abroad. It would have to stress performance over precept, showing first how things are done and explaining the beliefs behind them afterward. It would also have to focus primarily on the present, although it would, of course, still have to attend to the past because much of India's past survives into the present and has been of great importance in shaping it. I envisioned this introduction as an explorer's guide to Indian religion.

This book is a first step toward bringing this vision to reality. Readers may have noticed that I have talked thus far about Indian religion as a whole. In fact, the course that launched my initial process of reflection took on (almost) the whole of Indian religion. This text, however, addresses only that part of the Indian tradition commonly known as Hinduism. Its readers should not slip into the common error of assuming that Indian religion equals Hinduism. At least six more religious traditions have been of major importance in India.

When I first started my own studies of Indian religion, I worked primarily with Indian Buddhism, a tradition that began in the sixth or fifth century B.C.E., spread widely throughout India until the sixth or seventh century C.E., survived in some regions until the twelfth or thirteenth century, and then died out, returning only during the twentieth century. Buddhism was a major force in India while it lasted, and its impact on Indian religious history dare not be underestimated.

A second tradition of great influence was Jainism, a major rival to Buddhism thriving during roughly the same time. Unlike Buddhism, it never died out in India and still is quite important in some regions.

Thirdly, no one who has spent as much time in the Delhi area as I have dares ignore the major impact of Islam in India. My first breakfast in India was eaten overlooking tombs built by the Lodis, a Muslim family of Afghan descent who ruled a large chunk of North India between 1451–1526 C.E. When I taught at the University of Delhi, my taxi took me past the massive walls of the Red Fort, royal citadel of the still more extensive Mughal Empire that followed the Lodis. I encountered Muslims daily, in shops and businesses, at the university, and in the very household where I was living, which had a Muslim servant and a Muslim boarder.

That same household was capably managed by an elderly Sikh cook who left to worship at her *gurdwara* each morning after making sure that I was fed properly. Her community, strongest in northwest India, has existed since the fifteenth century.

Finally, we must not forget the Christian community of India, with one very old southern branch that claims it was founded by the Apostle Thomas, a Roman Catholic community dating from the sixteenth century, and many churches, schools, and hospitals started by Protestant missions during the time of the British Raj.

All of these religious groups, even the Buddhists, have many disciples in today's India. If I were able to do so, I would have written about all of them in this book. However, Hinduism alone is so complex that I have stretched every gift I have as an organizer and writer to talk coherently about this one tradition. Still, I hope that by writing this book I will start a trend in which other scholars will do for India's other traditions what I have tried to do for Hinduism.

GETTING STARTED: DEFINITIONS

Why begin such an effort with Hinduism?

There are three good reasons to do so. The first is that Hinduism is India's largest religious tradition. Some 80 percent of India's population is said to be Hindu. That translates into more than eight hundred million Hindus, a number that does not include the large number of Hindus living outside of India. The second good reason is, as mentioned, that a text grounded in practice *can* be written. Enough fine studies based on field research exist to make this possible. A third good reason is that the problem of discrepancy between standard models of religion and religion as it is practiced is most pressing for Hinduism. Hindu practice incorporates much orally transmitted lore that gets left out when an exclusively text-based approach is used, thereby hugely distorting the picture of the whole.

My decision to take up Hinduism has presented me with one huge problem: A good book on any topic should begin by defining its subject matter. What boundaries is it setting on the subject it means to explore? No religion has boundaries agreed on by all of its subcommunities. There are always some groups within it who want to set tighter boundaries than others between "us" and "them," between people they accept as authentic practitioners of their tradition and others whom they do not accept and often call heretics. Heated contests frequently go on within a tradition about which groups' boundary definitions will hold. Such a contest is going on today among Hindu communities; this contest is one of the problems this book addresses in its final section.

Such contests of definition are not merely academic. Territorial issues are at stake. One such issue important today is "Who has the right to speak for Hindus? Who is an authentic 'Hindu' representative?" The existence of this contest means, among other things, that the problem of defining Hinduism has become politically loaded. Any group offering a definition would love to see an American textbook writer take up the one it has offered, in effect, endorsing its claim that it speaks for every Hindu. We shall seek a more neutral ground, acknowledging the claims of all, while striving to favor none.

Our problem of definitions is complicated still more by the fact that the word "Hindu" itself offers little help. Historically, it is an "everything else" term. In the earliest known records of its use, it seems to have meant simply Indian. Under Muslim rule, India was called Hind, and a Hindu was someone who lived in India. The term first acquired a religious spin when it became necessary for Muslim rulers to draw a line between Indians who practiced Islam, their own religion, and those who followed the older traditions existing in India. At that point, a Hindu was anyone living in India who was not Muslim. As Europeans entered India with their knowledge of other traditions of the world, they subtracted additional groups from this definition. Buddhists, Jains, Sikhs, Christians, India's handful of Jews, and the Zoroastrian Parsees (Persians) in and around Bombay were considered "not Hindu." Hindus were whoever was left, excluding perhaps people of small hill tribes who had religions of their own. The term remained one used mostly by outsiders. Most so-called Hindus did not consider themselves part of one single tradition. They were Vaishnavas or Shaivas or Shaktas or even just Bengalis or Gujaratis who practiced their old regional traditions. To think of one's Shaiva self as practicing the same religion as one's Vaishnava neighbor required a major shift in thinking still in process in India.

So whom shall we call a Hindu? I am going to cut this Gordian knot by adopting a simplistic tactic. I shall call anyone a Hindu who accepts the label. In effect, this means I have taken the theoretical stance that there is more than one Hinduism, that the Hindu tradition is made up of multiple groups with multiple valid self-definitions. This is the main reason why I have chosen to call this book *Living Hinduisms* rather than keeping the title in the singular. I shall use the plural in this book when I want to call special attention to the variety of viewpoints and forms of observance being covered. At other times, I shall speak of Hinduism in the singular as I have done here. I am more used to speaking of it in this way. Moreover, as we shall see, like most of the world's great religions, Hinduism is both many traditions and one.

STRATEGY AND ORGANIZATION

Practice is contextual; it occurs in certain places, at certain times, among certain groups of people, in response to certain kinds of situations. Therefore, this book is also contextual; it looks at varieties of practice in a range of contexts. Two criteria were used in choosing the contexts discussed. Either they are very typical, so that students are likely to come across Hindu practice in such contexts; or they are very important for helping students grasp what is met in other contexts or for helping students understand controversies going on among Hindus right now. Twelve such contexts are presented, subdivided into four sections.

The first context taken up is time. We shall look at four types of teaching traditions that have developed and intermingled over time to give rise to much of the Hindu practice encountered today. Each has its own special leaders, literatures, and organizational structures, and addresses somewhat different concerns and audiences. The first traditions to be taken up are those carried by householder Brahmins, intellectuals of a very ancient type whose example and teachings have shaped much Hindu social and ritual practice. Second are the traditions of *sadhus* and *swamis,* explorers and teachers of spiritual disciplines. Third will be those of *bhaktas,* who showed ways to find God through ecstatic devotion. Fourth will be initiatives of samajists, more recent leaders of reform and revival who set in motion changes sweeping all previous traditions. This first section is the one most like older history-oriented textbooks because much of what makes these traditions distinctive is a product of the historical circumstances in which they emerged. It is difficult to make sense of them without understanding how they came into being and what concerns they were addressing.

In contrast to this first section, the second will look at the context offered by three different kinds of spaces in which practice from multiple traditions comes together. One such context is the home, blending ancient Brahman-borne rites of passage with devotional practice as well as occasional hosting of *swami* or *sadhu* visitors. A second is the temple, where Brahman rites blend with expressions of devotion, as well as other practice from family and local traditions. The third setting taken up here will be the pilgrim road, where devotion, discipline, and renunciation come together.

The third section's contexts are those of social level. This section pays special attention to two ends of the complex social ladder offered by India's intertwining systems of caste and class. One of its chapters examines ways in which bottom caste groups, the Hindu poor and oppressed, have responded to traditions that in the past were cited to justify their less-than-desirable standing. The second samples forms of practice taken up today among English-educated, high-caste groups of two regions in India. These activities show the imprint of an important series of initiatives that have strived to reshape Hindu thinking and practice during the last century.

The book's fourth and final section addresses the context of challenge, the challenge posed by the huge set of changes that have swept India and the entire world during the last century. It discusses new forms of Hinduism that have emerged to address that challenge. The first of its chapters looks at new movements, often with international outreach, that have taken up old themes and institutions and put them together in new kinds of ways. The second examines a complex triad of Hindu groups that are addressing the challenge posed by India's newly democratic political structure. The final chapter speaks to the challenge posed by new cultural and physical environments as Hindus and their practice move throughout the world.

As promised, each chapter is anchored in a concrete example, a description of some encounter that introduces crucial themes relating to the context to be taken up. All but one portray experiences I have had myself; the exception is a sequence from a documentary film. Each chapter asks what is behind its opening scene, explaining Hindu concepts or history that will help the reader make sense of what is found there. Finally, the chapter supplements that scene with examples of other kinds of practice that can be found in similar contexts. For example, when I talk about Hindu practice in homes, I begin with a scene portraying a friend preparing a meal, then talk about concepts of purity and pollution that underlie the clothes she is wearing and other precautions she has taken. Then I move on to other rites and observances found in homes, some grounded in these same concepts, others based on different premises found in a Hindu home context. My intent in setting up chapters this way is to provide a template, a master model to which someone newly arrived among Hindus can compare his\her own experience and find enough similarities to realize: "Oh, that must be what I see going on here."

No text can cover everything; this one, like others, relies on sampling. Any student heading for India or enjoying Hindu friends is bound to encounter forms of practice or teachings not covered in this book. But I have tried to address at least those aspects of Hindu life that are most common or conspicuous. This is the book I wish I had had before I first began to venture among Hindus.

ON SOURCES AND VOICE

I have already written briefly about the kinds of sources on which this text is based and why I have chosen to work from these kinds of sources. At this point I must list them a little more systematically. One important source has been my own experiences among Hindus, both in India and in America.

I have had four extended stays in India, ranging in length from two and one-half weeks to ten months. The earliest, in 1967, was a summer seminar on the humanities that took its participants to more sites, lectures, and performances than most visitors in India could manage within several years. The next three, in 1984–85, 1991–92 and 1998, based me in the New Delhi neighborhood described in Chapter 9, although here, too, I had ample chance to travel. In the interims, I have for many years tracked various Hindu groups and projects in my own region.

To supplement these experiences of my own, I have drawn extensively on field studies, most of them done by cultural anthropologists or by researchers in my own discipline. Cited on these pages are works by Lawrence Babb, Ann Gold, Akös Astör,

Brenda Beck, S. M. Bhardwaj, Mary Hancock, Lindsey Harlan, David Haberman, Diana Eck, and several others. Historical studies, too, have been important—not only of traditions with ancient roots but also of recent movements, such as Saurabh Dube's work on Satnamis, Eleanor Zelliot's on Dalit movements of Maharashtra, Rosalind O'Hanlon's on non-Brahmin movement origins, and Christophe Jaffrelot on Hindu nationalism.

A last important category of resources, consulted whenever available, has been first-person accounts by Hindus of their own experience and practice. Especially important to this volume have been memoirs by Ramabai Ranade, Shudha Mazumdar, Iravati Karve, D. D. Mokashi, Vasant Moon, Kancha Ilaiah, and Swami Tapovanam. These, I must admit, are my own favorite kind of reading about things Indian. I hope that readers of this textbook will follow up on and explore further those cited in the chapter reading lists.

One problem I have had to resolve in using so many kinds of sources has been the problem of voice. From what vantage should I speak? In textbooks, the author's vantage is often an impersonal one. He or she floats over materials described like a TV commentator doing voice-overs for an audience. Because I have often been present in scenes described in this book and because my presence has sometimes affected the scene's unfolding, I have decided to be as honest as possible about my role. I shall break with textbook tradition, using the word "I" wherever such use seems appropriate. Sometimes this means I shall use it not only to indicate that this is a scene I have viewed or is based on research I have done myself, but also to talk about decisions I have made about terminology or theoretical models. At other times, when using the work of others, I shall cite their names and works in the text and footnotes according to standard usage.

MY TEACHERS

It is the custom among Hindus for a teacher to certify credentials by reciting a line of masters whose teachings have shaped his own. My own shaping has been eclectic; several different scholarly lines have influenced my interests and techniques, and I have had several principal masters.

Burr C. Brundage, Professor of Ancient History at Cedar Crest College, where I did my B.A. work, majoring in History. Burr Brundage was an Egyptologist by training, a student of the famed John A. Wilson of the University of Chicago's Oriental Institute. By the time I knew him, he was developing a second expertise in the study of Aztec and Incan religion. He left me with a lifelong interest in ways religion is used to achieve political legitimation.

Mircea Eliade, Professor of History of Religions at the University of Chicago, where I completed my M.A. and Ph.D. Eliade drew on several strands of European intellectual history, including work by Emile Durkheim and Carl Gustav Jung. He also studied in India under Historian of Philosophy S. N. DasGupta and for a few months was a resident of the Shivananda Ashram. I acquired from Eliade much of my understanding of how sacred space and time work, and also of how ritual transforms and structures human experience. I also gained the conviction that the question most interesting in the study of religion is "What can this teach us about ourselves and our fellow human beings?"

Joseph M. Kitagawa, also Professor of History of Religions at Chicago and student of Joachim Wach, founder of the Chicago department. Kitagawa instilled in me Wach's interest in social dimensions of religion and taught me to note who is doing the talking or leading in religion and what group interests are being served.

Charles H. Long, another Chicago Historian of Religions and Wach student, with later incursions into Foucault, Derrida, and postcolonial theory. Long taught his students to pay close attention to the preconceptions we bring to our study. He taught me also to attend to hidden agendas underlying scholarship, such as the need to persuade subject peoples that their subjection is appropriate.

Johannes Van Buitenan, Chicago Sanskrit Professor and student of famed Dutch Sanskritist and Indologist Jan Gonda. While studying Sanskrit with Van Buitenan, I also learned a great deal about how language molds and limits thought. Furthermore, I gained from him a conviction that students will not grasp a concept unless they know the word for it in its own language, with its full range of overtones and connections.

Rita M. Gross, longtime friend and sometimes collaborator. Rita tugged me into feminist studies in religion. She taught me to attend to things that women do in religion, no matter how undramatic, and in general to be aware of the many ways in which gender intersects with religion. Rita was with me during two of the episodes described in scenarios opening this book's chapters.

Several Indian scholars of postcolonial bent who sometimes sound a great deal like my old mentor Charles Long. They have convinced me of the usefulness of concepts such as hegemony and contest used as a verb, despite my distaste for jargon that is stylish. They have also taught me a great deal about hegemony and contest during the colonial period and about that period's impact on untouchables. Of special influence on me have been Kumkum Sangari, Uma Chakravarti, Tanika Sarkar, Saurabh Dube, and Partha Chatterjee.

All of these influences will surface in this volume, along with other insights gained from various social and political scientists. I work with no single method, preferring to use whomever's insights help me make sense of the phenomena before me. A religion is a highly complex entity, like a human body or tree, an ocean or a continent. I believe that no single approach can unlock the whole of it. Different levels of exploration call for differing strategies of investigation.

Students who take my course on India often ask me whether I am a Hindu. I tell them "I don't think so." My parents were Protestant Christians of German Reformed heritage. India is not my holy land, although I love many of its people and places. Nor am I an initiate of any Hindu guru-disciple lineage, although I have known several gurus and have learned a great deal from them. I do use the field method called participant-observation, which means that I practice to some extent what I study so I can feel its impact on emotion and muscle. I have no problems doing this because I do subscribe to one teaching common among many present-day Hindu groups: that all religions are rooted finally in the same basic reservoirs of human potentiality and that all strive to enhance human insight, empowerment, and community. Nonetheless, I have formal ties to only one religion; I was baptized, raised, and confirmed in my parents' church, which has by now merged into the United Church of Christ. My church supported my efforts to understand what it was about, even when I asked sticky and difficult questions. My many years spent within it were overall a happy and constructive experience. I nonetheless found some downsides in my tradition and in other Christian churches I saw around me. This led me to expect that other religions of the world might have similar mixes of the uplifting and the problematic. I have tried to show both in this analysis of Hinduism, just as I would expect a Hindu scholar to do in writing an introduction to my own Christian heritage. I would truly love to read such an introduction.

AIDS TO THE READER

Documentation

As in most scholarly writing, other people's findings have contributed to this volume at differing levels. Some are in its foreground, made conspicuously visible because various chapters quote from them or summarize them. Others hover in the background, less obvious in their influence but important nonetheless because they have furnished helpful insights or comparisons that have helped me see what is special to examples cited and what reflects more general patterns. I have tried to do justice to both kinds of sources in my documentation. Direct quotes and summaries are acknowledged in conventional footnotes, located at the bottom of pages for optimal convenience. Influential background sources can be found in Additional Sources, located at the end of each chapter. The Additional Sources also contain some new materials published since the chapters were written. They are annotated to help readers further explore the practices and movements introduced in each chapter.

Glossary

Another aid offered is a glossary, located at the end of the volume. Unfortunately for those seeking an easy read, texts introducing religions new to the reader must use terms in unfamiliar languages. Along with names of people, deities, practices, movements, and works of literature, there are many concepts that have no one-on-one equivalents in English. Despite my best efforts to keep new terms to a minimum, they sprout a bit thickly during the initial chapters. To help readers recall them and sort them out, the Glossary not only offers the usual brief definitions, it also marks in boldface those that should be learned because they are used repeatedly in the volume.

The Glossary also offers aids intended to help readers deal with the difficult problem posed by alternative forms and transliterations. Any writer who uses Hindu terms faces three immediate problems: languages, script, and capitalization.

The first problem with terms is the multiplicity of languages. In today's India alone, at least nineteen different regional languages are spoken, depending on how one counts. Any study of Hinduism must also take into account a twentieth, the ancient tongue Sanskrit in which many scriptures, liturgies, and philosophical works are written. What version of a religious term does a writer use?

Making this problem still stickier is the fact that all Indian languages use scripts different from the Roman script used for most European and major American languages. The Indian Devanagari script used for Sanskrit and most modern North Indian languages have symbols for forty-four distinct sounds (forty-six in Hindi), plus two more symbols that modify certain vowels. Needless to say, the English alphabet cannot make all these distinctions. Linguists have worked out systems of equivalences using diacritical marks to modify Roman letters: lines and accents over letters and dots beneath them. These can be daunting for students, and are mostly useless when students go to India, where a different set of transliterations is common. Often, neither system matches what students see in books published for Western use by Indian religious movements. How does a writer transliterate terms in a way that will help the reader steer a course between these several systems?

Finally, when does a writer capitalize and when not? Indian scripts have no capitalization; English usage has quite a lot. Hence the distinction between proper and common nouns so dear to English is blurred in Indian languages. The name for a genre—a type of writing, such as *upanishad, purana, dharmashastra*—can also serve as a category of scripture. An occupational description such as "gardener" or "barber" becomes the name for a *jati,* one of the many "communities" that make up the Indian caste system. To capitalize a Sanskrit or vernacular Indian term can have the effect of exaggerating its distinctiveness and importance. To leave it in lower case can mislead. There are "gardeners" in India who do not garden; "barbers" who do not cut hair.

The following, often arbitrary, solutions to these problems are listed below:

1. Sanskrit versus vernacular terms If I introduce a term in the context of Sanskrit writings, I use the Sanskrit version of that term. I then continue to use the Sanskrit form throughout the text, so that the word remains recognizable to readers. If the term is first used in the context of some present-day practice, then I use the vernacular form most appropriate to that practice (in most cases, this is Hindi or Tamil). This will be less confusing than it sounds, because most Hindu terms used today in India are derived from Sanskrit, and the changes they have undergone are very minimal. The most common is loss of an "a" at the end of a word or middle of a compound. Hence, "*dharma*" becomes "*dharm*" or "Shivaratri" becomes "Shivratri." Transformations in South Indian languages are more complex; for example, Sanskrit *puja* becomes Tamil *pucai.* When vernacular versions of Sanskrit terms are used in the text, Sanskrit equivalents are provided in the Glossary.

I have broken my own principles of usage for two terms. I use the old English spelling "Brahmin" for a member of the Hindu intellectual caste. Strict transliteration of this term in most modern languages would yield "Brahman," whereas the Sanskrit term for this caste is "*brahmana.*" To use Brahman confuses the term with the supreme power Brahman important to many Hindu philosophical teachings. To use brahmana confuses it with an important category of ritual texts. Many writers, including myself, have turned to Brahmin to avoid these problems. I have also used both "Rama" and "Ram" to name the same ideal prince and ruler. He is discussed first in the context of Sanskrit texts, and hence should continue to be Rama throughout. But in today's Hindu politics, he would never be called by the Sanskrit version of his name; indeed, his political prototype is the hero of a Hindi retelling of his story, in which his name is Ram. Hence Rama becomes Ram when we talk about him in the always explosive context of politics.

2. Transliteration I solicited a great deal of advice on transliterations, and finally decided that *The Chicago Manual of Style* offered the best advice of all: When writing for a nonspecialist audience, keep it simple, but also try to get as close as possible to actual sounds in the transliterated languages. In the main text of this volume, I have done away with all diacritical marks or contortions likely to become stumbling blocks for readers. On the other hand, if adding a letter will make a term sound more like its actual pronunciation, I have done this. Please see the appendix for more detail on the decisions I have made on transliteration.

As a matter of general principle, whenever a given transliteration has become common in English works, I have used that transliteration even if another would be more consistent. Thus I use *purdah* for women's seclusion, even though the form consistent with actual spelling is *parda*. Also as a matter of general principle, I defer to usages preferred by authors whom I quote directly or summarize extensively. This has caused some slight discrepancy when I have referred to two studies of Tamil village practice that use different systems of transliteration. This discrepancy is corrected in footnotes.

For those readers who prefer accuracy to ease, all terms listed in the Glossary are shown both as written in the text and with full diacritical markings.

3. Capitalization Early versions of the manuscript for this volume tried very hard to hold out against what I consider to be the over-capitalization of Hindu terminology. Watching precedents set by my colleagues, however, I have finally caved in. All categories of Sanskrit texts are in capitals, hence Veda, Upanishads, Puranas, Itihasa, Dharmashastra, Agama. All *jati* names are in capitals, even when translated into English—Gardeners, Barbers, Drummers, Washermen.

ADDITIONAL READINGS

Any student aspiring to take up serious study of Hinduism will need to have some acquaintance with the history of European scholarship on it and the problems generated by this scholarship's assumptions and values. A fine place to start is P. J. Marshall, *The British Discovery of Hinduism in the Eighteenth Century* (Cambridge: Cambridge Univ. Press, 1970). Bernard S. Cohn takes up the methods of knowledge gathering under the British in *Colonialism and Its Forms of Knowledge: The British in India* (Princeton: Princeton Univ. Press, 1996). Ronald Inden points to the biases introduced by Indological method in *Imagining India* (Oxford: Blackwell, 1990); for this problem, see also Carol A. Breckenridge and Peter Van der Veer, eds., *Orientalism and the Postcolonial Predicament: Perspectives on South Asia* (Philadelphia: Pennyslvania Univ. Press, 1993). Uma Chakravarti shows how European distortions in turn have affected Indian scholarship and attitudes in her "Whatever Happened to the Vedic *Dasi*? Orientalism, Nationalism, and a Script for the Past" in Kumkum Sangari and Sudesh Vaid, eds., *Recasting Women: Essays in Colonial History* (New Delhi: Kali for Women, 1989), pp. 27–87. Richard King shows how colonialist inquiry played into Western conceptions of Hinduism in "Orientalism and the Modern Myth of 'Hinduism,'" *Numen* 46 (1999): 146–83.

Offering a useful typology of attempts at defining Hinduism is Brian K. Smith, "Exorcising the Transcendent: Strategies for Defining Hinduism and Religion," *History of Religions* (August 1987): 32–52. Smith also offers a definition of his own. Arvind Sharma examines Indian attempts at definition in his "On Hindu, Hindustān, Hinduism and Hindutva," *Numen* 49 (2002): 1–36. Driving much of the controversy over definitions is Hindu nationalist leader Vinayak Damodar Sarvarkar's *Hindutva: Who is a Hindu?,* 5th ed. (Bombay: Veer Sarvarkar Prakashan, 1969). This controversy will be discussed more extensively in Chapter 11. Indian historian Romila Thapar assesses nationalist assertions in "Imagined Religious Communities? Ancient History and the Modern Search for a Hindu Identity," *Modern Asian Studies* 23:2 (1989): 210–29. A special issue of *History of Religions* addressed the question "Who Speaks for Hinduism?" in December 2000 (Sarah Caldwell and Brian K. Smith, eds., vol. 68, no. 4).

Results of two important European conferences on constructions of Hinduism have been published in Günther D. Sontheimer and Hermann Kulke, eds., *Hinduism Reconsidered* (New Delhi: Manohar, 1989) and Vasudha Dalmia and Heinrich von Stietencron, eds., *Representing Hinduism: The Construction of Religious Traditions and National Identity* (New Delhi: Sage, 1995). von Stietencron's article "Hinduism: On the Proper Use of a Deceptive Term" (*Hinduism Reconsidered,* pp. 11–28) argues for a multi-strand approach such as the one taken in this volume, as does Julius J. Lipner's "Ancient Banyan: an Inquiry into the Meaning of 'Hinduness,'" *Religious Studies* 32: 109–26.

PART I

Hinduisms over Time:
Four Teaching Traditions

Europeans writing about Hinduism during early years of its exploration liked to compare it to a jungle. This was not a compliment. The jungle simile suggested that Hinduism is tangled and impenetrable, that it sends tendrils into everything, that it is exotic and garish and raucous, and that it has snaky ramifications that can easily trip up the unwary. Yet if one screens out negative overtones, parts of the image become appropriate. Hinduism *is* many branched and colorful. Sometimes it does, quite intentionally, assault the senses, especially during big festivals or peak hours at popular temples. Moreover, its intertwining traditions can indeed resemble the growth in a lush forest where stems twist around one another and vines stretch between trees to link them into a greater whole.

Yet this Hindu forest is quite penetrable. A few simple distinctions can help sort it out. Let us start with the premise that, like all major religions, Hinduism is less a single tradition than a cluster, sharing some features in common but also differing. Furthermore, it grew up in a landscape where until recently literacy was not extensive and many regions were cut off from the rest of the country by physical barriers. Complicating regional divisions in India is the very old north\south split caused by both topography and major language differences. A range of rugged hills, the Vindhyas, cuts India in half at just about the point where its triangular peninsula juts out from the rest of Asia. Above these hills, most languages are of

Indo-European origin, while below them most belong to the Dravidian family of languages.[1]

In a context so divided and with limited literacy, a great deal of religious lore is handed down orally, by means of stories, rituals, folk art, and drama. People who master special techniques such as healing or exorcism learn these from parents or local teachers and often practice them as a sideline while earning their living in the same way as other people around them. The famed anthropologist Robert Redfield called oral and informal traditions like this "little traditions" because they have few adherents and most often are highly localized in a family, a clan, a village, or small region. They can be compared to the underbrush that grows in a forest, the smaller trees and vines that sprout in clearings or hang from branches.

Overshadowing them are the major trees, what Redfield called "great traditions." These are traditions with large followings that have devised some long-term means of preserving their most precious stories and teachings. Although this means of preservation is usually writing, some Indian traditions have stored their scriptures by memorization. Along with such formal means of preserving teachings comes a class of designated experts whose principal job is interpreting and spreading those teachings—and often leading in ritual. Institutions such as learning centers and pilgrim sites, fixed liturgies for worship, and calendars that schedule ritual events are also created. Great traditions can last a long time and may spread through huge areas, even crossing political or cultural boundaries.

Many people who have heard this great tradition\little tradition distinction tend to identify great traditions with the complex entities normally called religions. If readers stop to think about how great traditions have been defined, however, they will realize that all major religions have multiple great tradition subdivisions. Most of the world's best known religions have acquired these subdivisions through splitting. Christianity, Buddhism, and Islam, for example, all had single founders; sectarian subdivisions of those traditions sprouted from those founders' teachings and examples as great branches do from the roots and stem of a single tree. Hindu subdivisions have been more like trunks rising side by side from shared soil. They have had multiple founders who drew upon a shared fund of ideas, symbols, and experiences, but put these together in distinctive ways with distinctive interpretations. Like subdivisions within single-founder religions, Hindu traditions have responded to and sometimes challenged one another. Furthermore, once established, they themselves have sometimes split and branched in more than one direction.

---

[1] Except for Marathi, the principal language spoken in the state of Maharashtra. Marathi is a Sanskrit-based language like those of North India. North India has a few tribal languages not of Sanskrit origin, as well as one small pocket of Brahui, a Dravidian-based language.

The complexity thus established has been complicated still more by the fact that some Hindu traditions have engaged in a counterprocess of knitting. Traditions initially separate are looped together in ways that encourage people to think of them as one. One can do this in several ways—from the top down, for example, by asserting theologically that many apparently separate deities are ultimately just aspects of a single supreme power or that different kinds of practice lead in the end to the same goal. The famed text called *Bhagavad-Gita* that is so popular among Hindus makes both these assertions and is a wonderful example of top-down knitting. But knitting can also occur at other levels. Indian anthropologist M. N. Srinivas has described a process that he calls Sanskritization, entailing a bottom-up, grassroots-level type of knitting. In this process, local groups sharing common oral traditions link themselves to great traditions by claiming caste niches, taking up "approved" practice, and identifying their deities with those celebrated in great tradition texts. Certain teachers of Brahmin heritage seem to have promoted such grassroots knitting with special zeal. It became an important means through which Brahmin influence expanded.

This volume's first part introduces these Brahmins and other teachers who presided over the splits and knits that produced today's Hinduisms. It looks at four kinds of teaching traditions developed over time that have been especially important in shaping the Hindu whole and in holding it together. These are all traditions of the great type, carried on by specialists with their own distinctive ideas and literatures. These traditions are introduced through their specialists because today these specialists are the traditions' most visible components. They often, but not always, have special dress, hair styles, styles of behavior, and symbols that set them apart. In such a person, an entire heritage of ideas comes to a focus. Among Hindus, as in many other religions, the specialist is expected to exemplify those ideas, to show how to enact them, as much as he or she is expected to preserve and teach them.

The Brahmins, introduced in Chapter 1, produced much of the social and ritual framework that has so well enabled Hindu knits. Brahmins are unique among the teachers introduced because they are a caste; they acquire their special standing by birth. One can claim membership in the Brahmin community only by showing that one has had Brahmin ancestors. Brahmins of the past were guardians and teachers of Sanskrit, India's principal literary language in ancient times. They claimed a monopoly over certain kinds of religious lore recorded in that language. Included in that lore are hymns and ritual chants that are the oldest surviving components of today's Hindu practice. These are part of the heritage called Veda, a word that simply means "knowledge." According to Brahmins themselves, all the other knowledge they carry has been derived from Veda. These teachings are so rich and of so many types that many scholars once equated Hinduism with Brahmin teachings, treating all other teaching traditions as afterthoughts. Certain modern Hindu teachers would make this claim as well, especially those deeply involved in the Hindu nationalist movement. This book assumes, however, that other teachers have also been crucial, as shown in Chapters 2 through 4.

Chapter 2 introduces the Hindu teachers called *sadhus,* specialists in spiritual discipline. A sadhu's role is not acquired by birth. It must be chosen and usually entails some significant break with ties to blood kin and property. Taking the place of these blood ties is adoption into a spiritual lineage by means of a guru-given ritual of initiation. The earliest-known sadhu lineage called Hindu today was that of the Pashupatas, founded around the second century C.E. But precedents for sadhu-style disciplines go back much earlier. The Brahmin texts called Upanishads suggest that renouncing worldly ties is the best way to gain spiritual insight, while early communities of Buddhists and Jains in India were so important as sadhu models that Chapter 2 describes them before turning to more explicitly Hindu lineages. Sadhu teachings were directed toward individuals rather than toward the whole communities that occupy so much of the attention of Brahmin teachers. They aim at self-transformation rather than at preserving the life-supporting *dharma* that is so often at the center of Brahmin concerns. Like sadhu traditions, the *bhakta*-centered devotional traditions described in Chapter 3 also focus on individual choice and spiritual transformation. Sadhu and bhakta methods are compatible enough that some bhaktas have taken up sadhu vows and become founders of sadhu lineages. But this is an add-on to their practice, not an essential. One need not join anything to become a bhakta, nor must one go through any ritual of initiation. Nor does a would-be bhakta have to be born into any particular caste. All the bhakta must do is love God and sing God's praises. Any God can become the focus of a bhakta's devotion, although India's main devotional movements were centered on a just a few deities: Shiva, Vishnu, the Goddess, and the two descents of Vishnu named Krishna and Rama. Although devotional movements existed in India at least as early as the second century B.C.E., the ones that lasted longest and became most famous were those launched by singing saints beginning in southern India during the fifth or sixth century C.E. These were largely lay-based movements; leaders who strived to keep up the founding saints' heritage often were householder gurus passing their roles on from father to son.

Until the early nineteenth century, Brahmins, sadhus, and bhaktas of many subvarieties were the most prominent Hindu leaders. A good way to learn what they did and what Hindu life was like before that momentous century is to read travelers' accounts by early missionaries and British officials. Although these accounts are often scornful of what they report, they furnish an essential baseline for assessing just how very much Hindu practice has changed since their times. Important initiators of that change were the final group of teachers introduced in Chapter 4. Historians of Indian religion have thus far not come up with a good collective name for these teachers.

Hence this text has assigned them a name of its own; it calls them samajists, after the type of organization that they founded. *Samaj* means merely "society," an organization of like-minded people, usually brought together to accomplish a common purpose. The like-minded people of samaj movements were mostly high-caste Hindus educated in schools where the English language was the principal medium of instruction. These schools were set up to train Indians to help British colonial rulers govern their land. The purpose shared in common by *samaj* founders was to remold their tradition to meet the needs of their own century—as they themselves perceived those needs. They redesigned women's lives, asked important questions about caste, and breathed new life into those parts of the Hindu tradition that favored knitting over splitting and stressed the unity of religion.

Other important Hindu leaders and movements are described later in the book. Much of the final section, in fact, is devoted to developments that occurred during the twentieth century. Various chapters also have more to say about oral traditions. But the materials presented in Part I offer the most basic equipment for a Hindu excursion. Those who read this analysis will be able to recognize central characters in scenes resembling the ones described. They will know the names of literatures important to those characters and the central ideas that molded their behavior and teachings. Finally, readers will come away with a sense of present-day Hinduism's historical background, the hidden dimension present in every situation they encounter in today's India.

1

The Brahmins

He looked like a scholar, this frail old man with the enormous turban and knee-length black coat covering close-fitting white cotton trousers. I knew that the Indian government had once awarded him a prestigious medal for his contributions to the study of Sanskrit, India's ancient sacred and intellectual language. Now he was telling me about his wife's objections to his joining this midwinter pilgrimage to the village shrine honoring his guru-friend's guru. "She wept," he said, "as she tied this scarf around me. She was afraid that she would not see me alive again. You must realize that we have been together for a very long time. Our parents got us married as children." Then a student stepped up with a question about a passage from a Sanskrit work she had been studying. "Come," he said, and the two sat down on a nearby rug, facing one another. He began to recite the problematic passage from memory, line by line, explaining its words and the grammar that linked them together.

One of the many terms that our English language has gained from India is "pundit," from *pandit,* the Hindi term for Sanskrit scholars such as the one described above. A pandit of high degree is in effect a living library, for he has committed to memory not only Sanskrit vocabulary, rules of grammar, and principles of interpretation, but also the texts that he has studied. In times before printing presses made possible widespread access to complex learning, pandits were the main guardians of knowledge in Sanskrit. For centuries, they produced and preserved a huge body of literature covering topics as varied as right behavior, statecraft, heroic exploits, logic, and metaphysics. The most accomplished among them were protégés of kings, who gave generous grants of land and cattle to support their studies and teaching. Many served as court advisors. Even the humblest who knew just a handful of texts and rituals were still prized residents in villages, where they could be called on to chant proper Sanskrit verses at household rites and to offer advice and arbitration during village quarrels.

Pandits were also India's most exclusive group of religious specialists, for to become a pandit one had to be born a Brahmin, a member of a group thought to possess special abilities to summon sacred powers by means of ancient chants. Brahmins claimed to be the highest-ranking and most pure among what today are called "Hindu castes," groups that strive to marry their children only to members of their own community, and who likewise once held monopolies over certain trades or services.

Brahmin attempts to keep their monopoly over Sanskrit lore and learning rested on their belief that their ancestors had been *rishis,* "seers," of the distant past. Rishis were people with special abilities to cross the divide that separates two worlds: the world of ordinary human activity that most of us see and live in and the world of superhuman powers that were believed to give the human realm its life and fertility. In that superhuman realm, the rishis "saw" the chants that could summon powers from the superhuman world to this one and stole secrets of the sacrifices that first brought immortality to the *devas,* "heavenly beings."[1] They brought these precious chants and rites to humans—or at least to Aryas, "Noble Ones," who were qualified to receive and use them. In this human world, protected by Aryas, the rishis' children and grandchildren guarded their findings, memorizing the chants from generation to generation, while applying and extending the ritual teachings.

In other words, Brahmins were religious experts serving a group of people called Aryas who claimed special status and privilege because they had access to sacred knowledge brought by the rishis. Part of this knowledge, called Veda, taught this group how to *be* Aryas, that is, how to keep up proper rituals and lifestyles so they would deserve to continue using Veda. Most high-caste Hindus believe today that the Aryas were high-caste Hindus' own ancestors. Honoring Brahmins and behaving as they teach is, therefore, one of the best ways to show that one has and deserves this very noble ancestry.

THE ARYAS

Who were these Aryas? According to Brahmin-preserved accounts, the Aryas, or at least their kings, were descendants of a human known as Manu, survivor of a great flood that once destroyed the earth. From two children born as the result of a sacrifice done by Manu came the two major Aryan lineages of the sun and the moon. The solar lineage settled and ruled the divide between the Indus and Ganges river systems in northern India, as well as the Ganges-Jumna valley, the region between and beside two great rivers that flow side by side across much of north central India. Descendants of the lunar lineage spread out in a semicircle to the east, south, and west of their solar cousins. From these two royal lines and their subjects derived the Aryan tribes who divided their holdings into sixteen tribal territories.

Histories of the Aryas offered by contemporary research are more puzzling. The rishis' chants, later gathered into four collections, are the main resource scholars have for reconstructing Aryan origins. The oldest chants of all are those assembled in the collection known as *Rig-Veda.* Verses of *Rig-Veda* chants suggest that the earliest-known Aryas were a mobile people skilled in breeding and herding domesticated animals, including cattle, goats, sheep, and horses; they also knew how to plant and raise barley and wheat. Aryas could weave, smelt metal, and build spoke-wheeled vehicles to which they harnessed horses. They prized generosity and hospitality to guests, but

---

[1] The word most commonly used in very ancient chants to describe how these were received is *drish,* meaning "to see." This, of course, designates a special kind of seeing, the kind of visionary insight that people think of when they use the word "seer." Later texts used the term *shru,* "to hear," to describe the same process. This is the base of the term *shrauta;* see p. 29.

perhaps not peace, for their chants celebrate cattle raiding and pray for heroic sons and victory in battle. Geographic references in *Rig-Veda* chants do not locate Aryas in later Aryan heartlands, but rather in a region called Saptasindu, the land of seven rivers. This is thought to include the region of northwest India now called the Punjab (five waters), plus the valley of a now-dry river that once flowed between the Punjab and the Ganges/Indus divide.[2]

Rig-Veda chants were preserved in a language that is clearly a parent to later classical Sanskrit, but also has strong affinities to Avestan, the priestly language of ancient Persia. Both languages belong to the Indo-European language family, which includes European tongues such as Greek, Latin, German, and English. All languages of this family are thought to stem from one common ancestor called Proto-Indo-European. Many linguists think this was first spoken somewhere near the Black Sea, in western Turkey or southern Russia. Looking at this evidence, early European Indologists concluded that the Aryas also came initially from central Eurasia. They had been warrior tribes, nomadic herders who for unknown reasons invaded Persia and northwest India sometime during the second millennium B.C.E.

Scholars who painted this picture of Aryan origins did not yet know that ruins of a great civilization lay scattered throughout the area supposedly conquered during Aryan invasions. These ruins were first discovered only in 1921, when the British were laying railroad beds in the Punjab region. This Harappan civilization, as it is now called, reached its height during the third millennium B.C.E. but then began to fade. Most of its settlements were abandoned after 1600 C.E. It had been a highly sophisticated accomplishment, extending from the Himalayas to the Arabian Sea, and along that sea's coast lands from present-day Maharashtra well into Iran. Its walled cities, towns, and villages were built from fired bricks of standardized sizes. Harappans used uniform weights and measures, even somewhat uniform tools. Their artisans fired large pots, fashioned exquisite jewelry, skillfully carved stone images, and molded images out of bronze. One surprising feature of the largest Harappan cities is the system of water conduction that allowed filling and draining of great public pools, as well as smaller baths and latrines in some of the bigger homes. Harappans raised sheep and humped cattle like those still seen in India today. They grew grain and built granaries for storage between harvests. Goods found in their homes and public structures show that they traded with sister civilizations of the ancient Near East.

Like those sister civilizations, Harappans had a writing system; samples of this exist on seals most likely intended to stamp marks of ownership into clay. But Harappans left no libraries inscribed in clay like their Near Eastern neighbors, and the Harappan writing found on seals is too sparse to be deciphered. Hence, nothing is known about them other than what can be learned from their material creations. What kind of religion did they have? How did they order their social system? Who built the Harappan settlements and pulled them together into one remarkably uniform culture? Most importantly of all for some of today's Hindus, what connection might they have had with the people who called themselves Aryas? All these questions remain unanswered.

---

[2] Many Hindus believe that the dry river was the Sarasvati, a stream often praised in the *Rig-Veda* chants. The seventh stream may have been the Indus, the river in which the Punjab's five tributaries unite. The once-mighty Sarasvati started losing its waters sometime around 2000 B.C.E. after climactic changes and earthquakes shifted the course of its headwaters.

It seems unlikely by now that Aryas caused Harappan collapse. Archaeological research has failed to find evidence of the once-postulated invasion.[3] Harappa's fall was more likely caused by a drying climate that meant such a large population could less easily be fed. Were Aryas latecomers on the scene, moving in among Harappans who stayed in the region after their culture's greatness had faded? This is what I was taught in graduate school. If it is so, Aryas nonetheless seem to have absorbed important aspects of Harappan culture: concern with purity, for example, and perhaps a prototype for the deity later called Shiva. Or were the Aryas Harappans perhaps a Harappan ruling class? The word *Arya* means "noble." Later in Indian history, it clearly referred to members of certain dominant clans rather than to a particular tribe or people. Certain new Hindu groups would love to be able to show that Aryas were Harappans, largely for political reasons. There is more about their efforts to prove this theory in this book's final section.

Luckily, this chapter needs only to recognize the problem, not to solve it. It is clear that sometime before Buddhists and Jains surfaced in India, people who called themselves Aryas did claim tribal territories across North India. They were served by Brahmin pandits and priests, who performed the sacrifices and spread the social theories on which their prestige and claim to prominence rested. As Aryan influence spread in India, Brahmin influence spread with it. Moreover, it seems likely that peoples initially outside the Aryas' sphere of influence bit by bit knit themselves into it by accepting Brahmin authority and adopting Brahmin teachings and practice.

THE WRITINGS OF THE BRAHMINS

For much of the rest of this chapter, I shall summarize these teachings and practice as described in hundreds of Brahmin-transmitted teachings and writings. Readers should understand that this description is much simpler and more consistent than the actual body of Brahmin teachings. Brahmins were intellectuals, and intellectuals love nothing more than to argue with one another and to develop new interpretations and perspectives. In addition, they were divided into different *shakhas,* or schools, depending on which Vedic collections they studied and which lineages of teachers had trained them. They also evolved many specialized roles. Some served as family chaplains; others became temple priests; still others became astrologers, healers, legal experts, and reciters of heroic tales. Many Brahmins performed no specialized religious roles at all, but simply strived to live according to pandit-developed codes and hence to serve as examples to those around them. To make things still more complex, Brahmin teachings were not static; they developed over time as the pandits who studied them applied their knowledge to new problems and new milieus. Brahmin teachings reported here are by no means complete and represent only fully developed versions of Brahmin concepts.

---

[3] Thirty-seven bodies found in the ruins of the city Mohenjodaro have been cited as proof of invasion, but it now appears that they did not come from a military conquest. See Edwin Bryant, *The Quest for the Origins of Vedic Culture: The Indo-Aryan Migration Debate* (New York: Oxford Univ. Press, 2001), 159–60. Bryant's book is the most helpful analysis to date of arguments about Aryan origins and travels.

The most important Sanskrit sources for Brahmin teachings summarized here fall into four categories. The first of these, simply called Veda, or "knowledge," is the oldest body of Brahmin-transmitted literature and the part believed to stem directly from the rishis. Brahmins claim that all their teachings are based in some way on Veda, which today consists of four collections of works: *Rig-Veda, Yajur-Veda, Sama-Veda, and Atharva-Veda.* Each collection once belonged to a particular group of ritual specialists, who used its contents as its working materials. As mentioned, the *Rig-Veda* is thought to contain the very oldest of the rishis' chants. The *Yajur-Veda* is probably next oldest, and the *Atharva-Veda* the youngest. However, all Vedic collections contain both older and newer materials because each was built up in strata consisting of four types of teachings. The oldest of these were the basic Samhitas, "collections" of chants to be recited during fire sacrifice. Next came Brahmanas, prose commentaries laying out sacrificial rituals and justifying materials used and actions taken during them. Then came Aranyakas, reflections on the secret meanings of certain rituals. Finally came Upanishads, consisting of more advanced and independent secret teachings. These texts were composed over many centuries; some chants could be more than 4,500 years old, whereas the last major Upanishads appeared around the beginning of the common era.[4]

The second oldest and most influential category of Brahmin-transmitted literature is Dharmashastra, "teachings about appropriate duty." Like Veda, Dharmashastra is a collection of literature, not a single piece of work. Its contents are somewhat more consistent than those of the four Vedas because Dharmashastra consists almost entirely of teachings about how proper Aryas should behave. The two most prestigious Dharmashastras are *Manusmriti,* often translated "Laws of Manu," assembled sometime between 100 B.C.E. and 100 C.E., and *Yajnavalkyasmriti,* assembled around 400 C.E. But many other *dharma* works exist; Dharmashastra became a major area of Brahmin specialization, and pandits who study it have added to it straight on through until the present century.

The third and fourth categories, Itihasa and Purana, are more popular in nature. Itihasa, "history," includes most notably India's two huge Sanskrit epics, *Ramayana* and *Mahabharata,* stories of ancient kings and wars still retold all over the Hindu world and reenacted in many different kinds of popular theater. Purana, "lore," covers multiple subjects extending from mythology to instructions for carving and honoring images. Brahmin tradition identifies eighteen major Puranas, as well as other minor ones. Scholars think that Brahmin pandits who assembled the epics and stories of the Puranas based them on sagas produced in courts by royal bards. The epics seem to have come close to their present shape by the fourth or fifth century C.E. Major Puranas were pulled together during a time span extending from perhaps the fourth through the eleventh centuries C.E.

From time to time in this text, there are references to materials from three other types of Brahmin literature. Upavedas and Vedangas were appendixes to Veda, extending and detailing Vedic inquiry; because these were composed in oral sayings called *sutras,* they are also sometimes called Sutra literature. Most important among these for us are Kalpa and Grihya Sutras, dealing with the greater and lesser forms of Brahmin

---

[4] Bryant has the best summary of evidence on *Rig-Veda* dating, ibid, 238–66. For a summary of recent findings on Upanishad dates, see the introduction to Patrick Olivelle's Upanishad translations: *Upaniṣads: A New Translation* (New York: Oxford Univ. Press, 1996).

sacrifice, and Dharma Sutras, predecessors to Dharmashastra. These have been dated between roughly the sixth and third centuries B.C.E. Later works of religious importance were the Agamas, guides for temple practice and ritual; most Agamas date after the eighth century C.E. A final important body of Brahmin literature was the writings produced by *darshanas,* philosophical traditions that began emerging during the early centuries C.E. These systematized Brahmin thought and ranged in coverage from logic and physics to ritual theory and metaphysics. One such darshana, called Vedanta, has become especially important to contemporary Hindu teachings.

BRAHMIN TEACHINGS

Let us turn now to the Brahmins' teachings themselves. Discussion of these teachings is divided into five sections. The first two concern precepts that, at least in theory, are directed toward all Aryas. These tell Aryas what rituals they should sponsor and how they should act from day to day. The third section looks more closely at practice proper for kings, always a subject dear to Brahmin hearts. The fourth looks at basic beliefs and premises underlying Brahmin teachings. The last takes up the fascinating theme of "secrets" that weaves through Vedic literature. The conclusion then asks what effect Brahmins had as would-be teachers in India. Who put their teachings into practice? To what extent were these observed? What long-term influence did Brahmins have?

AN ARYA'S RITUALS

Already in very ancient Vedic sources, it becomes clear that Aryan identity was tied closely to performing the right sorts of rituals. Aryas uphold the way of proper rites, *Rig-Veda* chants tell us; the *dasyus,* despised others, are riteless. Central among proper rites was the practice of making offerings to fire, an element that, like rishis, could move between the human and superhuman realms. Fire itself, Lord Agni, was a superhuman power, a deva, who showed himself not only on the hearth and in wildfire but also in lightning and the sun. Being close to humans in his hearth-bound form, Lord Agni could serve as a mediator, carrying offerings to other devas in more distant realms.

In the times of the rishis and Aryan ancestors, procedures for fire sacrifice seem to have been simple. Sacrificers installed Lord Agni on a proper hearth, chanting verses brought by the rishis to ask for Lord Agni's aid in bearing their gifts into divine realms. Other chants invited various devas to gather by the fire, seating themselves on heaps of grass laid out to receive their divine presence. Food was placed in the fire, using wooden ladles and forks. Some offerings were liquid: milk, melted butter, and *soma,* a drink made by steeping dried portions of the sacred plant *soma* in water. Other offerings were solids such as cakes made from barley and the meat of slain animals. The sacrifice fed the devas and, therefore, strengthened and sustained them. It also sought their favor so they would use their strength to benefit the humans who fed them.

A fire offering could be as small as a bit of milk poured into a home's cooking fire at daybreak and sunset. Fire rituals could also be hugely complex, providing feasts for devas and humans alike and adding several kinds of contests—gambling matches, chariot races, or poetry and riddling competitions. For reasons hotly argued by experts, such exciting features began to disappear or be tamed down around the time Aryas claimed and settled their tribal territories. The sacrifice became a technical apparatus used to control the devas and the powers they represented. More and more stress was placed on the chants, recited not for their meaning but for the mysterious power called *brahman* activated by their vibrations. The chants evolved into different types: *Rig-Veda* verses still summoned the devas, but now added to them were prose lines muttered to sanctify ritual actions, songs to celebrate soma, and spells that could mend the sacrifice if some part of it was performed wrongly. Priestly specializations evolved as different families developed expertise in their own bodies of chants and ritual practice. Even the fires became specialized; some sacrifices featured as many as seventeen hearths, each serving a different ritual purpose. In addition, any potential source of disruption was dropped from the ritual or changed to remove the disruptive parts. Contests were formalized to predetermine winners or were carried out symbolically; for example, displaying a chariot wheel could substitute for a race. Killing and eating were removed from the sacrificial enclosure. Even at a distance, animals were killed not by shedding blood, but by the more tidy means of suffocation.

Instead of satisfying the devas's needs and wills, these revised rites stressed the existence of hidden links between components of the rituals and the greater world. The sacrifice became a control system intended to adjust the world by manipulating these links. Its work was done for the benefit of a single pair of persons, the sacrificial sponsor and his wife. An adjustment made at one point in the rites could bring a child to the sacrificing pair if they had not produced one; slight changes at other points brought wealth, victory over enemies, or long life. Certain advanced and complex sacrifices claimed to accomplish still more. They pulled a special, invisible, "self," or *atman,* out of the sacrificer, then opened a path to deva realms and sent his atman venturing along that path. Having found his way once to a deva realm, this wandering self could return there after its body was burned away after death in fire. Because she was ritually fused with him through marriage, the sacrificer's wife shared this heavenly benefit.

Such opportunities were not for everyone. A sacrificer had to be twice-born, that is to say, he had to undergo during childhood a special ritual that prepared him to use Vedic knowledge. He had to be married, with a living spouse; all higher sacrifices required a wife to participate along with her husband, in part because they drew on her links to generative powers.[5] A sacrificer had to be wealthy. Even the daily milk offerings required him to own at least one cow, whereas a middle-sized sacrifice of the type called *agnistoma* required gifts of at least one hundred cows to assisting Brahmins. A potential sacrificer likewise had to be both persistent and ambitious. Fire sacrifices were cumulative; to perform a large ritual, one had to first do other ones preliminary to it. For example, before he could sponsor the midsized agnistoma mentioned above, a sacrificer had to set up three special hearths, maintain them with daily milk

---

[5] An important work exploring this issue is Stephanie W. Jamison, *Sacrificed Wife, Sacrificer's Wife: Women, Ritual, and Hospitality in Ancient India* (New York: Oxford Univ. Press, 1999); see especially Part III.

offerings, perform more complex offerings at times of the new and full moons, and complete at least one round of still more complex rites performed at the changing of India's seasons. There was an after-effect too: an agnistoma sacrificer had to keep up daily milk offerings throughout the rest of his life.

In fact, the larger ritual system became too elaborate for its own creators to sustain it. Around the sixth or seventh century B.C.E., pandits split the sacrificial complex into two components. The first, called the *shrauta* system, consisted of the complex rituals just described. *Shrauta* means "heard" and thus communicates the belief that these were the rites the rishis brought from the deva-world. This system was aimed mostly at the elites among the elite—heads of Aryan clans who wished to establish their claims to supremacy among others or Brahmins seeking a particularly exalted standing. Several of the most complex rituals described in the ritual teachings were clearly designed for use in consecrating kings.

The second system, known as the *grihya* system, consisted of rites that could be offered at the domestic hearths of ordinary householders. *Grihya* means simply "of the hearth." Some grihya sacrifices were daily prayers and offerings to devas. Some were offerings made on behalf of *pitris,* departed ancestors. Like many ancient and tribal peoples, Aryas believed that their ancestors could live on in another realm after death if proper rituals were done on their behalf. Sponsors of certain great sacrifices expected to ascend to deva-realms after their earthly deaths and cremations. Aryas who practiced only grihya rites were also cremated at death and sent to alternate realms by means of this "final sacrifice." But they traveled to the lesser ancestral realms, where male descendants kept them alive by means of monthly and yearly food offerings.

The third and largest component of the grihya rituals were a series of rites known as *samskaras,* "perfectings." These are rites of the type that scholars of religion call "life-cycle rites" or "rites of passage." Such rites exist in many cultures and function mainly to carry people safely through major transitions that occur during life. They separate people from a condition in which they existed before—childhood, for example, in the case of the puberty rituals common among such rites. They ritually remake their subjects, drawing on gods or ancestors as witnesses or assisting powers, and then reintegrate those remade subjects into a new level of life. Life-cycle rites are usually public rites, performed at least with other family members present so that not only the person going though the ritual, but all who attend it, will acknowledge that person's changed standing.

Brahmin pandits added to this basic structure the idea that samskaras shaped and perfected the people who progressed through them. Only a person perfected in such a way was truly an Arya. A samskara series began with a rite performed to secure a child's conception, continued with rites to shape and protect the fetus in its mother's womb, and progressed after birth through a number of childhood firsts: first naming, first outing, first solid food, first haircut, first earrings, first introduction to letters.[6] They came to a climax with a more elaborate ritual that made a child twice-born and introduced him[7] to Vedic learning, and then peaked again with the marriage that

---

[6] Some of these rites are older than others; the ceremony of first letters, for example, was not introduced until after Brahmins had begun to use writing extensively.

[7] In ancient times, this ritual, called *upanayana,* seems to have been performed for girls as well as for boys, but later it became restricted to boys only.

joined a man and woman and made them into potential performers of the great shrauta rituals. According to some sacrificial theorists, the shrautas themselves were just a higher level of samskara.[8] For all Aryas, the progression of samskaras ended with the funerary cremation rituals that sent an Arya to the pitris and placed his or her spirit under the care of ancestral rites.

ARYADHARMA

One concept of great importance to early Aryas was *rita*. Composers of *Rig-Veda* chants called Aryas preservers of rita, whereas non-Aryas were *anrita,* "without rita." This term "rita" is one of many Sanskrit words that have cognates in Western languages.[9] One English cognate of rita, mentioned earlier, is the term "rite," a ritual action. Another cognate is the term "right," which evokes correct behavior of any kind. Even the most ancient Vedic chants imply that a life lived according to rita does not consist of rites alone; it also entails adopting a code of right day-to-day behavior. A proper Arya had to be generous, sharing wealth gained by good fortune with others who were less lucky. Also important was hospitality, giving proper honor and sustenance to guests. Both of these values are still an important part of Hindu culture, to the great benefit of many a Western scholar doing field research among Hindus.

By the time their teachings were standardizing domestic rituals, Brahmin pandits were also compiling lists of precepts that taught followers how to live daily as proper Aryas. By this time, however, their terminology had shifted. Instead of using the term "rita" to talk about proper behavior, they used another closely related term, *dharma.* This word comes from a root that means "to bear or sustain," so dharma means, basically, "that which sustains." The word *dharma* first shows up in a chant of the later *Rig-Veda* that developed an image often cited later in Brahmin writings about proper Aryan behavior. This chant, called "Purusha-Sukta," or "Hymn of the Person," is one of several ancient Sanskrit accounts about how the world came to exist. It states that the world arose from the sacrifice of a giant person, the Purusha of its title.

The sacred fire in this sacrifice was time itself—the seasons. Many essential aspects of the Aryan world were produced by this sacrifice: the world's three layers: heaven, atmosphere, and earth; the principal devas such as Indra and Vayu, lords of storm and wind; the sun and moon; the four basic types of chants; and the domestic animals offered in sacrifice. One very important product of the Purusha's sacrifice was a four-fold human social order, in which each division of society corresponded to one portion of the sacrificed being. Out of the mouth of the great being's mouth came the Brahmins, custodians of Vedic chants. Out of its arms came Rajanyas, Aryan chiefs and aristocratic clans. Out of its thighs (that is, its sexual parts) came Vaishyas, the great mass of common Aryas whose lives were devoted to the increase in herds, food, and offspring that would make all Aryas prosperous. Finally, out of the Purusha's feet

---

[8] Brian K. Smith, "Ritual, Knowledge, and Being: Initiation and Vedic Study in Ancient India." *Numen* 33:1 (1986): 82.

[9] Cognates are words in different languages whose closeness in form and meaning shows that they have developed from a common stem.

came the Shudras, laborers and craftspeople on whose services the Aryas depended. The chant closes with the assertion *"tani dharmani,"* "These are the dharmas," that is, these are the basic structures on which the world depends.

This hymn later became the basis for a comprehensive social theory. According to this theory, the world should be imagined as a great organism, whose various parts are meant to work together like limbs and organs of a body. So long as they do so, the world as a whole will prosper. If they betray their proper natures and functions, their dharmas, then the world's sustaining order will deteriorate and collapse. Integral to this organic functioning are differing dharmas assigned to human beings, who come in the hymn's four basic types. Their respective origins from the mouth, arms, thighs, and feet of the Purusha point to the tasks that they must perform: the Brahmins chant and preserve sacred words; Rajanyas (later called Kshatriyas) take up arms to protect their people; Vaishyas maximize the powers of fertility; Shudras support the others and facilitate their work.

Brahmin pandits first developed this theory of interdependent human functions in Dharma Sutras, oral teachings put together about the same time as the Grihya Sutras. The theory became a central feature of later Dharmashastra writings, which added some crucial new features to thinking about dharma. Dharma was understood to be a kind of talent as well as a function—a warrior, for example, was a man who had a special gift for fighting. This talent was hereditary, passed on through the blood of a family. Therefore, preserving dharma came to mean not only performing the roles assigned to one's group, but also preserving proper bloodlines. One had to breed for dharma, marrying Brahmin men to Brahmin women, warrior men to warrior women, and so on. Without proper breeding, the abilities special to one's own function would be lost and dharma could not be upheld. Thus the four human types became four hereditary classes, called *varna*s by Brahmin writers, and writings on dharma spun out rules about what each varna could and could not do and whom it could and could not marry.

In addition, certain varna functions were valued more highly than others. Brahmins writing the codes valued their own roles as keepers of knowledge most, so they assigned their own varna the highest status. Brahmins had to be honored, and their lives protected, above all others. Warriors and clan chiefs were next, then common Vaishyas, and finally the servant Shudras. All three higher varnas were designated privileged groups in contrast to the Shudras. Shudras, in fact, were not true Aryas and hence were denied all access to Brahmin knowledge and rituals. They were called once-born, in contrast to twice-borns who had been through the perfecting rites and Vedic initiation.

The system of varnas was also linked to rules about ritual purity. Each varna had a range of foods that it could and could not eat, as well as stipulations about which other varnas could offer it water and prepare its food. Other rules specified how members of high-status varnas were to maintain their kitchens, eat, have sex, and even handle their morning baths and bowel movements. Brahmins had to be purest of all and hence surrounded themselves with the thickest hedge of regulations.

Finally, varna was gendered. Men were to uphold the basic varna functions. Women's most important purpose in life was to bear sons who would uphold a family's dharma. Dharma for any woman, therefore, meant to be married into an appropriate family, to serve her husband, to bear his children, and to maintain a kitchen whose purity was appropriate to her family's status. Although Aryan women in ancient times underwent the Vedic initiation and had access to Vedic learning, this was discontinued by the time of the Dharmashastras. From that time on, except in matching for marriage and rules for observing purity, all women were assigned the varna status of Shudra.

Upholding varna was not the whole of dharma. Dharmashastra taught that a proper male would structure his entire life in a way appropriate to Aryas. An ideal life progressed through four stages. These began with the initiation into Vedic knowledge that first brought a young Aryan male to the level of full twice-born status. Ideally, this ritual gave the boy over to a preceptor who took the boy into his home for eight or more years of Vedic instruction. During this time, the boy was to serve and obey his teacher, while observing complete sexual chastity. This chastity became so closely associated with the student stage that the term *brahmacarya,* used for this stage, came to mean "chastity" in later years.

When the young Arya had learned as much as the teacher judged him capable of receiving, the student was given a ritual bath, another "perfecting" ritual, and returned home to marry a girl whom his parents had chosen. Marriage brought him into the stage of *grihastha,* "hearth-holding," in which he fathered children, earned wealth for his lineage, made offerings to devas and ancestors, honored guests—especially Brahmins—and continued Vedic study. When his children were grown and could take charge of a household, he was to enter the stage called *vanaprastha,* retiring with his wife into the forest. There they would live together without sexual connection, while he intensified his study and service to the fire. Toward the end of his life came a final option of *sannyasa,* total renunciation. Having his funeral rites performed, he renounced all ties to his former life and embarked on unceasing pilgrimage to holy places. Properly observed, this fourfold arrangement ensured that an Arya would attain all the ideal aims of a twice-born's life: *kama,* sexual pleasure, and *artha,* worldly wealth and power, during the house-holder stage; dharma, responsible action, during all of the first three; and *moksha,* final release, by means of the stage of sannyasa. As will be clear later, real Aryan lives rarely turned out so neatly.

BRAHMINS AND KINGS

One reason why real practice rarely matched this ideal life is that not all Aryas were Brahmins, and the system of four life-stages clearly presupposes a Brahmin lifestyle of study and teaching. For other Aryas, such as the Brahmins' all-important royal patrons, there had to be somewhat different teachings.

The special connection between Brahmins and kings in precolonial India has been mentioned earlier. It began with the high status that Brahmin varna teachings assigned to the aristocratic clans and chiefs called Rajanyas. Most of the very high-level sacrifices were designed for Rajanyas. Itihasa literature was largely concerned with Rajanya adventures and lineages, and the epic *Mahabharata* features a huge section on the dharma special to Aryan rulers. As North Indian political structures evolved from control by tribal lineages to states based on centralized kingship, Brahmins became fixtures in many royal courts, serving as family priests, tutors, and royal advisers.[10] In effect, they provided for kings the function that political theorists call legitimation. They created an ideological and ceremonial framework that said to a king's subjects, "This person, more than anyone else, is fit to be your ruler."

According to these teachings, a king was a person who had a strong capability for *kshatra,* dominion. This was the inborn dharma (meaning both duty and talent) of Aryas born to the Rajanya varna. The king's talent for dominion allowed him to keep his subjects observing dharma and, therefore, to ensure that they lived in peace and prosperity.

To accomplish these goals, a king had to know dharma and had to be able to discern what kinds of actions would uphold dharma or threaten it. Hence he had to keep learned Brahmins near him and had to give them generous support and protection. Not only that, he should appoint one Brahmin to serve as his personal advisor and priest. In fact, the land's true ruler was the combination of a dharma-protecting warrior-king and a knowledge-possessing Brahmin, a classic combination of brains and brawn.

Moreover, the Brahmins knew shrauta sacrifices that could guarantee victory to a king and bring the extra vitality that he needed to rule effectively. Recall that some Brahmin pandits taught that shrautas were higher levels of the life-cycle rites that moved Aryas toward perfection from the first moments of their lives. By means of these great sacrifices, a king could continue perfecting himself until he reached a truly superhuman status. Brahmins taught, in fact, that kingship is achieved at differing levels. Some kings are fit only to rule their own people. Others are fit in addition to rule other kings who are their neighbors, client kings who should accept their advice, support them in war, and pay homage and tribute to them on public occasions. Some kings are even fit to rule over kings who themselves are kings over kings; today these super kings would be called emperors. Brahmin rites could move a king from one such status to another. Of course, royal sacrifices offered wonderful occasions to invite other kings to come and pay their host tribute and homage. By watching who sponsored and attended them, a king's subjects could determine their own ruler's status. Because prominent subjects also attended these public gatherings, the king could, in addition, show, through the honors he gave them, which guests enjoyed the highest place in his favor.

Giant fire sacrifices went out of style in later India, but Brahmins then designed large festivals to offer similar opportunities. Temple construction also became a new way to move upward through royal hierarchies. Kings aspiring to be kings over kings could declare themselves to be clients of deities who themselves were kings over kings among the deities. Building huge temple compounds for their divine masters, early kings endowed these with enormous wealth, perpetual gifts, and even dancing girls to serve as the deity's junior wives and entertainment. Centers for Brahmin learning were built within or near them, and village revenues were gifted to support pandits based at these centers as well as priests who kept up the temple rituals.[11]

---

[10] A good book tracing this process is Romila Thapar, *From Lineage to State: Social Formations in the Mid-First Millenium B.C.E. in the Ganga Valley* (Bombay: Oxford Univ. Press, 1984).

[11] Even today in India, a strong distinction is drawn between Brahmins who study and teach sacred texts and those who serve as temple priests. The priests are far lower in status; in fact, priests for some Hindu temples do not have to be Brahmins. This is especially true for temples whose deities are honored mainly by low-caste groups.

BRAHMIN BELIEFS

Readers may have noticed by now that this chapter has said very little about beliefs, something usually assumed to be central to any religious system. Discussion of beliefs has been purposely delayed in order to point to an important aspect of Brahmin teachings. Confessing to some specific body of tenets in the way that most Christians confess to their creeds is *not* required of someone who aspires to be an Arya. Practice is far more important. Therefore, scholars of religion describe Brahmin-taught religion as one of orthopraxis, or right practice, rather than orthodoxy, or right teaching.

Brahmins, of course, did have beliefs. The practice they advocated rested on basic premises about the nature of the world and the place of humans in it. One premise underlying all the rest, that the world surrounding humans is more than its surface, is common to all religion. Many forces operate within the world that ordinary people recognize only by seeing the effects these forces bring about. Some of these forces presupposed by Brahmin teachings have been mentioned. It is now time to treat them more systematically. They will be grouped into two categories: the personal and the impersonal.

Personal forces are those imagined as beings and described in more or less human form. These are the beings that most religion texts call "gods," "spirits," "demons," "ghosts," and so on. Most important in Brahmin-transmitted texts were the beings known as devas and *asura*s. The term *deva,* meaning "shining ones" or "belonging to the heavens," is usually translated "god" in English. But note the lower-case "g." Most devas are more like the gods of ancient Greece and Rome than like the God of Christianity, Judaism, or Islam. Devas are multiple and limited, intelligent, and creative. They control, or perhaps pervade, various arenas of the natural and human worlds that make it possible for life to survive. The Vedic chants and the sacrifice belonged first to the devas; human rishis acquired these from the deva-realms. One wishes to have the devas on one's side; therefore, devas are always invited to a sacrifice. Nevertheless, they are part of the world, not beyond it; hence higher powers can constrain and override them.

Opposed to devas are asuras. Although *asura* is usually translated "demon," this translation is misleading because asuras are not forces of evil like Western demons. Instead they are obstructive and chaotic. They take things apart rather than pulling them together. For example, they foul up creative forces set in motion by sacrifice and so are kept away from sacrificial proceedings. Asuras are so innately contrary that sometimes they act in ways contrary to their own natures. Brahmin-told stories loved to contemplate the possibility of asuras who break with dharma by refusing to be destructive.[12] Asuras fortunately tend to be less bright than devas and, therefore, usually lose when the two come into conflict. They are nonetheless quite powerful and can drive the world into major crises before devas figure out how to overcome them.

A third category of personal force important to Brahmin practice is the *pitri,* or ancestor. Pitris are dead Aryas, converted by funerary rites into vaguely beneficial beings. For the most part, they stay in their own realm, except when called to receive offerings from males of their lineage. If such offerings fail, they disappear from the

---

[12] For examples, see Wendy Doniger O'Flaherty, *The Origins of Evil in Hindu Mythology* (Berkeley: Univ. of California Press, 1976), 94–138.

universe altogether. If the dead are not made into pitris by proper funeral rites, they become destructive ghosts that can possess a family's members and ruin its good fortune.

Beings with even fuzzier functions than the pitris are *apsarasas,* female heavenly dancers who appear in Indian stories, seducing kings and powerful hermits and giving birth to remarkable children. Apsarasas have masculine counterparts known as *gandharvas,* heavenly musicians summoned in spells and rites intended to increase human fertility. These are not the only lesser beings appearing in Brahmin tales. Surfacing both in later Brahmin writings and in the literature of other teachings are a host of additional beings, many of whom may have come initially out of local traditions of India: flesh-eating *rakshasa*s who threaten people venturing into the wilderness; *yakshas,* who may be dangerous but also protect settlements and grant wealth; snake-bodied *nagas* who dwell in ponds and rivers; and tree-dwelling *devatas* who make mischief but also grant small wishes.

As numerous as such beings were in the Brahmin universe, most seem of lesser interest than the impersonal powers, perhaps because the latter were the Brahmins' special secrets and the means by which they maintained their special edge in the world. The most important impersonal power by far for Brahmins was the power from which their own name was derived: *brahman,* the power channeled by *mantras,* ritual chants. This power was rooted in mysteries at the source of the world, discussed in a later section of this chapter. A cousin to brahman was *tapas,* a power of creative heat that was linked to sexuality and fire. Tapas could be raised and channeled in two ways: by lighting and feeding fires and by physical austerities, especially sexual abstention. It became especially important to Brahmin thinking about ascetics, also discussed later.

Brahman and tapas between them furnished much of the raw energy that made it possible for sacrifice to work transformations. Still another form of energy important to sacrifice that scholars are just beginning to study is the sexual power resident in sacrificers' wives.[13] This is sometimes raised in startling ways, for example, at the climax of the elaborate royal horse sacrifice, when a queen lies down and simulates sexual intercourse with a consecrated horse that has just been slaughtered. This idea of special sexual power residing in women seems to be one important source of later thinking about *shakti,* a creative and awesome energy strong in goddesses and women.

Even this far too brief summary of beings and powers mentioned in Brahmin literature reveals the second important premise, which is the naturalness of hierarchy in the world. For Brahmin pandits, a basic and unquestioned fact of life was that some things and beings are more important than others and deserve more protection and respect. Superhuman powers come in varying degrees of significance. The brahman power raised by sacrificial chants is more important, or at least more potent, than the devas; devas are more important than the other hosts of beings; and certain devas and asuras are more important than others. Similarly, among humans, Brahmins are more important than kings, kings than ordinary Aryas, and ordinary twice-born Aryas are more important than once-born servant Shudras. Subgroups within these classes were similarly ranked so that, for example, there were higher and lower classes of Brahmins, aristocrats, ordinary Aryas, and Shudras. Kingship, too, came in varying degrees on

---

[13] Studied by Stephanie W. Jamison, *Sacrificed Wife, Sacrificer's Wife,* op. cit.

both the divine and the human levels. The premise of hierarchy was vital to sacrificial theory, for it underlay the idea of hidden links, mentioned earlier. Such links exist in the world because the world's power and objects are arranged in hierarchies. One important link often manipulated in sacrifice was the link between things belonging to different categories located at the same levels in the world's various hierarchies.[14]

A third premise central to Brahmin thinking is very common among peoples who speak Indo-European languages: the premise that our world is a place of struggle. Brahmin writings are full of stories about struggles between devas and asuras. One very prominent tale in the *Rig-Veda* recounts how the deva chief Indra battled the asura Vritra who was holding back the life-giving waters. Later stories often feature the super-god named Vishnu in stories of deva–asura battles. Vishnu is one of two divine beings that epics and Puranas locate at the very top of deva hierarchies. In fact, the term deva became too weak a term to be used in referring to Vishnu. He is a super-deva, a king of kings among the deities, a being so very potent that he sends mere fragments of himself called *avataras* into the world when he needs to fight bothersome asuras. Lord Shiva, the other male super-deva whose followers contested Vishnu's highest-ranking seat, likewise battles asuras, but he does this in a somewhat different way. Either he takes on asuras themselves, slaying hosts of them at a time, or he fathers a child who kills them. More will be said about Vishnu and Shiva as well as a super-*devi*, a goddess, when Hindu devotional movements are discussed in Chapter 3.

The struggle between devas and asuras in Hindu stories is equivalent to a struggle between rita and *anrita,* dharma and adharma. That is to say, it is the struggle that eternally goes on in the world between life-supporting order and life-threatening chaos. Devas do not win this struggle automatically. Humans must take it up within their own earthly realms. To offer sacrifice is to struggle on the side of the devas. To honor Brahmins, support their studies, and observe one's dharma is to stave off asura victory for a little while longer.

Eventually the struggle will be lost. According to epic and Puranic literature, our universe goes through alternating cycles of existence and dissolution that last for huge spans of time. At the beginning of each cycle, a fresh new world comes into being, populated with beings who fully know and observe their dharma. As time wears on, some of these beings fall away from dharma, and the world order begins to crumble. Steps must be taken and institutions created to maintain proper dharmic balance. This process continues through four ages. By the end of the first age, one-fourth of dharma has been lost. By the end of the second, one-half is gone. By the end of the third, three-fourths has vanished. By the end of the fourth age, all dharma is gone without hope of recovery. The devas are defeated, and asuras reign. But this is chaos, which cannot sustain life, and, therefore, the world collapses. It burns in the fires of Lord Shiva. Its ash dissolves in the waters of Lord Vishnu. Then it rests, like a seed buried in the earth. And it recongeals and reorganizes itself, until it is ready to emerge fresh and perfect again. Humankind is currently in the fourth and final stage of the current world cycle; hence most of the world's sustaining dharma has been lost. According to Brahmin teachings, this is why the contemporary world is in such fragile and self-destructive shape.

---

[14] See Brian K. Smith, *Classifying the Universe: the Ancient Indian* Varna *System and the Origins of Caste* (Oxford: Oxford Univ. Press, 1994).

The epics and Puranas are fairly late, as Brahmin literature goes. Furthermore, their stories of grand cycles seem to be among the later parts of the bardic traditions gathered to compose the epics and Puranas known today. They presuppose teachings called Upanishads that arose as a product of a fourth and final premise of Brahmin thinking. In ancient times, this premise was perhaps not held by all Brahmins. But at least some of them acknowledged and explored it, and eventually it became quite widely accepted. This is the premise that the world holds secrets even more profound than those revealed in most public Brahmin teachings.

BRAHMIN SECRETS

Even during the period when *Rig-Veda* chants were still being brought to the human world, some Aryas were fascinated by the idea of deep mysteries lying at the very roots of existence. Certain chants are clearly intended as riddles, using elusive and dreamlike images to point to these mysteries. One such image is that of the Purusha, "person," who was sacrificed to establish dharma. That this Purusha image was intended more as a question than an answer is shown by the fact that other chants use different images to point to the same mystery. One chant hints that creative works attributed elsewhere to separate devas may in fact all be the product of one single entity, whom it calls Prajapati, "Lord of Offspring." Another, even more elusive in its language, asserts that "That One Thing" existed before the world's start, and its desires somehow brought the world into being. Precisely how this creation occurred cannot be known because the creation occurred first and the devas came afterwards. (Remember, the devas were the source of the rishis' knowledge.)

Vedic teachings on sacrificial practice retained this idea of One Thing that existed prior to the world. Sometimes they named it Prajapati, and sometimes they simply called it Brahman, thus making the claim that their chant-power tapped the world's very deepest source of energy. Portions of the Veda called Aranyakas and Upanishads carried this idea farthest and exploited it most profoundly.

What were these Aranyakas and Upanishads? The Sanskrit word *aranyaka* means "forest" and *upanishad* seems to mean "connection" or "equivalence." Both terms imply that these teachings were not intended for ordinary ears. Forests were places of secrets in ancient India, and connections are what most Brahmin secrets were concerned with.[15] The Aranyakas and Upanishads were not supposed to be heard by ordinary Brahmins. A teacher about to impart one drew his student aside, away from other hearers deemed too ignorant to learn them. Even Upanishad style reflects continuity with the riddling tradition. Upanishads are not systematic works, but rather collections of dreamlike tidbits: stories about origins and about the discovery of secrets, conversations between teachers and disciples, guided visualizations. The Aranyakas and Upanishads seem to have come rather late to the Vedic collections; the oldest Upanishads date from about 700 B.C.E. whereas Aranyakas are a bit older. Both clearly began in speculations about the mysteries underlying sacrificial theory.

---

[15] I have followed the translation of *upanishad* accepted by Patrick Olivelle in his 1996 book *Upaniṣads,* op. cit. An older meaning offered for this term was "sitting up near," which also connotes an idea of secrecy.

The Aranyakas, which served as a kind of intellectual bridge to the Upanishads, tend to be closely linked to special portions of the rites, whereas Upanishads break free of these and set up a system of teachings that offer an alternative to the rituals. Upanishads seem initially to have been shaped by a fairly small group of people. They mention several teachers by name; the most famous are Yajnavalkya and Uddalaka.

Upanishad teachers asserted that a mysterious One does indeed lie at the source of all existence. Sometimes they called this Brahman and sometimes Paramatman, "Supreme Self," or Sat, "the Real." Supremely intelligent, unlimited, and undying, this One resides within forms of the world as well as beyond them. In particular, it resides within human beings: one famous story of the Upanishads describes how the Supreme Self shaped humans and then entered them. This entry implies that humans have within themselves a hidden, undying, reservoir of unlimited power and intelligence. Upanishad teachers usually called this hidden aspect of humans either *purusha,* "person," or *atman,* "self." Readers should note that they have met this term "purusha" previously, referring to the cosmic person sacrificed to make the world. Beware of letting these two uses of this term become confusing.

The inner purusha or atman is the true source of human life and intelligence. Ordinary humans do not come close to tapping its full potential. Different teachers offered different explanations for this limitation. Uddalaka taught that ignorance holds us back; humans simply do not know their own full potential. Yajnavalkya blamed desires, which make people attempt to control the world around them instead of seeking to understand themselves. Whatever the reason might be for this loss of touch with our divine inner person, the result is a shortfall in intelligence, power, and will, much painful frustration, and a repeated illusion of dying.

This last secret, the discovery that death is illusory, was an important innovation of Upanishad teachings. It did not mean that people do not experience death in the ordinary sense. Bodies do age and drop away. Individual life spans come to an end. Atmans continue, however, taking on new forms according to the *karma,* "works," that their bodies have carried out in the past. This idea of rebirth according to one's karma recurs in other religious teachings of India. But one of its earliest interpretations occurs in a sacrificial context. Texts on sacrifice use the term "karma" to designate rites, the actions performed during sacrifices. Therefore, the Upanishads seem to be saying that ordinary deluded people are reborn in accordance with the rites they perform. Such a claim would have been quite consistent with the older Brahmin system. New in the Upanishads was the claim that people are reborn again and again. Our lives move in cycles of birth, death, and rebirth, a claim that prefigures Brahmin teachings about the world's own cycles of birth, death, and rebirth.

Upanishad teachers who believed that desire causes human limitation also taught that no actions driven by desire could have a permanent result. Brahmin teachings about sacrifice had assumed that people sponsored the large and expensive shrauta rituals in order to gain desired benefits: children, wealth, lordship, rebirth in a deva-realm. Upanishad teachers did not deny that shrauta rites could yield such benefits, but they did deny that such benefits could be lasting. Even a king of kings who sponsored a horse sacrifice and gained deva status through it would reenter the rebirth cycle when the force of this deed ran out.

Therefore, sacrifices do not accomplish all that much good for humans. They are a sop for the ignorant. Picking up on an old Brahmin image that called sacrifices boats that ferry their sponsors to heaven, one Upanishad teacher declared that the boats were leaky. People in the know would choose a different kind of practice, rooting out the desire and ignorance that obscured their atmans. This might require them to give up everything ordinary Aryas valued. One story about Yajnavalkya claims that, after winning great wealth by means of his knowledge, he gave it to his two wives and told them he was going off to live in the forest. His younger wife Maitreyi asked him if wealth should be dear to her. When Yajnavalkya said no, she should hold the atman dearer, Maitreyi gave his other wife her share of the wealth and went to study with her husband.

The cost of the new quest was high, but the benefits were great. Aryas who knew their true selves and desired nothing else were able to free those selves from bondage and to release all of their latent power and knowledge. Living, knowers of the atman became virtually superhuman beings. Dying, they returned to the world's hidden source and stayed there in permanent bliss without future rebirth.

Note that these secret teachings set themselves up as alternatives to emerging forms of classical Brahminism. At first such teachings must have been threatening to mainstream Brahmins, who gained much of their prestige and income from presiding over various forms of sacrifice. Some scholars have suggested that the system of proper life stages was designed to counter the Upanishads because it insisted that Aryas had to spend most of their lives as hearth-holders before they set out on any higher quest. If this is true, the strategy worked. Upanishad teachings came to be understood as a truly integral part of the Brahmin system. But they were viewed as teachings for very special advanced learners, not for ordinary householders.

THE BRAHMIN IMPACT

Many Brahmin teachings seem aimed at special groups of people rather than at Indians in general. Before closing this chapter, it is necessary to ask who took Brahmin teachings seriously enough to live the full Brahmin-recommended life.

For the most part, Brahmins observed their own rules. As noted earlier, not all Brahmins became ritualists or high-powered scholars. Nonetheless, most did try to acquire some Sanskrit and to study the texts of their own heritage. Many Brahmins still are careful to marry their children to proper partners, to observe samskaras, and in general to uphold dharma teachings. Many even today maintain high standards of purity, especially in caring for kitchens and in choosing and cooking food. Some Brahmin men still know how to perform shrauta sacrifices, and a few have even sponsored multiple shrautas. This high ritual knowledge is disappearing, however; other kinds of rites have been more popular for centuries.

Some Brahmin males, too, still aspire to renounce worldly ties at the end of their lives and to immerse themselves in a full-time quest for the atman. Around the eighth century C.E., the Brahmin philosopher and Upanishad expert Shankaracharya set up a monastic order intended for high-caste renouncers. Many pious Brahmin males still retire into this order. The forest-dwelling stage of life, however, has virtually disappeared as an option for Hindu living. People who call themselves *vanaprasthis* are usually retirees who study and practice religion in their own homes. Forest retirement and full renunciation, in fact, seem always to have functioned more as alternative options rather than as successive stages in a Brahmin life.[16] Furthermore, despite Dharmashastra insistence on hearth-holding, many young men inclined toward religion have moved directly from studenthood to renunciation. As for women, Shankaracharya's order was intended only for men. Full-time spiritual practice became an option mainly for widows, who could not remarry and hence had little to do other than practice religion. Women lost access to Vedic initiation at an early phase of Indian religious history. Indeed, most lost any chance to study. For a Brahmin woman, religion came to mean marrying, obeying her elders and husband, and carrying out the vows called *vratas*. Many women, even Brahmins, turned to forms of popular devotion to fill religious vacuums in their lives. Only during the last two centuries have these patterns changed.

And what of non-Brahmin men? Indian rulers of the past aspiring to high power and prestige very often did appoint Brahmin family priests and advisors, and did support "colleges" of Brahmin scholars. Such royal sponsorship was an important means through which Brahmin teachings spread across India. Some ambitious kings underwent complex Brahmin rites of royal investiture, and inscriptions and archaeological research suggests that some went so far as to sponsor the top-level horse sacrifice. When sacrifices lost popularity and temple construction became "in," kings funded huge temple compounds that are still important centers of Hindu pilgrimage and devotion.

As for nonroyal Kshatriya and Vaishya families, it is hard to say how faithfully they followed Brahmin teachings because scholars of Indian history have not paid great attention to these social strata. Some mid-ranked groups are known to have broken with Brahmins to follow other religious teachers. Others at least partly accepted varna categories and hence claimed Aryan status and privileges. They brought in Brahmins to conduct marriages and funerals, gave them appropriate gifts and honor, and upheld the Aryan code of generous hospitality.

The vast majority of Indians, those labeled Shudras, found themselves in a strange position because Brahmin teachings had included them only to exclude them. Brahmin teachings taught Shudras their duty, but offered few rewards for performing such duty. Most once-born groups cautiously conformed to the Brahmin system, accepting more powerful peoples' claim to privilege and claiming the latter's protection in exchange for performing the services that dharma teachings assigned. Many low-level groups developed their own versions of Brahmin samskaras, especially for marriage ceremonies and funerary rites. Some even found hungry Brahmins who would assist them with these rites, although these were then despised by other Brahmins.

Shudras likewise accepted freely the Brahmin vision of social order based on occupational groups that married internally. In fact, they took to this social vision so well that some scholars think that precedents for this kind of social order must have existed in India even before Brahmin varna teachings spread in India. The social system called caste in India today consists of two layers. Below the four *varnas* laid out in Brahmin teachings, there are a large number of social groups known as *jatis*, "birth-communities." Like varnas, jatis marry internally and claim hereditary rights to certain occupations.

---

[16] See Patrick Olivelle, *The Āśrama System: The History and Hermeneutics of a Religious Institution* (New York : Oxford Univ. Press, 1993).

Often Western writings translate varna as "caste" and jati as "subcaste," suggesting that the second is just a subdivision of the first. But in fact, jati is the more important category for Hindus, who always can tell researchers their jati but not always their varna. Some scholars, therefore, think that jatis came first in India and that Brahmins developed the varnas as a simple way to classify jatis and hence to put them in order. Jati divisions seem especially important to low-ranked groups, who use them to set up their own hierarchies and standards of caste purity.

Meanwhile, Indians from all social levels picked up snippets of Brahmin teachings and told and retold Brahmin stories until some were altered almost past recognition. They freely interknit these and their shreds of Brahmin practice with customs and stories preserved in old local and regional traditions. Brahmins in turn picked up parts of this composite tradition and knit them back into their own precepts and sacred lore. The result, when added to developments encountered in the next two chapters, became the tradition known today as Hinduism.

In sum, Brahmin teachings were indeed an important force in shaping today's varieties of Hinduism. It is not surprising that Western scholars assumed for many years that they needed to talk only with Brahmins to find out what Hinduism is. Brahmin accomplishments have been considerable in India. Brahmins were India's first civilizers. They instilled a stable social and political order that functioned well for more than two thousand years. By making their brighter descendants into living libraries, they developed an effective system for storing past knowledge long before the invention of paper, printing presses, or computers. In addition, Brahmins were important social integrators. With flexible Aryan genealogies, legitimating rites, and their practice of knitting Vedic with tribal deities, they brought India's peoples together within a common cultural system. By means of their treasure trove of stories, they also transmitted important moral and social values.

As a result of Brahmin teachings, moreover, an entire subset of people in Indian society were trained so successfully in intellectual discipline that men born and bred as Brahmins became major thinkers and leaders for many Indian traditions, even those deeply critical of classic Brahmin teachings. The pages to come show how often people of Brahmin caste emerged as important leaders of renunciant movements, Hindu devotional movements, and the movements of regeneration that emerged in India during the past two centuries. The Introduction spoke of the great dynamism and creativity of India's various traditions. It is hard to imagine such dynamism evolving without the contributions of Brahmin caste intellectuals.

Brahmins also shaped and preserved a beautiful and complex language that not only could express deep emotions, humor, and precise reasoning but also served for centuries as a lingua franca that helped leaders in India's regional cultures to communicate with one another. Nor should Brahmins' contributions as diplomats, middlemen for trading arrangements, and conveyors of ideas from one region to another be underestimated. Brahmins were also a vital means for conveying ideas from rulers to their people—and very likely also from the people to their rulers. A Brahmin village in the hinterlands, indebted to a king for the land it had been given, was an important source of the information that allowed rulers to rule and an important means of implanting the political and social values that let rulers minimize use of force in ruling. Thus Brahmins helped Indian rulers preserve the peace, and peace in turn brought prosperity to both the rulers and their subjects.

Brahmin teachings nonetheless did have drawbacks. Brahmins' blatant promotion of their own privilege drew snide commentary from rival groups for centuries. Although some Brahmins were deeply respected, others came to be charged with greed and arrogance. Furthermore, the hierarchy of worth laid out in the Brahmin-defended caste system meant that many people came to be treated as substandard human beings. Even for people of high caste, Brahmin teachings could become problematic. By demanding so firmly that people follow the dharma to which they were born, these teachings left few options for those unable to carry out their precepts. What became of a woman who could not bear children, a Brahmin with a faulty memory, a Kshatriya boy born with a club foot or twisted arm? What happened to the rebel needing more challenge in life than was available in his village or family business?

Finally, Brahmin practice and teachings offered few of the three "e's" that give human existence its spice: excitement, emotion, and enterprise. There was little wonder in the Brahmin system. It offered few emotional highs or chances to vent anger or frustration. Nor was there much incentive for anyone not a king or a Brahmin to strive for self-improvement or a higher standard of living. If Brahmin teachings had stood alone in India, if they had been the only foundation for Indian culture and civilization, they would have been too stifling to last for long. They worked because they did not stand alone. Other traditions offered the alternatives and spice that were missing from them.

ADDITIONAL SOURCES

Any conventional textbook on Hinduism will offer extensive discussion of basic Brahmin texts and concepts. Klaus K. Klostermaier, *A Survey of Hinduism,* 2nd ed. (Albany: State Univ. of New York Press, 1994) makes a good reference for quick checks. Readers wishing to sample important Brahmin literature might try Wendy Doniger O'Flaherty, *The Rig Veda: An Anthology* (Middlesex: Penguin, 1981); Patrick Olivelle, *Upaniṣads: A New Translation* (New York: Oxford Univ. Press, 1996); and Cornelia Dimmitt and J. A. B. van Buitenen, *Classical Hindu Mythology: A Reader in the Sanskrit Purāṇas* (Philadelphia: Temple Univ. Press, 1978). Indian novelist R. K. Narayan has published excellent summaries of the two Indian epics *Rāmāyana* and *Mahābhārata* (New York: Viking Press, 1972 and 1978 respectively). A standard reference on Dharmashastra is Pandurang Vaman Kane, *History of Dharmaśāstra,* 5 vols. (Poona: Bhandarkar Research Institute, 1968–77). Important dharma texts in recent translation are Patrick Olivelle, *Dharmasūtras: The Law Codes of Ancient India* (Oxford: Oxford Univ. Press, 1999); and Patrick Olivelle, *The Law Code of Manu* (Oxford: Oxford Univ. Press, 2004). A Vedic fire ritual can be viewed on the video *Altar of Fire,* Robert Gardner and Frits Staal, producers (Berkeley, CA: Univ. of California, Extension Center for Media and Independent Learning, 1994).

Sources on Brahmin history are surprisingly hard to come by. Rajendra Nath Sharma's *Brahmins through the Ages: Their Social, Religious, Political and Economic Life* (Delhi: Ajanta Publications, 1977) surveys references to Brahmins in Sanskrit literature. Michael Witzel has attempted the far more difficult job of tracking the history of Brahmin schools in ancient India. See his article "On the Localisation of Vedic

Texts and Schools," *India and the Ancient World: History, Trade and Culture before C.E. 650,* Professor P. H. L. Eggermont Jublilee Volume, Gilbert Pollett, ed. (Leuven: Department Oriëntalistiek, 1987), 173–211.

Field studies of Brahmin priestly practice are also rare. To follow the rounds of *purohita*s (household priests), see K. Subramaniam, *Brahmin Priest of Tamil Nadu* (New York: John Wiley, 1974). C. J. Fuller has two excellent studies of temple priests: *Servants of the Goddess: The Priests of a South Indian Temple* (Cambridge: Cambridge Univ. Press, 1984) and its follow-up volume *The Renewal of the Priesthood: Modernity and Traditionalism in a South Indian Temple* (Princeton: Princeton Univ. Press, 2003). Old and biased, but still useful for insights into Brahmin household practice is Margaret Sinclair Stevenson, *Rites of the Twice-Born,* 2nd ed. (New Delhi: Oriental Books Reprint Corp., 1971). A good survey of different kinds of Brahmin religious specialists living in a single city is Milton Singer, "The Social Organization of Sanskritic Hinduism in Madras City," in his *When a Great Tradition Modernizes: an Anthropological Approach to Indian Civilization* (New York: Praeger, 1972), 81–147. Insight into the elite world of Brahmin gurus is offered by Glenn Yocum, "The Coronation of a Guru: Charisma, Politics, and Philosophy in Contemporary India," *A Sacred Thread: Modern Transmission of Hindu Traditions in India and Abroad,* Raymond Brady Williams, ed. (Chambersberg, PA: Anima, 1992), 68–91; see also G. R. Welbon, "Person, Text, Tradition: India's Ācārya," *History of Religions* 25:4 (May 1986): 368–77.

The vast majority of India's Brahmins are not ritual specialists. To learn about these more ordinary Brahmans, try R. S. Khare, *The Changing Brahmans: Associations and Elites among the Kanya-Kubjas of North India* (Chicago: Univ. of Chicago Press, 1970). A Brahmin male of the mid-twentieth century describes his training, practices, and attitudes in Morris Carstairs, *The Twice-Born: A Study of a Community of High-Caste Hindus* (Bloomington: Indiana Univ. Press, 1961).

2

The Sadhus

He was squatting on the terrace, wearing only a loincloth despite the chill January air, when my friend and I reached the top of the stairs to the small Shiva temple we had found during our hike in the Himalayan foothills. With his black ascetic's top-knot, flowing beard, and necklace of wrinkled brown *rudraksha* seeds, he looked liked someone dropped there from another dimension. He seemed lost in meditation. We walked on past him, our interest caught by a small roofed structure in front of the temple proper. "I wonder what this is," said my friend. From behind us came the answer, in fluent English. "It's the *dhuni,* the hearth of the Nath Yogi who lived here before me. I don't get visitors very often. Can I offer you ladies a cup of tea?"

Our host, we learned during the long conversation that followed, was a disciple's disciple of the famous twentieth-century guru Swami Shivananda. He had come to this remote place looking for quiet in which to practice his *sadhana,* spiritual discipline. The tea with milk that he served us, the small gas stove on which he cooked it, his beads, the orange robes he slipped into, the small pot he used for cooking, and the few other possessions in his small room behind the temple had all been gifts, because he may earn no money and lives only on offerings made to him. He had broken all ties with his family, with caste identity, and with status. Although still a young man, he will never marry. Even his old name was gone: a new one was taken at the initiation that brought him fully into the circle of his guru's closest disciples.

Today the most common term that Hindus use for people such as our host is *sadhu* (feminine *sadhvi*), a word usually translated "good person." Based on a very old Sanskrit root that describes a hurled object moving straight toward its target, sadhu means "good" in the sense of being able to accomplish one's aim. Had my friend and I been traveling with a Hindu on that day, we might have heard other words used to address or describe our new acquaintance. He could have been called *swami,* a polite form of address roughly comparable to the English term "Lord." Any fully ordained initiate of his guru's order of Dasanami Sannyasis is able to claim this title, which is also used to address members of northern India's old landed aristocracy. We could also have called him a *yogi,* because he practiced and sometimes taught the types of spiritual method known as *raja* and *hatha yoga.* His guru's guru Swami

Shivananda had been the teacher most responsible for modern India's great revival of interest in these disciplines. A fourth term appropriate to our host is *yati*, "ascetic," because of the rigorous self-denial that he was observing. If we had met a sadhu from a different order, or *sampradaya*, we might have heard different terms. A number of sadhu orders have existed in India. Although some ideas and practices are common to them all, they differ sharply regarding others.

Three major sadhu-based heritages survive in Hindu India today: the Dasanamis or swamis, to which our host belongs; the Naths, also often called yogis because of their hatha yoga practice; and finally a cluster of groups from the Vaishnava tradition known collectively as *vairagis*. Other important sadhu-type figures are *nagas*, militant ascetics linked to the Dasanamis, yet often resembling the Naths in practice. These living traditions, as well as several that came before them, are a focus of this chapter, which will also look more closely at *yoga* and the closely related set of teachings and practice called *tantra*, important to several sadhu traditions. But the first focus is on the ideas and practice that sadhus hold in common.

One set of ideas most sadhus share is a premise that humans are beings held in a special type of bondage that limits their potential and subjects them to rebirth. The mechanism of this bondage is karma, a force that people set in motion through past thoughts and deeds. Within each person lies a center of power and intelligence, usually called a soul in English, that can bring freedom if only that person can tap into it or separate it from karma. To do this, people must understand the sources of their bondage and\or must put into practice a proper spiritual method.

Methods used by sadhus to break the hold of karma vary from physical austerities to forms of mental retraining, such as study and meditation. But all entail some form of renunciation. At the most extreme, this may be a break with all forms of civilized behavior: wearing clothes, grooming one's hair, eating cooked or cultivated foods, speaking politely. At the least, one may simply renounce some attitude that normally accompanies an action, for example, the expectation that one should always gain some payback for one's good behavior. Most commonly, sadhus renounce the social institutions that consume human energies and bind us with attachments: marriage, family, property, caste, or class status.

In exchange for the social ties they have given up, sadhus commit themselves to a *sampradaya*. This word, usually translated as "order" or "sect" in English, literally means "transmission," with a double implication. On the one hand, this transmission is a body of teachings first given shape by a sampradaya's founder, then developed and handed on by the founder's followers. These teachings explain the nature and causes of human bondage, the method or methods that bring freedom, and the nature of that freedom when it is won. Sampradaya teachings usually also justify the authority of the transmission's founder: Where did he get his teachings? How did he receive them? What makes him so special that other people should listen to his message?[1] These teachings function as a kind of sampradaya Bible. They are its raison d'etre, its purpose for being. In theory, all members should know them and should strive to protect and spread them. In fact, as in Western churches, most sampradaya members know only fragments of their heritages.

---

[1] The pronouns "him" and "his" are not used generically here. No sampradaya founder has been a woman, although several do initiate women members.

In fact, a sampradaya member does not have to know any teachings at all. One becomes a sampradaya participant with full privileges simply by being joined to the transmission in its second sense, the series of bonds between people forged by initiations that gurus of the tradition give to their disciples. A guru is a spiritual guide, usually a highly accomplished teacher, who is usually granted this status by his or her own guru or by other acknowledged masters of the community. The guru should be able to trace his or her spiritual lineage through a succession of recognized gurus all the way back to the sampradaya founder. Such a lineage, in Sanskrit a *guru-parampara,* is thought to transmit not only the knowledge that is the sampradaya's heritage but also a portion of the charisma, the power, of the founder and successor gurus. Being initiated by a guru and hence attached to the guru's parampara is to participate in a transforming power that will help make one's spiritual methods successful.

Once initiated, the new sadhu will take up the sampradaya's symbols, including a name that identifies the sampradaya or its subgroup to which the sadhu belongs. He will honor sampradaya gurus, especially his own. He will acquire his lineage's privileges—the right, for example, to stay at certain temples, monasteries, or camping grounds in a holy city. He will also assume its responsibilities, such as teaching lay disciples, if the sampradaya follows such a practice. A sadhu will be buried with his sampradaya's rites (sadhus are usually not cremated), and his remains will be placed in a tomb in its own graveyard. Dead or alive, the sadhu can never return to his or her original family. Some sampradayas go so far as to include funeral rituals in a sadhu's initiation to remind the new renouncer that the person he or she has been is gone completely.

SADHU ANTECEDENTS

Where did all of this come from? How did sadhu traditions get started? Scholars have identified at least four likely sources for sadhu teachings and practice. One has already been encountered—the tradition of forest-dwelling, mystery-probing Brahmins who developed Veda's secret teachings and taught them to disciples. According to Brahmin theories about the four stages of life, such forest-dwellers were the equivalent of retirees who moved away from their villages when they had finished with household life. But descriptions found in ancient texts seem more complex, as if many were people pursuing an alternative lifestyle. They lived in small settlements known as *ashramas,* "hermitages," sometimes along with wives, dependent children, and disciples who had come to them for instruction. They tended sacred fires and lived off forest produce such as berries and nuts, covering themselves with cloth made of pounded bark or leaves.

Added to these, or perhaps just representing one extremist branch in their tradition, were forest ascetics, often called *yatis,* "reined-in people," or *tapasvis,* "people who command inner heat." Every so often a text introduces us to a figure who has stood upright without sleep for years while wearing few clothes and exposing his body to the elements. Or perhaps he stands on one leg observing a vow of silence or practices the "discipline of five fires" sitting between four blazes with the sun beating down upon him. Such figures are usually loners or clustered in small groups in austerity groves, regions within forests. Some tend fires; some do not. Most eat hardly anything. Some are clearly of Brahmin origins; others had a broader range of backgrounds. According to Buddhist legends, the Buddha, born a *kshatriya,* followed this type of extreme practice before discovering his path of moderation. The forest ascetics' practice was based on theories that such tortures raise inner heat called *tapas* that burns karma from a soul much as a good refiner burns impurities out of metal. Given the importance of heat and heat imagery to such practice, it was probably an offshoot of the fire-based Vedic ritual complex.

Other possible antecedents to the sadhus were the wandering ascetics called *munis,* "sages," or *vratyas,* "vow-takers," in ancient Sanskrit texts. Several types of such figures may have existed in ancient India, because words used to describe them differ. Some are "hairy"; some wear "turbans"; some are clothed in "dirty yellow"; others wear black. Some seem linked to Rudra, an early form of the yogi-god Shiva who is lord of poisons and healing herbs. The wandering ascetics practiced out-of-body trances, perhaps induced by means of breath manipulation. They did not use sacred fires, nor is any fire imagery used to describe them. Some scholars, therefore, suggest that they were not of Aryan origin, but instead came from tribal groups knit into the Aryan complex. Whether Aryan or non-Aryan, they closely resemble the trance-traveling shamans who were religious leaders among ancient peoples of central and eastern Asia.

Final sadhu predecessors of great importance were the wanderers known in ancient texts as *shramanas,* "strivers." Perhaps these were simply descendants of the ancient trance-travelers, seen more clearly in later sources. They are known in far greater detail because two shramana groups survive and have preserved their own literatures. In classical India, these were known respectively as Jainas, "descendants of conquerors," and Bauddhas, "descendants of the Enlightened Ones." Today, they are called Jains and Buddhists.

Jains and Buddhists were not the only shramana groups of ancient times; they were merely the groups that survived longest. Buddhist stories name five other shramana leaders who taught in the Buddha's region during his lifetime. One, named Makkhali Goshala, founded a lineage of naked shramanas called Ajivikas that competed with Jains and Buddhists for more than a thousand years before dying out. Shramanas shared much of the teachings and practice that remain current among sadhu groups of India. They believed in rebirth and karma and taught that karma keeps humans in bondage. They followed teachers who had unlocked the secrets of this bondage and offered methods by which disciples might escape it. Such methods required practitioners to renounce, to break ties that bound them to the world around them. In the beginning, all shramanas followed a wandering lifestyle, moving from town to town begging for their living, although, like sadhus, some Jains and Buddhists modified this into year-round living in monasteries. All also observed, during the wandering phase of their lifestyles, the custom of "rain retreats," staying fixed at one site during the Indian rainy season when roads become impassable.

Shramanas differed from sadhus mainly in two particulars. They were organized somewhat differently, calling their communities *samghas,* "assemblies," rather than sampradayas and swearing allegiance to their path and community rather than to individual gurus. They also approached Brahmins somewhat differently than do sadhus. Sadhu sampradayas by and large live in peace with Brahmins; in fact, the most prestigious, the Dasanami Sannyasi Sampradaya, consists largely of former Brahmins and has many Brahmin lay-initiates. The shramanas were fierce Brahmin rivals, to the point where one famous Brahmin grammarian compared this rivalry to the enmity between snakes and the mongoose, a small snake-killing mammal.

JAINS AND BUDDHISTS:
THE NASTIKA TRADITIONS

Perhaps because of this rivalry, Brahmin pandits created a category that defined shra-mana groups outside of proper religion. All Indian religious communities, they declared, could be separated into one of two divisions. Some were *astikas,* believers in a supreme reality. Astika corresponds roughly to the Western term "theist." Others, including Buddhists and Jains, were *nastikas,* "atheists." Like their counterparts of today, these two terms cannot be taken too seriously as descriptors of the teachings thus labeled. Instead, they are "us and them" terms. *Astikas* were "ours," that is, Brahmins felt they could live with them. *Nastikas* were "not ours." Brahmins wished they would shut up shop and go away. As a result of this division, later writers from Western traditions eventually classified Jainism and Buddhism as separate religions. But they did not seem so wildly different in their time. Nor do they seem very different to many Hindus of today, who often regard Jains and Buddhists simply as early sadhus. As a matter of fact, today Indians call Jain renouncers sadhus, just like those in orthodox sampradaya lineages. Moreover, certain new temples built to promote Hindu unity include Jain and Buddhist shrines along with those for classical Hindu deities.

In this chapter, Jains and Buddhists are treated as if they were early sadhus, and they are studied to see how they understood the relationship between karma and human bondage. This relationship is important to sadhu traditions because it deter-mined which methods various sadhus followed. In essence, Jains defined the karma–bondage relationship in materialist terms and hence offered a materialist method of winning freedom. Buddhists defined the relationship psychologically and hence offered a psychological method. Once this major distinction was established, it set precedents for later groups, which can be categorized as either materialist or psycho-logical in their basic orientation.

Jains

Jainism may well have been the oldest of the shramana traditions. Jains can trace their teachings back at least to Mahavira, a man who lived in northeastern India during the later sixth and early fifth centuries B.C.E. But Jains claim that Mahavira was just a bril-liant re-interpreter of teachings extending back to Parshva, who lived two centuries earlier. Furthermore, Parshva himself is linked to a still earlier line of teachers.

All stories told of Jain teachers follow the same pattern. Some crisis occurs in the teacher's life, leaving him weary of worldly living. He renounces his old life and hits the road, subjecting his body to many harsh practices. Finally, he has a breakthrough that grants him full knowledge of our entire world system and how it works. He sees in a vision how rebirth occurs, how karma affects this, and how karma's hold on humans can be broken.

Jain ideas about rebirth are the most far-reaching in all of the sadhu traditions because they claim that any form of existence on earth can be reborn into any other form. A man can become a rock or a water or a fire molecule. This is because every form of existence is built up around an entity called a "life," a *jiva.* A jiva is like a Western "soul," in the sense that it is undying, immaterial, the source of a body's vitality, and able in its unborn state to know anything it wants to. However, it extends throughout a body rather than dwelling at some fixed point inside it. It has acquired its embodiment not through some divine gift, but rather as the result of contamination. Its contaminant is karma, which, according to Jain teachings, is a kind of physical substance attracted to the jiva as a result of its actions. Karma comes in different varieties, and all actions attract some subtypes. But the worst types of karma are pulled in by acts of violence and aggression.

Once drawn to a jiva, karma materializes and limits it, giving it a body and set of physical characteristics, a lifespan, and a determined level of basic luck and intelligence. All these have natural lifetimes and hence gradually wear out, only to be replaced by karma drawn in by subsequent actions. To liberate the jiva, one must, therefore, accomplish two aims: purge from one's jiva all the karma that infects it and prevent further karma from attaching to the jiva. To accomplish the former, Jains have used ascetic techniques: fasting, standing or sitting still for long times, and exposing themselves to the elements, as well as milder practices such as confession, study, meditation, and service to senior members of their communities. To accomplish the latter, they observe thorough-going forms of five moral restraints: avoiding harm to others, lying, sex, stealing, and ownership.

One special feature of Jainism, like other sadhu-based traditions, is that nonrenouncing Jains could also practice moderate forms of the Jain discipline. These householding disciples became quite important because they furnished food and other supplies that allowed the renouncers to keep up their practice. Any sadhu tradition that grew to any size had to attract and hold a solid base of lay disciples. This meant that few renouncers could turn their backs on the ordinary human social world completely. Between periods of retreat, they taught and advised disciples much as did learned Brahmins. Like Brahmins, they too became potent sources of "merit"—the good karma that a pious person gained by offering gifts to a person of spiritual worth. Some even used the knowledge of the world gained in the course of their wanderings to carry on worldly pursuits such as spying for benefactors, guiding trade caravans, or even running their own trade networks.[2] It is no wonder that they, like Brahmins, often drew generous support from kings.

Buddhists

Even more successful than Jains in attracting royal support were the several subgroups of shramanas today called Buddhists. Their name came from their founder, known popularly by the title of Buddha, "Enlightened One." He lived sometime between the sixth and fourth centuries C.E., probably somewhat later than Mahavira.[3] Like Jains, later Buddhists believed that the Buddha who lived at this time was just the most

[2] An important work citing evidence of sadhu business dealings is Suraji Sinha and Baidyanath Saraswati, *Ascetics of Kashi: An Anthropological Inquiry* (Varanasi: N. K. Bose Memorial Foundation, 1978); see especially pp. 79–81. See also D. H. A. Kolfe, "Sannyasi Trader–Soldiers," *Indian Economic and Social History Review* 8 (June 1971): 213–20.

[3] Older scholarship located his birth date during the second half of the sixth century, but work done by German scholar Heinz Bechert challenges this. See *The Dating of the Historical Buddha,* Vol. 3, Abhandlungen der Akademie der Wissenschaften in Gottingen Philologiasche-Historische Klasse Dritte Folge, 189, 194, 222 (Göttingen: Vandenhoeck & Ruprecht, 1991–97).

recent in a long line of teachers. However, he was not someone else's disciple; he gained his whole teaching by means of his own discoveries. Like Jain founder stories, Buddhist legends claim that the Enlightened One was born a Kshatriya in a powerful family. He hit a crisis—an obsession with the existence of human pain—that led him away from home on a religious quest in which he tried out but rejected teachings and paths of other shramanas. Finally, sitting alone under a tree, he experienced a series of visions that brought him understanding.

Rebirth and its causes were as important to the Buddha's teachings as they were for Jains. Life's transformations could bring a migrating being into any of six rebirths: into the human, animal, *deva,* or *asura* realms, into a series of hells where one was punished for bad deeds, or into a realm where one became an ever-hungry being who suffered as a result of not doing good deeds when a chance to do them had arisen. Karma determined where one found oneself at the time of rebirth. But here Buddhists hit a snag. Alone among shramana groups, they denied the existence of an eternal self or soul, holding that such an idea leads to egotism and that egotism is a major source of humanity's problems. So instead of portraying rebirth as a process by which a soul acquires one body after another, they imagined it as a chain reaction in which one self sets off another and the new one another, each imprinted with something of the old self's past.

Because there is no permanent substratum for this process, Buddhists also could not portray karma as a thing affecting another thing. They had to think of it as a force, an impetus, that propels a person through life and from one life into the next. This impetus is maintained by psychological attitudes, mostly by the greed that keeps people pursuing desires left unfulfilled in their lives. This greed, they pointed out, is itself maintained by other forces, such as self-centered thinking and ignorance.

Because the causes of bondage for Buddhists were principally psychological, the path that Buddhists evolved was psychological also. It involved three components. The first was cultivating moral, nongreedy behavior—that is, learning to live one's life in a basically self-controlled way and learning to use only what one needed. Buddhists rejected Jain austerities because these had no purpose, but still cultivated a lifestyle that avoided sex and property, life's greatest temptations to greed. The second component of the Buddhist path was meditation, viewed as a discipline that would help a person calm, understand, and control an always restless and self-aggrandizing mind. Finally, a third important component was study, which helped Buddhists both master their own difficult teachings and re-perceive the world in such a way that they would be less likely to cling to it and keep themselves trapped by greed.

Buddhists called their path a "middle way" and rejected other shramana paths as extremist. Buddhist renouncers wore saffron robes, shaved their heads, allowed lay disciples to invite them for meals, and swiftly left behind much of their wandering lifestyle in favor of year-round living in monasteries. In contrast, one branch of Jains, the Digambaras, wore no clothes. Jains pulled their hair from their heads by the roots, accepted only leftovers for their meals, engaged in prolonged fasts, and remained wanderers for much longer than the Buddhists, although they too became monastics at some points in their long existence. (Today, Jains have returned to a wandering ideal.)

Both Jains and Buddhists must have seemed extremist to neighboring Brahmins, because they admitted to their communities not only twice-borns, but also members of despised groups, such as shudras and even outcastes. Moreover, their renouncers included women, some of whom became famous and honored teachers. This and their dangerous claim that worth is gained through achievement rather than birth are what labeled them *nastikas*—not wanted, on Brahmin terms. On the other hand, the success they gained and the model they established by organizing prompted some Brahmins to organize groups of renouncers less hostile to their traditions.

Pashupatas and Their Successors Even some very ancient Sanskrit literature mentions loner ascetics living in ancient India, but Vedic references to such figures are so sparse and fuzzy that it is impossible to tell what traditions these figures came from or how they might be connected to Brahmin-preserved traditions. One especially intriguing figure mentioned in *Rig-Veda* chant is a *kesi,* "hairy man."[4] The hairy man is a soul-traveler who drinks "poison," probably a drug to aid him in his trances. He is clothed in dirty yellow or perhaps in yellow dirt, signifying that he might be naked. Moreover, he is connected to the deva Rudra, an early form of Shiva. Rudra is a problem figure in the study of the Vedic tradition. Although recognized as a deva, he is often treated as an unwelcome outsider. Chants associate him with death and ask him to stay away. A famous story from ritual writings recounts how he once attacked and scattered the sacrifice; now he must be bribed to leave it alone. In epic stories, Rudra wanders the wilderness dressed as a tribal hunter. He sometimes seems more an asura than a deva, more inclined toward dissolution than toward saving order.

The reason why Rudra's hairy devotee is so interesting to scholars is that centuries after his chant found its way into the *Rig-Veda,* a group of male ascetics looking much like the "hairy man" showed up as pioneer figures of Hindu sadhu traditions. These early Shiva ascetics were the Pashupatas, devotees of Shiva as Pashupati, Lord of Creatures. Pashupatas wore long, matted hair during some stages of their practice. They coated their bodies in ashes, recalling the yellow dirt of the chants. Cultivating trance and crazy behavior, they were no friends to orthodoxy, even though some sources claim that all Pashupatas were Brahmins. Although today Pashupatas are listed among Hindu lineages and are considered important forerunners of Hindu Shaiva traditions, in their day many Brahmins disliked them as much as they disliked Jains and Buddhists. Hence Pashupatas too were often labeled *nastika* or "outside the Vedas."[5]

According to their own legends, the Pashupatas were founded when Lord Shiva descended into a Brahmin corpse and brought it back to life—a way of claiming that this Brahmin, named Lakulisha, was Shiva in a human body. Lakulisha attracted four disciples and taught them a path of freedom and self-transformation. He seems to have been a real person, although nothing of his life is known other than this legend. He most likely lived some time during the second century C.E. in the region of western India that is now the state of Gujarat. His followers spread throughout India and became important enough to be noted in many writings and inscriptions.

Although the Pashupata tradition is now extinct, a few sources describing it have survived. According to them, Pashupatas believed that three kinds of reality exist in the world: *pati,* the Lord and Creator (that is, Shiva), *pashu,* or "creatures," that is, souls, and *pasha,* "fetters," the bonds of karma and matter. The Lord is all-knowing

---

[4] *Rig-Veda* 10:36.

[5] See David N. Lorenzen, *The Kapalikas and Kalamukhas: Two Lost Saivite Sects* (Berkeley: Univ. of California Press, 1972), 10–11.

and all-powerful, but he creates by shaping the world, not by transforming his body into it as Prajapati does in Vedic teachings. The Lord descended into the world in the form of Lakulisha to bring to creatures the path that will bring them freedom.

Because the fetters binding creatures are real and material, the Pashupata path, like the Jain path, required harsh austerities at its higher levels. It was divided into five stages, of which the first two are the most distinctive. In the first stage, a Pashupata disciple went to live with a guru and other disciples on the grounds of a Shiva temple. There he lived nearly naked, bathed daily in ashes, took instruction from his master, and spent much of his time in acts of worship to Shiva. In the second stage, he put on ordinary clothes and went back to live in the midst of everyday society. But while doing so, he acted crazily, snoring when awake, twitching his limbs, staggering while walking, talking and acting nonsensically, and making "amorous gestures" toward women. He did this so that people would avoid and abuse him. According to Pashupata teachings, abusers absorbed his bad karma, while he acquired the good karma they had earned for themselves. After this period of courting abuse, he returned to his ashes and ascetic's symbols and went off to live alone, first in a cave and then in a cemetery. Meditating constantly and eating only food that came to him without asking, he passed through three remaining stages of self-transformation. At the highest stage, he won freedom from all pain and karmic bondage and was linked to Shiva eternally. Because this state also entailed winning perfect power and intelligence, he became in effect a duplicate Shiva.

One characteristic of sadhu traditions has been their vulnerability to splitting. One can easily see from their organization why this is so. Each disciple of the tradition strives to become an enlightened guru. Each guru, having attained a very high level of insight, is thus qualified to add his or her own special "spin" to the tradition. If the spin is distinctive enough to break from the old tradition, a new sampradaya separates from the old one. Pashupata lineages split several times, with spin-offs moving in opposite directions. Some grew more respectable, shedding crazy behavior, studying Brahmin writings, and settling down year-round in monasteries. One such spin-off, the Kalamukha lineage, became a major force in central South India until the thirteenth century C.E, when it lost out to competition from devotional movements.

Other offshoots of the Pashupatas moved toward greater radicalization, increasing anti-social behaviors and building a reputation that cast them as "bad guys" in many a Sanskrit story. Kapalikas, for example, were said to use skull-bones for begging bowls and to perform human sacrifice.[6] They hung around cremation grounds and practiced magical rites in which they reawakened corpses and turned them into servants. How much of this is true is anybody's guess. But they did dress in a way that identified them with some of Shiva's more frightening aspects. Moreover, they did tinker with rites intended to bring them earthly power rather than liberation.

Much of the responsibility for this shift comes from increasing interest among more radical Shaivas in teachings called Tantras that began spreading in India after the sixth or seventh century C.E. These affected a number of renunciant communities,

---

[6] Lorenzen, ibid., is the best source on both these Kapalikas and the Kalamukhas; see also his "New data on the Kapalikas," *Criminal gods and demon devotees: Essays on the Guardians of Popular Hinduism,* Alf Hiltebeitel, ed. (Albany, NY: State Univ. of New York Press, 1989), 231–38.

including some Jains and Buddhists. But they became most highly developed among the more radical Shaivas. Their most important living offshoot is the sampradaya of Naths, also known as Nath Siddhas, Kanphata Yogis, or Nath Yogis. This is the group behind much of the yogi lore that has spread to the contemporary Western world. It is also the group whose mountaintop yogi maintained the hearth that set off our encounter with the sadhu described at the beginning of the chapter. Because yoga and Tantric teachings were so important to the Naths, they will be discussed later, after these teachings are taken up.

The Dasanami Sannyasis During the years 630–644 C.E., India had a distinguished visitor—a Chinese Buddhist monk named Hsuan Tsang, who had come to see the Buddhist holy places and to seek teachers who could help him understand the Yogachara tradition of Buddhist philosophy. Hsuan Tsang traveled widely during his long stay in India and wrote an extensive memoir after returning to China. His account is a treasure for scholars of Indian religious history because it allows us to assess the strength of various shramana and sadhu groups of Hsuan Tsang's time.[7] Hsuan Tsang, of course, was interested mostly in Buddhists; he recorded many Buddhist establishments, especially in northeast and southeast India. His memoir shows that Buddhism was declining. Some pilgrim sites were abandoned, and many monasteries had far fewer renouncers than they had been built to hold. Rival renunciant communities were quite visible, however; descriptions he gives of their hair and clothing suggest that he met both Jains and Shaiva sadhus. Apparently Brahmins of Vedic heritage faced a great deal of competition during the early seventh century.

At some time between Hsuan Tsang's visit and the beginning of the ninth century, the Brahmin philosopher Shankara set out to reassert Brahmin prestige and to put shramanas and Shaiva radicals in their places. Shankara was born in South India, in what is now the state of Kerala, according to his best-known biography. Even when very young, he showed great intellectual talent and took the vows of a *sannyasi,* a Brahmin renouncer. Traveling north to the Narmada River, Shankara found a teacher of the Advaita Vedanta tradition. According to this teaching, which is based on the Upanishads, all forms of existence are transformations of the one reality brahman. After Shankara's teacher taught the young genius all he could, he sent Shankara on to Banaras, an ancient holy city of northern India famed as a seat of Brahmin learning. Later Shankara moved again to the pilgrim center of Badari in the Himalayas, where he wrote commentaries on various Upanishads, on the famous philosophical work called *Brahma-Sutra,* and on the *Bhagavad-Gita,* another famous scripture. For the rest of his life, he traveled and taught in defense of his own very strict interpretation of Advaita Vedanta, which holds that nothing exists outside of brahman. Liberation consists of knowing in the deepest fiber of one's being that this is true and that therefore one is already united with brahman. Shankara's work on Advaita Vedanta brought him the title of Shankaracharya, "Shankara the Master Teacher."

The biography that furnishes this information does not tell us how Shankaracharya became a founder of monasteries. But other accounts report that during his travels, Shankara got the idea of organizing sannyasis along the lines established by other renunciant communities. Although Brahmin renouncers had existed since ancient

---

[7] Hiuen Tsiang, *Si-yu-ki: Buddhist Record of the Western World,* trans. Samuel Beal (Delhi: Oriental Books Reprint Corporation, 1969).

times, they had not come together in organizations and were disadvantaged when competing with organized renouncers for disciples and patronage. Shankara set up four head monasteries in the north, south, east, and west of India and installed disciples there to organize the sannyasis of their regions. The result was the sampradaya of Dasanami Sannyasis. *Dasanami* means "having ten names" and reflects a peculiar feature of this sampradaya. It is divided into ten subdivisions, each of whose cluster of lineages adds a distinctive surname to the religious names of its members. Each head monastery has two or three subdivisions affiliated with it. Three of the ten subdivisions take only Brahmins as members, whereas the rest accept all twice-borns. Brahmin influence remains strong throughout the whole, and Dasanamis follow mostly teachings of Shankara and his Advaita Vedanta teaching.

What does this mean for practice? Dasanamis are closest to the Buddhists in their outward observance. They shave their heads and beards periodically and do not let their hair become matted. They wear saffron robes and live on gifts. Many carry distinctive staffs. Like our host of the mountain temple, many also wear the Shiva rosary-necklace of *rudraksha* seeds, for Shankaracharya was a Shiva devotee as well as a Vedantist, and Dasanamis today are classified as Shaivas. They are addressed by the title Swami, "Lord," reflecting the high status of the *varnas* from which they were formed. Today, many people simply call them swamis, rather than using the more inclusive term sadhu.

Many Dasanamis wander during some periods of their lives, following the precedent set by ancient Brahmin renouncers. But most also spend extended periods living in communities called *maths*, or monasteries. This is because their method of gaining liberation is study. According to Dasanami teachings, ignorance is what separates human beings from their true nature and destiny. Knowledge is what frees us. But this is deep knowledge, full realization, not just the conceptual knowledge that human beings acquire from reading books. Therefore, like Buddhists, Dasanamis have to change delusive mental habits. To accomplish this end, they may make use of yoga meditation, especially the "eight-limbed" form developed by the Brahmin teacher Patanjali.[8] Also like Buddhists, Dasanamis avoid severe austerities.

Their learning, moderation, and large Brahmin membership won them support among the middle and upper-caste groups that had patronized Buddhists. As Dasanami fortunes rose, the Buddhist decline quickened. After the thirteenth century C.E., Buddhism vanished from India; Buddhist sects existing there now were all reintroduced in the twentieth century.

Vaishnava Sampradayas

The Dasanamis are so prestigious in India that a number of new Hindu organizations have connected themselves to Dasanami subdivisions. This is how our tea-serving yogi acquired the right to call himself a swami; his guru's guru Shivananda took initiation from a Dasanami guru. If one counts all such newer affiliates, Dasanamis may by now be the largest community of Hindu sadhus. They vie for this standing, however, with Ramanandis, another group whose origins require further explanation.

Around the time Hsuan Tsang toured India and the young Shankaracarya began his rise to fame, a movement was stirring in South India that would change the direction and focus of much Indian religion. Fuller description of this devotion-based

---

[8] See pp. 55–56.

movement must wait until the next chapter, but for now readers must know that it was centered on the super-gods of the Sanskrit epic and Puranic traditions and it asserted that devotion to God could by itself bring devotees to liberation. One advantage of the devotional path was that it did not require its followers to renounce families or economic activity. The ideal of the renouncer-saint nonetheless remained strong, and several devotional movements did give rise to renunciant orders. Among Shaivas, one that became quite successful was the Virashaiva movement, whose renouncers supplanted earlier Kalamukha sadhus in much of their previous territory.[9]

Among Vaishnavas, several groups established lasting sadhu orders. The first and most prestigious of these was the Shri Vaishnava Sampradaya, founded in the eleventh century by the Tamil philosopher Ramanuja. Others of importance were the Nimbarkis, Brahmas, and Gaudiyas, founded respectively by Vaishnava philosophers Nimbarka and Madhva and by the great Bengal saint Chaitanya. However, the most numerous and influential Vaishnava sadhus are the Ramanandis. Legends say they were founded by a sadhu saint named Ramananda, who lived and taught in Banaras during perhaps the fourteenth century C.E. Stories told about Ramananda's life are so vague and contradictory that ethnologist Richard Burghart has argued that he may have been an invented figure. Burghart suggests that the order bearing Ramananda's name started as a coalition of earlier groups too small to withstand larger groups' competition.[10]

One striking feature of Ramanandis is their inclusiveness; like the ancient shramanas, they accept both women and low-caste males as sadhus. Ramanandis usually wear white or yellow robes and their rosary-necklaces are carved of light brown wood from the *tulsi,* or "holy basil," Vishnu's sacred plant. Their hair may be long and matted or twisted in a bun, and their foreheads are painted in some combination of white centered on red: the white for Lord Vishnu and the red for Shri Lakshmi, Vishnu's consort-goddess.

Ramanandi practice varies hugely. For some sadhus, it consists solely of devotion to the epic hero Rama and his wife Sita, believed by many Hindus to have been gods living on earth. These devotee-sadhus spend much of their time performing services of worship in which they act out the roles of servants tending a royal prince and princess. Other Ramanandi sadhus combine devotional practice with ancient forms of austerity. These may look and act very much like radical Shaivas, going about naked, for example, and bathing themselves in ash. One seeming paradox of Ramanandi sadhus is that some are married. This is allowed, they say, because true renunciation means breaking attachment to the world around them, not turning one's back on life in the world itself. Because they stress breaking attachment, Ramanandis and other Vaisnavas also prefer that people call them *vairagis,* "passion-free people," rather than using the category sadhu.

The Nagas

Before leaving this listing of sadhus, mention must be made of one category of groups that are technically suborders, but important because they are highly visible—and highly problematic. These are nagas, militant ascetics, most of whom are affiliates of the Dasanami Sannyasi order. Nagas wear loin-cloths or go naked and have long

---

[9] Kalamukhas were discussed on p. 51.

[10] "The Founding of the Ramanandi Sect," *Ethnohistory* 25 (1978): 121–39.

matted hair like radical Shaivas. Often drawn from lower caste groups, they were first recruited during the sixteenth century to protect the higher-caste order. That century was a time of frequent warfare in India, which raged not only between Mughals and rival rulers, but also between sectarian groups such as Shaivas and Vaishnavas.[11] Naga recruitment gave the Dasanamis a comfortable edge over rival Ramanandis until the Ramanandis organized militants for themselves. Naga lines were probably not created from scratch, but rather wooed from small Shaiva groups whose histories have been lost. In North India's unstable medieval period, it was not unusual for people pushed off their lands to attach themselves to bands of ascetics. These in turn sometimes hired out as mercenary soldiers to gain a source of income. An alliance with the prestigious Dasanamis would have been a step toward acceptance and stability.

Nagas often carry tridents or spears and bathe in ash like older radical Shaivas. They live together in mother houses called *akhadas,* training centers, and the discipline acquired there still includes martial arts, although naga battles ended under British rule in India. In other practice, many naga subgroups are close to the Naths, the surviving line of radical Shaivas. For example, like Naths, some nagas practice hatha yoga and maintain Nath-style *dhunis,* hearths with perpetual fires. Some even wear the massive earrings acquired during high-level Nath initiations. Together with the Naths themselves, these Nath-like nagas are an anomalous subgroup among sadhu traditions. Their aims and worldview differ in significant ways from those of mainstream sadhu orders.

Yoga, Tantra, and Naths

Naths are often called yogis in popular Indian usage, although they dislike this title because it seems to connect them with a very low caste group, the *jogis.* In Sanskrit, the term *yogi* means "one who follows a yoga, a spiritual method." In this sense, virtually any sadhu can be called yogi. Why, then, should Naths in particular be called yogis when most other sadhus are not? The answer is that Naths practice a special kind of yoga, one developed by their founder Gorakhnath. This is the method known as *hatha yoga,* which needs to be put in the context of India's yoga traditions.

The term *yoga* will be familiar to many readers. They may have very different ideas about its meaning, depending on the context in which they have encountered it. Some have learned about yoga by reading *Yoga-Sutras,* teachings that are popular among several new Hindu movements exported to the West during the last century. These teachings are attributed to a Brahmin named Patanjali who lived in India around the start of the Common Era. He calls his yoga a method for stilling mental turbulence and is careful to say that it is not his own invention, but just an attempt to put together existing practice. This would have been Brahmin practice, developed in the tradition that based itself in teachings of the Upanishads. The amount of attention given to breath in very early Upanishads suggests that Brahmin forest teachers induced trance by using techniques of breath manipulation. Patanjali put these

---

[11] For materials on sadhu battles, see Richard Burghart, ibid., and David N. Lorenzen "Warrior Ascetics in Indian History," *Journal of the American Oriental Society* 98:1 (1978): 61–75. Peter Van der Veer discusses Ramanandi nagas in *Gods on Earth: The Management of Religious Experience and Identity in a North Indian Pilgrim Center* (London: Athlone Press, 1988), 130–40.

techniques together with others and offered the world an "eight-limbed method," very likely intended as a Brahmin alternative to the "eightfold path" of Buddhists.

Like the Buddhist path, Patanjali's method can be divided into three components. First come *yamas* and *niyamas,* basic training in self-restraint. Yamas parallel Buddhist and Jain moral restrictions: harmlessness, truth, chastity, respect for property, and non-coveting. Niyamas add classic components of Brahmin discipline: cleanliness, austerity, equanimity, study, and devotion. Next in Patanjali's method come a set of three physical disciplines: *asana,* quiet sitting; *pranayama,* breath restraint; and *pratyahara,* withdrawal of sense activity from the outer world. Finally came three states of high-level mental discipline: *dharana,* focus; *dhyana,* opening; and *samadhi,* total concentration. Patanjali's exercises had the same purpose as other sadhu-based disciplines; they sought to free the human soul from the matter that has entrapped it. But entrapment is viewed as mental; people are caught by their own distractions. Therefore, Patanjali aimed at producing an undistracted person.

Although Patanjali left no lasting sampradaya of his own, his teachings were known and studied among several sadhu traditions. Dasanamis certainly knew and used his work, as did some more conventional Shaiva lineages. Patanjali's method was probably also known to the Bhagavatas, the Vaishnava sect that compiled the poem known as *Bhagavad-Gita.* Bhagavatas nonetheless gave the term *yoga* a different spin, the second form in which many readers have met it. The *Bhagavad-Gita* is quite popular among Hindu groups of the West and is important both to Vedanta and to Vaishnava devotional teachings.

The *Bhagavad-Gita,* or "Song of the Blessed Lord," is part of the *Mahabharata,* India's longest and most complex epic.[12] It consists of teachings given by Krishna, a human "descent" of God, to the mighty warrior Arjuna, who falters on the battlefield because he becomes confused about how to choose the proper course of dharma. Shall he fight and kill his gurus and his cousins, who are lined up against him in the opposing army? Or shall he escape his agonizing situation by becoming a sadhu and seeking wisdom? Krishna rejects renunciation as it is known by sadhus and tells Arjuna that he must cultivate a higher form of yoga. He should not renounce the actions demanded by his warrior's dharma—which in this case entail killing his gurus and cousins. But he must instead renounce attachment to the karmic fruits of his actions, by giving his thoughts and will over to God.

In the course of making this argument, Krishna lists three forms of yoga appropriate to those who are followers of dharma. The first, *karma-yoga,* is the path of sacrificial rites and proper behavior prescribed in *dharmashastra* teachings. The second, *jnana-yoga,* is the quest for secret knowledge carried out in Brahmin forest-teaching traditions. The third, *bhakti-yoga,* is a path of devotion to God, which includes the other two when they are carried out with proper knowledge and attitudes. The whole suggests that a proper yogi is someone who seeks to know God and to act according to the path that God has laid out—that is, the path of orthodox Brahmin dharma. The *Bhagavad-Gita's* yogi is therefore a person "in the world but not of it," to steal a famous line from the Christian tradition. The single thread connecting him to Patanjali's yogi is the premise that both aspire to master their own turbulent, wayward minds.

---

[12] Many *Bhagavad-Gita* translations exist. I use Winthrop Sargeant's, which includes a text and word-for-word gloss (Albany: State Univ. of New York Press, 1994).

Both Patanjali's yoga and the *Gita's* may seem very alien to readers acquainted only with the "exercise yoga" taught in gym and TV classes, which stresses control of the body rather than the mind. The postures that this cultivates are part of the hatha-yoga tradition, which is rooted in the same heritage as Patanjali's yoga, but take it in a different direction. These postures are elaborations of the phase of Patanjali's practice *asana,* proper sitting, which ensures that the body is quiet and withdrawn from the world's activities. Hatha-yoga exercises aim at an external control of the body that in turn precedes efforts to harness and unite internal energies. To understand its efforts, it is necessary to take one more detour and look at the Tantric theories that underlie its practice.

Tantra is a category of secret religious teachings of India that began to gain popularity among religious elites during the fifth or sixth century C.E. It is not known exactly how these teachings got started; they appear to blend Brahmin and tribal traditions, with perhaps a dash of influence from Chinese Taoist Masters.[13] Tantra takes its name from the texts that guide it, which themselves are called Tantras, meaning "looms," that is, frameworks upon which a fabric of meaning is woven. Tantras are deliberately ambiguous writings, phrased in symbolic language that must be unpacked by oral commentary to make sense. They are written this way to keep uninitiated readers from trying to use them and misdirecting their power. Tantras claim to be divine revelations, given directly by God to a gifted disciple-initiate or sometimes "overheard" by someone eavesdropping on a divine conversation. They distinguish themselves from Veda as a source of religious knowledge, and some Hindu sects consider them even higher than Veda in spiritual authority.

One striking feature of the Tantric movement is that it affected virtually all religious communities of its time. Buddhists and Jains evolved their own forms of Tantric practice. Vedanta-based Brahmins produced Tantric lineages. Tantric subgroups exist among India's Vishnu-centered communities, and much of India's temple ritual has been influenced by Tantric theories and Tantric forms of practice. Tantric teachings flowered especially among Shaivas of the old radical traditions. These are the versions scholars usually cite as models when they write introductions to Tantrism in general.

Much Tantric theory is based on a premise that energies flow through the human body and the world that are scattered and weak under everyday circumstances, but potent and transforming if brought into proper balance with one another. Instead of striving to free some part of themselves from these bodily energies, Tantric yogis tried to raise and harmonize them. By doing so they believed they could become god-like, existing in the world without normal human limits. Tantric practitioners called up these energies by means of techniques of meditation such as visualizing deities and placing them in one's body, chanting special sound-sequences, imitating divine gestures, altering breathing patterns, and drinking special "life-extending" potions. The most extreme and notorious Tantrics practiced techniques of ritualized sex aimed at changing sexual fluids into immortalizing "nectars" or ingesting items usually forbidden to strivers, such as intoxicants and meat.

---

[13] For evidence of Tantric-Taoist connections, see David Gordon White, *The Alchemical Body: Siddha Traditions in Medieval India* (Chicago: Univ. of Chicago Press, 1996), 61–66. White is principally interested in exchanges of alchemical materials and methods, but where methods and materials change hands, ideas can transfer also.

Extremist Tantrics acquired a reputation for magically raising corpses at cremation grounds, use of human bones as ritual implements, and worship of horrific female deities. In Tantric art, male gods were portrayed with female consorts, and, especially in Shaiva Tantras, a goddess is often the source of the new Tantric revelation. In Tantric theory, this goddess is *shakti,* the creative energy that brings the world into being. Because shakti is strong in all females, many Tantric lineages were more open to women teachers than were most other sadhu lines. In fact, many Tantric groups classified as Shaiva are actually Shakta in orientation. In Shakta sects, female deities and powers are more important than the masculine. The Naths themselves had important Shakta antecedents, most notably a so-called Yogini Kaula, a phrase that translates "lineage of female yogis."

Most Nath lineages name as their founders either of two Tantric teachers: Gorakhnath, master of hatha-yoga, or Gorakhnath's guru, known as Matsyendra or Matsyendranath. Matsyendranath and Gorakhnath have been dated anywhere from the first to the seventeenth century C.E.[14] Their history is extremely hard to unravel, because both have become hugely popular folk heroes of North India. It is said that they lived for centuries, roaming the countryside with bands of yogi disciples and getting themselves and their followers into and out of trouble. Their magical feats are prodigious in these stories, as are the scrapes they get into. In one tale, for example, Matsyendranath becomes trapped in a land of women sorcerers and drained of his memory and sexual power. Gorakhnath goes to rescue him disguised as a female musician and shocks his guru back to awareness by killing, skinning, and then restoring Matsyendranath's son. When the women attack, Gorakhnath turns them all into bats.[15]

It is hard to know whether any memory of real events remains in these often-hilarious stories. Matsyendranath may be a wholly fictional figure, but Gorakhnath seems more tangible, because the Naths preserve books signed with his name. Religion scholar David White has argued that Gorakhnath lived in the twelfth or thirteenth century and was a reformer of Tantric practice, whereas Matsyendranath represents earlier Shakta groups who became "prisoners" of their passion for Tantric sexual ritual.[16] Like other Tantric works, Gorakhnath's writings on hatha yoga include a great deal of sexual imagery. But the union that Gorakhnath's writings talk about is a union of energies within one individual, not an actual sexual union between male and female yogis.

Gorakhnath's hatha-yoga practice begins with the Tantric premise that the central problem for humans is not how to escape existence, but rather how to acquire super-human power while still enjoying one's life and world. The main way to do this is by uniting cosmic energies that reside within all human bodies. Three categories of energy are especially important. The first consists of "hot" energies linked to fire and the sun. These are understood to be female and located in the right side and lower end of the body, especially around the sex organs. The second consists of "cool" forces linked to the moon and to water, located in the head and left side and understood to be masculine. Mediating between these are forces of breath and wind, having

---

[14] For a summary of arguments about their dating, see George Weston Briggs, *Gorakhnath and the Kanphata Yogis* (Calcutta: YMCA Publishing House, 1938), 228–50.

[15] As retold in White, *op.cit.*, pp. 136–37.

[16] *Ibid.*, pp. 234–5.

indeterminate gender and traveling through the body by means of three channels running along the human backbone. The outer two channels carry the inflow and outflow of normal human breathing. The middle one is usually empty. A skilled yogi, however, by stretching out breaths and stopping them between in-breath and out-breath, can pump up a column of inner breath along this central channel. As it rises, it penetrates *chakras,* energy centers strung out along it like wheels mounted along an axle. Each chakra is a site where the body's male and female energies can be brought to awakening and union.

Linked to all this is a theory of sexual fluids which claims that a person's life and power depend on retaining these fluids. During an ordinary lifespan, sexual fluids drain away, and their loss causes the process known as aging. Hatha yogis visualize this process by saying the fluids are drunk by a female power Kundalini, portrayed as a snake curled at the base of the body's central channel. Kundalini's mouth is wrapped around the organ that produces the fluids; her body blocks the channel's entrance. Although in most human beings she is fast asleep, her mouth nonetheless drains the body's life force.

All of these channels, centers, and energies belong not to one's physical body, but to a "subtle body" of energy centers that one's physical body overlays. One cannot see chakras or Kundalini in a dissected body, but a yogi feels them as they awaken. Practice begins by pumping the breaths to awaken Kundalini, shift her position, and open the base of the central channel. Then she rises along it toward the head, lifting a drop of the precious sexual fluid. As she ascends, she wakes one chakra after another, finally reaching the highest, where the body's store of male energy awaits her. Male and female energies unite, changing the sexual fluid into a drop of the nectar of immortality. Now the yogi redirects this throughout his\her body, in this way negating all karma and aging. The yogi who can do this is a *siddha,* "successful one."

Naths claim that a yogi good at this process can live for hundreds of years, as did Matsyendranath and Gorakhnath. He\she will also acquire a long list of *siddhis,* superhuman powers. Villagers of North India who have Nath yogis living nearby ask them for help in controlling the weather, driving off snakes, keeping well-water sweet, and curing barrenness in women. Naths, they say, know other people's thoughts and are aware of events going on far away. Some can travel like the wind from one place to another, can be in two places at one time, can see even when blind, and can stop film from registering their images. When Nath siddhas decide to die, they can set the time when they will do it. As that point, they have a choice. They can proceed straight to liberation or they can relax in the paradise of the siddhas, a place between earth and heaven through which high mountains extend. From here they return to earth at will, to play among humans during as many lives as they like. Such stories of siddha paradises are most likely the source of tales heard in India about yogis who live in the mountains for thousands of years and descend now and then to check up on humans.

Not all Naths are sadhus. Many married "householder Naths" live in northwest India, where the Nath order is strongest.[17] These are not mere advisees and donors like the householder disciples of most other sampradayas. Householder Naths go through

---

[17] See Daniel and Ann Grodzins Gold, "The Fate of the Householder Nath," *History of Religions* 24:2 (November 1984): 113–32.

at least some Nath training and, like sadhus, may serve villages as resident wonder-workers. In addition, male sadhus at times take consorts, a custom most likely derived from their Tantric origins. Nath sadhus can be recognized by robes dyed in *gerua,* a rusty, bloody-looking red. Like other Shaivas, they wear rudraksha rosary-necklaces and smear themselves with ashes or draw horizontal lines in ash across their foreheads. Many Nath subgroups wear huge clay earrings inserted into a slit cut through their ears' central hollows. Some also cut the membrane between the tongue and floor of their mouths so they can roll their tongues far back into their throats. Both the cut tongues and the split ears are said to help them circulate drops of immortality through their bodies.

A Nath staying in any place will always keep nearby a *dhuni,* a small fire-pit whose flames are kept going day and night. This fire pit is a kind of alter ego; when a Nath dies, it is often kept up as a memorial. Such a fire pit, protected by a small roof, set off the sadhu encounter described at the start of this chapter. Another familiar memorial linked to Naths is the *samadhi,* a tomb consisting of a small dome on a square base that looks a bit like the Buddhist monuments known as *stupas. Samadhi* is the Sanskrit term for the highest level of yoga trance. Calling tombs samadhis suggests that Naths do not die, but just pass into very long trances. Like many other sadhu*s,* Naths are buried, not cremated. This practice, too, suggests that death is quite different for them than it is for an ordinary person.

EFFECTS OF SADHU TRADITIONS IN INDIA

It is time to turn to the question that ends all of the chapters in this part. What did the sadhus accomplish in India? How did they help shape Indian religion and culture? Answering such questions is not easy because sadhu traditions are so disparate. Nonetheless, several contributions stand out clearly.

First, sadhu paths provided an outlet for the restless and those needing to know what lay behind the borders of their own valleys. If in one sense a sadhu renounced the world, in another sense he or she embraced it. Becoming a sadhu meant leaving one's village and traveling to places that few people one knew had ever visited. Some sadhu and shramana communities offered education to people with no chance to secure it otherwise. Sadhu paths also brought a second chance to those who had botched previous lives, to misfits, or to those who fell between society's cracks: orphans left without care from relatives, sons whose families did not have enough land to support them, daughters widowed young, rejected childless wives, girls too plain or rebellious to be easily married.

Second, sadhu achievements checked Brahmin pretensions, disparaging arrogance, while offering models of purity and quests for self-perfection that prodded Brahmins to live up to their own standards of behavior. Competition from sadhu and shramana philosophers also must have spurred Brahmin creativity. As noted earlier, kings whose lands held rival Brahmins and shramanas loved to sponsor debates between those groups' learned thinkers. Facing such tests periodically must have challenged all groups to keep intellectual skills growing. Like Brahmins, shramanas and sadhus became leaders of India's intellectual life. During the first millenium B.C.E., Buddhists ran India's most famed universities.

Third, sadhus were connectors, especially sadhus who followed wandering lifestyles. As they traveled, they carried news of the places they saw and the people they met.[18] Like Brahmins, they spread common values through India. People who shared such values could live, trade, and work together while avoiding the feuds that tear social systems apart. Like Brahmins, sadhus and shramanas brought intelligence to kings that helped the kings rule effectively. Often, too, they were valued guides to traders. Some became important traders themselves.

Fourth, sadhu traditions introduced a principle of merit and an avenue of mobility into the Indian social order. At least in principle, sadhus were honored not for what their families had been, but for their own spiritual achievements. With pasts wiped out, they remade themselves and were honored for what they became as a result of this process. In some sadhu orders, a person could enter as a low-caste nobody and end life as a beloved teacher with hundreds of disciples vying to touch his feet.

Finally, sadhus brought a sense of wonder to India. Sadhus were India's substitute for Superman—not all of them, to be sure, but those who were advanced in their disciplines. Although the stories of wonder that grew up around Naths have been stressed, all sadhus of high level were and still are believed to be wonder-workers. They add sparkle and mystery and the hope that miracles can happen to the worlds of ordinary people whose day-to-day lives are humdrum and boring. I have heard Hindus tell stories about holy sadhus who came to their village for a while and then disappeared. Always such accounts convey a feeling that something amazing happened, that the storyteller was brushed by a life-altering presence.

This could not be accomplished easily. Sadhu and shramana paths were harsh. One could not enter them lightly; and once given a full commitment, they demanded all of a person's time and energy. This made them still inaccessible to all but the rarest persons at the lowest of India's social strata. For the most part, they remained an option only for India's three highest caste groups. The movements that would firmly join humbler people to Hindu symbols and practice are the *bhakti* traditions of the next chapter.

ADDITIONAL SOURCES

Western readers will find a good entree to sadhu traditions in Austin B. Creel and Vasudha Narayanan, *Monastic Life in the Christian and Hindu Traditions* (Lewiston, NY: Edwin Mellen Press, 1990). A famous essay on the renunciant ideal is Louis Dumont, "World Renunciation in Indian Religions," *Contributions to Indian Sociology,* n.s. 4 (April 1960): 33–62; see also Romila Thapar, "The Householder and the Renouncer in the Brahmanical and Buddhist Traditions" in *Way of Life: King, Householder, Renouncer,* T. N. Madan, ed. (New Delhi: Vikas, 1982). Patrick Olivelle has translated several important Sanskrit texts relating to renunciation; see his *Samnyāsa Upanisads: Hindu Scriptures on Asceticism and Renunciation* (New York: Oxford Univ. Press, 1992); also *Renunciation in Hinduism: a Medieval Debate* (2 vols., New Delhi: Motilal Banarsidass, 1986–87); also his translation of Yādavaprakāśa, *Yatidharmasamuccaya:*

---

[18] I am indebted to the late and much-missed Kendall Folkert for pointing out to me this important sadhu function, which he observed during field studies in Jain villages of Gujarat.

Rules and Regulations of Brahmanical Asceticism (Albany: State Univ. of New York Press, 1995); and his article "Ascetic Withdrawal or Social Engagement," *Religions of India in Practice,* Donald S. Lopez, Jr., ed. (Princeton: Princeton Univ. Press, 1995), 533–46.

The best source on Kapalika and Kalamukha history is David Lorenzen, *The Kapalikas and Kalamukhas: Two Lost Saivite Sects* (Berkeley: Univ. of California Press, 1972). Ramanandi history figures prominently in William Pinch, *Peasants and Monks of British India* (Berkeley: Univ. of California Press, 1996). Ramanandis are also covered in several important field studies. Richest is Robert Lewis Gross, *The Sadhus of India: a Study of Hindu Asceticism* (Jaipur: Rawat Publications, 1992); see also Peter Van der Veer, *Gods on Earth: The Management of Religious Experience and Identity in a North Indian Pilgrim Center* (London: Athlone Press, 1988), and Richard Burghart, "Wandering Ascetics of the Rāmānandī Sect," *History of Religions* 22:4 (May 1983): 361–80. Sadhus at a single pilgrim center are studied in Suraji Sinha and Baidyanath Saraswati, *Ascetics of Kashi: an Anthropological Inquiry* (Varanasi: N. K. Bose Memorial Foundation, 1978). European-born sannyasi Agehananda Bharati recounts his own experiences in *The Ochre Robe: An Autobiography* (Garden City, NY: Doubleday, 1970). David M. Miller and Dorothy Wertz explore monasteries of several traditions in *Hindu Monastic Life: the Monks and Monasteries of Bhubaneswar* (Montreal: McGill-Queen's Univ. Press, 1976).

Two classic studies on yoga are Mircea Eliade, *Yoga: Immortality and Freedom* (Princeton: Princeton Univ. Press, 1958) and Jean Varenne, *Yoga and the Hindu Tradition,* Derek Coltman, tr. (Chicago: Univ. of Chicago Press, 1976). David Gordon White has done fine work on Tantra. See *The Alchemical Body: Siddha Traditions in Medieval India* (Chicago: Univ. of Chicago Press, 1996) and his anthology *Tantra in Practice* (Princeton: Princeton Univ. Press, 2000). White and George Weston Briggs, *Gorakhnath and the Kanphata Yogis* (Calcutta: YMCA Publishing House, 1938) offer the best historical resources on Naths. For an entertaining sample of Nath lore, try Ann Grodzins Gold, *A Carnival of Parting: The Tales of King Bharthari and King Gopi Chand as Sung and Told by Madhu Natisar Nath of Ghatiyali, Rajasthan* (Berkeley: Univ. of California Press, 1992).

Fine photographs of sadhus can be found in Dolf Hartsuiker, *Sādhus: India's Mystic Holy Men* (Rochester, VT: Inner Traditions International, 1993), although this book emphasizes their more sensationalist aspects. A more straightforward photographic collection portrays the Kumbh Mela, a great meeting of sadhus that occurs every three years: Jack Hebner and David Osborn, *Kumbha Mela: the World's Largest Act of Faith* (La Jolla, CA: Entourage Publishing, 1990). Sadhus of very different traditions are portrayed in Denis Whyte's three-video series, Sadhu*s: India's Holy Men* (Princton, NJ: Films for the Humanities and Sciences, 1995).

Readers wishing to learn about women sadhus can start with Catherine Ojha, "Feminine Asceticism in Hinduism: Its Tradition and Present Condition," *Man in India* 61–63 (September 1981): 254–85; also [as Clementin-Ojha] her "Outside the Norms: Women Ascetics in Hindu Society," *Economic and Political Weekly* 23:18 (April 30, 1988): WS34–36. See also Lynne Teskey Denton, "Varieties of Hindu Female Asceticism," *Roles and Rituals for Hindu Women,* Julia Leslie, ed. (Delhi: Motilal Banarsidass, 1992), 211–31, and Ursula King, "Effect of Social Change on Religious Self-Understanding: Woman Ascetics in Modern Hinduism," *Changing South Asia: Religion and Society,* K. Ballhatchet and D. Taylor, eds. (London: Univ. of London, 1984), 69–84.

3

Bhaktas and Shaktas

She sat cross-legged in the old armchair crammed into a corner of the tiny apartment she shared with her teenage son and daughter. Although she worked very hard, it was all she could do to keep this modest roof over their heads. Now tears slid from her closed eyes as she sang for me the song she had written casting her troubles at the feet of her beloved goddess. Filling a niche in another corner was the miniature "temple" at which she offered daily devotions to that goddess, Vaishnodevi. Crowding it were framed pictures of Vaishnodevi, both in her quasi-human form of a lovely young woman with a tiger behind her and in her self-manifestation as the three stalagmite stumps seen by pilgrims who make the twelve-kilometer climb to Vaishnodevi's mountain shrine. My friend has made that climb many times, although she admits that the trail becomes harder as she and her knees grow older. "The singing carries me," she says. "We sing all the way as we go up there." "We," in this case, means the group of devotees who pool funds to rent a bus for the long trip to the start of the pilgrim trail.

My friend's sister is guru to a circle of Vaishnodevi devotees and runs a small Vaishnodevi temple and ashram near the ancient holy city of Hardwar. This sister has never married, preferring to live like a female sadhu. But my friend is the more classic devotee because even while "in the world," she yearns all the time for her goddess like an impassioned lover. And it is she who, like the great saints of old, composes songs to pour out her longing. She, in fact, represents two important traditions in India. She is a *bhakta,* one whose religious discipline consists of giving herself over in love to her deity. She is also a *shakta,* one who worships a female form of divinity.

Her tradition of yearning devotion to a single god goes back to at least the sixth century C.E. Like the sadhu traditions, it is a complex heritage, the product of many teachers and groups that can differ widely. All, however, share the trait of having an intense personal relationship with some deity whom they call their source and savior and who will one day end their pain. Most celebrate that deity in poetry and song in languages spoken by ordinary people. Many are ordinary people themselves, with spouses, children, and jobs, although some devotional movements have also produced important sadhu lineages. Some bhaktas are of high caste; others are lowly. Some are men and others women. Most believe that God values devotion above caste distinctions. Unlike Brahmins and major sadhu lineages that have diffused through the whole of India, devotional movements tend to be regional. The songs and following of a particular saint or saints spread principally in lands where their songs' language is best understood. Thus in this chapter, it is necessary to pay close attention to geography.

DEVOTIONAL ANTECEDENTS

To locate the most ancient roots of devotionalism in India, one must go back to the time when India's most visible religious teachers were Brahmins and their shramana rivals. Most descriptions of India's religious history create the impression that the teaching and practice of these two groups was the only religion of their era. This impression is quite distortive; in fact, disciples of these two groups were probably not even a religious majority. Much religion of the time consisted of doing honor to local and tribal spirits. Buddhist and Jain accounts of their founding years often mention such spirits. Some are *devatas* who live in certain species of trees and grant small favors in exchange for offerings. Some are *nagas,* snake-spirits who guard hoards of wealth at the bottom of forest lakes and springs. Some are bloodthirsty *rakshasas,* who seize careless travelers in wilderness regions. Others are *bhutas,* restless ghosts of the dead whose kin have not brought them to proper rest. The most complex are *yakshas,* who sometimes are man-eating jungle-dwellers like rakshasas and sometimes are tutelary spirits who protect human settlements or particular family lineages. Unlike Vedic devas, these beings were territorial, bound to specific places and people. Some had stone or wooden images carved of them, worshiped via the series of offerings called *puja.* Although their usual shrine was a fenced-in sacred grove, some were housed in richly decorated temples surrounded by gardens and high walls.[1]

As Brahmin and shramana traditions spread across India, they absorbed deities of local traditions rather than attempting to erase their worship. Buddhists told tales about how the Buddha converted this or that local deity. Brahmins identified locals with Vedic deities or located them within divine families and entourages.[2] The compilers who assembled the epics and Puranas were especially good at doing this. Two devas of the old Vedic tradition—Vishnu and Shiva—became especially popular foci for such absorptions and evolved into super-devas.

Vishnu began as a deity mentioned just a few times in the *Rig-Veda.* His most famous *Rig-Veda* hymn celebrated three giant steps that carried him into the highest heaven. Later ritual texts on ritual called the sacrifice Vishnu. This identification with sacrifice may explain why Vishnu grew so important in later writings. By the time of the epics and Puranas, he had become a God beyond all others, except for Shiva and the Goddess. Not only was Vishnu identified with other beings who had once been independent deities, he also acquired lists of *avataras,* descents, who came to earth to rescue dharma whenever it was threatened. Some avatara stories are clearly remakes of older Vedic stories about Vishnu, such as the tale of a dwarf avatara who turns into

---

[1] See Ananda K. Coomaraswamy, *Yakṣas,* 2nd ed. (New Delhi: Munshiram Manoharlal Publishers, 1980).

[2] Undoubtedly often in response to local initiatives; see references to the process called "Sanskritization" in the introduction to Part I, p. 17.

a giant and takes three huge steps that re-win the earth from a conquering demon. Others recast stories that must have been widely known in Asia, such as the tale of the fish avatara who saves Manu, ancestor of humans, from a world-covering flood. Other avataras are epic heroes, such as *Ramayana*'s Prince Rama or the *Mahabharata* figure Rama Jamadagni. Even teachers who are rivals to Brahmins can be avataras; the Buddha appears on several lists as do some Jain Tirthankaras. The most famous avatara is Krishna, a cowherd and epic prince so important that one sect devoted to him drops the avatara identity and simply calls him Supreme Deity.[3]

The super-deva Shiva, like Vishnu, is mentioned only rarely in the *Rig-Veda,* which knows him by the name Rudra, "Howler." Even in the *Rig-Veda,* Rudra displays the ambivalent nature that shows up in later tales of Shiva. On the one hand, he is a master healer and lord of medicinal herbs, and on the other, he is a killer: people beg him to keep his sharp arrows at a distance. In ritual texts, Rudra acts like an asura, threatening to break up the sacrifice. Yet the *Shvetasavatara Upanishad,* composed before the turn of the Common Era, gives Rudra the alternate name Shiva, "Beneficent," and calls him the One God who is source of all life. Later stories of Shiva stress his awesome power, used to destroy demons, to father a child of incredible might, and to catch the Ganges River in his hair as the river descends from heaven to flow upon the earth. Shiva always remains an outsider, hovering beyond life's normal boundaries. He lives in jungles or on high mountains, especially the Himalayan peak Kailasa. He wears the garb of a hunter or yogi, and is often called Pashupati, "Lord of Animals."

In classical Sanskrit literature, Shiva has no avataras, although at times humans encounter Shiva himself on earth.[4] Other gods were attached to Shiva by finding a place in his family. One important god connected to Shiva in this way was Murugan, worshiped by Tamil-speaking peoples of South India. Tamils honored Murugan well before Brahmins and shramanas carried their teachings from the north to the Tamil region. Brahmins absorbed Murugan into their catalogue of deities by identifying him with Skanda, a son of Shiva born after Shiva married the mountain goddess Parvati. Even as a child just three days old, Skanda\Murugan was so mighty that he killed a terrible asura whom no other god could defeat.

Parvati herself was a third nexus knitting local deities together. Even today, along the slopes of India's northern mountains, in the eastern states of Bengal and Assam and old western desert kingdoms, along the wild hills dividing north from South India, and on through thousands of southern villages, goddesses are the principal local and tutelary deities. Like Shiva, these goddesses are not always kindly; some manifest in disease and receive worship to keep it away. Others are powerful warrior-women who take up weapons and fight against evil; many of these are guardian-deities for Kshatriya clans. To their worshipers, such goddesses seem independent of one another. And yet they are also one, because all are identified with Parvati, bride of Shiva. Some local goddesses are even married to Lord Shiva during annual festivals— or they return to their home towns with great fanfare, making their annual visit from their marital home where they live with Shiva.

---

[3] The Pushti-Marga or Vallabhacarya sect, discussed on page 81.

[4] Now, however, people sometimes speak of teachers considered Shiva avataras. Many attributes of Hindu divinity that have "taken" over the years are now used freely for almost any divinity.

Trying to track relationships between these various deities can be tricky because their stories were put together by different groups, not all of whom understood those relationships in the same way. Some of the texts containing these stories were produced by Brahmins called Smartas, famed for their efforts to pull many traditions into synthesis. It may have been Smarta Brahmins who first came up with the idea that all Hindu deities are "faces" of a single power that extends beyond them. Other texts portraying relationships between various deities were products of sectarian groups promoting worship of one god to the exclusion of others. These told stories and produced writings that called their own god Supreme Deity and made all others subordinate. At least two such groups were active by the early centuries C.E. One, already introduced, was the Pashupata sampradaya, devoted to Shiva. It was probably founded during the second century C.E. The second, whose members called themselves Bhagavatas, "those who belong to the Blessed One," was devoted to Vishnu and probably started a few centuries earlier. An ambassador from the Greek colony of Bactria, northwest of India, declared himself a Bhagavata in the year 115 B.C.E. It is not known who founded the Bhagavata movement or how it was organized and led. Brahmins must have played an important role because the movement produced literature in Sanskrit, the language sacred to Brahmins. Moreover, it did not challenge classic Brahmin teachings, but rather conformed them to its own devotional viewpoint.

This viewpoint is most visible in the most celebrated Bhagavata product, the *Bhagavad-Gita*, the interlude in the Sanskrit epic *Mahabharata,* discussed in Chapter 2. The *Mahabharata* tells the story of Kshatriya kings of the lunar lineage and focuses on a destructive war fought between two branches of this lineage. Two heroes of this epic are Prince Arjuna, third oldest of the five Pandava brothers, who win the war but lose most of their family in the process, and Arjuna's brother-in-law and best buddy Krishna. The hero tales that make up the epic's main story line most likely were Kshatriya legends woven together by court bards. But the story was reworked several times before reaching its present form.[5] Bhagavatas did one such reworking, asserting that Krishna was Vishnu's avatara and inserting the *Bhagavad-Gita* into the epic just as the war is about to begin. Arjuna is in crisis, having realized that the war will require him to kill not only his cousins, but also two revered teachers. He asserts that he will not fight, because killing family and teachers is contrary to dharma. Krishna sets about to convince him that he must listen to a higher dharma, the warrior's dharma that demands he must fight to protect what is right. As they talk, Krishna tells Arjuna the Upanishads' secret about the undying atman in every person, then denounces beliefs that a person seeking such knowledge must renounce all action. Instead, he suggests to Arjuna that truly insight-bringing action is action given to God, done only because it is right and because God wants His devotees to do it.

Krishna then reveals that he himself *is* God, come as a human avatara to save the dharma that Arjuna's enemies threaten. While revealing this, he reviews all prior modes of religious practice and asserts that, through his own doing, each brings its practitioners to their intended goal. In this context, he describes the three yogas discussed previously: karma-yoga, the method of rites advocated by classical Brahmins: jnana-yoga, the method of the Upanishad sages, and bhakti-yoga, the

---

[5] It remains a living oral tradition in India and is still being reworked. Therefore, the phrase "present form" here means only the form that it has in manuscripts that Western scholars study.

method of devotion. Krishna's teaching includes all three because it reveals the highest knowledge to be had, knowledge of God's power and existence. Such knowledge calls forth proper action, namely action done in the spirit of devotion. Therefore, everything turns on God. Those who know this fact and act upon it go in the end to Him, shedding their burden of rebirth and karma.

It is hard to overestimate the importance of this small work for later Hindu devotional thinking. Nearly every writer who ever tried to shape a devotional theology wrote a *Bhagavad-Gita* commentary, especially writers in Vaishnava traditions. In addition, every teaching, including Shaiva and goddess-centered traditions, imitated the *Gita's* basic technique, which was to encompass and co-opt rival teachings by claiming, "They are valid as far as they go, but they do not go far enough. We have the highest knowledge that will result in the best achievements." Nonetheless, neither the *Gita* nor any other teachings in Sanskrit can claim the principle credit for the huge spread of god-centered movements after the sixth century C.E. The first of these movements was set in motion by two groups of Tamil saints who loved their own land and language and managed to exalt both while singing the praise of God. In making devotion patriotic, affirming the gods of their own sacred places, they took back initiative in religous leadership from both shramanas and Brahmins.

SINGING OF A PLACE:
NAYANARS AND ALVARS

By the sixth century C.E., the region that is now Tamilnadu in southeast India had grown tired of interference from outsiders. This lovely land evolved independently of India's northern kingdoms, making the transition from rule by warlord-headed clans into three small kingdoms while the North grouped and regrouped into a series of larger empires. Its people spoke Tamil, one of four regional Indian languages derived from a Dravidian, rather than an Indo-European, base. By the first century C.E., this language had a growing body of literature, lush poetry about love, heroism, and the relation of both to the landscape.[6] Even while those poems were being written, influences from the north were slipping in. Brahmins brought fire sacrifices and Sanskrit genealogies to legitimate the new kings and began integrating Tamil deities with their own. Then Buddhist and Jain shramanas moved into caves in western Tamilnadu's hill regions. At first they adapted well, and the Tamils accepted their presence. In fact, a Jain monk wrote the Tamil poem *Cilappatikaram,* "Ankle Bracelet," which has become the Tamil people's national epic.

By the third century, however, Tamil kingdoms were falling apart.[7] Finally, they were conquered by rulers called Pallavas, who had built a large empire north of Tamil lands. The Pallavas imported more Buddhists and Jains, some more arrogant than their predecessors. By the start of the sixth century, many Tamils had come to resent them.

---

[6] Examples can be found in George L. Hart, III, trans., *Poets of the Tamil Anthologies: Ancient Poems of Love and War* (Princeton: Princeton Univ. Press, 1979).

[7] Very little is known about the period the third and sixth centuries C.E. in Tamilnadu, largely because of a shortage of literature and inscriptions dating from this time.

Some responded by reaffirming their landscape, language, and religion, using devotional song as their medium.

Nayanars

The earliest composers of such songs were Shaivas who lived in and around the delta of the Kaveri River. These were the first of 63 male and female saints later known as Nayanars, "masters," who sang their love for God in Tamil between the sixth and ninth centuries C.E. Although they came from various caste levels, many were Vellalas, a farming group classed as Shudras that nonetheless had great influence in Tamilnadu. Vellala Nayanars included Appar, one of the four Nayanars whose songs became the most famous (ca. sixth to seventh century). The other three most famed were from Tamil Brahmin families: Campantar (sixth to seventh century), Cuntarar (seventh to eighth century), and Manikkavacakar (ninth century).

Nayanar songs praise the deeds of Shiva, described as a mighty king, and celebrate holy places where the Lord has shown himself to Tamils. Each of these sites reveals a different aspect and power of God; hence, each must be visited and treasured. Appar, Campantar, and Cuntarar describe themselves as pilgrims who go from one shrine to another, striving to meet Shiva in all of his myriad aspects.[8] At each place they visit, they sing at least one song that praises the beauty of that place, its rites and festivals, and the deeds that God has done there:

> Sing the town where the Lord dwells with the Goddess,
> as his servants praise him,
> crying, "He gives us release! Age does not touch him!
> Dweller in Kanrappur, three-eyed god,
> the beggar who smashed Daksha's sacrifice!"
> Sing the town where the gardens flow with pure honey
> from blossom clusters swarming with bees,
> and the temple resounds with devotional songs—
> O tongue, sing the shrine of Pacupatiyiccaram in Avur![9]

The pilgrim singers also recount their own experiences. In the Lord's presence, they taste ambrosia. They dissolve in longing to see Him and babble with joy when He is near. They tell devotees to "dance, weep, worship."[10]

> I love him who dwells in the hearts of his lovers,
> whose great self is love itself.
> Desiring to see him, I melt;
> melting, I waste away.
> How shall my heart,
> ant trapped on a two-headed firebrand,
> join my Father, the great Lord?[11]

---

[8] They are atypical. Other Nayanars stayed at one particular shrine.

[9] *Tevaram:* Campantar, I.80.7; Indira Viswanathan Peterson, trans., *Poems to Śiva: the Hymns of the Tamil Saints* (Princeton: Princeton Univ. Press, 1989), p. 154. © 1989 Princeton University Press. Reprinted with permission.

[10] *Tevaram:* Appar, V.177.8; trans. Peterson, ibid., 259.

[11] *Tevaram:* Appar IV.75.6; trans. Peterson, 227.

The Tamil poets knew stories and concepts from the northern traditions: note how the first poem cites Shiva's attack on the sacrifice, cited earlier in this volume.[12] Claims that devotion brings release from karma and suffering show that the poets also were quite familiar with central themes from shramana and sadhu traditions.

The poets' response to rival traditions is twofold. Brahmins and their rituals find cautious acceptance, perhaps because some Nayanars themselves were Brahmins. The sound of Vedic chant, they sing, brings sweetness to a shrine, and the Lord himself has "the Veda on his tongue."[13] Nevertheless, festival drums and songs in Tamil are praised just as highly, and the poems make no surrender to claims of Brahmin or Sanskrit precedence. Jains and Buddhists, however, are scathingly condemned. Appar, a Jain monk before he converted to Shaivism, calls his former companions "base" and "ignorant."[14] Other epithets for Jains and Buddhists in Nayanar songs range from "stupid" to "filthy." One can readily imagine the power of harsh language such as this, once it spread through the region in songs any Tamil could understand.

Alvars

Shaivas were not the only singers composing Tamil songs that affirmed the Tamil land's holiness and its claim on Sanskrit gods. By the seventh century, a parallel movement emerged among Tamil devotees of Vishnu. Less is known about the personal backgrounds of these Vaishnava saint-singers, called Alvars, "Divers." There seem to have been far fewer of them; Vaishnava tradition records only twelve Alvars, who composed some twenty-three works altogether.[15] Only seven identify their castes in their poems. Two were Brahmin temple priests, one a Brahmin woman; two were local chiefs, one a landlord, and another a bard. According to legend, the other five were low-caste bards or yogis.

Alvars did not restrict their affection to Vishnu alone, but also addressed a great deal of poetry to the two avataras Krishna and Rama. Krishna's story and cult had been brought to Tamilnadu from the north sometime around the third century C.E., most likely by settlers who named the inland city of Madurai—this name is a Tamil equivalent for the northern Mathura, which, according to legend, was Krishna's birthplace. Stories told about his youth among cowherds swiftly linked Krishna to Mayon, a Tamil cowherd deity. According to these stories, Krishna was born a prince, but then was hidden among cowherds until he was old enough to destroy his evil asura-uncle. He grew up charming his tribe, while conquering demon-servants his uncle sent to search for him. Especially delighted with Krishna were the tribe's younger women, who dropped everything and ran to dance with him when he played his flute to call them. These young women, called *gopis*, "cowgirls," were said to be his ideal devotees.

When Alvars sang of Vishnu, they at times followed Nayanar examples and celebrated their lord's holy places. But they also put themselves into the place of characters in the avatara stories, pouring out love and longing for the gods taking birth on earth. Conventions from older Tamil love poetry were reworked into an imagery of

---

[12] Page 65.

[13] *Tevaram:* Campantar II.192.5 and I.71.5; Peterson, ibid., 183.

[14] *Tevaram:* Appar IV.5.9; Peterson, ibid., 292.

[15] However, there may well have been both Alvars and Nayanars whose songs were lost before others tried to collect and record them.

religious adoration. Tamil love poets had especially liked to portray the emotions of women waiting for husbands away at war and young girls longing for meetings with their lovers. Such scenes could readily become metaphors for a soul's longing when it seeks for God:

> You were gone the whole day grazing cows, Kanna![16]
> Your humble words burn my soul,
> Evening tramples like a rogue [elephant]
> and the fragrance of the jasmine buds,
> unleashing my desires, blows on me.
> Embrace my beautiful breasts
> with the fragrance of the wild jasmine
> on your radiant chest.
> Give me the nectar of your mouth!
> Adorn my lowly head
> with your jeweled lotus hands.[17]

Or the poet could stand in the place of a loving companion or parent, as in the following poem addressed to Rama:

> The other day,
> As a baby on the banyan leaf,
> You swallowed the worlds.
> You killed Vali
>   and gave the kingdom to his brother
> O dark gem of Kanapuram
>   Where the waves wash gems to the shore.
> O ruler of the city called Ali,
> O you who abide in Ayodhya!
> Talelo.[18]

The Nayanars and Alvars did help renew Tamil culture and drive Jains and Buddhists away from their region. But soon their heritage began disappearing. They had not founded groups that would preserve their songs. The songs circulated orally for a time and then began to fade. Legend claims they were all but lost when scholars managed to recover them and collect them in anthologies. The most important Saiva collection is the *Tevaram;* the most important for Vaishnavas is the *Nalayira Divya-Prabandham, The Sacred Four Thousand.*

During the next two centuries, Alvar and Nayanar anthologies in turn were taken up into the literature of a pair of sampradayas that ever since have dominated the religious life of Tamilnadu. Perpetuating Alvar devotion was the Shri Vaishnava sampradaya, tracing its origins to Nathamuni, compiler of *The Sacred Four Thousand,* who

---

[16] Kanna or Kannan is the South Indian equivalent of the Sanskrit Krishna.

[17] Nammalvar, *Tiruvaymoli* 10.3.5. As translated in John Carman and Vasudha Narayanan, *The Tamil Veda: Pillān's Interpretation of the Tiruvāymoli* (Chicago: Univ. of Chicago Press, 1989), p. 171. © 1989 University of Chicago Press. Reprinted by permission.

[18] Perumāḷ *Tirumoli* 8.7. Translated by Vasudha Narayanan, *The Way and the Goal: Expressions of Devotion in the Early Śri Vaishnava Tradition* (Washington, DC: Institute for Vaishnava Studies, 1987), p. 31.

lived sometime during the ninth or tenth century C.E. Its most influential teacher was the celebrated Brahmin philosopher Ramanuja, who lived from 1017–1137 C.E. Ramanuja is best known for his challenge to the Advaita, "non-dualist," Vedanta teachings of Shankaracharya. Ramanuja argued that souls bound in rebirth are similar to but not identical with God; hence, they will know God's bliss when liberated, rather than being absorbed in Him. Intense and steady love brings the devotee to God; *prapatti,* "surrender," enables such devotion.[19] In addition to philosophical works, Ramanuja wrote hymns in Sanskrit and worked to standardize Vaishnava temple ritual. The Shri-Vaishnava heritage that he passed on to later disciples joins Tamil and Sanskrit expression, Brahmin philosophy and devotion. The lineage that continues his practice and thinking includes both renouncers and lay disciples.

The thirteenth-century Velalla-caste philosopher Meykantar knit Nayanar devotion together with teachings of a ritual tradition known as Shaiva Siddhanta. Grounded in Tantra-influenced Sanskrit writings called *Agamas,* Shaiva Siddhanta had strongly influenced Shaiva temple practice in India during the tenth through twelfth centuries.[20] Meykantar's writings in Tamil shifted its emphasis more toward devotion as a means of salvation; he stressed even more than Ramanuja the soul's separation from God and the need for God's grace to save it. Successors in his lineage continued to write extensively in Tamil, and today Shaiva Siddhantists are largely a Tamil-based community.

DISSOLVING BOUNDARIES:
VIRASHAIVAS AND WARKARIS

Raising pride in local identity is not the only reason why Tamil poet-saints became important. They were also trendsetters, inspiring movements like their own in other regions. Such movements also began when poets or singers used a local language to praise some deity, usually Shiva, Vishnu, or Vishnu's avatara Krishna or Rama. Some poet-saints were loners whose memories survive only because their poems and songs grew popular enough to become a lasting part of their region's lore. At times, however, their disciples started a sampradaya or *panth,* a "path," that purposefully carried on their memory and their teachings. Such organizations developed their own collections of teachings, designed their own liturgies and iconographies, and established their own temple and pilgrim sites. Some of these remained wholly networks of householders, headed by men who married and passed the privilege of initiating new members through their family lines. Others founded lineages of sadhus who combined devotional teachings with older techniques of spiritual discipline.

One question that proved vexing as new sectarian groups emerged was the relationship between the new groups and the caste system promoted by Brahmin teachings. According to caste teachings, people of low castes should always defer to those

---

[19] For a fuller summary of Ramanuja's thought, see Narayanan, ibid., 79–93.

[20] Evidence for its pan-Indian history is summarized by Richard M. Davis in *Ritual in an Oscillating Universe: Worshiping Śiva in Medieval India* (Princeton: Princeton Univ. Press, 1991), 14–18.

ranked higher. Furthermore, members of different caste groups should keep separate when it comes to intimate matters such as marriage and eating. The new saint-derived groups often flouted such teachings. Lists of revered saints included both low-caste figures and women. Additionally, even high-caste saints proclaimed that devotion to God was the sole measure of human worth, not a person's status within worldly social systems. Groups inspired by such teachings had an uncomfortable tendency to draw devotees across caste lines and to blur social divisions within their regions. As such groups evolved into formal organizations, they had to decide where they stood on enforcing common marks of social distinction. Would initiates intermarry? Would they eat together?

Virashaivas

When a devotional group rejected caste distinctions and gathered a cross-caste following, one solution was to treat it as a jati in and of itself. This is what happened to the next devotional movement that emerged in southern India. This movement of Virashaivas, "heroic Shaivas," first became prominent during the mid-twelfth century in the north of the present-day state of Karnataka, which is several hundred miles northwest of Tamilnadu. Virashaivas taught in the Kannada language, which, like Tamil, has a Dravidian base. The saints' main mode of expression was the *vachana*, "saying," a short free-verse poem very rich in metaphor. Some vachanas, but not all, were set to music.

Like Nayanars, the Virashaivas were Shiva devotees. Virashaivas knew about the Tamil Shaiva saints, but also drew on concepts and prototypes from the Kalamukha sampradaya that was strong in their region. Like Nayanars, Virashaivas believed that Shiva reveals different aspects of himself at different localities. Thus, particular poets liked to address Shiva by the name used for him at the shrine where they received their own special calling. Basavanna's Shiva was "Lord of the Meeting Rivers" because Shiva entered Basavanna at the temple at Kudalasangama, "the Meeting of Rivers." Allama Prabhu, initiated by the Lord in a mysterious underground shrine, called his Shiva "Lord of Caves." The woman poet Mahadeviyakkha's Shiva was "The Lord White as Jasmine," the Shiva of the temple where she was initiated as a child.

Yet all Virashaiva poets insisted that the Lord is One, and they were far less temple-oriented than their Nayanar predecessors. The body, they said, is the only temple a devotee needs:

> With a whole temple
> in this body,
> where's the need
> for another?
> No one asked
> for two.
> O Lord of Caves,
> if you are stone,
> What am I?[21]

---

[21] Allama Prabhu, *Allama Vacane Candrike* (Mysore, 1960) 213, translated A. K. Ramanujan, *Speaking of Śiva* (Middlesex: Penguin, 1973), p. 153.

Virashaiva saints did not live at temples but wandered and begged for handouts like sadhus, calling themselves *jangamas*, "travelers." The famous woman saint Mahadeviyakkha wandered without clothes, covered only by her hair.

When Virashaivas evolved an organization, sadhu sampradayas became their model. Each devotee is initiated into connection with one of several Virashaiva *matha*s, monasteries, each headed by an *acharya,* master teacher. Moving between this spiritual master and ordinary devotees is the class of *jangamas,* who sometimes function like sadhus and sometimes like Brahmin priests. Every Virashaiva is also to some extent a sadhu or priest in his or her own right, wearing around the neck a tiny *linga,* Shiva's chief symbol, and worshiping it twice daily, as well as following a strict moral code. At death, each is treated like a sadhu, receiving rites of burial rather than cremation. No restrictions of death pollution are observed.

This structure blurs the lines between home and monastery, so that jangamas may be either celibates or householders. Virashaiva practice likewise blurs divisions of caste and gender. Famous Virashaiva saints have included a Brahmin court treasurer, a chief's wife, a temple drummer, a woodcutter and his wife, a washerman, a barber, and a scavenger. About one third of the best-known saints were women, responding to the teaching that the soul within humans is not gendered:

> If they see
> breasts and long hair coming
> they call it woman,
> if beard and whiskers
> they call it man:
> but, look, the self that hovers
> in between
> is neither man
> nor woman
> O Ramanatha![22]

As for hierarchy-promoting Brahmins and their ancient fire rituals, the Virashaivas scorned them:

> In a brahman house
> where they feed the fire
> as a god
> when the fire goes wild
> and burns the house
> they splash on it
> the water of the gutter,
> and the dust of the street,
> beat their breasts
> and call the crowd.
> These men then forget their worship
> and scold their fire,
> O lord of the meeting rivers![23]

---

[22] Dēvara Dāsimayya, Haḷakaṭṭi edition (Bijapur, 1955) 133, trans. Ramanujan, ibid., 110.

[23] Basavaṇṇa, S. S. Basavanāḷ, edition (Dharwar, 1962) 586, trans. Ramanujan, ibid., 85.

Warkaris

Roughly a century and a half after the period of the greatest Virashaiva poets, the neighboring state of Maharashtra produced a movement similarly scornful of classic ritual, caste, and gender boundaries. It went one step farther, however, challenging also the boundaries dividing Shaivas from Vaishnavas. Nominally, this movement was Vaishnava; in fact, its most distinctive feature over the centuries has been its pilgrimage to the temple of an old local god named Vitthal or Vithoba, said to be a form of Vishnu. This pilgrimage, described in a later chapter, has given its devotees their name of Warkaris, "pilgrims" (Sanskrit Varkari).

The Warkaris' God nonetheless extends well beyond Vithoba. As the maidservant Janabai put it:

> i eat god
> i drink god
> i sleep on god
> i buy god
> i count god
> i deal
> with god
> god is here
> god is there
> void is not
> devoid of god
> jani says:
> god is within
> god is without
> and moreover,
> there's god to spare.[24]

This Vedantic-sounding concept of a God who transcends all distinctions was taught by the Warkari founder, the young man Jnaneshvar, whose probable dates are 1275–1296 C.E. Jnaneshvar was the son of a Brahmin with Nath connections. According to legend, the father took vows of renunciation, but then was sent home to his wife after his guru learned he had not completed his obligation to father children. Because he was then made an outcaste for breaking his vow of renunciation, his children grew up in social isolation. Jnaneshvar, the second and brightest of the four children, became a student of teachings by the Vaisnava philosopher Madhva, who lived in the neighboring state of Karnataka (1238–1317 C.E.). Knitting Madhva's teachings together with Nath components from his own background, Jnaneshvar developed his own highly unitive philosophy. Although he lived for only 22 years, he composed a commentary on the *Bhagavad-Gita,* a second book on devotional philosophy, and more than one hundred *abhangs,* devotional songs.

Like those of many devotional saints, Jnanadeva's songs celebrate a personal relationship with God, who transcends all dualities, yet still loves his disciples and reaches

---

[24] Translated by Arun Kolatkar, *Poetry India* I (1966); reprinted in *Palkhi, an Indian Pilgrimage* by D. B. Mokashi (Albany, NY: SUNY Press, 1987), 40–41.

out to save them from samsara. Yet Jnaneshvara's God does not have a clear sectarian identity. Jnanadeva draws on both Shaiva and Vaishnava imagery when he tries to communicate his mystical visions. "In my body, I have seen this Lingam of light," he sings, "and have embraced it without hands. . . ."

> I have seen the linga whose basin is the heaven;
> whose water-line is the ocean;
> which is a fixed as the Sesha;
> which is the support of all the three worlds;
> which fills the whole universe;
> on which the clouds pour their water;
> which is worshiped by means of flowers in the form of the stars;
> to whom the offering of the moon as a fruit is to be made;
> before which the sun is waved as a light;
> to whom the individual self is to be offered as an oblation.
> I have worshiped it with ecstatic bliss. I have meditated upon that Lingam of
>   light in my heart.[25]

The central image of this song refers to a Puranic story in which Shiva appears to Brahma and Vishnu in the form of an endless column of light. They had been quarreling about which of them was the greater; but the linga of light shows that Shiva is greater than either.

Jnaneshvar's only guru was his older brother Nivritti, who himself was initiated by Gaininatha, a saint of uncertain connections. The two brothers' first disciples were their other brother and sister. Toward the end of his life, Jnaneshvar met and won over the tailor's son Namdev (1270–1350 C.E.), an ardent Vithoba devotee who wove pilgrimage to this god into the new group's practice. Namdev in turn became spiritual anchor for a group of devotees that included a potter, Namdev's own maid Janabai, and at least one other woman. All of these low-caste and uneducated devotees left songs of their own. The tradition they started went quiet for a time, then was revived by the Brahmin Eknath (ca. 1533–1599 C.E.) and the Vaishnava sadhu Tukaram (ca. 1598–1650 C.E.), who became the movement's greatest poet. Tukaram in turn had a large and multicaste group of disciples, which included Bahinabai, another woman who composed many well-loved songs. Even this very brief list of Warkari saints shows both the movement's disregard for caste boundaries and its openness to women.

A GOD WITHOUT IMAGES: ISLAM
AND THE NIRGUNA SANTS OF NORTH INDIA

Research into regional devotional movements of India is still fairly new to Western scholarship. One problem still needing attention is the movements' connections to one another. Despite differences in language and huge distances between their locales, saints of one region often knew and were influenced by songs and teachings from

---

[25] From Abhang 65 and 66, trans. R. D. Ranade, *Mysticism in India: The Poet-Saints of Maharashtra* (Albany, NY: SUNY Press, 1983), 172; reprint of a 1933 work.

other areas. Thus, devotees from North India called Sants, "True Ones," celebrated a God who transcends sectarian boundaries, much like the God adored by Warkaris. However, the Sant's God beyond Gods included not just Shiva and Vishnu, but Allah, God of Islam, a tradition new to India.

Islam was an import religion, brought in by several waves of northern invaders. Northern India had always been easier to penetrate than the south. Strangers came to the south in traders' ships. Until well-armed fleets of Europeans arrived, these trade ships were small and vulnerable enough not to pose a threat to the southern kingdoms. Much of the north was also well protected: in the east by Assam's jungle-entangled hills and from Bengal to Kashmir by the wall of the Himalayas. But the western mountains of Afghanistan are pierced by several passes well known since ancient times, through which armies were able to travel. At various points in history, northwest India experienced invasions by Greeks, Shakas from Persia, and Kushans and Huns from the deserts west of China. Each left colony kingdoms that survived for a time and then fell and were reabsorbed into native empires.

Islam did not exist yet when these earlier conquerors came. It was born in 622 C.E. when the prophet Muhammad led his circle of disciples from their native city of Mecca in western Arabia to Medina, 250 miles to the north. Muhammad's Meccan relatives were unhappy with him because he was spreading a teaching that threatened their wealth. He said an ancient God named Allah had told him that Arabs must shed tribal gods and divisions and unite in the worship of Allah alone. They must throw away their idols, take care of their poor, and follow the commandments that Allah gave through Muhammad. Muhammad's relatives had grown wealthy by exploiting their control over an old tribal shrine that attracted many pilgrims and traders. Allah's orders implied they should strip this of its divine images.

Muhammad was a gifted leader, and Medina, in need of leadership, invited him to come just when his relatives moved to kill him. His rule there was successful, guided by revelations that Allah continued to utter through him while he was in a trance-like state. When Mecca sent an army to unseat Muhammad, Allah told his Muslims to defend their faith. The Muslims won and soon conquered Mecca. By the time Allah's Prophet died, he had built a community that was simultaneously a new religion, a utopian state, and a support base for a powerful series of armies. Within a century, these armies spread the Prophet's teachings from Spain and the Atlantic coast of Africa through Persia and the desert trade routes west and north of India. About 1000 C.E., an Afghan Muslim, Mahmud of Ghazni, began raiding deeply into India each year at harvest time. One of his targets was the wealth of large temples and Buddhist centers, which he justified taking by pointing to Islam's ban on image worship.

A century and a half later, in 1185, another Afghan, Muhammad of Ghuri, began incursions that carved out a kingdom centered at Delhi, the site of India's present capital. Several Muslim kingdoms followed in Delhi and other parts of North India, some also controlled by Afghans, others by Turks, and still others by Arabs. These, in turn, vied against one another, until finally all were conquered by Babar, a descendant of the famous Mongol Genghis Khan. At its peak, the Mughal empire that Babar founded stretched from Afghanistan to Bengal and through all but the southernmost part of the Indian penninsula.

Each new wave of conquests brought its own forms of Islam to India. At one extreme was pure Sunni Islam, which evolved largely in Arabia and regions further to the west. Sunnis based their practice on the revealed words of the Prophet, recorded in the Qur'an, their Holy Book. When they needed guidance beyond what the Qur'an could give them, they turned to *hadith,* stories about the Prophet's life and words that he had uttered while not in a state of direct revelation. When hadith could not help them, they turned to their own scholars, who built up a code of sacred laws by drawing out implications from these sources. Especially important to Sunni Islam were its codes governing family and ritual practice. Central rituals were prayer five times per day, pilgrimage to the city of Mecca, and fasting during the Muslim month of Ramadan. New institutions supporting this practice were the mosque, or house of prayer, and the *madrasa,* the Muslim university.

Other Muslims in India were Shias, adherents of a Muslim branch strong in Iraq and Persia that had split from Sunnis due to a leadership struggle after the Prophet's death. Shias continued much Sunni practice, but added rites of mourning for Shia martyrs, who included the Prophet's son-in-law and grandsons. Shias brought to India their Muharram festival, during which Shia males lashed themselves in public and wailed to remember those who died unjustly. Still other Muslims were *fakirs,* members of Sufi brotherhoods who taught that love of God is more important than law or ritual and celebrated their love through dance and song, like the Hindu bhakta*s*.

Little of this practice gave much pause to Indians. They were used to living in a society where many religious communities existed side by side, each with its own leaders, teachings, and customs. The Muslim teaching that all who commit themselves to God are equal was new to some, but not to those who knew about the southern saints' teachings. The belief that God is beyond all form was familiar to both Vedantists and Naths. Once secure in their holdings, Muslim rulers left temples alone; some even gave wealth and land to develop pilgrim sites.[26] Three Muslim practices remained sources of occasional tension. Muslims killed and ate beef, whereas many Hindus who followed Brahmin teachings honored cows as special symbols of prosperity and dharma.[27] Muslims also encouraged conversions, helping despised subcastes escape polluting tasks assigned to them by Brahmin teachings. Finally, and most crucially, Muslim rulers gave gifts and patronage to their own scholars, schools, and saints rather than to Brahmins or shramana monasteries. The resulting loss of royal donations killed Buddhism completely and left Jain communities in only four western states. Brahmins survived by farming land inherited from ancestors or by working for the new Muslim administrations. Many fled south to remaining Hindu kingdoms.

---

[26] Temple destruction was far less widespread than Hindu nationalist groups have claimed. Richard M. Eaton examines its incidence and motives in "Temple Desecration and Indo-Muslim States," *Beyond Turk and Hindu: Rethinking Religious Identities in Islamicate South Asia* (Gainesville: Univ. of Florida, 2000), 246–81. See also Chapter 12, footnote 2.

[27] Hindus have good reasons for respecting cows. Not only do Indians eat many milk products, they use sun-purified cowdung to plaster their homes; they use cow urine in medicines (for its antiseptic qualities); and poor Indians burn cowpatties mixed with straw as an inexpensive and handy source of fuel. But Brahmins doubtless also had their own interests in mind when promoting cow protection: An ancient mode of paying Brahmins for ritual services was to offer them cows, and many had large herds.

Nirguna Sants

These developments left a vacuum in religious leadership into which new bhakta saints swiftly stepped. Those most compatible with the new Muslim context were the nirguna Sants. As noted previously, *Sant* means "True One" and is roughly equivalent to the English word "saint." *Nirguna* means "formless" and refers to nirguna Sants' teachings that God cannot and should not be reduced by imagining Him with a form or making images of Him. Sants of the north in general were more independent of one another than were saints of the southern movements. Some, but not all, produced lasting groups that evolved into panths or sampradayas. Scholars commonly draw a distinction between nirguna Sants and saguna Sants, who worship God through images. This should not be considered absolute. Most saguna theologies teach that God has both formed and formless manifestations; and some Sants celebrate God at both formed and formless levels.

Teachings of the nirguna Sants were much like those of Warkaris, and some scholars have suggested that they, like the Warkaris, have a strong streak of Nath influence in their backgrounds.[28] God is One, they taught, and hence sectarian tensions are senseless because all sects worship the same Supreme Being. God loves his disciples and actively works to save all who call on his name and sing his praises. Because God is everywhere, a devotee need not seek Him out through pilgrimage. Nirguna Sants tended to affirm household life rather than set up sadhu lineages. Many were poor and of humble caste. Kabir, who became very famous, was born a Muslim weaver, and the panth that claims him as founder became a haven for outcastes. The following quote from a song attributed to him shows his contempt for religious divisions:

> Hindus, Muslims—where did they come from?
> Who got them started down this road?
> Search inside, search your heart and look:
> Who made heaven come to be?
> Fool, throw away that book and sing of Ram.
> What you're doing has nothing to do with him.
> Kabir has caught hold of Ram for his refrain,
> And the Qazi?[29] He spends his life in vain.[30]

Note the use of the word "Hindu" in this poem. Kabir's poetry is one of the very first places where Hindu is used to include all non-Muslim Indians. Note, too that Kabir used the name "Ram" to refer to God. Rama worship was common in Banaras during Kabir's lifetime, and Kabir legends claim he was an initiate of the Ramanandis' founder. Kabir's God nonetheless was no epic hero or avatar, but rather a pool into which the Sant dove, "a flame without a lamp . . . an unsounded sound that sounds without end."[31]

---

[28] See Kabir scholar Charlotte Vaudeville, *A Weaver Named Kabir* (Delhi: Oxford Univ. Press, 1993), 70–78.

[29] A Qazi is a Muslim judge and legal scholar.

[30] As translated by John Stratton Hawley and Mark Juergensmeyer, *Songs of the Saints of North India* (New York: Oxford Univ. Press, 1988), p. 55. © 1988 by Oxford University Press, Inc. Used by permission of Oxford University Press, Inc.

[31] Ibid., p. 57. Vaudeville points out that "Ram" is commonly used as a general name for God in India, sometimes even by Shaivas, *A Weaver Named Kabir*, op. cit., p. 90.

Sikhs

Although most nirguna Sant movements were tiny eddies in the huge tide of events that was medieval North Indian history, one devotional community—the Sikhs—became a major force. The Sikhs, whose name means "Disciples," were based in the Punjab region of northwest India. Stories about the Sikh founder Guru Nanak claim that he met Kabir and was inspired by him during a pilgrimage to Banaras. This is possible, but not probable; much depends on Kabir's dates, which are highly uncertain (Kabir, fifteenth century, Nanak 1469–1539). Nanak taught, like Kabir, that God is formless and can be known only by listening to His voice within the heart.

From a young age, Nanak had experience in crossing religious boundaries. Born a Punjabi Kshatriya, he worked as steward for the local Muslim governor and led *kirtans,* devotional sings, with a Sufi Muslim musician. One day Nanak disappeared while bathing in a local river. When he returned, he said that God had taken him to heaven and told him he must teach humans how to adore God's holy name. Insisting "there is no Hindu; there is no Muslim," Nanak wandered on pilgrimage to many sacred places. Later, however, he returned to his family, living with them and disciples at the town of Kartarpur.

Nine other Sikh gurus after Nanak developed the community that he had started.[32] The second standardized the group's daily worship and started a *langar,* community kitchen, where Sikhs ate together to show disregard for caste divisions. The third designed a system of administration and funding. The fourth built Amritsar, the Sikh Holy City. The fifth, Guru Arjun, gathered songs of Sikh gurus and other Sants into the Sikh Holy Book, the *Guru Granth Sahib.* By Guru Arjun's time, Sikhs had become a major force in the Punjab region, made wealthy through their hard work and mutual support of each others' undertakings. The great Mughal emperor Akbar admired Sikh enterprise and teachings and gave Sikhs the land on which they built Amritsar. But after Akbar died, his successor Jehangir turned against the community. Soon Arjun was arrested and died from torture. Under successive gurus, the group became militaristic, until Sikhs were in effect a rebel militia.

Several more gurus died as martyrs, until the tenth announced that no more would follow. He reorganized his community into the *khalsa,* a group to be led by the words of the Holy Book. Khalsa members undergo a special rite of initiation and wear the five symbols that make Sikhs familiar to Westerners: uncut hair and beards, a comb to tend these,[33] a steel bangle worn on the wrist, a white undergarment, and a sword to be used in defending the faith. All Sikh men take the name Singh (lion) and all women the name Kaur (princess), thus stressing that they belong to a single family of commitment. Mughal emperors kept trying to exterminate Sikhs until the Mughals themselves became too hard-pressed to do so. Sikh general Ranjit Singh then founded an independent Sikh kingdom in the Punjab that lasted for a time. After the British conquered the kingdom in 1849, Sikh warriors became the backbone of the British army in India. Many Sikhs now deny that they are Hindus, preferring to think of themselves as members of a separate religion.

---

[32] For a brief summary of Sikh history, see W. H. McLeod, *The Sikhs: History, Religion, and Society* (New York: Columbia Univ. Press, 1989).

[33] This comb distinguishes them from sadhu groups, who usually leave hair and beards unkempt.

NORTHERN SAGUNA SANTS

Image-affirming Sant traditions of the north by and large continued patterns initiated in the south, so they can be reviewed more quickly. They subdivide into three categories: Krishna bhaktas, Rama devotees, and Shaivas.

Krishna Bhaktas

Krishna devotees were perhaps the first Hindus in the north to adopt the new style of ecstatic devotion. Already during the twelfth century, Bengali court poets writing in Sanskrit took up the Alvar practice of writing in the voice of characters from the Krishna story. The most famous of their products was the poem *Gita-Govinda,* based on a popular belief that Krishna had a special girl friend, his cousin Radha.[34] The poem describes an episode in their relationship in which the two quarreled, parted, suffered, and reunited. It made Radha a special prototype for the Krishna devotee, who was expected to pine for the Lord as she did. But it also implied that God needs and loves His devotees just as much as they need Him.

Soon after the turn of the sixteenth century, a young Brahmin, later named Chaitanya, met a Krishna devotee while on pilgrimage to perform funeral rites for his father. Returning to his home town, Chaitanya started nightly kirtans, which often ended in processions where the singers danced and sang through the streets. Chaitanya himself identified so ecstatically with Radha that he sometimes dressed as a gopi, one of Krishna's cowgirls, and fainted with longing for Krishna. The group's behavior alarmed the local Muslim authorities, and soon Chaitanya found it wise to remove his group from the city. He had already taken vows of renunciation, affiliating with Madhva's Brahma Sampradaya. Now he went to live as a sadhu in the holy city of Puri, in Orissa, the state just south of Bengal.

First, however, Chaitanya and his disciples journeyed to the district of Braj near Mathura in north central India, where Krishna had lived with the cowherds and danced among his cowgirls. Chaitanya left disciples in Braj to develop the sacred sites and to make Braj an active center of Krishna worship. Many temples of Braj and Mathura are still controlled by Chaitanya's Gaudiya Vaishnava lineage, which includes both sadhus and householders. One branch is the group known today as the International Society of Krishna Consciousness or, more popularly, Hare Krishna.

A second northern devotee of Krishna left a heritage defined more by a legend and songs than by organizations. Mirabai (sixteenth-century C.E.) was a princess of one of the Rajput warrior clans that dominated the west Indian desert region Rajasthan. At an early age, she became a devotee of Krishna, taking as her guru, according to some accounts, the low-caste saint Ravidas (Rohidas). When her parents gave her in marriage to a more powerful Rajput family, she refused to consummate her marriage, insisting that she had already wed Krishna. She soon lost her parents and, according to some accounts, her husband. One famous song charges that her father-in-law tried to give her a cup of poison, angered at the disgrace she had brought to his family. Somehow, however, she escaped his fortress and wandered the

---

[34] The finest translation of this poem by far is Barbara Stoller Miller, *Love Song of the Dark Lord: Jayadeva's Gītāgovinda* (New York: Columbia Univ. Press, 1977).

countryside as a devotional singer, ending her days at the pilgrim center of Dwarka in western India. Over a thousand devotional songs are attributed to her; many, however, seem to be about her rather than by her.[35]

Braj itself gave rise to another important Krishna movement. One saint who either settled there or visited during the sixteenth century was the blind singer Surdas. Many of his songs are in the "cowgirl's longing" genre. But others focus on the paradox of Krishna's becoming a child. How could the great Lord of All become a naive and unsteady baby? The following verse speaks in the voice of Krishna's mother:

"If you drink the milk of the black cow, Gopal,
  you'll see your black braid grow.
Little son, listen, among all the little boys
  you'll be the finest, most splendid one.
Look at the other lads in Braj and see:
  it's milk that brought them their strength.
So drink: the fires daily burn in the bellies
  of your foes—Kans and Kesi and the crane,"
Sur says, Yasoda looks at his face and laughs
  when he tries to coax his curls behind his ear.[36]

At some point, Sur and his poetry were claimed by the movement of Vallabhacharyas, principal rivals to the Gaudiyas for control of Krishna devotional sites in North India.[37] The Vallabhacharyas also based themselves in the Braj region, founding a circle of devotees that stretched from Braj as far as Gujarat and Maharashtra. Their founder was a Telegu Brahmin named Vallabha (1479–1571) who spent his youth in Banaras and most of his life on the road as a pilgrim. Vallabha was a philosopher more in the mode of Ramanuja and Madhva than an ecstatic devotee. Nonetheless, he aimed his teaching at householders, rejecting sadhu renunciation, and taught that devotion alone is a practice fit for the present degenerate age. His most distinctive teaching was the assertion that Krishna and Radha are supreme deities, thus denying that Krishna is a mere avatara.

Rama Devotees

Banaras (Sanskrit Varanasi, or Kashi in ancient texts) is one of India's oldest cities. It is also a holy city and important pilgrim center. Puranic texts teach that anyone who bathes in the Ganga at Banaras will attain liberation at death, regardless of caste or spiritual discipline. Although Banaras is best-known as Shiva's city, it is also a major center for Rama devotion.

This Rama adoration, it is said, was started by Ramananda, founder of the Ramanandi sadhu lineage. Although Ramananda's historicity has been questioned,[38]

---

[35] Especially in North India, it was not uncommon for devotees to attribute their own compositions to a famous saint; this seems especially true in the case of both Mirabai and the weaver Kabir.

[36] Trans. Hawley and Juergensmeyer, op. cit., p. 105. © 1988 by Oxford University Press. Reprinted by permission.

[37] Their movement is also known as the Pushti-Marga.

[38] See page 54.

by the sixteenth century C.E. it is clear that Banaras had an active circle of Ram bhaktas because the poet Tulsidas (ca. 1532–1623 C.E.) belonged to such a circle. Stories about Tulsidas claim he was orphaned as a child and reared by Ramananda disciples. Tulsidas is most famed for his long poem *Ramcaritmanas,* which retells in Hindi the older Sanskrit epic about the deeds of the hero Rama. Drawing on techniques of Krishna-centered devotion, Tulsidas portrayed *Ramayana* characters as models of types of devotion that can be paid to Lord Rama. He also greatly stressed Rama's avatara identity, a concept less developed in the original epic. Tulsidas's *Ramcaritmanas* is the *Ramayana* version best known in India. It has been retold in comic books, dramatized in a famous TV series, and is still enacted each year during weeks leading up to Rama's Dusshara festival.

Shaivas

One surprise in northern India, given the importance of Shaiva devotion in the south, is the absence of Shaiva devotional movements in North India. The north does not lack Shiva worship per se; it is full of Shaiva pilgrim sites. But these are largely tied to sadhus and their disciplines. Shaiva devotion was strong, however, in the mountainous northern province of Kashmir, long a center of Tantric thought and practice. Kashmiri praise songs to Shiva are largely in Sanskrit and far more formal than the hymns of southern singers. One woman yogi known as Lal Ded (fourteenth century C.E.) did produce popular songs of Shiva devotion written in the vernacular. Her stories say she was born a Brahmin and married at a suitable age, but left her husband's home after her mother-in-law mistreated her. Lal Ded had a guru from the Trika Tantra tradition, a monistic and restrained form of Tantra popular in her region. She had little use for image-worship, and her hymns use a language of absorption in God much like that of nirguna Sants.

THE SHAKTAS

This chapter began by describing a woman who is both bhakta and shakta, whose central religious practice is loving surrender to God and whose God is actually a Devi, a goddess. In the classic devotional movements described here, figures like her are rare. All famous panths and sampradayas of devotional movements were centered on male deities—even those whose saints included many famous women. Yet today in India, one often meets goddess devotees, as well as women saints said to be goddess-manifestations. Before leaving the heritage of devotional saints and movements in India, it is necessary to ask where this goddess enthusiasm came from.

Goddess worship in India is a compilation from at least seven sources. The first might be called the "primordial feminine," a nearly universal human tendency to perceive certain caves and cracks in the earth as wombs where the earth's powers of life and death are concentrated. India is full of earth-wombs, not necessarily called this, but readily recognized as such by anyone who sees them. Vaishnodevi herself is an earth-womb, a cave high on a mountain into which pilgrims slither through a narrow and winding crack, their feet bathed in a tiny stream that flows from the mountain's interior. Priests waiting inside to collect pilgrims' offerings say that three broken and dressed-up stalagmites are the goddess's three forms Durga, Lakshmi, and Sarasvati. Those who enter know nonetheless that the goddess is all around them. Vaishnodevi exists throughout the cave; she is in the temple at the cave entrance, in the nearby pilgrim quarters, on the entire mountain, and on the path that winds up it. She is there in such concentrations that no one dares climb her path wearing shoes of leather. Vaishnodevi is a "pure" goddess, unlike some wilder sisters, and she may not be touched with substances such as leather that are made from something dead.

Primordial goddesses are site-linked. A second class of deities coming together in the Indian Goddess is group-linked: tutelary deities protecting a village or town, a specific family lineage, or a *kul,* the greater network to which several families belong. Ammas, village goddesses, are found throughout southern India. Female lineage and kul protectors are found especially among two types of communities: warrior jatis such as the Rajputs of Rajasthan and very low jatis such as the Chamars of central India. Female tutelaries are also common among India's many "tribals." Village and low-caste goddesses are often frightening and not of the pure type, receiving offerings of liquor and blood sacrifice. Some goddesses were once humans, such as kul-guarding *satis,* women burned on the funeral pyres of their husbands.

A third type of goddess contributing to today's Devi is a figure once associated with royal thrones. One comes across her in ancient folklore, housed in a tree shading a royal stone seat that is much like a yaksha altar. She whispers advice to the king she protects and is his *shri,* his royal luck. If a king offends his shri, she deserts him and his kingdom falls. As myths and images of the great Sanskrit gods evolved in India, the great king Vishnu was assigned as consort to the goddess Shri or Lakshmi, "Luck." Sitting on a lotus and sprayed with rain by white elephants, Lakshmi is the Brahmin version of the old throne goddess.

A fourth source of goddess prototypes is Vedic literature, although it had less influence in goddess constructions than for those of great male gods. Vedic hymns praise several goddesses, especially Usha, goddess of the dawn. Nonetheless, male gods dominate, and today just one major goddess has clear origins in Vedic imagery. Sarasvati, goddess of knowledge, is a present-day combination of the Vedic river goddess Sarasvati and Vak, goddess of speech, important in Vedic ritual texts. When Brahmin super-gods were paired with consorts, Sarasvati was paired with Brahma, personification of the "spoken" power behind the chants.

The next two extremely important components of today's Devi—Parvati, wife of Shiva, drawn from Puranic mythology, and *shakti,* the Tantric conception of the female power that activates the gods—have already been introduced. Shakti is the main concept unifying today's goddesses; many Hindus now would say that India's many goddesses are "faces" of one *shakti,* in much the same way that they know all local Shivas are ultimately one.

Finally, added to Shakti's role in unifying the goddess are two constructs from three rival systems of philosophic systems. The dualistic Samkhya philosophy contributed its concept of *prakriti,* the web of material nature in which souls become entrapped. In Samkhya teachings, prakriti is mindless, only appearing to have intelligence because she "reflects" the soul. Tantric teachings took the next step, making prakriti into a divine power with intelligence and will. In a parallel development, the goddess absorbed *mahamaya,* the concept of duality-shaping illusion central to Vedanta-based philosophies.

Originally, all the female powers and concepts listed above were separate. Just what group or thinker first knit them together is an unsolved mystery of Hindu history. The first joining of goddesses found in Sanskrit literature is in the poem *Devi-Mahatmya,* "Greatness of the Goddess," now part of the *Markandeya Purana,* which dates from around the sixth century C.E.[39] This poem, which has little to do with the rest of the *Markandeya,* celebrates a series of battles in which goddesses overcome asuras. In its most famous episode, a buffalo-shaped asura, Mahisha, conquers an army of devas, who run to Vishnu and Shiva in terror.[40] In anger, the two superdevas wrinkle their foreheads, out of which burst great beams of *tejas,* "fiery splendor." Other gods follow their example, and the beams coalesce into a fiery woman riding a lion. The gods give her their weapons, emblems of their powers, and she plunges into battle wielding all of these. Asuras fall by the thousands, and soon she confronts Mahisha. He changes form as she fights him, but she kills one body after another until finally he is conquered.

The woman on the lion is the goddess usually called Durga, often a tutelary goddess for warrior families. But the poem also calls her by other well-known goddess names, such as Ambika, Chandika, Shri, and Gauri, and during other gory battles described in the poem, she transforms into Lakshmi, Parvati, Sarasvati, and the black and blood-lapping goddess Kali. At one point in the battles, all the male gods' Shakti-consorts emerge from the gods' bodies to join the fight. The poem's preface calls all of these female powers Mahamaya. By the end, the work has assembled virtually all female powers known to Sanskrit mythology, along with several others from Tantric and local traditions. All of these, it asserts, are alternative forms of one single and all-powerful Devi.

The *Devi-Mahatmya* is well known in many regions of India because goddess devotees read it aloud from beginning to end during the Nine Nights festival held to honor Durga. So it is not surprising that many Hindus share its belief that a single super-goddess underlies other goddess figures. More surprising is the fact that goddess devotion has taken so long to emerge in India. Tantra's reputation for extremism may be to blame because many Shaktas are also Tantrics.

India's current fascination with goddesses seems a product of Bengal and especially of three Bengali men who lived fairly recently. Bengal was an old center for Tantric Shakta practice, but much of this was kept secret until two saints affirmed their love for Kali, the most awesome and frightening aspect of the Tantric goddess. Ramprasad Sen was born in 1720 into a Vaidya Shakta family[41] and was a brilliant student, studying not only Sanskrit but also Persian and Urdu. Stories about him say that he took a job as an account clerk for a wealthy landlord, but filled his account books with Kali's name instead of numbers. Then his boss saw a song he had written in one book and paid Ramprasad a stipend to become a full-time devotional writer. A Maharaja heard him sing and gave him land to grow food for his family, but he managed it badly, losing himself in ecstatic visions. One day his wife thought she saw

---

[39] Another name for this poem is *Durga-Saptasati,* "Durga's Seven Hundred Stanzas."

[40] Remember that Brahmin-told stories are full of deva–asura battles. The struggle between these forces of order and disorder is one of the most frequent themes of Sanskrit mythology.

[41] Vaidyas are often Ayur-Vedic doctors, as was Ramprasad Sen's own father.

Ramprasad's Kali statue breathing. When he learned of this, Ramprasad took the statue away and worshiped his wife in its place. He outlived both her and his Maharaja, but drowned in 1766 while immersing a Kali image during her annual festival. His poems celebrate the sheer lunacy of his love for the daunting goddess:

> She's playing in my heart.
> Whatever I think, I think Her name.
> I close my eyes and She's in there
> Garlanded with human heads.
> Common sense, know-how—gone.
> So they say I'm crazy. Let them.
> All I ask, my crazy Mother,
> Is that You stay put.
> Ramprasad cries out: Mother, don't
> Reject this lotus heart You live in,
> Don't despise this human offering
> At your feet.[42]

Ramprasad's act of offering puja to his wife was echoed by the Bengali Brahmin Ramakrishna, who lived from 1836–1888, during Britain's most triumphant period of rule in Bengal. Ramakrishna inherited the job of priest in a Kali temple from his brother, who himself was appointed by a wealthy Shudra woman. At first, Ramakrishna avoided the Kali image, preferring to serve at a Krishna chapel on the Kali temple's grounds. But he came to love the goddess, whom he called his "loving Ma." He prayed for a vision of Kali, but she withheld it until he threatened to kill himself with her sword from the temple wall. Later he had more visions, not only of Kali but also of Krishna, Jesus, and Muhammad. Ramakrishna became famous in Calcutta when Hindu reformer Keshub Chandra Sen became impressed with his mystical vision and wrote about him in a paper published by the group Keshab headed. Then Ramakrishna's disciple Vivekananda spread his fame much farther, carrying word of his Master to England and North America.

The Bengali writer Bankimchandra Chatterjee (1838–94) may be the man most responsible for the Devi's current fame. By 1882, many Bengalis were unhappy with their British rulers' behavior and policies. Bengali Hindus were galvanized, therefore, when Bankimchandra wrote the novel *Anandmath* that covertly encouraged them to organize and revolt. Central to its imagery was a portrayal of India as the Devi, presently a gaunt and blackened Kali, but promising she could be changed into a Lakshmi-like beauty. "Rise up!" she says to her children. "Give yourselves over to setting me free!" This and other portrayals of Bharat Mata, "Mother India," made goddess-devotion respectable. To love the Devi was to love India, in all her craziness and need—and in all her difference from her rulers with their patriarchal deity. New forms of Hindu nationalism today have called more attention to the ideal prince Rama. But the Devi's popularity is still strong.

---

[42] As translated by June McDaniel in *The Madness of the Saints: Ecstatic Religion in Bengal* (Chicago: Univ. of Chicago Press, 1989), p. 142. © 1989 The University of Chicago Press. Reprinted by permission.

EFFECTS OF DEVOTIONAL TRADITIONS

How did devotional movements change India? Psychologically, they added both comfort and color to India's emerging mix of traditions. They promised that ordinary, humble, people are not alone in the world. Awesome beings look out for devotees and reach out to save them. Devotional movements also produced a treasure trove of songs and stories that offered not only instruction but also popular entertainment. Hindus still love to gather for devotional singing, both in remote villages and in sophisticated cities.

Devotional traditions also became an important bridge between the intellectualized teachings of Brahmins and shramanas and the god-and-experience-centered traditions of India's masses. They gave poor and lowly peoples a stake in high-caste religion, promising that even humble people had access to high and pure gods. Moreover, they made such access easy; it could be gained by singing and prayer within one's own home. People aspiring to salvation no longer had to go to the woods and spend half their life in meditation or fry bodies in the midst of rings of fire. Devotional movements also offered an outlet for women's religious aspirations. Respect for women increased somewhat as a result of teachings that all devotees should "become women" in their attitude toward God. Such teachings, nevertheless, did not change women's social standing because the quality they most praised in women was submission.

Devotional movements may have helped Brahmins and their teachings to survive, even in regions where movements challenged Brahmin claims to religious supremacy. Devotional challenges weakened shramana movements that had been rivals to Brahmin teachers. The new enthusiasm for devotion also brought Brahmins a lucrative source of income. Especially when movements were closely tied to old sacred places, the new influx of pilgrims to such places meant that they could be greatly expanded and developed. Wealthy donors set up temples in the holy spots and then turned them over to Brahmins to maintain them. Kings, too, found that developing sacred places was an immensely successful way to bring themselves honor and legitimation. Some temples of Vishnu and Shiva evolved into huge divine palaces with wealth lavished throughout and hundreds of retainers appointed to serve them. Not all of the latter were Brahmins, but Brahmins were put in charge.

Devotional movements also redrew India's religious and cultural boundaries. Religiously, the great dividing line between communities was no longer the boundary drawn between astikas and nastikas, but the line between Vaisnavas and Shaivas, and later between Hindus and Muslims. Meanwhile, crossregional identities produced by Brahmin and shramana teachings began to be counteracted. Devotional movements produced strong regional identities—love for local pilgrim centers and for locally-spoken language. Low-caste people who shared the same shrines and tongue became "us," whereas people across the wastelands or mountains were "them." Indeed, the fission set in motion by the saints would most likely have left India a collection of small states like Europe, if conquerors had not forced her back toward union.

Finally, devotional movements prepared the way for the massive changes in Hindu culture that brought about the movements studied in the next chapter. Nineteenth-century leaders who tried to rethink Indian religion and society could not have challenged gender and caste roles as they did without precedents set by India's bhaktas. Keshab Chander Sen's movement in Bengal peaked in popularity when he added Chaitanya to his list of great prophets. M. G. Ranade of Maharashtra drew inspiration from Tukaram and Jnaneshvara as well as from the Western philosophers he studied. Hindu nationalists who challenged reformers also borrowed both mobilizing techniques and symbols from devotional movements.

ADDITIONAL SOURCES

Recent literature on devotional movements is massive. Helping sift through it is Philip Lutgendorf, "Medieval Devotional Traditions: an Annotated Survey of Recent Scholarship," *The Study of Hinduism,* Arvind Sharma, ed. (Columbia, SC: Univ. of South Carolina Press, 2003), 200–60. For earlier sources, see Eleanor Zelliot, "The Medieval Bhakti Movement in History," *New Essays in the History of Religions,* Bardwell L. Smith, ed. (Leiden: E. J. Brill, 1976), 143–68. Other than these essays and chapters in textbooks, comprehensive coverage of bhakti movements remains rare. An exception is the collection edited by Diana L. Eck and Françoise Mallison, *Devotion Divine from the Regions of India: Studies in Honor of Charlotte Vaudeville* (Groningen: Egbert Forsten, 1991). Researchers are otherwise advised to work through specific movements.

For Tamil Nayanars, an excellent start is Indira Viswanathan Peterson, *Poems to Śiva: the Hymns of the Tamil Saints* (Princeton: Princeton Univ. Press, 1989). For Alvars, see Vidya Dehejia, *Slaves of the Lord: The Path of the Tamil Saints* (Delhi: Munshiram Manorharlal, 1988). Poet A. K. Ramanujan offers fine translations of Alvar poetry in *Hymns for the Drowning* (Princeton: Princeton Univ. Press, 1981). Linking Alvars to later Shri Vaisnavas is Vasudha Narayanan, *The Way and the Goal: Expressions of Devotion in the Early Śrī Vaishṇava Tradition* (Washington, DC: Institute for Vaishnava Studies, 1987). See also her work, with John Carman, *The Tamil Veda: Piḷḷāṇ's Interpretation of the Tiruvāymoḻi* (Chicago: Univ. of Chicago Press, 1989). A. K. Ramanujan, *Speaking of Śiva* (Middlesex: Penguin, 1973) offers superb selections of Virashaiva poetry. Dan A. Chekki describes contemporary Virashaiva organization and practice in *Religion and Social System of the Vīraśaiva Community* (Westport, CT: Greenwood Press, 1997). V. Raghavan introduces a famed Telegu poet-saint in *Tyāgarāja* (New Delhi: Sahitya Akademi, 1983). R. D. Ranade, *Mysticism in India: the Poet-Saints of Maharashtra* (Albany, NY: SUNY Press, 1983), a reprint of a 1933 work, remains a useful overview of Maharashtrian poet-saints; the collection *Religion and Society in Maharashtra,* Milton Israel and N. K. Wagle, eds., includes more recent studies of several saints by Western scholars (Toronto: Univ. of Toronto Centre for South Asian Studies, 1987). More of Arun Kolatkar's fine translations can be found in his "Translations from Tukaram and Other Saint-Poets," *Journal of South Asian Literature* 27:1 (1982): 109–14.

For northern Sant traditions, the best start is John Stratton Hawley and Mark Juergensmeyer, *Songs of the Saints of North India* (New York: Oxford Univ. Press, 1988). Karine Schomer and W. H. McLeod have compiled a useful essay collection: *The Sants: Studies in a Devotional Tradition of India* (Delhi: Motilal Banarsidass, 1987). The standard introduction to Kabir is Charlotte Vaudeville, *A Weaver Named Kabir*

(Delhi: Oxford Univ. Press, 1993). Another saint inspiring a major low-caste panth was Raidas (Ravidas); see Winand M. Caelwaert and Peter Friedlander, *The Life and Works of Raidās* (New Delhi: Manohar, 2002). Exploring Sant reverence for gurus is Daniel Gold, *The Lord as Guru: Hindu Sants in the Northern Indian Traditions* (New York: Oxford Univ. Press, 1987). Extensive work has been done on Sikhs; readers wishing to sample Sikh gurus' songs can do so through Nikky-Guninder Kaur Singh, *The Name of My Beloved: Verses of the Sikh Gurus* (San Francisco: HarperSanFrancisco, 1995).

John Stratton Hawley has the best introduction to Surdas in *Sūrdās: Poet, Singer, Saint* (Seattle: Univ. of Washington Press, 1984). For the Vallabhacharya [Pushti-Marga] tradition that claims Surdas as its own, see Richard Barz, *The Bhakti Sect of Vallabhācārya* (Faridabad: Thomson Press [India], 1976); see also Mrudula I. Marfati *The Philosophy of Vallabhācārya* (Delhi: Motilal Banarsidass, 1979). Asking who sings Mirabai songs and why is Parita Mukta, *Upholding the Common Life* (New Delhi: Oxford Univ. Press, 1994); she finds that Rajputs don't, but low castes do. The best entree to Rama devotion is Philip Lutgendorf, *The Life of a Text: Performing the Rāmcaritmānas of Tulsidas* (Berkeley: Univ. of California Press, 1991); for a well-translated sampling of *Rāmcaritmānas* poetry, see Lutgendorf, "From the *Rāmcaritmānas* of Tulsidas, Book 5: Sundar Kand," *Indian Literature* 45:3 (2001): 143–81. A low-caste tradition of Ram devotion is superbly portrayed in Ramdas Lamb, *Rapt in the Name: The Ramnamis, Ramnam, and Untouchable Religion in Central India* (Albany: State Univ. of New York Press, 2002).

To sample Bengal's highly ecstatic devotion, a fine start is June McDaniel, *The Madness of the Saints: Ecstatic Religion in Bengal* (Chicago: Univ. of Chicago Press, 1989); for goddess devotion, see Malcolm McLean, *Devoted to the Goddess: the Life and Work of Ramprasad* (Albany: State Univ. of New York Press, 1998). Showing how drama evokes devotion is David Haberman, *Acting as a Way of Salvation* (New York: Oxford Univ. Press, 1988).

Many sources cited above include materials on women saints. Readers with a specific interest in women can add to these Vidya Dehejia, *Āntāl and Her Path of Love: Poems of a Woman Saint of South India* (Albany: State Univ. of New York Press, 1991); Vijaya Ramaswamy, *Walking Naked: Women, Society, Spirituality in South India* (Shimla: Indian Institute of Advanced Study, 1997); and Madhu Kishwar et al., *Women Bhakta Poets, Manushi* special issue 50–52 (January–June 1989).

4

The Samajists

Her back was as straight as a military cadet's. Not a hair was out of place in the bun of snow-white hair at the back of her neck. Her twisted hands lay still and folded in the lap of her simple white cotton sari. She quietly but articulately answered my questions about roles of women in her branch of the Arya Samaj, the religious organization she had served for most of her life. Her own career showed the opportunities that it offered to women. She began as a teacher in one of its colleges, became head of her college, and rose through governing committees of her branch of the Samaj. Finally, now retired, she was this region's vice-president and highest ranking female officer. Never before had I met a woman with so much dignity.

Her distinguished career was the by-product of an accident of history—the bone disease that crippled her hands when she was twelve years old. This handicap made it hard for her family to arrange the marriage with a well-placed husband that was usual for a girl of her high caste. Her grandfather and his sons were prominent members of the Arya Samaj, which was working hard to build a system of schooling for women, so her family decided not to make a marriage search but instead to give her the best education available.

One meets so many poised and learned women in today's India that it is hard to realize that, as few as seventy-five years ago, a woman with a higher education was rare in India.[1] One hundred and sixty years ago, just a handful of schools offered even basic literacy to women. In fact, a belief then widespread among high-caste Hindus held that a woman who learned to read would bring an early death to her husband. In the nineteenth century, a new breed of religious leaders turned this situation around.

These men—and, later, women—drew on religion to change religion, while at the same time challenging social practice that religion had protected. The movement they started will be called the *samaj* movement, after the type of organization that it created. It began among people of Hindu descent and upbringing, and only the

---

[1] Even rarer than in Europe and the United States, which by that time had many women's colleges and women who had undergone teacher's training.

forms it took among Hindus will be studied here. But it was not restricted to Hindus; both Sikhs and Muslims had important parallel movements. Nor did all Hindu-descended samajists consider themselves Hindus after they had joined the new organizations. In fact, the degree to which they were willing to depart from Hindu norms was a source of controversy that often split the movement and kept it from reaching all its goals.

What was a *samaj?* The word itself just means "society," a group of people who have banded together to accomplish a common purpose. Such societies were cross-caste organizations; in theory, at least, they accepted as members anyone willing to work for their cause. Most members were, nonetheless, from upper-caste groups, and the famous Prarthana Samaj of western Indian was almost entirely Brahmin. Unlike disciples of new religions arising in other countries, samajists did not depend on inspired prophets or even gurus for their teachings; for the most part they just figured things out, drawing on their stock of knowledge and powers of reasoning. Most samaj leaders were working men with families, although some groups did support paid full-time *acharyas,* a word they translated into English as "minister." Samajists were usually highly educated; many first joined their societies as college students. Older samajists often were people of social influence: government officials, professors, and doctors. They banded together to work for change both in religion and in society. Samajists founded presses, ran newspapers and journals, set up schools, lobbied the British government for needed laws, mounted demonstrations, studied other religions, rethought their own religious heritage, and designed new ways to worship together. This chapter tells their story and examines their accomplishments.

SAMAJ ORIGINS

In each previous chapter, some ancient strand of the Indian religious heritage set the stage for the movements or figures discussed. Here it is necessary to shift strategy. Samajists did, indeed, continue their Hindu heritage, especially the part of it that had so skillfully absorbed new ideas and practices and made them its own. However, the new ideas and practices being absorbed were not born on Indian soil; they were products of the British colonial presence.

The British presence in India started inconspicuously. A few trading stations, or "factories," run by a consortium, the British East India Company, were set up along India's coastline around the beginning of the seventeenth century. These were nothing unusual in India, which had traded with the West since the time of the Roman Empire. The Portuguese, French, and Dutch all had trading bases in India when the British established their factories. During the next century and a half, the British expanded their holdings while suppressing competition from European rivals. In 1757, the British defeated the French, their last major competitors, at the Battle of Plassey in Bengal. They then began the process of buying or undermining local rulers that changed a group of trading stations into an empire.

By the turn of the nineteenth century, the British East India Company held three large colonies, each based at a port that the Company had developed. The Bengal colony surrounded Calcutta on a mouth of the Ganges River, near the head of the

Bay of Bengal in eastern India. The Madras colony surrounded Madras city on the southeast coastline in Tamil-speaking country, and the Bombay colony extended inland from Bombay, an island city just off the western coast.

About the same time, the British Parliament began to take an active interest in these colonies, demanding that the Company bring benefit to its colonized subjects as well as to its own investors. In attempting to do this, the Company took three steps that had a major impact on subsequent Hindu history. The first was launching a massive information-gathering project. The second was creating schools and colleges that taught the English language and introduced Indians to British thought and culture. The third was giving Christian missionaries access to the British colonies in India.

The Indology Project

It is hard to rule or even trade with people about whose customs one knows nothing. The British had been alert to this problem from the very start of their trade with India and constantly asked visitors to India to send back records of their observations. In fact, the East India Company often intentionally hired scholars to serve as administrators, knowing they would gather valuable information about the new colonies. In the beginning, much of their work was haphazard, carried out during spare time between more official duties. This situation changed at the turn of the nineteenth century when the Company founded the College of Fort William in Calcutta.

Fort William College was assigned two principal tasks: It had to systematize collection of information about Indian customs, languages, and history; and it had to train new administrators to do their jobs, using the knowledge being gathered. It went about its assignments with zest, hiring Indian scholars to help and giving them access to its findings. It developed grammars for local languages and explored their literatures, while helping Indians publish new writings to aid in standardizing style and usage. It collected Sanskrit grammars, dictionaries, and texts from Brahmins willing to share them and deputed experts to find Brahmins who could still recite Vedas and would let them be recorded on paper. It also studied *Dharmashastra*, trying to adapt dharma codes into a consistent legal system. In addition, bit by bit, drawing on both these findings and archaeology, it and its sister college Haileybury in England pieced together a portrait of India's past: its Vedic Age, so far distant in the past that it rivaled the Biblical patriarchs in antiquity; its breakaway shramana movements and the first great Indian empires whose rulers had been their patrons; its later classical empires when Brahmins recaptured their sway over rulers; and finally its troubled medieval period, when Muslim rulers controlled much of the land and battled Hindus and one another.[2]

Much of that history was previously known only in a very fractured form. Epics and Puranas recounted tales and genealogies of ancient kings, and Sanskrit inscriptions on copper plates and the walls of religious foundations offered brief glimpses into ancient realms. But no one had put these pieces together into one coherent story, assigned them dates, or compared them with the histories of other civilizations.

---

[2] These developments are described in David Kopf, *British Orientalism and the Bengal Renaissance; the Dynamics of Indian Modernization, 1773–1835* (Berkeley: Univ. of California Press, 1969).

This reconstruction of the Indian past was a revelation for most Indians, especially for those whom the British were calling "Hindus." It held that the Vedic collections that Brahmins guarded so carefully were as old—and thereby as precious—as was the Old Testament of the British rulers' own Bible. The epic heroes had lived before the start of Christianity. Moreover, India's past had been a Golden Age, like that of the Greeks and Romans in the West. Wisdom had flourished; caste was less binding; men and women lived together as nearly equal partners. Wealth abounded, and rulers of native Indian descent held huge empires together successfully. This portrait of their past brought Hindus tremendous pride, as did the praise that Westerners heaped on translations of major Upanishads and the *Bhagavad-Gita*. It also began to implant a new sense of Hindu unity. Once a group of communities has a story of common origins, it becomes able to think of itself as a single people.

English Language Education

One justification for founding the College of Fort William had been that people will accept foreign rule more readily if it does not hugely disrupt their own culture. The Company sponsored its study of India so that its personnel could communicate in India's languages and work within Indian structures, changing them only minimally. Quickly, however, it learned that this was a daunting undertaking and required more adjustments than Company representatives were able to make. So it changed its tactics and set about instead to create a class of Indians who would adjust to the Company. They were to learn British language and customs and to help the Company keep the peace and reconcile Indians to foreign domination.

Fortunately for the British, this project coincided with a decision among some Indians themselves that learning the language and thought of their new masters would be a good way to gain advantage in the new colonial world. The push for English education started among upper-class Calcuttans who controlled much of their city's property and trade. Most were Hindus, many of them Brahmins whose income came from land and commerce rather than older Brahmin vocations of teaching and ritual supervision. By 1817, the British agreed to open Hindu College in Calcutta as a place where young men of respectable background could study English language, literature, and science.

This move opened a Pandora's box. It did accomplish the Company's aims. Graduates of Hindu College and others like it provided an invaluable cadre of civil servants, vastly extending their rulers' reach and effectiveness in India. English-educated Indians took over most of India's middle management in courts, the revenue system, government offices, trade centers, and the railroad and postal systems. But the new schools also gave those competent middle managers a language in which they could speak to each other across India's regional boundaries. Furthermore, the schools exposed their students to ideas that had been radical even for cultures that produced them: the ideas, for example, that humans have certain basic rights and can overthrow governments that do not honor these rights or that all people are humans, even women, the poor, and dark-skinned peoples from half a world away. At first English-educated Hindus admired their new rulers because their culture had produced such noble concepts. Later, they started to notice that the rulers did not always practice what their books had preached.

The Missionaries

Christianity was not new to India when the East India Company began admitting missionaries to its colonies. Christians observing the Syriac rites of the old Eastern churches had settled in South India already during the early centuries C.E. Legends of their community claim that it was started by Jesus' apostle Thomas. Ships carrying French and Portuguese goods and traders later brought Catholic missions to work in India. Although not hugely successful, these missionaries did win converts among low-caste Hindus and peoples who serviced the French and Portuguese colonies. Danish Lutherans also established two tiny mission footholds on the west coast of India at the same time that the British were solidifying their presence. The Danish mission at Serampore near Calcutta later became an important base for the first British missionaries to enter the Bengal colony.

Before 1813, missionaries had to work from outside Company territories because the Company did not let them settle within its holdings. In general, it had avoided interfering with native religions on the premise that disrupting something as dear to people as religion was likely to win it more enemies than friends. However, Britains back in the homeland soon called this policy into question, telling the Company it had a duty to "civilize" India. In return for extracting India's wealth, the Company was to give Indians a system of just government, access to Western ideas and science, and the chance to hear and be saved by the good news of Christ. The difficulties the Company had in staffing schools where children could learn the English language added another motive for letting missionaries enter the Company's colonies. Missionaries eager to win young souls were far more willing to come to India as teachers than were young people merely in need of a job.

When the missionaries came, they arrived in many varieties. There were not only Anglicans from England proper and Presbyterians from the Scottish north but also Baptists, Unitarians, and American Methodists. Some went about their work unobtrusively, made Indian friends, and did their best to help and heal India's people. Others were pushy and intolerant, preaching that Hindu traditions were ignorant and degenerate. When the latter became teachers, they deeply alarmed Hindu parents because they often tried to turn students against their families.

One Christian assertion the Company swiftly adopted was that Indians needed British rule and missions because they behaved so badly when left to their own devices. One proof of Indian barbarism, according to missionaries, was the way Indian Hindus treated their women. Hindus burned widows or made them live in perpetual mourning, gave young children in marriage, made women live secluded in dark inner rooms of their houses, and refused them access to education. Making these practices even more offensive was the fact that many were sanctioned by Hindu religion. The missionaries proclaimed that God had brought the British to India to enlighten Hindus and lead them to abandon such practice.

Unfortunately, these charges were just true enough to make some Hindus quite uncomfortable. The old custom of sati was enjoying a renaissance among upper-caste Bengalis: living women sometimes burned on cremation pyres with their husbands' corpses believing that this act of sacrifice would make them family-protecting goddesses. Upper-caste widows who did not do this were forbidden from remarrying and were expected to dress and behave as if they were sadhvis, with shaved heads, no adornments, plain white saris, simple vegetarian eating, and no attendance at family celebrations. Many widows were very young girls because *dharmashastra* precepts taught that girls should be given in marriage before first menstruation. Seclusion of wives and older women was common among high castes in some regions. Furthermore, girls' education was rare and was thought to endanger prospective husbands.

SAMAJIST IDEALS

The samajists began their movement in order to show that Hindus could solve their own problems by mounting effective responses to these and other social issues. They wanted to counter missionary incursions, although they also took what they liked from Christianity and knit it into their own teachings and organizations. Most samajists came from the cadre of young men with an English-language education who had read and taken seriously the works of Western literature. One of the ideas they would use most effectively was the Indologists' vision of a Golden Age in the Hindu past that could be set up as standard for correcting the present.

This was not the only idea they used because the samaj movement was really a series of undertakings, like the sadhu and bhakta movements described in earlier chapters. Various groups emerged with different ways of promoting and carrying out change. Two tensions in particular caused much of the movement's differentiation. The first tension was between those who made social reform their first priority and those who were principally interested in religious reformation. The group stressing social reform was composed largely of highly educated young men enthused by the new moral philosophies coming out of Britain. They wanted to see Indian social practice become based on principles of rationality. To accomplish this, they believed they had to make religion more rational also. At the very least, they wished to subject religion to rational critiques that would break the hold of pandits and sadhus who resisted rational change. People most interested in religious reform were more mixed in background. Some were highly educated, others less so. They shared a conviction that something had gone out of kilter in Hindu religion. It had lost contact with its spiritual mainsprings, and therefore, something had gone wrong as well in the ways Hindus treated their own people. To set things right again, Indians needed a basic transformation of spiritual vision. The difference between these two groups was mainly in style and priorities because they agreed that both society and religion needed changing.

The second major tension cut through both these groups, and was a how-to do-it tension. One group of reformers thought that change was best accomplished by looking to the wisdom of India's Golden Age, especially that of the Vedic collections that Brahmins and Europeans were calling the principal roots of Hindu tradition. These reformers are often called revivalists because they thought Hindu religion and social practice could best be renewed by reviving older values and forms of practice. Many revivalists wished to avoid angering the more traditional Hindus who surrounded samaj communities. They hoped to catch other Hindus up in their renewal projects, not to alienate and distance them. Opposed to them were people who wanted something new that could connect Hindus spiritually to the overseas religious groups that were becoming more and more a part of their own world. They thought they would find the resources to change their own society by drawing on humankind's cumulative religious vision. Writers on India usually call these people universalists because they sought to create a form of religion that could embrace not only Hindus, but all other peoples. They knew they were breaking with tradition and angering older Hindu leaders. But they believed they had launched such an exciting project that it would draw supporters through its own merits.

Much of the rest of this chapter is spent tracing the history of these tensions in the samaj movement and showing how they were expressed in various organizations and accomplishments. All the groups examined were founded in the nineteenth century, and the focus here will be mostly on their nineteenth-century alternatives. The final group studied, formed at the century's very end, did not call itself a samaj and departed from the samaj model of organization. But it preserved samaj ideals, and its changed structure gave it a way to reconcile earlier samaj tensions. Its fusion of sadhu traditions and service, revival and global outreach, would be imitated by many new Hindu groups of the twentieth century.

SETTING THE PRECEDENTS: RAMMOHAN ROY

Tensions in a religious movement are often a product of disciples' different ideas about how to carry on the example of the founder. However, the pulls in different directions that characterized Hindu samajists were already present in the work of the founder himself. Bengal-born Rammohan Roy (1772–1833), sometimes called "the Father of Modern India," was a social and religious reformer who believed that both types of reform had to go on simultaneously to produce effective change. Religiously, he was also both a revivalist and a universalist, believing that teachings from India's past, especially the Upanishads, preserved the common core of spiritual insight that Hinduism shared with the world's other great religions. Rammohan's[3] work for social change included several projects in support of English-language education and a famous campaign against widow-burning. His work on behalf of religious renewal included writings against idolatry, translations of the *Vedanta Sutra* and five Upanishads, studies of Christian moral teachings, and the founding, with several friends, of India's first samaj. This Brahmo Samaj was universalist in vision, honoring the one, all-powerful, all-knowing and personal God that it believed to be at the core of all religions. But it was revivalist in particulars, anchoring its worship in the Vedas and its preaching in the Upanishads.

It is hard to understand how one man could have moved in so many different directions without looking at Rammonhan's life. He came from a high Brahmin family, but was not of classic Brahmin upbringing. His father's family had been Gaudiya Vaishnavas, members of the sect founded by the Bengali saint Caitanya. Although she converted to his father's faith, his mother was the daughter of a prominent Shakta priest. Like many north Indian Brahmins of the post-Muslim era, Rammohan's immediate male ancestors had been administrators for Muslim rulers rather than pandits or priests.

---

[3] I am following standard Bengali practice of referring to people by their given rather than their family names.

Rammohan's father, therefore, gave his brilliant son a dual education. On the one hand, Rammohan studied Sanskrit, as was proper for a Brahmin boy of his time. But he also learned Persian and Arabic, the languages he would need to work for a Muslim government. One experience deeply affecting Rammohan as a teen was a time when his father sent him away from home to study at a Muslim college. There he came to accept the Muslim teaching that God is one and too sublime to be lessened by giving Him form in images. When Rammohan returned home, he wrote an essay against image worship that his father found and interpreted as an attack on the family's religion. The two quarreled, and Rammohan headed out into the world on his own, instead of living at his family homestead.

He traveled for three years, claiming later that he had reached Tibet and conversed with Tibetan Buddhists. His father finally found him and called him home, only to quarrel again with Rammohan soon after. Now Rammohan moved to the old holy city of Banaras. Here he studied more Sanskrit and acquired some English, for by now it was clear that the English were becoming the major power in his region. Rammohan moved at least twice more, found a job in the British revenue service, and then worked for several years as assistant to a British tax official. As a result of this service, he became much more fluent in English. He used most of his earnings to make land investments, building himself a tidy independent income.

By 1814, at the age of 42, Rammohan was rich enough to retire and live on his investments. He moved to Calcutta, gathered a circle of like-minded friends, and set them to thinking about how they could improve Bengal society. Education was one of their projects. Although Rammohan's own name is not on the charter for the Hindu College, most of his friends signed it, and Rammohan himself did support the college. He also donated funds for a missionary-run, English-medium elementary school and helped raise funds for a second one. At a time when the government had not yet decided what kind of education it should back most strongly, Rammohan wrote a powerful defense of young Indians' need to have an education that would let them move freely in the world.

Most of Rammohan's reform efforts arose out of his own experience. He had struggled to learn English and knew the difference that command of it made in his own life. When he wrote at one point about the evils of multiple marriage among Kulin (very high-caste) Brahmins, he spoke as a Kulin who as a child had been forced to marry three small girls. When he charged that women's innate intelligence was being stifled by lack of access to education, he seems to have been thinking about his own bright and forceful but opinionated mother. When he launched his campaign against sati in 1814, it was the memory of a sister-in-law's sati that drove him. She had been his older brother's wife, and in Bengal an older brother's wife often develops a strong friendship with the next brother down. It is not known for certain if Rammohan was close to the sister-in-law burned with her husband. It is known that this action sickened and horrified him and that he was furious because his family did not stop her. Even before, he had campaigned for a total sati ban. He had gone to cremation grounds where satis were expected and tried to persuade the widows not to carry out their vows.[4]

---

[4] Two such incidents are described in Sophia Dobson Collet, *The Life and Letters of Raja Rammohun Roy* (Calcutta: Sadharan Brahmo Samaj, 1962), p. 89.

Rammohan's move toward a more active anti-sati campaign was fueled by signs from the British that they, too, would like to find a way of imposing a sati ban. Between 1813 and 1817, the Bengal Governor had tried several ways to cut down on satis. This backfired. The number of satis rose, and several prominent Hindus charged the government with breaking its own policy against interference with religion. Rammohan's response was to publish and distribute a pamphlet arguing that sati was not truly sanctioned by religion. He cited texts that later samajists would cite again and again as sources for the norms of "real" Hinduism: the Upanishads, the *Bhagavad-Gita*, and the *Laws of Manu* (*Manusmriti*). When this pamphlet raised a storm, he followed it with a second one, and then lobbied his British contacts until a new governor banned sati in 1829.

While his sati campaign was getting under way, Rammohan launched another enterprise that again landed him in the middle of public controversy. He translated into Bengali a central Vedanta text and five of the shorter Upanishads (published 1815–17).[5] One reason why he did this was to challenge idol worship. He had never lost his conviction that making divine images was destructive and kept humans from realizing the true nature of God. His very first published work, issued around 1804–05, had been a tract against idol worship written in Persian. Rammohan was convinced that idol worship helped cause the social customs that he found evil. Degraded religion leads to degraded moral standards, he wrote, citing stories about Krishna's affairs with his cowgirls. Therefore, one could not heal social ills without also cleaning up religion.

One reason religion becomes degraded, Rammohan taught, was that priests seize upon humanity's "pure" religious instincts and exploit these for their own profit. He believed that all humans are naturally inclined to worship a single God as the world's creator. He believed, moreover, that every God honored in the world's religions was at heart the same God as every other. When Rammohan studied Vedanta and the Upanishads, he became convinced that they preserved Hinduism's original "pure" teachings and that the power they called "brahman" was the one true God.[6] So he published them to show that India's ancient Veda held the religious teaching that he believed was valid.

The Upanishad publications drew criticism more for what he had done than for what he had said. Over the years, Brahmin authority to issue religious teachings had been eroded both by sadhu and bhakti traditions. But Brahmins still monopolized Veda, which they said they alone could study. Moreover, only the purest renunciant Brahmins were allowed to study Vedanta and the Upanishad texts on brahman. Rammohan was out of line on at least two counts. Although he was a Brahmin and thus able to study Veda, he was a householder and thus should not have studied the Upanishads or Vedanta. Moreover, not only had he studied these, he had also translated them into a language in which any literate person could read them. In short, he had challenged the Brahmin monopoly on India's most ancient texts and had given Hindus resources for challenging custom without withdrawing from their own tradition.

---

[5] The works were *Vedantasutra* and the *Kena, Isha, Mundaka, Katha*, and *Mandukya Upanishads*. All but *Mandukya* were also translated into English.

[6] Encouraging Rammohan's belief was the fact that scholars had not yet separated out the internal stratifications of the Veda. A Brahmin of his time would have assumed that the Upanishads were just as old as any other part of the Veda's known texts.

By 1816, Rammohan was part of another controversial project. He began to study Christianity with Baptist missionaries at Serampore, helping two of them translate the New Testament into Bengali. His collaborators hoped to convert him, but soon he was trying to convert them. At issue was the Christian doctrine of the Trinity, which Rammohan charged was polytheistic. Christians would be more consistent, he argued, if they would use the term "God" only for the world's creator and would understand Jesus solely as God's chosen instrument. Rammohan's arguments on behalf of this unitarian doctrine won over one translator and frustrated the other to the point that he fled the project. Later, in 1820, Rammohan drew on this project to publish an English compilation of the "pure and sublime" moral teachings of Jesus. Although he planned also to issue Bengali and Sanskrit versions, his missionary acquaintances blocked these translations. They were upset because the first publication told Bengalis that they should heed Christian moral teachings, but ignore the rest of Christian doctrine. On the whole, Rammohan's excursions into Christianity brought him more enemies than friends.

Nearly all the initiatives discussed thus far took place before the Brahmo Samaj first began meeting in 1828. Twice before Rammohan had tried to start an organization that would carry out his ideas. When he first came to Calcutta, he had started a "Friendly Association" that met at his home to discuss reforms. Although this did not last, some members became close friends of Rammohan and later helped him with many projects. In 1821, he tried again, this time working with the missionary William Adam whom Rammohan had convinced to reject Trinitarian doctrine. After the Baptists expelled Adam, Rammohan helped him gain approval from American Unitarians to start a Calcutta Unitarian congregation. Rammohan and his friends hired a meeting house for Adam, who conducted services based on a fusion of Rammohan's teachings with Christianity. But this proved too strange for Rammohan's friends to swallow, and soon Adam was preaching to an empty hall.

Rammohan's third attempt succeeded. This time he and his friends formed a "theistic society" that would be grounded in Indian teachings and forms of worship.[7] They used what had worked best in the Unitarian experiment: a regular weekly meeting for worship, following a format much like a Christian service: chanted scripture from the Upanishads, followed by explanation and preaching, and ending with hymns in Bengali composed by Rammohan and his friends. Any person of pious intention could enter the Brahmo meeting house and worship, and no image or sacrifice was allowed on the premises. No other religion was to be slighted; this was a place for positive models and not for polemic.

From the Christians, Brahmo Samajists also borrowed the idea of appointing a permanent acharya who would tend the community like a Christian minister. They gave this job to a Brahmin named Ramchandra Vidyavajish, whose brother was a sadhu and a long-time friend of Rammohan. This group at first met and worked out procedures in a small house they had jointly rented. Two years after their first meeting, they bought a meeting house of their own and signed a formal charter of incorporation. Then they lost Rammohan, who traveled to England at the end of 1830 to carry a request from the last Mughal emperor and to defend the ban on sati before a

---

[7] The principal source for Brahmo Samaj history and practice is David Kopf, *The Brahmo Samaj and the Shaping of the Modern Indian Mind* (Princeton: Princeton Univ. Press, 1979).

Parliamentary committee. Neither England's food nor its climate agreed with Rammohan; three years later he died there, leaving his Brahmo Samaj without its strongest proponent. His friends kept the society going for a while, and it had an endowment that let Ramchandra keep holding services even after it lost most of its congregation. He struggled to keep the samaj alive until the early 1840s when the son of one of its founders discovered and revived it.

SUCCESS AND FIRST SPLIT: THE ADI BRAHMO SAMAJ AND THE BRAHMO SAMAJ OF INDIA

The young man who rescued the Brahmo Samaj ideals was Debendranath Tagore, son of Rammohan's close friend Dwarkanath Tagore. Debendranath had attended Hindu College, where he fell into the group Young Bengal, made up of early graduates from the college. Many had been students of a teacher there, Henry Louis Vivian Derozio, a young half-Indian greatly impressed by the West's new philosophical teachings. Derozio taught his students to challenge tradition and to listen only to reason. These teachings so badly alarmed Hindu College parents that they forced the school to fire him. But the damage was done; for years after graduation, Derozio's students stuck together, sponsoring lectures and debates on Indian social issues. One issue that they picked up and kept alive was the maltreatment of Indian women, especially in widowhood and child marriage. They did not have many listeners because their behavior and ideas were too extreme. Many had taken to British hairstyles and dress, eating meat, and drinking alcohol, and they grounded most of their arguments in Western theories about human rights, rather than in values familiar to Hindus.

Debendranath himself was uneasy with Young Bengal and never became a member of its inner circle. But he did make friends there who later joined him in a venture of his own. As Debendranath passed through college and beyond, he rebelled against the Westernized context in which his father had raised him. He drew close to his deeply religious grandmother, whose 1835 death sent him into a crisis that convinced his family he had gone crazy. Rejecting the comforts of his rich home, he took up an austere lifestyle, neglected his role in the family business, and began to obsess about missionary incursions. In 1833, the East India Company had lifted its last restrictions on missions in its territories. Soon after, Christians made several conversions that stirred up a great deal of public protest. Now Debendranath turned to Young Bengal friends to launch a society—the Tattvabodhini Sabha—that would work to stop these conversions.

The Tattvabodhini Sabha proved to be far more successful than Young Bengal at pulling together well-to-do Bengalis. Soon it had several hundred members. It bought a press and founded a newspaper that challenged claims made by missionary propaganda. It also started a school that used Bengali as a teaching medium, and it began to publish textbooks in Bengali. It explored the religious meaning of the Upanishads and Vedanta philosophy and it took up again the social issues pursued by Rammohan Roy and Young Bengal, most notably the problem of female oppression. Pushing this issue especially were *Tattvabodhini* newspaper editor Akshoy Kumar Dutt and Dutt's friend Ishwarachandra Vidyasagar, a brilliant Sanskritist and principal of Sanskrit College, a sister school of Hindu College that offered studies in Sanskrit literature. In 1855 and

1856, Vidyasagar published two tracts based on Dharmashastra research that argued that dharma teachings allowed widow remarriage during the present age.[8] These won popular backing far more swiftly than Rammohan's anti-sati tracts had done. In 1856 the Bengal government passed a bill allowing Hindu widows to remarry.

Adi Brahmo Samaj

These aspects of his society's work did not interest Debendranath, whose passion was religious reformation. During the early 1840s, he rediscovered the Brahmo Samaj that had been founded by Rammohan and his father. Talking with its minister, Debendranath came to believe that he and the Brahmo Samaj shared a common purpose. By 1843, he had nineteen Tattvabodhini friends interested enough to take vows of formal Brahmo Samaj membership. By 1859, membership in the two groups overlapped so extensively that Debendranath merged them. Although Vidyasagar and a few others rejected this merger, others came gladly, bringing the Brahmo Samaj a solid and growing base of membership.

Meanwhile, Debendranath found a protégé even more successful at winning recruits than he was. In 1857, Debendranath went to hear a talk given by a young man of Vaidya caste named Keshab Chander Sen. Soon they were friends, and Debendranath swiftly drew Keshab into Brahmo Samaj activities. In 1862, Debendranath proposed to initiate Keshab as a Brahmo Samaj acharya, or minister. This startled older Brahmos because Keshab was just twenty-four years old and would be the first acharya not born a Brahmin. Moreover, they considered him a social radical. But Debendranath had his way, and soon Keshab was a full-time Brahmo Samaj leader.

Soon the charismatic Keshab was pulling in college students whom he fired with visions of working for massive social transformation. High-caste students began burning the sacred threads that set them apart from their Brahmo brothers, eating meals with lower-caste members, arranging intercaste and widow marriages, and preaching against the oppression of women. Keshab also organized a band of young missionaries eager to carry the Brahmo Samaj into other towns in Bengal. In every town where they preached, they made converts, especially among students and employees of the British. Some paid dearly for their conversions when families outcasted and disinherited them.[9] For these, Keshab founded a support society and a Brahmo commune in Calcutta where they could live.

Keshab himself traveled farther afield, using the railroads recently built by the British. In 1864, he gave talks in Madras, where enthusiasts founded a small group called the Veda Samaj. From Madras, he continued to the Bombay colony in western India. His contact with English-educated leaders in Bombay laid the base for their founding a Prarthana Samaj, "Prayer Society," three years later in 1867. Like the Brahmo Samaj of the east, this society soon spawned branches throughout its region and became a reform center for western India.

---

[8] Ishwarchandra Vidyasagara, *Marriage of Hindu Widows* (Calcutta: K. P. Bagchi, 1976 reprint). See also Brian A. Hatcher, *Vidyasagar and Cultural Encounter in Bengal* (Calcutta: Oxford Univ. Press, 1976).

[9] An outcaste experiences total ostracism. Relatives and caste-mates will not speak to or aid outcastes; other castes will do no work for them.

Despite all these successes, Debendranath's friends had been right about Keshab. He was too different from Debendranath for their two groups of Brahmos to go on working side by side. Keshab's radical social initiatives alarmed Debendranath, who wanted to change fellow Hindus gradually and not to offend them. Even more alarming, however, were Keshab's attempts to reconcile Brahmoism with Christianity. Debendranath had always stressed the part of Rammohan's teaching that claimed that the Upanishads were the best foundation for reconstructing a pure Hinduism. Careful study had shown him that not all Upanishads were equally up to this task. One day, however, while he was praying intensely, God showed him which Upanishads to use. Recorded in his book *Brahmo Dharma*, these had become the official collection of Brahmo scripture.[10]

Keshab, in contrast, was most interested in that part of Rammohan's teaching that stressed the universal component in Brahmo Samaj religion. When Rammohan translated Upanishads and made them available for study, he had done so believing they reflected a religious vision that was central to all religions. Stripped of myths and theologies and fanciful icons, all religions came down at last to simple belief in God, a belief in life after death that would reward good actions, and a moral impulse to take care of others. When he started preaching, Keshab too drew on this notion that Brahmo religion represented the essence of all faiths. But he took this idea one step farther. He began to draw on other faiths as well as Hinduism for the scriptures he used in teaching and the figures he cited as worthy examples for Brahmos to follow. He especially admired the Jesus he found after having stripped him of two thousand years of theological interpretation. To Keshab, Jesus was a heroic prophet who taught people to love and look after one another.

Brahmo Samaj of India

This was too much for Debendranath, who had founded his first society to counter the work of Christian missions. The two groups agreed to split at a Brahmo General Meeting on November 15, 1866. Debendranath's supporters took the name Adi Brahmo Samaj, "first Brahmo Samaj," and kept the founding Brahmo Samaj property. Keshab's faction became the Brahmo Samaj of India, quickly raising the money to build a temple of its own. The split freed Keshab's energies, and 1866–72 became his most productive years. He expanded Brahmo missions into the countryside, using the devotional saints' old methods of putting religious messages into songs and attracting attention through singing street processions. These began winning Bengali members outside the original English-educated circles. Keshab himself became so famous that thousands came to hear him speak, even though his talks at times went on for two or more hours.

In 1870, Keshab was invited to visit Britain, where he was hailed as a great religious leader. Inspired by social programs sponsored by Christians in Britain, he returned to launch a whirlwind of projects. One group, the Indian Reform Association, worked for "uplift" of low-caste and poor people, starting an industrial school to teach crafts to laborers, a night school for teaching adult literacy, and a highly successful one-cent paper to bring news and instruction to the working classes.

---

[10] *Brahmo Dharma of Maharishi Debendranath Tagore* (Calcutta: Brahmo Mission Press, 1928).

Another group started a girls' school and a normal school for training women teachers. Keshab organized a Brahmo Samaj women's society, launched "Bands of Hope" to fight alcohol addiction among students, and encouraged followers to assemble libraries and to establish savings banks for workers. Brahmo Samaj branches in the countryside became small colonies of institutions: a central meeting hall, often flanked by one school for boys and another for girls, a night school for laborers, a library, a bank, and a press to disseminate Brahmo Samaj teachings and news.

In 1872, Keshab's Brahmos also won a major legal victory: the Brahmo Marriage Act passed by the British government recognized the legality of the Brahmos' simplified marriage rituals and of intercaste marriages performed within their community. The same act forbade marriages of children under sixteen and polygamous marriage within the Brahmo community. There was only one catch; to be covered by this act, people marrying under its provisions had to declare that they were no longer Hindus. In law, the Brahmo Samaj was now a separate religion.

MORE SPLITTING AND FURTHER TRIALS: SADHARAN BRAHMOS, THE NEW DISPENSATION, THE PRARTHANA SAMAJ AND HINDU NATIONALISM

The year of greatest triumph for Keshab's samaj was also the beginning of its fall. After 1872 came two decades of crisis that weakened both the Brahmo Samaj and the Prarthana Samaj, its Maharashtrian cousin. In 1872, moreover, a new samaj began that displaced Brahmos in a large swath of northwest Indian territory. This rival Arya Samaj will be discussed later during this chapter. This section will look more closely at the trials of the older societies.

The first crises were internal, fracturing Keshab's Brahmo Samaj along an old fault line. In 1872, Keshab quarreled about women with the faction among his Brahmos that was most deeply committed to social reform. Since the time of Rammohan Roy, all samaj social reformists had made women's emancipation one of their primary goals. Keshab was no exception, but he differed from younger followers concerning how far women's emancipation should go and how quickly it should be accomplished. Keshab's ideal woman was a loyal Brahmo wife who would work beside her husband toward India's transformation. Brahmo radicals wanted women who could move about freely in society, think for themselves, and choose their own direction in life.

Their first quarrel with Keshab was about seating at Brahmo services. The radicals wanted their wives beside them, thus showing that they had fully rejected purdah, the seclusion of women. Keshab preferred to seat all women upstairs in the meeting hall's balcony, but finally agreed that wives could sit with husbands if the wives themselves so chose. The second and more serious quarrel concerned curriculum in the new Brahmo school for women. Both the radicals and a woman teacher who had come from England wanted Brahmo women to study the same subjects as men. Keshab preferred an emphasis on literature, morals, and home economics. This time,

Keshab held his ground, and the teacher and the school's principal, a radical Brahmo, left to start a rival school of their own.

Stung by these challenges to his authority, Keshab pulled back from Brahmo social reform projects, turning his attention to religious reformation. He went into an extended retreat with his missionaries and assigned them to do research on other religions, looking for better ways to merge multiple teachings and practice together into the universal Brahmo path. Now the social reformers were stung and recalled other features of Keshab's religious reforms that they found bothersome. They did not like the increasing emotionalism of Brahmo practice, especially the singing processions derived from Krishna-centered devotion, which they believed was degenerate. Nor did they like the direction that Keshab's sermons were taking. Keshab had a theory of progressive revelation. The world's religions, he taught, had been founded by a series of prophets, each of whom God called to address a problem or problems special to his age. This teaching seemed to suggest that Keshab himself was a prophet for his own age, as did repeated hints that he was receiving divine inspiration.

Brahmo tensions came to a crisis when Keshab agreed to a request that he give his daughter in marriage to the young ruler of Kuch Bihar, one of India's semi-independent principalities. Because the Brahmo Marriage Act did not hold in Kuch Bihar, in theory it did not matter that the bride was fourteen years old. But to Brahmo social reformers, Keshab had abandoned his own principles. Keshab most likely agreed to the marriage in the hope that his daughter would influence her husband to spread Brahmo reforms in Kuch Bihar—as indeed she did in later years. But he would only tell his followers that God had told him to allow the marriage. The social reform contingent now broke off, forming a separate Sadharan Brahmo Samaj. Two years later, Keshab announced that he was indeed his age's new prophet and regrouped his following into the Nava Vidhan, "New Dispensation." For three more years, his group tried out both ritual and organizational innovations that they believed would become the religion of the future. Then Keshab died of advanced diabetes, leaving no one who could carry on the process he had begun.

Prarthana Samaj

Meanwhile, initiative in combining social with religious reform was shifting west to the Prarthana Samaj. Three brothers named Pandurang founded this group, responding in part to proddings from Keshab. Its most famous leader, however, was Judge Mahadev Govind Ranade, who joined the Samaj in 1869 and worked for the most part out of its Pune Branch, set up one year later. Prarthana Samajists cooperated with the Calcutta Brahmo Samaj and often received visits from Keshab's cousin P. C. Majumdar, a leading Brahmo Samaj missionary. Prathanists were, nonetheless, careful to keep their organization separate. Like Debendranath's Adi Brahmos in Calcutta, they did not want to offend too greatly the orthodox Hindu community surrounding them. Their samaj had an almost entirely Brahmin membership. Like Ranade, most members were Chitpavan Brahmins, a group that had held many government positions during the Maratha reign that preceded the British. As Chitpavans, they had a great deal of influence that could help them bring about change if they did not alienate people. Also, Brahmin pandits were well organized in Maharashtra and had caused a major setback for a group that worked for widow remarriage before the Prarthana Samaj was organized.

Hence, the Prarthanists were more cautious than Keshab's Brahmos. They kept their sacred threads, avoided conspicuous breaking of caste rules, and in general paid more attention to education and women's issues than to thornier and more difficult efforts like uplifting the poor or challenging caste. Prarthanists organized schools, libraries, and lecture societies, backed the widow remarriage effort, promoted women's education and helped their women to form western India's first women's society. Many members were active in a group that fought child marriage during the 1880s, and Prarthanists led in organizing the first all-India National Social Conference (founded 1887). For several years this conference met conjointly with the Indian National Congress, the first nationwide group of Indian leaders set up to advise the British rulers (founded 1885). As a group, Prarthanists were more deeply committed to social and political change than to religious experimentation. They borrowed most of their founding principles from the Brahmo charter, asserting that they would worship only the One God who was creator of all, would not use images, would not recognize any sacred book as infallible, but would not abuse any book or object held sacred by another community. But when Prarthanists wrote justifications for reform, their language was often revivalist. Ranade, for example, liked to refer to the "venerated Vedic past," asserting that "false Puranas" had corrupted this.[11] He even combed Dharmashastra writings to find support for reform initiatives. For the first twenty years of their existence, this caution brought Prarthanists tolerance from most orthodox Hindu leaders.

Hindu Nationalists

This tolerance started to fray in the late 1880s. In this case, damaging pressures were mostly external, products of India's changing political context. During the first half of the nineteenth century, relationships between Indians and their British rulers had been cordial. The drive to study and develop Indian culture had won many friends, while the government created new and well-paying jobs, promoted schooling, introduced technological advances, stabilized the legal system, and improved travel via the railroad system. Unfortunately, it also drained wealth from the Indian economy, reserved many business opportunities for its own people, and enacted a system of taxation that worsened effects of the famines that were frequent in India. Administrators and their policies furthermore changed so often that India's people found the changes unnerving.

In 1857, a combination of dissatisfactions set off a mutiny in the Indian Army that killed many British officials, together with their wives and families. Realizing that the East India Company could no longer maintain control, the British crown took over its holdings and reorganized India into a single crown colony. New administrations proved even less flexible and more racist than their predecessors. Meanwhile, fallout from the mutiny changed government policy toward Indian landlords, who were

---

[11] See citations from writings of M. G. Ranade in Richard P. Tucker, *Ranade and the Roots of Indian Nationalism* (Chicago: Univ. of Chicago Press, 1972), especially 319–23. Unfortunately the Prarthanists have not been studied nearly as thoroughly as the Brahmos; their writings are hard to find and few are available in English.

allowed to get away with greater exploitation of tenants. The new colleges soon produced too many eligible candidates for the jobs available, and attempts by Indians to gain jobs reserved for the British prompted decisions showing that the British would not share any power or advantage. In fact, the more cosmopolitan and able Indians became, the more the British in India seemed to despise them.

These changes in turn produced a wave of backlash, especially among Hindus, who focused most of their anger against samajists. Samaj efforts had always produced some backlash. When sati was banned, for example, Rammohan's opponents founded a group called Dharma Sabha to try to undo his work and protect Hindu practice from government interference. Each new reform initiative that depended on the legal system for enforcement crystallized further opposition. As British rulers grew more oppressive, some young men from the educated class they had created began calling for a united stand of Indians against them. These young radicals charged that samajists were collaborators and that their reforms should be rejected because they divided Hindus.

Both Bengal and Maharashtra became centers of nationalist protest, and in both regions, Hindu symbols crystallized this protest. In Bengal, these symbols were goddess images: India herself was portrayed as Bharat Mata, a chained and broken goddess, whose own sons and daughters must strive to free her. The black and frightening Kali was made an image of the *shakti*, "power," that was rising in Hindus who would liberate her. College students in Bengal organized terrorist cells teaching that murder of British officials was a fit sacrifice to Kali. In Maharashtra, the principal symbol became the elephant-headed god Ganesh worshiped by Shivaji, founder of the Hindu Maratha dynasty. The forceful young writer and editor Bal Gangadhar Tilak reorganized Ganesh's festival into a protest march, whose bands of singers wove messages of resistance into devotional songs.

Tension between reformers and Hindu nationalists came to a head when Prarthana and Sadharan Samajists united to back a law that would raise to the age of 12 the limit at which a girl could consent to sexual congress. This law's initiator, Parsee reformer Behramji Malabari, intended to make this law an initial step toward raising the legal age for marriage. Thus, he made sure it stipulated that sex with an underage girl would be illegal even if the girl and her partner were married. He and samaj backers thought it would pass easily. They did not count on the nationalists, who whipped up a frenzy of Hindu anger against it. Tilak won national prominence by running a press campaign that demanded "No more government meddling in Hindu religion!" The law was passed, but afterwards its backers found they had lost most of their credibility.[12]

After this point, nationalists captured much of the energy of young people working for change in India. Attention was deflected away from social and religious issues and focused instead on efforts more explicitly political. Two more samaj-style groups were, nonetheless, successful in carrying on earlier samaj endeavors. They achieved this success by working with nationalist sentiments rather than against them, encouraging Hindus to take pride in their traditions even as they changed them.

---

[12] See Meera Kosambi, "Girl Brides and Socio-Legal Change: Age of Consent Bill (1891) Controversy," *Economic and Political Weekly* 36 (August 3–10, 1991): 1857–68.

TRANSFORMATIONS: FROM ARYA SAMAJ
TO RAMAKRISHNA MISSION

The last two movements described in this chapter differed from their predecessors in several important ways. Both were led by swamis rather than the well-to-do house-holders who led earlier samaj groups—although one of these swamis had first been a college student and Brahmo Samajist. Both were strongly revivalist in tone, stressing the need to restore glories of the ancient Hindu past. Both were nationalist to the extent that they questioned the legitimacy of British colonial rule. Moreover, both remain major religious forces in today's India, unlike their predecessors, who today have only a tiny presence.

Arya Samaj

Swami Dayananda Saraswati, the Arya Samaj founder, was a Gujarati-born Brahmin of Shaiva background who ran away from home to become a sannyasi when he was 22 years old. His autobiography tells how, already as a child, he began to question image-worship after watching mice crawl about on a Shiva-linga.[13] Dayananda wandered from teacher to teacher for several years until he found an expert on Veda who claimed that commentaries used to study it had applied an incorrect method of translation. Using the new techniques developed by his teacher, Dayananda came to believe that the Vedas allowed worship of just one God and did not support image-making or worship. His impressions were strengthened, he found, when he treated Veda as layered, in the approach being used by contemporary textual critics. The oldest parts of Veda, the chant collections, seemed to support his position most strongly. Dayananda finally decided that only the chants were truly authentic Veda; anything not prefigured in these was a product of later false insertions. Moreover, true Hindus should act only as the Veda taught them; all later sacred teachings were like-wise false.

Dayananda's first efforts to find an audience followed classic Brahmin sadhu procedures. Wearing only a loincloth, he walked from village to village challenging local pandits to debate him in Sanskrit. He argued that they should study Veda using his method and throw all divine images into rivers. As time went on, he added a third message about caste. The varna system, he taught, was just a classification of professions. A given varna's privileges should belong only to those who did its work. This was too strong a challenge for most of Dayananda's hearers. For nearly ten years almost no one accepted his teachings.

Then Dayananda met a Brahmo Samaj leader who encouraged the dissident swami to present his ideas in Calcutta. The year was 1872. The Brahmos were at their peak; they were happy to show this man who attacked idolatry and caste how to build a broader following. When he left Calcutta, Dayananda put on robes, used trains to travel, and began to speak in Hindi. He addressed his talks not to pandits but to the new educated classes and sprinkled in references to topics they found appealing. The Vedic seers knew science, he claimed; they could build telegraphs and steam engines.

---

[13] *Autobiography of Dayanand Saraswati*, K. C. Yadav, ed. (New Delhi: Manohar, 1976), 24–25.

Moreover, they taught women Sanskrit, gave them sacred thread initiations, had them marry only as adults, and let widows remarry. As for varna status, people should claim it only as adults, after their deeds revealed their talents.

Dayananda's style was often abrasive, and he had little patience with rivals. One favorite method he had for gaining an audience was to issue a challenge for public debate with local experts, whom he tried to show the error of their ways. At one famous two-day debate in 1877, he took on two distinguished Muslim legal experts and four Christian missionaries.[14] Dayananda approached all rival religions in the same way. Each of them, he said, had begun with the same original revelation, which was the teaching found in the Vedas. Over the centuries different events had degraded this teaching, leaving only shards of Vedic truth scattered through their Holy Books' pages. Like other samaj leaders of his century, Dayananda studied other religions, but he studied them only to refute them. Roughly one-half of his main summary of his teachings, the *Satyarth Prakash,* "Light of Truth," refutes Muslims, Christians, Buddhists, Jains, and thirteen other sects of India.[15] Sects attacked did not always accept his portrayals; one group of Jains sued him for libel.

At the same time, Dayananda's pugnaciousness attracted disciples. In 1875, during his second visit to Bombay, a group of Dayananda enthusiasts started the first Arya Samaj to keep his teachings going locally. This was based on the Brahmo and Prarthana samaj model: members held weekly meetings centered on scripture, preaching, and song. Image worship was banned, social service affirmed, and control was kept in the hands of the local community. Services included *havans,* nonbloody offerings to a sacred fire, because Dayananda taught that these were "scientific," cleansing noxious influences from Indian air.

The new Arya Samaj's greatest success, however, was in the Punjab or Northwest India and the United Provinces to its east.[16] These had not been part of the original Indian colonies. The British won the Punjab from descendants of the Sikh king Ranjit Singh only in 1849, bringing in Bengali civil servants to help organize the region. The Bengalis brought along their Brahmo Samaj and tried to spread its teachings, but the Punjabis resented both because the Bengalis held all the best jobs. Punjabis knew by this time that their region had been the original Aryan motherland. Hence, when Dayananda arrived there in 1877 to present "pure Aryan" teachings, many Punjabis welcomed these as something of their own. By the time he left a few months later, the Punjab had eleven Arya Samaj branches. When Dayananda died while preaching in Maharashtra five years later, the Lahore branch in the Punjab founded the first Arya Samaj College in his memory.

Like Brahmos, Arya Samajists were prone to splitting, and the Punjab Samaj soon split into two branches. One worked principally to establish and fund schools that would educate Aryas toward social reformation. The distinguished woman educator

---

[14] This debate is summarized in Bawa Chhajju Singh, *Life and Teachings of Swami Dayananda,* 1st ed. (New Delhi: Jan Gyan Prakashm 1903) I, 124–42. Although clearly biased by its author's enthusiasm for the Swami, it conveys a good sense of the Swami's teaching style and debating methods.

[15] *English Translation of the Satyarth Prakash,* Durga Prakash, tr., Vaidyanath Shastri et al., eds. (New Delhi: Gyan Prakash, 1970).

[16] My principal source on Arya Samaj history has been Kenneth W. Jones, *Arya Dharm, Hindu Consciousness in 19th century Punjab* (Berkeley: Univ. of California Press, 1976).

at the start of this chapter was a product of this "College" branch.[17] The other branch continued Dayananda's aggressive missionizing, setting up Arya Samaj chapters in South India and among many Indians living outside their country. The Arya Samaj was often controversial, and at odds with non-Hindu groups of India. But it did make peace with Hindu nationalists and worked by their side in the struggle for Indian independence.

Ramakrishna Mission

In a sense, Dayananda's Aryas were the last of the true samajists because the Ramakrishna Mission abandoned both the samaj form of organization and the prohibition of image worship that had been the most common feature of samaj practice. Nonetheless, the young man later known as Swami Vivekananda started his religious career as a Brahmo Samajist and carried over several Brahmo ideals into the group he started. Vivekananda's Ramakrishna Mission thus was both an ending and a beginning. It ended Brahmo dominance in eastern India as well as samaj-based forms of religious organization. It began a series of new Hindu groups that fused samaj concerns with more classically Hindu forms of organization. In effect, it was a bridge tradition, setting in motion the process samajists had hoped for, penetration of samaj ideals into the greater Hindu community.

The instrument for this accomplishment was a reimagined sadhu, and its inventor was a young man born in Calcutta in 1863. His birth name was Narendranath Datta, and his caste was Kayastha—once a scribal group but by then part of the Bengal upper classes. His father was a well-to-do Calcutta lawyer. Young Naren attended the Presidency[18] and Scottish Church Colleges, graduating from the latter in 1884.

Like many of his classmates, Naren joined the Brahmo Samaj in college, first attending meetings of the Sadharan Brahmo Samaj and then switching to Keshab Chander Sen's New Dispensation. But then he was called to be the disciple of a local Kali priest who had recently become a protégé of Keshab. This priest was the devotional saint Ramakrishna.[19] Ramakrishna claimed he had proved the unity of religion by practicing each of India's traditions for a time and achieving its culminating experience. Many Calcuttans, including Naren, thought at first that he was crazy. But Keshab thought Ramakrishna was a truly enlightened saint, and so the Brahmos gave him publicity that drew disciples to him. When Keshab died in 1883 and Naren's father followed one month after, Naren turned to Ramakrishna for consolation. He became one of Ramakrishna's "boys," a group of male students who often sat through the night with the saint, listening to his songs and stories and sometimes joining him in ecstatic dancing. At first Naren held back from Ramakrishna's image worship, but finally the saint persuaded him that it did no harm.

---

[17] However, the other, more conservative, branch was the first to found Arya Samaj schools for women.

[18] Presidency College was the former Hindu College renamed and remains to this day the most prestigious college in Bengal. Naren transferred after an illness that made him drop out of school for a time.

[19] See Chapter 3, p. 85.

Then came another wrenching loss for Naren. In 1886, Ramakrishna died of throat cancer. He had pleaded with Naren to keep his boys together. After his death, the young men decided to become a brotherhood of renouncers, claiming that Ramakrishna had given them secret initiation.[20] They dressed like Dasanami sadhus and lived together for a time in a run-down house in Calcutta. Then each began moving off in his own direction, searching for a religious path that would make sense of his experiences. Naren himself used Vedanta teachings to put his insights together, treating Vedanta as a capstone toward which other religions pointed. For a while he corresponded with a swami in Banaras, trying to resolve questions about Vedanta. Then he found a Nath to train him in techniques of yoga. Finally, he left Bengal altogether and set off on a two-year walking tour of India.

One conviction Naren acquired from his Brahmo heritage was that religion was worth little if it did not express itself in service to one's fellow humans. Walking through India let him see the struggles of India's poor people. It also brought him news of a coming World Parliament of Religion soon to be convened by Unitarians in the American city of Chicago. He thought that if he went to America, he might be able to find the expertise and funding that would help him link religion more effectively to projects of social reformation. He was bright and charismatic and by now had wealthy supporters who offered him funding for the journey. One even suggested a new name for him: Swami Vivekananda.

Vivekananda's trip to America started bumpily. He arrived too early, ran out of money, and discovered he needed an invitation to become a Parliament delegate. Chance encounters and sheer charm brought him helpers to solve these problems. He addressed the Parliament, became a darling of the press, and soon was in great demand for lectures. He used this chance to thunder against missionaries, to defend Hinduism's glories, and to teach American disciples his own version of Vedanta. One disciple skilled at stenography turned his lectures into books, which spread his fame farther. Now he began writing to his guru-brothers in India, telling them that they should gather and dedicate themselves to social service. The poor are God, he asserted. One must bring them basic physical security to help them find the God who lies within them. His guru-brothers at first resisted, but Vivekananda's growing fame and his promise of support for their new order persuaded them.

In 1896, Vivekananda returned to India, bringing with him several U.S. disciples and a few gathered during a stop in England. Several of these gave money for purchase of land at Belur Math, on the riverbank opposite from Ramakrishna's old Kali temple. In 1897, Vivekananda and his guru-brothers reorganized themselves as the Ramakrishna Math and Mission: *Math* meaning "monastery," and "Mission" declaring their intention to give themselves over to forms of service. Burned out and suffering from several ailments, Vivekananda himself died in 1903 after a second trip to America. But his guru-brothers carried out his purpose, founding schools of all kinds, college hostels, libraries, medical centers, and various slum, tribal, and rural development projects. In 1957, after Indian Independence, the Math and Mission realized an old dream of Vivekananda, establishing a parallel women's Math and Mission named

---

[20] This claim is problematic because Ramakrishna himself was a householder whose wife lived within the temple precincts. He never had sexual relations with her, however, preferring instead to revere her as an incarnation of the goddess.

for Sharada Devi, wife of Ramakrishna. Like the men's order, the Sharada Math and Mission focuses on service, especially service to women. Many of Vivekananda's foundations abroad have also survived under the name "Vedanta Societies." These focus on spreading Vedanta teachings and promoting inter-religious cooperation. The Ramakrishna Mission continues to carry on its founder's precedent of carrying his message into new regions; it now has centers not only in India, Bangladesh, the U.S.A., Canada, and England but also in France, the Netherlands, Switzerland, Argentina, Sri Lanka, Singapore, Mauritius, Japan, and Fiji.

THE SAMAJISTS' IMPACT

It is time to ask the question that has ended all chapters thus far. So what? How did the samaj movement affect the shape of Hinduism? How does it live on today? Several layers of impact must be considered. Nearly all the societies described here still survive, although some are just pale shadows of their former selves. The Arya Samaj and Ramakrishna Mission continue to be major influences in modern India; the Sadharan Samaj, although much smaller in membership, continued to work for social improvement well into the twentieth century.

One major product of samaj efforts has been India's active and vocal women's movement. By the end of the nineteenth century, many men left the women's cause to put their energies into the push for political self-determination. By then, however, women had found enough of their own voice and talents to run their own women's uplift organizations. Women's groups were not the only samaj efforts carried over into the present. India now has hundreds of schools, colleges, libraries, widows' and orphans' homes, dispensaries, hospitals, and relief and rural centers that can trace their origins back to one or another samaj.

In addition, samajists left children, grandchildren, and great-grandchildren, men and women alike, who prized education and kept up samaj ideals even after drifting away from membership in samaj organizations. Many became educators, social activists, and community leaders working quietly and persistently toward creating a more humane and self-reliant India. Many joined the freedom movement under Mohandas Gandhi, working to achieve his goal of winning national independence by practicing nonviolent resistance. Although Gandhi himself did not come from a samaj family, his calling to his disciples echoed longstanding samaj motifs. God and Truth are one, he asserted, and God's Truth calls from within human beings in the form of human conscience. Humans are one also and must care and work for each other. Religions may be different, but they are complementary, calling people to move toward the same transcendent goal.

The spirit of the samajists continues as well in the many secular, grassroots projects that search for locally managed solutions to rural and low-caste problems throughout India. It is hard to imagine even Marxist movements gaining so strong a foothold in India if India had no precedent for well-to-do young men and women giving up their comforts to work for people suffering from hunger and oppression. India's strongest asset today is its many social idealists putting minds and bodies to work on issues such as healing and empowering the poor.

Finally, samajists did, indeed, point at least one sector of Hinduism in a new direction, which is still unfolding. Since the beginning of the twentieth century, India has experienced a spate of new religious movements, paralleling a similar trend in other countries. Most are run by leaders who look very much like teachers from India's past: sadhus and gurus claiming links to ancient sampradayas and drawing disciples who believe they have powers derived from deep spiritual transformations. But these teachers proclaim a God who is One and advocate paths that they see as a capstone to teachings of other religions. The books they recommend to disciples for study are often the same books said by samajists to hold the keys for restoration of Hindu religion: the Upanishads, *Bhagavad-Gita*, and often Patanjali's *Yoga-Sutras*. They establish *ashrams*, "hermitages," that run schools, charitable dispensaries and programs of outreach to the poor. Finally, they are mission-oriented, sending workers and literature anywhere they think they may find fertile ground, be this Bombay, Delhi, Madras, New York, Buenos Aires, or western Michigan. More will be said about them in this book's final section.

ADDITIONAL READINGS

Two good general sources on movements discussed in this chapter are Robert W. Baird's collection *Religion in Modern India,* 3rd ed. (New Delhi: Manohar, 1995) and Charles M. Heimsath's older *Indian Nationalism and Social Reform* (Princeton: Princeton Univ. Press, 1964). Studying the broader colonial context is David Kopf, *British Orientalism and the Bengal Renaissance: the Dynamics of Indian Modernization, 1773–1835* (Berkeley: Univ. of California Press, 1969). Kenneth W. Jones introduces a broader range of movements in *Socio-Religious Reform Movements in British India,* The New Cambridge History of India, Vol. 3: 1 (Cambridge: Cambridge Univ. Press, 1989). Kopf and Jones have written the two principal scholarly studies of the Brahmo and Arya Samaj: Kopf, *The Brahmo Samaj and the Shaping of the Modern India Mind* (Princeton: Princeton Univ. Press, 1979); Jones, *Arya Dharm, Hindu Consciousness in 19th century Punjab* (Berkeley: Univ. of California Press, 1976). Richard Tucker's *Ranade and the Roots of Indian Nationalism* (Chicago: Univ. of Chicago Press, 1972) remains the best entree to the Prarthana Samaj.

Readers are strongly encouraged to look at writings from this period. Available in reprint are Ram Mohan (Rammohan) Roy's two tracts against sati: Satī: *a Writeup of Raja Ram Mohan Roy about Burning of Widows Alive* (Delhi: B. R. Publishing, 1989). Also readily secured is the original *History of the Brahmo Samaj* by Shivanath Shastri, founder of the Sadharan Brahmo Samaj (Calcutta: Sadharan Brahmo Samaj, 1912). Bipin Chandra Pal, *Memories of My Life and Times* (Calcutta: Bipinchandra Pal Institute, 1973) is also a fine entree to the period. Contemporary accounts of Swami Dayananda are cited in Bawa Chhajju Singh, *Life and Teachings of Swami Dayananda,* 1st ed. (New Delhi: Jan Gyan Prakashm, 1903). Disciples' accounts of Ramakrishna and Swami Vivekananda are found in *Life of Sri Ramakrishna, Compiled from Various Authentic Sources* (Calcutta: Advaita Ashram, 1948) and *Life of Swami Vivekananda by His Eastern and Western Disciples* (Calcutta: Advaita Ashram, 1912). News reports on Vivekananda are cited extensively in Marie Louise Burke, *Swami Vivekananda in the West: New Discoveries,* 3rd ed., 6 vols. (Calcutta: Advaita Ashram, 1983–87).

An even more fascinating way to approach this period is through writings of the women whose lives it changed. For Bengal, try Malavika Karlekar, *Voices from Within: Early Personal Narratives of Bengali Women* (Delhi: Oxford Univ. Press, 1991); also Srabashi Ghosh, "Birds in a Cage: Changes in Bengal Social Life as Recorded in Autobiographies by Women," *Economic and Political Weekly* 21:43 (October 25, 1986): WS88–96; and Ghulam Murshid, *Reluctant Debutante: Response of Bengali Women to Modernization, 1849–1905* (Rajshahi: Sahitya Samsad, Rajshahi Univ., 1983). For Maharashtra, Ramabai Ranade's account of her husband is a good start: *Ranade: His Wife's Reminiscences,* Kusumavati Deshpande, tr. (New Delhi: Government of India Publications Division, 1963). Meera Kosambi has done extensive research on woman reformer Pandita Ramabai; see especially her *Pandita Ramabai through Her Own Words: Selected Works* (New Delhi: Oxford Univ. Press, 2000); see also Uma Chakravarti, *Rewriting History: the Life and Times of Pandita Ramabai* (New Delhi: Kali for Women, 1998). Another outspoken woman of Maharashtra was Tarabai Shinde; see Rosalind O'Hanlon, *A Comparison between Women and Men: Tarabai Shinde and the Critique of Gender Relations in Colonial India* (Madras: Oxford Univ. Press, 1994).

For women's experience in the Arya Samaj, see Madhu Kishwar, "Arya Samaj and Women's Education: Kanya Maha Vidyalaya, Jalandhar," *Economic and Political Weekly* 21: 17 (April 26, 1986): WS9–24; also her "The Daughters of Aryavarta," *Women in Colonial India: Essays on Survival, Work and the State,* J. Krishnamurty, ed. (Delhi: Oxford Univ. Press, 1989), 78–113. On Arya Samaj women today, see John E. Llewellyn, *The Legacy of Women's Uplift in India: Contemporary Women Leaders in the Arya Samaj* (London: Sage, 1998).

PART II

Hinduisms in Space: Home, Temple, and the Pilgrim Road

ll of the traditions described in Part I have places special to them. A visitor
to India can still find Brahmin schools where children learn by echoing
verses chanted by their teachers—or newer styles of academies that train
would-be priests in Vedic chanting and techniques of fire sacrifice. Monasteries in
many regions offer shelter to sadhus, maintain libraries, and serve as administrative
centers for their lineages. Devotional movements often control their own centers and
temples at major pilgrim destinations. Surviving samaj organizations have schools and
meeting houses. A full introduction to Hindu practice would venture beyond the
doors of such places and describe what is going on within them. The present text
cannot offer nearly so rich a coverage. It introduces just three kinds of spaces, chosen
because they are often entered by visitors to India. These are spaces where ordinary
Hindus practice, often while drawing on the expertise of ritualists or teachers such as
those described in Part I. They are also spaces where multiple strands of Hindu tradition meet, complementing and enriching one another.

One space central to Hindu practice is the home, taken up in Chapter 5. Much of
Hindu practice is home practice; in fact, one can be a good Hindu all one's life without ever leaving home.[1] Ancient Brahmin texts on fire sacrifice assumed that the

---

[1] This important point was made in one of the first films on Hindu practice made for
American student viewing: H. Daniel Smith's *Pilgrimage to a Hindu Temple* (New York:
Syracuse University, 1969).

hearth fire in the home would receive the most fundamental offerings and that the rites by which an Arya became an Arya would be done at home with the domestic fire as witness. A Hindu home is understood to be a kind of temple, in which the head of the family that lives there serves as chief priest. Like a temple, a high-caste home is protected by rules maintaining its purity, especially in certain special places. One such special place is the kitchen; another is the *puja* room where deities are housed and worshiped daily. Most rites for ancestors are carried out in homes. Many festivals are based there or have special home components. Women observe their own cycles of home-based vows, and homes may also host devotional sings or offer speaking platforms to visiting sadhus with spiritual insights to offer. In fact, all Hindu great traditions can be met at one time or another in Hindu homes, often enhanced or modified by traditions special to a caste or local area.

A second center of importance to Hindu practice is the temple, explored in Chapter 6. Temples are spaces structured in distinctive ways, with special meanings. They are also concentration points for deity, fixed at that site by means of consecrated images. Although the primary mood in a temple is devotion, temple worship has also been strongly influenced by the Brahmin heritage. Chapter 6 discusses symbolism, images, and worship that are common to many Hindu temples. It then goes on to distinguish four different types of temples, three of which are rarely mentioned in textbooks: clan temples, shrines of village deities, and royal temples. Because much of the uniqueness of a temple resides in the festivals it sponsors, Chapter 6 also offers examples of festivals tied to each type of temple. Such festivals offer a fine way to see how local and family traditions come to be knit together with great traditions by means of temple worship.

Local traditions and great ones also meet on the pilgrim road, covered in Chapter 7. This is an odd kind of space, in effect, a space between spaces, the kind of space that anthropologist Victor Turner called "liminal."[2] In India's past, sadhus and shramanas claimed such spaces as their special province. Hence, even when ordinary householders venture into such spaces, they take up some of the sadhu's language and lifestyle. They may add *tapas,* austerity, to their journeys by going barefoot. They talk about journeys in a language of loosening, emptying, and thinning, all suggesting relaxing of ties to the everyday world. Not all will use such language, however, for many types of pilgrim journeys exist in India, and different people who undertake them may have different understandings of what they are about. Chapter 7 samples variations both in the types of pilgrim journeys undertaken and in the interpretations given them. It concludes by introducing two "perpetual pilgrims," sadhus who have

---

[2] See, for example his *The Ritual Process: Structure and Anti-Structure* (Chicago: Aldine, 1969).

embraced a life of perpetual religious wandering. They are of the same teaching lineage, but different generations: The first did most of his wandering during the early twentieth century; the second is living now. The contrast between their stories points to a striking change taking place in sadhus' pilgrim journeys.

Evidence of this change introduces an important caution into conclusions that readers may want to draw from the present section. Most of Part II's practices are of the type that scholars often label traditional Hinduism. Such practices are called "traditional" because one can readily see connections between them and older Hindu traditions such as those of the Brahmins, sadhus, and devotional movements. Readers will notice that chapters here make very little mention of the samaj movements and the changes they introduced into Hindu practice. Patterns of home and temple practice and pilgrimage were well established before samajists began their teachings.

"Traditional," however, can be a loaded label that often leads to misconceptions. The tendency is to assume something traditional has existed for a long time, that it is stodgy and change-resistant. It is implicitly contrasted with the term "modern," which suggests something up-to-date, forward-looking, and adaptable. Holding to such assumptions can greatly confuse people trying to understand the dynamics of today's Hinduisms. In the first place, Hindu teachings and practice changed a great deal in the past, as chapters in Part I have shown. In fact, one can argue that Hindus had a tradition of adapting to change with great skill and flexibility. American anthropologist Milton Singer made this point nearly fifty years ago in his pioneering studies of the relationship between religion and change in Madras city;[3] yet it continues to be overlooked and forgotten.

In the second place, one often finds that Hindu practices called "very traditional, very old" are not very old at all. One excellent example is the pilgrimage to Pandharpur described in Chapter 7. To be sure, it is based on a very old precedent. Devotional saints of Maharashtra celebrated such pilgrimage in their songs; indeed some of the most famed saints first met their own gurus in Pandharpur. Pandharpur had a great temple housing a god named Vitthal or Vithoba. Its popularity is attested by the fact that several kings made additions to its buildings. But when Mughal kings made conquests in its region, they saw this temple as a threat to their authority and tore it down. Vitthal's image alone escaped, carried away to another city. The current temple is a modern reconstruction, housing the returned image. The pilgrimage that carries the saints' sandals to it started only during the later 1800s.

---

[3] In his book, *When a Great Tradition Modernizes: an Anthropological Approach to Indian Civilization* (New York: Praeger, 1972).

Complicating matters still more is the fact that "modern" Hindus are now asserting pride and identity by returning to tradition and using its models and resources to address problems they meet today. A massive Hindu revival has been taking place in India—especially among the cosmopolitan classes who are present-day heirs to the nineteenth-century samajists. Traces of this revival appear just briefly in this section. Parts III and IV will have more to say about these issues.

5

In the Home

She sat on the floor in the middle of her kitchen, sliding a fat squash over the blade of the upright slicer in front of her. Sweat beaded her face because the silk sari she wore to protect her food from pollution was hotter than the cotton worn outside at this time of year. Nonetheless, the shower she had taken before entering her kitchen had cooled her, as did the memory of her beloved dawn prayers and meditation, carried out in the family puja room whose entry stood beside her kitchen door. Hence, her mood was calm and centered, her movements swift and sure. The meal she was cooking would be pure and charged with constructive attitudes when she served it to the two guests watching from outside the room.

In their introduction to *House and Home in Maharashtra*,[1] editors Irina Glushkova and Anne Feldhaus point out several meanings of *ghar*, the Marathi word translated "home" in English. A ghar is a house, a physical structure. It is a family, a social unit of people related by blood ties who live and work within a house's confines. It is also a household, a center of social and economic activity. And finally, like Hindu homes elsewhere in India, the ghar is a site of religious practice. In fact, the very name *ghar* is derived from a Sanskrit term, *griha,* which means "hearth," the ancient center of an upper-caste Aryan household's practice.

This chapter focuses on the final meaning of ghar, exploring several ways a home functions as a religious center. But here there is an instant problem: the huge variation able to occur in a physical structure that is also a social, economic, and religious unit. In Maharashtra, as elsewhere, the layout of a home varies according to the economic resources of those who built it, the constraints placed upon it by its locale, and the means of livelihood of its inhabitants. Some ghars are sprawling multiroomed structures, laid out around one or more central courtyards. Others are more compact and entirely roofed over, sometimes with multiple stories and additional outbuildings.

As families, Maharashtrian ghars are normally patrilineal, reckoning descent through the male line, and patrilocal, meaning that women move into their husband's homes at marriage. Although common in India, this pattern is not universal. In several jatis of South India, family descent is matrilineal, traced through the female line. At least one matrilineal jati, the Nayars of Kerala, was matrilocal until quite recently.

---

[1] New York: Oxford University Press, 1998.

Sisters and brothers lived together in the family's homestead, whereas fathers of a family's children lived with their own kin and came to wives on visits. The economic structure of households also varies widely in India. Once upon a time, it was standard practice in many regions that well-to-do landowning households were, in effect, joint corporations; several generations living together owned virtually all property in common, sharing it out as needed. In other places and in poorer households, some approximation of a nuclear unit was more frequent. Nuclear households are becoming more frequent today, although variations on the joint form are still common.

Religious practice in homes across India is even more varied, with caste an important factor shaping differences. A very high-caste family, especially an orthodox Brahmin family, is likely to observe more household rites and rules of purification than a lower caste family. It is also more likely to "go by the book," conforming its practice to norms laid out in the pandits' dharma literature. Lower caste practice is freer in form, and practices guarding purity may vanish altogether.

Family wealth also causes differences. A well-to-do family may regularly pay a Brahmin priest to oversee rituals and carry them out in elaborate form. A poorer household may do without the priest and eliminate some rites or carry them out much more perfunctorily. Simple custom, specific to a region, a caste, or a family, adds more variations. One reason often given in the past for swiftly moving young girls into marital families was that this helped them adjust to a new family's rites while they were still pliable.

If household religion among Hindus is so varied, how can a single chapter even begin to describe it? Luckily, field studies done in various areas of India reveal widespread standard patterns beneath the welter of variations. These studies also offer a fairly standardized set of classifications that can help organize discussion of these patterns more coherently. However, one warning must be issued. Most studies of household religion have looked at practice in higher caste homes, not necessarily homes of Brahmins, but of groups high enough in the social ladder to pattern their practice according to Brahmin-established norms.[2]

In homes of this type, virtually all over India, household religious practice subdivides into four basic types: daily observances, consisting mostly of early morning (and sometimes early evening) worship and precautions taken to uphold household purity; *samskaras,* rituals of "perfecting" that occur at transitional points in a human's life such as birth, marriage, and death; calendrical rites that respond to points of danger and opportunity in the cycles of time; and optional observances, done because a family wants to achieve some special purpose or to celebrate some special accomplishment. They are taken up here in the order listed.

DAILY OBSERVANCES

The brief sketch that began the chapter describes a woman who is taking great precautions to guard the purity of a meal she is preparing for her guests and household. We also learn through the sketch that even at mid-morning, this housewife has already gone through a significant period of daily worship. The particular scene described

---

[2] An important exception is Ravindra S. Khare, *Culture and Reality: Essays on the Hindu System of Managing Foods* (Simla: Indian Institute of Advanced Study, 1976). Khare compares Brahmin and low-caste practice in northern India.

here occurred in Bengal, a state in easternmost India, but I have come across similar scenes in the Indian south and have read about them as far to the west as Maharashtra.

To understand what is happening in these household practices, it is necessary to understand two premises common in popular Hindu thought. The first is that the human world, as most people know it, is separated by only a very thin veil from another that is much more real and powerful, one which can be called the realm of the sacred or, in the language of ordinary people, the realm of the gods. Powers from the other side of that veil can penetrate it and intervene in human affairs. Some humans too can pierce it through ritual or spiritual discipline and draw on the resources that the sacred world offers. However, certain forces in this world prevent this from happening. Sophisticated teachings such as those of India's sadhu-borne traditions point to human factors such as selfishness and ignorance as causes of such blockage. Ordinary Hindus, following teachings especially of Brahmin-transmitted traditions, tend to trace their problems to pollution. Pollution separates humans from God. The higher and more exalted the God, the worse the problem becomes. Very high deities such as Vishnu and Shiva cannot stand pollution at all. Certain goddesses are an exception. (They are discussed in a later chapter.)

Food Preparation

What is the nature of this pollution? It can be thought of as a kind of spoilage that comes about via contact, much like the rot that affects a piece of fruit when another bad piece sits next to it. The worst kind is produced by contact with death and human effluvia: blood, saliva, snot, urine, feces, and sexual fluids. Most bodily-produced substances pollute, unless they come from some extremely pure source like the cow, whose feces and urine are actually beneficial. Dirt in the streets pollutes because it is often mixed with saliva, urine, or feces, but ordinary dirt, as from working in fields, does not. Even attitudes can be pollutants of sorts, passing from people into food and then on to those who eat it. Pollution does not require literal touching; it can come floating through the air. It readily penetrates food, especially foods such as rice that are cooked in water and absorb it. So long as pollution mars a person, that person is blocked from access to the gods and their sacred power.

The solution to this problem is to get pollution off one's body and to keep it away. One can remove minor pollution by bathing—not in a tub because standing water simply absorbs the pollution and returns it to the body, but by means of flowing waters that will carry it away: a stream, a shower, or simply a bucket of water poured over the head and then shunted off through a drain. More drastic pollution requires special rituals for its dissolution, like the cleansing rituals high-caste Hindus once faced to restore them to their castes after they traveled overseas and met polluting foreigners. As for keeping pollution away, one simply takes precautions. People who deal in death and its products must be avoided: outcaste groups who clean waste-cluttered streets, remove dead animals from them, or turn the skins of dead animals into leather. Menstruating women must be kept away from food preparation—and sometimes, in very strict homes, away from most other family activity. Food intake in general must be guarded; a Hindu aspiring to high purity watches both what is eaten and how it is prepared.

Hence, the care taken by the housewife of our opening anecdote. Her precautions were at the strictest level. She had taken a shower before she entered her always-spotless kitchen. She wore a special sari of silk, which absorbs and transfers pollution much less easily than cotton. She let no one not of her own caste level or above enter her kitchen—and let no one at all enter it without first bathing. She kept her mind calm and peaceful and, of course, wore no leather shoes in her kitchen and took no leather into it. The one further precaution she might have taken was to leave outside her cut and sewn blouse and underskirt. The strictest rules of ritual purity insist that one wear no garment that has been cut and sewn because it has passed through the hands of a low-caste and impure tailor.

The precautions of my hostess were unusually strict for a household not of Brahmin caste. Her husband told me she was observing them so strictly because she was feeding guests, and "in a Hindu house, a guest is god." The fact that one guest was a religion professor studying Hindu practice was also a factor; she was showing me how to prepare the meal correctly. Brahmins have kept the rules of purity most strictly through the ages because their hereditary charge is to deal with deities and with all other sacred forces that help to keep life real and powerful. Nonetheless, even among Brahmins, the level of observance varies nowadays. A learned pandit's family may still keep kitchen rules of purity very strictly indeed.[3] The family of a Brahmin government servant, teacher, or businessman is more likely to soften them for convenience.

Nevertheless, even in a non-Brahmin household, an upper-caste woman is likely to know standard procedures for kitchen purity. She will also be an expert on several other kinds of food lore. She knows which foods go along with the rites of the many *vrats,* or "vows," that a woman may take up as part of her calendric practice. She knows what special foods are offered to which deities in *pujas,* rituals of offering. She knows about "heating" and "cooling" properties inherent in certain foods and about the circumstances in which they should be served: a woman who has just given birth, for example, has cooled enormously and hence must be served foods that will warm her. But a festival where a goddess receives blood sacrifice is hot, and hence foods served there must be cooling. In fact, Hindu food preparation and service is so laden with implications that its study has become an entire subdiscipline.

Puja

Food preparation and expertise are only part of our exemplary woman's discipline. She has also taken part in her household's morning puja. Understanding this puja requires explanation of a second premise common among Hindus. This is the premise that certain things, people, periods of time, or entities belonging to the world beyond this one are charged with qualities that make them auspicious or inauspicious. "Auspicious" means that having them near will enhance a person's happiness and well-being or will help make sure that a crucial undertaking will turn out rightly. "Inauspicious" times, things, people, and entities are likely to make life turn sour. Among Hindus, the dichotomy between auspiciousness and inauspiciousness is so important that the two qualities have their own presiding goddesses. Their names Lakshmi and Alakshmi are cognates of the English terms "luck" and "unluck."[4]

---

[3] See Khare, ibid., for detailed examples of strict kitchen purity.

[4] A good work with which to begin the study of purity and auspiciousness is John B. Carman and Frédérique A. Marglin, eds., *Purity and Auspiciousness in Indian Society* (Leiden: E. J. Brill, 1985).

Like the dichotomy between purity and pollution, the auspicious\inauspicious opposition underlies several aspects of Hindu practice. For now, it will be considered only in relationship to two components of a daily routine, timing and place. As shall be seen in the discussion of calendric rituals, different times have differing qualities, according to most Hindus.[5] Periodically, there are auspicious or inauspicious moments—that is, times of opportunity and danger. Transitional times, such as dawn and twilight, are especially charged. Of the two, dawn is the more auspicious because it falls in the day's "bright half," the portion of the day when the sun's light is increasing. Dawn is a time when the human world and the divine world beyond it are in close connection. Therefore, in writings of Brahmin pandits, dawn was set aside as a time for a twice-born man's morning bath and prayers, prayers addressed to the rising sun that asked for enhanced understanding. Many Brahmins still start their day with the Gayatri mantra, the central and most sacred prayer of this ancient set of morning rites.

They are likely to supplement this prayer, however, with a practice common among many other Hindus, that of worshiping their families' gods in the household's *mandir,* or domestic temple. Virtually all high-caste Hindu homes have some kind of mandir. Even a friend of mine who insists she is irreligious keeps a collection of small divine images on the night stand beside her bed. In some homes, the mandir may be just a shelf in a room used for other purposes—although this is usually one of the home's more private rooms, not open to the casual public. For others, it is a niche specially built into the house or a free-standing cabinet made especially to hold divine images. If a house is spacious or has very pious inhabitants willing to crowd themselves, a whole room may be set aside as a puja room, another name for the household mandir. Often such a room is next to the kitchen, and both are located in the deepest and most private sections of the home. This is because, like the kitchen, the puja room must be kept very pure, and because food prepared purely for worship is carried from the one room to the other.

The images in a home mandir may be freestanding statuettes or the brightly colored lithographs, "god posters," that have been widely sold in India since the mid-twentieth century. The home mandir may hold just one or two images: a movie made in the sixties in a Shri-Vaishnava Brahmin home in Madras (now Chennai) shows a mandir with one metal image of Krishna and a *shalagrama* stone, a smooth round rock with a whorl in its center that is a common aniconic image of Vishnu.[6] In contrast, most mandirs that I have seen in Hindu homes were packed with images, sometimes stuffed in so tightly that I could hardly distinguish one deity from another. In the center of such a shrine, at least in theory, is the family's *kuldevta,* a deity that protects its lineage. Others may be *ishtas,* preferred deities, of family members or sometimes just mementos of a pilgrimage taken by some family member or friend. I myself have taken such mementos to Hindu friends and seen them swiftly tucked into corners of home shrines.

Divine images in a home mandir are also sites of auspiciousness—spatial equivalents of the positive times in which their rituals are located. Their auspicious effect can be sullied by impurity. No one should enter the deities' space without bathing, and a very strict home will keep ritual clothing for use in its puja room. Procedures for

---

[5] Or for most religious human beings, for that matter, as argued by my own teacher Mircea Eliade. See especially the second chapter of his famous book *The Sacred and the Profane* (New York: Harcourt Brace, 1959).

[6] A kind of ammonite fossil found in a river of northern India.

image worship are known collectively as *puja*. The texts known as Agamas that prescribe puja liturgies structure them like rituals used since ancient times to welcome
honored guests into a home.[7] The "divine guest" is invited in and offered a seat. Its feet
are washed, and it is offered water for washing its face, rinsing its mouth, and taking a
cooling drink after its "journey." Then, it may be bathed and wrapped with a cloth signifying clean new "clothing." It is anointed with cooling sandalwood ointment and\or
decorated with red kumkum powder applied to the center of its forehead. Next, it is
decked with flowers, while sweet-smelling incense burns before it. Finally, a burning
lamp is waved before it, and food is offered, including the family's intended breakfast
or supper. The food is returned to the family as *prasad,* a manifestation of divine grace.
All worshipers present do *namas* or *pranam*. The first is a gesture of pressing both palms
together and raising them before the face. In the second, the worshiper drops to the
knees and touches his or her forehead to the floor or stretches out full length with
palms pressed together and extended in front of her or his head. All are gestures of reverence used in many contexts in India; the closer the body comes to the ground, the
deeper the respect expressed. After pranams, the god is bade good-bye, and the family
can turn to other pursuits. Family members may return at twilight for a repetition of
this service—or they may go instead to pay respects at a neighborhood temple.

An everyday puja, however, is rarely as long or formal as the one described above.
It may consist of little more than a muttered invocation, flowers draped on the deities,
powder applied to divine foreheads, the waved lamp, food offering, final bows, and
farewell. It may also be extended by acts of an individual worshiper's choosing:
singing devotional songs; chanting a favored deity's names; reading selections from a
beloved book such as Tulsidas's *Ramcharitmanas;* sitting in quiet meditation; or doing
japa, which entails repeating a mantra given by one's guru a prescribed number of
times while telling the beads of a *mala,* the Hindu equivalent of a rosary. An entire
family need not participate in puja room observances. One adult alone may conduct
them for everyone's benefit. Or worshipers may move into and out of the room,
entering, perhaps, just to receive the morning's prasad and bow.

Prasad

Like namas, pranam, and puja in general, prasad is a basic component of Hindu worship, by no means confined to homes. Therefore, it is necessary to examine the ideas
behind it more closely. As discussed earlier, purity of food is very important, especially
to Hindus of high caste. "You are what you eat" is an idea found in very ancient texts,
especially of the Brahmin-borne traditions. This principle was closely tied to ideas
about caste. According to Brahmin pandits, the divisions of caste reflected, at least in
part, degrees of bodily purity.[8] Brahmins were extremely pure, second in purity only to
the deities they approached via their ritual works. Outcastes were outcastes precisely

---

[7] See my own entry "Pūjā: Hindu Pūjā" in *The Encyclopedia of Religion,* vol. 12 (New York:
Macmillan, 1987), 83–5. A fine description and explanation of puja in practice are in
Lawrence A. Babb, *The Divine Hierarchy: Popular Hinduism in Central India* (New York:
Columbia University Press, 1975).

[8] "In part" because the caste system, as a living reality, always to some degree escaped the neat
idealized images that the pandits provided to justify it. Hence Kshatriyas, classed as high by
Brahmin standards, have always eaten meat, which is otherwise considered highly polluting.

because they were so deeply impure that their impurity could not be taken away. These levels of purity in part were inborn; one reason why caste groups practiced marriage within their own groups was to maintain their caste group's appropriate level of purity.

However, purity can always be lost; one has to maintain it. Therefore, a high-caste group must eat only pure foods. And pure means in part that food has been prepared purely and only by pure people. To have a person of lesser purity touch or, worse still, taste a pure person's food is to contaminate it and render it unfit for the purer person's consumption. Moreover, even slipping a spoon into a pot to test spicing counts as a taste—or spooning out a portion from a common bowl or stealing a cookie from a common tray. Doing so converts the remaining food into "leavings," which are then fit only for persons of the taster's level or less. On the other hand, eating leavings of someone very pure and good can actually be of benefit. The person's qualities are conveyed through the food. A guru wanting to bestow blessings on a disciple may feed the disciple a little food from the guru's plate. To show respect for her husband, a wife will take her own meal after he eats so that she receives his leavings. The same is true of a god, whose purity and auspiciousness passes into food of which the god has partaken. When food is offered to a god during a puja, the god is believed to eat its spiritual essence. Thus, the food becomes the god's leavings and conveys its benefits to the lucky worshipper who acquires the privilege of eating it. Any meal in a devout home thus is first offered to the deities—if not the entire meal, then at least token parts of it. Eating in a devout home therefore ensures that one's own body is enhanced little by little by infusing it with food first tasted by the home's deities.

Who can receive such food? Who is entitled to dine after deities? Who is fit even to approach them in the sanctity of the puja room? Not everyone is positioned to make use of such benefits. To do so one must be "perfected," the purpose of the samskara rites, the next category of practices in the home.

SAMSKARAS

Samskaras are Hindu versions of a type of ritual recorded in virtually every society of the world, the so-called life-cycle, or life-crisis, rite. These are rituals designed to help both individuals and their surrounding communities get past critical points of transition in human life, such as birth, the onset of adolescence, marriage, and death. These transition points are often seen as times of great vulnerability. It may be said that a person at such a time is more open to attacks from malevolent powers, such as the angry ghosts or witches that figure so prominently in local traditions of India. But even people who do not believe in such beings can readily see that the life crises are at least points of physical or psychological vulnerability—either vulnerability for the person going through them, such as a fragile newborn child, or vulnerability of kin and community, such as those suffering the loss of a loved and respected member. Nowadays, highly secularized Westerners rely on medical specialists and counselors to help them get through such times of crisis. But in earlier times, and still today in many religious communities, ritual has been the chief means of support in making such crossings.

All Hindu communities practice some form of life-crisis rituals, from the most despised groups of outcastes to the most orthodox and exacting Brahmins. As is the case with daily observances, life-crisis rites become more numerous and more elaborate at higher levels of the caste ladder. Outcaste families may ritualize only birth, death, and marriage. Learned Brahmins can cite up to forty life-cycle rituals described in their household and dharma literatures, and their families will regularly enact at least a dozen.

In many Hindu communities, especially those of the first three varnas, the principal model for life-cycle rite practice is the one offered by Brahmins.[9] Families of non-Brahmin castes imitate what Brahmins do, insofar as their means and knowledge allow this. They may also add customs special to their own castes. Even though Brahmin texts themselves state that no priest is required for these ceremonies, most families aspiring to "correctness" will try to have a Brahmin present if one is available and they can afford to pay him. I suspect this is because the Brahmin version of these rituals became a mark of Aryanness very early in Indian history. Because samskaras are fairly simple, carrying them out in the same way as the Brahmins did became a way of showing that one accepted at least to some degree the Brahmins' claim to religious authority.

Because the Brahmin model is so prestigious, it will be followed throughout this section. The Sanskrit term "samskara" itself reveals the intended purpose of Hindu life-cycle rites. The word is composed of two elements: *kara,* from a verb meaning "to make," and the prefix *sam-,* meaning "full, whole, perfect." A samskara is a rite that perfects, completing a person. Ancient pandits viewed this "perfecting" in part as a process of especially deep purification. Hence, for example, the *Manusmrti* asserts, "By performing the *samskaras* ... seminal and uterine impurities are washed away."[10] Such rites also address the dangers and possibilities inherent in life's transitions: the dangers, by taking steps to avert them; the possibilities, by making sure that the subject's first steps into a new state of life are taken in the purest possible way, while surrounded by auspicious forces and presences.

Let us see how this works. An optimal course of samskaras begins with initiatives taken by a child-to-be's mother and father. Until recently, among Brahmins, as well as many other castes, especially in northern India, a girl was married before or during puberty. Such very early marriages still take place in some rural areas. One argument put forth by pandits to justify early marriage is the need to perform a samskara called *garbhadhana* during the three-day period believed to be optimal for conceiving that immediately follows a girl's first menstruation. The garbhadhana is sexual intercourse preceded by a ritual bath and sanctified by mantras that link the uniting couple to the powers of earth and sky. Any child conceived by a couple thus perfecting their first union is thereby given a boost toward its own process of completion.

Because Hindus, like most other people, keep their sex lives private, the garbhadhana ritual is not open for viewing by the couple's family, let alone by invited Brahmins. After it, however, comes a long series of rites witnessed at least by relatives and sometimes also by guests from beyond the family. In the mid-1960s, Professor Daniel Smith of Syracuse University filmed a number of samskaras connected to childhood as performed by a Brahmin family in the city of Madras (now Chennai) of South India.[11] His portrayal will be followed. But again, readers should remember that non-Brahmin families perform fewer samskaras than Brahmins and do them in

[9] A good source for the textual version of these rites is Raj Bali Pandey, *Hindu Saṁskāras: Socio-Religious Study of the Hindu Sacraments,* 2nd ed. (Delhi: Motilal Banarsidas, 1969).

[10] Manusmrti 2.27; as cited ibid., 29–30.

[11] *Hindu Sacraments of Childhood* (New York: Syracuse University, 1969); see also Smith's *Hindu Sacrament of Thread Investiture* (New York: Syracuse University, 1969).

lesser detail. Brahmin practice itself differs somewhat according to region, financial means, and the family's level of orthodoxy. Still another important factor is whether a rite's central figure is a girl, who will one day shift through marriage into a different family, or a boy, who is considered more a family's "own"—at least in the patrilineal families found in most of India. In general, a boy undergoes more samskaras, and they are done more elaborately.

The rites filmed by Smith all had present the family *purohit,* a Brahmin learned in household rituals whose family is usually linked by heredity to a number of client families whom it helps to perform its rites. All but one of the rites Smith filmed also had present a sacred fire into which offerings were placed. The presence of such a fire is a clear indication that a rite has historical roots in the complex of Vedic rituals that were always the special prerogative of Brahmin priests in India. Its meaning is very close to that of an image in a puja room; when it is lit with the proper summoning chants, divine forces become present through it. When the fire is fed, these forces are strengthened and made content, and hence good fortune descends on the makers of the offering. A sacred fire is rarely lit inside a puja room; hence Smith's filming was done mostly in a family living room. Moreover, the names of the forces summoned when such a fire is lit are not usually those called on during a family's daily worship. This is because the fire rites come out of a different ritual heritage than do everyday pujas, which are more closely related to the devotional complex.

Samskaras filmed by Smith also share several other features common to rites done under Brahmin supervision. All participants have bathed first, and all wear proper ritual dress: silk saris for women and *dhotis,* raw silk cloth draped below the waist, for men. The rite always starts with a declaration of the rite's purpose by the presiding senior household male. Often gifts are offered: to the subject of the ritual, to attending guests, and always to the officiating Brahmin. My students are always struck by the fact that samskaras often entail rice-throwing. In India, as in the West, rice is a symbol of abundance and fertility. Finally, many samskaras include use of sanctifying designs drawn in rice powder on areas of the floor or items focal to the rite. These designs, drawn by women, are common to both samskaras and pujas; skill in drawing them is a housewifely art prized by all respectable Hindu women.

Added to these features common to samskaras is one or more central acts that signal and complete its main intention. Smith's film starts with two samskaras performed for a pregnant woman. These are both protective rituals, but the first also helps the mother produce a boy, whereas the second prepares her for her coming delivery. In the first, the father-to-be squeezes banyan juice into his pregnant wife's nostril; this juice is said to have properties that influence gender and prevent miscarriage. In the second, the husband uses a feather wrapped in a spray of mango leaves to trace an invisible line up the center of his wife's body. This "splits" her symbolically and signals her body to release the baby that it holds inside.

Next among classic samskaras are rites surrounding birth. Smith could not film the birth rites per se because most take place in the delivery room, where mother and child and attending household women are secluded. This shields the rest of the household from the polluting fluids that emerge from a mother during birth. One striking feature of birth seclusion is the presence and aid of a traditional midwife, usually of low barber caste. The midwife's expertise includes not only mechanics of delivery, but also techniques for pollution removal and additional rites to open a mother's body. After birth, too, many precautions are taken to remove residual pollution and bring mother and child safely back into the family.[12] The first public rite after birth filmed by Smith introduces the baby to its new relations. Its father dips a coin into a bit of honey and feeds it, showing that the family from now on will share its wealth and food with the child.

As the child grows, it passes through other ritualized first occasions. During the rite "name-giving," the father whispers the child's formal name into its ear. In the rite "beginning food," it receives its first solid food from its father. During "first haircut," childhood locks are shorn, first, in token, by the child's father inside a consecrated room and then more fully by a barber waiting outside—another low-caste specialist in removing pollution. In "start of learning," the boy of Smith's film is shown the alphabet, written before him in sand by his father. Then his family proudly accompanies him to his first day of school.

Among the Brahmin families filmed by Smith, a boy's next big occasion is the rite of *upanayana*, "leading near." This preserves echoes of older times when a family gave its son over to a teacher for instruction in Vedic learning. Dressed like a young man in the pure student stage of life, the boy is taught how to beg food properly for himself and his master. Then, he is draped with a sacred thread signifying Vedic learning. The father consigns the boy to a Brahmin teacher, who takes him outside and shows him how to recite the Gayatri, the prayer to the sun that should start his mornings. Upanayana is a major celebration crowded with family guests.

In times of the past when many Brahmin boys really did leave home to study Vedic lore for years, they ended their studies with a special ritual bath that is also listed among the textual samskaras. Then they came home for their marriage, by far the most festive and lavishly done samskara for a Hindu of any caste. Marriage customs today come in seemingly endless variation; I have never quite gotten straight even those I have encountered among my closest Indian friends, whose weddings often go on for days.[13] But the heart of a Brahmin-model wedding is simple. A boy's family seeks out a girl suitably matched to him and works out an agreement with her family—usually entailing a generous dowry of household goods that she will bring to her husband's home, representing her claim on her family's property.[14]

---

[12] Interested readers can find an excellent description of birth rites in a village of North India in Doreanne Jacobson's "Golden Handprints and Red-Painted Feet: Hindu Childbirth Rituals in a North Indian Village," *Unspoken Worlds: Women's Religious Lives*, Nancy A. Falk and Rita M. Gross, eds., 3rd ed. (San Francisco: Wadsworth Press, 2001), 83–102.

[13] For a good description of a full set of marriage rites and customs, see Lina Fruzzetti, *The Gift of a Virgin: Women, Marriage, and Ritual in a Bengali Society* (Delhi: Oxford University Press, 1990).

[14] The custom of giving dowry to a girl is now causing major problems in India because girls may now inherit and their brothers argue, with some justification, that their dowries are an unfair claim on their families' wealth. Moreover, only a small part, her jewels and clothing, remain her own once she joins her husband's household. Dowries become a way for a family with sons to increase its wealth, whereas a family with several daughters is drained. Obsession with consumer goods in India has also produced a new problem, the "dowry death." A young wife may be saddled with demands for additional dowry payments from her natal family until she commits suicide to protect them. Or she is killed by her in-laws so they can keep her wealth and seek new brides for their sons. Such abuse of the system of course horrifies most Hindus as much as it does Europeans and Americans; women's groups fight it vigorously.

When the wedding day arrives, after preparatory rituals in his home, the groom goes to the bride's house[15] in a festive procession. At an auspicious time preselected by astrologers, he enters and is greeted by his bride to be, while each hangs a large floral garland around the neck of the other. Later, he takes a seat by a fire, opposite a chanting Brahmin priest. The girl's father leads in his daughter, dripping with gold and dressed in an elaborate silk sari. Then he asserts his intention to give the bride away with all her adornments. Ancient Brahmin texts acknowledged seven licit types of marriage, but this form, called "gift of a girl," was considered the most auspicious for the father and family that gave her.

After the bride is given, the couple is symbolically bound together in several ways. The bride and groom's hands and then their clothing are tied together. Next they circle the fire three or seven times—both auspicious numbers. If the wedding is in South India, the groom may tie a pendant called *tali* around his wife's neck, to symbolize his family gods who have by now claimed her. If it is in the North, he traces a line of red kumkum powder in the parting of her hair, a mark that only married women with living husbands may wear. The guests are feasted, and the bride is taken home, to be incorporated by more rites into the groom's family. Soon, with the garbhadhana, their sexual life begins. With luck, they soon find themselves cycling through childhood samskaras again, now from the perspective of the child's parents.

One set of major samskaras still awaits them. At death, each will be washed, dressed in new clothes, and carried on a bier to the local cremation ground, where their oldest son will light the torch that sets off their funeral pyre. Then, family members will bathe and begin a period of seclusion and mourning, whose duration varies in accordance with caste, age, and sex. In the meantime, after the fire has cooled, a member of the family collects bone fragments from the ashes, later to be "sunk" in a sacred river. On the eleventh day after death, the dead receive a rice-ball offering to strengthen them and ease their transition to the next stage of their existence. Rice-ball offerings may continue through the mourning period, and for many years after, on the date of death, the family sponsors small fire-rituals in remembrance of the loved one.

CALENDRICAL RITUALS

When several generations and their families live together in a joint Hindu household, daily rituals and samskaras for children alone can give it a very active religious life. That life is made still more complicated by times occurring periodically that offer occasions for special observances and rites. Some of these are widespread and festive public holidays, like Christmas or Hanukkah in the West. Others are small in scale and may be performed only by certain groups: members of a particular caste; devotees of a certain deity; people pursuing a certain aim. Many of the latter kind of rites have become the special province of women, who usually perform them to seek some benefit for male members of their families.

---

[15] Or a place selected by her family. Weddings today may be in temples, hotel banquet rooms and gardens, special tents erected over streets, or parks maintained especially for such purposes in well-to-do urban neighborhoods.

The focus here is on this latter type, usually called vrats in Northern India. To clarify the thinking behind them, it is necessary to explain Hindu thinking about time a little more fully. First of all, there are two types of time measurement: solar time and lunar time. Indian solar time pretty well matches the timing of the West: days and nights are demarcated by the sun's rising and setting, and seven days make up the week that determines the standard cycle of business openings, school days, etc. There is one significant difference between Hindu and Western weeks: a Hindu week does not have just one holy day. Every day is a holy day of sorts, although different people may choose different days for special observance. Days of the week have special links to planets considered to be sources of auspicious or inauspicious influence. Especially when such influence is inauspicious and dangerous, specific gods may be called on to help a devout worshiper contend with that day.

The exact associations of any given day vary throughout India. The understanding of the week recorded in Chhattisgarh state in south central India by anthropologist Lawrence Babb is summarized below.[16] Babb's description is consistent with one given to me in New Delhi by my Punjab-born and raised hostess. Sunday (Itvar) belongs to the sun and is auspicious. Although sun worship is appropriate for Itvar, Babb says it is rarely performed in the region he studied. Monday (Chandravar) belongs to the moon and to Shiva, and is auspicious. Wise Hindus, nevertheless, worship Shiva on Mondays. Tuesday (Mangalvar) belongs to Mars; it is inauspicious and a bad day for travel. Tuesdays call forth worship of certain scary but very powerful goddesses or of Rama's monkey devotee Hanuman, who is extremely strong and hence can offer special protection. My hostess fasted until sundown every Tuesday, while lines at the Hanuman temple in downtown New Delhi grow very long on this day. Wednesday (Budhvar) belongs to Mercury; it is auspicious and a very good day to start a journey. Thursday (Guruvar) is Jupiter's and also auspicious. Friday (Shukravar) belongs to Venus and is auspicious; lines at temples of kindly goddesses grow longest on this day. Saturday (Shannivar) belongs to Saturn and is extremely inauspicious. The deity needing worship to counter its influence is Saturn himself.

Paralleling this pattern, and probably older, is a lunar method of thinking about time that determines the occurrence of monthly, semi-annual, and annual ritualized days. A *tithi,* or lunar day, is the period of time from one moonrise to another (or from moonset to moonset; Indian astrologers differ somewhat about this). A lunar month extends from full moon to new and back again (or the converse). A year consists of twelve lunar months of thirty tithis each and is adjusted periodically to match the solar cycle.

Overlying both solar and lunar systems are beliefs about the qualities of particular kinds of time units. "Bright halves" and "dark halves" of time units are auspicious and inauspicious, respectively. A bright half is a time when light increases: in a day, it is the morning; in a lunar month, it is the period when the moon's illumined portion increases in size; in a year it is the time between the winter and summer solstices. Within any given month, individual tithis also have auspicious and inauspicious qualities, and may be assigned to particular deities. Finally, India's three seasons—hot, rainy, and cool—have qualities of their own, which may counteract or reinforce the

---

[16] At the time of Babb's studies, Chhattisgarh was the southeastern region of the huge state of Madhya Pradesh; it now a state in its own right.

power of light and dark halves. The hot season is a time of passion, the rainy, of torpor, and the cool, a time for reconstructing order.

The interplay of these qualities infuses various points in time with challenge and opportunity. A certain tithi during a certain lunar half in a certain season may become optimal for one or more major festivals of a specific deity. Vaishnavas, for example, tend to hold their most important celebrations on "elevenths," because the eleventh tithi of a dark or bright half belongs to Vishnu. Moreover, just as during the week some days are full of peril that must be countered, whereas others offer a special chance to gain what a person desires, so it is during the month: some days hold special danger, others special opportunity.

Vrats

Vrats are prescribed ritual sequences that take advantage of the calendar's opportunities. Why so many are special to women and why so many are done for men's benefit are thorny questions. Social scientists usually answer by pointing to women's insecure position within their marital families. Given the patriliny, patrilocality, and patriarchy of most Indian families, a woman is an alien in the household where she lives most of her life. She must earn her way into its confidences, and even while there, she depends upon her links to males within it to back up her claim to its resources—her husband at first and then her sons. Meanwhile, her brothers are her principal link to her natal family because they are go-betweens who bring gifts for her children and in-laws and because they escort her to her natal home for welcome visits. She has abundant motivation to keep her menfolk healthy.[17]

Another important consideration is Hindu thinking about women's power. As pointed out earlier, women are often perceived as repositories of special power, shakti, that is closely linked to their life-sustaining abilities. When left in its "natural" state, unchecked by social and religious discipline, such power becomes dangerous—the reason why pre-nineteenth century Hindus found widows so threatening. When disciplined by marriage, household rites, and austerities such as those found in vrats, women's power gains protective force. India has special names for such disciplined and protective women. Most start with the prefix *su-,* meaning "auspicious, good." Such a woman may even be called the Lakshmi, "luck goddess" of her home. Hence, women also do vrats to protect family members because they can. Linking their power to that of the vrat's patron deity, women themselves become centers of auspiciousness in their homes.

Like samskaras, some vrats are very old. Prototypes of some done today are summarized in Puranas, and several are based on stories appearing in the Sanskrit epics. They are not found in Vedic texts, however, and so most likely entered the Hindu weave from old local and oral traditions. In the founding tales told during performance of many vrats, a deity appears to a woman caught in a predicament and tells her how to resolve her problems by performing a given set of actions on a particular day or days. Actions prescribed include ritual bathing, fasting, and puja to the deity who presides over the fast day—that is to say, purification, austerity, and worship, standard

---

[17] See Susan S. Wadley, "Hindu Women's Family and Seasonal Rites in a North Indian Village, *Unspoken Worlds,* op. cit., 103–13.

components of virtually all Hindu practice. Women's studies scholars have lately taken great interest in vrats and have described many examples in different regions of India. Although not all regions or castes observe the same rites, some are quite widespread. Let us look at three vrats that give some idea of the range of their focus and style.

Vrats in Practice

The first example is drawn from an autobiography reflecting practice at the beginning of the twentieth century.[18] The woman recalling the vrat was Shudha Mazumdar, born in 1899 as daughter of a wealthy Bengali landowner. Mazumdar was raised among women in *purdah,* seclusion. No man who was not a relative could look upon them. As she herself points out, vrats at that time were not just a way for women to gain some desired end, they were also an important way to instill a family's values in children. However, Shudha was raised in a changing world, and hence, during her younger years, she was also sent to school.

When Shudha was eight, her mother had her undertake a vrat of Shiva Puja, intended to bring her a husband like the stern but devoted super-god Shiva. This puja is based on a popular Sanskrit story telling how the goddess Parvati won Lord Shiva as her husband by worshiping his linga and practicing austerity. Shudha performed her vrat every morning during the month of Visakh (April–May) for four years, until she was twelve and ready to marry. Well before her time to leave for school and before she ate or drank anything, she got up, bathed, put on a silk sari, and gathered flowers and *darva* grass for her puja. In the family puja room, she poured Ganges water into a small copper urn and then washed the flowers, grass, and some leaves of the *bel* tree, said to be much loved by Shiva. She rubbed sandalwood mixed with water into a paste and put it on a plate, washed uncooked rice and put it on another, and peeled a banana and put it on a third. Next she took Ganges mud kept in a pot of earth in the room's corner, molded a Shiva linga from it, stood this on a dish on a sprig of bel, lit a small lamp, and put this, the flowers, and the plates of food beside it. She bathed the linga by sprinkling it three times, said "I salute thee, o Shiva,"[19] dipped a few flowers and leaves in the sandalwood paste, recited a little prayer asking the Lord to accept them, and offered the items she was holding, again doing this three times. Then she tried to visualize Lord Shiva, imagining him in the form of a picture hanging in her family home. Having disciplined herself in this way and fixed her mind on God, she ended her rite, ate her breakfast, and headed off to her daytime classes.

Although Mazumdar's vrat entails only a short and simple fast, fasts during vrats can become quite complicated and intense. They may restrict food intake to a certain category, as in the vrat associated with the goddess Durga's "nine nights" festival. In this case, fasting women may only eat foods that grow beneath the ground.[20] In the *karva chauth* vrat popular in northwest India, the fast is total. No food or water is taken from dawn until first sighting of the moon. This vrat is done to bring long life

---

[18] Shudha Mazumdar, *Memoirs of an Indian Woman,* Geraldine Forbes, ed. (Armonk, NY: M. E. Sharpe, 1989).

[19] This was probably "Namah Shivaya," a common mantra of homage to Shiva.

[20] At least in the city of New Delhi; I have not verified this type of fast elsewhere.

to a husband. As performed in New Delhi, where I encountered parts of it, women intent on fasting get up before dawn, hurry to take some food and drink before the light breaks, and bathe, dress, and pray in their usual daily way. At dawn, all intake of food and drink ceases, as does all normal household work. In the meantime, a young wife's mother will have given her in-laws money to be used for buying food to break the fast, as well as special flat pastries and sometimes other sweets. Displays featuring these treats are a common sight in New Delhi markets just before the karva chauth fast day. Around 4 PM of that day, fasting women bathe again and dress in fancy silk saris. Then they gather in someone's home, bringing with them food trays bearing pastries and food purchased with their mother's gift. Now they fashion images of Gauri, another form of Shiva's wife, placing them in the center of the trays. They offer puja to Gauri, sit in a circle, and tell the first half of the karva chauth story. Next, they pass their trays around the circle and announce, "We shall do no work today." They tell the story and pass their trays five times, then wait for the moon, often chatting and telling more stories until the time comes to break the fast. When the moon appears, they first drink water. Once upon a time, this was taken from a silver tumbler given for the occasion; today it is more often drunk from stainless steel. Finally, the fasting women take food, always starting with the fast's special pastries.

The weather is still warm at the time of karva chauth, which falls on the "bright fourth" of the month of Kartik (October–November). For a young and active woman, a warm day without food or liquid can be an ordeal. I sat one karva chauth night with a friend who is separated from her husband and hence does not perform this vrat. Her recently married daughter, however, was doing her first karva chauth in the joint household of her in-laws. As moonrise approached, she kept phoning her mother: "Mummy, I'm starving." "Mummy, I have such a terrible headache."

Not all vrats are this demanding. Just twelve days later, on dark Kartik 2, my New Delhi friends celebrate the vrat of *bhai dhuj,* "brother's second." This is a rite of protection for one's natal brother, and the same friend with the suffering karva chauth daughter took me along on her ritual visit to the family homestead where her two brothers still live. She took a box of sweets for each, and a small vial of red kumkum powder. Now she climbed the stairs to the second floor apartment where her younger brother waited. She dabbed his forehead with the powder, presented him with the sweets, and accepted the token amount of money that he offered as a return gift. Next, she went downstairs to her older brother, where she followed the same procedure. Her vrat over within minutes, she headed for the rear room where her bedridden mother still lived. Two sisters were already there, and two more soon arrived. All lay around on their mother's large bed, swapping in-jokes and family gossip.

These latter occasions show yet another important function of women's vrats. They offer chances to socialize, and sometimes to bring scattered families together. They build community among women who gather to observe them. One widow told me that her second greatest sense of loss after her husband's death came when her karva chauth companions told her she could no longer join their gathering. In addition, by suffering through a fast for her husband or dabbing kumkum on her brother as she would on a household god, a woman shows that she values and honors these male relatives. In the meantime, she enhances her own spiritual discipline and reasserts her own claim to be a center of household auspiciousness. It is no wonder that such rites survive, even in the midst of extensive social change.

ADDITIONAL OPTIONS

This chapter has looked mainly at routine household practice. Sometimes a visitor to an Indian household finds himself or herself in the midst of some practice that is done simply because the family wishes to host it. These practices can be called "boosters," for they raise a household's general level of auspiciousness. Many times they are done in celebration of a special occasion: a forthcoming wedding, a graduation, a move to a better house or apartment. Alternatively, they are done because the household has had bad luck—a series of mishaps, an ailing child. Unlike calendrical rites, most can be done at any time, although some are tied to special seasons or are done more often in connection with special holidays. These are summarized only briefly.

Perhaps the most common form of occasional practice is the *kirtan,* a devotional songfest. Devotional traditions of India left Hindus with a rich heritage of songs, many of which have been popular "hits" since the time of their creation. Indian devotees constantly add to these, and whereas some of their songs remain known only to themselves or to groups in which they function, others attain regional or national distribution. Many of India's new guru- and ashram-centered groups also compose new songs for kirtan, as do astute professional singers, who sometimes adapt popular songs from films, giving them devotional words and sentiments. Many Hindus love to sing these songs or to hear them sung. They may invite friends in to sing them together. I know women in New Delhi who do this weekly, just as American women might invite friends for a bridge club. For a special occasion, they may pay a singer and instrumentalist to come to the house and lead a kirtan, perhaps setting up a temporary shrine to their favorite deity in the place where the kirtan is done and concluding the songfest with a puja. Or a kirtan may be a private concert. I attended one given before an only daughter's wedding that featured one of New Delhi's finest artists. The audience did not sing that night; it listened with rapt attention.

In New Delhi, too, during the season of multiple festivals occurring each fall, guests are often invited to *jagrans,* all-night vigils which are a cross between a kirtan and a vrat. The jagrans I have encountered are special to Vaishnodevi, a goddess of the Jammu-Kashmir region popular among Punjabis who fled their homes during Partition and resettled in New Delhi. Vaishnodevi jagrans have become so popular that special groups of jagran singers crop up for hire each fall, arriving complete with portable shrines, instruments, and amplifiers. I attended one given as a housewarming by a family that had recently acquired a new and much better apartment. It was set up in a tent pitched in an alcove of their complex that clearly had been designed so that residents could use it for such celebratory purposes. A large paper-mache image of the goddess, glittering with gilt sparkles, rode a "lion" with a mane and stripes at the center of a temporary mandir set up on a table at the front of the tent. A bowl with a burning flame was at Vaishnodevi's feet, to be kept burning throughout the night. The evening started with dinner; then, guests gathered for invocations offered by a prominent local religious leader, who next applied kumkum to foreheads of the fifty to sixty guests.

Then, the musicians began to sing, with a loud and infectious beat. They sang until about three in the morning, then took a break while the audience sang on, led by a group of teenagers among the guests. After an hour or so, the musicians returned and sang on until just before dawn. The head singer next told the story of how the jagran was founded. Then puja was conducted, ending with an *arti,* a frequent conclusion of group rituals in which a lighted oil lamp is waved in circles before the deity. This arti entails group participation: the lamp is passed from one participant to another—and then carried through the crowd so its purifying smoke can be caught and brushed back over faces. Host and hostess distributed the goddess's prasad, sweets and a black lentil curry. Finally, exhausted, we broke up at dawn.[21]

Yet another practice common on special occasions is reading a holy book from beginning to end in a single session. Such a reading will always be done as part of a larger puja, much as the jagran's singing is part of its larger vrat structure. If in Sanskrit, the reading is likely to be done by a specialist. *Devi-Mahatmya* is a popular text for such readings in the center and south of India.[22] More popular in the north is the Hindi *Ramcharitmanas,* written by the sixteenth century devotional poet Tulsidas. I have heard about groups of women who undertake this on their own, reading in tandem throughout a night. An alternative is to bring in a professional reader or a commentator whose artistry consists of relating a text's tales to the foibles of everyday life.[23]

Finally, a family may invite a holy guest, a pandit or sadhu, perhaps just for a meal and conversation, or for the more formal religious discourse called *satsang*. A guest, let us remember, is a god in one's home. But a holy guest is a special god and receives special honors. I have seen a swami stopped on a doorstep to stand on an auspicious design while a housewife washed his feet, heaped rose petals on them, and then sang a song of welcome while waving a tray with a lamp in arti. Inviting holy guests for a meal is a very ancient means of bringing merit to a household, well recorded already in Buddhist texts more than two millenia old. Having the guest deliver a religious discourse is a practice equally old. Some family's willingness to sponsor satsang in its home and invite friends to attend has given many a new teacher important public exposure. This text will return to this practice of hosting satsang in Chapter 8, when it introduces disciples of a modern sadhu.

THE HINDU HOME:
A FOUNDATION STONE

What sense can be made of all this? What is the purpose of religious practice in a Hindu home? Recall, first of all, that a home is a holy place. It even incorporates a temple within its boundaries. If its rules for maintaining purity seem excessive to some readers, they should recall that they themselves would probably hesitate before contaminating a church or synagogue. During each daily puja, divine guests are invited into the home's

---

[21] Kathleen Erndl describe this same ritual as practiced in the Kangra Valley of North India in her "Fire and Wakefulness in Contemporary Panjabi Hinduism," *Journal of the American Academy of Religion,* 59 (Summer 1991): 339–60," and in her book *Victory to the Mother: the Hindu Goddess of Northwest India in Myth, Ritual, and Symbol* (New York: Oxford University Press, 1993).

[22] Lawrence Babb has described a very elaborate form of such a reading in east central India in his *Divine Hierarchy,* 39–46.

[23] Hindi scholar and religionist Philip Lutgendorf has written an excellent book on the many versions of Ramayana performance: *The Life of a Text: Performing the Rāmcaritmānas of Tulsidas* (Berkeley: University of Chicago Press, 1991).

holy place, guests who demand proper respect and reverence. Treated properly, they will come, protect the reverent family, and keep it prosperous; treated badly, they may not bother to make the next day's stop at the household when summoned.

Furthermore, a home is a foundation stone in the greater edifice that Brahmins call dharma. Again, it is necessary to remember that the longstanding Brahmin ideal for building a healthy society has been to maintain a proper balance or harmony in existence. Humans and deities must be in a proper relationship with one another; humans and humans must get along; husbands and wives, sisters and brothers, parents and children, even the living and the dead, all must reaffirm and value their interdependence. If all homes maintain proper dharma, it becomes more likely to flourish in the greater world and hence to benefit all society.

Like homes in any other culture of the world, a Hindu home is also a place where values are instilled. Even a superficial review of practices covered in this chapter will show how many instill qualities that are prized in family members. Often these are instilled without a single word having to be spoken about what these qualities are or why family members should prize them. Not only do the rituals teach cleanliness, reverence, and respect, but also reciprocity, industry, early rising, self-restraint, hospitality, and even grace and beauty of movement, which many women especially try to perfect in themselves while performing their pujas.

Finally, household rites and purifications are important forms of preparation for later, higher, varieties of spiritual discipline. The deep cleansing or perfecting undergone through samskaras as well as the basic discipline a Hindu acquires while carrying out a well-regulated household life are essential prior steps for movement onto higher paths of renunciation or yoga. This does not have to occur in the present life—although it may well do so, especially if the practitioner is a Brahmin. But at least there is always the promise that it will carry through, that in the next life or the next the disciplined householder will gain a chance to practice at that higher level.

ADDITIONAL SOURCES

A good general introduction to Hindu domestic values and concepts is T. N. Madan's *Non-Renunciation: Themes and Intrerpretations of Hindu Culture* (Delhi: Oxford University Press, 1987). The most extensive research on Indian food customs and values has been done by Ravindra S. Khare; see especially his *Culture and Reality: Essays on the Hindu System of Managing Foods* (Simla: Indian Institute of Advanced Study, 1976); see also his edited collection *The Eternal Food: Gastronomic Ideas and Experiences of Hindus and Buddhists* (Albany: State University of New York Press, 1992). Lawrence Babb's *The Divine Hierarchy: Popular Hinduism in Central India* (New York: Columbia University Press, 1975) is the best introduction to household puja and time cycles. Portions of household pujas can be viewed on the short video *Pūjā* (Washington, DC: Smithsonian Institution, Arthur M. Sackler Gallery, 1996). A full household puja is shown on the unfortunately much older film *How a Hindu Worships: At the Home Shine,* H. Daniel Smith, producer (Syracuse: Syracuse University, 1969). Raj Bali Pandey's *Hindu Saṁskāras: Socio-Religious Study of the Hindu Sacraments,* 2nd ed. (Delhi: Motilal Banarsidas, 1969) is the best general resource on Hindu rites of passage; to learn how they work in a specific context, see Ralph W. Nicholas, "The

Effectiveness of the Hindu Sacrament (*Saṁskāra*): Caste, Marriage, and Divorce in Bengali Culture," in *From the Margins of Hindu Marriage: Essays on Gender, Religion, and Culture,* Lindsey Harlan and Paul Courtright, eds. (New York: Oxford University Press, 1995), 137–59. Lina Fruzzetti's *The Gift of a Virgin: Women, Marriage, and Ritual in a Bengali Society* (Delhi: Oxford University Press, 1990) and Janet Chawla's *Child-Bearing and Culture: Women Centered Revisioning of the Traditional Midwife: the Dai as Ritual Practitioner* explores the ritual roles of midwives (New Delhi: Indian Social Institute, 1994).

An excellent place to begin the study of women's vrats is Anne Mackenzie Pearson, *"Because It Gives Me Peace of Mind": Ritual Fasts in the Religious Lives of Hindu Women* (Albany: State University of New York Press, 1996). See also June McDaniel, *Making Virtuous Daughters and Wives: An Introduction to Women's Brata Rituals in Bengali Folk Religion* (Albany: State University of New York Press, 2003); Mary McGee, *Feasting and Fasting: The Vrata Tradition and Its Significance for Hindu Women* (Harvard University Ph.D. dissertation, 1987); and Holly Baker Reynolds, *To Keep the Tali Strong: Women's Rituals in Tamilnad, India* (University of Wisconsin Ph.D. dissertation, 1978). The latter also describes life-cycle rites from a woman's perspective. Nancy A. Falk and Rita M. Gross's edited collection *Unspoken Worlds: Women's Religious Lives,* 3rd ed. (San Francisco: Wadsworth Press, 2001) includes several essays on Hindu women's domestic practice, as does Julia Leslie's collection *Roles and Rituals for Hindu Women* (Delhi: Motilal Banarsidas, 1992). Leslie's translation of Tryambakayajvan's *The Perfect Wife (Strīdharmapaddhati)* (Oxford: Oxford University Press, 1989) lays out a day's daily tasks and rituals for a proper Hindu wife. Susan S. Wadley's collection *The Powers of Tamil Women* (Syracuse, NY: Syracuse University, Maxwell School of Citizenship and Public Affairs, 1980) explores the relationship between shakti and women.

6

At Temples and Temple Festivals

At shops lining the road, each of us bought one coconut, four pieces of fruit, a garland of marigolds, and one small red, gilt-trimmed version of the wide scarf called a *chuni* in New Delhi. We were ready to pay our respects to a goddess. Leaving our shoes in the car, we rinsed our mouths and splashed ourselves with water from faucets just inside the compound's entrance. From here we could see lines of worshipers high on the temple's side, snaking in and out of doorways to peripheral shrines. This was a full-moon day and a Friday; so this palace for deities was quite busy. "This place is well organized; we won't wait long," my friend's neighbor assured us. She had been here before and had volunteered to guide us through our visit.

She was right; when we arrived at the staging area, worshipers were moving briskly up the ramps and stairs leading into the central complex. As we ascended, some devotees bent to brush fingers in dust left by others' feet and then touched those fingers to their foreheads. As they passed the temple's several peripheral deities, they made the gesture called *namas* and tucked small bills into offering boxes. Our path took us first past shrines of Shiva and Shakti, then Ram, then Krishna and Radha. All were richly decked in silks, gilded crowns and jewelry, and multiple strands of fresh flower garlands.

When we reached the shrine of an eighteen-armed goddess labeled "Shakti," our guide headed for a gate in the railing that separated the deity from the line of devotees filing past her. "They are with me," she said to the attending priest, who clearly knew her. At first, he had moved to block our entrance; now he let us in. We laid the offerings brought with us on a tray at the Devi's feet, stuffed larger bills than usual in her cash box, and did *pranams,* bows to the floor. The priest marked our foreheads with dots of red powder, touched a bowl-like object to our heads, and presented us with *prasad,* offerings the deity has touched: half a coconut, a banana, an orange, a single marigold. This shrine had an antechamber, a space big enough for a group to sit down in. "We have to sit for a few minutes, or the effect will not be so strong," my friend whispered. So we settled on the floor to reflect a bit on the *darshan,* view of the deity, that we had just experienced.

The main shrine was anticlimactic: a larger, brightly decked goddess, more cash stuffed into boxes, more prasad in the form of tiny white candies. This shrine's anteroom was a large one with a platform at one end; on it sat a group of women fervently chanting Om. We sat here for a while again, then rose and made our exit, pausing to look at some of the temple's other wonders: magnificent carvings in stone, paintings of deities adorned with gold and silver leaf, fluted white marble columns soaring up to domes carved like inverted wedding cakes. Outside the temple's main door, our guide showed me a tree with small red scarves tied on its branches, along with other gifts of the type that a goddess likes. "If you want something," she said, "tie a gift for the goddess on this tree." But she would tie on nothing and wanted nothing, she told me. It was enough for her just to have this chance to visit with the Devi.

Hindu temples can have as many different personalities as the deities within them. Huge new divine mansions like the one described above are very popular in India now. Some come complete with high-tech laser and audio-visual shows portraying the deities' great deeds to eager visitors. Hindu India also has awesome temple-mazes, drawing walkers to sacred centers through shadowy pillared halls; sublime temple towers soaring skywards; cheerful mid-sized temples so teeming with colorful deities that they seem transplanted from a Disney theme park; and thousands of much simpler one-room structures, some barely large enough to hold a small image and a single worshiper. A temple can be peaceful enough to let a devotee sit before its image for hours in meditation. It can be so supercharged with throbbing music from drums and blaring instruments, with brilliant colors of deities' clothes and flowers, with overpowering smells from burning incense, that a person entering feels immediately shifted into highest gear. A temple is clearly intended to be not just a place but an experience. It should work a change on those who visit it and celebrate the deities within its walls.

This chapter shows what kinds of experiences are shaped by temples and what changes they produce. To do so, it is first necessary to examine three elements central to temple worship: the temple itself as an architectural and symbolic structure, the image or images housed in a temple and their significance; and the *pujas,* acts of worship, addressed to these images. It then introduces four different kinds of temples important to Hindus and explores the purposes they each serve. Distinguishing these four types points to links between deities and communities that often are ignored in textbooks on Hinduism. Recognizing these links should help readers understand better why Hindus put so much effort into building and keeping up temples and also why temples can be major issues in Hindu politics.

THE TEMPLE

In its most minimal form, a temple is merely a marker for a place where divine power is concentrated. A Hindu deity does not have to be housed in a complex temple structure. A simple low wall or platform is enough to mark off a deity's *sthan,* its place. Deities found at such simple sites are usually those of local and orally carried traditions. Central to the sites is the belief that the deity itself chooses where it will make itself available. This is also true for larger and more famous temples. Virtually all have stories connected to them telling how their deity chose the temple's location or how the temple founder discovered a god was at this place.

Even when a deity chooses its own site, that site must still be consecrated by a host of rites carried out at carefully calculated auspicious times by Brahmins who special-ize in such rites. One such ritual of great importance is the drawing of a diagram called a *vastumandala* to establish the temple's power center. It is a square divided into smaller squares, usually nine by nine, cut from corner to corner by diagonals that cross in the central square. Into this diagram are invoked creative and protective deities such as Brahma, maker of the world, the planets, and guardian deities of the direc-tions. The diagram as a whole may also contain a sketch of a sitting man with his head in one corner, feet with soles together in the corner opposite and outstretched elbows and knees poking into the corners remaining. This represents the Purusha, the single cosmic Being whose sacrifice made the world as we know it. In this place, his image suggests, the world's divisions will be overcome, its differences reconciled into a new place of harmony.

Harmony is important as well in planning the structure, all of whose proportions are laid out in Brahmin-developed texts called Shilpashastras. Although temple build-ings may be elaborated in various ways, a series of shared ideas is expressed through elements common to their structures. One is the presupposition that God is imma-nent, a force within the world, empowering it and holding it together. Two others are portrayals of God as world center and world axis: a center that gives the world its focus and bearings and an axis that stretches from earth to heaven and holds together differ-ent levels of existence. Another important concept is the more familiar expectation that God is Lord: a figure of high authority who deserves to live in lovely surround-ings and be richly served, with other deities who stay nearby as friends or entourage.

From the presupposition of divine immanence comes an association between temples and wombs or caves. Some temples of the past were actual caves hollowed out of hillsides. A famous example is the rock-cut temple of Shiva at Elephanta, one of the islands that protects Mumbai's huge harbor. The cave motif is also carried out in freestanding temples. The inmost shrine of the temple, called the *garbha-griha,* or womb-room, in older temples was often made to look and feel like a cave: window-less and cramped, with bare stone walls, its only light the oil lamps flickering around its central image. To walk from India's glaring light through shadowed porches up to the threshold of such a womb-room is like probing into the heart of a daunting mys-tery. But this mystery is clearly within the world, not soaring somewhere beyond it.

Portrayals of God as center and axis shape the temple's exterior. Viewed from the outside, a Hindu temple is identified with a mountain, usually either Meru, the mountain at the world's center, or Mount Kailash, the Himalayan peak whose invisi-ble upper slopes hold Shiva's paradise. Again, this identification is not solely theoret-ical; many Hindu temples do indeed look like mountains or mountain ranges, whose *shikara,* central peak, rises directly over the temple's central womb-room. Styles of such peaks may differ: in northern India, they often look like a huge cylinder whose sides curve inwards at the summit; in the south many look like a steep-sided A-frame. The peak's top always holds a finial, a crowning arch or stone said to represent the part of God that always remains beyond human reach or imagination. Sides of temple shikharas often squirm with carvings of heavenly beings; Meru, like Kailash, houses divine realms in its upper reaches. Temple foundations may include sculptures of animals such as elephants, once said to hold up the foundations of the earth. One feature making certain medieval temples notorious is the sculpting of dozens of loving couples at temple entryways and on temple sides. What these signify is not fully understood; at the least, they express the life-enhancing power that streams from within.[1]

The conception of God as Lord most certainly underlies the huge medieval temple-as-palace complexes found especially in South India—with their high surrounding walls, massive towers over their gates, and dozens of shrines within, as well as swimming-pool-like tanks for bathing, halls for talks and dance performances, and sometimes Sanskrit colleges, hospitals, and kitchens to feed Brahmins and the needy poor. This theme also dominates in temples built today, although today the concept of God-as-Lord sometimes seems to morph into God-as-Celebrity. Deities in modern temples are dignified but accessible; they stand on brightly lit stages, like film stars posed for a photo-op. Often a number of deities are housed under a single roof. This practice, too, has a special concept of God behind it. As discussed later, many new Hindu movements teach that all deities are aspects of just one single formless power. This means that from an enlightened perspective, all deities housed in a temple are One, just like the single roof that shields them. (The new Hindu movements and their beliefs are discussed in Chapter 10.)

THE IMAGES

Much of the symbolism described above shows that a temple is a point of juncture, a focus, where divine energies come together in a highly intense form. The center of this center, focus of its focus, is the temple's principal image. Images come in different degrees of sanctity. Most revered of all are those called self-revealed images. Like temple sites, these are acquired through divine initiative. Some vision or sign has led a devotee to the image, which may be a rock that looks like a face or a Shiva-linga, or even a log washed out of the sea, like the one from which the Jagannath image at Puri was first carved. Self-revealed images need no special rituals to call God into them because God is already there. Some of India's largest and most famous pilgrim temples have been built around self-revealed images.

More frequent and slightly less potent are images carved by artisans. These are not works of art in the sense of being products of the artists' own creativity. Divine images are, in effect, collections of symbols that evoke the power of a god and display that god's qualities. Every inch of such an image bears meaning. Hence, those who carve them must follow rules, codified also in Shilpashastras. These specify what materials the image can be made of, the proper proportions for its body, how facial features and hands should be shaped, how many arms hands are attached to, what those hands must hold and how they gesture, and which attendants and animals must accompany the image.

---

[1] Much of the preceding description comes from George Michell, *The Hindu Temple* (Chicago: Univ. of Chicago Press, 1988). An earlier work of great importance to temple studies is Stella Kramrisch, *The Hindu Temple,* 2 vols. (Calcutta: Univ. of Calcutta, 1946).

Every deity has symbols special to itself: Vishnu wears a royal crown and carries a conch shell, a flaming wheel, and often a royal mace or club; warrior goddesses carry tridents or great curving swords; Lakshmi holds a lotus flower and sometimes a fruit; Sarasvati rests a *vina,* Indian lute, across her lap. Each deity also has at least one special animal, called a mount because the deity sometimes rides astride it. Shiva rides a bull; Vishnu a giant snake or Garuda, a man-bird combination; goddesses often sit upon some form of giant cat. Divine images do not necessarily look like people; the most common temple image of Shiva is his linga, a short post often rising from a ladle-like pedestal, called a *yoni,* that represents his goddess-consort. This linga has complex associations ranging from immortality won by uniting male and female energies to Shiva's *tapas,* ascetic power, that undergirds all of the worlds. Especially in the case of great super-deities like Shiva, no image can portray all aspects of the deity simultaneously. Therefore, many deities can be carved in several different forms: Shiva can be a dancer, a yogi, a beggar, or a fiery figure with fangs and multiple arms tromping on a pile of hapless demons.

Once carved, a divine image is called a *murti,* face. Such a murti is a bit like a radio or TV receiver; it draws its deity to it when proper prayers and invocations "turn it on." Many Hindus place smaller murtis into puja rooms at home with no further level of installation; one can pray the deity into such an image at will, with no need for concern if its puja is missed for a day. If an image is to be placed into a temple with broader access, the image-maker will often leave its eyes unfinished. When the image is installed and consecrated, he goes to the temple with his tools and "opens the eyes of the image" by completing them. This makes the image into a full-time channel for deity, a much stronger level of manifestation. One can do this in a home-shrine also, but once an eye-opening ritual is performed, the deity must be honored daily. It also receives another name; it is now called *pratima,* a term that most Hindus translate "idol," with none of the negative overtones that this term has in Christian countries. Yet another level and even stronger level of ritual joins a deity to its idol so firmly and potently that a deity installed this way must have at least one permanent priest to attend to its needs; this would not be done in a home. In this rite, an attending priest calls the deity first into his own body and then transfers it into the image. Once that is the case, the temple becomes a site of continuous presence. The deity may sleep, but it does not leave.

Often in temple festivals, for one reason or another, a deity exits its temple compound to make a journey outside. Most temples own moveable forms of their images that can be mounted on a cart or carried in a palanquin. To transport the deity, one invokes it into its moveable image, which can then be transported wherever it needs to be. Some deities bathe in the sea; some visit other deities or wage war with attacking demons; some simply go out to move among their adoring subjects. Yet they are not absent while doing this. The moveable image is a clone; although it travels, the original deity still empowers its temple. The concept of image as receiver can help one to understand such doubling. If one TV is receiving a broadcast and a second is turned on, activating the second does not switch off the first; both can receive the same program at the same time. The same concept helps to explain how a single deity can be present in many temples at the same time.

The idea of divine image as receiver does not work fully, however. A receiver can be turned off easily, whereas an image once activated is permanently "on." After a time the deity moving through it fades and needs restorative reconsecration, but this takes years to occur, and during all this time, the image must be cared for as faithfully as one would care for an honored human guest living within one's home. Furthermore, a receiver merely recreates an image of something whose reality is at a distance. Central to Hindu understanding of a temple image is the belief that the deity is present in the image, seeing through its ritually opened eyes, looking back at the devotee who is looking at the deity. This mutual exchange of *darshan,* "viewing," is the central act and purpose of a temple visit. One goes because God is there, at a special, heightened level of intensity. And one goes there to place oneself before God, to show commitment, to be accountable.[2]

PUJA

If God is really present in the image before a worshiper, then merely looking at it like a statue in a museum is hardly enough to accomplish a proper viewing. Something must be done to express reverence toward that deity. Puja was introduced in Chapter 5 when describing devotions in Hindu homes. The main difference between home and temple pujas is that temple pujas have two kinds of participants. On the one hand there are ordinary worshipers, people like me and my friends in the temple visit described at the beginning of this chapter. Such worshipers rarely officiate at a temple puja, as a household head or his wife does in a puja performed at home. Ordinary worshipers are restricted to the basics: gestures of homage and prostrations, offerings, and acceptance of prasad. Most bring tangible gifts: flowers and colored powders, incense, fruits and items that the deity likes, such as the bright red scarves and coconuts we took to the goddess. All deities accept money, which helps feed, house, and clothe the priests who serve them, as well as funding other projects that a temple may maintain. Song, too, is an appropriate offering. The most electrifying moment I have known in a Hindu temple occurred when the friend escorting me suddenly burst into devotional song before the Rama image we were visiting in a nearly empty temple. She has a lovely pure soprano voice of a type much admired in India; by the time she finished, a worshiper standing behind her was so moved that he had tears running down his face.

Unlike ordinary worshipers, temple priests serve a deity again and again throughout the day. Their pujas are based on the guest-rituals standard to all pujas, but often add elaborate variations. Anthropologist Fredrique Marglin has summarized the round of priestly pujas during an ordinary day at the very famous Jagannath temple in Puri.[3] This temple has three central deities: Jagannath himself, considered a form of Krishna, his brother Balarama, and his sister Subhadra. At dawn, five temple servants check and break mud seals placed on the temple's door the previous night. Temple priests wake the temple's three central deities, who have been "sleeping" on

---

[2] A very helpful source in explaining this concept is Diana L. Eck, *Darshan: Seeing the Divine Image in India,* 3rd ed. (New York: Columbia Univ. Press, 1998). Offering important insight into the concept of divine embodiment are essays in Joanne Punzo Waghorne and Norman Cutler, eds., *Gods of Flesh, Gods of Stone* (Chambersburg, PA: Anima, 1985).

[3] In *Wives of the God-King: the Rituals of the Devadasis of Puri* (Delhi: Oxford Univ. Press, 1985), 185–91.

beds placed in front of their images. The beds are removed; lamps and candles are offered; and the previous day's garlands and flowers are removed from the deity. The deities have a bath and their teeth are brushed: priests performing these services apply them to reflections of the images appearing in mirrors that are set before them. Then, the public is let in to have the day's first open darshan. Next, the deities are adorned with further cloths and jewelry. Preparations by now have been started for their morning meal; these include a fire offering made in the temple's kitchen as well as uncooked food presented to the deities. Then a very long and elaborate breakfast is served. Doors to the inner shrine are closed at this time because the public may not see the deity eating. The public may, however, see the dancing girl who performs in an audience hall in front of the shrine.

Next, the temple is cleared of all visitors while food is offered that will be taken to nearby monasteries or sold to pilgrims at a stand in the temple's outer courtyard. During this quiet time, the deities have their midday meal. Beds arrive for their midday nap and doors to both their inner shrine and the outer hall are sealed. Around 5 PM, seals are rebroken, the deities waken, beds are removed, and lamps are waved as in the morning's service. The deities get a clothes change and fresh flowers. They have an evening meal, another public audience, and another change of clothes. They are rubbed with cooling sandal paste and other sweet-smelling items. Next, they are decked with the day's most extensive flower offerings, served a light evening snack, and offered songs from the *Gita Govinda*, a twelfth-century song cycle depicting the love of Radha and Krishna. After the meal, the area is purified by water sprinkling. The deities' beds are returned to the room. A small image called the "sleeping lord" is brought to the bed, placed on it briefly, then taken out to the main hall, where it receives offerings of lamps and flowers. It comes back to the beds and touches them, then returns to the room where it is kept throughout the day. Meanwhile, a dancing girl sings to please and soothe the Lord. Finally, doors are closed again and again sealed.

Temple routines vary somewhat. Every deity has its own *agama*s, manuals of worship; many temples, too, have routines special to those temples. Some take moveable counterparts of their deities out on tours of their temple grounds, transporting them in palanquins or stretchers. Many temples, too, perform private pujas for individual sponsors, scheduled when the temple is closed to the general public. As at Jagannath, some temples close between pujas, treating visitors' hours of worship like the daily audiences once granted to their subjects by Hindu kings. Others stay accessible throughout the day, their gods available like hosts at a perpetual open house.

On some temple days, celebrations become more intense, as priests carry out extra rituals specified for days especially important to their deity. These periodic rites range from simple additions to regular rites noticed only by temple priests to grand celebrations in which deities and worshipers take to the streets and preempt the attention of an entire surrounding town or region. Sometimes these celebrations are observed in all temples housing the same deity: Krishna's birthday, for example, or Shivaratri, "Shiva's night." Certain temples also have celebrations distinctive to them, for example, the great chariot festival associated with Jagannath, the deity whose daily rites were just described. In this festival, Lord Jagannath and his brother and sister go to visit his Garden House, another temple a mile away. Devotees haul the three deities to this temple in three massive cloth-covered wooden carts that look like moving palaces; Jagannath's "chariot," the largest, is forty-five feet high. A unique feature of this procession is that the temple images themselves ride on these chariots, instead of the more usual substitutes.[4]

A MULTITUDE OF TEMPLES

What is the point of all this? Why shower a temple's deity with such lavish attention? On the surface, a temple's purpose is to help a devotee express adoration for a divine Lord or Lady. A divine Lord does not ask for much. Krishna says in his *Bhagavad-Gita*: "If a person offers to me with devotion a leaf, a flower, fruit or water, I accept the devotion offered by that pious self."[5] Why then mount huge processions or construct palatial mansions for a deity? Furthermore, if grand displays are proper, why bother to build temples that are small and inconspicuous? Why do Hindus build and maintain so many, many temples?

To answer these questions, it is necessary to ask another pair. Who constructs temples, and why? At first glance, these questions may seem silly because a fully appropriate answer is "anybody, for any reason." Any Hindu who has means to do so and can find priests to perform the needed rituals is free to build a temple. "The means to do so," however, must cover not only the cost of the structure but also the ritual entailed; and additional provision must be made for priests and attendants to maintain the structure once it is built as well as for materials needed to carry out its daily and periodic pujas. Kings who built great palace-temples used to endow them with lands whose income supported their priests and the artisans who produced their puja equipment. Although kings were the principal patrons for large temples in the past, inscriptions show that wealthy merchant guilds were also frequent donors.[6] Today, a great deal of temple-building money comes from industrialists; the very wealthy Birla family, for example, has constructed several of India's new palace-temples. Low-caste standing does not prevent would-be patrons from temple building. Calcutta's impressive Dakshineshwara temple was built in the early 1800s by a Shudra fisherwoman who married a wealthy man of much higher caste.[7] Her story offers one caution. She discovered that no Brahmin would tend a temple for a Shudra. A poor and hungry Brahmin pandit suggested a way out; if she signed the temple's title over to her guru, the pandit could serve the temple's deities for her. He took his younger brother along to help him. When he died prematurely, that younger brother took over his duties— and became the famed saint Ramakrishna. Temples built by low-caste Hindus more usually are staffed by priests who themselves are of lower-caste standing. Such a priest is discussed later in this chapter.

Why build a temple? Devotion is a frequent reason offered for building temples today. One concept strong among today's Hindus is that of the *ishta,* the

---

[4] Stephen H. Huyler, *Meeting God: Elements of Hindu Devotion* (New Haven: Yale Univ. Press, 1999), p. 173.

[5] Bhagavad-Gita 9:26; author's translation.

[6] See Michell, op. cit.

[7] The story of this remarkable woman is told in an article in *Manushi* magazine: "Rani Rasmani: a Philosopher and a Rebel," 78 (Sept.–Oct. 1993): 2–7; no author is given.

"chosen" deity. This is a deity selected by an individual to be the center of that person's worship. The "choosing" deity might be a better expression of that deity's role because one usually acquires such a deity through some event suggesting that the deity has chosen its devotee. It may help overcome some huge problem, for example, or rescue the devotee from danger. It may appear in a dream or vision—or may just tug on its devotee's consciousness. A chosen deity is honored at its devotee's home shrine. The devotee may wear some symbol of it constantly, put its picture on the dashboard of a motorbike or car, place a sticker of its image in a window. She or he will go on a pilgrimage to its centers, visit and support its temples, and, if means are available, may go so far as to build it a temple.

If one looks at the vast range of Hindu temples in India today, however, one finds that they generally fit into one of four categories reflecting purposes distinctive to groups that have built or maintained them. Because these purposes vary, the temple rites themselves and reasons for doing them also vary. The first type of group likely to build temples is, not surprisingly, a devotional sect, the sampradaya or panth that cultivates a special relationship with a deity. The second is the blood lineage, a group that claims descent through a common ancestral line. A third is the settlement, people inhabiting a common territory. The fourth is the realm, people controlled by a common political center. Often, the difference between them is best reflected in the main festivals centered in their temples. The rest of this chapter concentrates on these festivals. I have chosen temples and festivals from very different parts of India, once again to remind readers of India's regional differences.

Sectarian Temples: Krishna at Puri and Vrindaban

Chapter 3 described a series of regionwide devotional movements that established themselves in India starting in the sixth century C.E. Many of these movements evolved into longstanding religious communities held together by guru–disciple relationships. Because their main discipline was devotional practice, it is hardly surprising that many had temples built for them by devotees. Often, too, such groups took over control of existing temples. A good example of a temple takeover occurred at Jagannath's temple in Puri. Originally built as a royal temple by an Orissan king, after the sixteenth century Jagannath came under the control of devotees of the Bengali saint Chaitanya. Although his image dates from a time before Krishna worship was widespread in Orissa, today most Hindus would say that Jagannath is Krishna. Krishna's songs are sung before Jagannath's image, and Jagannath's sister and brother bear the names of Krishna's sister and brother Subhadra and Balarama. Their chariot journey to the Garden House is said to commemorate Krishna's journey to Mathura to kill his evil uncle Kansa. Sectarian groups often have their own liturgies for divine worship, including songs composed by their saints recounting deeds of their principal deities.[8] Their festivals also tend to stress themes from stories central to their own traditions—stories either of their deities or of their saints. American religionist David

---

[8] See, for example, Whitney Sanford, "Painting Worlds, Tasting Sound: Visions of Krishna in Paramānand's Sixteenth-Century Devotional Poetry," *Journal of the American Academy of Religion* 70:1 (March 2002): 55–81; also Vasudha Narayanan, "Srī Vaiṣṇava Festivals and Festivals Celebrated by Srī Vaishnavas: Distinctive and Cosmopolitan Identities," *Journal of Vaiṣṇava Studies* 7:2 (Spring 1999): 175–94.

Haberman provides a fine example of a festival observed on Krishna's birthday at another temple controlled by Chaitanya's Gaudiya Vaishnava sampradaya:

> The focus of the Janmashtami celebrations for the Gaudiya Vaishnavas in Vrindaban is the temple of Radharaman. Radharaman, the "Pleaser of Radha," is a form of Krishna said to have manifested directly from a sacred black shalagrama stone, due to the devotional power of the sixteenth-century saint Gopal Bhatt Goswami. After entering the temple compound through a massive and elaborately carved sandstone gateway and following the lane which passes between the homes of the temple priests, the pilgrims are welcomed at the temple by the music of a drum and *shenai* and by the inviting shade of a patchwork awning. All participants fast for the morning of Janmashtami. During that time, Radharaman is bathed with gallons of Yamuna water and a liquid made of five substances: milk, honey, yogurt, butter, and sugar. Throughout the bathing, Sanskrit mantras are intoned amid the clanging of temple bells. When the birthday bathing is finished, this liquid mixture is distributed to all as prasad, grace in an edible form, and the fast is broken with food prepared from this sacred substance.[9]

This Radharaman festival is fairly simple to interpret. Vrindaban is the linchpin of the magical land of Braj, where Krishna spent most of his youth and played among the cowgirls. (Braj is covered in Chapter 7.) Goswami was a disciple of Chaitanya and an important figure in the stories that justify Gaudiya claims to be special guardians of Braj.[10] The drum and shenai are instruments prominent in pujas all over India; the *shenai* is a loud and penetrating reed instrument that sounds like a souped-up oboe. A fast is a purifying discipline, often used in preparation for major Hindu events. The bathing, clearly the central event of the birth in this temple, recalls the cleansing done for a newborn child. But it has additional overtones: milk, yogurt, and butter are all products of cows. Krishna grew up as a cowherd and loves cows and cow products. Stories of his butter stealing as a child are favorites all over India.[11] Honey and sugar are both sweets, and Krishna is known for his sweetness. According to ancient Hindu beliefs about food, "you are what you eat." This combination *is* Krishna, in a sense, and so makes an especially fitting prasad. The Yamuna River, too, is special to Krishna. It flows through Braj and many of his adventures took place on its banks or even in its waters. (Perhaps I should say *her* waters; all Indian rivers are female.)

Nonetheless, like many Hindu celebrations, even this fairly straightforward one holds at least a double layer of meaning. Why would a bath, in particular, be chosen as the most important moment of Krishna's birth? Baths held deep significance in ancient India. Rulers were consecrated by baths called *abhishekhas,* the same term used whenever an image is bathed. Krishna's bath at birth therefore also reminds participants of his royal status. Although swiftly hidden with his cowherd foster parents, he is born in a palace as a prince and later returns to his birthplace to reclaim his royal

---

9 David Haberman, *Journey through the Twelve Forests: an Encounter with Krishna* (New York: Oxford Univ. Press, 1994), 11–12.

[10] Two major Krishnaite sects claim Braj; the second is the Vallabhacaryas, also known as the Pushti-Marga.

[11] See John Stratton Hawley's fine study of this theme: *Krishna, the Butter Thief* (Princeton: Princeton Univ. Press, 1983).

status. The bath also evokes another status enjoyed by Krishna. For Gaudiya Vaishnavas, Krishna is the most complete and important earthly avatar, or descent, of Vishnu, Lord of the Universe and supreme protector of dharma. Hence, Krishna as baby, prince, cow-protector, and God are all called to mind by this one simple act of bathing him in sweet and milk-derived liquids.

The next three temple\festival pairings are harder to understand because most readers do not think of blood lineages, settlements, and realms as religious entities.[12] In ancient times, however, and in much of the world, such social and political groups were anchored in religion. Throughout Asia, this anchoring took the form of a special relationship between the group and a deity of a type that used to be called tutelary. A tutelary deity has a group under its special protection, and the group in return has a special obligation to help its deity maintain its strength and achieve its aims. In ancient North India, beings called *yakshas* seem to have been the principal tutelaries. Buddhist texts tell of towns protected by yaksha shrines, and a well-known Buddhist story tells how the yaksha who guarded his family bowed to the baby Buddha-to-be when his father presented the child at the family shrine. Such guardian deities have always been important to India's local and oral traditions, although they are often linked to India-wide traditions by the processes of knitting described earlier.

Deities of blood line, settlement, and realm are present-day Hindu versions of the old tutelary deities. Not all such deities are female in India, but many are. Indeed, all three examples below feature female deities. Although these examples come from different regions of India, they share some strikingly similar characteristics. The deity honored is a sometimes-fierce being said to be a local form of either Durga or Kali. She slays a chaos-maker, a being who attacks proper order. In order for her to do this, her community must help her, an enterprise that affirms its ties and binds it more tightly together.

Lineage Temples and Festivals: A Rajput Example

Several times previously, this text has mentioned the institution of caste. To understand the practices described below, it is important to recall that the English term "caste" covers two institutions. One is varna, the fourfold division of society laid out in dharma teachings. For many Hindus, varna is largely an abstraction, too broad a category to affect most actual caste-based behavior.

The caste unit that matters most to Hindus is the jati. It is jatis that strive to marry within their own communities and that claim hereditary monopolies over certain skills and ritual functions. In fact, often the true working units are subdivisions within jatis that differ in rank and avoid marriage connections with one another. Often, too, several groups in different regions share the same jati name and functions, but still think of themselves as separate communities.

The term *jati* comes from a Sanskrit root meaning "to give birth." This root is an important clue to the way Hindus think about jati. People in a given jati bring about births for their community by exchanging marriage partners with one another. But

---

[12] Portions of the remainder of this chapter have been previously published in my essay "Mata, Land, and Line: Female Divinity and the Forging of Community in India," *Invoking Goddesses,* Nilama Chitgopekar, ed. (New Delhi: Har-Anand, 2002), 140–64.

they also tell stories about having some linked or common origin. In theory at least, they are tied together by blood. A jati can, therefore, think of itself as a very large family, a group of people who are blood relatives of each other, even if the blood link is very distant. Perhaps even more importantly, a jati thinks of itself as made up of interlinked lineages, lines of people descended from shared ancestors.

The jati described in the next few pages is the Rajput jati, distributed across much of northern India but strongest in the western desert state of Rajasthan. The term *rajput* means "son of a king," and some Rajputs were indeed kings for many centuries in their regions, controlling lands won through military victory and distributing these as estates among their bravest warriors. Not all Rajputs hold large estates or wealth today. But some still do and claim Kshatriya status. In the early 1980s, American religion scholar and anthropologist Lindsey Harlan studied Rajputs of Mewar, a state of Western Rajasthan. These were middle-ranking Rajputs, families with estates, but not royal lines. Harlan published her results in the fascinating *Religion and Rajput Women: The Ethic of Protection in Contemporary Narratives.*[13] As its title reveals, Harlan's work focuses mainly on Rajput women, concentrating on their "ethic of protection," that is, their efforts to protect the men they live with. In the course of exploring this problem, Harlan learned a great deal not only about how women protect their men but also about how goddesses protect their lineages.

Rajput women protect men by observing rigorous self-discipline, which for many still includes some degree of seclusion, staying out of the sight of men not their relatives. For some Rajput women in the past, this discipline culminated in acts of self-immolation; if a husband died before them, they would ascend his funeral pyre to die beside him. Such women were known as satis, true or faithful women. By performing such an act, they became household deities, able to protect their families' descendants from harm. Despite laws passed against sati burning during the nineteenth century, satis are still admired by Rajputs today, and from time to time sati immolations are done illegally. In 1987, the burning of the young bride Rup Kanwar caused a huge controversy and protest in India. Many Rajput families have satis in their heritage, honored at household shrines.

Sharing some qualities of satis but far more powerful are the beings called *kuldevis. Kul* is a category of Rajput relationship that corresponds roughly to the English term "clan." All members of a kul trace their family lines back to a common source, some famous hero-Rajput who made a name for himself and acquired the lands that became his kul's kingdom or estate. Many kuls preserve stories about how their kuldevi rescued this hero from some dire strait. The following is a typical example:

> Naganecha Jhi came with our ancestors when they journeyed from Idar [in Gujarat]. While they were fighting for Nagor, Naganecha Jhi became their kuldevi. At Nagana they built a temple for her. . . . She appeared to Cumda Jhi Rathaur, who had prayed to her because he was losing a battle. She manifested herself as a snake and from then on was always with him. Because of this the Rathaurs were able to conquer Marwar.[14]

---

[13] *Religion and Rajput Women: The Ethic of Protection in Contemporary Narratives* (Berkeley: Univ. of California Press, 1992).

[14] Ibid., p. 56.

In the past when Rajputs still fought as warriors beside their kings, kuldevis traveled with them to battlefields and fought beside them. Today, when Rajputs no longer fight, the kuldevi brings healing to household members or success in a family's business.

Most Rajput families whom Harlan met had a kuldevi temple on the grounds of their family estates. This is a small structure with a single room housing the kuldevi herself, in the form of a richly clothed female image, and perhaps also images of some companion local goddesses. Its most distinctive feature is a trident that tops the structure. Daily worship is not usually held at kuldevi temples. One pays respect at them when going on a trip or arriving home, during family samskaras, at the birth of a boy, and especially at marriage. A daughter takes leave of her family's kuldevi and goes with her husband to meet his own when she comes as a bride to his family. Such leave-taking and greeting are especially important for brides because they enter new kuls when they marry. Rajputs may not marry within their own kuls; they take spouses only from families outside their kuls, who therefore honor different kuldevis.

On the other hand, kuldevis are not entirely different from one another. The trident on their temple crests gives them away. All are forms of the goddess Durga the Buffalo Demon Slayer. This goddess is celebrated in one of India's most widely observed festivals, the so-called Durga Puja or "Nine Nights" observance. According to the story behind this festival, a terrible *asura,* chaos being, was born into the world with the form of a huge fierce buffalo and the ability to change shape at will. Soon he has the world so terrorized that even the mightiest gods are afraid to confront him one-on-one. Hence, they come up with a way to kill him collectively. Standing in a circle, they project into its center their shares of *tejas,* fiery energy. This crystallizes as a woman, a multi-armed warrior woman riding a mighty lion. Her divine creators then present her with their own weapons. Grasping Shiva's trident in her main fighting arm, she rides off to meet her opponent. She kills him after a terrible struggle in which one new form after another emerges out of his body as soon as the preceding form has been slain. Durga Puja festivals vary a great deal from region to region in India. In the days when Rajputs were warriors, their Durga Pujas were full of military themes and included events such as blessing of weapons and troop reviews. Their culminating event was a buffalo sacrifice performed by the Rajput king, who was expected to take the animal's head off with one mightly blow of his sword.

Durga Puja is an especially important festival for Rajputs because Durga is the entire Rajput jati's guardian deity, just as kuldevis are guardians for individual kuls. Durga Puja is therefore observed in all Rajput temples. Durga's story, the *Devi-Mahatmya,* is read at kuldevi temples as well as in the goddess's public temples. Kuldevis are dressed as Durga during her festival; and according to Harlan, the buffalo sacrifice characteristic of Durga Pujas was done at kuldevi temples as well as the king's own shrine. A warrior of the kul wielded the sword of decapitation.[15]

So the Durga Puja carries out and forges a complex set of links. It links kul to jati. Just as a kuldevi is distinctive and yet part of the greater whole that is the buffalo-slaying goddess, so the kul is distinct and yet part of the greater whole that is the jati. It also links kul members to the jati's greater mission: Rajputs are warriors; their jati-assigned task is to aid the goddess who clears chaos from the earth, in all its ever-changing forms. For a moment during her festival, they stand in her place.

---

[15] Ibid., p. 88.

They do what she did. They not only remember and worship her; they assist her. To do something together, at the same time and in the same way, can be a powerfully unifying experience. To go through Durga Puja together makes Rajputs one, just as it makes their kuldevis one goddess.

Settlement Shrines and Festivals: A Tamil Example

Their specific kuldevis are special to Rajputs, but Rajputs are not the only jati in India that has kuls and deities special to those kuls. Kul deities are not universal among Hindu jatis. They seem to predominate among groups tied together by the system known as *jajmani,* in which various caste groups perform services for landowning patrons in exchange for living space on the land and a share in its produce.[16] Jajmani ties figure prominently in the next example.

It too describes a community unified through its shrine and festival. But this is a community brought together initially not by blood but by proximity. Its members share a common living space, a settlement. Many kinds of settlements have protective deities in India, and often these deities are goddesses. Unifying a group of people who merely live next to one another is more challenging than unifying blood relatives because people who simply live together may have somewhat different goals and interests. This may explain why deities connected to settlements are often more testy and explosive than kul deities, and their festivals have a strong atmosphere of danger and crisis.

Especially prominent in South India are goddesses linked to the thousands of villages that farm South Indian lands. Many villages have some story of how their goddess came to this spot and helped or commanded their village to be founded. Usually, a village goddess's power does not extend any farther than the borders of the village-worked fields. Within this reach, the goddess protects not just one dominant kul or jati, but all residents of the village. This same deity may cause disease and other disasters. When smallpox was still a frequent plague in India, village goddesses were often smallpox deities, whose pustules were seen as signs of goddess possession. Village goddesses can be as unpredictable and capricious as life itself seems to be in most Indian villages. Nonetheless, residents address them as "Amma," Mother.

At the start of the twentieth century, Henry Whitehead, a British bishop, made a valuable survey of village gods and goddesses of South India.[17] He noted that most of the time these deities stayed dormant. When life went well, no one mentioned or approached them. Their shrines were tiny and rough enclosures. Often their "image" was little more than a rock or a pot filled with water and daubed with red kumkum powder. Villagers came to the goddess when things went wrong: epidemics, failing harvests, runs of bad luck. Then the villagers put on festivals whose most outstanding feature was abundant blood sacrifice of buffalo and goats. During these festivals, village deities possessed festival ritualists, or *pujaris,* who were usually low-caste potters, barbers, washermen, or untouchables. Villagers also underwent ordeals during some of these festivals, such as walking over hot coals or letting themselves be suspended from hooks driven through muscles of their backs.

---

[16] Jajmani is explained in Pauline Kolenda, "Toward a Model of the Hindu Jajmani System," *Human Organization* 22:1 (Spring 1963): 11–31.

[17] *Village Gods of South India* (Calcutta: Oxford Unversity Press, 1921).

Village goddesses today are changing rapidly. They have lost some of their feroc-ity. Many now accept only pure vegetarian offerings, delegating lesser deities to receive blood offerings when these seem necessary. Pumpkins have become stand-ins for sacrificial animals. The red powder kumkum substitutes for blood; and when blood still flows, smaller offerings of chickens or goats substitute for older buffalo sac-rifices. Village goddesses are acquiring temples, sometimes attended by priests, and some receive visits by pilgrims who come from areas well outside the goddess's home settlement. Village deity festivals are gaining regular places on ritual calendars and are incorporating motifs that knit local beings to deities of the great traditions.

Many of these trends can be seen in the following example, which comes from Tamilnadu, India's southernmost state on its eastern shore and the region where India's tradition of ecstatic devotionalism started. The source used is a series of stud-ies done by anthropologist Brenda Beck in the Konku region of Tamilnadu during the 1960s and 1970s.[18] The most inland region of Tamilnadu, Konku is a bowl carved out of the western mountains by headwaters of the Kaveri River. Beck describes it as a place of rocky, sandy soil, often plagued by droughts and housing inhabitants known for their hard work. Until the tenth century or so, it was heavily forested and peopled largely by hunters and herders. This changed when the Tamil region's Chola dynasty sent colonists to develop it for agriculture.

For administrative and tax purposes, the Cholas divided the lands they ruled into districts known as *natu*. These in turn were subdivided into units called *kirima,* a word derived from the Sanskrit term *grama.* This is the term commonly translated as "village" for Tamilnadu, although strictly speaking a kirima is less a single village than a clus-ter; each kirima holds within it several smaller settlements called *urs.* A kirima's lands were taxed as a single unit by its rulers, who placed an official over it to keep track of its accounts and collect its income. Today, a Tamil kirima is the unit of Indian gov-ernment that elects the local council known as a *panchayat.* In Konku, it is also a small holy land, for each kirima has its own kirima goddess.[19]

When Beck studied Konku, much of the local land was controlled by a subcaste of the Vellalar jati known locally as Kavuntars or Goundars, "Farmers." These claim to be descended from the first Konku colonists. Kavuntars lived near their land holdings and farmed their lands themselves as well as managing them. They exchanged jajmani services with Barbers, Washermen, Potters, Toddy-tappers, Drummers, and Pantarams, who served as cooks and also as priests for lineage and village goddess temples. Other caste groups of the region included Artisans, Merchants, Weavers, Builders, Tax col-lectors, and Brahmins.

A major focus of Beck's early work was a split in overall caste structure within the region into two divisions: a "right" division, consisting of all caste groups linked to one another via jajmani, and a "left," consisting of land-free groups such as Artisans and Merchants who worked on a fee-for-service basis. Right and left divisions did not

---

[18] Brenda E. F. Beck, *Peasant Society in Konku: A Study of Right and Left Subcastes in India* (Vancouver: Univ. of British Columbia Press, 1972); "Colour and Heat in South Indian Ritual," *Man,* n.s. 4:4 (1969): 553–72; "The Goddess and the Demon: a Local South Indian Festival and Its Wider Context," *Purusartha* 5 (1981): 83–136.

[19] This may be something special to Konku. Anthropologist Valentine Daniel, studying a dif-ferent Tamil region, has asserted that the kirima is never a sacred unit. Only the ur is sacred. *Fluid Signs: Being a Person the Tamil Way* (Berkeley: Univ. of California Press, 1984), 72–79.

always get along with one another and also had important differences in custom. Castes of the right had strong ties to local deities and were far more likely to have strong kuls and kul deities. Castes of the left were more often linked to religious sects with centers based outside of Konku. Brahmins and Tax collectors bridged the right-left distinction, although castes of the left tended to link more closely with Brahmins. This is an important observation because it suggests that the sectarian type of Hinduism best known to outsiders may really be only a Hinduism of certain social divisions.

Village deity festivals in Konku were unusual among such festivals because *only* castes of the right were deeply involved in them. All right-division castes had representatives playing prominent roles in village goddess festivals; all right-division families contributed to mass offerings. Beck found evidence suggesting, on the other hand, that women of the left were once actively barred from making offerings during such festivals or from entering temples while a festival was in progress.

Mariyamman

Beck studied the goddess festival of a kirima named Kannapuram, one of the older areas of settlement in the region. The name of this kirima's deity was Mariyamman, a frequent village deity name throughout Tamilnadu. Mariyamman is a figure of great potential interest to Indian religionists, for she seems to be even now undergoing the process by which many little figures fuse into bigger ones. On the one hand, some Mariyamman temples in Tamilnadu are drawing worshipers from areas well beyond their village boundaries—thereby suggesting that a single Mariyamman underlies the many smaller ones. On the other, Mariyamman is developing tenuous connections to Sanskrit goddesses. Mariyamman's temple in Kannapuram shares a wall with a temple of Kali, who has a festival of marriage that overlaps in time Mariyamman's own annual celebration. Mariyamman herself is said to be married to Shiva at the ending of her festival, although during that festival she weds and sheds a different husband. Her temple also has extensions within the several urs that make up her kirima. Although Mariyamman's rites are practiced at these smaller temples, their central images are given names belonging to the Sanskrit goddess Kali.

Mariyamman's temple is in a style typical for village temples: a covered porch leads into its small shrine room and a layered peak covers the site where the deity stands enshrined. It is part of a larger complex that includes not only Mariyamman's temple and the Kali temple fused to hers, but other structures for Shiva and Parvati and their sons Murukan (identified with Skandha) and Vinayakar (Ganesha). It enshrines an image, not a rock, but Beck does not describe details of that image's appearance. Mariyamman's temple is served by a priest of the Pantaram caste, considered lower in purity and status than Brahmins serving the Shiva temple.

The most important event at the Mariyamman temple is its annual festival, which is open to outsiders, unlike some other Tamil village festivals. This festival officially lasts for eight days and nine nights and occurs in the month of Chittrai, which is mid-April to mid-May on Western calendars. This is the peak of India's hot season, a time often connected with goddesses, who are said to be naturally hot in their tempers and powers. Thus, they need cooling and recognition during this often-harsh season. It is also a time of frequent sickness, which can be read as a manifestation of the goddess's presence.

Kannapuram's festival reenacts a story of inappropriate union. Mariyamman, it is said, was once a human being, the adopted daughter of a Brahmin. An untouchable claiming to be Brahmin tricked her into marriage, but she discovered his true status when she saw the drums hanging in his parents' home. Drums are made of polluting leather; hence drummers of south India were usually untouchable. When she realized that her husband had married her improperly, she killed him in a fury. In this story, the false husband substitutes for the demons who are normally fought off in village goddess festivals. As Beck points out, however, an untouchable passing as Brahmin *is* a demon, a being who upsets right order in the world.

Mariyamman's festival is more complex than others described earlier and takes more time to describe. It unfolds in four stages. In the first, after initial preparations, the goddess leaves her temple and travels to a field not far from the temple, where a village marries her to her deceitful fiancee, using a simple but standard marriage rite. Her traveling image for this trip is a pot filled with water topped with margosa leaves, a common symbol of the goddess used in many rites. Her husband's image is a tree, located earlier by the villagers, chopped down and stripped of its branches, and left for a time to soak in the water of a well in the field where the marriage takes place. This must be a "milk hedge" tree, one that exudes a sticky white semen-like sap when cut. It must also have three main branches emerging from its trunk at the same height. These branches are cut at some distance above the fork, so they can hold a pot securely between them. Before the goddess arrives, the tree-groom is pulled from his well and waits beside it to greet his intended.

After the wedding, the Brahmin retreats, and the goddess's Pantaram priest takes over; Brahmins may not officiate where blood is going to be shed. In the next state, the goddess takes her new husband "home," and they live together for a week within the grounds of her temple.[20] Two motifs dominate this phase. The first is Mariyamman's frightening ferocity, shown during the trip to the newlyweds' home. After a goat sacrifice performed soon after her wedding, Mariyamman possesses her Pantaram. While inhabiting his body, she picks up her tree-bridegroom and hauls him back to her temple compound, stopping along the way from time to time to bite off the heads of live chicks that an attendant is carrying. As her procession moves homeward, villagers ask her questions about the year to come, such as prospects for village crops and families. When they reach the temple, the bridegroom is upended into a hole in front of the temple kept for this occasion. This hole functions like a Christmas tree stand, holding the tree erect with its branches in the air.

Now the second motif is introduced: the goddess's oscillation between a hot, angry, and possibly also sexually aroused form during the night and a calmer, cool form taken up by day. Her hot form is a pot with coals kept burning in it; her cool form the more familiar pot filled with water and margosas. During most of the couple's short time together, she is literally mounted atop her husband, her pot of either type sitting among the lopped-off branches of his tree. By night the burning fire pot is attended in its cleft by a man of the untouchable Peraiyar, Drummer, caste—the same caste as the lying husband. Like the Pantaram, this Peraiyar has undergone special advance preparation for the duties that he undertakes during the festival.

---

[20] Note that this marriage reverses the common pattern of localization in Hindu marriages. Normally a bridegroom takes the bride to *his* home.

Before the festival starts, both Pantaram and Peraiyar bathe, have all body hair shaved off by a barber, and give up all cooked food and all sex. They sleep every night at the temple until the festival is over.

Each dawn, after the fire pot has burned all night in its tree cleft, the Pantaram comes, worships the goddess, becomes possessed, takes the fire pot from the tree, and carries it around the temple clockwise, accompanied by drummers and a flutist. Again people question him about the future. Then he returns to the tree, the goddess leaves him, and again he places her pot on the tree. But now she is the cool pot filled with water and leaves. At sunset, the fire pot is lodged in the tree cleft again.

The climax of the festival comes on its eighth day, which must always be a Thursday before a full moon. Now the village helps the goddess shed her unwanted husband. In the morning, a special visitor comes to the temple, a representative sent by the most influential kul of the Kavuntar jati that controls much of the land in the kirima. After a thread is tied on his wrist, he lifts a tray filled with small lighted oil lamps made of flour and water onto a supporting ring placed on his head and carries it around the temple, again accompanied by noisy drumming. Like the pots, these lamps represent the goddess, and placing them on the head is a gesture of reverence like prostration. A man of the Toddy-tapper caste beheads a goat in front of the tree trunk. Its cooked meat will later be fed to three lesser male spirits who guard the goddess. Now the goddess herself receives a meal of cooked rice, her first relief from the raw-food diet that she has had since the festival's beginning. This change suggests both that she is moving away from her former wild state and that she accepts the community and support being offered by her worshipers.[21] A light is waved before her image in the temple, and her worshipers receive prasad in the form of sacred ash.

Later in the same day, women from all right-caste families bring trays of lighted lamps and pots of boiled rice and cooked vegetables and offer them to the goddess, while right-caste men carry water from the river to bathe her. This is poured at the roots of the tree trunk and around the outside of the temple until everything becomes a sea of mud. This water suggests some cooling of the goddess's hot temper, but perhaps also a dissolving of her marriage bonds. Around two in the afternoon, the fire-pot is relit and placed back on its tree trunk. However, late that night, around 10 PM, the Pantaram priest lifts the pot, becomes possessed again, and circles the temple with it. As he does so, helpers loosen the tree trunk within the hole that has kept it on end. When the Pantaram priest returns, he hands the pot to a helper and yanks the trunk out of its hole while yet another goat is beheaded. He jams the goat's head into the hole, smashes it down with the tree base, then runs back to the well in the fields with the tree trunk, and sinks the tree in the well. Then he takes off his wrist-thread, throws it in the well, bathes, changes his clothes, and floats on the water a little camphor lamp, representing the by now much calmer goddess. Meanwhile, in the temple, the image of Mariyamman is stripped of her jewelry and changed into white clothes, both actions signifying that she has become a widow.

The celebration's final phase is a brief one. On the following morning, devotees who come for morning worship find their goddess dressed again in clothing appropriate for a married woman. But she now has a different husband, the great Lord Shiva.

---

[21] Cooked food means togetherness among Hindus; very strict renouncers eat only wild food, while normally only members of the same family or jati eat cooked food together.

A chicken is killed this morning to honor her guardian deities. Members of the crowd throw turmeric water onto each another. With this joyous act, the festival is over.

Several features of this festival must be noted to make sense of its events. First, it is very bloody. Blood is a power substance used in religions all over the world to jump-start processes that are lagging: rains that don't fall; fields that need to start bearing; deities who have been sleeping and need to move swiftly into action. Second, this festival is a drama, designed to draw participants into its flow of emotions. It moves toward a climax in which all people of the village become involved—and get wet and joke and release a great deal of tension. Using a different means than those of the Rajput Durga Puja, it generates a shared, community-building experience. Once again, an important part of that experience is helping the goddess, working with her, becoming one in a shared relationship to her. Finally, as noted earlier, every caste group crucial to the village system of exchanges has some conspicuous role to play within the festival. Thus, it affirms in a very dramatic way the importance of each sub-community. All castes are needed for the community's survival. Nonetheless, it also carries a warning: no caste should try to usurp another's place. To do so is to become demonic—and to awaken a fearsome deity's anger.

Temples of King and Realm: a Royal Goddess of Bengal

The last example combines features of both lineage and settlement. Like smaller Hindu communities, kingdoms in India's past had guardian deities for whom they built temples and with whom they celebrated festivals that banished chaos beings and reaffirmed order. In such festivals, kings played a focal role, both as sponsors who paid for activities and as ritual actors appearing at crucial moments. Remember that a king had a special charge to protect his people and the dharma that kept them prosperous.[22] Keeping them in a proper relationship with their lands' guardians was one important way to do this. The old kingdoms are now gone, but some of their temples and festivals remain, still led by descendants of old royal lines. They can teach a great deal about the relationship between temples and political dynamics in modern India.

Just as kul and village protectors are not necessarily goddesses, royal temples are not necessarily goddess temples. Jagannath began as a royal temple, and many themes associated with such temples underlie its later emphasis on Krishna devotion. In fact, it remains a royal temple, to which heirs of former kings still contribute daily offerings and services during its festivals.[23] Most of the South's great temples were also royal establishments, enshrining such male Lords as Shiva and Vishnu. Indeed, much of the pomp and extra display at grand temples such as these reflects the larger-than-life stature that had to be displayed by kings in all their undertakings. Kings had to do things in the best and grandest ways. If they did not uphold this standard, they did not deserve to be kings.[24]

---

[22] See pp. 31–32.

[23] See Marglin, *Wives of the God-King*, especially pp. 156–84.

[24] This was true on a double level; the human king had to give lavish gifts, whereas the divine king had to be housed, clothed, and fed on a lavish scale. For the special connection of deities and kings in South India, see George Hart, "The Nature of Tamil Devotion," *Aryan and Non-Aryan in India*, Madhav M. Deshpande and Peter E. Hook, eds., Michigan Papers on South and Southeast Asia 14 (Ann Arbor: Center for South and Southeast Asian Studies, 1979), 11–33.

Even though kings often linked themselves to the high and pure super-gods, goddesses too served as realm protectors. Some of the richest studies of royal temples and festivals have centered on those with female deities. Perhaps the best-known of all is Menakshi of Madurai, another Tamil goddess. However, because this book uses examples from different corners of India, a less-famed Lady will be described. The chosen site is the city of Vishnupur in the state of Bengal, a state in love with goddesses, largely because of its medieval Shakta heritage. Vishnupur today is a small and unpretentious city, known best for its fine silk weaving and terracotta temples, medieval temples built from clay in a Bengali style quite different from the usual ones described in this chapter. It has these unusual temples because for more than eight hundred years, from the tenth through early eighteenth centuries C.E., it was the capital of a thriving small kingdom ruled by the Malla line of kings. Although Malla lands eventually were swallowed by a neighbor, the Malla line still survives and so do the temple and festival founded by Malla ancestors. Harvard-based anthropologist Ákos Östör studied this temple and festival in the late 1960s. The summary that follows is based on Östör's book *The Play of the Gods,* published in 1980.[25]

Vishnupur's royal goddess was a form of Durga named Mrinmoyi Debi, "Goddess Made of Earth." According to Malla legend, her special connection with Mallas began when the nineteenth king in the Malla line sent his trained hawk to seize a heron perched in a tree while hunting in the Vishnupur region. The usually-mild heron instead killed the hawk, leading the king to suspect that some supernatural power was at work. Then the goddess appeared before him and told him to set up his royal city where this had happened. The site of the tree should house its temple. He would find the goddess's image buried in the soil below. He dug and found a rock later made into the head of an image of Durga the Buffalo Demon Slayer.

This legend sounds much like kuldevi stories told by Rajputs of western India. Yet the temple's past and festival also echo themes from southern village goddess festivals. According to Östör, before the twentieth century the Vishnupur royal temple was a simple mud hut sitting beneath the heron's tree. The goddess herself foiled royal efforts to make it more splendid. Until recently also, Mrinmoyi Debi's festival held special roles for representatives of each of Vishnupur's several resident caste groups. Until the seventeenth century, it was bathed in blood, including not only animal but human sacrifice. However, in that century a Malla decreed that henceforth it must be "Vaishno," pure. Since then, the festival's sacrifices have been offerings of pumpkins and rice cooked with legumes.

The festival is a Durga Puja, and part of it is very much like Durga Pujas elsewhere in Bengal. Families, neighborhood groups, and merchants' associations set up clay images of the goddess in the streets, throw a grand party for them, and dissolve them in "living waters" when the festival ends. The images portray Durga in the act of killing the shape-shifting buffalo, and this grand celebration honors her struggle and victory.

The royal temple's share in the festival comes before this, and the part of her story it celebrates seems to be the goddess's summoning rather than her battle. Piece by piece, the king's priests call together her lesser manifestations until, at the crowning moment, she appears in fullest glory in the midst of her people. One special feature

---

[25] Chicago: Univ. of Chicago Press.

of the temple-based celebration is a subdivision of the goddess into three "Ladies," called respectively, "Big Lady," "Middle Lady," and "Little Lady." The Bengali words used for "big," "middle," and "little" are used in much the same sense that Americans speak of "big" and "little" sisters or brothers—that is, they carry overtones of "elder," "middle," and "younger." The significance of these forms remains hazy in Östör's description, but the "elder" has overtones of the ancient, primal shakti that is the life-force in all living things, whereas the "younger" has closer connections with the specific royal protectress who is Mrinmoyi Debi.

The ritual at the king's temple starts six days before the "nine nights" sacred to the goddess during which Durga Pujas are normally held. Like Mariyamman's festival, it divides into four segments. During the first, which lasts for eleven days and involves only temple priests, Big Lady is called, brought into the temple, and worshiped. Most of the action in this part occurs on the first night and second morning. Late in the night, the temple's chief priest along with another trained in Tantric rites go to a place outside the temple that holds the remnants of an old tree sacred to Shiva. By means of a long series of rites, they call the goddess out of the tree and worship her, then escort her back and install her image, a painted scroll, in the temple. The next morning, they go to the temple pond and call her again. This time she comes out of, or "over," the water. Her presence in plants is also stressed at this time. An important image of her honored now and later during the festival is a bundle of nine plants tied together, each of which has food or medicinal value and each of which is one manifestation of the goddess. The remaining days consist mainly of pujas for the Big form of the goddess, although one curious incident occurs on the ninth day when Middle Lady arrives and receives worship for a time, but then leaves again at the end of the day.

The second phase of the festival, lasting for two days, multiplies forms of the goddess summoned and sets in motion public involvement in the festival. Its starting event is the arrival of the Middle and Little Ladies, both of whom are fully installed in the temple. To do this, the priest performs a rite usually done for permanent temple images. He calls the deity into himself and then transfers her into each of the three scrolls now representing the Big, Middle, and Little Ladies. Other forms of the goddess also receive large and elaborate pujas during this transitional festival phase. For example, Lakshmi is worshiped in the form of two huge kettles of rice. Worshiped too are Ganesha, Brahma, Vishnu, Shiva, and Surya, the five major deities who are family gods for most Brahmins. Meanwhile long lines of townspeople come to the temple for darshan and homage. Townspeople also pay respects to the Malla "king," who receives them in his home next door. This king is the still-living Malla heir, standing in for his forefathers.

During the third festival phase the goddess appears fully. This is completed in one day, the third from the last in the festival's full time span and is marked by two major events. The first occurs during the day, when a very old image owned by the king is brought out for worship. This Devi engraved on a golden plate has eighteen arms, which mark her as an extremely powerful and ferocious figure. During the daytime puja, this golden image is bathed in multiple sacred substances and then set up on top of a *yantra* drawn for this occasion. A *yantra* is a diagram common in Tantric practice in which subforms of a deity are arranged in an order reflecting that deity's distribution throughout the world.

At night, just before midnight, the golden image becomes the central focus of a grand climax. When the doors open for this midnight puja, crowds pack the temple.

Those lucky enough to have a good view see the Devi in the midst of huge pots of food, with a mountain of flowers piled in front of her. During rites preceding the climactic moment, the four major festival deities are worshiped: Big Lady, Middle Lady, Little Lady, and the king's golden goddess. Each receives thirteen plates of the food, as well as flower offerings that become more and more generous. Meanwhile, fire offerings are made at the temple's fire pit. Then the king makes a grand entrance wearing a silk *dhoti,* the seamless cloth draped around the waist and through the legs that Hindu men wear for their purest worship. The king takes hold of the priest's shawl, showing that the priest is now acting as his stand-in. At precisely midnight, the priest picks up a massive bunch of flowers, the crowd gives a huge shout, a cannon is fired outside, waiting musicians burst into loud music, the priest lays his flowers before the goddess, and everyone bows to the ground. At this moment the goddess appears. Her devotees claim that the most committed among them will see her image moving.

After this event, the crowds start to disperse, although lesser pujas continue. Priest and king go around the temple, circling each altar and image. After the temple has cleared, the king distributes the food to all priests, musicians, and other temple servants involved. The festival will continue for two more days and nights. For the public, these are devoted to the gala goddess celebration now going on in the streets. The king and temple priest have one more task to complete, a secret puja in the temple honoring deities so frightening that their images must stay wrapped in scrolls, not to be seen even by the priest who presents their offerings. Finally, on the third morning, a special mantra releases the goddess from her many temporary images. Devotees carry her images to the river and immerse them there to dissolve back into clay. They will keep a small pot of water collected at her immersion site in household shrines through the following year.

If this festival and the experience it structures are seen as a whole, two powerful themes dominate. The first is the reassembling of power diffused into many places and its transformation into a greater whole. The power reassembled is the Goddess herself, whose energy normally is extended into the world's trees, waters, plants, foodstuffs, and lesser deities. Her reassembling correlates with the moment in Durga's myth when Durga is assembled from the tejas of the deities who project her. But it also reflects Bengal's longstanding Tantric heritage, in which goddesses were central creative powers and adepts worked to transform themselves into superhuman beings by reuniting energies scattered throughout their bodies and world. This Durga Puja clearly has Tantric connections: a Tantric priest must be present during its opening ritual; a Tantric yantra serves as base for the golden image; and the secret rites of the festival's final days also seem intended to control and pacify some of the darker aspects of the goddess recognized in Tantric traditions.

The festival's second most striking theme is the role of the king. The king is the festival's sponsor. Before Indian independence took away royal incomes, the king would have paid for all festival expenses and offerings. He supplies the golden image, the final and most crucial piece of the reassembled goddess. The king's dramatic appearance and ritual actions are the catalysts bringing the goddess into full manifestation. Finally, his secret rituals calm and tame her dangerous dark side. The king is as vital to her ability to work in full strength for his kingdom as she is vital to his kingdom's prosperity and protection. Like royal fire sacrifices of ancient Vedic tradition, the Durga Puja of Vishnupur's royal temple is a ritual of royal legimation. Yet, like other rituals explored in this chapter, it also unites a community's will and effort. The Devi, her temple, and her festival are Vishnupur's glue, the extra something that binds individuals and groups into a greater whole.

WHY BUILD TEMPLES?

Why build so many temples? Why spend so much effort and money adorning them richly and carrying on seemingly endless pujas? Certainly, temples are centers for devotion. The veil that separates humans from deity is pierced in such places. People come face to face with God there, and their experience is heightened by the fact that their gods do have faces, even if these cannot reflect the full reality that lies behind them. Devotees respond to the deities found in temples as anyone would to another person who is held in high awe, or loved and respected.

At the same time, temples are lightning rods that pull into the world powers essential to human survival. The deities present there sustain human life and stand as bulwarks against the forces that make for communal disintegration. A community with a temple is an anchored, empowered whole. The very layout of a classic temple whose peak pierces the sky and base spreads out to grip the earth evokes such anchoring. Its image is the channel through which divine power flows.

Moreover, at least when they run smoothly, the festivals that go on within and around a community's temples pull that community together and make it into a whole. Such unity is not merely theoretical or symbolic. Subcommunities work together to plan and enact such festivals. Their contributions are affirmed. Leaders are recognized, and their authority underscored. Often, too, the festivals include climactic moments that leave participants feeling charged and exhilarated, ready to face whatever challenge next faces them. I do not mean to suggest that this always happens. Temple and festival studies are full of accounts of festivals gone awry or temple boards split because of squabbling.[26] But this is a very human phenomenon and occurs in institutions of all the world's religions.

A TEMPLE REVISITED

I had an "aha" experience when writing this chapter, one of those moments when pulling materials together yields an insight not initially expected. Return for a moment to the New Delhi temple visited at the chapter's outset. I know very little about this temple except what I saw and what my friends told me during my single visit. A sizeable complex going up around it will host subsidiary institutions much like those of old temple complexes in southern India. Our guide said that one of its outbuildings has a Sanskrit library with a resident pandit and that a college is planned for its grounds. Its central image is Katyayani, an aspect of the Goddess who, according to

---

[26] Good examples of such squabbling are in William Sax, *Mountain Goddess: Gender and Politics in a Himalayan Pilgrimage* (New York: Oxford Univ. Press, 1991) and Arjun Appadurai, *Worship and Conflict under Colonial Rule: a South Indian Case* (Cambridge: Cambridge University Press, 1981).

my friends, "looks out for people's well-being." Money to build it has come mostly from wealthy industrialists, but my friends claim the vision behind it and the effort to raise its funding came from a "Tantric *bawaji*," a Tantric adept and teacher.

A Tantric teacher launching a massive and pricy temple complex like those of ancient kings—housing a goddess who looks out for people's welfare with an eighteen-armed shakti beside her? It all fits together nicely. New Delhi is hardly a royal seat, but it is the capital city of the world's second largest nation. Katyayani's temple lies on its southern border, almost due south of the Indian Parliament building and the surrounding structures that house India's government offices. A Tantric teacher would know all about the ancient, deeper functions of temples described in this chapter—how they protect and empower and glue together communities. He would know about goddesses, too, and how they fight off forces of chaos and destruction. And he would know that the south is the direction of the dead, out of which ghosts and angry forces can boil forth to disrupt a city and keep it from working in ways that will benefit its citizens. I wonder about Katyayani's brand new temple and the motives that put it where it is. I am sure it was not merely meant to be a nice place where goddess devotees can come to worship and wonder at its beauties.

ADDITIONAL SOURCES

The most thorough discussion of temple construction and symbolism is still Stella Kramrisch, *The Hindu Temple,* 2 vols. (Calcutta: Univ. of Calcutta, 1946). George Michell's *The Hindu Temple* (Chicago: Univ. of Chicago Press, 1988) is the most recent and convenient. For a neo-Hindu interpretation of temples, see Srikant, *Power in Temples: A Modern Perspective* (Payyanur, Kerala: Integral Books, 2002). Gregory D. Alles shows how a classic group of temples structured the experience of worshipers through their layout and design: "A Fitting Approach to God: On Entering the Western Temples at Khajuraho," *History of Religions* 33:2 (November 1993): 161–86.

Elizabeth U. Harding's *Kali: The Black Goddess of Dakshineswar* (York Beach, ME: Nicholas-Hays, 1993) has a vivid description of a daily Kali puja. Technical explorations of puja liturgy of Maharashtra are in Gudrun Bèuhnemann's *Pūjā: A Study in Smārta Ritual* (Vienna: Gerold, 1988). Carl Gustav Diehl's older *Instrument and Purpose: Studies in Rites and Rituals in South India* (Lund: CWK Gleerup, 1956) portrays southern practice. Richard M. Davis's *Ritual in an Oscillating Universe: Worshiping Śiva in Medieval India* offers a clear explanation of the relationship between Shaiva Siddhanta temple practice and theory (Princeton: Princeton Univ. Press, 1991). Hillary Peter Rodrigues compares Banaras- and Bengal-based liturgies for the great goddess festival in *The Liturgy of the Durgā Pūjā with Interpretations* (Albany: State Univ. of New York Press, 2003). A lively description of worship special to Krishna in North India is in Margaret H. Case, *Seeing Krishna: The Religious World of a Brahman Family in Vrindaban* (New York: Oxford Univ. Press, 2000). Temples and pujas of the Vallabhacarya sect are described in Peter Bennett, *The Path of Grace: Social Organization and Temple Worship in a Vaishnava Sect* (Delhi: Hindustan Publishing, 1993). Paul Younger describes practice at a famous Shaiva temple of Tamilnadu in his *The Home of Dancing Śivan; The Traditions of the Hindu Temple in*

Citamparam (New York: Oxford Univ. Press, 1995). Younger's "Singing the Tamil Hymnbook in the Tradition of Rāmānuja: the *Adyayanōtsava* Festival in Śrīraṅkam," *History of Religions* 31:3 (February 1982): 272–93, records a festival of the Tamil Shri Vaishnava heritage.

Readers wishing to explore village goddess rites might start with a dissertation: Richard Brubaker's *The Ambivalent Mistress: A Study of South Indian Village Goddesses and Their Meaning* (Chicago: Univ. of Chicago, 1978). The collection *Wild Goddesses in India and Nepal,* Axel Michaels et al, eds. (Bern: Peter Lang, 1996) describes both village and Tantric practice. Superb photographs of village, temple, and household worship are featured in Stephen P. Huyler's *Meeting God: Elements of Hindu Devotion* (New Haven: Yale Univ. Press, 1999). A more academic study of village ritual is Alf Hiltebeitel's *The Cult of Draupadi*; see especially Volume II, *On Hindu Ritual and the Goddess* (Chicago: Univ. of Chicago Press, 1991). Hiltebeitel's video *Lady of Gingee: South Indian Draupadi Festivals* shows festivals central to this study (South Asia Center, Univ. of Wisconsin–Madison, 1987). Sarah Caldwell records a Kerala village festival in the video *Ball of Fire: The Angry Goddess* (Berkeley: Univ. of California Extension Center for Media and Independent Learning, 1999).

Descriptions of older Durga Pujas and much popular practice are in C. J. Fuller, *The Camphor Flame: Popular Hinduism and Society in India* (Princeton: Princeton Univ. Press, 1992). Fuller has also studied the royal Minakshi temple at Madurai. See his "The Divine Couple's Relationship in a South Indian Temple: Mīnākṣi and Sundareśvara at Madurai," *History of Religions* 19:4 (May 1980): 321–48. William P. Harmon analyzes rites of Minakshi's marriage and coronation in *The Sacred Marriage of a Hindu Goddess* (Bloomington: Indiana Univ. Press, 1989). Minakshi's marriage is portrayed in the video *Wedding of the Goddess* (South Asia Center, Univ. of Wisconsin–Madison, 1987), along with a closely linked festival of the nearby temple of Aligarh (Vishnu).

7

On the Road:
Pilgrim and Sadhu Journeys

We had trudged for hours up grueling switchbacks, our destination a small cave high on the back of this mountain spur said to focus and hold the presence of the goddess Vaishnodevi. As we climbed, a stream of returning pilgrims flowed down the twisting trail toward us. Most had spent the night at the pilgrim center on the slopes surrounding the shrine—as we ourselves and our guide intended to do. Around the heads of many were tied the red scarves bordered in gold tinsel that the goddess gives to pilgrims who reach and worship at her shrine. They shouted when they met us: "Jai Mata-Di!", "Victory to the Mother!" Several stopped to ask if we would pose with them for a photograph. Portly middle-aged American women are rare on this shrine's approaches, rare enough that a pilgrim group with a camera might want a record of the occasion.

Now we were nearing a crucial transition point on the trail. In just a few more moments, the trail would slip over the mountain shoulder we were climbing, then level out and descend a bit as it circled behind the mountain on its final approach to the shrine. We reached the turning point, rounded it, and found ourselves face to face with a friend—a *sadhvi,* woman renouncer, in bright saffron robes whom we had met on another pilgrimage completed a few days earlier. She and her two disciples had made the climb the day before, doing it the hard way, shoeless, in chill January weather. Now they stopped to tell us of the wonders ahead: the snow-covered high ranges soon to be seen from the pilgrim path, the beehive-like pilgrim center hung on the mountainside, the goddess's cave itself into which we would slither at an angle, our bare feet washed by the icy streamlet running through it. Soon a crowd of pilgrims gathered around us, mouths gaping in astonishment. Who were these Western women on the goddess's mountain? How had we come to know a sadhvi?[1]

---

[1] An extensive description of this pilgrimage can be found in Kathleen M. Erndl, *Victory to the Mother: The Hindu Goddess of Northwest India in Myth, Ritual, and Symbol* (New York: Oxford Univ. Press, 1993); see especially pp. 38–44, 62–68, 80–81.

The two preceding chapters paid a great deal of attention to Hindu practices that establish boundaries and nourish the groups within them: families, jatis, sects, local and political communities. It is time to turn to a practice that addresses itself to the spaces between and around communities. Some readers may find it strange that a religion so strongly affirming life in community also produces a bumper crop of pilgrims. But pilgrimage—religious journeying—is as common among Hindus as pujas and life-cycle rites. Like these, it is also a very old practice, going back to a time well before pilgrims had planes, trains, and busses to speed up travels. The *Mahabharata* contains a list of pilgrim sites, laid out in an itinerary that would have circled a pilgrim going from one to the next through much of the territory of today's India.[2] Several Puranas, too, praise particular pilgrim centers and cite the merit gained through visits to them. Pilgrimage is a practice common to all Indian sects. Indian Buddhists, Jains, Muslims, Christians, and Sikhs all have sacred places that they aspire to visit, sometimes sharing the same site with members of another religious community.[3]

Like temple festivals, Hindu pilgrimages come in many forms and often acquire different meanings in different contexts. It is easiest to make sense of this multiplicity by distinguishing between three basic components of pilgrimage, all reflected in the example that starts this chapter. First, a pilgrimage has a destination, a place toward which the pilgrim is heading, believed to be in touch with divine presence and steeped in miraculous, transforming qualities. One goes there, at least in part, to be there—to be in the deity's presence at least for a few moments, to be touched and changed by the powers concentrated in that place. Second, a pilgrimage is a journey—sometimes one of just a few miles, but sometimes an arduous trip that begins in a long flight or train ride and culminates in an exhausting trek to reach some riverbank or spot high on a hillside. As such it is a form of *tapas,* austerity, analogous to the austerities that sadhus practice when they resolve not to sit or to hold one arm in the air for years. Third, a pilgrimage entails one or more pilgrims—people who make the journey, with some intention in mind.

In most pilgrim journeys, the destination seems the most important part. The discipline of the journey and the loosening of ties that it entails prepare the pilgrim to receive the power that is in the place. Many pilgrims travel to gain some benefit or to fulfill some religious duty. Readers will find examples of this standard pattern in this chapter. But the chapter also shows variation: pilgrimage where the journey means more than the goal, pilgrimage where the goal is a state of mind rather than a location, pilgrimage where the benefit to be gained is full salvation, pilgrimage transforming itself into mission. How can one practice hold so many possibilities? It is necessary to look more closely at the three pilgrimage components.

THE DESTINATION

In Sanskrit literature, a pilgrim destination is commonly called a *tirtha,* "crossing." This term can also be used to designate a "ford," a place where travelers can safely walk or ride across a river. When used with reference to a pilgrim site, it indicates not a crossing place of this mundane world, but rather a site of crossing between

---

[2] For analysis of these sites, see Surinder Mohan Bhardwaj, *Hindu Places of Pilgrimage: A Study in Cultural Geography* (Berkeley: Univ. of California Press, 1973), 42–57.

[3] A number of examples can be found in J. J. Roy Burman, "Shivaji's Myth and Maharashtra's Syncretic Traditions," *Economic and Political Weekly* 36:14–15 (April 14, 2001): 1226–34.

planes of existence. It offers transit between the ordinary, earthly plane, where humans reside and do everyday work, and the realm of the divine or sacred, where powers exist that are more than human and that can be drawn upon to support and empower human effort. Attached to every Hindu tirtha is some story about what my teacher Mircea Eliade called a hierophany, a "sacred showing." A saint won enlightenment there, or a miraculous linga revealed itself to some king or cowherd through a dream or vision. Perhaps some crucial event occurred on that spot during the battles between devas and asuras that populate so much of Indian mythology. Or some piece of the goddess Sati fell to earth here as her grieving husband Shiva roamed through India carrying her self-burned body in his arms. Vaishnodevi came to her cave, it is said, fleeing an unwanted lover, whom she eventually destroyed there. Once such an event happens someplace, that place can never be the same. It becomes a permanent site of access to the power or powers that once moved on that spot.

Stories of past sacred showings nonetheless do not account fully for the nature of Hindu tirthas. Hindu deities, especially the great ones, can show themselves anywhere they please. Yet most tirthas occur at just two kinds of places. They are either by water, on a river or seacoast, or they are in some wild place, perhaps in a forest or, like Vaishnodevi, near the summit of a hill or mountain. Such siting is rooted in ancient premises about the nature of the world, premises that were seen operating in the last chapter. According to these premises, this world is a place where two kinds of forces struggle for supremacy. The first are forces that create and preserve order, enable settlement, and bond humans together into supportive communities. Brahmin teachers call these forces of dharma; the beings who defend them are the devas. The second type of forces are those of *adharma,* anti-structure or chaos, and the beings promoting them are *asuras,* a word often translated into English as "demons," although "anti-god" is more accurate. Many stories of clashes between devas and asuras are told in Brahmin-transmitted literature, especially in the Puranas. We have seen how festivals of settlement and realm develop themes of the battle between order and chaos. In these stories and festivals, asuras are usually "bad guys" who must be trounced for human existence to be sustained.

Nonetheless, if one examines closely the way Hindus act in relation to chaotic forces, one realizes that such forces are not wholly negative. After all, structure must be challenged and broken from time to time if creative change is ever to take place. The demon who attacks a village or kingdom's goddess—or conceals his true nature to win her in marriage—brings vitality into the community he enters even as it unites to battle and overcome him. Furthermore, the demon-riddled places of India, the wild forests and hills that lie outside of settled areas, are precisely the places where people go to seek spiritual breakthroughs and transforming power. To be redone, one must be undone, such behavior seems to suggest. To become fully creative, one must encounter dissolution. Once the importance of such occasional undoing for the emergence of growth and creativity is recognized, certain themes in Indian religion that otherwise would seem crazy and incoherent begin to make sense. The Indian super-god Shiva, for example, has oddly asuric twists in his stories and symbolic makeup; he attacks and breaks up sacrifices, seduces *rishis'* wives, roams forests and mountainsides dressed in wild animal skins, and is sometimes identified with the buffalo asura Mahisha who is slain by Durga at the time of Durga Puja. This same Lord Shiva is Lord of Yogis, the patron god of spiritual growth and transcendence. Again, the message comes through in his stories: remaking entails unmaking.

An occasional splash of chaos in a world, god, or human life is not just unavoidable, but necessary.

This same theme is found again at pilgrim sites.[4] Most are places whose very nature evokes unmaking, places where boundaries turn fluid. Either they are wilderness sites per se or places of flowing waters, long associated in India with dissolving and remaking. Furthermore, even within such places, many are at locations where the dissolving of boundaries seems most intense: on hills where earth heaves upward to penetrate sky; at river confluences where streams mingle waters; at peninsulas on seacoasts where land ventures into water. Most pilgrim visits also entail rituals of unmaking: bathing, for example, which at riverine tirthas is *the* pilgrim ritual par excellence. Bathing in a tirtha's waters, the pilgrim unmakes and is remade; disabling karma disappears, letting the site's blessings flow into a cleansed and receptive body and spirit.

THE JOURNEY

The pilgrim bath itself is a completion of a cleansing process already begun when the pilgrim leaves home. Brahmin writings on dharma prescribe a small unbinding rite for the leave-taking moment. The would-be pilgrim has his or her hair cut entirely or partially, undertakes a daylong fast, worships Ganesha, Lord of Thresholds, along with home shrine deities, and makes the declaration of intention required at the beginning of any Hindu ritual. He or she puts on special pilgrim's dress: distinctive reddish cloth wrapped around the body, a copper ring and bracelet. Only then can the pilgrim set out, breaking his or her fast only when at least two miles from home.[5]

Several of these actions resemble the behavior of a religious renouncer: hair removal, fasting, wearing clothing in the yellow-to-red range of the color spectrum. Like renouncers, pilgrims of the past expected to live while traveling on gifts made by those who believed that feeding pilgrims would bring merit. Moreover, some writings assert that a pilgrimage yields greater merit when it is done with maximal *tapas,* austerity. Hence, it is better to travel on foot than in a conveyance such as a wagon or litter.[6] Such expectations are echoed today at Vaishnodevi in beliefs that climbing her mountain on foot is better than riding a rental pony and ascending in bare feet is still better. More meritorious still is doing it in the manner called *dandoti*—measuring one's length on the ground in a full prostration, moving to the end of that prostration and prostrating again, for the full distance between pilgrim and goal.[7]

Similarly, the most esteemed pilgrim sites are often the least accessible, for example, Gomukh, at the mouth of the Ganges high in the Himalayas, or the four sites

---

[4] Anthropologist Victor Turner has argued that it is a central theme of pilgrimage throughout the world, appearing not only in spatial values but also in social dynamics. See "Pilgrimages as Social Processes" in his essay collection *Dramas, Fields and Metaphors: Symbolic Action in Human Society* (Ithaca: Cornell Univ. Press, 1974), 166–230; also, with Edith Turner, *Image and Pilgrimage in Christian Culture: Anthropological Perspectives* (New York: Columbia Univ. Press, 1978).

[5] The distance given is one *krosha,* roughly two miles.

[6] As cited by Pandurang Vaman Kane, *History of Dharmaśāstra,* Vol. IV (Poona: Bhandarkar Research Institute, 1973), pp. 376–77.

[7] I have seen pilgrims doing this in India, but not at Vaishnodevi.

"every Hindu should aspire to visit," as I was told by New Delhi friends: Badrinath in the north, on another Himalayan Ganges feeder; Jagannath-Puri on the far eastern sea-coast; Rameshwaram in the far south on the chain of islands stretching between India and Sri Lanka; and Dwarka on the far west coast of Gujarat's Kathiawar peninsula, where the Arabian Sea mingles its waters with the Gulf of Kutch. A pilgrim making the rounds of these four sites in one trip would encircle nearly the whole of India. Of course, exceptions do exist to this general rule of difficulty. The city of Banaras, a pilgrim magnet for centuries and one of the most prestigious, is on the central Ganges plain. It can be easily reached today by air, rail, highway, or even river-going vessel.

THE PILGRIM

Who can make a pilgrim journey? Even Brahmin texts of the past stipulated that pilgrimage is for everyone, including women, foreigners, people of mixed caste, and lowly Shudras. A pilgrim site is one of the few places where contact with an untouchable is not polluting.[8] This does not mean, however, that the same mix of pilgrims is drawn to every site. Surveying pilgrims at northern hill sites during the late 1960s, geographer Surinder Mohan Bhardwaj discovered that pilgrims sift themselves out according to caste, level of wealth, and level of education.[9] At Badrinath, famed throughout India, Bhardwaj found mostly high-caste and well-to-do pilgrims familiar with Sanskrit literary traditions. At shrines known mostly locally, he found high concentrations of poorer and less educated local villagers. People of low caste congregated at goddess-centered sites where blood sacrifice was offered; people of high caste gathered at those of pure gods celebrated in Sanskrit texts.

Pilgrims interviewed by Bhardwaj also reported a wide range of motives for their journeys. Some came to complete vows made in pursuit of worldly benefit: the birth of a son, success in finding a proper marriage partner, profit in business, good crops, or victory in lawsuits. In a pilgrim vow, one in effect says to a deity, "Honor my request and I shall go to your holy place." If the desired goal is achieved, the vow-maker must fulfill the promise. Certain pilgrim sites of India have gained fame as places where particular kinds of vows are often successful. The same is true concerning particular types of ritual: Bhardwaj found, for example, that goddess-linked sites in the region he studied were often visited by families intending to perform the life-cycle rite of first haircut for a child.[10] But he also found many pilgrims who said they had come to a site just for "merit," that is, just for general spiritual benefit. As is seen in other studies described in this chapter, a pilgrimage can also be an expression of devotion, an attempt to move nearer for a time to a beloved deity. Or, especially for the sadhu, often portrayed as a permanent pilgrim, religious journeying can be an important part of the process of life transformation that brings one finally to *moksha,* liberation. By now, it should be apparent that Hindu pilgrimage is just as varied in form and intent as practice in Hindu homes and temples.

---

[8] Kane, op. cit, 569–70.

[9] Bhardwaj, op. cit., see especially pp. 163–200.

[10] Bhardwaj, ibid., pp. 156, 160.

Once again, the best way to appreciate its diversity is to look more closely at a series of examples. The remainder of this chapter subdivides into three sections. The first describes pilgrimages of ordinary people who are principally concerned with raising families and day-to-day survival. The second samples pilgrimages of devotees who have chosen, at least in theory, to put God at front and center of their attention. And finally, the third takes up pilgrimages of renouncers, those who have made their pilgrimage permanent.

ORDINARY PILGRIMS

Many studies of pilgrimage in India locate their research at noted pilgrim centers, asking why pilgrims come to these places and what they do after they arrive. One noteworthy exception is a book by anthropologist Ann Grodzins Gold, who based herself in a village in the northwestern state of Rajasthan and asked what kind of pilgrim journeys her friends and neighbors went on. The book she wrote, *Fruitful Journeys,* pays special attention to three types of pilgrim intentions.[11] Some villagers journeyed in search of specific "fruits," often the healing of some illness or, in the case of women, conceiving a child or reversing some child-linked misfortune, such as a string of miscarriages or first-year deaths. Some journeyed to complete rituals, most notably the ritual process called *shraddha* that separates the dead from the living and releases them from clinging to their old life so they become free to seek another rebirth. Finally, like pilgrims whom Bhardwaj interviewed in the Himalayas, some went on pilgrimage just because it was a good thing to do.

Like Bhardwaj, Gold found that journeying for fruit was usually a local pursuit. Pilgrim sites in India tend to sift themselves out according to the distance that people will travel to reach them. Some are famous throughout the country; would-be pilgrims often go to great effort and expense to visit such sites at least once during their lifetime. Other sites, like Vaishodevi, are popular in specific regions. Vaishnodevi visitors come mostly from states north and west of Delhi, although in recent years her catchment area has been growing. Others draw pilgrims only within a single state or former kingdom, and others still draw merely from a circle of nearby villages. In Gold's case, most journeying for fruit moved toward shrines quite near her base village. Some shrines attracting pilgrims were so unpretentious that they were not even called temples. Gold has described one at the village where she stayed:

> The primary icons of Puvali are installed at the back of a large raised platform. These are Dev Narayanji's "bricks" (*ī̃ṭ*) as well as a carved icon of Devji riding his famed mare Lila Ghori. The flat stone plank directly beneath these is said to belong to Pipal De Rani, Devji's wife. Behind the bricks are stones representing the couple's twin son and daughter known as Bila-Bili. . . . The "essential" shrine is also embellished with framed colored pictures of the gods, and small, ornate, silver umbrellas donated by pilgrims to shade and honor the icons. The bricks

---

[11] *Fruitful Journeys: The Ways of Rajasthani Pilgrims* (Prospect Heights, IL: Waveland Press, 1988).

themselves are kept nicely "dressed" with sheets of colored, patterned foil. Overspreading the shrine from its right side is a nim tree, beneath which resides one of the compound's several Bhairujis.[12]

Such an open shrine is likely to honor a deity well-known only in its specific region; Dev Narayanji is the hero of a Rajasthani oral epic. The local shrine's ability to draw pilgrims arises from its reputation for helping people solve specific types of problems. Gold describes treatments at Puvali of two men suffering from mental illness plus a woman experiencing constant pain, with a history of losing children. In each case the shrine priest, possessed by the god Bhairuji, Dev Narayanji's "agent," identifies the cause of the problem and prescribes a course of action that should solve it. For the woman, the cause is a witch who has attached to her. One of the men is afflicted by a jealous goddess, whereas the other has failed to keep promises to Dev Narayanji and has treated disrespectfully another local god's shrine. Gold also describes "pouch-filling" that goes on at this shrine. When a woman wants a child, she and her family petition Dev Narayanji for it. She then must come to the shrine for a special ritual in which a coconut wrapped in red cloth is placed in a pouch she makes with the front of her sari, suggesting the child that she wishes to form in her womb. If this rite produces a healthy child, the family returns again to give cash to the shrine and hang from a nearby tree a basket holding that coconut. This attests that the shrine's power has been effective. The child itself is later brought to honor Dev Narayanji, who then becomes that child's lifelong protector. Pouch-filling is an example of the transaction called a "vow," where the supplicant in effect strikes a bargain with the deity: if you do x, then I shall do y in return.

Divining by possession or seeking aid by means of vows are folk practices common in many regions of the world. Gold notes that even the villagers who perform them do not consider them unusual or special. Nor do they set them apart or classify them in the same way as other journeys they make of a religious nature. To go to a nearby shrine to seek aid from its deity requires no preliminary pilgrim rites. Such a shrine is not called a tirtha, although, like a tirtha, it is a place where sacred power has revealed itself. Nor is the journey a full *yatra,* the Sanskrit term most North Indians use when they talk of making a pilgrimage. Instead, Gold's villager friends use the term *jatra,* the Rajasthani version of yatra, when they talk of such lesser pilgrimages. But still they retain the sense that these require a journey. Gold points out that Dev Narayanji's petitioners come mostly from other villages, not his own. When residents of Dev Narayanji's village have needs of a sort that might take one to his shrine, they will often travel to a shrine at a greater distance.

As for pilgrimage of the yatra type, both the ritual detail and distance involved increase sharply in such an undertaking. Yatra sites are also more likely to have connections to widely known Sanskrit-recorded literary traditions. Gold describes three pilgrimages of the yatra type, two done to "sink flowers" of the dead and one completed just for the sake of doing pilgrimage.

According to Gold, "sinking flowers" seems a custom relatively recent to her region, a product of increased access to sacred rivers through development of public

---

[12] Gold, ibid., pp. 162–63.

transportation systems. It consists of the following. When an adult Hindu of caste—that is, high caste—dies, his or her body is cremated at a local site. After this, the dead person's family goes through a series of rituals known as *shraddhas,* which have two intentions. One is to separate the dead from the living cleanly, while cleansing blood kin of the pollution resulting from contact with death. The second is to unite the dead with the *pitris,* family ancestors, from whom they will later separate to enter another life. The union with pitris is accomplished by breaking a ball of rice, called a *pinda,* into pieces and merging these with other pindas representing ancestral figures.

The dead do not always separate from the living easily. In fact, ailments taken to local shrines are often caused by spirits of dead children or adults unwilling to move away from the home of their last birth. The cure in this case consists of setting them up as local or family deities and ensuring that they receive proper worship. Nonetheless, sinking flowers usually helps the dead to move on smoothly. If the departed is a parent, his or her eldest son gathers a few of the ashes left after the parent's cremation and puts them aside in a special pot. When able to do so, the son goes on pilgrimage to a tirtha that is auspicious for such a ritual and sinks the pot in its body of water. In Rajasthan, the tirtha usually visited for such practice is the city of Hardwar, where the river Ganga (Ganges) emerges from the Himalayan foothills. The Ganga has an old and special connection to death rites. Stories told about this famed goddess and river claim that she first agreed to descend to earth so her water could bring peace to warrior princes who died while helping their royal father perform a horse sacrifice. To sink flowers, the son travels to Hardwar, identifies a priest whose family does these rites for one's home settlement, and has the priest guide him through a series of rites that entail worshiping the river, sinking the ash pot within her waters, and immersing pindas within the river. As Gold reports it, this ritual also entails carrying water from the river back to the village. The Ganga herself is an important Rajasthani deity, and a central ritual in the village Gold studied was "Celebration of Ganges Water," in which the pot thus returned is opened and its water offered to guests. Actions accompanying this rite suggest that, through its performance, life supplants death.

Gold also observed a longer version of the pilgrimage for the dead, which took its travelers through several sacred sites of North India until they sank their flowers at Gaya, said to be the most potent spot in India for performing ancestral rites. In this case, the pilgrims traveling for their dead were part of a larger group, some of whose members journeyed just for the sake of doing pilgrimage. Most flower bearers of this group came from a single village, but were of different village jatis. Doing pilgrimage for its own sake were a dozen Brahmins from a nearby town, all relatives of one another. The group traveled by chartered bus, a common practice among pilgrims of India. Often a person or group intent on pilgrimage gathers a bus group from family and friends and then networks for other riders until all seats on the bus are sold.

Gold's longer pilgrim tour had an ambitious reach, lasting a full month and making stops at twenty-four sites, including the famed pilgrim centers of Mathura, Prayag, Banaras, Gaya, Ayodhya, and Hardwar. In the east, it reached as far as Kalighat Temple in Calcutta and the great temple of Jagannath at Puri on the Bay of Bengal, easternmost of the big four sites. It did not attempt the heart-stopping mountain travel that would have taken it to Badrinath or the source of the Ganges in the high hills, nor did it venture south of the Ganges valley to any site other than Puri.

Like the shorter pilgrimage to Hardwar that Gold describes, this tour began with the local rites considered proper for a pilgrim tour's opening. At a time judged auspicious by a local astrologer, the pilgrims gathered at the shrine of Path Mother, a local manifestation of the Ganga. With them were women who would stay behind in their households, bearing pots in which they had planted sprouts to be carefully tended as a symbolic stand-in for the pilgrim kin. As long as the sprouts flourished, the pilgrims would do well. The Brahmin priest of the shrine offered pujas to the goddess and her attendant Bhairuji and dotted foreheads of the pilgrims with red powder.

While on the road, Gold's fellow travelers sang devotional songs, told stories of the gods, discussed their own needs and plans, and quarreled over seat allocations. At sunset every evening, they sang a special praise song for Vishnu while their bus-master lit sticks of incense at a small shrine on their vehicle's dashboard. At night, they usually camped around their bus, but at Puri they stayed at one of the pilgrim hostels that many wealthy Hindus maintain at pilgrim sites as acts of charity. When visiting tirthas, they bathed, went to temples for darshan, offered pujas, and gave money to priests and sadhus. Upon reaching home, they first returned to Path Mother's shine, staying there overnight while celebrated by a *bhajan* party from the village. In the morning, their households' women brought the sprouts tended during their absence. Now, with a series of rituals, the priest released them from pilgrim commitments and their families sang for them and gave them gifts. The women circled Path Mother seven times with their sprouts; then all went to Vishnu's temple in the village where they bowed, made small offerings, and separated.

According to Gold, this journey's high point was its bath in the sea at Puri, which her fellow pilgrims enjoyed so much that they returned to the shore to repeat it before leaving Puri. She vividly describes the self-abandonment with which usually staid and modest villagers threw themselves into the waves fully dressed, tangled up with one another, and clung together. This self-abandonment then became a clue in her efforts to understand the significance of this journey for those who underwent it. Loosening, emptying, and thinning are three central images through which Gold articulates this significance. Her fellow travelers loosened ties to the villages left behind, with their tangled webs of social expectations. They emptied their pockets, knowing they reap no immediate benefit from this action as they would have, for example, if they had given a gift in the village where everyone could see and admire it. The rigors of their journey thinned their bodies. They proved sceptical about claims that one can wash away bad karma by bathing at sacred places, but they did expect to be different after making the journey.

The motif of loosening becomes pervasive enough in the pilgrimage done for its own sake to make one ask what connection this loosening accomplished through pilgrimage has with the ultimate loosening accomplished via the ancient Hindu ideal of *moksha,* release. When Gold tried to find out how her fellow travelers might connect pilgrimage to moksha, she found only one pilgrim willing to claim that she had traveled in search of deliverance. Nonetheless, the pilgrimage done for its own sake seemed at least to be a preparation for moksha. As one woman pilgrim put it, "Sweeping the road ahead, then Brother, moksha happens well."[13]

---

[13] Gold, ibid., p. 228.

PILGRIM DEVOTEES

One clue that may help explain why Gold's fellow pilgrims were so modest about the goals they sought to attain through pilgrimage is provided by British ethnographer Alan Morinis, who has compared three types of Hindu pilgrims and pilgrim sites in the state of West Bengal, on the opposite side of India from the village Gold studied.[14] Morinis describes two separate understandings of the role and value of pilgrimage that circulate in India's sectarian traditions. One, strongly anchored in the school of thought called Advaita Vedanta, classifies pilgrimage, along with other rituals, as an inferior practice set up to aid people not spiritually advanced enough to carry on the Advaita quest for higher understanding. The pilgrimage done to attain worldly goals is especially devalued. Only those who do ritual without seeking gain from it can hope to attain any high spiritual goal. Gold's fellow pilgrims seem to have drawn on this set of expectations.

The second understanding, anchored in teachings of bhakta saints, views pilgrimage as a form of devotion, and devotion as a direct route to God. Pilgrims tied to devotional groups following such teachings believe that pilgrimage and other forms of worship can bring them to full salvation. The next portion of this chapter studies two unusually ambitious pilgrimages that approach their journeys from this second perspective.

First, however, one more component must be added to the list of pilgrimage basics: time. Although most journeys to pilgrim centers bring benefit whenever one makes them, most powerful tirthas have certain times that are better for pilgrimage than others. Or to put it more precisely, such times are better for fulfilling certain types of pilgrim aims. At some pilgrim centers, times of such special efficacy become an occasion for holding periodic *melas,* fairs, where ritual practice is mixed with business and entertainment. Attendees bathe, take darshan of temple images, trade livestock, buy and sell at temporary markets, and enjoy carnival rides, all at the same occasion.

The Warkaris and the Pandharpur Journey

Certain times also offer occasions for great mass pilgrimages, when people gather and travel across long distances to reach a site at an especially auspicious moment. One famous mass trek is a journey taken during the bright half of the month of Asadh (June–July) by Marathi-speaking people in the state of Maharashtra in western India. The tirtha on which it converges is the temple of the god Vithoba (Vitthal), usually identified with Krishna\Vishnu, in the town of Pandharpur on the Bhima River, on the southeastern border of the Marathi speakers' area. Although anyone who wishes may join this journey, the main group of pilgrims who sustain it are devotees known as Warkaris (Varkaris), "those who come and go." Initiated by gurus of the Warkari Panth founded in Maharashtra during the thirteenth century, Warkaris make a commitment that they will journey to Vithoba at least once per year wearing the special *tulsi* necklace given them at the time of initiation.[15] Going twice is even better; if taken, the second journey occurs during the month of Kartik (October–November).

---

[14] E. Alan Morinis, *Pilgrimage in the Hindu Tradition: A Case Study of West Bengal* (New York: Oxford Univ. Press, 1984).

[15] Tulsi is the plant sacred to Vishnu. This necklace is the Hindu equivalent of a rosary.

Some Warkaris go four times a year, and a few hundred souls make the journey continuously, cycling between Pandharpur and whatever town or village they once called home. Making this annual journey *is* their spiritual path, the central expression of Warkari devotion.

The Pandharpur journey in Asadh consists of multiple pilgrim groups, accompanying conveyances known as *palkhis* (palanquins), Indian versions of sedan chairs. These palkhis bear the Warkaris' most precious symbols: the wooden sandals said to have been worn by great saints of Maharashtra's devotional movement. Often palkhis are quite elaborate; the palkhi of the founding saint Jnaneshwar is wholly encased in silver together with its sandals, which rest upon a jewel-studded throne within it. Jnaneshwar's palkhi is so heavy it must travel most of its distance by bullock cart, using the human bearers usual for a palanquin only when moved to a tent during nighttime stops.

For the duration of the pilgrimage, the sandals are the saint, come back to life to make this journey with the devotees who are the saint's descendants. Each palkhi departs from the town or village that holds its saint's tomb and travels to Pandharpur along a route set by past tradition. Often, it joins with other palkis along the way. Their collective paths resemble rivers converging. Attending a saint's palkhi are one or more *dindis*, groups that celebrate the palkhi's passage with continuous singing of devotional songs. Dindis are usually made up of people who know each other, residents of a single village or subcaste. They pool contributions to buy supplies for the journey, secure tents in which they will sleep, and hire trucks or carts to haul their luggage. The journey can be a long one, over three hundred miles for pilgrims coming from the most distant departure point. It can take as long as a month because a truly devoted Warkari walks the entire way, starting at 6 or 6:30 each morning, walking until time for the midday meal, then hiking again until just before nightfall.

Three writers have described this journey. Maharashtrian sociologist Irawati Karve published a short account of her own pilgrim experience in Marathi in 1951.[16] Jesuit priest and scholar G. A. DeLeury made his pilgrimage in the same year, describing it in a long monograph ten years later.[17] Maharashtrian writer D. B. Mokashi published his own account in 1964.[18] All three traveled with Jnaneshwar's palkhi, the oldest and most prestigious.[19] Departing from Alandi, twenty miles north of Poona, this procession crosses a ridge, then follows the valley of the Nira river to its confluence with the

---

[16] "Watcal," in the book *Paripurti* (Pune: Deshmukh and Company); translated as "On the Road" in the *Journal of Asian Studies* 22:1 (1962): 13–29; later reissued in *South and Southeast Asia*, Association of Asian Studies 30th Anniversary Commemoration Series 3 (Tuscon: Univ. of Arizona Press, 1972) and again in Eleanor Zelliot and Maxine Berntsen, eds., *The Experience of Hinduism: Essays on Religion in Maharashtra* (Albany: SUNY Press, 1988).

[17] *The Cult of Vithoba* (Poona: Deccan College Postgraduate and Research Institute, 1960).

[18] *Palakhi*; translated by Philip Engbloom as *Palkhi: an Indian Pilgrimage* (Albany: SUNY Press, 1987).

[19] No palkhis date back to the time of the saints themselves. Although the custom and vow of pilgrimage to Pandharpur appear in Warkari saints' songs, early pilgrimages were probably far less structured. They may also have been interrupted during the time of Tughlaq rule, when Hindu shrines of the region were razed by Muslim rulers. According to DeLeury, the Asadh pilgrimage acquired its present form of organization from merchant devotee Haibatrao Arphalkar in the late 1800s. The latter donated the Jnaneshwar palkhi, its first horses, and other equipment. He also organized the first dindis and set a prescribed order for singing the *abhangs*. Subsequent palkhis followed the precedents he had set.

Bhima and thence on into Pandharpur—a fifteen-day trek of 150 miles. Although each account reflects its own writer's take on the Jnaneshwar palkhi pilgrimage, agreement on its route, order, and events is substantial. Mokashi translator Philip Engbloom reports just one major change between 1951 and the mid-1980s. Dindis made up of untouchable caste groups, once forced to march ahead of the main procession, now have won the right to take a place within it.[20]

The event these writers describe is as much a festive parade as it is a devout journey. A bystander watching a palkhi progress along the road first sees two horses bearing poles with saffron pendants, one with a rider, one without. Like the palkhi, the riderless horse bears the invisible saint himself. Next come several dindis, ranging in size from twenty to several hundred members, who march from five to twelve or more abreast, depending on how near they are to Pandharpur and hence how large the procession has become. At least one member of each dindi carries a *vina*, a large lute-like instrument. Another beats the South Indian double-headed drum, the *mridangam;* and still others play small cymbals or bear more saffron banners. All sing the songs of Warkari saints. Next, its silver casing glittering in the sunshine, comes the palkhi itself, pulled along on an oxcart while the procession is moving and accompanied by attendants from its home temple. When it makes rest stops, these attendants conduct pujas to it and supervise the lines that wait for darshan. After the palkhi come more dindis, banging drums and cymbals and singing more saints' songs. Like bands in a U.S. parade, these are not necessarily in sync with dindis before and after; each unit sets its own rhythms. Women in the procession may carry water pots on their heads or other small pots of *tulsi,* the "holy basil" plant sacred to Vishnu. Before and after the central procession come baggage carts and trucks, as well as many poor pilgrims who travel without dindis, relying for food and shelter on the generosity of people they meet along the road.

Most pilgrimage procedures are set by custom and preliminary agreement, including the order of the dindis, the songs for each day and occasion, and the order of palkhis as processions meet and join. Many other customs have become standard. When the palkhi stops at night, it must be removed from its cart and carried at a run to the tent that will house it while singing increases in intensity. Then, it receives an *arti,* a common form of worship that includes singing and waving a lighted lamp before it. Lines form for darshan, both of the palkhi and of the saints' horses. At night kirtans occur, which in Maharashtra include not only singing of religious songs, but also stories, sermons and dancing. Dindis of the procession take turns organizing such kirtans, usually aided by gurus traveling with them.

At certain points in the journey, stops are made to allow for more lighthearted entertainments. Both Karve and Mokashi describe a custom in which a palkhi procession's two horses race one another down a straight or circular track. Mokashi also reports the excitement of a "run" occurring close to Pandharpur: the pilgrims race over the brink of a steep hill and plunge down it together, many tumbling and losing sandals as they go. He is less happy with a game played by male and female participants in which they stuff puffed rice into one another's mouths, then pair off in couples, interlock hands, and whirl around in circles together. Sometimes, too, pilgrims enact folk dramas, in which handy saris or blankets are captured to use as props.

---

[20] *Palkhi,* ibid., p. 7.

Evening housing is usually in tent camps thrown up in fields beside the road. When halts occur in sizeable towns or villages, well-to-do dindis secure sleeping space in local halls or residents' homes. At such a stop in a populated area, the procession's visit itself becomes an occasion for local festivity. Locals offer pujas and entertainments before the palkhi and sponsor mass feedings for pilgrims who cannot pay for their own meals. Extra visitors flood into town to take darshan of pilgrims and palkhis, to view shows, and to join in with the travelers' songs and sermons. Any pilgrim on the way to Pandarpur is a temporary saint and manifestation of God, whether or not that pilgrim is a necklace-wearing Warkari. Just to be in the pilgrim's presence is a blessing. Any occasion that draws people together in India also draws merchants and peripheral entertainments. Thus, a simple pilgrim stopover becomes a fair and a focus of intense local excitement.

The peak of the pilgrims' own excitement comes at the end of the journey when all palkhis join together and enter Pandarpur in a grand procession. Most assemble first on the bright ninth of Asadh in the little town of Wakhari, where each has been assigned its own staging place. On the next day, bright tenth, comes the climactic procession, with Jnaneshwar's palkhi in the final and climactic position. All palkhis must enter the city by 4 PM. Afterwards, anticlimactically, the pilgrims split up and go their own ways. All eventually bathe in the Bhima and take darshan of Vithoba in his temple, standing day and night in lines so long that regular puja patterns are suspended to accommodate pilgrims seeking to get in. Most pilgrims stay in town until Purnima, the night of the full moon. Then they return home by train or bus. Just a few attendants escort palkhis home on foot, making fewer stops and at twice as fast a pace.

How can one make sense of an event like this? One feature seems clear: the significance of the Warkaris' trek lies less in arriving than in making the journey. Three aspects of the journey seem especially important. The first is the experience of self-loss in a larger whole fused into a single unit by singing and moving together. Karve has expressed this the most poetically:

> I was walking on and on in a space filled with color, sound and wind. When I looked down, I saw innumerable feet moving up and down, onward to the rhythm of tal and mrdangam. I felt I was a drop in this vast stream of human beings; that instead of walking, I was being carried forward by the surrounding motion."[21]

Elsewhere she describes the pilgims as "intoxicated with happiness."[22] Even the more detached Mokashi from time to time is caught in the euphoria of the group experience:

> The entire procession is immersed in the gaiety and liveliness of the *bhajans*. The *abhanga*s pour out with ever increasing vehemence. Even men and women in their fifties and sixties jerk their bodies ungracefully as they dance to the rhythms of the music, and they look at one another and laugh with happiness. Just look! This is the joy of the *palkhi!* This is why we come along.[23]

---

[21] Karve, op. cit., Zelliot and Berntsen, p. 151.

[22] Ibid., p. 159.

[23] Mokashi, op. cit., p. 135.

A second and somewhat contrasting experience is the tapas that is so often a valued component of pilgrim journeys. The month of Asadh occurs in the midst of Maharashtra's rainy season. Both Mokashi and DeLeury tell of the downpours that afflict pilgrims, turning roads into seas of mud and sending streams into flood across them. During Mokashi's journey, floodwaters carried a woman away after she lost her footing crossing such a stream. Poor people with no housing or tents wind up sleeping in puddles, and all experience impromptu fasting when storms make it impossible to light cook fires. When the rain stops and clouds part overhead, the sun bakes pilgrims black and leaves them parched for water. Feet protected only by sandals blister, crack, and bleed. Sanitation is minimal; bathing is available only in ponds and streams, often fouled by the presence of thousands of other people. Yet pregnant women make the journey, parents bring their children, and many travel who are past sixty. Mokashi met one pilgrim in his nineties, hanging onto a servant's arm, but determined to walk the whole distance as usual.

A third important component of the trip is religious education. With a few exceptions, the pilgrims are not educated people. Most are of modest means and come from rural areas. Mokashi, who financed his trip by securing a grant to take a survey, noted how very few middle-class or professional pilgrims he met. The theology and values of the Warkari saints are transmitted to most pilgrims principally through songs they sing and sermons and theater they encounter during the procession's nighttime stops. For pilgrims, the trip becomes an intensive multiweek retreat. For local villagers coming to honor and join with pilgrims, at least one night per year is spent in absorbing pilgrim views and values. Thus, the pilgrimage feeds on itself, drawing new pilgrims into its circle. If it challenges and exhilarates them enough, some will make the commitment to come back year after year.

Ban Yatra

Even longer and more demanding than the Maharashtrian journey is one to the north that has no destination. This pilgrimage describes a rough circle of more than 200 miles through a tract of sacred territory—a circle that carries its pilgrims through sites of the story most focal to their Krishna-centered sects. This journey, called the Ban Yatra, the "Forest Journey," takes place in Braj, the land of Krishna's youth. In mundane space, Braj surrounds the ancient city of Mathura, located 60 miles south of India's capital New Delhi. Like the Warkaris' pilgrimage, the Ban Yatra must be made at one specific time, beginning just after Krishna's birthday on the eighth bright day of Bhadon, or August–September, which puts it in the midst of its own region's rainy season.

Although any devotee of Krishna may take this journey, most who do it belong to one of two sectarian groups: the Gaudiya Vaishnavas, based largely in eastern India, and the Pushti Margis or Vallabhacharyas, based largely in the northwest. These two groups have been the most active in developing Braj as a pilgrim center, a process begun during the sixteenth century by their founders Shri Chaitanya and Vallabhacharya.[24]

---

[24] Although Vaishnavas agree that Braj was Krishna's land in ancient times, they say that he left it in later life to establish his Yadava clan in and around the city of Dwarka, on India's westernmost shoreline. Several kings restored the Krishna sites for would-be pilgrims. But all sites were eventually lost, and the city fell under Buddhist and Jain dominance. When Chaitanya and Vallabhacharya made their own journeys to the city, they rediscovered the sites with the aid of divine guidance.

Priests of these two sects control most of the sites and pilgrim events in Braj today. Each sect mounts its own Ban Yatras; differences of emphasis and structure in the journeys reflect differences in the groups' own organizations and theology. According to Ban Yatra pilgrims, the principal purpose of their journeys is to join Krishna's *lila,* "play" and hence to taste the joy that this play produces. The concept of lila is central to many Krishna-centered groups. Like its English equivalent, "play," the term conveys a double meaning. On the one hand, lila is "play" in the sense of "child's play," that is, spontaneous activity done just for the sheer delight of doing it. Among his several other roles in Hindu mythology, Krishna revealed the *Bhagavad-Gita,* the important Hindu text mentioned several times earlier in this book. During this revelation he says to his friend Arjuna, "I have nothing at all that I must do in the three worlds\ Nothing not won that I have to win;\ Nonetheless I engage in actions. . . ."[25] Arjuna is told to act like Krishna; goal-free action is liberation. According to Krishna-sect teachings, the devotee who attains Krishna's playfulness will one day play forever in God's presence.

On the other hand, lila is also "play" in the sense of drama—the drama that tells of God's goal-free action and shows disciples *how* to emulate this. So Krishna-lila is the phrase used to describe Krishna's life, recounted most fully in the fourth book of the tenth-century Sanskrit text *Bhagavata-Purana* (or *Shri Bhagavatam*), but also in other poems, songs, folk tales, and dramas enacted yearly at Braj and other Krishna centers. This lila-as-drama begins with Krishna's birth in the palace of Mathura, overshadowed by his uncle King Kansa's determination to kill him. The newborn Krishna tells his father Vasudeva to exchange him with the new daughter of Nanda, chief of a cowherd tribe camped on the opposite bank of the Yamuna River. Thanks to Krishna's *maya,* power to befuddle the mind, neither Nanda nor his wife Yashoda recalls that their child was a girl, and they accept little Krishna as their own son.

He spends his childhood and teenage years in the forests of Braj among the cows and cowherds. Stories told of these years fall into three categories. Those of the first portray Krishna as an adorable and mischievous toddler who steals butter and stuffs dirt in his mouth, but also kills demons and performs superhuman feats. He makes friends and parents forget these wonders by using his maya. Stories of the second category portray him as a daring friend who saves his beloved companions from many dangers, including a forest fire, a devouring snake-monster in the river, and an angered Indra who pounds the cowherds with deadly storms. The third set of stories portrays him as an adolescent charmer, adored by all the *gopis,* young cowgirls of his community. When gopis bathe in the river as part of a vow to attract Krishna's attention, he steals their clothes and makes the girls emerge nude to reclaim them. Then he regrets his act and promises to spend a night dancing and making love with the girls beside the river. Krishna has one special girl friend, Radha by name, with whom he carries on a more extended affair. One major difference between the two sects dominant in Braj concerns Radha's status. Vallabhacharyas say she became Krishna's wife by means of a secret marriage; Gaudiyas say she was married to another.[26] All these actions and relationships have "transcendent" meanings, showing how devotees (the parents, friends, and cowgirls) need to lose themselves in the love of God.

---

[25] *Bhagavad-Gita* 6.25.22.

[26] A second and even more major difference concerns his status. Gaudiyas say he is first among avatars; Vallabhacharyas say he is God.

In the *Bhagavata-Purana* version of his stories, Krishna's idyll in the forest is inter-rupted when King Kansa learns where he is. Kansa plots to lure Krishna and his brother Balarama into a trap in Mathura. Krishna takes the bait, but foils Kansa's efforts to kill him. Instead, he kills Kansa and enthrones his birth father, the husband of Kansa's sister Devaki. Krishna spends the rest of his life as a reasonably well-behaved prince and king living within cities, the places of dharma. The high point of this royal phase of his existence is his participation in the war described in the *Mahabharata* and his instruction of Arjuna in this epic's *Bhagavad-Gita*.

Despite the respect most Krishna sects give to the *Gita,* the bulk of their atten-tion falls on the forest years of Krishna's story. For this reason, the Forest Pilgrimage holds the greatest prestige of those occurring in Braj.[27] Even though most of its forests are now gone, Braj is full of sacred sites where Krishna's forest adventures sup-posedly occurred. Many are richly developed, with pavilions and temples and ponds for pilgrim bathing. The latter are often said to have been dug and filled by Krishna himself. The Ban Yatra circle visits more than forty such sites, taking in all the most famous events of the *Bhagavata*'s Krishna story, plus a number known only via Braj's own oral traditions.

In September 1988, American scholar of Indian religions David L. Haberman made the Ban Yatra trek in the company of "five to six hundred" Gaudiya Vaishnava pilgrims. Six years later, he published *Journey Through the Twelve Forests,* an engaging reflection on his adventures.[28] Haberman's book is too long and too rich to be sum-marized fully, but a few important contrasts and comparisons between his trip and the Warkari pilgrimage can be made.

First, in keeping with the ideal of attaining "goal-free action," the Ban Yatra is a journey without a destination. In a sense, its pilgrim goes nowhere; he ends where he has begun, with the provision that his perspective on that beginning point should have changed. The ritual structure of the pilgrimage itself reflects this "going nowhere" orientation. The journey to get to Braj for Ban Yatra is not ritualized. Its formal beginning is in Braj itself, in the little town of Brindaban, where Haberman takes a vow to accept a local Brahmin as his "pilgrimage guru," and makes his pledge to complete the pilgrimage ritual.

In keeping with its central motif of spontaneous "play," the Ban Yatra is far less structured than the Warkaris' pilgrimage. Of course, five hundred people cannot trek two hundred miles without *some* form of organization. As in the Warkari pilgrimage, ox carts carry tents and supplies ahead of the trekkers and set up camps for them at night. At one point, Haberman also mentions the banner bearers, drummers, and cymbal players that accompany any sizeable pilgrim parade in India. Ban Yatra pil-grims are clustered into groups, each with its own guides to point out sites and explain them. Otherwise, variation reigns. Departure and arrival times shift from

---

[27] It is not the only one, or even the longest. The latter honor goes to a trek called Braj Yatra, which takes four months and covers 662 miles.

[28] *Journey Through the Twelve Forests: An Encounter with Krishna* (New York: Oxford Univ. Press, 1994). Haberman also later joined a portion of the Pushti Marga version of the Ban Yatra and sometimes compares the two journeys in his book. To avoid confusion, I shall refer only to the Gaudiya version.

day to day. Pilgrims are often awakened as early as 2 or 2:30 AM. They may arrive at a destination by early morning, or at 11 PM. The trek itself has no set procedures. Some pilgrims sing; others walk in silent meditation or talk with one another. Night camps are set up in no discernable order. Nor is there any order to the Krishna life unfolding before the pilgrims; sites of his love affairs come during the early and middle phases of the trip, adventures of his babyhood and childhood toward the end. Even the mode of pilgrimage itself changes at one point, as guides for Haberman's journey decide they will load their pilgrims on boats and float them down the Yamuna to riverbank sites, rather than have them walk as usual. According to Haberman, no two Ban Yatras are alike. Moreover, some of their dissimilarity appears to be intentional.

Although such play is a central feature of Ban Yatra, tapas is also crucial. Many of Haberman's fellow pilgrims walked the entire circuit barefoot. "Fifty to sixty" rode in horse-drawn carriages, but these were mostly people too old or ill to go on foot. Although Haberman's pilgrimage guru let him wear tennis shoes, his feet nonetheless swiftly blistered and bled. During much of the journey, the daytime temperature was over 100° Fahrenheit. The blistering heat was the principal reason why pilgrims were awakened so early; walking before sunrise was cooler. At one point, when the trek moved into the dry and rocky Aravalli Hills of easternmost Rajasthan, Haberman speaks of pilgrims vomiting from heat stress. At another point, he himself was covered with heat rash. Barefoot pilgrims stumbled on rocks while walking in the dark. All were sleep-deprived, and many fell ill from lack of rest, poor food, and poor sanitation. When the rains finally arrived, pilgrims were soaked and chilled, then steamed in the sun. A third of them gave up at some point and abandoned the journey. Oddly enough, this very struggle contributed to acceptance of the journey's play, even for Haberman himself. At the beginning of the journey, suffering from blisters and missing his family, he notes other pilgrims' euphoria with detachment. At the "village of Radha's maternal grandmother," he describes women pilgrims weeping, rolling in the dirt, dancing, and crying out "Radhe, Radhe!" as though their excitement is something alien and incomprehensible. But gradually he enters into the spirit of the pilgrimage.

At one point, he has an unsettling visionary experience. Early in the pilgrimage, near a site called "Radha's Pond," he meets a mysterious Bengali widow named Maya who lives full-time in the settlement at the site. After questioning Haberman and mocking his scholarly pretensions, she joins the trek and several times engages him further. During one encounter soon after the difficult hill trek, she guides him to a pond called Prema Sarovar, "Pool of Love." When she tells him to watch the pond's surface with "lila eyes," he sees in the waters a forest scene where a golden-skinned woman and dark-colored man decked with flowers first face one another trembling, then touch, and finally embrace. Maya later tells him that this pool "is where Krishna and Radha first experienced love for one another."[29] Acquiring such visions of God is another reason for doing pilgrimage in Braj. Braj is more than a common tirtha; to Krishna devotees it is God's dwelling place. God is always in Braj, beneath its surfaces, for those who are blessed with the eyes to see Him.

---

[29] Haberman, ibid., p. 179.

Finally, during a rainstorm, Haberman learns to play. A ridge of earth on which he is walking beside a flooded path gives way and he slips into the mud:

> Something inside me burst, and I could hold on no longer. I let go and surrendered to the water. The most wonderful thing then happened. Exploding with laughter, I realized that this *was fun*. I looked around and suddenly became aware that many others were laughing and playing in the rainy water, joyfully shouting 'Radhe, Radhe!' One man fell flat on his ass. He laughed. What a riot![30]

Haberman *was* changed by his pilgrimage, at least enough to understand what motivates other pilgrims to walk over stones in rain and sun for 200-plus miles. Like many other pilgrims, he was tested in the ascetic fires of the journey and found himself "loosened," able to let go and enjoy whatever the trek brought him. He was also educated into Krishna's life drama, as are all the many pilgrims who arrive in Braj, visit its sites, and hear their stories or view the Krishna plays performed there.

PERMANENT PILGRIMS

Given the sense of freedom that Haberman, a foreigner, won by means of his journey, one can finally comprehend why some Hindus opt for lives of permanent pilgrimage. We have already met these permanent pilgrims, the sadhus, in Chapter 2. Here we shall look at just two examples of their journeys. Both men to be described are swamis of the same lineage; the first taught a teacher of the second. But they lived in different times, separated by half a century. Their lives show not only the different directions that sadhu journeys can take, but also the change now affecting sadhu journeys in India.

Swami Tapovan

The first of the two lived during the first half of the twentieth century. The boy who would become Swami Tapovan Maharaj[31] was born in 1889, the oldest son of a well-to-do Nair caste family from the Malabar region of South India, now part of the state of Kerala. Like many well-to-do, upper-caste males of his time, he was sent to a local English-medium school to study in hopes that he would one day win a good job as a government servant. But he disliked the school and became a dropout, continuing his studies on his own. He studied Sanskrit and the texts of India's own classical heritage, as well as Vedanta philosophy and the lives of India's great modern saints. His mother died when he was still young, and his father when he was twenty-one, leaving him head of his family's household. Although relatives urged him to marry, he refused, concentrating on getting his younger brother through college and law school. For a while he was an editor, then a sought-after public speaker on religious and political subjects. His greatest love, nonetheless, was traveling to places where he could discuss religion with learned and saintly men.

Visiting the city of Madras, he met the head of the local Ramakrishna Mission, then later accepted an invitation to visit Mission headquarters in Calcutta. From

---

[30] Haberman, ibid., p. 198.

[31] Tapovanam Maharaja in Sanskrit.

Calcutta, he went to Banaras, then to Hardwar, Rishikesh, Mathura, Vrindavan, Pushkara, and Dwarka—all famous pilgrim centers. He began to fast strenuously and to withdraw from casual social contact. When his brother completed a law degree in 1923, Tapovan took a train north, telling his brother he wished to go on pilgrimage. He never returned. After studying for a time with a swami in Maharashtra, he took a vow of renunciation.

Now wearing a swami's robes, he went to the pilgrim centers of Prayag and Ayodhya, and then once again to Rishikesh, which he had come to love during his previous visit. There an ashram head initiated him into the Dasanami Sannyasi order. In the summer, he moved higher into the mountains, into Uttarkashi, a region that includes several major Himalayan pilgrim centers. He began trekking from tirtha to tirtha, even walking over the mountains into Nepal and Tibet, reaching the fabled Lake Manasarowar and Kailash, the mountain whose upper reaches are said to hold Shiva's paradise. Gradually, he evolved an annual pattern, spending winters in Rishikesh, then moving higher during the summers, hiking from one pilgrim site to another but stopping wherever he pleased to spend days in meditation. During winters he taught and wrote, acquiring considerable fame for his learning and his teaching skills. He never again descended farther from the mountains than Rishikesh, where the Ganga breaks through the Himalayan foothills. Although the life he had chosen was rigorous and he often suffered from illness, he lived to be nearly 68 years old, dying in January 1957.[32]

A collection of Tapovan's musings on his pilgrim travels has been published in English as *Wanderings in the Himalayas*.[33] The book can be frustrating to read because it does not order his journeys sequentially and often shifts suddenly from travelogue-style descriptions to reflections on classic Vedanta topics. Nonetheless, it yields a fine sense of this distinguished swami and his motivations for keeping to his wandering lifestyle. First of all, Tapovan clearly loves the mountains. Nearly every description of a mountain scene includes the word "beautiful," and his vivid depictions pull readers into the vistas he is recalling. Secondly, mountains are not just mountains for him. Just as the sites of Krishna's play are places of access to God for the devotee who travels to Braj, so the mountains are a gateway to God for Tapovan. Those who have eyes to see will recognize God within them. Recalling a failed attempt to reach the site where the epic hero Yudhisthira was carried to heaven, Tapovan breaks into verbal ecstasy:

> My heart was dancing with joy at the divine splendour all around me. . . . God himself shines here as this mass of spotless snow, as lakes and springs, as these powerful tall trees and these powerful cold blasts and these crystalline streams. All I see is God. The Himalayas are God. The entire earth is God. Everything exists in Him. Everything shines because of his brightness.[34]

The site he was trying to reach at this time reveals a third aspect of his fascination with the Himalayas. They are steeped in Hinduism's legendary history, touched by famed ancient sages and heroes. Near the temple of Badrinath, Tapovan describes a rock

---

[32] According to Nancy Patchen's bibliography of his famous student Swami Chinmayananda: *The Journey of a Master: Swami Chinmayananda* (Bombay: Central Chinmaya Trust, 1989), p. 201.

[33] Sri Swami Tapovanji Maharaj, rev. ed. (Mumbai: Central Chinmaya Mission Trust, 1990).

[34] Tapovan, ibid., p. 59.

where the Rishi Gaudapada composed his commentary on the *Mandukya-upanishad*. Twenty-four miles north of the town of Kullu, he finds the hot spring where Rishi Vasishtha spent much of his time doing austerities. Every place Tapovan reaches puts him in touch with the sacred past, makes him a part of its precious legacy.

Finally, his writings reveal the spirit of an adventurer who ventures into challenging circumstances in part because they *are* a challenge. Like all swami*s*, he travels light, wearing only his robe, sandals, and shawl, taking for protection only the walking stick customary for swamis. He eats whatever is offered along the way, sometimes fasting in places without human residents or living on buttermilk given in villages of herders. He sleeps on the ground and often reports shivering from cold at night, struggling to ford freezing currents in mountain streams, or tending fires all night to keep away wild animals. Several times he makes dangerous transits over high and snow-clogged passes, often despite warnings that these are currently too treacherous. He says of one, "Crossing the Lutang Pass was like passing through the terrible gate of hell."[35] Yet in that "gate of hell," he becomes so absorbed in the pass's splendor that he nearly loses track of the traders with whom he is traveling.

In short, Swami Tapovan was a classic sadhu, meeting the expectations spelled out in classic texts. He devoted himself to pilgrim travel, meditation, and study; sought out wilderness and ascetic hardship; avoided civilization, family ties, and property. Tapovan was not a loner; often he traveled with other sadhus or traders. He stopped to talk with pilgrim temple priests and mountain hermits, as well as the villagers who fed him. In Rishikesh, he taught disciples who came to him for instruction. But by and large, he did not look for hearers or view himself as a man with a teaching mission.

Today in India, many sadhus still walk the mountains and pilgrim routes like Swami Tapovan. They crowd great pilgrim centers, which often have special buildings and camping areas for them to stay in. They join pilgrim tours; several made the Ban Yatra with Haberman's group. Offering gifts to sadhus at tirthas is a common means of "loosening" pilgrim purses. Several Dharmashastras cite the chance to make such gifts as an important source of the merit that pilgrimage brings. Yet a new kind of sadhu is also emerging—one who seeks out audiences and population centers where potential listeners congregate. Sadhus of this new type ride in trains and planes, and their "pilgrim routes" may take them as far from the Himalayas as Kalamazoo, Michigan.

Swami Bodhananda

I first learned about Swami Tapovan from one of his spiritual descendants, a very modern swami named Bodhananda who had studied with a Tapovan disciple. Like Tapovan, Bodhananda was born in Kerala of Nair descent. But he grew up in a newly independent India and took on his orange robes because he believed that by doing so he could help fellow Hindus find their way through a changing and confusing world.

I met Swami Bodhananda in New Delhi in the fall of 1991. He was then teaching morning "classes" on alternating weekdays in the living room of a small rented house in back of the local market. One class was on the *Bhagavad-Gita* and another on *Viveka-Chudamani*, a difficult work by the Vedanta philosopher Shankaracharya. On some evenings, Bodhananda repeated his *Gita* lectures; early in the mornings he

---

[35] Tapovan, ibid., p. 131.

led guided meditations. A small fee charged for his classes paid for his teaching space. Collecting it was the head of the Sambodh Foundation, a local group established to support him. At that time, Bodhananda taught in a style classic to India—verse-by-verse commentary on his texts, spiced with witty observations on the life around him, all used to clarify his texts' terminology and concepts. He taught in English because few Delhi residents can understand Malayalam, his native language. Most of his morning-class students were college-educated housewives. Wondering what might attract housewives to a text as difficult as *Viveka-Chudamani,* I sat in on a class and was hooked, attending it whenever I was in the city. Little by little, I came to know Bodhananda. When he learned that I planned to travel in South India, he arranged for me and my aide to visit with his disciples in Kerala's capital city of Trivandrum. Later his own travels brought him to the United States. I taped his life story in my Kalamazoo living room.[36]

Bodhananda was born in a Kerala village, the oldest son of young parents who lived in their own household at some distance from their parents—an arrangement unusual in upper-caste India at that time, but more common today. He was a difficult, rambunctious child; U.S. counselors probably would have called him hyperactive. Knowing little about child rearing, his father tried to beat him into obedience. Several times he ran away from home to escape such punishments. Usually he went to his grandparents, but once, when he was older, he stayed with Ramakrishna monks at a Kerala branch of the Mission. At that time, he feared he had earned a poor grade on an important set of school exams. Instead, the relative who found him told him he had passed at the highest level, and so he returned home to enter college. His school was one of the many in India founded and led by Christians; ironically, many Hindu leaders of today's India are graduates of Christian schools and colleges.

Bodhananda's B.A. degree was in economics, and he emerged a Marxist, like many young Indians who wish to see India's social problems addressed and believe Marxist-style organizing offers a viable way to do this. Now, he moved to Delhi, hoping to gain admission to a prestigious graduate program in economics at the University of Delhi. This proved harder than he thought, and by the time he was successful, his father had tired of his absence and refused to advance him the funds that he needed to study. His life went into a tailspin; refusing to go home, he lived hand to mouth, picking up income through occasional copyediting and tutoring students. When he could, he rode buses north to the mountains, hiking them alone while he tried to figure out what to do with the rest of his life.

One day a friend with whom he loved to argue challenged him to attend talks by a swami of the Chinmaya Mission. This group had been founded by a man much like him: Swami Chinmayananda was an atheist and radical news columnist until he met Swami Shivananda at Rishikesh.[37] There, he became persuaded that Hindus wishing to live constructively in today's world could best accomplish this by tapping their own roots. Like Shivananda, Vivekananda, and others among India's "new gurus," Chinmayananda studied the Upanishads, *Bhagavad-Gita,* and Vedanta texts to see what guidance they could bring to Hindus now. He traveled the country making fiery

---

[36] Swami Bodhananda has reviewed my retelling of his life story as well as all other portions of this book that relate to his work in the United States and India.

[37] More is told about him in Chapter 10; see pages 251–53.

speeches that called Hindus to take pride in their spiritual heritage, then designed a training program for *sannyasis* who would be willing to follow his example.

Bodhananda became a regular attendant at Mission talks, then a highly successful apprentice instructor, and then a trainee in the Chinmaya program. Taking his vow of renunciation, he was sent back to Kerala to teach and began winning his own disciples. But he disliked the Chinmaya practice of building up new centers by sending star teachers and then reassigning those teachers elsewhere after formative work was done. He wanted to keep on guiding disciples who had begun their studies with him. Hence in 1989, just two years before I met him, he broke with the Chinmaya Mission and struck out on his own. By 1991, he had three centers, two in Kerala and one in New Delhi. Twelve years later, he had eleven ashrams and centers in India, had another underway in the United States, and was making regular U.S. teaching tours each summer. Two of his Indian centers also run small social service projects—in Trivandrum a residence center for the aged and in Kollam a vocational training center for handicapped girls.

When I returned to India for research in 1998, the Swami invited me to join a tour of *Bhagavad-Gita* lectures that he was planning in Bombay, Bangalore, and Trivandrum. His pattern of work in India had changed by then, adapting itself to the several types of conditions that he found locally. Needing to acquire greater flexibility, he had abandoned the regular "classes" in New Delhi and instead taught disciples in homes when he was in the Delhi area. Such informal meetings, called *satsangs,* "assemblies of the faithful," remain an important means through which teaching sadhus find new audiences. (Chapter 9 says more about them.)[38] Bodhananda also taught via household satsang during the Bangalore portion of his tour, offering nightly talks in the home of his host and hostess. This he could do comfortably, because his Bangalore following is small. In Bombay, he taught in a meeting hall of a large ashram with facilities for holding several such meetings simultaneously. Here he had taken a risk, for Bombay was new recruiting ground. His support group paid for news advertisements to draw an audience—not an uncommon practice these days for religious teachers trying to expand their reach. In Trivandrum, his much larger following had the resources to hire and fill a sizeable public auditorium.

He had changed his teaching style, too, picking up the American technique of approaching his topic as a whole and organizing it by nightly themes. Thus, he did not lecture on the *Gita*'s text itself, but rather on the messages that he perceives within the text. His central theme was one of "self-unfoldment"—learning to tap the inner resources of power, joy, and creativity that lie within all human beings, according to many Hindu religious teachings. Although surely something they had heard before, this nonetheless inspired his hearers. Most returned to hear his entire series. His wit and keen observation of human quirks continue to be an important feature of his presentations.

Bodhananda has also found a new audience, business managers. While touring, he held three "management seminars" at large companies, each lasting about two hours and involving both upper- and middle-level managers. In these seminars, his concept of self-unfoldment was transmuted into advice that managers should look for and encourage such self-unfolding creativity in employees—rather than the bootlicking that too

[38] See pp. 217–18.

often has carried over from India's old hierarchical and colonial systems. The *Gita's* message to work without regard for the fruits of actions became advice to middle managers that they should quit fretting about perks and focus on getting jobs done so their whole company and nation could benefit from their work. One manager who has become his disciple confided to me that the Swami's teachings had indeed changed his leadership style. Now he was getting much better cooperation from employees.

The perpetual pilgrimage of sadhus like Bodhananda is changing beyond the wildest imaginings of religious wanderers of the past. Not only is this taking them around the world but also into the very bastions of secular and materialistic values. And it is changing the roles of sadhus. Once holy "dropouts" seeking principally their own transformation, they have become missionaries, seeking to spread transformation throughout the world. Indeed, Bodhananda's tour reminded me far more of the tours of American circuit riders and evangelists than of the Himalayan wanderings of Swami Tapovan.

WHY GO ON PILGRIMAGE?

Many Hindus, of course, have more than strictly religious motivations for leaving home to go on pilgrimage. It allows them to separate themselves from their daily grind, to take stock of their lives, to visit new and interesting places. If a pilgrim site is high in the mountains like Vaishnodevi or on a great river or a seacoast, it can also be a place of breathtaking beauty.

Pilgrimage also offers the pilgrim a chance to meet new people and explore new ideas in places where the usual social walls are at least partially lowered. Recall that Swami Tapovan first started going to holy places to talk with the scholars whom he found there. The saint Chaitanya's career was launched by a guru he found while on pilgrimage to perform funeral rites for his father. Pilgrim journeys and sites are generators of informal education carried through songs and talks, textual recitations and plays. Pilgrim centers have for centuries been places for exchange between regional cultures. Exchanges between pilgrims have been one of the principal means through which news of devotional movements and their songs traveled from one region to another. As was seen in this chapter, pilgrimage offers hope. Power resides in pilgrim sites—at least as pilgrims themselves perceive these. It can heal, reverse bad luck, or offer a fresh start to those who have been stumbling. In addition, a pilgrim journey itself can be a challenge and a discipline that transfigures the pilgrim.

Finally, for the householder, a pilgrim journey offers a chance to try out for a time the discipline and stripped-down lifestyle of the renouncer. Life stories of many renouncers have shown that their vocations began with one or more pilgrim experiences. It is less common to find accounts of would-be renouncers who learned through pilgrimage that a wanderer's lifestyle was not for them, but I strongly suspect that this, too, is not uncommon. As for renouncers themselves, perpetual pilgrimage offers a way of structuring a life truly free of ties while not slipping into total aimlessness. There is always another holy place to visit—or another city in the world to which to carry one's message.

I do not mean to suggest that pilgrimage is always an exalting experience. The pilgrims with whom Ann Gold traveled encountered their fill of guides and priests haggling to raise the price of fees offered for their services. I have had the same experience myself. Pilgrim priests and guides must feed their families, and loosened purse strings for pilgrims mean opportunity for those who serve them. Large amounts of money flow through pilgrim centers and temples. They can be cash cows for the sectarian groups that control them, to the extent that some groups have come to blows over them. But again, greed at pilgrim sites is a global phenomenon, unique neither to Hindus nor to India.

ADDITIONAL SOURCES

There is no comprehensive study of pilgrimage in India. Surinder Mohan Bhardwaj's *Hindu Places of Pilgrimage: A Study in Cultural Geography* (Berkeley: Univ. of California Press, 1973) comes the closest. Readers are strongly encouraged to explore more fully the individual accounts discussed in this chapter: Kathleen M. Erndl, *Victory to the Mother: The Hindu Goddess of Northwest India in Myth, Ritual, and Symbol* (New York: Oxford Univ. Press, 1993); Surinder Mohan Bhardwaj, *Hindu Places of Pilgrimage: A Study in Cultural Geography*; Ann Grodzins Gold, *Fruitful Journeys: The Ways of Rajasthani Pilgrims* (Prospect Heights, IL: Waveland Press, 1988); E. Alan Morinis, *Pilgrimage in the Hindu Tradition: A Case Study of West Bengal* (New York: Oxford Univ. Press, 1984); Irawati Karve, "On the Road," *Journal of Asian Studies* 22:1 (1962): 13–29; G. A. DeLeury, *The Cult of Vithoba* (Poona: Deccan College Postgraduate and Research Institute, 1960); D. B. Mokashi, *Palkhi: An Indian Pilgrimage,* Philip Engbloom, trans. (Albany: SUNY Press, 1987); David L. Haberman, *Journey Through the Twelve Forests: An Encounter with Krishna* (New York: Oxford Univ. Press, 1994); and Sri Swami Tapovanji Maharaj, *Wanderings in the Himalayas,* rev. ed. (Mumbai: Central Chinmaya Mission Trust, 1990). Also recommended are Valentine Daniel's account of his own experiences as part of a popular and painful all-male trek to the shrine of Lord Ayyappan in South India in *Fluid Signs: Being a Person the Tamil Way* (Berkeley: Univ. of California Press, 1984), 245–87, and William S. Sax's *Mountain Goddess: Gender and Politics in a Himalayan Pilgrimage* (New York: Oxford Univ. Press, 1991).

The concept of tirtha itself is explored more fully in Diana Eck's "India's Tīrthas: 'Crossings' in Sacred Geography." *History of Religions* 20:4 (May 1981): 323–44. Eck's *Banaras, City of Light* (Princeton: Princeton Univ. Press, 1982) offers a detailed introduction to a major pilgrim center. Peter Van der Veer's *Gods on Earth: The Management of Religious Experience and Identity in a North Indian Pilgrimage Center* (London: Athalone Press, 1988) introduces the people who live and work at the pilgrim center of Ayodhya.

David R. Kinsley explores the emergence of the lila concept in *The Divine Player: A Study of Krsna Līlā* (Delhi: Motilal Banarsidass, 1979). William S. Sax's edited collection *The Gods at Play: Līlā in South Asia* (New York: Oxford Univ. Press, 1995) explores both the concept of lila as play and examples of sacred dramas. Examples of dramas strongly linked to pilgrim centers can be found in Sax's "The Ramnagar Ramlila: Text, Performance, Pilgrimage," *History of Religions* 30:2 (November 1990): 129–53, and John Stratton Hawley and Shrivastava Goswami, *At Play with Krishna: Pilgrimage Dramas from Brindavan* (Princeton: Princeton Univ. Press, 1981); also see Norvin Hein's *The Miracle Plays of Mathurā* (New Haven: Yale Univ. Press, 1972). Sacred dramas plus the life of a guru's family at Vrindavan (Brindavan) are described by Margaret H. Case, *Seeing Krishna: The Religious World of a Brahman Family in Vrindaban*. (New York: Oxford Univ. Press, 2000).

The tension between wild and settled areas is discussed in my own early essay "Wilderness and Kingship in Ancient South Asia," *History of Religions* 13:1 (August 1973): 1–15; see also French scholar Charles Malamoud's essay "Village et forêt dans l'idéologie de l'Inde brahmanique," in his *Cuire le monde: rites et pensée dans l'Inde ancienne* (Paris: Éditions la Découverte, 1989), 93–114.

PART III

Hinduisms of Caste and Class

Hindus of today often use the term *sanatanadharma,* "eternal dharma," to refer to their bundle of traditions. One should never make the mistake of assuming from this terminology that Hinduism is static and unchanging. If Hindu dharma has survived a long time, this is because it has adapted so skillfully to new conditions and challenges. The last 150 years have been a time of especially turbulent change for India, and India's Hindu traditions have experimented with a number of different ways to absorb and adapt to this change. Change has been most profound at the lowest and highest social levels, the two contexts to be examined in this section.

Change within them has been driven by somewhat different concerns. At low social ranks, a central motivation for change is the hope of improving social respect and economic mobility. This may not seem an appropriate subject for a religion text, but in India, as in many other regions of the world, various groups have struggled to attain respect and mobility through religion. At high ranks, concerns driving change have been more complex. The effort to deal with change coming from below is one such concern, but this is complicated by a matching need to address pressures coming from outside—pressures to "modernize," that is, to adopt Western intellectual systems and values. Once again, one might ask "What does this have to do with religion?" The answer is "A great deal," because religion is one of the principal means through which high-class Hindus maintain their own integrity while responding to such pressures.

A concept often used by Indian social analysts to interpret processes seen in this section is "hegemony." The literal meaning of this term derived from ancient Greek is "leadership" or "domination." Indian theorists as well as many Western social scientists use it with a special spin added by the Italian Marxist theorist Antonio Gramsci. Like all Marxists, Gramsci assumed that the central driving force of human history is class struggle: the effort of elite groups to dominate others and control the goods they produce and the effort of the dominated to break elitist yokes. Gramsci realized that two important means by which elite groups gain and maintain power are force of arms, that is, command of police and military forces, and economic power, the ability to give or take away access to livelihood. But he added a third, the power of hegemony, by which he meant the power to control thinking by means of messages beamed out by culture.

Gramsci compared the culture that surrounds humans—the stories, songs, sayings, rituals, art forms, advertisements, and so on—to a huge school that continually teaches people what to value, how to behave, and how to locate their place in the entire scheme of existence. The most effective and longest-lasting ruling classes, he said, were those who gained enough control of the cultural "school" surrounding them to insert into it a vision of the world that says their own preeminence is right and proper. If this message goes out in enough ways and makes enough sense to those who receive it, the hegemonic class will rule by consensus and does not have to apply more painful forms of coercion to back up its position. Gramsci argued that when a group achieves hegemony of this type it becomes very hard to dislodge. The only way to break its hold is to take apart the hegemonic vision and offer an alternative to replace it.

The four examples described in Chapter 8 illustrate a series of challenges to an existing hegemony. When the British established their colonies in India, the principal hegemonic system among Hindus was the system of Brahmin social teachings that defended caste hierarchy and reinforced caste standings by means of rules concerning purity and pollution. The first example described in Chapter 8 portrays a context in which this Brahmin-defined hegemony remains very much in place. Rules of purity and pollution structure the behavior of very low-caste Tamil villagers even though such rules operate to the low-caste group's disadvantage. The disadvantage is questioned only in the mildest of ways. The author of the study described argues that this is because the disadvantaged group has absorbed the values behind the rules; it perceives itself as lowly.

The second example, whose study is based on a longer historical sequence, also begins with the same hegemonic system firmly in place. In this case, low-caste villagers do challenge their low standing, but they do not question the rules and values that govern that standing. Instead, they try to use these to change their location within the system. Note, by the way, how nicely their effort dovetails with the find-ings by M. N. Srinivas described earlier in this volume.[1] In his writings on "Sanskritization" Srinivas argues that groups seeking to become "Hindu" adopt the rules and practice of Brahmin-transmitted Sanskrit-based culture; in effect, they opt into the Brahmin-transmitted hegemony. If a group is already "Hindu," but of lower-caste standing, it will attempt to shift its standing by adopting the practice of a group ranked higher in the caste system's pecking order. This is exactly what the Satnamis, the group in the second example, did first. But in the middle of their struggle they shifted tactics, a shift possible because the hegemony holding them in place had been weakened by changes in India's political structures.

Chapter 8's third and fourth examples portray the kind of revolutionary dynamics that Gramsci hoped his writings would foster in Europe. The groups described there have broken out of the greater consensus that kept them in place and have replaced its hegemonic vision with alternatives of their own. Enabling them to do this were changes occurring in India resulting from British colonial practice. One such was the chance for a few low-caste Indians to gain an education. Both the great low-caste leaders Jotirao Phule and Bhimrao Ambedkar began their remarkable careers in English-medium schools.

Another important development under British rule was the entry of British gover-nors and legal codes into Indian power structures. In effect, this deprived upper castes of the power to enforce the social norms their hegemony had created. Still another important shift in power allocation was the small experiment in democratic gover-nance for India that the British launched during the 1920s. This offered low-caste groups a chance to covert their numbers into power. They have continued to do this, bit by bit, as that experiment expanded to become independent India's system of par-liamentary democracy.

One alternative vision that has helped low-caste Indians garner the self-respect to claim power has been the teachings of Buddhism, taken up by followers of Ambedkar. Other bottom-caste groups not discussed in this chapter have turned to Christianity or Islam to help them shape their counter-hegemonic vision. Perhaps the most brash countervision has been the one first crafted by Phule and then taken up by Tamil Adi-Dravidas. It was also a product of efforts by British and European scholars to reconstruct India's earliest history. Early Indologists believed that the people called Aryas first entered India as invaders. Drawing on this construction of history, Phule and the Adi-Dravidas wove stories about how evil Aryas conquered their ancestors and stole their lands. Now the Brahmins whose lore helped them make this conquest had to be resisted.

---

[1] See the Introduction to Part I, p.17.

No counter-hegemonic account like this has taken hold among Hindus other than those who stand to benefit from it. Instead low-caste groups' accounts of their place in India's world are contending today with alternatives favored by groups of higher caste and class. Members of these more privileged groups have thus far been the principal beneficiaries of the struggle for Indian independence whose beginnings we saw in the chapter on the samajists. Many are blood descendants of the samajists themselves. All are samajist cultural heirs in the sense that their own practice presupposes the new values that the samajists implanted in Hindu India. They educate women and send their children to schools that provide English-medium education. They support the idea that low-caste groups should have access to the schooling and jobs that will let them change their standing. Virtually none would say that a person can be so polluted that he or she must not walk the same pavements as others, ride on the same buses, or enter the same temples.

Yet the same process of social change that samajists set in motion has plunged their descendants into an even bigger and more buffeting world than the one samajists tried to knit together with their own. Since Indians gained independence in 1947, what began as a bicultural class, part Indian, part British, has now become a community of full-fledged cosmopolitans. Upper-class Hindus travel and study abroad, watch CNN in their neighborhoods, and communicate by computer with business contacts around the world. They are battered by new ideas and new demands for their attention and commitment. Many of these new demands come from America, for in recent years the entire world has been subjected to the lure of a new hegemony spreading out of the United States. Its buzzwords are familiar terms: freedom, progress, development, modernity, globalization. These are attractive to upper-class Hindus, but also frightening. American exports and experts often come with them, promoting forms of dependence that—as upper-class Hindus know well—can easily turn into new forms of colonial subordination.

This means that upper-class Hindus are caught in a double squeeze. On the one hand, they are pushed from below, by groups no longer impressed by older worldviews that once validated their dominance. On the other, they are pressed to surrender to new views coming from outside of which they are rightfully suspicious. The system through which earlier Hindu elites validated their own worth has come apart in crucial places. Nonetheless, it still contains teachings and practice that many find meaningful and pleasing. Small wonder then that the upper-class and upper-caste Hindus described in this chapter are turning back to those teachings and practice to help them reassert their own value and identity.

Chapter 9 shows two different forms that this return has taken among the high-class, high-caste Hindus studied. It calls the women of New Delhi examined in its first case "seekers." Many formerly had little interest in religion. But now they are reexploring older traditions. Some attend lectures on sacred texts, chant Sanskrit together in homes, or gather for sessions of devotional song. Many are disciples of new Hindu movements that bridge sectarian divisions and sponsor ambitious programs of social service.

The second group of women surveyed in the chapter is the "keepers." Of Brahmin descent, they have a stronger vested interest in saving what is left of the old hegemony than the New Delhi women of the chapter's first part. They affirm their Brahmin heritage proudly and assertively. Nonetheless, while doing so, they are making quiet changes that expand their own role as women and that reach out toward connection with symbols important to caste groups below them. The author who did the research on these Brahmin women traces part of the initiative behind this change to the Hindu nationalist movement that has become a powerful force on the Indian political scene. Part IV will discuss both the new cross-sectarian movements and the Hindu nationalists at greater length. Hence the two studies described in Chapter 9 also serve as an introduction to these important new forces reshaping the practice and choices of Hindus.

One warning must be issued about the studies in Chapters 8 and 9. Among Hindus, two factors interact to determine who is of high or low social standing. One is the old factor of caste, transmitted by descent. This is what sociologists call an "ascribed" status; it is granted by the surrounding society because one has been born into a particular family lineage. The second is the factor of class, based on such factors as earning power, education, and prestige of office or occupation. This is an "achieved" status, implying that those who hold it have earned it by means of their own effort. In today's India, caste and class operate somewhat independently of one another. A few individuals or groups of low-caste standings have raised their class standings through education, successful entrepreneurship, or political office. Not all untouchables are poor, although many remain so. A somewhat different situation is true for high-caste Hindus. A fair number achieved high-class standing; indeed, the majority of socially and economically advanced Hindus are also descendants of high-caste families. On the other hand, many high-caste Hindus are of middle income or even slipping into the ranks of the poor. Indeed, this downward social mobility of once-advantaged groups is one of India's main sources of social friction. Groups described in Chapter 8 are both low in caste and poor. Chapter 9, however, first describes a group that is high in class but mixed in caste, then turns to a group high in caste but mixed in class. Some of the differences seen in this chapter reflect not only differences in the regions of the two groups described, but also differences in the groups' caste\class mix.

8

Among the Poor and Oppressed

At 7 AM in the fall and winter, a wealthy New Delhi neighborhood is a busy place. The last early morning walkers are still on the streets, while outside workers who tend homes, cars, and gardens are already starting to appear. One such worker I came across often during a recent visit was a woman, perhaps in her fifties, whose flattened nose and missing front teeth suggested she had led a less than easy life. Her job was to sweep the preceding day's trash from the street. Like other Indian sweepers, she did this squatting, using as a broom a bundle of flexible twigs bound together. When other walkers passed her, she kept her face down, looking like little more than a bundle of rags fallen from some truck to the ground and stirred by a morning breeze. But each time I came by, she looked up, smiled, and pressed her palms together before her in the gesture called *namas*, homage. When the time came for giving gifts to servants during the Diwali holiday period, there she was also in the part-timers' line, waiting for the small tip my landlady gave her. I never spoke to her, never did more to establish a bond between us than to *see* her and hence to acknowledge the tiny space she occupied within my world.

The woman of my morning walks was of the Sweeper jati, one of the lowest of the many very low-ranking Hindu communities that used to be given the collective name "untouchables." Today, it is more correct to call them "former untouchables" because the ritual exclusions once practiced against them are now forbidden by India's constitution. By law, all former untouchables can now enter temples to worship, walk on roads leading to holy places, sit in schoolrooms beside high-caste classmates, draw water from public wells, own land, and in general move about without warning others of their polluting presence or trying to be invisible. In practice, especially in villages, most still experience multiple forms of discrimination, enforced by social consensus and unable to be resisted because of their usual poverty and economic dependence on groups ranking above them.[1]

The New Delhi Sweeper woman's tip from my much higher-caste landlady was a relic of the old system that once kept her fellow caste-mates in their much-scorned place.

---

[1] For examples of continuing problems, see Sukhdeo Thorat, "Oppression and Denial: Dalit Discrimination in the 1990s," *Economic and Political Weekly* 37:6 (February 9, 2002): 572–78.

In the agricultural villages that for centuries held most of India's population, the system of *jajmani* ensured that those who controlled the land received essential services. Its central premise was *jati,* an institution that reserved certain functions for specific groups who retained a monopoly over them by practicing internal marriage. Each village was usually dominated by a single landholding jati, often a remnant of a tribe that once controlled the region or descended from some family once sent by a nearby ruler to settle in that place and develop its lands for cultivation. Settled also on village lands were satellite families whose inherited specializations were needed to keep a settlement thriving: priests, scribes, healers, accountants, potters and other artisans, washermen, barbers, oil-pressers, village watchmen, tanners and shoemakers, sweepers, and the drummers essential to all festivals. In exchange for providing the services to which jati membership assigned them, such families acquired shares in produce from the village lands, as well as access to portions of those lands, such as common grazing areas for village goats and cattle.

As noted elsewhere in this volume, not all jati-inherited functions were equally valued, even though all were essential to village well-being. Correspondingly, the respective jatis that fulfilled them came to be ranked hierarchically within village social systems. All but the topmost jati had others above them to whom they showed deference by various means. All but the very lowest had jatis below them from whom deference was expected. Much of this ranking of jatis and exchange of jati-based services still survives in today's India, even though the landholding system on which it was based has changed.

In 1970, French sociologist Louis Dumont published an ambitious analysis of the principles upon which jati and varna ranking were traditionally based.[2] Underlying this system, he claimed, was the same deep-set opposition between purity and pollution that affects so much Hindu ritual life. Groups whose services required them to maintain a high state of purity gravitated to the top of caste rankings. Those whose services and lifestyles enmeshed them deeply in pollution sank to the bottom, whereas others with lighter pollution burdens were strung out in between.

Dumont's study has been much criticized by Indian sociologists, who point out the many examples of groups whose place in social rankings cannot be accounted for by so simplistic a measure as the purity\pollution dichotomy; high-caste warrior groups, for example, eat meat, drink alcohol, and shed blood, all pollution-producing activities. Nor can the dichotomy explain the differences in mid-caste rankings that often occur from village to village. The purity\pollution dichotomy nonetheless does seem to account for the caste system's extremes. It explains, for example, how Brahmins who follow strict rules of ritual purity have been able over the centuries to claim the very highest status despite their economic dependence on lower-caste patrons and donors. It also shows how certain groups in various regions of India acquired untouchable standing and sank to the very bottom.

Such bottom-caste groups have experienced a peculiar dilemma within the complex of practices and beliefs now called "Hindu." On the one hand, services of several low-caste jatis are integral to maintaining the Hindu ritual system. Without their interventions to receive and remove pollution, high-caste practice cannot survive.

---

[2] *Homo Hierarchicus: an Essay on the Caste System,* Mark Sainsbury, tr. (Chicago: Univ. of Chicago Press, 1970).

On the other hand, performing these same essential services often pollutes low jati members to such an extent that they themselves cannot fully join into practice of the system. They are included, it would seem, only to carry out functions that exclude them. In the past, such exclusion was so thorough that many higher-caste Hindus did not classify the lowest jatis as Hindu at all. They were outcastes, outside the reach of dharma and its categories. Only recently, and often for political reasons, have many Hindus considered them part of the Shudra varna.

Most past academic studies of Hindu thought and practice have played a similar game of simultaneous inclusion\exclusion when the time came to discuss groups of very low caste. On the one hand, a text might acknowledge their despised status as an unfortunate negative by-product of the Hindu system. Its reader might learn that even the mere shadow of a polluted untouchable falling across a high-caste Hindu could require the high-caste Hindu to go home, bathe, and change clothes, or that such untouchables could not enter temples—but sometimes became great saints. The text might point to untouchables' low education levels, their poverty, and efforts by high-caste reformers to raise their status. Nonetheless, they were mostly portrayed as recipients of definition and actions. Only rarely did any study approach them as agents shaping their own roles, defining or at least trying to define the direction of their own lives.

This chapter is an attempt to rectify that situation, showing how bottom-status Hindus have responded to their places within the hegemonic "Hindu system." Four different kinds of responses are studied. The first, exemplified by villagers of the Drummer caste in Tamilnadu, is simple conformity to the prevailing system's norms. Over the centuries, this has been the most common response to caste discrimination. Readers should never assume, however, that conformity means acceptance. Often, differences of power and economic resources are so great between high and low castes that challenge to the system is not an option. The second response, exemplified by a sect called Satnamis in central India, entails appropriation of high-caste values to challenge status. Taught by their surrounding community that low status is a result of polluting habits, Satnamis changed their habits. This, unfortunately, accomplished little other than exposing the hypocrisy of their high-caste neighbors. Satnamis did later alter their status somewhat by taking advantage of changing political structures. The third series of movements examined, so-called non-Brahmin movements of western and southern India, offered adherents an alternative way to account for structures that oppressed them. So they could reject the older system's values and attempt to instill others in their place. Again, this was made possible in part by shifts in existing power structures. The last group considered, followers of the Maharashtrian leader Bhimrao Ambedkar, at first tried to change their circumstances via politics, but later turned to mass religious conversion. These latter three movements have by no means been the only three efforts among low-caste Hindus to take on the structures that keep them subordinate. More will be mentioned along the way. And others are beginning to surface via new studies.[3]

---

[3] One study I would have summarized had I found it soon enough is Ramdas Lamb, *Rapt in the Name: The Ramnamis, Ramnam, and Untouchable Religion in Central India* (Albany: State Univ. of New York Press, 2002). Ramnamis did not challenge the system so much as transcend it via intense devotion to the name of Ram.

CONFORMING TO HIGH CASTE NORMS:
DRUMMERS OF TAMILNADU

To help readers understand the practice described below, the premises behind it must be explored more fully. What services offered by one group of people to another could be so polluting that simply to perform them locates the doer on the bottom of the social pile? Recall that the worst pollution stems from two types of activities. The first removes bodily outflows: excreta, menstrual flows, blood from childbirth. Cut or shaved hair is also polluting. Before the introduction of flush toilets, a Sweeper such as the woman I encountered in New Delhi would have removed night soil from city latrines, a major source of her caste's very intense pollution. The second set of deeply polluting tasks puts the doer into contact with death and its by-products: corpses, cremation rites and grounds, any form of animal slaughter, pelts stripped from dead animals and tanned into leather. Performing such services is so contaminating that groups who do this are considered unpurifiable.

Remember that pollution is also transmitted through contact. High-caste Hindus of the past therefore would not risk any contact with someone from a deeply polluted group—hence the label "untouchable" assigned to such groups. Nor could members of deeply polluted groups live near persons at a higher level of purity. For this reason, a classic Hindu "village" included at least two hamlets: one where touchable caste groups lived and went about their business, and another for untouchables who entered touchable boundaries only to remove the contaminants within them.

In 1972, American ethnologist Michael Moffat set out to study the culture of a once-untouchable hamlet in Parangudi village in Tamilnadu. Initially, Moffat followed the participant observer method popularized by ethnologist Bronislaw Malinowski. For three months, he lived for several days each week in a hut at the edge of the bottom-caste settlement, sharing as much of its everyday activity as he found bearable and his higher-caste neighbors found tolerable. That proved too awkward and stressful an arrangement, and finally Moffat left without completing his research. A year later, he returned to work in another Tamil village named Endavur. This time he lived at a local hospital and visited the low-caste hamlet with a Tamil research assistant to help him conduct interviews. Although the earlier experience gave him a sense for the feel of bottom-caste life, the work that he finally published draws most of its data from the latter experience.[4]

Moffat especially wished to learn to what extent the bottom-caste groups he studied drew on values and models prevalent in the higher caste culture surrounding them. He concluded, somewhat to his own surprise, that the low-caste groups seemed to accept the high-caste system. They even structured their own social rankings in accordance with its values. "The cultural system of Indian untouchables does not distinctively question or revalue the dominant social order. Rather, it continuously recreates among Untouchables a microcosm of the larger system."[5]

---

[4] Michael Moffat, *An Untouchable Community in South India: Structure and Consensus* (Princeton: Princeton Univ. Press, 1979).

[5] Moffat, ibid, p. 3.

Moffat supports this claim by analyzing two aspects of village life where values are reflected: caste ranking and interaction with deities. To follow his argument, it is necessary to learn three terms describing the spaces within which he worked. According to Moffat's description, Endavur itself was a *kiraamam,* a settlement taxed as a single unit, like the kirama of Kannapuram described earlier in this volume.[6] Endavur's hamlet of touchable residents was known locally as an *uur,* a unit of distinctive identity for Tamils because all who live within one uur are said to absorb and reflect its character.[7] Its untouchable hamlet, in contrast, was called a *ceeri,* "colony," a term that conceded its status as an outpost of the "real" village, the uur. Entry to either of these two units was restricted for residents of the other. In former times, ceeri residents had to stay off uur streets entirely, unless they were there to fulfill a traditional duty, such as removing a dead animal. When Moffat conducted his studies, uur residents still cleansed themselves after going within boundaries of the ceeri. Living beyond even the ceeri were a few families so low that even other bottom-ranked jatis refused to let them dwell within their own colony's boundaries.

Caste Rankings and Pollution

Regarding caste ranking and practice within this complex of spaces, Moffat found that low-caste groups did not stop at merely conforming to the system that said they were lowly and forced them to live outside uur boundaries. They also generated internal ranks among themselves that were ordered according to the high-caste premise that doing polluting jobs will pull rank down. The overall kiraamam caste hierarchy consisted of some nineteen jatis distributed among 295 households. In the three highest ranks, representing members of only nine households, Moffat found one Brahmin family, three of Accountants, and five of Reddiyars, who once controlled all village lands and still own much village acreage. In the next ten rankings were groups identified with special skills, such as Weavers, Merchants, Herdsmen, Florists, Artisans, Basketmakers, Washermen, and Barbers. All from these thirteen rankings resided within the uur and hence could be considered the village's base community.

Of the thirteen caste-groups described above, four were especially affected by the pollution\purity dichotomy. The Brahmin claimed top ranking by virtue of the purity he maintained to serve the local Shiva temple and to lead life-cycle rites for high-caste residents. Moffat notes, however, that this same Brahmin held lesser rank among Brahmins outside the village. This was because he served a temple and hence had to accept gifts from castes ranked below him. Far lower in rank than he, however, in positions eleven through thirteen, were three jatis whose services entailed pollution acceptance. A member of the village Basketmaker jati also served as *pucari,* or priest, for the uur's goddess, a Mariyamman. Others of this group served as pucaris during the annual festival for the kiraamam goddess Selliyammam, an alternate form of Mariyamman. Pucaris are of low rank because they become possessed by dangerous and polluting aspects of the goddess; they also perform the blood sacrifice

---

[6] See p. 150. Kiraamam and kirima are the same term, transliterated differently by different authors.

[7] As described by anthropologist Valentine Daniel in *Fluid Signs: Being a Person the Tamil Way* (Berkeley: Univ. of California Press, 1984). Again, ur and uur are the same term.

required by the goddess in her terrible manifestations. The single Washerman family, ranked just below them, provided the uur's laundry services, whose tasks included accepting cloths stained by menstruation and childbirth. Next came two Barber families. Men of these families shave heads and body hair for ritual occasions and perform as an "auspicious band" during upbeat uur celebrations such as weddings. Performing in such a band is downgrading because of contact with drums whose heads are made of leather. Furthermore, Barber women serve as midwives to higher caste families, a function such women fill in most Indian regions. Midwifery brings them in contact with childbirth blood, a highly polluting and dangerous substance.

Just one single group lower than Barbers had access to the uur—five families of Forest Persons who hunted small game and sold it to village meat eaters. Below these came jatis so low that they had to live in the ceeri and even families who received pollution from higher castes would not serve them. The highest of these were Velluvar Pandarams, astrologers whose services were often sought by members of caste groups above them.[8] Yet they were outside the uur because one member of their jati served as a surrogate Brahmin for untouchable families, who were so polluted that a true Brahmin could not come near them. Like the uur's Brahmin, this surrogate officiated at life-cycle rites and served as "pure" priest during the annual festival of the ceeri's goddess. He had even adopted the symbols and dress of a Brahmin, shaving his head except for a Brahmin-style topknot, baring his chest and covering it with ash, and wearing a sacred thread and a clean unstitched waistcloth. Nonetheless, he used no Sanskrit mantras in his rituals.

Below the Velluvar Pandarams came the Drummers. By the time of Moffat's research, these were calling themselves Harijans, "children of God," a name Mohandas Gandhi coined for untouchables during the struggle for Indian independence. Their original name Paraiyans, "drummers," had been derived from the name of a drum called *parai,* whose head is made of stretched calfskin. This drum was played for inauspicious occasions, such as funerals, blood sacrifice, angry goddess possession, and processions that pass through places where spirits of the dissatisfied dead congregate. Below the Paraiyan Harijans were the Harijan Washermen, duplicating functions of the uur-dwelling Washerman jati, but lower in status because they accepted pollution from untouchables. During colony goddess festivals, Harijan Washerman served as pucaris, thus matching roles taken by Basketmakers at uur and kiraamam celebrations. Even lower than these very low groups and excluded even from the ceeri were families of two other jatis: three households of Leatherworkers and two of Crow Catchers, scavenging trappers so despised that they were untouchable even to other untouchables.

Most important to Moffat's argument were the Velluvar Pandarams and Harijan Washermen, who performed for bottom-ranked jatis the services done for uur-dwelling families by the local Brahmin and the Washermen proper. According to Moffat, the standing of the Astrologers within their community shows that even bottom-ranked jatis prize ritual purity and seek out the purest officiants they can find when they themselves have need of ritual services. The status of Harijan Washermen shows that even caste groups deemed hopelessly impure feel a need to

---

[8] These are equivalent to the Pantarams of Chapter 5.

have others take impurity from them. Moreover, those called untouchable may have others whom even they will not touch, as shown by the miserable status of Crow Catchers.

Even divisions within jatis evaluated their rankings according to criteria of purity and pollution. By far the largest caste group in Endavur at the time of Moffat's study was the Drummer jati, whose 98 households outnumbered even the 69 Weaver households, the most from a single caste among uur residents. Although most so-called Drummers earned their living through field labor, this jati had to delegate members to carry out six duties that were special to the caste. These duties, in turn, were allocated according to three internal Drummer subdivisions. These divisions, in turn, were ranked, and one determinant of their rank was the pollution entailed in the assigned duties. The highest-ranked subdivision furnished an assistant to the local police inspector—a position entailing a fairly low level of pollution. The middle-ranked furnished "announcers" to the village; because these announced village deaths, their pollution level was higher. The third and lowest-ranked group provided parai drummers and cremation ground attendants. Bottom-ranked Drummers also carried away dead cattle that fell within the village and acted as village night watchmen, a duty that risked encounters with night-roving dissatisfied dead. All three of their services were considered highly polluting.

A second important factor in determining lower ranking was eating habits among the three Drummer divisions. This calls attention to an aspect of untouchable status left out of our discussion thus far. Higher castes claim that untouchables are polluted not just by the duties they perform but also because they eat beef, ordinarily forbidden to Hindus. Many poor people do eat beef in India, mostly because it is cheap and hence the only meat the poor can afford. Drummers studied by Moffat told him that part of the reason some ranks were lower was because they had less desirable beef-eating habits. The highest ranked Drummers did not eat beef at all. The middle ranked ate only beef that was freshly killed. The lowest ate flesh of the already-dead cows that they cut up and removed from village streets.

Interaction with Deities

When interacting with deities, too, Endavur's bottom-caste residents acted in ways consistent with higher caste beliefs and values. Like people in many other areas of India, Endavur residents believed that their world held a broad spectrum of superhuman beings. At one end of this spectrum were the deities called super-gods in this book. They were very exalted, pure, well-intended gods with extremely wide-ranging and vaguely defined powers, in short, they were the deities central to Hindu sectarian practice. In the middle of the spectrum were deities of mixed nature: more accessible to humans and with powers more clearly defined, but also less predictable, swinging between calm good favor and demands for blood. They were deities such as the goddesses of lineage, settlement, and realm described earlier in this book.[9] At the opposite end from the super-gods were beings almost wholly lowly, impure, chaotic, and dangerous to humans. In Endavur, these were called *peeys* and *pisasus*. As elsewhere

[9] Chapter 6, pp. 146–58.

in India, such dangerous beings were often said to be ghosts of people who had died by accident or suicide. Possessing some unfortunate who crossed their paths, they revealed their presence by bringing persistent bad luck and unexplained physical or mental illness. Unlike the beings of higher standing, rituals done for such beings aimed at driving them away from the performers' presence.

Among pure or mixed-nature deities, each Endavur adult singled out at least five for special attention. One was the "chosen" god, usually a high or semi-high sectarian deity who in fact had "chosen" the worshiper by manifesting its power, for example, by curing a persistent illness. The second was a household deity, usually the spirit of a wife who had died auspiciously, with her husband still alive. Like satis of Rajasthan, such departed wives of Tamilnadu act as family protectors. A third type of deity honored by all Endavur residents was a deity of family line, comparable to the kuldevis described in Rajasthan. The fourth was the hamlet deity, who in Endavur was a Mariyamman with two manifestations, one guarding the uur and the second the ceeri. The fifth was the kiraamam goddess Selliyamman, said to be a form of Parvati once trapped into servitude by a demon after making a rash promise. Mariyamman and Selliyamman festivals described by Moffat both emphasize themes of cooling and reintegration somewhat like those of the Mariyamman festival described in an earlier chapter. But they differ in detail; even within the same region of India, local goddess festivals vary considerably.

Most important to Moffat's argument was his finding that all caste groups, even lowly Drummers, claimed access to and considered "theirs" all levels of deity. Moffat concedes that he found few worshippers whose chosen gods were the very pure deities Vishnu or Shiva, and he found these only at Parangudi, the first village he studied. At Endavur, the chosen god most prevalent among low castes was Murugan, a god popular throughout the Tamil region. Moffat concedes, too, that none of the bottom-caste Hindus he studied would have dared attempt worship of their chosen deity at any local temple where their caste might be recognized, despite their constitutionally granted right to do so. One teacher reported going on pilgrimage once a year to a Murugan temple at some distance from the village. But even there, when asked his caste, he answered Adi-Dravida, claiming affiliation with a movement usually supported by higher-caste Shudras.[10]

Moffat found only four significant differences between high- and bottom-caste practice relating to deities. First, when bottom castes needed a priest, they called on the Velluvar Pandaram, not on the mantra-reciting Brahmin. Second, the deity worshiped at the annual hamlet goddess festival was the Mariyamman of the ceeri, not the uur. Her ceeri temple served as focus of the festival, and the ceeri's Washermen acted as pucaris, even though rites performed were much the same as those in the uur. Third, during the festival of the kiraamam goddess Selliyamman, untouchables stood at a greater distance from the temple than uur residents. Also, during her procession from "wilds" to "village," she never actually entered the ceeri's space, waiting outside for its residents to come and meet her. Fourth, and perhaps most importantly, whenever impure peeys and pisasus had to be driven back to their own wild spaces, men of the Drummer jati did this. All castes shared the premise that the Drummer

---

[10] See the discussion of Adi-Dravidas later in this chapter, pp. 208–09.

jati could best handle this job because such beings are managed best by the humans closest to them in nature.

In sum, Moffat argues, the low-caste Hindus he studied acted much like Hindus of higher castes, and the practices they engaged in were based on the same values. He concludes from this that the two groups viewed the world in the same way and hence, in effect, the low-caste Hindus concurred with their own subjugation. Here, many critics argue that he went too far. One argument raised against him is that he failed to take into account the importance of power discrepancies within the villages he studied. When one group holds a great deal of power over another, the second will act in accordance with the first group's expectations. But this is a matter of sheer self-preservation; it does not necessarily mean that both *think* the same way. A subjugated group may well question inwardly the behaviors forced upon it and often expresses such questioning in covert ways. A second critique of Moffat is that his research was not structured to pick up such covert questioning. He did not look at songs low-caste people sang when high castes were not listening or at sayings they might have used to comment on their standing. Nor did he ever ask them directly what they thought of their own pollution.

Indeed, two of Moffat's findings show that his subjects did question their low status to some extent. The first was the name that the Drummer jati chose for itself. "Paraiyan," the old caste name, is loaded with negative connotations; in fact, the English term "pariah," scorned one, was derived from this Tamil word. The alternative "Harijan," adopted by Moffat's subjects, was promoted by Gandhi. Meaning "children of God," it was intended to raise untouchable self-respect and to promote unity among India's many untouchable jatis. The latter purpose remains unaccomplished; Moffat himself notes that "Harijan" is becoming simply a caste label in Tamilnadu. If one local caste takes it up, others use it just for that group. Still, the very fact that the name is claimed implies some rejecting of the denigration entailed in other caste titles.

A second indication of dissent is the story Drummers told to account for their status. They are descendants, they said, of the oldest son of Shiva and Aadi, the world's first woman. One day the older brother volunteered to cook while the family was preparing beef. When a piece fell out of the boiling pot, he hid it under the ashes, to avoid being charged with carelessness. But the others found it and accused him instead of selfishly hiding it for himself. Hence, he was disgraced and forced to live separately from the rest of his family. Untouchable status, this story suggests, is a fluke, the result of an ancient mistake never rectified. The cast-out brother should really be honored. After all, he was the oldest! His exclusion is not fair. He may have acted poorly, but the punishment is out of proportion to the wrong.

Another Tamilnadu ethnologist, French scholar Robert Deliége, asserts that stories such this are common among former untouchables throughout India.[11] Drawing on his own studies, Deliége modifies Moffat's assertions. As a general rule, he argues, "Untouchables have never challenged caste values and the behavior they engender. What they do contest is their own position in the system. They legitimize untouchability,

---

[11] See his discussion of "Untouchable Myths of Origin," *The Untouchables of India*, Nora Scott, tr. (Oxford: Oxford International Publishers, 1999), 71–80.

but refuse to accept that their own caste is polluting and degraded."[12] This may or may not be true of the Drummers studied by Moffat. But it does describe accurately the stance taken by the sect called Satnamis in central India.

APPROPRIATING PURITY: SATNAMIS OF CHHATTISGARH

The Satnami challenge to untouchability dates to the beginning of the nineteenth century. The best source through which to trace it is *Untouchable Pasts,* written by India-born ethnohistorian Saurabh Dube.[13] The Satnamis were a religious sect founded around 1820 in the region of Chhattisgarh, now the state of the same name.[14] It drew most of its membership from the Chamar jati, Chhattisgarh's largest untouchable community, constituting about one-sixth of the region's population. Traditionally in central India, Chamars had been leatherworkers, charged also with the duty of removing dead cows from village streets. In Chhattisgarh, however, Dube points out, most had become agricultural field workers. Before the Satnami sect was founded, a combination of economic and political factors had even made it possible for some Chamars to become landlords who controlled their own villages. By 1820, however, these external factors were changing and local Chamar fortunes were deteriorating.

Satnami Beginnings

The Satnami founder Ghasidas was himself a Chamar and an agricultural laborer.[15] Stories of the sect's founding say that from the time of his childhood he showed signs of miraculous abilities. One day his master saw Ghasidas's plough moving on its own; Ghasidas's hand merely hung in the air above the plow's handle. The founder's decisive moment of calling came after two bullocks he used for ploughing wandered from their pasture onto a nearby mountain. Pursuing them, he encountered a pure white figure who said to him: "I had sent you to reform the lineage, but you have forgot and have started working for others. This entire Chamar lineage has got spoilt. Have you forgotten this? Intoxicated by meat and liquor, these holy men have got ruined. You spread the name of *satnam.* I am *satnampurush,* know me."[16]

When Ghasidas failed to carry out this charge, Satnampurush caused the deaths of his wife and children. (He later restored them.) In his grief, Ghasidas fled into the hills and tried to destroy himself, but Satnampurush pursued him. Finally, Ghasidas accepted his calling. After purifying himself through austerities for six months, he returned to his former home and began to preach and initiate disciples. He threw his

---

[12] Ibid., p. 77.

[13] Saurabh Dube, *Untouchable Pasts: Religion, Identity, and Power among a Central Indian Community, 1780–1952* (Albany: SUNY Press, 1998).

[14] Encountered previously in Chapter 5, p. 128.

[15] Two preceding sects called Satnamis are recorded in northern India, one founded in 1657 and another at the start of the eighteenth century. Although they share a few common characteristics, no direct connection has been shown between them. Dube, op. cit., pp. 36–39.

[16] Dube, op. cit., p. 120.

people's deity images on the village rubbish heap, saying they must worship only *satnam,* "True Name," the God without form. He also told them not to eat meat, remove dead cows, or deal in hides, and not to use tobacco, intoxicants, or a number of red vegetables associated with blood: tomatoes, chilies, eggplant, and red lentils. His disciples were not to use cows for plowing, not to plow after midday meals, and not to mix or eat with low-caste people who did not follow Satnami injunctions. If others did take up these injunctions, however, Satnamis had to treat them as equals. Satnamis were not to recognize caste distinctions that had divided them in the past: neither internal rankings among Chamars themselves nor distinctions between Chamars and other castes. A few non-Chamars did join the Satnami community, mostly from other groups of comparable caste ranking.

To mark their new-found unity and commitment, Satnamis wore a black string with wooden beads called a *kanthi,* tied on them at the time of initiation. They remained householders, but rejected many standard household practices. Their only journeys to sacred places were the ones they made to their own meetings of the pious. They observed three sacred days from the Hindu ritual calendar but redesigned these to celebrate their gurus. They retained rites of passage such as name-giving, marriage, and funerals, but invited as officiants only their own guru-appointed priests. During his lifetime, Ghasidas himself was guru to his community. After his death around 1850, his older son replaced him. By this time the Satnamis were well established, with an estimated membership of 250,000.

As Dube has pointed out, much of Satnami practice was a refusal of Chamar caste status. In effect, Satnamis challenged their neighbors to take seriously the principle that purity meant high standing. Hence, they ended all polluting activities: handling dead cattle, eating meat and other suspect foods, drinking intoxicants, and associating with people who indulged in such activities. Swearing to worship the formless power satnam, they linked themselves to the highest and purest form of Hindu deity. By refusing to honor images, they also removed themselves from ritual situations in which their low-caste standing had to be acknowledged. Setting up their own priesthood, they sidestepped all contexts in which Brahmins could refuse to serve them. They likewise avoided all dealings with non-Satnami Barbers, Washermen, Confectioners, or Graziers—other castes that in their region performed ritual services for caste groups above them.

Claiming to be purer than the very pure high castes, Satnamis later began wearing sacred threads after they came of age. They marked Satnami settlements with "victory pillars," high bamboo poles topped by white triangular flags that resemble the standards mounted in Hindu temples and carried before kings. Also entailing claims to high-caste standing were the elephants and horses that accompanied Satnami gurus out on tour. Normally, these animals took part only in royal or divine processions. Another innovation that promoted internal coherence was the addition of two levels of organizational hierarchy mediating between the guru and priests who serviced individual settlements. *Diwans* served as guru advisors and aides, whereas *mahants* supervised districts of between five to one hundred villages. Other village officiants besides the bhadari priests were *sathidars,* functioning much as barbers did in orthodox Hindu villages.

How did these efforts affect Satnami status? Initially, they brought mostly ridicule and resistance. Higher castes made a point of calling Satnamis Chamars and treating them as the despised caste from which most Satnamis had come. If anything, Satnamis' "uppity" pretensions increased the likelihood that other Hindus would abuse and cheat them. High-caste Hindus challenged in court their claim to wear sacred threads, issued restrictions on what they could wear, and forbade them from riding horses, elephants, or palanquins, the sedan chairs carried by human bearers that were a common mode of nineteenth-century high-caste travel. Opponents took advantage of Satnami illiteracy to falsify records of loans and land claims and so to rob Satnamis of their property.

Conversely, the new identity brought pride, self-discipline, and group solidarity that gave Satnamis the strength to resist oppression. Dube collected stories told by present-day Satnamis about times when their predecessors united to bring down village landlords who exploited or cheated them.[17] Unfortunately, solidarity was often broken. Some Satnamis reverted to eating meat and red lentils, and images of Shiva and Draupadi reappeared in Satnami practice, together with several agricultural festivals. Intrigues among wives of the gurus split the community into two branch lines, each accepting a different descendant of Ghasidas as guru.

Satnamis and Politics

Disciples of one of these gurus, Agamdas, brought about the next set of community transformations, this time responding to changes in their historical context. By the 1920s, reforms launched by the British colonial government had created regional leg-islatures of limited power, made up of elected representatives. One by-product of this initiative was the founding of a Depressed Classes Association, intended to gain rep-resentation for low-caste groups. In 1925, with help from this group's leadership, two Satnami mahants joined with landholding Satnamis to found the Satnami Mahasabha, an organization designed to promote Satnami political interests. Shortly after, having won support from Guru Agamdas, they sent five delegates to that year's session of the Indian National Congress, meeting in the nearby city of Nagpur. There the five were accepted, "purified" by high-caste leaders, and confirmed in their right to wear the sacred thread.

The following year, with support from new Congress-based allies, Agamdas sent a petition to the provincial governor outlining grievances such as exclusion of Satnami children from schools, efforts to cheat community members of land and wages, and demands by landlords that Satnamis serve on free labor corvees. The peti-tion also asked the government to acknowledge that Satnamis were separate from Chamars, stressing that Satnamis did not do leatherwork, but instead served mostly as farm laborers and menials. Well attuned to its new upper-caste, reform-minded allies, the petitioning group did not stress Satnami claims to high ritual purity, but instead pleaded that Satnamis were exploited because of their lack of access to education. It claimed that they were, therefore, a Hindu "depressed class." Calling themselves Hindu was an unusual move for Satnamis. Earlier, the only people they called Hindus were the high-caste groups who opposed them.

In response, the government agreed to investigate their complaints and granted the separate caste status they had requested. The Mahasabha next founded a Satnami

---

[17] Ibid., p. 100–101.

school and launched a series of internal reforms, including a rule that Satnami women must wear blouses. Mahasabha supporters began trying to appear more Hindu, building Satnami temples and involving themselves in a regional cow protection movement.[18] By the time of independence, their efforts had paid off. Satnamis were enough of a force in the Hindu community that the Congress Party nominated Guru Agamdas to stand for a parliament seat in the 1952 national election.

Dube's account of Satnami history extends no farther than this election, in which Agamdas defeated his long-time rival Guru Muktawandas. An article written by anthropologist Lawrence A. Babb adds an important coda, showing how the Satnamis' entry into politics reunited the guru's office.[19] When Agamdas died soon after his election, one of his co-wives, Minimata, stood for the election to fill his seat, once again challenged by Guru Muktawandas. With Congress backing, she won by a large margin and was still winning regularly when Babb wrote his own Satnami essay. Because her political seat helped her win jobs for Satnamis, she became the de facto leader of the community. This allowed her to claim the original guru's *gaddi,* cushion, for a son of Agamdas by another of his wives. Thanks to her support, this son became "official" heir to the gaddi, despite the fact that Muktawandas's lineage had previously held it.

Hence, nearly two centuries after Ghasidas began preaching, his descendants finally achieved both communal unity and enough power to accomplish genuine change for the better in Satnami lives. Both Dube and Babb agree, however, that this has come at a cost. By the time of Babb's essay, Satnamis had become less a religious community than a caste-based voting bloc. Babb reports that even major celebrations such as the birthday of Ghasidas had now "become increasingly political in nature, providing public platforms for the new political elite."[20] This reflects a parallel trend within the greater Hindu community, as politicians strive to turn religious identities into "vote banks" that they can rely on during elections.[21] Vote-bank politics has also been an important factor in non-Brahmin movements and conversion, the two low-caste responses to Hinduism considered below.

AN ALTERNATIVE HISTORY: NON-BRAHMIN MOVEMENTS

Many ethnologists have held that low-caste Hindus are really members of separate cultures, grafted only through coercion onto the high-caste Hindu system. Michael Moffat claimed that his research in Tamilnadu repudiated this theory. Yet for years, certain low-caste Hindus have themselves made the same claim. It is, therefore,

---

[18] According to Dube, cow protection had been an issue for them even before the Mahasabha's founding. In fact, involvement in a mutual cow protection effort had brought the Mahasabha's two original leaders together. Dube, ibid., p. 149.

[19] "The Satnamis—Political Involvement of a Religious Movement," *The Untouchables in Contemporary India,* J. Michael Mahar, ed. (Tuscon: Univ. of Arizona Press, 1972).

[20] Babb, ibid., p. 150.

[21] See also Chapter 11.

helpful to ask on what experiences this claim is based and what kind of motives might lie behind it.

Perhaps the most accessible example of this claim is a small book entitled *Why I Am Not a Hindu*, published in India in 1996.[22] At the time of its writing, its author Kancha Ilaiah was professor of political science at Osmania University in Hyderabad, India. Ilaiah tells us that he was born into the Kurumaa, or Shepherd, jati of a small Telegu-speaking village in South India. This birth would locate him not at the very bottom of his region's caste hierarchy, but among lowly but "clean" Shudras who still have access to a village's Brahmins and barbers. Five hundred years ago, Ilaiah tells us, his people lived independently of the village economy like the hundreds of tribal groups still living in more remote areas of India. Now they are fully integrated into the village system.

Nevertheless, he argues, it is still inappropriate to call his people Hindus. When he was a child, he never even heard the word "Hindu." He was only vaguely aware of caste distinctions. He knew that he could be friendly with some children: Goudaas, whose parents were Toddy-tappers, and Kaapus, whose fathers drove ploughs in the fields. He helped tend village cattle with children of these groups, and sometimes ate in their homes or brought them to eat in his own, although always keeping proper ritual distance. There were other children he dared not approach—below him, untouchable Maadigas, drummers, and above him, the privileged children of Brahmins and Baniyas, Vaishya merchants. As for religion, his caste honored deities who kept children healthy and helped his village succeed in its daily livelihood: Pocamma, who protects from diseases; Kattamaisamma, goddess of water and protectress of the village tank; Pomimeramma, guardian of the village boundaries; Potaraju, who protects the fields from thieves; and Beerappa, a god specific to the Kurumaa caste who decides if sheep and goats will prosper.

"We knew nothing of Brahma, Vishnu, or Eashwara [Shiva] until we entered school," he asserts. "When we first heard about these figures they were as strange to us as Allah or Jehova or Jesus were."[23] He learned the classical Hindu stories only when he went to school, finding these as alien as Shakespeare and Milton. Not only were those stories themselves strange to him, but so were the ideals of human behavior that such stories held up before their readers. Women of his community were not submissive like Sitas. They quarreled with their husbands and sometimes were beaten. But they stood up for themselves and asserted their own value and dignity. If husbands displeased them too much, they could divorce and remarry, celebrating "with food and drink" both marriage and divorce.[24] Widows, of course, could remarry.

Nor did his community find it proper to live off the labor of others. They all worked hard to survive, pooling resources when needed for the whole community's benefit, offering others a hand when they met with misfortune. They prized expertise and knowledge, but this was the knowledge of their own economic specialties, not the arcane ritual knowledge monopolized by Brahmins. Kurumaas made little use

---

[22] Kancha Ilaiah, *Why I Am Not a Hindu: A Sudra Critique of Hindutva Philosophy, Culture and Political Economy* (Calcutta: Samya, 1996).

[23] Ilaiah, op. cit., p. 7.

[24] Ilaiah, ibid., p. 13.

of priesthoods in their rituals, approaching deities mostly on their own, encountering Brahmins mostly at marriage and death. "And then he [the Brahmin] comes not to educate them about the spirit that he visualizes as being embodied in God; not to talk in a language that people can understand. No mantra he recites is understood by anyone present there—not a word."[25] Kurumaa concepts of death also differ from Brahmin concepts. They have an idea of the soul, and call it *atma,* and the dead return as ghosts if not fed well while they are alive. But there is no heaven or hell: "All the dead live together somewhere in the skies."[26]

Ilaiah offers two reasons for low-caste concession to high-caste Hindus' insistence on their own superiority. The first is fear, which he attributes less to members of his own community than to those of the bottommost caste groups. Speaking of very low-caste communities, he says "At home they live as equals, eating, drinking and smoking together." But parents teach their children that "they must shiver and shake before the 'upper' caste master." This is not because they "have great respect or real love for the 'upper' caste landlord, the Brahmin, or the Baniya, but because there is always the fear of losing their jobs. They will say 'My son, be careful with that bastard, pretend to be very obedient, otherwise that rascal will hit us in our stomachs.'"[27] Hence children become obedient and obedience turns into habit, reinforced by the fear that disobedience will bring severe retaliation.

A second reason for accepting high-caste claims to superiority is pure brainwashing. Upper-caste children, Ilaiah asserts, are taught from childhood "that they are the greater race, and that they are better bred."[28] Such teachings are so constantly repeated from all directions that even low-caste children like himself come to accept them: "All this was proclaimed so consistently that it went into our psyches as if it might be true."[29] Because low-caste people even of his parents' generation did not have enough education to let them assess such claims, they had no means of countering their children's psychic subjugation.

This latter charge offers an important clue to Ilaiah's reasons for writing his book. Far more of it is a diatribe against Brahmin teachings than a description of low-caste belief. Ilaiah portrays high-caste Hindus as leeches out to strip the poor of rightful benefits from their own labor. Gods of classic Hindu stories are said to be little more than thugs, battering opponents into submission with their weapons. Ilaiah charges that Indra was a leader of ancient Aryas who led a mass extermination of Adi-Dravidians, India's original inhabitants.[30] Rama was a conqueror from the north, whereas Ravana, his "demon" opponent, was a powerful native leader in the south who resisted Rama's advance.[31] The *Ramayana*'s story "is also a means of subordinating women by establishing role models for them."[32]

---

[25] Ilaiah, ibid., p. 21.

[26] Ilaiah, ibid., p. 7.

[27] Ilaiah, ibid., pp. 10–11.

[28] Ilaiah, ibid., p. 19.

[29] Ilaiah, ibid.

[30] Ilaiah, ibid., p. 73.

[31] Ilaiah, ibid., p. 87.

[32] Ilaiah, ibid., p. 88.

All this rhetoric, plus his praise of the Shudra leader Jotirao Phule, locate Ilaiah within the tradition of a series of low-caste movements that from the nineteenth century challenged upper-caste hegemony by providing alternative views of low-caste culture and history. Such non-Brahmin movements often are built on a historical argument that Shudras are the original and true owners of India's lands. In the distant past, these first owners were overcome by an Aryan invasion that threw down original rulers and established present-day high-caste groups in their position of prominence. Movement teachings often assert as well that pre-Aryan culture valued desirable qualities suppressed in high-caste practice but surviving among lower strata: industry, egalitarian views, strong women, and an impulse to work for the whole of society rather than for individual benefit.

Phule and Non-Brahmin Origins

India has known several non-Brahmin movements, which are usually regional rather than nationwide. In Tamilnadu, for example, the Adi-Dravida movement is a powerful force in politics. Launched around 1917, it centered its ideology on the claim that Shudras who spoke Dravidian languages were India's original, or "Adi," peoples. In the north, the similar "Ad Dharm" and "Adi Hindu" movements spread among untouchables in the Punjab and Uttar Pradesh after the early 1920s.[33] But the first and most famous movement of this type was launched in the mid-1800s in Maharashtra by the Jotirao Phule so highly praised by Ilaiah. Historian Rosalind O'Hanlon's account of this movement follows.[34]

Phule was of the *Mali,* or Gardeners, jati, a group of middling standing in Shudra caste rankings of his region. His rise to prominence began with his education, first in a small village school and later in a school in Pune run by missionaries of the Free Church of Scotland. The Scottish Mission schools had been among the first in India to admit qualified boys of all castes. Through his schooling, Phule acquired a mixed-caste circle of friends who later joined in several of his early reform projects. They were inspired by the same European post-Enlightenment writings that would soon move young men of high caste to found samaj chapters. Phule himself, it is said, could recite from memory Thomas Paine's *Age of Reason.*

Soon after finishing school, Phule started a school of his own for low-caste and untouchable girls, aided by his wife Savitribai. He and his school friends launched further projects in untouchable education that soon brought him regionwide recognition and honor. But he was also concerned about the fate of low-caste peasant farmers, known as *kunbis* in Maharashtra. In 1873, he and other friends started the Satyashodak Samaj, "Truth-Seeking Society," to teach kunbis how to save themselves from exploitation. Through a series of ballads and plays, he spread his ideas about the sources of such exploitation.

At the root of low-caste suffering, he wrote, lay a conspiracy of the Brahmin caste that maintained its own supremacy by means of its monopoly over ritual and

---

[33] Unlike the Adi-Dravidas, however, these movements are no longer a significant force in India. For a study of the former, see Mark Juergensmeyer, *Religion as Social Vision: the Movement against Untouchability in 20th-Century Punjab* (Berkeley: Univ. of California Press, 1982).

[34] *Class, Conflict, and Ideology: Mahatma Jotirao Phule and Low Caste Protest in Nineteenth-Century Western India* (Cambridge: Cambridge Univ. Press, 1985).

education. Demanding high fees and privileged treatment in ritual, Brahmins stripped farmers of their small savings and immersed them in debts that caused them to lose their property. Blocking low-caste access to education, this same Brahmin elite deprived its victims of the knowledge that would help them fight such tactics. Yet Brahmins were an illegitimate presence in India. Drawing on the new views developed by European scholars, Phule charged that Brahmins were invaders who came with Aryas of the past to overwhelm and enslave India's first inhabitants. Present-day Shudras, he claimed, were descendants of pre-Aryan Kshatriyas who once protected and tilled their own lands. Untouchable jatis descended from groups that had resisted especially strongly. He called on low-caste groups to recover the courage of their heroic past, to perform their own rituals and hence guard their wealth, and to demand the education that could bring them freedom.

One concern motivating Phule was the number of Brahmins moving into civil service positions and roles of educational leadership within the British colonial government. He thought this was just a new variation of an old Brahmin strategy for capturing power by infiltrating administrative bureaucracies. He feared that the British regime might travel the route of Marathi kings, ceding power to Brahmin bureaucrats until those Brahmins became the effective rulers. On the other hand, he saw that, nudged in the right direction, the British could become a healthy check to Brahmin power structures. Already the new regime had refused to use state machinery to enforce Brahmin judgments on caste and ritual customs. This took away an important means through which high castes had kept low castes in their place.

But the British responded best to pressure groups with the weight of numbers behind them. Phule believed he could create such a group by forging an alliance between the lower and lowest caste groups of Maharashtrian society. For a while he seemed to succeed, through his education projects for untouchables. But courting Shudra peasants in addition proved too large a task. Eventually, his movement came to focus mainly on Shudra uplift, as did the parallel Adi-Dravida movement of Tamilnadu. Phule nonetheless had taught untouchables how to change their own lives by organizing and gaining education. One by-product of this discovery in Maharashtra was the last movement discussed in this chapter, which began as a quest for political power and culminated in a decision for conversion.

HOW MAHARS BECAME BUDDHISTS: CONVERSION AS PROTEST

Surely the most distinguished untouchable leader of pre-independence India was Dr. Bhimrao Ambedkar of Maharashtra's Mahar community.[35] Mahars are the largest of Maharashtra's once-untouchable groups; and there is an often-made claim that at least one Mahar family lives in every village where the Marathi language is spoken. Historically, Mahars functioned as all-purpose village servants, repairing village walls,

---

[35] The principal source for information cited on Ambedkar's life and work has been Eleanor Zelliot, *From Untouchable to Dalit: Essays on the Ambedkar Movement* (New Delhi: Manohar, 1992).

guarding gates and tracking thieves, carrying messages between settlements, caring for visitors' horses, making public announcements, and fulfilling the classic untouchable assignments of dragging dead cows from villages and gathering fuel for cremation grounds. One function distinctive to them has sometimes been cited as evidence that they were the original owners of Maharashtra's land: when land disputes arose, Mahars were called in to attest the land's true boundaries.[36]

By 1891, when Ambedkar was born, many Mahars had already moved away from home villages to pursue jobs offered by the British regime. Up to one-sixth of the Bombay Presidency army was Mahar before a military restructuring in 1893 cut off further Mahar enlistments. The railroads and shipping docks that serviced British colonial needs were also a frequent source of Mahar employment.

Ambedkar was an army child, the fourteenth and last child born to his parents. Unlike most untouchable children of his time, he had access to education because of his father's army service. In 1900, he began attending an English-medium school in the town of Satara, then moved to Bombay in 1904 with his family so that he could continue his studies. His conspicuous brilliance prompted a teacher to call him to the attention of Sayajirao Gaikwad, Maharaja of the princely state of Baroda and a frequent supporter of efforts devoted to low-caste uplift. When the prestigious Elphinstone College accepted Ambedkar as a student, the Maharaja offered a stipend that would pay for his tuition. After Ambedkar finished at Elphinstone in 1912, the Maharaja agreed to support him in graduate study at Columbia College in the United States (now Columbia University). Ambedkar studied economics at Columbia from 1913 to 1916, then secured an additional grant for a year of study at the London School of Economics. He returned to India for a few years, then went back to London for legal studies. By the time he completed his education in 1923, he had received an M.A. and Ph.D. from Columbia and a D.Sci. from London University and had qualified to practice law before the British bar.

Ambedkar and Politics

Ambedkar's involvement in Indian politics began in 1919, when he was called to testify before the Southborough Committee. This committee was seeking input on the proposed Montagu-Chelmsford reforms, an early British plan for beginning Indian self-governance. A new Legislative Council of one hundred seats was being established to participate in certain areas of decision making. Ambedkar asked the British to set aside nine seats for untouchables on this council, matching untouchable distribution in the Indian population. Only untouchables themselves could fairly represent their own interests, he argued. Furthermore, only when they held real power would they be able to change their dehumanizing situation. Ambedkar's testimony secured just a single seat, whose occupant was chosen by the government. Six years later, the government set aside a second untouchable seat, and in 1926 Ambedkar acquired it.

By this time his fame was increasing; he was a speaker in high demand at depressed class conferences. He also helped organize demonstrations for the so-called Temple Entry Movement, then striving to win untouchable access to major temples and roads leading past them. Later, however, he left this movement, calling it a misplaced effort.

---

[36] Ibid., pp. 56 and 87.

Ambedkar's most famous act of militant public leadership occurred during a conference held at the town of Mahad in March 1927. He led a procession to a tank (arti-
ficial lake) in the town's Brahmin section, and then stopped and drank its
water—thus, in Brahmin perceptions, polluting the reservoir. Nine months later, he
returned to Mahad and burned a copy of the dharma code *Manusmriti* before a gathering held there. In the meantime, he worked through the courts. After a battle that
took three years, he won a court judgement that untouchables did indeed have a
right to draw water from the tank.

He would soon take up a much larger battle. In 1930, under pressure from nationalist agitation, the British called for three Round Table Conferences in London to
plan the next stage in Indian self-governance. Ambedkar was a delegate to all three
conferences, arguing there for separate untouchable electorates. This meant that legislative bodies would have seats set aside for untouchables, to be elected only by
members of untouchable communities. In this effort, Ambedkar echoed and supported fellow delegate Muhammad Ali Jinnah, then seeking separate electorates for
India's Muslim communities. At the second Round Table Conference, Ambedkar
clashed sharply with delegate Mohandas Gandhi. Gandhi not only refused to support
proposals for separate electorates, but also claimed that he, not Ambedkar, represented
India's untouchables.[37]

Two years later, when the government unveiled its constitutional plan, it did
indeed provide for a modest number of separate electorate seats. Gandhi's response to
this plan was to announce a "fast unto death" in protest. By then, Gandhi had become
India's most visible and beloved nationalist leader; his death would have caused chaos
in India. As Gandhi grew ever weaker from his fast, Ambedkar succumbed to pressure.
He agreed to a compromise that would provide for seat "reservations." This meant
that certain elective seats would indeed be designated for untouchable candidates
only. But all voters in their constituencies would choose from among those candidates. This meant that candidates representing specifically bottom-caste interests were
likely to be rejected in favor of those answering to a broader base. Ambedkar was
infuriated by this episode and felt until the end of his life that Gandhi had used
grossly unfair tactics. Meanwhile, Gandhi swiftly organized an All-India Anti-
Untouchability League, dedicating to winning access for all castes to public wells,
roads, schools, temples, and cremation grounds. For the next several years, Gandhi led
a mostly high-caste following into intensification of the old Temple Entry campaign.
In 1939, this won a major victory when a precedent-setting Temple Entry Act passed
in Madras.

Ambedkar charged that this campaign was mere window dressing, deflecting
attention and energy from real untouchable needs: political voice, equal economic
opportunity, and respectful treatment in ordinary social intercourse. Like many
other untouchable leaders, he rejected as paternal the name that Gandhi coined
for untouchables—*Harijans,* "children of God." Tired of picking up political
crumbs dropped from high-caste Hindu tables, he announced before a conference in
1935 that, although he'd been born a Hindu, he did not intend to die one. He claimed

---

[37] Zelliot, p. 166, in a quotation from *Proceedings of the Federal Structure Committee and
Minorities Committee,* Indian Round Table Conference (Second–1931 London) (London:
H.M.S.O., 1932), p. 544.

that untouchables were treated badly only because they made the mistake of call-ing themselves Hindus: "If we were members of another faith, none would dare treat us so."[38]

CONVERSION

The following year a Mahar caste conference resolved to seek conversion to another religion. From then on, various Muslim, Christian, and Sikh leaders courted Ambedkar and his caste-mates. For a time, Ambedkar considered becoming a Sikh. But his following by then had won concessions from the government because of their oppressed-caste status, and he was afraid of losing these. The concessions set up quotas for bottom-caste access to certain government jobs and educational programs. Mahars were among the large number of scheduled (listed) castes able to benefit from these quotas. (This quota system still exists in India; one problem for would-be converts is that conversion often cuts them off from access to its benefits.)

Instead of immediately carrying through his threat to convert, during the later thirties and forties Ambedkar concentrated on organizing political parties that would pursue low-caste concerns. Although he founded three such parties before his death, none managed to dent the huge Congress Party majority. He also wrote two impor-tant books: *What Congress and Gandhi Have Done to Untouchables*, published in 1945, again pleaded for separate untouchable electorates. *The Untouchables*, published in 1948, argued that untouchables had once been Buddhists, pushed into subordination after Brahmin resurgence overwhelmed their religion.

By now, Ambedkar had begun to believe Buddhism was the religion best suited to untouchables. According to Zelliot, he wanted untouchables to have a religion born in India. He was also attracted by the egalitarianism that he saw in Buddhist writings. In 1934, he named a new house he had built Rajgriha, after the first city that welcomed the Buddha and his teachings. Later, in 1946, he named a college he had founded Siddharth, the Buddha's personal name. In 1948, he backed republica-tion of a classic Indian study of Buddhist teachings, Lakshman Narasu's *Essence of Buddhism,* adding his own introduction. In 1950, he visited Ceylon and began com-piling an anthology of Buddhist scriptures, *The Buddha and His Dhamma*. It would be published posthumously in 1957. In 1951, he named another college Milind, after a Greek ruler who became a Buddhist convert. In the meantime, Ambedkar followers began to read books and write plays about the Buddha. They set up Buddha images by temples, and discouraged fellow Mahars from observing Hindu celebrations.[39]

Before converting, Ambedkar accepted one further major national position. Despite his frequent challenges to the Congress Party, he was asked to fill a cabinet post in the first government of independent India. He became law minister, serving simultaneously as chair of the committee that drafted India's constitution. This con-stitution banned all forms of discrimination based on untouchability. To Ambedkar, however, this victory was hollow because the new government still refused to implement

---

[38] Cited in Zelliot, ibid., p. 206.

[39] These initiatives are described in Vasant Moon, *Growing Up Untouchable in India: A Dalit Autobiography* (Oxford: Rowman and Littlefield, 2001); see especially pp. 124–32.

structures that would grant despised peoples increased political power. When his proposed Hindu Code Bill failed in 1951, Ambedkar resigned from the cabinet. Five years
later, his health failing, he stood before half a million Mahars in the city of Nagpur and
received initiation as a Buddhist lay-disciple from the oldest Buddhist monk then present in India. Then he turned around and led the crowd in a ritual of mass conversion.
Two months later, following his death, another three million Mahars converted.

The Impact of Conversion

Today, virtually all Mahars are at least nominally Buddhist, along with a few converts
from other bottom-caste groups. As described by Ambedkar scholar Eleanor Zelliot,
Ambedkar Buddhists today follow a mix of practices drawn from Ambedkar's precepts, Buddhist texts, and teachings of non-Indian Buddhists whom they have met.
These latter range from Sri Lankan and Thai Theravadins to Tibetans, Western
Buddhists, and the Japanese Nichiren sect. Most Ambedkar Buddhists are lay disciples, although a few have become *bhikkus* (Buddhist renouncers), and some hold doc-
torates in Pali and Buddhist studies. They meet for worship in structures they call
viharas, opening each gathering by garlanding pictures of the Buddha and Ambedkar,
displayed side by side. They observe four annual Holy Days: Buddha's birthday,
observed throughout the world and believed to be also the date on which the Buddha
won Enlightenment and later exited from the world; Dhamma Diksha day, the date
of their first mass initiation; and Ambedkar's birth and death memorial days.

What difference has conversion made in Mahar lives? It has not erased Mahar
poverty; nor has it increased high-caste Hindu respect for Mahars. Conversion, even
mass conversion, by bottom-caste groups is nothing new in India. Muslim, Christian,
and Sikh communities have all at various times accepted bottom-caste converts. Each
time their old low status has followed converts into their new communities, just as
the label Chamar followed the Satnamis described earlier in this chapter. Change for
untouchable groups arrives very slowly. It usually results from social, political, and
economic forces affecting oppressed groups more generally.

On the other hand, as Zelliot points out, conversion has hugely enhanced
untouchable self-respect. One index of this self-respect is the large volume of literature produced by Ambedkar Buddhists since their conversion that is now considered
"a major contribution to Marathi literature."[40] Ambedkar editor Vasant Moon has
described in his autobiography how he and his own friends helped to launch this
outpouring of short stories, novels, drama, and poetry:

> In 1953 we decided to put out a handwritten magazine in the community. . . .
> Handwritten magazines were published in many communities like ours. . . . The
> boys in our community had no tradition of writing. However, after we decided
> to put out a magazine, many made the effort. Boys from eighth standard up
> wrote articles. I refined them. I myself wrote various poems, and stories for the
> magazine. I used different names such as Madhup or Shashi. From friends in

---

[40] Zelliot, op. cit., p. 293. Karnataka, too, has by now experienced a significant literary
movement among former untouchables. See Oliver Mendelsohn and Marika Vicziany, *The
Untouchables: Subordination, Poverty, and the State in India* (Cambridge: Cambridge Univ.
Press, 1998), p. 215.

college I obtained sketches and articles that I included. . . . Encouraging the
newly educated, bringing the ignorant into the light, fostering the writing of
students from the lowest classes to create a class of writers from them—this was
the aim of the handwritten journal.[41]

Another important achievement has been the gradual overcoming of subcaste distinctions once dividing the Mahar community. Moon's descriptions of his childhood
show how those distinctions once generated tensions and rivalry. Yet, soon after his
conversion, Moon decided to seek a marriage with a girl from outside his subcaste.

Unifying non-Mahar untouchables has been a stiffer challenge. One problem
dogging Ambedkar until the end of his life was his difficulty in drawing followers
from castes other than his own. Even Maharashtra's other large untouchable group
rejected him. Gandhi was thus not altogether wrong when he claimed that he rather
than Ambedkar spoke for *all* India's untouchables. Ambedkar did find admirers among
adherents of the Punjab's Ad Dharm movement. This movement's president Mangu
Ram supported Ambedkar by undertaking a counterfast when Gandhi launched his
"fast unto death."[42] Later, when the Ad Dharm movement folded, several of its leaders joined the Ambedkar Buddhists.[43] More recently, Ambedkar Buddhists have
gained a following in the state of Karnataka. One powerful new attractant is a name.
In the 1970s, a group of radical Mahar writers took the name "Dalit Panthers" for
itself. The "Panthers" part of the name was borrowed from the American Black
Panthers, admired by this group for their militant creativity. "Dalit" was a word initially used by Phule meaning "Ground" or "Broken to Pieces." Failure to find a name
that could embrace all oppressed groups had always been a barrier to bottom-caste
unity. "Dalit" seems to be taking. Its use is now common in western India, and it is
spreading into other regions.

BOTTOM-CASTE HINDUS: SIGNS OF CHANGE

In sum, India's bottom-caste Hindus have engaged in a complex dance with the tradition that first assigned them their unpalatable status. Some have bowed to it; some
have refused it; some have reshaped it to suit themselves. In the course of reshaping
it, they are changing even the high-caste traditions with which they tussle. Today,
former untouchables who do not convert are called low-caste Hindus, not outcastes.
Today, although they retain many disabilities, they can find many other Hindus who
will say that this is wrong and change must be made. Today, they have access to education and jobs that have begun to lift at least a few out of poverty. They can own
land, enter temples, and walk openly on the street. Perhaps most importantly, today
they are a force to be reckoned with on the political stage. Part IV shows how high-
caste Hindus are addressing this phenomenon. But first, it is necessary to look at
another extreme of the Hindu social spectrum, the well-to-do, cosmopolitan Hindus
who still control the system that low-caste groups hope to alter.

---

[41] Moon, op. cit., p. 143.

[42] Juergensmeyer, p. 128.

[43] Described ibid., pp. 159–68.

ADDITIONAL SOURCES

Readers wishing to pursue this chapter's topic further would be wise to start with sources described in the text. Robert Deliége's *The Untouchables of India,* Nora Scott, tr. (Oxford: Oxford International Publishers, 1999) is a fine general introduction. Michael Moffat, *An Untouchable Community in South India: Structure and Consensus* (Princeton: Princeton Univ. Press, 1979); Saurabh Dube, *Untouchable Pasts: Religion, Identity, and Power among a Central Indian Community, 1780–1952* (Albany: SUNY Press, 1998); Rosalind O'Hanlon, *Class, Conflict, and Ideology: Mahatma Jotirao Phule and Low Caste Protest in Nineteenth-Century Western India* (Cambridge: Cambridge Univ. Press, 1985); and Eleanor Zelliot, *From Untouchable to Dalit: Essays on the Ambedkar Movement* (New Delhi: Manohar, 1992) well deserve additional exploration.

An important topic not covered in this chapter is the relationship of untouchables to devotional movements. See the reference to Ramdas Lamb's *Rapt in the Name: The Ramnamis, Ramnam, and Untouchable Religion in Central India* (Albany: State Univ. of New York Press, 2002) studying the Ramnami movement. David Lorenzen describes the closely related Kabir Panth in "Traditions of Non-Caste Hinduism: The Kabir Panth," *Contributions to Indian Sociology,* n.s. 21:2 (1987): 263–83, and "The Kabir Panth: Heretics to Hindus," in Lorenzen's *Religious Change and Cultural Domination* (Mexico City: El Colegio de Mexico, 1981), 151–71.

Pauline Moller Mahar traces Arya Samaj impact on Sweepers in Uttar Pradesh in "Changing Religious Practices of an Untouchable Caste," *Economic Development and Cultural Change* 8:3 (April 1960): 279–87; see also her [as Pauline Kolenda] *Caste in Contemporary India: Beyond Organic Solidarity* (Menlo Park, CA: Benjamin\Cummings Publishing Company, 1978). Additional instances of challenge to untouchable standing are in R. S. Khare, *The Untouchable as Himself: Ideology, Identity, and Pragmatism among the Lucknow Chamars* (New York: Cambridge Univ. Press, 1984). Further coverage of Shudra-based non-Brahmin movements is provided in Eugene Irshick, *Politics and Social Conflict in South India: The Non-Brahman Movement and Tamil Separatism, 1916–1929* (Berkeley: Univ. of California Press, 1969); and Gail Omvedt, *Cultural Revolt in a Colonial Society: The Non-Brahman Movement in Western India 1873 to 1930* (Bombay: Scientific Socialist Education Trust, 1976). Sociologist André Béteille assesses their impact in his essay "Caste and Politics in Tamilnadu," in his *Society and Politics in India: Essays in a Comparative Perspective* (Delhi: Oxford Univ. Press, 1992), 79–121. For the Ad Dharm movement of the North among untouchables, see Mark Juergensmeyer, *Religion as Social Vision: The Movement against Untouchability in 20th-Century Punjab* (Berkeley: Univ. of California Press, 1982).

Several accounts of untouchable lives exist. Especially valuable is Vasant Moon's tale of his awakening under Ambedkar, *Growing Up Untouchable in India: A Dalit Autobiography* (Oxford: Rowman and Littlefield, 2001). A Muslim convert recounts his own gradual transformation in Hazari, *Untouchable: The Autobiography of an Indian Outcaste* (New York: Praeger, 1951). James Freeman records the story of a man damaged by limited options in *Untouchable: An Indian Life History* (London: George Allen and Unwin, 1979). To view the untouchable world from a woman's perspective, see Viramma et al., *Viramma: Life of an Untouchable* (New York: UNESCO Pub., 1997); Sumitra Bhave, *Pan on Fire: Eight Dalit Women Tell Their Story* (New Delhi: Indian

Social Institute, 1988); and Fernando Franco et al., *The Silken Swing: The Cultural Universe of Dalit Women* (Calcutta: STREE, 2000).

Writings by untouchables are increasingly available. For an Ambedkar sampling, see B. R. Ambedkar, *The Essential Writings of B. R. Ambedkar,* Valerian Rodrigues, ed. (New York: Oxford Univ. Press, 2002); Vasant Moon has edited Ambedkar's complete works. For recent Dalit writings, see Barbara R. Joshi, ed., *Untouchable! Voices of the Dalit Liberation Movement* (London: Zed Books, 1986); also Arjun Dangle, *Poisoned Bread: Translations from Modern Marathi Dalit Literature* (Bombay: Orient Longman, 1992); also M. S. S. Pandian, "Stepping Outside History? New Dalit Writings from Tamil Nadu," in *Wages of Freedom: Fifty Years of the Indian Nation-State,* Partha Chatterjee, ed. (Delhi: Oxford Univ. Press, 1998), 292–309; and Challapalli Swaroopa Rani, "Dalit Women's Writing in Telegu," *Economic and Political Weekly* 33: 17 (April 25, 1998): WS21–25.

9

Among the Well-to-Do
and Advantaged

Two silver-haired former generals rose to offer their seats to entering women. I was surprised to see one of them, my Hindi tutor, at this gathering, for a few weeks earlier he had told me he had no interest in religion. But word had gotten around that the swami offering this evening's *satsang* was an unusually gifted speaker. Hence the neighbors invited by our hostess packed into her living room until some in the audience were forced to stand.

She had taken care to make this a very special event. Sheets covered the carpet to accommodate floor-sitters. In the left corner of the room's front stood a chest-tall wooden shrine holding an image of Krishna, elaborately adorned with bright-orange marigold strands. To the right was a large armchair also covered with a sheet, waiting to receive the evening's guest of honor.

Now the swami entered from an inner room and took his seat, his orange robe and curling black hair and beard adding to the room's color and festive air. Pausing and bowing his head for a moment, he began to chant in Sanskrit. First came several Upanishad verses and a hymn of praise to his line of gurus. Next were the opening verses to Chapter 4 of the *Bhagavad-Gita,* announced as the subject for his discourse tonight. Now he began explaining these verses, line by line and phrase by phrase. He addressed his audience in English, for he was from Kerala and his native tongue was Malayalam, whereas his New Delhi hearers spoke mostly English, Hindi, and Punjabi. His interpretation of the *Gita's* message stressed the ideal of karma-yoga, acting constructively in the world without looking for constant rewards for one's actions. Humor sprinkled his talk: phrases with unexpected twists, classic stories with wry punch lines, comments on the human quirks that this highly perceptive man had observed among the disciples he counseled and crowds he watched when strolling in local streets and markets. Soon the room's overcrowding and stuffiness were forgotten. Although the swami's talk continued for nearly two hours, no one grew restless or checked a watch.

When I first attended satsang among Hindus of today's India, I was struck by the resemblance between this type of religious gathering and those described in Buddhist texts from two thousand years earlier. Meaning "assembly of the good" or "assembly to do good," a *satsang* is a gathering held for the sake of edification. A satsang host invites a speaker to deliver a religious discourse, often in the host's own home. Guests are then invited to share the occasion. Afterwards the speaker is fed, often together with disciples or guests who have come along in the speaker's entourage. Sponsoring satsang serves a double purpose, enlightening host and audience and bringing the sponsor or sponsors a great deal of spiritual merit. As in other optional practices such as pilgrimage, this merit can be channeled toward achieving a special purpose or simply left to promote the sponsor's overall religious good.

Sponsoring satsang requires considerable household resources: enough space to hold a sizeable group of people, enough food to put on a generous meal, and often transport for the guest and his or her disciples. In Buddhist times, the expense entailed often meant that gatherings of this sort were hosted by well-to-do merchant families. Today's Hindu satsang hosts also tend to be economically comfortable. They are members of India's new postcolonial elite: the college-educated, multilingual, and widely traveled officials, professionals, and entrepreneurs who today occupy the most privileged positions in Indian society.

Many members of this new elite are descendants of the samajists who challenged religious authorities during the nineteenth century.[1] Remember that samaj movement leaders arose from a class of English-educated Indians created intentionally by the British to mediate between colonial rulers and the people they sought to govern. Because they could speak English and were familiar with central ideas and customs of their British rulers, members of the new cadre moved easily into government posts open to Indians and into professions such as law, medicine, and education. After India gained independence, members of this same cadre not only retained dominance over posts they had monopolized under the British but also moved into command of emerging institutions in commerce and industry.

This new elite should be clearly distinguished from the caste-based elite groups of precolonial Indian history. In the categories used by social scientists, it qualifies as class-based rather than caste-based. People enter its circles via achievement, not via birth; they complete educations, secure desirable jobs, and amass enough in earnings to travel and acquire valued consumer goods and comfortable homes in prestigious neighborhoods. An important social transformation occurring in today's India has been a shift from a caste-based to a class-based flow of social respect and job opportunity.

But this transformation is slow, so it is also important to realize that a great deal of overlap remains between class standing and caste standing in today's India. High-class Hindus are almost always of high-caste birth. This is because, historically, high-caste Hindus were far more likely than members of low-caste groups to gain the education and connections that admitted them to prestigious jobs and elite social circles. As noted in previous chapters, Brahmins did well in negotiating the caste-class crossover. In the two regions of Maharashtra and Tamilnadu, for example, they gained a near monopoly over government jobs and business opportunities. As a result, in such regions the privileged class is composed of much the same cadre of people who are descended from

---

[1] See Chapter 4.

the older privileged-caste groups. The one important difference between their present and past status is that not all high-caste Hindus made it into high-class circles.

Why single out well-to-do and privileged people for special attention in an introductory textbook? There are three very good reasons. First, the privileged are trend-setters. Innovations they make and examples they set tend to trickle down slowly into the rest of Hindu society. For example, today in India it is far more common for a Hindu girl to go to school than it was a century ago. Secluding women is much rarer. Many widows keep their hair and jewelry. Although child marriage still occurs in some rural areas, girls as a rule tend to marry at ages well past their first menstruation. All these trends follow precedents set by the young samajists who were ancestors of today's privileged classes.

Second, the class of Hindus that can afford to sponsor satsang is the same class of Hindus that Westerners are most likely to meet first when going to India to study or to negotiate business deals. They are the ones whose values and viewpoints Europeans and Americans most urgently need to know because they are the ones who must be approached for help and cooperation. They are also the class of Hindus that non-Indian readers of this book are most likely to find among their fellow students and neighbors because this is the group in India most likely to study or travel abroad. It is the group most likely to have sons or daughters living and working permanently in another country. It is a highly cosmopolitan community. I am always surprised, when making new friends among well-to-do Indians, to learn how many come regularly to the United States. One benefit of working among this group is that good friends often show up on one's doorstep.

Third, the samajist ancestors of this group promoted wide-scale religious changes. Returning to them is a good way to learn what has become of those changes. Are they still an important force in people's lives? Have they set off additional change as well? And to what extent is this privileged cadre still promoting change in the Hindu traditions of India?

This chapter addresses these questions. This time the focus is on two studies: one based in the north, in India's capital city of New Delhi, and the other based in the south, in the great ocean-side city of Chennai, formerly Madras and once capital of the East India Company's Madras Colony. The first study is my own, conducted during three stays between 1984 and 1998 in the neighborhood of Defence Colony, New Delhi. The Chennai study was done by anthropologist Mary Hancock during three stays extending from 1985 to 1996.[2]

To some extent, these two studies seem very different. Defence Colony is a very urbane, cosmopolitan, and modern community by most of the measures described earlier in this book. The people with active religious ties whom I knew there were often devotees of new religious movements rather than of longstanding sectarian communities. Defence Colony is also decidedly a unit drawn together by similarities in educational level and economic standing rather than by caste identity. Indeed, I found a reluctance to talk about caste at all, as if it were dirty laundry that my

---

[2] See Hancock's *Womanhood in the Making: Domestic Ritual and Public Culture in Urban South India* (Boulder, CO: Westview Press, 1999); also her "Saintly Careers among South India's Urban Middle Classes," *Man*, n.s. 25 (1990): 505–20; and her "Dilemmas of Domesticity," *From the Margins of Hindu Marriage*, L. Harlan and P. Courtright, eds. (New York: Oxford Univ. Press, 1995), 60–91.

neighbors preferred not to display before the visitor who would go home and write about their community.

The community studied by Hancock is also highly cosmopolitan and modern in its openness to state-of-the-art education, science, gadgetry, and economic pursuits and methods. But its members are far more conservative religiously. Most are strong supporters of the sectarian tradition founded by the great Hindu philosopher Shankaracharya. As such, all pay reverence to the living successor of Shankaracharya who heads the monastery at nearby Kanchipuram, one of five central monasteries of Shankaracharya's Dasanami Sannyasi order. All have inherited such allegiance via family lineages, for Hancock chose to study not a neighborhood but a caste, the so-called Smarta Brahmins who are the majority among Chennai's more privileged groups.

One characteristic linking Hancock's study with mine is that both focus principally on women. In part, this is a result of simple happenstance. My own study was intended to concentrate on women. I had no idea that one day it would become part of a textbook. Mary Hancock's study simply seemed to mesh well with mine. I especially liked the fact that the developments we witnessed took place during much the same period. It is, nonetheless, particularly appropriate to focus on women if one wishes to understand contemporary religious change at high social levels. This is because both men and women at these levels still take seriously the idea, first floated toward the end of the nineteenth century, that women have special talent and responsibility for religion.

This idea many have come into India from the English-speaking West. In the West, it was a product of the separation of workplace from home that resulted from the Industrial Revolution. The workplace came to be thought of as a dog-eat-dog space that corrupted the men who had to deal with it. The more humane values of morality and religion had to be protected by women who could stay at home. In India, the workplace was believed to be corrupted by the values and bad habits of colonial masters. Home was a refuge; women who stayed at home were its guardians. Because the religion of upper-caste families was practiced mostly at home, women of India, as in the West, came to be appointed special guardians of religion.[3]

The growing popularity of this idea had some deeply ironic repercussions. Teaching Sanskrit to women had once been so frowned on that the Brahmin father of the woman reformer Pandita Ramabai had to defend himself before a caste council after he started to teach his wife Sanskrit.[4] Yet by the end of the nineteenth century, high-caste girls in Bengal from conservative Hindu families were taking classes in Sanskrit recitation as part of school instruction in household skills. Offering such instruction assumed that women might take the lead in household pujas, a role previously thought to belong to men in many regions. The idea that women have a special affinity for religion seems to have also been an important factor in the decision of a number of twentieth-century gurus to make women

---

[3] See Partha Chatterjee, "The Nationalist Resolution of the Women's Question," *Recasting Women: Essays in Colonial History,* Kumkum Sangari and Suresh Vaid, eds. (New Delhi: Kali for Women, 1989), p. 240.

[4] As recounted in her autobiography *A Testimony* (Kedgaon: Ramabai Mukti Mission, 1907), pp. 4–5.

their chief spiritual heirs.[5] It most certainly is one factor that motivates thousands of well-to-do, well-educated Hindu women to seek initiation from gurus and to flock to lectures by teachers who can bring them insight into ancient Hindu texts. Such activities can be found both among Defence Colony women and among the Chennai women whom Hancock studied. They bear testimony to a massive Hindu revival occurring among the middle and upper classes of today's India. Although both men and women are active in this revival, one of its most striking features has been its effort to capture women's attention and to engage women more fully in its endeavors.

ECLECTIC SEEKERS:
DEFENCE COLONY, NEW DELHI

New Delhi is India's national capital. When combined with its sister city Delhi, it is India's third largest metropolis. It is relatively new among Indian cities, having been established by the British in 1912 to serve as a new colonial capital after Calcutta proved too fractious and peripherally located to continue housing the colonial government.[6] Delhi proper, however, was once the ruling center of the great Mughal empire and scattered through New Delhi neighborhoods are ruins of six other royal seats of earlier Muslim rulers. Local legend says the site's connections to kingship reach back a millenia, that on it stood the city of Indraprastha built by Yudhishthira, oldest of the five Pandava brothers, heroes of India's Sanskrit epic *Mahabharata*. Roughly one hundred kilometers to the north of Delhi is the renowned Kurukshetra, "field of Kurus," where the Mahabharata's war is said to have been fought. Sixty kilometers to the south is Mathura, Krishna's birthplace and gateway to Braj, where Krishna danced and played with his adoring cowgirls.

Within New Delhi, roughly six kilometers south of the central shopping district called Connaught Circle, lies the neighborhood of Defence Colony. About one and one-half square kilometers in area, it is considered one of the city's better neighborhoods to live in, with its tree-lined streets, a number of small open parks, a residents' club, and a small but convenient neighborhood shopping area. My 1996 New Delhi map lists 1,548 street addresses for the area. When I first lived there, most were private homes ranging in size from modest duplexes to large structures of eight or nine main rooms designed to hold multigenerational families. In recent years, there has been an increasing tendency to subdivide larger homes as married sons move away to take jobs in other cities or countries. Many families, too, have "sold the roof" to developers who add additional stories to existing structures, then sell them or rent them as apartments.

Defence Colony's name reflects its origins. When British India was partitioned into India and Pakistan, many of the Punjab-born Indian military officers were cut

---

[5] I have discussed this phenomenon in "*Shakti* Ascending: Hindu Women, Politics, and Religious Leadership During the Nineteenth and Twentieth Centuries," *Religion in Modern India,* 3rd rev. ed., Robert Baird, ed. (New Delhi: Manohar, 1995); also 4th ed. (New Delhi: Manohar, 2000).

[6] Construction of the government center was not actually finished until 1929, and it was dedicated formally in 1931.

off from their families' lands, now within the borders of Pakistan. To compensate for their losses and to ensure that they would have retirement homesteads, the government set aside land south of the new capital that these officers could buy at a modest price. Today, many retired officers and their wives still have homes within Defence Colony. Other residents, often wealthy businessmen or merchants, have bought in as homes come up for sale. Many apartments hold younger professionals or business people living in nuclear families, some of whom came to New Delhi from other regions of India. There is even a small international contingent. Americans are the most common foreign-born residents, but I have also met Bangladeshis, Japanese, a Nigerian, a Jamaican, and an Italian in the neighborhood. The resulting neighborhood is quite mixed in social and sectarian background. Jains and Sikhs live side by side with Hindus from most of the higher-caste groups found in the New Delhi region. Religious centers within or near the Colony include three Sikh gurdwaras, a Jain ashram, at least six Hindu temples, an Arya Samaj meeting house, centers for other new movements, a Christian church, and a mosque. During my second visit, I found a Buddhist meditation center, but this has now moved to another neighborhood. Balancing this loss has been the opening of a meditation center run by the women-led sect of Brahma Kumaris.[7] The most significant social rift that I have found in Defence Colony is that which stretches between homeowners and servants. Most families have enough means to pay at least part-time help, and some homes still have live-in servants, although servants willing to live in are becoming more difficult to find in India. Live-ins usually occupy small upper-story rooms built in the rear of homes. Stairwells with exits from these spiral down to back alleys, whose pedestrians know a Defence Colony very different from that of residents who stroll front lanes. Many servants are Christian or Muslim; the church and mosque serve mainly the servant populations.

This attractive and upscale neighborhood became my Indian second home in 1984 when I won a Fulbright Fellowship to lecture for a year in the history department of the University of Delhi and several of its related undergraduate colleges. In that same year, my husband won a Fulbright to teach in Calcutta. To accept both awards, we had to separate temporarily. I planned to take our children with me to New Delhi, where they would have access to a fine American-style private school. An India-born friend in my home city learned of this plan and called me on the phone. She had a recently widowed sister living in New Delhi, she said. This sister was looking for someone willing to rent part of her home. She had a really comfortable house, my friend said, and trustworthy servants to take care of cleaning, cooking, and washing. She loved children and would make sure that mine were well cared for if I had to leave New Delhi for guest lectures. Was I interested? Of course I was.

We spent a splendid year in Defence Colony, making many neighborhood friends with the help of my generous hostess. I had come with plans for a small research project on the side. I wanted to learn what I could about the values that informed thinking and choices of educated, cosmopolitan Hindu women. I especially wanted to learn to what degree they upheld old Brahmin-taught norms that said women should defer to parents and husbands and that children must accept marriages set up by parents. So I did a great deal of listening. When I could, I sat in on conversations

---

[7] See Chapter 10, pp. 264–66.

taking place on our household's front stoop, which attracted neighbors like moths during afternoon tea-times. On days free of travel for teaching, I often parked myself in the in-house boutique of an enterprising neighbor who designed and sold stylish Punjabi-style "suits" to wealthy women and their daughters. My hostess took me to luncheons and various other affairs taking place among her social set. Meanwhile, my lecturing rounds took me to several women's colleges, where faculty members offered tea and conversation after lectures. I could not call this research; it was reeducation. I had carried in my brain an imagined India put together out of texts from the past. My new friends brought me into a very real twentieth century. I went home and changed the focus of my study, determined to learn more about changes shaping India in the last two hundred years.

In 1991–92, I returned to Defence Colony, this time alone and wanting to learn more about the religious affiliations of the women I had come to know earlier. This time I asked Hindu friends to take me with them to religious sites or occasions that they regularly attended. I attended meetings of groups attracting my neighbors, interviewed leaders and members, read group literature, and visited the national headquarters of several organizations.

During the fall of 1998, I returned once again, expecting to do follow-ups on my previous study. Instead, I found myself drawn more and more into the activities of a single circle of disciples. This group was facing a special problem. It had gathered around a gifted and charismatic young swami, the Swami Bodhananda introduced in Chapter 6. He had come to New Delhi shortly before my previous visit in 1991.[8] For several years, Bodhananda had been a regular presence in the Colony; he was the featured speaker of the neighborhood satsang described at the beginning of this chapter. But by 1998, he was spending much of his time on a mission in the United States. The group was struggling to deal with his absence, searching for ways to stay together and integrate the teachings he had given them into their lives.

Women between Cultures

What did all this teach me? Recall that the first question I brought to Defence Colony concerned the values held by educated Hindu women, especially the values affecting their own behavior and choices made in their families. Centuries before, Brahmin pundits had laid out rules for women in the literature known as Dharmashastra. A woman must never be independent, these stipulated. In childhood, she had to submit to her father's authority; in adulthood to her husband's. If she was unlucky enough to become a widow, then she must defer to her sons. She was to marry as soon as possible after puberty, via a match arranged by her parents. She had to remain in perpetual mourning if her husband died. I knew that upper-caste Hindu women had observed these rules for many centuries. But I had also learned through my graduate training to distinguish between "traditional" and "modern" women. Rules such as these were "traditional"; only uneducated women should be expected still to follow them. My informants, on the other hand, were "modern," well educated and savvy in the ways of today's world. I thought they would be reexamining those rules and discarding those that did not work for them.

---

[8] See Chapter 7, pp. 180–83; 310–12.

To some extent, I was right. The changes I found were especially great in areas that samajists had addressed. Widows such as my hostess moved about freely. They kept their long hair and jewelry, attended weddings and other auspicious occasions, and wore bright saris or Punjabi-style suits rather than the traditional widows' white. All the women I talked with assumed that girls of their class should be educated through college if at all possible and that they should wait until educations were finished before marrying. No trace remained of old customs such as veiling or seclusion. Many Defence Colony women drove their own cars, although the most wealthy hired chauffeurs to negotiate New Delhi's chaotic traffic.

In many situations, however, my new friends' talk and actions betrayed a curious ambivalence. They valued marriage, they told me—especially women of my own generation and older. All young women should be married by the time they reached twenty-five. Yet they pointed with obvious pride to the few women in their midst who had not married and had carved out successful careers or to girls who had persuaded parents to let them work after college and had thus far done well in their vocations.

Many Defence Colony women had combined careers with marriage: Two whom I met were successful designers, and another a doctor. Several were college teachers; another took over management of her husband's business after he became ill. My friends voiced skepticism about old rules of deference, but then told me how they felt compelled to say yes to a parent who sent them on errands day after day or called on them for chauffeuring services. Gossiping about some spat between a young wife and her husband, they would comment that a young girl should never talk back to her husband or fail to do what he asks. Older women were very skeptical about "love" marriages, talking on and on about cases where mismatched backgrounds had created problems for a couple. But younger women, too, would say, "We'd rather let our parents choose for us; they have more experience in knowing what makes a marriage turn out well." Then they would tell me about a boy they liked whom they had met in college.

It took me a while to figure out what was going on. Like male samajists of the previous century, my friends were products of two cultures, with two accompanying sets of values. One set of values had been acquired via upbringing in Hindu homes and exposure to popular sayings, stories, and festivals. Another came through educations which, like those of the samajists, used English as a language medium and exposed students to Western literature, with its ideas about human rights and the need for human self-expression. At times, those two sets of values came into conflict. When that happened, instead of trying to reconcile their claims or to replace one set of values with the other, my friends drew on both, jumping back and forth between one standpoint and the other.

When I wrote about this duality of values after returning home, I explained the persistence of old values by pointing out that the social needs that gave rise to them had not yet changed all that much.[9] Many young brides, for example, were still forced by economic need and lack of alternatives to live with their husbands' parents. Rules of deference were ways of drawing clear lines of authority so that people living together in multigenerational families would get into fewer arguments with one another. Arranged marriages, too, were a way of minimizing family tensions by

---

[9] "Women In-Between: Conflicting Values in Delhi," *Journal of Religion* 67:2 (April 1987): 237–74.

making sure that a bride would be raised with family customs similar to those of the family that she would be entering. Young girls dared not challenge parents too drastically, for fear of being cut off from families. Living without the support and aid of family networks remains very difficult for both young women and young men in today's India. When I try to explain to my students why older values have so much power in India, I point to the persistence of these needs. But I have begun to realize that ethnic and national pride are also at stake. That will be clearer as the rest of this book unfolds.

Let me turn to the discoveries of my second Defence Colony visit. What religious practices did Defence Colony women engage in? And what kinds of religious groups might they belong to? Some of my new friends had no interest in religion. India, like the United States, has a strong secular tradition, well established among its intellectual class. Although the term "secular" has somewhat different connotations in India than it does in Western countries, for some Indians it entails rejection of religion and an attempt to structure society according to wholly rational principles. For example, India has a tradition of Marxist critique and activism that perceives religion principally as a social opiate and an instrument through which privileged classes maintain control over others. One neighbor, a college teacher raised in central India, confided to me one day that her father and brothers had been Marxists. She had little experience of religion, let alone any sort of commitment to it. Once upon a time, a friend had taken her to visit the ashram of the famed holy man Sathya Sai Baba. But the first thing she noticed was that this guru seemed to invite only wealthy people to his private audiences. She had decided she had no need of holy men and did no more experimenting with religion.

Another close friend had little sympathy with Marxists, but told me firmly that she was an agnostic. Yet she collected Krishna images, conducted memorial rites for her deceased husband, fasted once a week, and loved to go on pilgrimage. Justifying this, she told me, "For me this is cultural, not religious—I just like to go to new places and see things valued by other Indians." This same friend kept up vrats affirming her ties to her brothers and celebrated the fall Diwali festival with the same zest as other Hindus. Until her husband's death, she told me, each fall she had observed the annual karva chauth fast to promote his good health, along with friends in the neighborhood. This, too, she said, was cultural; she had done the fast to be with her friends as much as to protect her husband.

During my first stay in Defence Colony, I had mistakenly come to believe that vrats such as karva chauth were no longer practiced there. Later, I realized that many were still kept up, but in an inconspicuous manner. I would come across evidence of them accidentally. At a luncheon party held during the fall Nine Nights festival, for example, a special fruit salad was available to meet needs of women observing the reduced-foods fast that accompanies the festival. Many other religious practices were similarly low-key. I heard of women who met weekly with friends in homes for an hour or two of *kirtan,* devotional singing, and of another woman of deep religious interests who offered regular talks in her home. One friend who ran a stressful business found respite by doing *japa,* repeating a mantra while telling beads on the Hindu equivalent of a rosary. She did this when taking breaks for walks, keeping beads and hand concealed in the handbag that she wore stylishly over her shoulder.

I discovered that many neighbors kept puja rooms in inner recesses of their homes, or at least kept a puja corner in a bedroom where a visitor such as I was unlikely to see it. Some told me of saying daily prayers or meditating for half an hour in the morning. A great many had gone on pilgrimage, usually to prestigious but accessible shrines such as Badrinath in the north or the great temple of Venkateshwara (Tirupati) in the south. Vaishnodevi's pilgrimage was newly popular.[10] Most had done their pilgrimages with husbands or friends, rather than joining the boisterous singing and dancing middle-class pilgrim bands who sometimes pooled money to hire busses from New Delhi. Religion did obtrude on the neighborhood from time to time. A few neighbors had large puja rooms complete with family priests who arrived periodically to lead services. We often heard the ding-ding-ding of their puja bells in the evening as twilight fell. One neighbor with such a shrine, a goddess devotee, was daughter-in-law to a wealthy Jain family that was not in the least disturbed by her persistent Hindu devotions.

My neighbors of course kept festivals—many festivals, given the several communities present in the neighborhood and the longstanding tendency in India for neighbors to celebrate each other's festivals as well as their own. The most elaborate by far was the Diwali festival honoring the goddess Lakshmi, who in this neighborhood seemed most strongly honored for her function of bringing wealth. Neighbors played an Indian version of poker before Diwali, sometimes staking just small coins and sometimes large amounts whose losses gave rise to much teatime gossip. They also gave gifts to family members, servants, and special friends. They told me, when I asked, "What is Diwali about?", that it is special to business people, who close the old year's books and open new ones on Diwali. As night fell on that special day, my neighbors lit small oil lamps or candles and lined these on railings of balconies in front of their homes, as do many Indians of all religions. Household chauffeurs and watchmen set off fireworks in the streets, to the delight of neighborhood children and grandchildren. Diwali in New Delhi is Christmas and the Fourth of July wrapped up in a single package.

Most of the practices listed above are common among many Hindu women of North India. The Defence Colony women who joined in them were not necessarily college-educated or English-speaking. Higher education for women is still new enough in India that even in an upscale neighborhood such as Defence Colony one finds women who have completed only high school or even primary school. One elderly wife of a highly successful businessman was barely literate.

Nevertheless, many college products resided in my Indian second home, especially wives of retired officers. Several friends of my hostess had been classmates at Kinnaird College, once a favorite place for progressive Punjabi families to send their daughters. Not all had finished their Kinnaird schooling because several were still in school when Pakistan and India were ripped apart. Kinnaird landed in Pakistan, and many of its Hindu or Arya Samaj students fled Pakistan along with their families. As I came to know my neighbors better, at times I heard harrowing stories of that time. One friend lost most of her relatives in a village massacre; others escaped mob attacks with only the clothes they had on, leaving beloved homes and all other property behind.

---

[10] See Chapter 7, p. 161.

Seeking New Paths

Such memories may be one reason why some of my new neighbors had turned into religious seekers. Few of my neighborhood friends seemed strongly linked to older sectarian traditions, unlike the Brahmin women of Chennai looked at next. Although several had been reared in Arya Samaj families, many had fallen away in adulthood; if anything, their Arya Samaj upbringing had increased their separation from the greater Hindu community. None were regular temple goers except the Sai Baba devotees, who went weekly to pay respects at the nearby Shirdi Sai Baba temple. All of my New Delhi temple visits were made with friends from other neighborhoods.

On the other hand, many Defence Colony residents were involved with one or another of the many cross-sectarian religious movements that have grown up recently in India, movements often rooted in older Hindu teachings and symbols but drawing together strands of multiple traditions. For example, on learning that I teach religion in the United States, many new acquaintances told me they were devotees of South Indian guru Sathya Sai Baba. This teacher, believed by many to be an *avatar,* God walking on earth, has a widespread and quite active organization in New Delhi. By the time of my 1998 visit, a grand center for this organization was under construction less than a mile from the Defence Colony border. One Sai Baba devotee in the Colony was a doctor who volunteered each week in free treatment clinics that Sai Baba's organization ran in poor Delhi\New Delhi neighborhoods. Once a month, she held an hour-long kirtan in her spacious home, open to anyone who wished to join its singing. Many Sai Baba devotees offer such in-home kirtans, inviting singers trained by the organization to lead them. Sai Baba tells them that attending and sponsoring such sessions will attune them to God and intensify their devotion. The New Delhi organization coordinates the kirtans, making sure they are spread throughout the month and publishing dates, times, and places for them in an annual program book. A devotee wishing to attend kirtan need only look in this book to find the next and nearest one available.

The doctor told me she had become a Sai Baba devotee because Sai Baba had cured her of a strange and crippling illness that she herself could not diagnose. Now she thanked Baba by offering her service. She also attended "camps" each summer at the Sai Baba central ashram. Another Defence Colony Sai Baba devotee had also hosted kirtans in the past and had taught *bal vikas* classes, a kind of Hindu Sunday school for children. She liked the organization, she said, because its people supported and looked out for one another.[11]

Another "new" religious organization well established in New Delhi is the Ramakrishna Mission. Although some of my contacts dismissed this as a "Bengali organization," others had embraced it. One was a friend of my hostess, raised, like her, in the Arya Samaj. As a young wife, she had lost her husband. Living with his parents, she found new meaning for her life through service to the Mission, whose New Delhi branch had just been started by a gifted young swami named Ranganathananda. After women of the central Mission in Calcutta fulfilled a long-term dream to build a parallel organization serving women and children, she helped bring a branch of this

---

[11] For more on Sathya Sai Baba, see Chapter 10, especially pp. 245–46 and 258–60.

Sharada Mission to New Delhi. Now, she headed the board of lay trustees that worked beside Sharada Mission's women renouncers to run the convent that housed them and the school they were running. Every Saturday, she and Colony friends piled into her car and drove to hear the school's principal deliver talks on Patanjali's *Yoga Sutras*. Often they took me with them. They loved Sharada Mission, they told me along the way, because its women were so bright and admirable, and so thoroughly devoted to serving others.

Most of the larger and well-established new Hindu movements described in the next chapter have flourishing branches in New Delhi. In various neighborhoods of the city, I met devotees of the Aurobindo Society, the Divine Life Society, the Chinmaya Mission, the woman saint Anandamayi Ma, the International Society for Krishna Consciousness, the Brahma Kumaris, and several other groups not described here. But smaller new groups are also significant. To my surprise, my explorations in Defence Colony turned up three devotees of Yogi Raushan Nath, a householder yogi and guru I had known for years via American connections. One married couple crossed the city every Sunday morning to join a group meeting at his home for meditation. Between my first and second visits, Yogi Raushan Nath himself had died. His group nevertheless went on meeting as usual, hosted by the yogi's wife and led by tapes of his powerful Om chanting.

Most of my religiously inclined friends in Defence Colony claimed allegiance to gurus. Many of these gurus had names I had never heard before; their unfamiliar faces often looked out at me from framed photos sitting on end tables of Western-style living rooms. Especially if gurus did not live close at hand, many of my friends also formed secondary allegiances to teachers more readily available. I found such dual allegiance often among Bodhananada devotees, the circle I knew best and interviewed most intensely. One such was the third disciple of Yogi Raushan Nath, who, by the time I met her, was enthusiastically attending Bodhananda's classes.

Another friend of my hostess had first led me to these classes, which met in the living room of a little house on a street just behind the Defence Colony market. The swami had set up three such classes, each meeting two days per week for two hours at a time. Two were on the *Bhagavad-Gita,* one meeting mornings from 10 AM until 12 noon and another in the early evening. A third, alternating with the morning *Gita* classes, was on the philosopher Shankaracharya's most famous treatise *Vivekachudamani,* a very dense and difficult work. Very early on weekday mornings, the Swami led guided meditations; on weekends, he addressed satsangs meeting around the city.

When I met Swami Bodhananda, he had been in the neighborhood for just a year; in fact, he had "gone independent" just two years before, breaking ties to the Chinmaya Mission that had trained him. I joined his *Vivekachudamani* class, taught with wit and sparkle, verse by verse in traditional Indian fashion. Bodhananda would chant a verse or two in Sanskrit, then take them apart for interpretation, sometimes word by word. A dozen or so women attended regularly, bringing copies of the text to class and paying small monthly subscriptions to cover the swami's expenses and rental costs for his center. They were barely a third of the way through their volumes when I started, and only slightly more than half way through when I left for the United States nine months later. Most were longstanding Colony residents, nonworking wives of retired military officers.

Like the yoga lectures delivered at Sharada Mission, the swami's talks were sprinkled with astute observations on human dilemmas and the psychological foibles that lead people into trouble. Underlying them was the classic Vedanta assertion that humans are at root brahman and hence we contain within ourselves all the resources needed to deal with problems. It is not surprising, then, that women attending this class told me they were learning through it how to "get on," working out solutions to problems for themselves instead of relying on others to do it for them.

Many religious teachers in India double as psychological counselors. As I grew to know Swami Bodhananda better, I realized that he too spent a great deal of time advising disciples on problems ranging from handling cranky spouses and in-laws, to making job decisions, to managing money problems. Learning to think through problems on one's own is not an important part of childhood or college training in India; deference to authority has classically been much more important.

The swami was out to change this. He would leave his Defence Colony protegees, he said, when they were ready to direct their own lives. He did leave them four years later, moving on to extend his reach to America. He now visits Defence Colony once or twice a year, staying no more than a month at a time. He teaches no more classes there, but still talks at frequent satsangs and at times leads disciples in pujas they have requested. When I returned to Defence Colony in 1998, he had not yet shown up for his annual fall visit. A group of women disciples had continued to meet twice a week at the home of one, a near neighbor to my hostess. It was hard to have Swami-ji go off like that, they told me. But he had, indeed, given them the strength to go on without him. They had gained confidence and courage from his teachings and had learned how to detach from family problems. If they needed help in thinking their way through obstacles, they brought them to one another and worked them out together. I saw the importance of their mutual support in one woman battling cancer. She attributed her long survival to the combined support of God, Swami-ji, and her friends.

Bodhananda's disciples also drew solace from two weekly practices that drew them together. During one weekly session, they chanted together the Sanskrit text *Vishnu Sahasranama,* the thousand names of Vishnu. This, they said, was a chant of empowerment. Swami-ji had suggested they do it before he left and had prepared for them the short puja that they performed before reciting it. They chanted swiftly and surely; questioning them, I learned that some had listened to tapes so they could chant more precisely. Their second weekly practice was *bhajan* singing. They had hired a teacher who came to the house to teach them devotional songs composed by North India's saints, especially those of nearby Braj, the holy land of Krishna. The bhajans they were learning are not the simple hymns usually sung during kirtans, where a leader sings out a line and the group repeats it afterward. They are complex compositions both in poetry and melody, usually performed by professional singers. "These are our heritage," they told me. "We want to know them." Ironically, the man they had found to teach them was a Muslim. They had decided this was okay because he had studied in Braj itself with a respected teacher. In India, it is quite common for Hindu and Muslim singers to learn and perform the music of each others' traditions.

Because Bodhananda's students had been so enthusiastic about studying their tradition's religious classics, I had thought I might find them conducting something like Christian Bible study groups, working through texts together and puzzling out their meaning. But they resisted this idea, saying "We aren't competent to do that." They did study, however, by going to lectures by other swamis. At several nearby centers, lecture series were held from time to time, often advertised in New Delhi papers. When the primary guru of one group member came to town for a week, her closest friends went by taxi together to hear the lectures he gave in a downtown auditorium.

Every so often something would happen that introduced me to another level of my friends' complex affiliations. One such event occurred just a few weeks before I left in 1998. We had been talking about the secular service organizations in which many upper-class Hindu women are involved. Then, I learned that several of my friends gave financial support to another guru whom they had never told me about before. This one was a school chum. A former Kinnaird classmate—an incredible tomboy, they said—had undergone a religious conversion. Now she is Param Pujya Ma, the "Universal Mother." She heads a large and successful ashram called Arpana, located to the north in a poor rural area. Drawing on volunteer labor and funds from well-to-do city dwellers, it serves its region with mobile clinics, job training programs, and a marketing outlet in the city for village-made handicrafts. My friends glowed when they told me this; they are proud of their former classmate. Once I learned of Param Pujya Ma, I discovered that she too has a generous circle of Defence Colony supporters.

In sum, Hinduism is alive and well among Defence Colony women, taking, as usual, many different forms. Old patterns like those described in Chapters 5–7 persist there: pujas and vows; kirtans and pilgrimage; visits by family priests to aid with household rites. But new ones are emerging alongside of them. Especially striking in our neighborhood was the active presence of swamis, bringing teachings once thought special to renouncers' traditions to householders deeply engaged in worldly activity. A history professor at Delhi University whom I know well assured me during my 1998 visit that this was indeed a new phenomenon. He noticed it only during the last decade, although my own digging has shown that the trend it reflects had been gathering momentum for at least the past half-century. Closely related to this trend are other departures from older traditions: women as well as men studying Sanskrit philosophy; women chanting in Sanskrit; women acting as ritualists, teachers, and gurus. The mixing of devotion and high philosophy was also a part of this new trend, explored further in Part IV. First, another group of modern and privileged Hindus whose practice sheds important light on this new trend are covered.

SUBTLY CHANGING KEEPERS: BRAHMIN WOMEN OF CHENNAI

India has recently gone through a spate of name changing to shed traces of its past domination by Britain. As a result, the Southern city once called Madras is now Chennai, reassuming the name of the fishing village initially on its site. In 1639 C.E., merchants established a trading center at this village, and that trading center evolved into the capital of the British East India Company's Madras Colony. Chennai is in the northeast corner of Tamilnadu, on the shore of the Bay of Bengal. Sixty kilometers to the west is the old royal city of Kanchipuram (or Conjeevaram), renowned for its temples and the great monastery that is one of five principal seats of the Dasanami Sannyasi order. Chennai currently has about five and a half million people, making it South India's largest urban center.

Despite its peripheral location in Tamilnadu, Chennai is very much a Tamil city. It shares its region's interest in goddesses and goddess lore.[12] The Tamil-speaking region also played a major role in the history of Hindu devotional movements. Remember that India's first "singing saints" were Tamils: first the Nayanars, devotees of Shiva, and then soon after, the Alvars, devotees of Krishna. Collecting their songs and extending their theologies were the famed Shaiva-Siddhanta and Shri-Vaishnava sampradayas. Nor did Tamilnadu's history of devotional enthusiasm stop with foundation of these movements. A major Krishna revival took place there in the seventeenth century. Chennai experienced yet another in the mid-1900s, described by anthropologist Milton Singer in a famous article, "Radha-Krishna Bhajanas of Madras City."[13]

The Radha-Krishna bhajanas described by Singer were groups that existed for the sake of singing songs and dancing to Radha and Krishna. Although they had some cross-caste membership, these groups were made up primarily of high-caste men. Especially active as both members and leaders were men of the Smarta Brahmin subcaste. This subcaste honors five, or sometimes six, main deities: Shiva, Vishnu, the Goddess, Ganesha, Surya, and sometimes Murugan, identified with Shiva's son Skandha. Yet it leans strongly toward Shiva because of its association long ago with Shankaracharya, the famed Hindu philosopher and sannyasi organizer. Singer was puzzled by the fact that a group with such a history would throw itself so enthusiastically into Krishna devotion. He was also struck by the groups' eclecticism. Along with devotional songs in Tamil, they sang songs by Hindi, Marathi, and Bengali saints in the languages in which these songs were written.

Mary Hancock says that she based her study in Chennai in part because of Singer's previous work there. She was especially interested in what he had to say about how modernization had affected the religious lives of Smarta Brahmins. By and large, Smarta Brahmins are every bit as modern as my Defence Colony friends. Their caste group benefited most from the English-medium schools set up by the British in the Madras Colony. Like Chitpavan Brahmins of Maharashtra and the *bhadralok* class of Calcutta, they captured the bulk of high-paying jobs and became the core of the rising new middle and upper-middle class. Singer suggested that, to some extent, bhajana movements reflected the modern experience of Smarta Brahmins themselves. On the one hand, Smartas were well traveled; Singer was able to trace how government workers stationed for a time in other regions brought back songs to add to bhajana groups' collections. On the other hand, they felt pressed for time and compromised by their jobs, which required them to relax many Brahmin restrictions

---

[12] See Chapter 6, pp. 150–54 and Chapter 8, p. 200.

[13] In Singer's edited volume *Krishna, Myths, Rites, and Attitudes* (Honolulu: Univ. of Hawaii Press, 1966), 108–18; this article is reprinted in Singer's *When a Great Tradition Modernizes, an Anthropological Approach to Indian Civilization* (New York: Praeger, 1972), 199–244. A companion essay in the *Krishna* volume by T. K. Venkateswaram describes the theological and historical background of this movement: "Radha-Krishna Bhajanas of South India: A Phenomenological, Theological, and Philosophical Study," 139–72.

guarding ritual purity. So they had taken up the path of bhakti, said to be the easiest and best path of spiritual discipline for the present degenerate age.

Another important factor in the new Krishna movements' rise was the Adi-Dravida movements mentioned in Chapter 8. Also called non-Brahmin or anti-Brahmin movements, these challenged Brahmin dominance over Tamil society and the hegemony maintained by Brahmin culture and teachings. Adi-Dravidas became and remain today a major force in Tamilnadu state politics. Using such instruments as caste quotas in hiring for government jobs, they have rolled back Smarta economic dominance. They are not always gentle in their methods. Brahmins no longer feel safe moving through Chennai streets. Many have been attacked by Adi-Dravida gangs. Singer postulated that one reason for Smarta support of Krishna movements was that these had cross-caste participation and professed at least the ideal of human equality under God. They could, therefore, help Brahmins reconnect with low-caste participants, undoing damage caused by the Brahmin\Adi Dravida split.

In a later Madras-based study, Singer interviewed high-caste industrial leaders to learn how they handled clashes between rules set down in their religion and the demands they faced in a modern workplace. He found that they did this via processes that he called compartmentalizing and delegating. In compartmentalizing, they acted differently in the workplace from the way they did at home or in religious spaces, treating the workplace as a neutral, nonsacred space where they could afford to be more flexible. Delegating meant that they resolved time conflicts between home and workplace by turning over home demands, including ritual demands, to other people. Some of Singer's subjects hired Brahmin priests to come in and conduct the household pujas that men were expected to do. Others turned responsibility for pujas over to their wives, together with other good works such as volunteering for charities and listening to swamis' talks.

Hancock wanted to know what had come of the changes Singer described and how those changes affected Smarta women. Like me, she began by finding out what sorts of values related to womanhood were being upheld by Smarta women. Then, she asked what kinds of practice they were engaged in. Finally, she did some important historical digging, uncovering initiatives by a major Smarta leader that influenced their values and their choices about practice.

Auspicious Wives

Values are the first consideration. Despite the fact that many held jobs and were often as highly educated as their husbands, the Smarta women Hancock interviewed consistently affirmed that they aspired to be *cumankalis,* auspicious wives. The Sanskrit equivalent of this term is *sumangali.* Cumankali comes very close in connotation to the term *pativrat* used in the north, "one who is vowed to her husband." A cumankali is a woman with a living husband who dedicates her life to keeping her spouse healthy, happy, and prosperous. She is modest, virtuous, restrained, and graceful in speech and action. She is a good household manager and acts according to her husband's wishes, doing nothing that would embarrass him. She adorns herself richly and tastefully to increase her beauty, for in Tamil belief external beauty enhances the beauty one carries within. The Tamil prototype for the cumankali is Lakshmi, goddess of wealth, good luck, and beauty. Her fortunate spouse is Vishnu, divine protector of dharma. An implication of their coupling is that the man who upholds dharma will enjoy wealth, good luck, and beauty, brought to him in large measure through the support of his virtuous wife. A virtuous wife is called the Lakshmi of her household.

Being a cumankali entails engaging in a broad range of religious activities. At one point or another in her book, Hancock mentions virtually every type of traditional practice that I encountered in Defence Colony: vows, called *nonpu* in Tamil; pilgrimage; festivals; devotional singing; hosting and attending satsangs; Sanskrit rites of passage guided by Brahmins. In striking departure from Singer were her findings concerning bhajans. At the time of Singer's research, bhajan groups had been led and organized mainly by men. Women and children sat on the sides and joined in on bhajan refrains. A few women's bhajan groups were forming, he noted, and he predicted that this trend would spread. It did; bhajan groups seemed as popular among Hancock's informants as they had been formerly among Smarta men.

Hancock also notes participation by both men and women in two "new" religious groups well established in Chennai. Sai Baba has a large and successful organization there as does the older Ramakrishna Mission. Smarta Brahmin disciples are found in both groups. Nonetheless, the main focus of Smarta women's attention appears to be their puja rooms. As in Delhi, some puja spaces described by Hancock were simple niches in apartment walls or small freestanding cabinets located in inner rooms. The latter were opened during worship, but closed away at other times to protect them from polluting contact. If space in a home was tight, for not all of Hancock's informants were wealthy, a puja space could even be a kitchen or closet shelf. But where space was available, Smarta homes often held large and richly adorned puja rooms, many equipped with expensive silver implements sharply contrasting with modest furnishings elsewhere in the home.

Women often performed a home's pujas, despite older precedents that assigned such tasks to men. They might spend as much as two hours on a single puja and still more on special occasions that required extras be added to the ritual. During one especially popular puja, an oil lamp was worshiped as Lakshmi, either daily, weekly, or for a pre-set period. Women often fasted on days when they did this lamp puja.

Going Public

One change in puja patterns that Hancock noticed over the years of her Chennai studies was a tendency for puja performance to become increasingly public. Puja rooms were moved from inner recesses of homes to boundary spaces where outsiders could reach and see them. Many wealthy homes even had private temples, built within the walls of a family compound, but not inside that family's living space. Another change was the mounting of public pujas featuring women. One variety begun in 1947 featured large groups of women doing lamp puja together, synchronizing their chants and gestures. Its first performance was set up to publicize an organization founded to fight harassment of women by "anti-Brahmin rowdies."[14]

Certain festivals, too, were increasing in profile. One highly popular among high-caste Hindus was Navarattiri (Hindi Navratri), the Nine-Nights goddess festival.

---

[14] Hancock, ibid., p. 40.

Once upon a time in this region, Navarattiri was a festival of warriors and kingship just as in the Rajput versions described earlier in this text.[15] In today's Chennai, however, it is a celebration mounted mainly by women and children, who build elaborate displays based on themes from Indian culture and then visit each others' homes to view them. During her 1996 visit, Hancock was invited to act as a judge in a newspaper-sponsored contest based on these exhibits. She saw exhibits on "shakti power," that is, womanpower; on Ganesha and the goddesses; on "marching bands, cricket games, weddings, and . . . merchants with their wares."[16] Models of Indian villages were popular, as were Disney scenes and models of Chennai city. Winners included the womanpower display, an illustrated history of India, and a display of South Indian handicrafts and agricultural products titled "Green Revolution." Many displays she saw filled one or more rooms.

Two other new activities unusual for Brahmin women were initiatives to restore goddess temples and leadership in goddess cults. One older Smarta woman from a home of modest resources had decided to clean up a dingy goddess shrine near her home. Gathering a large support group of neighborhood women, she raised money for improvements, including a new image. She and her friends then set a new precedent of meeting at this shrine for special Tuesday and Friday services, as well as mounting celebrations of several annual festivals. Another much wealthier woman set up a full goddess temple within her home. She not only led pujas there but also gave religious discourses. An initiate of the Tantric goddess-centered teaching called Shri Vidya, she had disciples to whom she gave Shri Vidya initiations.

Two Shankaracharyas

The temple-restorer and the Shri Vidya leader both served the goddess Kamakshi. This goddess was not only central to Shri Vidya teachings but also tied to lower-caste and village practice. Hancock found another Smarta Kamakshi devotee who underwent monthly possessions by the goddess, answering questions posed to her by other women in attendance; a *mataji,* goddess medium, of much lower caste had initiated her into goddess service. The Smarta medium had a Smarta protegee of her own, who in turn drew into her orbit another Smarta woman who met her when serving as Hancock's research assistant.

Unlike my Defence Colony friends, most of Hancock's Smarta informants observed practices that, like their values, were highly consistent with patterns seen in the past. How then can we account for the shifts noted above, especially the increase in women's public activity and their involvement in goddess practices linked to lower classes? The role played in their lives by their main spiritual adviser, the Shankaracharya of Kanchipuram, was one answer Hancock found. For many centuries, Smarta Brahmins have worked in close alliance with renouncers of the Dasanami Sannyasi sampradaya founded by the philosopher Shankaracharya. These are highly revered, usually orange-robed, swamis. Chief among Dasanami gurus are the heads of the sampradaya's five principal monasteries, one of which is located in Kanchipuram. Like the

---

[15] See Chapter 6, pp. 148–49.

[16] Hancock, ibid., pp. 248–49.

teacher who founded their order, these monastery heads are called Shankaracharyas. They are also known as *jagadgurus*, "teachers of the world." For many traditional Hindus of high caste, the Shankaracharyas represent the highest spiritual authority available in their tradition. In the past, they were often called in to resolve disputes Hindus could not settle within their own caste communities.

Most Smartas have special reverence for the Shankaracharyas. Both Singer and Hancock speak of the weight their word carries in the Smarta community. Chennai Smartas have been especially close to the Shankaracharya of Kanchipuram because he is located so close to their city. He is not a distant authority; Smartas visit him often, both for darshan and for advice.

During the period of Hancock's research, the Kanchi Shankaracharya was a sup-porter of the Hindu nationalist movement described here in Chapter 11. Both he and his predecessor were also initiates of the Shri Vidya teachings. These connections mean that both had an interest in promoting goddess worship. The current Shankaracharya's nationalist sympathies mean that he had also had an interest in promoting assertive public demonstrations of support for Hindu practice. Making Hindus and their prac-tice more conspicuous in India has been a consistent effort of the nationalist program. The Shankaracharya was, moreover, drawing on a strain of nationalist symbolism that touted women as preservers of Hindu religion and "spirituality." This symbolism often portrays India itself as a woman or goddess, so that images of virtuous Hindu woman-hood and nationalist pride come to be connected with one another.

Hancock cites several Shankaracharya initiatives that had promoted the changes she was seeing. "As early as the thirties,"[17] the Shankaracharya's predecessor began encouraging women to chant a Sankrit text called *Lalita Sahasranama* together. This text is a goddess-centered equivalent of the *Vishnu Sahasranama,* a litany of one thousand titles evoking the deeds and powers of the deity it honors. This same Shankaracharya also encouraged Smarta women to sing together prayers that he had set to music. During the 1950s, he advised Smarta women to form cross-sectarian bhajan groups and to participate in a vow honoring the Alvar saint Antal (Andal); for-merly, only Vaishnava women did this. The older Shankaracharya had also mentored the woman Shri Vidya guru described earlier in this chapter. Although he could not initiate a woman, he had found a guru for her. He also gave her a gold Kamakshi to install and serve in her home, a move that set in motion her priestly activities.

Many women with whom Hancock talked during the 1980s had at one time or another received personal instruction in performing public, collective forms of god-dess pujas from both the older Shankaracharya and his successor. It was the younger, however, who attempted to turn women's devotion into an expression of patriotism. In the 1980s, he founded an organization called Jan Kalyan, "people's welfare," to pro-mote nationalist themes and "Hindu culture," which in his understanding was Brahmin culture. Members were encouraged to found religion libraries, teach the culturally backward, clean up public spaces, perform public ceremonies, build new temples and monasteries, and establish "cow protection homes."[18] Although Jan Kalyan was intended for both men and women, he recruited women to organize its

---

[17] Hancock, ibid., p. 75.

[18] Hancock, ibid., p. 232.

meetings and promote it. One means of promotion was mass lamp pujas. A woman active in these told Hancock that one had featured one thousand eight women, all coordinating gestures so that all moved together as if they were one.[19]

The Jan Kalyan movement failed. By 1990, its organization had broken up and the Shankaracharya himself gave up on it. Nonetheless, the smaller changes he had promoted in women's lives remained, kept up by the Smarta women themselves.

Why did they support all this time-consuming activity? According to Hancock, they enjoyed it:"Over time, I came to understand that women derived great pleasure from these activities—emotional and aesthetic satisfaction, equanimity, the friendship of other women, and sometimes a reputation for piety."[20] Moreover, they accepted propaganda, such as the following, proclaiming women's special mission: "All the greatness of our land shines through our women. It is our country's greatest asset that women continue our traditional practices despite the rapid advance of civilization."[21] Hancock suggests that the prestige brought to Smartas in general as a result of their women's conspicuous piety is also a factor worth considering. Although non-Brahmin movements have weakened Brahmin prestige, they have not destroyed it. Women's public practice reasserts the claim that Brahmins deserve to continue as "culture brokers," standard setters with the right to tell others what is proper and in good taste.

A HINDU REVIVAL

Earlier in this chapter, I claimed that the activities it describes attest to a massive Hindu revival in today's India. What does this mean? The word "revival" suggests that something once flagging has acquired new energy and direction. The "something" being reenergized today is interest in a wide range of classic Hindu practice, symbols, and teachings. The bearers of this reenlivening process are often men and women wearing renouncers' robes. Their target audience most often consists of cosmopolitan Indians of Hindu birth disaffected with their religious heritage.

That much of the direction of today's revival *is* new is clearly shown by my findings among Defence Colony women, particularly the disciples of Swami Bodhananda. They had not chanted in groups before or gathered to sing bhajans, nor had they worked their way through religious texts, not even a text as well known the *Bhagavad-Gita,* now being drawn on to generate new insights. The very fact that my friends even felt free to study classical Sanskrit texts and to chant in Sanskrit is something new in Hindu India. As indicated earlier, in the mid-nineteenth century, the father of woman reformer Pandita Ramabai had to defend his decision to teach his wife Sanskrit before a local Brahmin council. My friends' interest in learning great devotional songs of the North also seems new to Hindus of their caste and educational levels; I suspect, in fact, that it is a northern echo of the bhajan respectability that has emerged in South India.

---

[19] Hancock, p. 234.

[20] Hancock, p. 90.

[21] Cited Hancock, ibid., p. 76.

As for Chennai's Smarta Brahmin women, even though their practice seems at first glance quite traditional, Hancock's digging shows that much of it is also a product of initiatives undertaken within the last two generations. Even household pujas were once a responsibility assigned to men, and any public performance was improper for Brahmin women. Synchronized lamp pujas by women are new transformations of older rites. A twentieth-century guru set in motion the now-popular group chanting of *Lalita Sahasranama*. His successor challenged high-caste women to clean up and restore services in neglected goddess temples. This successor promoted the women's bhajan groups so popular today.

Many scholars have called attention to the fact that traditions being promoted in the current Hindu revival are largely from the Brahmin heritage recorded in Sanskrit. Note the importance of Sanskrit chanting, the *Bhagavad-Gita,* the philosopher Shankaracharya, and complex pujas. Yet portions of Brahmin teachings are also being by-passed. In addition to rules restricting women, rules of purity and pollution have been relaxed. The very fact that Hancock, a foreigner, entered the spaces described in her book is evidence of such transformation. I myself have entered many a high-caste Hindu kitchen, even cooked in one or two, and eaten beside high-caste friends, including some who are otherwise quite strict in practice. This would never have been possible a century ago; during the late nineteenth century, Maharashtrian Brahmins outcasted several reformers for the simple offense of drinking tea with Christian missionaries.[22]

Still other relaxations are seen in the increased access of women to roles of religious leadership. Many women have become gurus, not only teaching, but also initiating disciples. A few Sanskrit centers have trained women to officiate at samskaras and serve as household priests.[23] Access of lay disciples, both men and women, to texts once restricted to renouncers is another important change. Yet another is the eclectic blending of traditions across both caste and sectarian lines. Such changes should not be misread as spillover from Western influence. Many are anchored in and promote deeply conservative values, such as affirmation of classic womanly ideals.

What is behind today's Hindu revival? Two converging forces promote it. One is the impact of a spate of new "spiritual" movements that have emerged since the beginning of the twentieth century, movements that built on precedents established by nineteenth-century samajists. Adapting old forms such as renunciant vows and meditation practiced in forest hermitages, they have used these to launch a massive reordering of Hindu religious priorities. Self-transformation, service to others, and the need to work for the good of all without seeking profit are among these movements' central themes. Also important is organization, coordinating efforts to pursue common goals. Recall that many Defence Colony women are involved in such new organizations, and some are also supported by women in Tamilnadu.

The second major impetus toward today's revival is a cluster of movements promoting Hindu nationalist sentiments. Their influence on the younger Kanchipuram

---

[22] This incident is described in Ramabai Ranade's account of her life with her famous reformer-husband: *Ranade: His Wife's Reminiscences,* Kusumavati Deshpande, tr. (Haridabad: Government of India Press, 1963), pp. 136–40.

[23] See my "Shakti Ascending."

Shankaracharya has been noted. Promoting Hindu pride and assertiveness, they are legacies of the Indian struggle for independence. Set in motion initially to fan resistance against the British, they now fight "pseudo-secularists" whom they claim have turned the Indian state over to its religious minorities. They, too, have learned to organize, becoming skilled both in spreading their own propaganda and in building an often-victorious political machine. These movements are covered in Part IV, as is a special challenge confronting them, the movement of Hindus overseas.

ADDITIONAL SOURCES

Surprisingly little research has been done on religious practice or commitment among India's cosmopolitan Hindus. An example of links across generations between samaj supporters and today's cosmopolitans is offered in Aparna Basu, "The Reformed Family, Women Reformers: A Case Study of Vidyagauri Nilkanth," *Samya Shakti: A Journal of Women's Studies* 4–5 (1989–90): 52–82; see also Basu's "A Century's Journey; Women's Education in Western India: 1820–1920," *Socialization, Education and Women: Explorations in Gender Identity,* Karuna Chanana, ed. (New Delhi: Orient Longman, 1988), 65–95. Rama Mehta shows how English-medium schooling alienated women from Hindu traditions in *The Western Educated Hindu Woman* (New York: Asia Publishing House, 1970). An unexpected asset I found in my studies of Kinnaird College graduates was Michelle Maskiell's *Women between Cultures: The Lives of Kinnaird College Alumnae in British India* (Syracuse, NY: Maxwell School of Citizenship and Public Affairs, Syracuse Univ., 1984).

One way to learn about the religious premises of cosmopolitans is to study the new spiritual movements in which they are often engaged. Several examples of these movements and relevant references are given in Chapter 10. A few works concentrating on gurus furnish insight into the guru–disciple relationships so often important in this group. Long excerpts from guru–disciple exchanges are quoted in Charles S. J. White's "Mother Guru: Jnanananda of Chennai, India," *Unspoken Worlds: Women's Religious Lives,* 3rd. ed., Nancy A. Falk and Rita M. Gross, eds. (Belmont, CA: Wadsworth, 2001), 43–65. Kirin Narayan, *Storytellers, Saints, and Scoundrels: Folk Narrative in Hindu Religious Teaching* (Philadelphia: Univ. of Pennsylvania Press, 1989) describes a guru's everyday exchanges with disciples; unfortunately, Narayan tells readers little about the class backgrounds of this teacher's clientele.

Milton Singer's studies of upper-class Hindus in Madras\Chennai still offer significant insight into cosmopolitan Hindus' methods of integrating Western influence with their own tradition. See especially his *When a Great Tradition Modernizes, an Anthropological Approach to Indian Civilization* (New York: Praeger, 1972). Mary Hancock's several studies are strongly recommended: *Womanhood in the Making: Domestic Ritual and Public Culture in Urban South India* (Boulder, CO: Westview Press, 1999); "Saintly Careers among South India's Urban Middle Classes," *Man,* n.s. 25 (1990): 505–20; and "Dilemmas of Domesticity," *From the Margins of Hindu Marriage,* L. Harlan and P. Courtright, eds. (New York: Oxford Univ. Press, 1995), 60–91. Readers can learn more about Kamakshi and the Shankaracharya of Kanchi through William Cenker, "The Sankaracarya of Kanci and the Kamakshi Temple as Ritual Center," *A Sacred Thread: Modern Transmission of Hindu Traditions in India and Abroad,* Raymond Brady Williams, ed. (Chambersberg, PA: Anima, 1992), 52–67.

Finally, readers wishing to explore further the knotty caste\class relationship in India can start with two works: André Béteille, *Caste, Class, and Power, Changing Patterns of Stratification in a Tanjore Village* (Berkeley: Univ. of California Press, 1965), and Edwin D. and Aloo E. Driver, *Social Class in Urban India: Essays on Cognitions and Structures* (Leiden: E. J. Brill, 1987).

PART IV

Hinduisms in the Making

Scholars who use the word "hegemony" a great deal also frequently use the word "contest" as a verb. To contest something is to challenge it, to question its validity. Several times during the last two centuries Hindu practices and values have been contested, often with the result that many Hindus disowned them and distanced themselves from traditional authorities who once promoted them. In effect, an old hegemony has come apart. There is no longer widespread consensus among even high-caste Hindus about which behaviors are acceptable and which are not—or who should lead and who should follow.

This situation is not unique to India or to Hindus. Old hegemonies have shredded in many regions of the world: some, as in India, as a result of innovations introduced by colonial regimes; others simply as a result of pressures from the too rapid pace of economic and social change. Whether desirable or not from the perspective of other people, such shreddings are painful for those who go through them. It is difficult to make choices in a world where one can no longer be sure of what—or who—is right or wrong.

A common occurrence, therefore, as old systems come apart is that new religious movements arise to meet the challenge of putting meaning and order back into the world. Literally thousands, perhaps tens of thousands, of such movements have arisen across the globe during the last century and a half, some tiny, others gaining worldwide prominence. It may be a mistake to stress too much the "newness" of such movements because much of their practice and teaching is a recovery effort. They take pieces of older religions still meaningful and precious and put them together in new ways, giving them new interpretations. This process isn't necessarily deliberate and reasoned. Leaders are often people who have undergone some sort of life-transforming experience, an experience of spiritual awakening or prophetic calling that shows them what must be done to bring about constructive change. It also gives them the authority to tell prospective audiences that parts of existing practice can indeed be set aside and new features adopted. If the teachings of such leaders resonate, if large audiences accept them, they may eventually win out over others and become the basis of a new hegemony.

During the last century, many such new movements have arisen in India. Two chapters in this final part show how some Hindus are meeting the challenge of restructuring their own systems of order and meaning. The process of restructuring has brought about the Hindu revival noted at the close of the preceding section. Recall that two somewhat different kinds of movements are behind this revival. The first consists of groups that describe themselves as spiritual. They teach messages and methods of individual empowerment, teaching disciples how to tap the "soul power" lying within them. Many also run active programs of social service. Significantly, many such movements also describe themselves as secular. In India, this term has come to mean "nonsectarian." Therefore, a secularist is a person who affirms the underlying unity of religions. Use of this term also implies that such movements incorporate secular values, such as the worth of all humans and the right of all to be educated and protected. In other words, by claiming this term, such movements also assert that they are modern and progressive.

Movements of this type are described in Chapter 10, entitled "In Ashrams" to call attention to a characteristic institution of these movements. In ancient times, an ashram was a hermitage; today, it is often the base for an international religious network. Many new movement ashrams are run by orange-robed swamis; both the names and the robes are ways of asserting connection between their movements and India's renunciant heritage. The challenges that tarred some older Hindu leadership were not aimed at the renunciant strands of Hindu tradition. It is not surprising, therefore, that early steps toward renewal came from and have claimed connection to these strands. Ashram-based movements are extremely varied. To give a better sense of their different styles and emphases, Chapter 10 discusses eight examples instead of the usual four. These choices are not exhaustive; many readers will know other movements that they would have liked included.

One of the many factors differentiating these new movements is the degree of their immersion in Indian politics. Readers may find it strange that a movement led by renouncers would have any ties to politics at all. And indeed, some new movements deliberately keep away from India's turbulent political scene, despite the number of political leaders who would be happy to receive their endorsement. Yet renouncers, like Brahmins, once advised kings in India, while retiring kings, at least in legend, often became renouncers. Even today, two of India's most prominent new movement founders began their rise to fame as revolutionary leaders: Swami Chinmayananda of the Chinmaya Mission and Shri Aurobindo of the Aurobindo Ashram. If they became gurus instead, that was a result of their conviction that building a new kind of India required a new kind of Indian. Their movements are among those that have not avoided political involvement.

Far more conspicuous on the political scene, however, are the groups described in Chapter 11. These Hindu nationalist organizations have actively strived to capture control of India's still-new democratic political machinery. Their goal is to establish a new Hindu hegemony in India, with their own leadership in the favored position. One of their several instruments has been a political party, the so-called Bharatiya Janata Parishad, or "Indian People's Party." Although this party has won elections and is a powerful force in India, it has thus far fallen short of nationalist expectations. Chapter 11 analyzes the historical and social sources of Hindu nationalist groups, their strategies for winning allegiance, and the reasons why the party they have backed and led has not attained its stated goals.

Readers should note that both ashram-based movements and nationalists share certain assertions and actions. All reject untouchability and seek support among India's low castes, although with varying success. Virtually all have placed women in positions of public visibility and prominence. All disparage sectarian fragmentation and offer messages of Hindu unity. All affirm the merits of spiritual quest and discipline, although nationalists tend to add to this strong reaffirmations of the value of Brahmin-transmitted ritual practice and devotional discipline. All teach that Hindus must more boldly assert their presence and values in today's world. Moreover, nationalists, like ashram-based movements, claim that they are secularists, often adding to this claim the charge that opponents are only pseudo-secularist. So, there are broad areas of overlap between nationalist movements and at least some that are based in ashrams. Many Hindus who are disciples of ashram movements also support the nationalists, with no sense of conflict between these dual allegiances. Other ashram supporters reject the nationalists, pointing out that their frequent baiting of Muslims and Christians belies claims of religious inclusiveness.

One additional characteristic that nationalists and ashram-based movements share is their avid pursuit of a new constituency, the hundreds of thousands of Indian emigrants and Hindu converts living outside India. These global Hindus are confronted with challenges of their own, adapting to rules and resources of alien cultures, struggling to hold the loyalties of their children. Chapter 12, the final chapter, examines the new Hinduisms being forged among these worldwide Hindus as they and initiatives from India interact with one another. The seven examples given in Chapter 12 are creations of my own neighbors, Hindus of Western Michigan and Chicago.

10

In Ashrams

The woman behind me had sharp knees. I was grateful for folds of her sari that partially padded them as one jabbed my kidney again and again. She could not help it. My own knees were jammed against neighbors as we sat cross-legged on the cold stone floor. Several times already we had all wriggled forward to make space for devotees pouring into the rear of the tent-roofed enclosure facing the ashram's temple. We had to cram into that space as tightly as we could, for people had come from all over India—indeed, from all over the world—to have this *darshan,* view, of the man who would soon enter. Like me, many had sat for an hour or more in line outside the enclosure's gates just to make sure they could get in when the time came to enter. They had been impressively patient, entering swiftly but quietly after the gates opened, moving into places pointed out by ashram volunteers.

Now a stir began behind me, and heads swiveled to see its source. Emerging from an entrance on our women's side was a short, slim man in an orange robe. A mane of gray and black hair surrounded his broad face. Sathya Sai Baba looked much older than he had seven years before when I last visited this remote place. He'd grown stoop-shouldered and walked as if his joints were painful; his trademark halo of curls had thinned to mere frizziness. But the crowd still sighed when he entered, and devotees still dived to touch his feet as he walked along narrow paths that the volunteers struggled to keep open. As before, he took the folded petitions handed to him, waved a palm from time to time, and gave whatever came into it to someone sitting before him. He was there for at most ten minutes, walking about among us, taking the crowd's requests, and choosing who would come upstairs for a face-to-face interview. Then, he was gone, and the crowd began dispersing.

The crush was greater going out than it had been coming in. I offered my arm to steady an elderly village woman struggling to keep her balance on a flight of stairs. When she turned to take it, her face was radiant. Why wouldn't it be? She had just seen God!

The scene described in the preceding paragraph occurred a few days after Christmas in 1998 at the ashram known as Prashanti Nilayam, "Abode of Peace." Christmas is a public holiday in India, the holiday granted by law to India's Christian community. Like legal holidays allotted to other religious sects, Christmas is widely celebrated by Indians of all persuasions. Thus, many disciples of Sathya Sai Baba had gathered at his ashram to "take his *darshan*" and win the recharging of spiritual batteries that such darshan entails. Some traveled thousands of miles to get there, for Sai Baba's disciples live all over the world. Those who can afford it think little of flying to India to see him several times per year. Some stay for weeks, sleeping on floors beside people they do not know in the ashram's dozens of dormitories, eating vegetarian meals prepared by ashram volunteers, and paying less than a dollar a day for the privilege of doing so. Many rise before dawn to join early morning events: chants before the Ganesha image that stands at the ashram's entrance, communal *samkirtan,* a singing procession that circles through ashram streets, and the morning puja within the ashram's temple. They gather again later for twice-daily kirtans, sessions of simple religious song. For all, the highest point in any day comes when Sai Baba walks among them and accepts the petitions for aid that devotees hand him. For a few, the joy of that moment intensifies, as Sai Baba calls them to a smaller group interview within the temple. Here he sometimes offers short talks, or simply listens to problems and materializes gifts presented to his guests.

Darshan holds special importance for Sai Baba devotees because his devotees believe he is a living manifestation of God. To see Sai Baba walk the narrow paths among his devotees is to see God and to be uplifted by divine presence. To touch his feet, meet with him, or receive one of his gifts is to come into contact with divinity.

Sai Baba's is one of the largest and most successful of a host of new religious movements that have arisen in India since the beginning of the twentieth century. New religions are proliferating in virtually all contemporary cultures. But their growth has been intense in Hindu India, and the movements themselves reflect distinctively Indian precedents and preoccupations. Almost all, for example, claim to be "spiritual," not "religious." To them this means that they bypass ritual and priestly mediation and instead teach devotees how to tap directly into the world's sacred energies. They identify most closely with ancient shramana- and sadhu-born traditions that taught methods of individual transformation. Like many of those traditions, they welcome all who wish to learn from them, regardless of birth or station. Most of their terms and literature are derived from sadhu-transmitted traditions, and the institutions that they set up are modeled on those of older paths. Nonetheless, they have transformed their models freely, adding three important components: organization, often on a massive scale; a call to service, usually by running schools and hospitals; and mission outreach, founding satellite branches around the world.

They have both continuities and discontinuities with their Hindu past. Often heads of such groups are called "gurus," especially in the Western press. Classically, a guru was a link in a spiritual lineage, a *parampara.*[1] His most important function was his authorization to give *diksha,* initiation, linking a disciple to that lineage. He became qualified to give diksha by achieving "realization." In other words, he had to show that he himself had achieved the spiritual transformation promised by his

---

teachings. This would be reflected, day by day, in his bearing, choices, powers, and personal charisma. Guruship also entailed responsibility. A guru was a disciple's spiritual guide, leading the disciple also to self-transformation.

Leaders of new spiritual groups meet many of these criteria. They are considered realized beings; their very example legitimates whatever teachings they offer. They are guides offering spiritual and sometimes secular advice. Often their devotees will not make any important decisions without first seeking their approval. Many, but not all, offer initiation, usually imparting a mantra that a disciple will repeat daily during devotions or meditation.

More questionable is their relationship to spiritual lineage. Some are indeed present-day initiates of old guru–disciple lines, adapting teachings they have received to the present-day context. Perhaps the most famous recent teacher of this type was Swami Bhaktivedanta, founder of the group known popularly as Hare Krishnas.[2] Bhaktivedanta was a renouncer of the Gaudiya Vaishnava lineage founded by the sixteenth-century Bengali saint Chaitanya.[3]

Other new movement leaders have belonged to no lineage at all. The popular "hugging mother," Mata Amritanandamayi, was born a lowly Fisher-caste girl. Her religious vocation began when she started falling into trances in which she seemed taken over by deities. Still other new movement leaders have had lineage connections, but ones of very tenuous nature. Stories told about such leaders report that they came to realization largely on their own. One day, however, a guru of an established lineage gave them initiation that let them wear his line's robes and symbols, then disappeared from their story after this event. Perhaps the most famed twentieth-century guru of this type, discussed later in this chapter, was Swami Shivananda, restorer of Hindu yoga traditions. Shivananda is especially important because he himself later initiated sannyasis and certain of these later founded new movements of their own. Shivananda's initiation affiliated him to the Dasanami Sannyasi order. So many new movement leaders of today claim formal connections to that order. Yet they owe far less allegiance to its gurus and centers than to their own movements and founders. To use a Christian phrase, they are "new wine in old bottles."

When new movements such as Shivananda's initiate sannyasis, these fuse old and new approaches to religious practice. They wear the same robes and symbols as older lineages and take vows of celibacy and homelessness. But the jungles into which they venture are more likely to be streets of modern cities than forests. When they "ascend to the heights," they aren't climbing mountain ranges, but crossing oceans in airplanes to preach to international audiences. Their life of "homelessness" means staying in ashrams and teaching centers or sometimes circulating between homes of disciples. "Renouncing the world" means renouncing an attitude that clings to things worldly, while carrying their message to housewives, public servants, and businessmen, and sometimes into factories and corporate offices. In effect, they are Hindu missionaries, spreading news of inner resources that can help devotees meet the challenges posed by a rapidly-changing world. Instructing these devotees, the new movements' millions of lay disciples, is far more the focus of these new sadhus than working out their own paths of spiritual self-polishing. Helping lay disciples work more constructively

---

[2] Devotees have also given him the honorary title Srila Prabhupadu.

[3] See Chapter 3, p. 80.

in the world is the central purpose of most such groups. Some consist almost totally of lay followers. In Sai Baba's centers and ashrams, the only orange robes seen are those worn by Sai Baba himself.

Perhaps the greatest tension between old and new in these new Hindu movements is seen in the ashrams. The term *ashram* means a "hermitage," a place to go for retreat. In classic Sanskrit literature, ashrams were small forest settlements occupied by men and women who had taken up the forest-dwelling third stage of life.[4] Unlike the monasteries that were headquarters for renouncers of the great medieval sampradayas, ashrams still preserved connections to the world outside them. Ashram dwellers retained family ties. A husband and wife might live together, although without sexual connection. A younger sibling might stay with them, as Rama's brother Lakshmana stayed with Rama and Sita during their forest exile in the epic *Ramayana*. In the famous story of Savitri, who outwitted Death to save her husband, the husband's exiled royal parents live in a forest ashram with their son. When Savitri marries the son, she moves to this forest ashram. Both this story and Rama's also remind us that an ashram retreat is not necessarily permanent. Both Savitri's in-laws and Rama return eventually to their respective kingdoms.

Today's ashrams, too, are better characterized as retreat centers than as housing for sannyasis. Although sannyasis may be based there, lay disciples also move about freely, staying for an afternoon or weekend, two or three weeks of annual vacation, a year of regrouping between jobs, or in permanent retirement. A modern ashram may be small; one I visited in Kerala consisted of a kitchen, four simple bedrooms, and a large main room with a shrine where devotees gathered for darshan and teachings. At the other extreme, a large ashram can resemble a small city. On the grounds of Prashanti Nilayam are dozens of dormitories, huge backup sheds for overload crowds to sleep in, meeting rooms of all sizes, public assembly areas, a temple, refectory, and bookstore, as well as shops selling keepsakes and supplies. Prashanti Nilayam even houses a sizeable museum. Other ashrams contain schools, clinics, or training centers for handicraft and work projects run in villages.

Another common feature of large ashrams is offices. A sizeable ashram can be as complex to run as a hotel or resort. Just keeping track of arrivals and departures busies two offices at Prashanti Nilayam: one for Indian visitors and one for foreign nationals. In addition, meals must be planned and served, structures cleaned and repaired, schedules and announcements made up and distributed, and guides trained and assigned to maintain crowd control. Ashrams work extensively with volunteer labor. Some devotees commit set blocks of time to stay at the ashram and work in its service; other volunteers reside full time on the ashram's premises. Such labor crews require skilled coordination, often provided by devotees who have retired from former lives in corporate management. A large ashram may also serve as national center for dozens of subsidiary ashrams or teaching centers scattered in other regions. It may host offices for one or more international organizations with outreach to

---

[4] Distinguished Sanskritist Patrick Olivelle has pointed out that this third stage seems initially to have represented an alternative to the fourth stage of constant wandering, rather than a preface to it, as classic dharmashastra texts most commonly represent it: *The Aśrama System: The History and Hermeneutics of a Religious Institution* (New York: Oxford University Press, 1993).

devotees around the world. Often an ashram has a press or publishing office, because a new movement of significant size issues newsletters or magazines plus volumes of works by its founder and leading disciples. And then there are tape recordings of talks and devotional songs, promotion videos, and CD-ROMs, and no self-respecting movement would fail to have a Web page.

In the next sections, several examples of the new movements housed at these bustling centers whose names connote quiet and simplicity are studied. Most ashram-based movements I have found during my studies can be grouped into three major types. Movements of revival recover spiritual paths and teachings of the past, reinterpreting them for present-day audiences. "Living god" movements such as that of Sai Baba draw devotees to the feet of teachers believed to be God walking about on earth. Prophetic movements work to prepare the world for a new order foreseen in the visions of a founder and devotees. Each of these types will be illustrated with examples well-known in India. Why movements like these have become so popular, why they place such stress on their spiritual character, and why women often have a special role within them are also issues that will be discussed.

MOVEMENTS OF REVIVAL

Movements of revival are the most common and also the most consistent with precedents set in the past. Most have adopted the model shaped by Swami Vivekananda, with its fusion of reworked ancient teachings, sannyasi leadership, aggressive outreach in the style of Western missions, and commitment to social service. They follow Vivekananda, too, in their frequent choice of English as their principal language medium. On the one hand, this gives them both pan-Indian and international outreach. On the other, it means that their principal supporters have been members of the same English-educated, bicultural class that supported samaj movements in the nineteenth century.

Revival movement founders are themselves often from this class, born into well-to-do families and of upper-caste background. Some, but not all, have been Brahmins. Accounts of founders' early lives reflect a common pattern. The founder is raised in a pious home and receives an English-medium education. He becomes disenchanted with religion and pursues some worldly calling that becomes increasingly hollow and unsatisfying. Then he rediscovers some part of India's religious past and becomes convinced that this holds an important message for the present. Because founders have worked in the everyday world, they often have a heightened sense of their audiences' needs. They are also more likely than traditional Hindu leaders to know and experiment with new modes of communication. Often, they are criticized by older leaders because they break so freely with tradition.

The teachings attracting the most attention from today's revival movements are those of yoga and Vedanta traditions. The remainder of this section will look very briefly at two twentieth-century teachers and movements that have rekindled interest in these traditions. It shall then turn to a less common type of revival, one based in a devotion-centered tradition.

Swami Shivananda and the Rebirth of Yoga

Swami Shivananda, guru's guru to the young swami described in the opening scenario of Chapter 2, was extremely influential in reawakening interest in yoga. His
short autobiography offers just a few details about his early life.[5] Born to a Brahmin
family in 1887 in a village in Tamilnadu, he was given the name Kuppuswami Iyer.
His father was a tax official who sometimes also served other families as a household
priest. Reasonably well off, he sent young Kuppuswami to a private English-medium
school and later to a Jesuit College. After college, Kuppuswami studied for several
years at the Tanjore Medical School. In 1905, he interrupted this study, for reasons not
given in his autobiography. Movement-published biographies have claimed that his
father died suddenly and his mother was ill. Returning home, he founded and wrote
for a medical journal, thus continuing his medical studies informally. Because the
journal brought him little income, he worked on the side at a local pharmacy.

In 1913, Kuppuswami took a job in Malaysia running a clinic at a rubber planta-
tion. After working there for seven years, he shifted closer to Singapore where he was
an aide to two doctors. Increasingly torn by the suffering he saw during this work, he
realized that he had to begin healing himself. He started studying the Upanishads and
Bhagavad-Gita, classics of his Hindu spiritual heritage. In 1923, he returned to India,
leaving behind his job and most of his possessions. After traveling to the holy city of
Baranas, he began living as a renouncer, walking westward across northern India
along the Ganga. When he reached Kailash Ashram in Rishikesh, where the Ganga
emerges from the Himalayan foothills, a swami named Vishnudevananda Saraswati
performed rites of sannyasi initiation for him. But Shivananda apparently had no further relationship to this guru. Instead, he took off on his own, living in a series of
huts, studying scriptures, and meditating intensely. In the meantime, he opened a
small free dispensary. The services this offered plus his intense practice soon won him
a reputation for saintliness. Rishikesh became his permanent base, although between
1925 and 1938 he also did many pilgrimages.

In 1929, Shivananda published his first book, the beginning of a series called *The
Practice of Yoga.* By the time of his death in 1963, he had published 340 books and
pamphlets. Although his written works addressed many topics, he returned again and
again to yoga. His yoga writings were eclectic, taking Advaita Vedanta as a philosophical base and citing freely also from Patanjali and from hatha yoga descriptions of
energy centers and flows within the human body. Such works were intended as
guides to practice, not scholarly studies. They offered readers tools that would help
them curb wayward minds without having to wander all over India in search of
teachers.

Many of Shivananda's published works were edited by disciples from transcripts
made during his talks, a technique first used by Swami Vivekananda and later widely
adopted by new movement teachers. Such publications are often crucial to a movement's
success, bringing needed publicity and attracting new disciples, who in turn provide
labor to help broaden the movement's outreach. Public appearance is also important.

---

[5] *Autobiography of Swami Sivananada* (Rishikesh: The Divine Life Society Press, 1958). See
also David M. Miller's "The Divine Life Society Movement," *Religion in Modern India,* 3rd
ed., Robert D. Baird, ed. (New Delhi: Manohar, 1995), 86–117.

By the early 1930s, Shivananda had developed speaking skills that could attract and hold large crowds. Inevitably, some readers and hearers came to Rishikesh for further instruction. Initiating the most determined as sannyasis, he made them his aides in evolving a larger set of enterprises.

By 1934, the popular new swami had convinced a local ruler to donate land for an ashram north of Rishikesh. There he adopted a routine observed in many ashrams. During the day he worked at writing, correspondence, and tasks of ashram management. Toward evening, he appeared in the ashram's main hall to talk with disciples, challenge them, and take their questions. Then he led worship consisting of chanting and bhajans and offered a discourse on a sacred text. Disciples loved his humor and attentiveness. A valuable picture of life in his ashram during the 1950s can be found in *Radha: Diary of a Woman's Search,* written by his disciple Swami Sivananda Radha.[6]

In 1936, Shivananda filed with the Indian government to set up a trust, calling his growing organization the Divine Life Society. The society sponsored a number of further enterprises: some temporary, some permanent. Among the former, perhaps the most prominent was a World Parliament of Religions, organized in 1956 and following the model of the American World Parliament that made Swami Vivekananda famous. Among his latter foundations were a Shivananda General Hospital, annual out-patient "camps" for people in need of eye treatment and surgery, three model villages for lepers, and a vocational training center for low-caste women. The Shivananda Publications League, founded in 1939, spreads the organization's writings around the world, as does its monthly *Divine Life Society Magazine,* begun in 1938.

To systematize training for a ministry that would continue after his death, Shivananda founded in 1948 a College of Yoga and Vedanta, later called the Yoga-Vedanta Forest Academy. Disciples of Shivananda and graduates of this academy were subsequently sent to North America, Europe, and South Africa, where they founded their own Divine Life organizations. So today, as far away as Kalamazoo, Michigan, one can take hatha yoga classes at the local YMCA taught by Janet Bhuyan, trained by Swami Vishnudevananda, who was sent to teach in Canada by Swami Shivananda. As of 2002, the Divine Life Society claimed overseas branches in eighteen countries. If the terms "yoga" and "ashram" are today a standard part of most English speakers' vocabularies, this is in part a result of Shivananda's efforts.[7]

Swami Chinmayananda Continues the Vedanta Revival

Many students from North America associate the term "Vedanta" with the Vedanta Societies founded here by disciples of Swami Vivekananda. But in India, another figure must receive more credit for bringing Vedanta philosophy to public awareness. The future Swami Chinmayananda was born in Ernakulam, Kerala, in 1916. His parents named him Balakrishna Menon.[8] His mother was of the dominant Nayyar caste,

---

[6] Palo Alto, CA: Timeless Books, 1981.

[7] See also www.divinelifesociety.org (Divine Life Society).

[8] I have followed the reconstruction of Chinmayananda's life in Nancy Patchen, *The Journey of a Master: Swami Chinmayananda, the Man, the Path, the Teaching* (Bombay: Central Chinmaya Mission Trust, 1989).

and his father was a younger son of the Nambudari Brahmin community.[9] His family was well-to-do, his father a local judge. When Balakrishna was five, his mother died after giving birth to his younger sister. Thenceforth, his aunts raised the boy and his two younger sisters in the ancestral joint-family household. As his father's sole son, he was royally spoiled. Nevertheless, each day he had to join the family's daily pujas: two hours at twilight singing bhajans, then offering flowers while chanting one thousand names for each of the three household deities. He hated these rituals and spent much of this time daydreaming.

Like many other new movement founders, he attended an English-medium school, where he also studied Sanskrit and his native Malayalam. At first a good student, he became increasingly restless and disruptive while moving through upper levels. His resulting low grades aborted his original intent to work in science. Although he did gain entry to an English major program at Lucknow University, he left school in mid-course to join the freedom struggle. Soon, he was running from police; then, he was caught and jailed, becoming so ill from typhus that his jailers dragged him out of town and left him for dead beside the road. A kind woman found and nursed him, sending him back to a cousin in Lucknow after he was well enough to travel. There he finished school, earned a Master's degree, and moved on to Delhi where he became a journalist known for his brashness and his calls for social justice.

During the summer of 1947, with Indian freedom on its way, Menon traveled to Shivananda's ashram at Rishikesh, intending to write an exposé of Hindu holy men. Instead, he was captivated and challenged by his host, and he stayed for a month. Then, ashram personnel asked him to edit a special volume that they were preparing to honor Shivananda's sixtieth birthday. Soon he was traveling often to Rishikesh, giving talks at the ashram, and reviewing Shivananda's writings for his paper. Eventually, he was at the ashram more often than in Delhi. After going with a cousin on a pilgrimage that moved him greatly, he asked for rites of sannyasi initiation.

Shivananda conducted these rites, thus becoming the new Swami Chinmayananda's guru. But soon this guru sent his protege into the Himalayas to study Vedanta with the famed Swami Tapovan.[10] Chinmayananda wanted to study the Upanishads and *Bhagavad-Gita* in Sanskrit. (Again and again these texts were identified as central by teachers wanting to renew Hindu traditions.) Like earlier samajists, he viewed Hindu history as a fall. Much of it he called "overgrowth," whose many branches and sproutings had hidden "the tiny Temple of Truth . . . hidden behind its own banners."[11] The Upanishads, *Bhagavad-Gita,* and Vedanta philosophy held these ancient deep secrets in need of recovery.

For two years, Chinmayananda hiked the mountains with Tapovan, receiving his teachings on the road and experiencing far more rigors than he had known previously. Then he began to dream of taking the teachings he was receiving back onto India's plains. He wanted to carry them to people like himself who had become

---

[9] In Kerala, it was customary for Nambudari younger brothers to take Nayyar wives; only oldest brothers married Nambudari women.

[10] See Chapter 7, pp. 178–80.

[11] Patchen, op. cit., p. 264.

alienated from their Hindu heritage. After six months of wandering in India as an unknown ascetic, he began working with contacts in Pune to plan an "Upanishad Jnana Yagna." This would be a one-hundred day series of Upanishad talks, accompanied by forty days' continual chanting of the Hare Krishna mantra. Hearers were asked to abstain from sex, movies, and rich foods while talks were in session. Added to sessions as audiences grew were bhajan singing and a concluding four-day *havan,* a sequence of fire offerings. Later add-ons offered early morning instructions in meditation. Understanding and practice must come together, he taught. Merely hearing about great teachings is hollow and useless.

The effect of this first extravaganza was much like that of a Christian tent revival. Attendance at first was small, but then crowds began pouring in. Part of Chinmayananda's success was his teaching technique. He would recite a verse in Sanskrit and then unpack it with down-to-earth explanations of technical jargon, lacing talks with humor, colorful metaphors, and stories. He challenged listeners to question his assertions and held informal morning and post-lecture sessions where he was staying so listeners could meet him and argue with his assertions. All this appalled some orthodox pandits. This swami was teaching Upanishads in English to householders who should not even hear them! But the audiences themselves loved the occasion, and soon invitations came to repeat the lecture series in other cities.

As demand grew, he shortened his programs, keeping features that worked, tossing out those that failed or became too clumsy to manage as crowds grew larger. Like Shivananda, he spread the effects of talks beyond his actual sessions by having them recorded and printed for distribution. He added *Bhagavad-Gita* lectures to his programs as well as intensive teaching camps and special group conferences.

Chinmayananda himself did not try to set up a permanent organization. A group of Madras Brahmins organized the first Chinmaya Mission, asking the swami to serve as its advisor. During his absence, it carried on weekly meetings of discussion, song, scriptural chanting, and group meditation. Women of the group formed their own auxiliary to set up special programs and classes for children. Soon, chapters followed in other cities, and the needs of this spreading organization became more than a single teacher could meet. Like Shivananda, Chinmayananda then started his own school to teach swamis "who will serve as missionaries to their own people."[12] Completed in 1963, this Bombay-based center offered three-year training programs in scripture and pedagogy, sending trainees out afterwards to found and head teaching centers. By 1968, Chinmayananda was touring areas as disparate as Thailand, the West Indies, South Africa, Mauritius, Malaysia, Switzerland, and the United States. By the time he died in 1993, he had built an organization with more than 300 centers in India and another 50 overseas, with 251 men and women serving as swamis or *brahmacaris.* Along with its centers for adults, it sponsors 62 schools for teaching children their Vedic heritage and a research center for studies in Sanskrit and Indology. Its most recent project, announced via the Internet, is an e-course in Vedanta.[13]

---

[12] Quoted ibid., p. 215.

[13] See www.chinmayamission.com (Chinmaya International Foundation).

Swami Bhaktivedanta Teaches the World to Chant
"Hare Krishna"

Most of today's exported Hindu movements emphasize yoga and Vedanta so strongly that students meeting Hinduism through them sometimes think that yoga is the only Hindu practice and Vedanta the only Hindu teaching. An important counterbalance to this assumption is the Krishna Consciousness movement launched in 1965 by Swami Bhaktivedanta, known also as Shrila Prabhupada. This movement has an unusual history; it started in the West in New York City and only later captured a following in India. Yet its founder was of Indian birth, lived in India until he was nearly seventy, and, although he too was of the English-educated class, spent most of his life as a lay devotee of a long-established devotional movement.[14]

Bhaktivedanta was a Bengali, born in 1896, and given the name Abhay Charan De. His father was a cloth merchant and Krishna devotee, a lay initiate of the Bengal-based Gaudiya Vaishnava lineage. The father taught his son as a child to play the *mridangam* drum so he could lead kirtan singing, and the child became enough involved in his father's devotion to ask for a Krishna image and to stage a miniature chariot festival in his neighborhood. Nevertheless, like many other English-educated young Bengalis of his generation, he later was caught up in the emerging nationalist movement and became critical of teachers who taught withdrawal from worldly and political life. Completing college in the fateful year 1920, he heeded Gandhi's call for noncooperation and refused to accept his degree. He became a businessman, selling pharmaceutics most of his life. He had married when in college and fathered children.

His return to religion began when he was twenty-six. A friend insisted that he come along on a visit to meet with Bhaktisiddhanta Sarasvati, then head of the chief monastery of the Gaudiya lineage. Young Abhay was unexpectedly impressed by this articulate man who defended so well his lifelong commitment to Krishna consciousness. In addition, Bhaktisiddhanta challenged him. According to International Society for Krishna Consciousness accounts, Bhaktisiddhanta told the two at that meeting: "You are educated young men. Why don't you preach Lord Caitanya's message throughout the whole world?" Abhay began to associate with devotees and to study Gaudiya teachings. Ten years later, he took initiation, accepting Bhaktivedanta as guru. To his wife's displeasure, he became increasingly ardent, founding and funding *Back to Godhead,* a Krishna-centered magazine.

Meanwhile, Abhay's guru died, and his disciples quarreled dismayingly over succession and control of Gaudiya property. India, too, was in disarray. During World War II, East India suffered terrible famines. The trauma of Partition followed as East Bengal became part of Pakistan. Abhay himself suffered business reverses and grew estranged from his wife and children. Finally, he abandoned both business and family, drifting first to Jhansi, then to Delhi, and then to Krishna's holy city of Mathura, begging here and there for money to keep *Back to Godhead* going. Finally, in a dream, his dead guru told him to take the vow of renunciation. Receiving the name Bhaktivedanta, the new swami began writing a commentary on the *Srimad-Bhagavatam.* Yet he was still haunted by his guru's early challenge: "Go preach Krishna throughout the world."

---

[14] Principal source for Bhaktivedanta's life is Satsvaru Das Goswami, *Prabhupada: He Built a House in Which the Whole World Can Live* (Los Angeles: Bhaktivedanta Book Trust, 1983).

By the time a chance came to do so, he was 69 years old. He met a businessman with a son in the United States who was willing to sponsor him for a visa. A woman admirer who owned a steamship company gave him passage on a cargo steamer. In 1965, he reached the United States, spent a month with his sponsor, and then made his way to New York City, surviving on help from contacts and sales of three completed *Srimad-Bhagavatam* volumes. In New York, he found himself in the midst of the emerging hippie movement, which quickly grew fascinated with the orange-robed, bead-wearing old man from India who taught people how to chant the names of Krishna.

The new guru's theology clashed with the little that most Americans knew of India. Bhaktivedanta taught that the world's supreme power is a God, separate in essence from the human souls He calls to Himself. The ultimate need of humans is to dwell with God, in the spirit of play and freedom that God models. Chanting God's names renders God present and infuses the chanter with the permanent, sustaining bliss that is God's nature. All of this meant little to the new disciples. But they did enjoy chanting and dancing themselves into ecstatic states. A handbill that they put out to attract new recruits advertised "Stay High Forever!" Food drew them as well; Bhaktivedanta taught them Bengali-style vegetarian cooking and at his meetings often offered prasad that amounted to full meals.

Once he had a small but persistent circle of admirers, Bhaktivedanta offered initiation. Then, he and his new disciples thought up new ways to spread his message. Especially effective was the Krishna Consciousness Be-in, a combination of hippie-musician jam session and simple talks on Krishna held in a New York park. He and his new disciples gained their first celebrity ally, beat poet Allen Ginsberg, whose lawyer helped disentangle visa problems for Bhaktivedanta. Next, they filed for incorporation, calling themselves the International Society for Krishna Consciousness (ISKCON for short). Most people, nevertheless, called them "Hare Krishnas" after the words of the chant they sang and danced to.

Hippies moved a great deal, and an ISKCON couple soon relocated to San Francisco, starting a Krishna center there. When Bhaktivedanta visited, he was made the star attraction at a great Mantra Rock Dance, featuring five popular new rock bands, including the Grateful Dead and Jefferson Airplane. In return, he brought Indian culture to the Bay City, launching the first North American chariot festival. He encouraged devotees to move out and start more centers in Boston, Buffalo, Santa Fe, and Montreal. Within two years, he sent a mission team to London, where the Beatles gave it crucial help. He then embarked on the first of the eight world tours that he would conduct over the next ten years. In the midst of all this activity, he continued to write, dictating his growing corpus of works into a tape recorder. These eventually included not only the *Bhagavatam* commentary, but others on the *Bhagavad-Gita* and *Life of Chaitanya,* as well as many smaller works. He would wake at one in the morning and work until four, when he and his disciples began their morning devotions.

Bhaktivedanta's world tours included several returns to India, where he left disciples to build three major centers: at Vrindavan, spiritual center of Krishna's holy land of Braj; at Mayapur near Chaitanya's birthplace Navadvip; and in Bombay, gateway to India, at the emerging Juhu Beach suburb. Here, Bhaktivedanta's business acumen proved critical. He helped his group acquire land in places that at the time were jungle, but later became prime locations. He also blocked several attempts to cheat or drive out U.S. devotees, who were often painfully naive about Indian ways of doing business. In the meantime, his groups courted Indian converts, mounting splashy festival celebrations and tent meetings. An especially successful strategy was selling life memberships. For a set fee, a member became entitled to stay at the guest house of any Krishna center around the world. At that time, the Indian government severely restricted the amount of money that any citizen could carry out of the country. Therefore, access to safe and clean stopping places became a powerful attraction. The prospect of finding tasty and sanctified food was also a major draw; by now ISKCON was famous for its cooking. Hindus at first were sceptical about the young Americans wearing sadhus' robes and chanting "Hare Krishna." Soon devotees won their favor by restoring pilgrim sites and by building attractive temples, centers, and schools to recall India to its heritage of Krishna devotion.

Bhaktivedanta lived for just twelve years after his first trip to America in 1965. During that time, he initiated more than four thousand devotees, published more than sixty books, and helped his society open more than one hundred centers in America, India, Africa, and Europe. His base in the United States today has faded since its peak, losing ground to New Age movements and newer Hindu groups. But in India, ISKCON is a major and still-expanding religious presence. Hundreds of visitors pour in daily to its colorful temples and ashrams.[15]

THE GURU AS GOD

The injunction to worship one's guru as a god is very old among Hindus. Throughout India, devotees stoop to touch gurus' feet or even prostrate at full length on the ground before them. A widely observed Hindu holy day is *guru-purnima,* when devotees flock to honor gurus and make the generous gifts that sustain their enterprises. Many devotees believe that their gurus have powers not available to ordinary humans; they will say that Guru-ji knows what they have in mind before they speak, that he strengthens the pen writing a crucial examination, or that he holds off foul weather until an important ritual has been completed.

Nonetheless, most Hindus still draw a clear distinction between a guru who is god-like because of spiritual realization and the guru who *is* God—an actual divine descent walking the earth in human form. Such teachers do not wander aimlessly in the world until they are thirty, forty, or sixty years old before they find their calling. Their divine nature manifests when they are young. Often, they are born into unpromising circumstances, which they transcend like lotus buds thrusting above murky waters. They need no gurus of their own, no initiations, no special practice to help them unlock inner secrets. They simply *are,* and the divinity revealed through their own behavior draws devotees to them. Nor need they preach inspiring messages or teach a complex spiritual discipline. When one has a chance to enter God's presence, just being there is enough. Disciples of deities in human form often compare the experience of being near one to having a spiritual battery recharged. Living-god

---

[15] See also www.iskcon.net (International Society for Krishna Consciousness).

gurus are empowering; their presence alone gives devotees the strength that they need to achieve their goals.

The most famous guru of this type is Sathya Sai Baba, whose ashram was described at the start of this chapter. While most of this discussion looks at Sai Baba and the massive movement he has created, a few words must be said about a type of living-divinity guru often overlooked in the shadow cast by Sai Baba's bright glare.

The Living God as Living Goddess

A striking fact of Hindu interaction between gender and religion is that women acquire the status of living deity more readily than men. This phenomenon seems to be a by-product of the ancient idea that a goddess is a crystallization of *shakti,* creative and life-giving power. Women have shakti in plenty through their power to give birth; therefore, less distance exists between women and goddesses than between men and gods. A different terminology is used to describe a woman-as-goddess than a man-as-god. He is an *avatara,* a divine "descent," whereas she is a Ma or Mata, a divine mother. This title links divine mothers to *matajis,* women possessed by female deities.[16] But if the divine Ma is a mataji, she is one taken to a higher level, summoned to her calling not by some local deity, but by the Supreme Shakti energizing the universe.

Probably the woman who has done most within the last century toward upgrading the status of women as living deities was Anandamayi Ma, who lived from 1896 to 1982. A Bengal-born Brahmin and village housewife married at 12, she started falling into spontaneous trances and chanting mysterious mantras. Although her husband first feared she was possessed by some demon, she was so artless and joyful that he decided she was a saint. Giving up all sexual claims on her, he became her first devotee. Because they moved around a great deal, she soon attracted other admirers. One renamed her "Mother Joyous" (Anandamayi Ma) and wrote an adoring book about her that made her famous.[17] As her episodes of divine seizure grew more intense, she came to accept the notion of her own divinity. While still in her early twenties, she announced that she was ultimate deity, "Purna Brahma Narayanan." Her growing fame exploded during the struggle for Indian independence when Jawaharlal Nehru's wife Kamala became her devotee. Other nationalist leaders soon followed, perhaps attracted by the idea of honoring a woman as Mother and Goddess while fighting to free an India also portrayed as such. A restless deity, Mother Joyous wandered constantly back and forth across North India, teaching devotees to chant God's name and leaving a string of ashrams behind her. Twenty-six of these remain active today, and an ambitious complex in her honor has recently been constructed in the pilgrim center of Hardwar. Her organization also runs at least two schools and a hospital, and it communicates with worldwide devotees by means of an extensive Web page.[18]

---

[16] See Chapter 9, p. 234.

[17] Bhaiji, *Mother as Revealed to Me,* G. Das Gupta, tr. (Varanasi: Shree Shree Anandamayee Sangha, 1962).

[18] www.anandamayi.org (Shree Shree Anandamayee Sangha). This site includes an extensive pictorial biography of Anandamayi Ma.

In twenty-first century India, however, one hears less about this earlier Mother Joyous than about her near namesake, Mata Amritanandamayi of South India. Her story begins quite differently.[19] Born in Kerala in 1953 to Fisher-caste parents, she was the fourth of nine children. She grew up scorned by her family because she acted strangely and had unusually dark skin. Worn down by arthritis and excessive child-bearing, her mother often beat her and forced her to work as a family servant. Finding solace in devotional song to Krishna, she began experiencing *bhavas,* trancelike states, in which she assumed Krishna-like postures and expressions. Goddess bhavas soon followed, as did devotees drawn not only by these signs of divinity but also by her loving and generous nature. Known best today by her shortened title "Ammachi," Mata Amritanandamayi has won renown as a "Hugging Mother." She does little preaching, preferring simply to hug devotees who line up before her or to join with them in devotional song and dance.

Ammachi's central Indian ashram is at Quilon, Kerala, the town of her birth. It houses a library and Vedanta school. Other charities listed by her organization include a dental college, medical center, AIDS hospice, two old-age homes, and a program offering free legal services to the indigent. Ammachi makes annual world tours in the United States, Europe, and Asia and has overseas devotees in twenty-four countries. She has a second large ashram in San Ramon, California.[20]

Sathya Sai Baba, Divine Magician

Despite the huge repute of such divine Mas, India's most famous living deity remains Sathya Sai Baba, the male guru described in this chapter's opening scene. According to publications put out by his movement,[21] Sai Baba was born in 1926 to a pious family of Raju caste in the village of Puttaparthi, next to which his central ashram now stands. The youngest of four children, he received the name Satyanarayana. His region is a poor one, stony and dry. Satyanarayana's family nonetheless had enough means to own a small brick house, send their son to a village school, and later to send him to high school ninety kilometers away in a town where he could live with a married brother. Satyanarayana took his schooling lightly; he spent much of his time singing kirtans with friends and putting on plays based on stories from Hindu mythology. Accounts of his childhood claim that even then he materialized objects, giving playmates candy and pencils pulled from empty schoolbags.

When Satyanarayana was thirteen, he fell into a seizure, attributed to poisoning from a scorpion sting. Although he recovered quickly, he began to act strangely—crying, laughing, fainting, and reciting scriptures. Although his family called in exorcists, they did no good. Then, he started pulling sweets and flowers out of empty air.

---

[19] As told in Swami Amritasvarupananda, *Mata Amritanandamayi: Her Life and the Experiences of Her Devotees* (San Ramon, CA: Mata Amritananda Mayi Centers, 1988).

[20] See her two Web pages: www.ammachi.org (Mata Amritanandamayi Center, U.S.) and www.amritapuri.org (Mata Amritanandamayi Math, India).

[21] I have followed the summary of these publications in Lawrence A. Babb, *Redemptive Encounters: Three Modern Styles in the Hindu Tradition* (Delhi: Oxford Univ. Press, 1987), pp. 162–66; Babb's account of Sathya Sai Baba and his organization takes up one-third of this volume; it is the best Western study of this movement that I have found.

He announced that he was Sai Baba, from the ancient *rishi* lineage of Bharadvaja and then told friends and family: "I am come to ward off all your troubles; keep your houses clean and pure." Soon, attending school became unbearable for him. Saying he had to complete an unfinished task, he went to live in a temple near his village. Stories of his miracles drew others to see and hear him.

Both the name he had taken and his reference to an "unfinished task" hinted at a connection to an earlier saint. Shirdi Sai Baba had been a saint from the village of Shirdi in Maharashtra who dressed as a Muslim fakir, but spoke and taught as if he were Hindu. Like Sathya Sai Baba, he was a wonder-worker, famed especially for his healings. First appearing as a teenager in 1854, he died in 1918, eight years before Sathya Sai Baba was born. Sathya Sai Baba later asserted that he was Shirdi Sai Baba's reincarnation. He also predicted that he will take birth once more as a teacher named Prem Sai Baba after he leaves his present body. He will live for 96 years during his present birth.

Acting on his own authority, the new boy-guru began initiating disciples soon after he left his family. By 1944, his devotees had built him a new residence near Puttaparthi, now called the Old Shrine. On his twenty-fourth birthday in 1950, they gave him the building called Prashanti Nilayam, now the heart of his ashram of the same name. Like other famous gurus, he did not stay there permanently, but toured often in India's great urban centers. Soon, he had satellite centers in Bangalore, Madras, and Bombay, with circles of devotees all over India. By the late sixties, his reputation was spreading around the world, first among Indian emigrants, then to non-Indians via books, recordings, and films. I first heard of Sathya Sai Baba through a recording of his kirtan singing that I picked up at a local record store during the early seventies. Soon after, I received mailings on a film made about him. By ordering it and showing it in my classes, I inadvertently became part of his widening circle of publicity.

Sai Baba gives public discourses throughout India, usually in his native Telegu language, using translators when addressing non-Telegu-speaking audiences. He has done less international travel than other gurus of worldwide fame. Themes of his talks are little different from those of most teachers steeped in Upanishad and *Bhagavad-Gita*-based traditions. His principal mission to the world, he says, is to reestablish Vedic and Shastric teachings. The Veda is the true source of all religious authority. It teaches that God is one, and lies latent within all human beings. The difference between Sai Baba and other humans is not that he is God and others are not, but rather that he knows he is God and others do not. Ego and selfish desires stand in the way of God-realization. Truth, righteousness, peace, and love are the four pillars of eternal dharma. Sai Baba's talks are peppered with snappy aphorisms. I have seen devotees pull out small notebooks recording these and read them to one another: "Life is a journey from 'I' to 'We.'" "Love lives by giving and forgiving; Self lives by getting and forgetting."[22]

Nonetheless, as anthropologist Lawrence Babb has pointed out, when devotees are asked about Sai Baba, they usually talk about the miracles that he performs.[23] They tell of rings, necklaces, and watches that he materializes for them, saying these

---

[22] Seema Kundra, compiler, *Facets of the Divine Diamond* (New Delhi: Kanwar Kishore, 1990), pp. L-6, L-19.

[23] Babb, op. cit., pp. 159–201.

gifts will help them remain in contact with him. They say that he heals, sometimes through sacred ash that he has materialized or sometimes from a great distance, by appearing in a dream. He saves his faithful from danger. One devotee has described how Sai Baba befuddled two men intent on hijacking a plane that she was on, thus preventing them from accomplishing their mission.[24] Books of testimony to such deeds are an important means of spreading the word of this master; Sai Baba himself encourages literate disciples to write them.

A greater miracle may be the immense worldwide organization that Sai Baba and his devotees have built together. Founded in 1965, the Sri Sathya Sai Seva Organization claims twenty million members in 137 nations. It has branches in virtually every Indian city. In New Delhi, where I know its work best, it sponsors lectures, coordinates and publicizes kirtans in homes of devotees, trains singers to lead kirtans, conducts free medical clinics in slum areas, and runs a number of *bal vikas* programs, comparable to Christian Sunday schools. Like other guru-centered organizations, Sai Baba's began as a grassroots enterprise, beginning with local circles of devotees. A world conference of devotees held every five years helps coordinate and standardize these groups' activities. Plans for the future are laid there and information traded about strategies that have helped local Sai Baba circles reach their goals.

Note that Sai Baba's organization is called a "Seva," service, organization. Sai Baba has always asked his devotees to do service. Like other guru-centered groups, his organization runs not only clinics and children's programs, but also free schools, offering programs from first grade through college level. With a by-now formidable institutional machinery to rely on, Sai Baba has stepped up his call to service since his sixtieth birthday. Devotees have constructed a large research hospital near Prashanti Nilayam, where all treatment is free. They have installed a massive project to bring fresh drinking water to 750 villages in the district surrounding Puttaparthi. Devotees offer both money and labor for such projects. Their guru tells them not to wait for government to solve India's problems. Working together, they can do it themselves. Criticized in the past for being a "rich man's guru," Sai Baba has become perhaps India's most successful leader at persuading the rich to put their money and skills to work on behalf of the poor. Moreover, the followers seen working at projects in films and publicity releases are clearly middle-class as well as wealthy, and young as well as aging. Sai Baba has the most broad-based following of any guru I have encountered. But today, he is also troubled by would-be imitators and an extensive Web-based debunking effort.[25]

HERALDS OF A NEW ORDER

One new religious movement common throughout the world is the prophetic movement, based on a message given its leader during an experience of divine summoning. Often, this message asserts that group or world renewal will come about if certain prescribed disciplines or rituals are followed. Although less frequent in India than

---

[24] Phyllis Krystal, *Sai Baba: The Ultimate Experience* (Mangalore: Sharada Press, 1985), pp. 111–15.

[25] For additional materials, see www.sathyasai.org (International Sai Organization).

elsewhere, several prophetic movements have occurred there in the past. A good example is the Satnami movement described earlier.[26]

Two twentieth-century Indian prophetic movements are especially interesting because of the way they have merged Indian and Western themes, those of world progress and evolution, in teachings of Shri Aurobindo, and the theme of world apocalypse, in teachings of Dada Lekh Raj. Striking, too, has been the importance of women to their efforts toward world transformation. I have stretched categories a bit to include these two movements in this volume, for neither describes itself as "Hindu." Aurobindo's following insists on calling itself "secular," in the nonsectarian, inclusive sense described in this section's introduction. Brahma Kumaris, too, refuse to call themselves "Hindu." Yet the symbols, values, and practice of both are clearly Hindu in origin and offer fine illustrations of an ancient tradition's capacity for self-transformation.

Sri Aurobindo Announces a New Stage of Human Evolution

Several twentieth-century Hindu leaders were skeptical of their own traditions during their youth. None, however, grew up as divorced from his Hindu heritage as Aurobindo Ghosh, the revolutionary turned prophet who proclaimed the imminent breakthrough of a new level of human consciousness. Born in Calcutta in 1872, Aurobindo was the son of a Scotland-trained physician convinced that the best way to turn his sons into great men was to have them educated in Great Britain. When Aurobindo was seven, the father escorted him and two older brothers to England. Leaving them with a Christian pastor, he asked their new mentor to arrange for their education and to make sure they did not undergo any Indian influence.[27]

Aurobindo proved a brilliant scholar. To his father's joy, he qualified for Oxford University's difficult training program for the Indian Civil Service. But the young exile already dreamed of leading his people to freedom. Failing a crucial exam on horsemanship, he did not show for a retest and so gave up the Civil Service opportunity. Returning to India in 1893, he became an aide to the Maharajah of Baroda and a teacher and administrator of Baroda College. He also made contact with Tilak followers, began writing nationalist articles, and started to study Bengali and Sanskrit.

By 1906, he was a highly regarded member of the extremist faction struggling for control of the National Congress. He moved to Bengal that year to become principal of the new Bengal National College, arriving at the peak of agitation over the proposed Bengal partition. Soon he was writing for the nationalist magazine *Bande Mataram*. He wrote the famed pamphlet "Bhawani Mandir" to help his brother Barin recruit students for terrorist cells. Like Tilak and other extremists, Aurobindo soon became a target of British efforts to break the nationalist movement. Accused of complicity in an attack carried out by Barin's recruits, he was charged with treason and jailed, remaining in jail for a year in 1908 and 1909.

Somewhat earlier, in 1903, Aurobindo had started practicing the yoga discipline of breath restraint. He claimed this helped him stay focused for his demanding round

---

[26] See Chapter 8, pp. 202–05.

[27] Many accounts of Aurobindo's life have been written. I have followed a scholarly study by Peter Heehs, *Sri Aurobindo, a Brief Biography* (Delhi and New York: Oxford Univ. Press, 1989).

of activities. After a serious illness in 1907 interrupted his work, he asked a Maharashtrian yogi to help him with yoga practice. Soon after, he had a break-through experience of the "passive Brahman."[28] He later claimed that this had helped him stay detached during his treason trial; to defend himself, he simply let the power of Brahman speak through him. His time in jail let him do still more intensive prac-tice because he spent much of his time in solitary confinement. Studying a copy of *Bhagavad-Gita* that he had been given, he had an experience of Krishna pervading everything. He determined that henceforth he would surrender completely to divine guidance.

Acquitted of charges against him, Aurobindo resumed his nationalist writing, only to be warned that the government would soon arrest him for sedition. Heeding a "command from above," he fled to the colony of Chandernagore. Although only twenty miles from Calcutta, this town was under French control, so that British authorities could not reach him. Soon after, he moved again, to Pondicherry, another French colony south of Madras. From there, he sent a message back to former asso-ciates: he would not do any more political work. His mission from now on would be to change himself more fully so he could work more effectively to change the world. He spent his time in meditation, writing, and study of sacred texts, sharing household tasks with four students who had moved south with him.

Soon after arriving in Pondicherry, Aurobindo had met Paul Richard, a visiting French lawyer, who thought Aurobindo might be the spiritual guide for whom Paul and his fiancee Mirra had been searching. In 1914, Richard returned with Mirra to help Aurobindo launch a magazine of spiritual guidance called *Arya*. Six months later, Richard and Mirra had to leave because Richard had been drafted by the French army. Aurobindo nonetheless continued to issue *Arya,* pouring onto its pages his new understanding of world history and his own calling.

He claimed that his articles wrote themselves, that he just let his pen record whatever divine revelation was showing to him. The world, he wrote, had its source in brahman, which devolved into form at the time of creation. But then, for its own joy, the world began re-evolving toward reunion with its absolute source. First it produced matter, then life, then mind. Now it was on the verge of receiving what Aurobindo called Overmind, a level of heightened consciousness that would help humans live in greater integrity, peace, and harmony. Aurobindo was making him-self the first channel for its descent by means of his spiritual experiments. He was also working out the specifics of an "integral yoga" based on the underlying princi-ples of all spiritual methods used in India previously. In six years, writing at a frantic pace, he produced virtually all the essays that he later assembled into his four most famous works: *The Life Divine, Synthesis of Yoga, The Human Cycle,* and *The Ideal of Human Unity.*

In 1920, Paul and Mirra Richard returned to Pondicherry. Soon Paul left again, but Mirra stayed behind with the man she had taken as her spiritual master. Mirra herself was a person reared between cultures. Born in 1878 of a Turkish father and Egyptian mother, she grew up in Paris, studying art and socializing with the Paris art community. She had no religious training because both her parents were atheists.

---

[28] Heehs, p. 89.

Nonetheless, at an early age she began having out-of-body experiences. As a young adult, she moved to Algeria for two years to seek instruction from an occult master named Max Theon. When she met Aurobindo, she believed he was the mysterious teacher whom she had seen during earlier visions. Aurobindo himself believed Mirra was an incarnation of Shakti, activating Mother of the universe. Soon she became his partner in his spiritual experiments, while he withdrew almost totally from interaction with the outside world.

In the meantime, Aurobindo's growing reputation as a holy man had drawn a small group of disciples to Pondicherry. He came to look upon them as potential further recipients for the descending Overmind. In 1926, he assembled these disciples, about two dozen in number, and told them that "the Mother"—that is, Mirra—would now guide them. She organized them skillfully into a working ashram and directed their spiritual practice. Aurobindo intensified his practice, study, and writing, pulling his books together and writing first drafts of a long, symbolic poem called *Savitri*. He gave darshan three times per year and for a time answered disciples' letters. But the Mother became the ashram's effective leader, leading collective meditations and offering talks, counseling, and darshans much like her counterparts at other ashrams. After Aurobindo's death in 1950, she became the ashram's sole head, firmly controlling its affairs until her own death in 1973.

Aurobindo's ideas spread largely by means of his writings. He, too, gained an international following, which in turn organized branch ashrams, meditation centers, and schools. These in turn drew more disciples to Pondicherry, which today has been virtually taken over by the spreading ashram. Two master organizations coordinated these institutions: the Sri Aurobindo International Centre of Education, established in 1952, and the Sri Aurobindo Society, established in 1960.

One project important to the Mother toward the end of her life was her plan to found a model international city, intended to furnish a context in which the Overmind could take hold and grow. Such a city would be a model and light to illumine the rest of the world. During a visit to Pondicherry in 1967, I was shown an architect's model for that city, named Auroville, with its planned zones for integrating differing types of activities. The Mother was already screening applications for residence. In 1968, the city's foundation was consecrated and would-be residents began to arrive and settle. Unfortunately, the Mother had not designed a method of governance, believing the Overmind would solve all city problems. Instead, residents wrangled with the ashram board that controlled their financial resources. Finally, the Indian government intervened, assuming control of the city and its financing. Auroville is still growing; I last heard a report on its progress at an international conference during 2003. Aurobindo's ashram also remains a significant force in India, gaining most of its support from well-to-do and powerful English-educated Hindus. It claims fifteen hundred residents in the main ashram alone, and large and well-fitted branch ashrams exist in several major cities. One that I visited in New Delhi includes not only housing for disciples and visitors but also a large and much-in-demand private school. The Sri Aurobindo Society claims to have fifty branches and three hundred centers in India and overseas.[29]

---

[29] See www.sriaurobindosociety.org (Sri Aurobindo Society, Pondicherry).

In many ways, the Aurobindo movement strongly resembles others that I have called revival movements. Aurobindo himself often cited the Upanishads and *Bhagavad-Gita*. His *Integral Yoga* claimed only to unify older spiritual methods by locating and stressing their common elements. Yet the interpretation he gave to classic Hindu teachings in effect superceded these by remolding them in accordance with his own vision. Furthermore, he never saw his work as an attempt to restore something called "Hinduism." He did not consider his teachings to be an "ism"; he did not even consider them to be religious. They offered a new set of facts discovered about the world. When the Indian government took over administration of Auroville, much of its discussion centered on whether or not this city was a religious project. The Supreme Court eventually ruled that both the city and Aurobindo's teachings were secular.

Dada Lekh Raj Foresees a World Ending

If Aurobindo took his followers to the fuzzy borders of Hinduism, Dada Lekh Raj led his own disciples firmly beyond those borders. His Brahma Kumaris and Kumars define themselves as non-Hindu and have broken with or redefined many Hindu concepts and symbols. Yet their movement has such conspicuously Hindu origins, values, and motifs that it must still be considered part of the Hindu orbit. Originally persecuted, its leaders scorned and abused, it has become one of India's fastest growing and wealthiest new movements.

The Brahma Kumari story begins with a businessman trading in fine jewelry. Based in Sind, the broad valley surrounding the lower Indus River, Lekh Raj was a multimillionaire whose business network stretched throughout northern India. He was so noted for honesty and straight living that native princes gave him access to the apartments where royal wives lived in seclusion. Although he was deeply pious, no one would have predicted that he would turn into a controversial religious leader.[30]

But when he turned sixty, in 1935, he underwent a series of disturbing visions. First, he saw the deities Vishnu and Shiva, and then terrible events: nations lobbing fiery explosives at each other, followed by tidal waves, floods, plagues, and general chaos as the planet itself ran amok. Last, he saw a wonderful world full of gods and goddesses. A light and power surrounding him told him he had been chosen to make this wonderful world come about.

He began holding *satsangs,* religious gatherings, in his home, telling neighbors and friends about his visions and leading them in songs and dancing. Soon, his visions became contagious; listeners, too, began seeing the terrors and the new world that came after them. Gradually, he worked out a complex world view that made sense of his calling and experiences.

He began with several premises familiar to many Hindu communities. Within all humans are undying, intelligent souls that gain happy or painful rebirths as a result of deeds they have done. These rebirths locate them at moments of huge recurring

---

[30] The principal source on his life remains his movement's book by Raj Yogi Jagdish Chander, *Adi Dev: The First Man,* 2nd English ed. (Singapore: Prajapita Brahma Kumaris, 1983). Both his life and a good summary of Brahma Kumari teachings are in Babb, *Redemptive Encounters,* pp. 93–155. See also www.bkwsu.com (Brahma Kumari World Spiritual Organization).

cosmic cycles that begin with worlds made fresh and perfect, then pass through four ever-deteriorating ages until they collapse from internal chaos. Transcending this process, but engaging with it, is one Supreme Soul, whom Lekh Raj called Shiv Baba, which holds resources of power and intelligence for lesser souls that can tap it. Lekh Raj also recognized lesser deities, whom he called by familiar Hindu names such as Vishnu, Lakshmi, Krishna, and Shankar [Shiva].

Yet he gave all these teachings distinctive twists. Souls, he taught, are many and separate from one another, as in Jain teachings or ancient Samkhya and Yoga philosophies. Souls are also finite in number; just five and one-half billion such souls exist. Cosmic cycles are short; each lasts only five thousand years. The ending of the last one was the *Mahabharata's* war. Most souls remain unborn during early phases of a cosmic cycle; they enter the cycle at junctures appropriate to their karma. Pure, good souls enjoy the times of golden perfection, whereas souls of lesser character experience only the ages of suffering. Once a soul has been born, it is reborn again and again, so that even souls initially pure undergo degradation. As for the deities, only Shiv Baba remains untouched by the cycle. Others are, in fact, reborn souls of the Golden Age, remembered in distorted form by stories told in later times.

The most urgent of Lekh Raj's teachings was his insistence that the current time hovers at the brink of the present cycle's collapse. It will become a time of terror. Wars will erupt using hideous instruments of destruction, followed by natural convulsions such as earthquakes, volcanic eruptions, and tidal waves. But this is also a time of opportunity because all souls that have lived are now flooding into births where they can hear a message that can change their fates as the world enters its next cycle. If they purify their souls and straighten out their lives, they will be deities of the coming Golden Age. The divine power called Bap Dada can aid them, if they learn how to re-attune their minds to him. He has descended into the human body called Lekh Raj to bring this saving message and to teach souls how to accomplish such re-attuning.

The practice taught by Lekh Raj had three central components. Disciples learned to link themselves to Shiv Baba via a simple form of meditation that Brahma Kumaris call Raja Yoga. They also had to maintain absolute purity, which meant abstaining from sex and intoxicants, eating vegetarian food, and eating only food prepared by pure persons, i.e., themselves. Finally, they had to cultivate a list of some twenty virtues. This included the virtue of "packing up," shedding meaningless customs and conventions and staying open to new ways of getting things done.

Among the Sindi community of traders where Lekh Raj began teaching, men are often absent for long portions of the year; stay-at-home wives raise families and maintain households. Lekh Raj's first audience was, therefore, mostly female. When husbands came home from traveling, they were astonished to find wives who refused to have sex with them or to cook meat for their meals. Many of their daughters refused to marry or bear children. In outrage, some Sindhi men launched a long persecution of Lekh Raj, who finally moved his followers to Karachi to escape them. Even in Karachi, his group lived in a quasi-monastic condition. Lekh Raj had already turned most of his wealth over to a trust formed to support his movement. Having mostly female disciples, he appointed women trustees. One girl in her twenties named Om Radhe was a gifted organizer. She became the group's "Mama," second in command only to Lekh Raj himself.

After Britain placed Sind in Pakistan during Partition, Dada Lekh Raj moved his community to India. Now it settled in Mount Abu, a hill station nestled amid peaks of a low mountain range in the desert state of Rajasthan. There he prepared group members to carry his message into the streets of Indian cities. He would send only women, clad in white saris to signify their commitment to purity. Since the death of Lekh Raj in 1969, women have remained the group's principal heads and teachers. A few men of the group's central committee manage mundane jobs at Mount Abu, such as managing construction and heading kitchens at retreat and conference centers. Currently, three women working in close collaboration head the organization. All were members of the original community.

When I first learned of Brahma Kumaris in the early 1980s, they were a tiny group preaching on Indian street corners, mocked by the society around them.[31] Today, they are highly respected with thousands of supporters and money pouring into their projects. What has brought this transformation? Much of their attractiveness comes less from their teachings than from the way they exemplify the promise of a new order. It is as if they *are* the new world they speak of, already cropping out amid the garbage of the old. I have often heard Indians say that they practice what they preach. They do not lie, cheat, bribe, or waste money on ostentation; they are efficient, cheerful, neat, and attentive to others' welfare. They work to bring beauty and simple pleasure back into the world, planting flowers, playing silly games, handing out homemade candy to crews on trains. Moreover, they have not only stood Indian patriarchy on its head, they are also undoing classic Hindu hierarchical structures. They do not touch anyone's feet or stretch out in pranams before leaders; instead they gaze straight into each other's eyes in an exchange of self-baring that they call *drishti*. They do not use fancy titles such as "maharaj" or "Her Holiness." Their most senior leaders are addressed as Dadi, "Grandmother"; all others are "Sister" or "Brother," or simply *brahma kumari* or *kumar,* meaning "pure miss" or "pure mister." Like several other groups described in this chapter, they are scornful of the pretense, narrowness, and greed sometimes surfacing in conventional forms of religion. Hence, like the others, they do not call their undertakings "religious," but rather "spiritual" and "educational." The formal name for their organization is "World Spiritual University."

This Brahma Kumari University now claims more than 3,200 branch centers in seventy countries and every region of India. Most are equipped with the latest communication technology: faxes, cell phones, and computers. Like other new spiritual movements, the World Spiritual University owns and runs its own press and sponsors several large service projects. A research hospital in Mount Abu offers free treatment to anyone who cannot pay. Mobile clinics visit more than a thousand Rajasthan villages. An agricultural outreach program helps Rajasthan villagers increase their sparse fields' productivity. As a nongovernmental affiliate of the United Nations, the World Spiritual University has for years promoted programs that work for world peace. When I once asked a Brahma Kumari how she could work so hard to improve the world while believing it would soon end, she shrugged her shoulders and said, "Maybe things will work out differently."

---

[31] I am grateful to Lawrence Alan Babb, who first called my attention to them.

A QUIET REVOLUTION

This chapter on new spiritual movements could easily be a book. It does not even begin to cover all the creative efforts now going on to recover and reinterpret Hinduism's rich spiritual heritage. Readers will know the names of many teachers not described here: Meher Baba, Maharishi Mahesh, Swamis Rama, Muktananda, and Yogananda, or the women gurus Godavari Mataji, Mrinalini Devi, Swami Chidvilasananda, and Mother Mirra.[32] Many other new teachers in India with deeply committed disciples are barely known outside the areas in which they teach or run service projects. A few were mentioned in other chapters of this book: Yogi Raushan Nath;[33] Swami Bodhananda;[34] and Param Pujya Ma.[35] Together, remarkable people such as these are bringing about a quiet revolution in India: generating can-do attitudes, easing human pain, reversing social habits that once encouraged advantaged Hindus to perceive the disadvantaged as little more than animals. The importance of their work is too often ignored by scholars seeking to understand how India is transforming itself in today's world.

What makes the new spiritual movements so attractive? Especially, why would urbane, sophisticated Indians with secular educations be drawn so extensively into their followings? What is at stake in their calling themselves spiritual rather than religious? Finally, why have some shown so much interest in promoting women in roles of leadership? The charisma and teaching skills of leaders is one obvious answer to the first question, and it certainly explains what attracts disciples to such movements in the first place. But what holds those disciples and keeps them together? At least four factors are important:

1. *The promise of peace*   Almost any movement's description of its ashrams will portray them, like Sai Baba's Prashanti Nilayam, as "abodes of peace," islands of quiet and restoration in the midst of a frantic world. Almost all also have one or more points in their daily routine when devotees stop to collect themselves. They may do this through devotional singing, as at Prashanti Nilayam; by repeating mantras of homage to God's name, advocated by Anandamayi Ma; by practicing some form of structured meditation, as at Shivananda's ashram; or by a combination of all three. One practice I always enjoy at Brahma Kumari centers is the "traffic stop." At certain times each day, calming music wafts through the building and all present drop what they are doing to observe quiet for one minute. It would be a mistake to assume that the world's ashrams are always peaceful; they have their share of disruptions and internal quarrels. Nonetheless, in today's normally stress-filled lives, the calming techniques they teach can be great stress-breakers.

2. *Empowerment*   New movement teachings assert that their knowledge and practice will bring not only calm but also the intelligence, power, and energy needed to sift through problems in a complex world. The older teachings that they draw on

---

[32] Not to be confused with The Mother Mirra Richard of the Aurobindo movement, although her devotees claim she is a reincarnation of the latter.

[33] See Chapters 9 and 12, p. 228 and 309–10.

[34] See Chapters 7, 9, and 12, pp. 180–83, 228–30, and 309–12.

[35] See Chapter 9, p. 230.

usually begin with the premise that humans have hidden within them a bit of God or a supremely intelligent soul whose potential they can release to transform their own lives. Living-god-centered movements add the reassurance that a deity within reach looks out for devotees and lends them strength to aid their efforts. India today is a hugely complex culture, buffeted by more change than most human beings can handle easily. Most buffeted of all are the well-educated, well-placed Hindus attracted to spiritual movements. Movement teachings reassure them that they have the strength and smarts needed to work their way past challenges. Movement disciplines also help them acquire the detachment needed to think their way through new situations.

3. *Coordination*   Spiritual movements also empower by the old Indian technique of yoking, pulling small energies together and into coordination so that much larger tasks can be accomplished. In this case, the energies yoked are those of movement members themselves, working together to carry out the movement's many service projects. Well-to-do Hindus are very much aware that government initiatives alone cannot help their country solve all of its many problems. At the same time, obstacles like poverty, bad water, and insufficient health care and schools are too large and daunting for most people to tackle single-handedly. Service projects launched by new movements offer venues in which individuals with social concerns can feel and be useful by pooling talents and money to address their country's ills.

4. *Networking*   Offering a different level of advantage are the networks of social connections woven by all newer movements. One kind of change that began in India during colonial times and has accelerated since independence is the breakup of complex families as sons move away to work in new regions and daughters move farther from homes with emigrating husbands. Once again, this change has particularly affected higher class families in India. New movements offer friendships and through them support networks to supplant the kin networks that in the past helped well-placed Indians accomplish their aims. Friends made through the movements provide ears to listen to trouble, help in setting up marriage matches, links to needed business connections, and sometimes short-term loans. In the meantime, teachers and movement heads provide family and job counseling, and ashrams may solve the problem of old people left alone by taking them in as permanent ashram residents.

What is at stake in calling them spiritual movements? The description of the Brahma Kumaris given above offers one key. Classifying themselves as spiritual helps provide distance from aspects of older traditions they would rather not claim. Adherents often explain that, although religion has a spiritual core, unscrupulous priests and other leaders of the past have managed to corrupt it. This is how sectarian division came into being as well as destructive practices such as untouchability. Their movements are not like that; they are reaching once again into the energies that are true religion's wellspring.

This same assertion that they are going straight to the source of religion allows these movements to sidestep old sectarian loyalties. In a large ashram such as Sai Baba's, devotees of Shiva, Krishna, and the Goddess rub shoulders with one another. One can even spot a few turbaned Sikhs, Christians, and Muslims. Claiming that their movements are spiritual rather than religious avoids conflicts with older groups. The movements say: "Keep your own religion; use our teachings and practice to enrich it."

Or to those determined to have nothing more to do with religion, they may say: "Our movement is not religious; we are just helping you realize your own potential." In fact, it is not unusual for new movements to claim that their methods are scientific, based on experimentation.

Finally, sheer pride is an important factor, responding to the way Hindus see themselves mirrored by the rest of the world. Let us not forget that, already at the beginning of the twentieth century, educated Hindus could read in newspapers about the reception of their ideas abroad. Religious leaders from India even traveled overseas. Ram Mohan Roy and Keshab Chander Sen traveled on speaking tours in England; and as early as 1883, Keshab's cousin Pratap Chander Mazumdar preached to Unitarians in the United States. With his fiery defense of Hinduism and his orange robes and turbans, Swami Vivekananda attracted extensive press coverage during his two American tours. He himself may have invented the spirituality\religion distinction; if not, he at least did a great deal to publicize it. He asserted that spirituality was India's great strength, a gift that the rest of the world would do well to explore. Seeing the Western converts he won and brought back to help with his mission and reading of other swamis and yogis invited to travel abroad and teach, it is no wonder that some Hindus began to value more highly the part of their own tradition that those traveling teachers put forward. And it is no wonder that newer teachers strive to float their own undertakings upon those more valued streams of their Hindu religious heritage.

Pride is surely also a factor in the increase of leadership options assigned to women. Assigning women a place of high prominence is one way to show that a movement is progressive, that it affirms changes made within Hinduism during the last two centuries. Nonetheless, it is striking to note that more conservative undertakings also put women forward into prominent positions. Another expectation is also coming into play. Late in the nineteenth century, a face-off occurred between two types of new leaders in the Hindu community. One type criticized aspects of older practice and sought reform. As already seen, reformers often made the status of women their central focus and tried to create more space for women outside their homes. The leaders who opposed them were Hindu nationalists uneasy because reformers were splitting the Hindu community. To keep that community together and focus it on resisting the British, nationalists stressed the rosy side of past traditions. Women who had stayed at home became heroines to them, pure because they evaded Western influence, spiritual and a source of pride because they kept up customs of devotion when men were abandoning them. At a time when religion was coming apart, it made sense to hand such pure women a prominent role in the task of knitting it back together. There have been several passing references in this book to these nationalists and their impact. It is time to look at them and their present-day descendants more closely.

ADDITIONAL SOURCES

Two old but still useful depictions in English of new movement gurus are G. S. Ghurye and L. N. Chapekar, *Indian Sadhus* (Bombay: Popular Prakashan, 1964), and Marvin Henry Harper, *Gurus, Swamis, and Avataras* (Philadelphia: Westminster Press, 1972). Deeper in analysis is Lawrence A. Babb's more recent *Redemptive Encounters: Three Modern Styles in the Hindu Tradition* (Delhi: Oxford Univ. Press, 1987); it studies the Sathya Sai Baba movement, the Brahma Kumaris, and the Radha Soami Samaj (not described in this chapter). Robert Baird's collection *Religion in Modern India* (New Delhi: Manohar, 1995) includes chapters on Shivananda's Divine Life Society movement and on Aurobindo. Karen Pechilis has edited a fine collection of studies on women gurus: *The Graceful Guru: Hindu Female Gurus in India and the United States* (Oxford: Oxford Univ. Press, 2004); see also Linda Johnson's *Daughters of the Goddess: The Women Saints of India* (St. Paul, MN:Yes International, 1994).

Most founder biographies mentioned in this chapter have been published by their respective movements and take a hagiographic (glorifying) approach to their founders. An exception is Peter Heehs' well-balanced study *Sri Aurobindo, a Brief Biography* (Delhi and New York: Oxford Univ. Press, 1989). An interesting in-group supplement to this is Kireet Joshi, *Sri Aurobindo and the Mother: Glimpses of Their Experiments, Experiences, and Realisations* (New Delhi: Mother's Institute of Research and Motilal Banarsidass, 1989). The most lively movement biography is Satsvarūpa Dāsa Goswami, *Prabhupāda: He Built a House in Which the Whole World Can Live* (Los Angeles: Bhaktivedanta Book Trust, 1983). The author was one of Bhaktivedanta's original hippie disciples; once his guru arrives in New York, the book is rich in often-amusing reminiscences. Examining ISKCON's establishment and impact in India is Charles R. Brook's *The Hare Krishnas in India* (Princton: Princeton Univ. Press, 1989). Sai Baba's practice of collecting testimonies has resulted in several works offering insights into the mind-set of devotees; in addition to Phyllis Krystal, *Sai Baba: The Ultimate Experience* (Mangalore: Sharada Press, 1985), see Diana Baskin, *Divine Memories of Sathya Sai Baba* (Prashanti Nilayam: Sri Sathya Sai Books and Publications Trust, 1990); and M. R. Kundra, *Twenty-Five Years with Divinity* (India: Sai Shriram Printers, n.d.).

All ashrams of any importance have Web pages with lists of founders' writings. For some samples of these writings, try Swami Shivananda, *Mind: Its Mysteries and Control*, 11th ed., (Shivanandnagar: Divine Life Society, 1990); Swami Chinmayananda, *A Manual of Self Unfoldment* (Mumbai: Central Chinmayananda Trust, 1975); and Canto I, part 1 of Swami Bhaktivedanta's translation and commentary of the *Śrīmad Bhāgavatam*, 10 vol. (New York: Bhaktivedanta Book Trust, 1972–1986). Robert McDermott has edited a handy collection of Aurobindo samples, *The Essential Aurobindo* (New York: Schocken Books, 1973). Movements whose leaders inspire more by being experienced than by being read often have inexpensive videos available for purchase. In classes, I have used Sathya Sai Baba's *The Song of Service* (Laxmi Films, 1999); the Brahmo Kumaris' *Companion of God, Interview with Dadi Janki* (no producer or date given); and one of several "World Tour" videos put out by Mata Amritanandamayi's organization.

Finally, a good way to gain insight into ashram-based movements is through disciples' reminiscences about their own ashram stays. Unfortunately, these are not common. A very fine one is Swami Sivananda Radha's *Radha: Diary of a Woman's Search* (Palo Alto, CA: Timeless Books, 1981) telling of her stay with Shivananda. Another, by a disciple of the famed Ramana Maharishi, is Suri Nagamma, *My Life at Sri Ramanasrama* (Tiruvannamalai: Sri Ramanasram, 1974). Author John Ittner has published a description of practice within an American Shivananda ashram: *Lighting the Lamp of Wisdom: A Week inside a Yoga Ashram* (Woodstock, VT: Skylight Paths, 2002).

11

In Politics

Through the streets of the city moves a bus decorated to simulate a large golden chariot, with a speaker's platform mounted behind its cab. A silver-haired man wearing glasses and an Indian-style suit stands waving from the platform. Mounted above his head is the revered Hindu syllable "Aum"; to his right flutters a triangular flag of the yellow-orange color that Indians call "saffron." A large lotus outlined in blue is painted inside a circle on the "chariot's" side. As the vehicle moves, its riders shout out the phrase "Jaya Shri Ram!", "Victory to Lord Ram!" When it stops, the silver-haired man promises the crowds that gather to hear him: "At the place in Ayodhya where Lord Ram was born no power can stop us from building a temple. And it will be built at the very same spot!"

This scene described above is from the movie *Ram Ki Nam*, "In the Name of God," produced and directed by Indian filmmaker Anand Patwardhan.[1] *Ram Ki Nam* is a documentary, and the scene was real, enacted in dozens of Indian cities and towns. The chariot's point of departure was Somnath, site of a famed Hindu temple destroyed by eleventh-century Turkish raids. Its destination was Ayodhya, city of Lord Ram [Rama in Sanskrit], divine descent and royal hero of India's famed epic *Ramayana*. The bus-turned-chariot was meant to evoke Ram's own war chariot, rolling across India to confront demon enemies. The name of Ram himself evokes both his victory over chaos and the kingdom that he ruled after that victory was won. In the Ramrajya, Ram's kingdom, it is said, no fire, flood, nor wind brought destruction, no thieves preyed on the unwary, and all people were healthy and happy and had enough to eat.

The chariot tour and temple promotion were projects of a coordinating organization for religious leaders called the Vishva Hindu Parishad, known in India as the VHP and elsewhere as the World Hindu Council. The silver-haired speaker was a politician, L. K. Advani of the Bharatiya Janata Parishad, or "Indian People's Party" (henceforth called BJP). The saffron flag to his right was the BJP banner, and the lotus on the chariot's side is the party's symbol, marked on voters' ballots in this land where some voters still cannot read well enough to identify a party's name. The promise implicit in his journey is that Advani's party will work to bring Ramrajya back again.

---

[1] Filmed in 1990; released in 1992.

As its first step toward achieving this goal, it will build a temple at Ram's birthplace in the Indian city of Ayodhya. Unfortunately, when this scene was enacted, this "very same spot" was covered by a sixteenth-century mosque, a house of prayer for the Muslim community.

The struggle over this site has been long and complicated. It began with the emergence of a cluster of groups known collectively in India as the Sangh Parivar, "Family of Organizations." The three central groups of this cluster are the VHP, the BJP, and a Hindu youth organization, the Rashtriya Svayamsevak Sangh, "National Volunteer Organization" (henceforth RSS). One goal of the Sangh Parivar, especially its RSS and VHP, is to liberate three sites important to Hindus that have been covered by mosques since the Middle Ages: Ram's birthplace at Ayodhya, Krishna's at Mathura, and the original location of the Vishvanath Temple, the central temple of Shiva at Banaras. Those who push for this goal believe that the sites first held Hindu temples, destroyed by the Muslim rulers who conquered sizeable chunks of India during the medieval period. Some of those rulers indeed destroyed temples and constructed mosques on their ruins; at Banaras, the old temple's foundation remains clearly visible beneath the mosque that covers it. Other Sultans and Muslim governors promoted pilgrim centers and gave lands and money to develop them, a fact ignored by would-be temple liberators.[2]

The temple liberation project has been mostly a VHP initiative. The "Ram's birthplace" campaign, a first step in this project, started in 1949, when a small group of Ayodhya religious leaders broke into the mosque at night and installed a Ram image there, later spreading the rumor that it had come there through a miracle. After the image appeared in the mosque, the government ordered the structure closed to all religious groups. In 1984, the VHP launched the first of a series of "chariot pilgrimages" intended to win support for razing the mosque and building a huge new Ram temple in its place. By 1986, the campaign had achieved the goal of getting the mosque's gates unlocked—to allow Hindu worship. In 1989, the VHP began raising money for the Ram temple, asking donors to finance bricks for use in temple construction. It also performed the first of a series of rituals intended to consecrate the temple site.

Although Advani's BJP party tacitly supported this campaign from its beginning, it played an open role in the chariot pilgrimage only in 1990, the year of Patwardhan's filming. That year Advani's chariot was stopped in the state of Bihar, when the state's chief minister had him arrested to prevent Hindu\Muslim clashes swirling in the chariot's wake. Nonetheless, crowds gathered in Ayodhya on the date set for the temple's start, broke through police lines, planted flags atop the mosque, and attacked its walls with crowbars before police finally stopped them. After another chariot campaign the following year, temple supporters again scaled the mosque's central dome and planted a saffron flag there. The next year, defying a new law that forbade

---

[2] David L. Haberman has described Muslim rulers' support of Krishna's pilgrim center at Mathura in his *Journey to the Twelve Forests*, op. cit., pp. 33–37; *In the Name of God* includes an interview citing Muslim rulers' donations to Ayodhya. Richard M. Eaton argues that protection of Hindu sites was far more common than destruction; destruction occurred at royal temples and was aimed at stripping rival kings of the structures that validated their authority, "Temple Desecration and Indo-Muslim States," *Beyond Turk and Hindu: Rethinking Religious Identities in Islamicate South Asia* (Gainesville: Univ. of Florida, 2000), 246–81.

transferring a place of worship from one religion to another, temple supporters attacked the mosque again and totally demolished it. Police did not try to stop them because the state's government had changed, and BJP members now controlled it. Subsequent clashes between angry Muslims and temple supporters left more than two thousand people dead across India.

How did all of this happen? Why would a political party in a secular democracy engage in a temple building campaign—especially one that left such a trail of blood behind it? There were four contributing factors. The first is India's well-established history of precedents for drawing on religion to offer political legitimation. The second is unhappiness among certain Hindus with the decision taken at independence to make India a secular state, rather than establishing Hinduism, as its rival Pakistan had established Islam. The third is a problem facing all Indian political parties: how do they build enough unity in a hugely divided India to put their candidates in office—and then to govern? The fourth is the anger that simmers among many of India's Hindus, anger with a world that has too few jobs to support them and anger with the shredding social structures that once brought security and affirmed their own value.

THE PRECEDENTS

Mixing politics with religion is a practice longstanding in India. Already in Vedic times, rulers legitimated claims to govern by sponsoring sacrifices transforming them into would-be gods.[3] Later, village leaders and kings fought alongside deities in rites to drive away demons and restore beneficial order. Royal temples channeled deities to earth so that their powers could prosper human realms.[4] A politician crusading on a god's behalf is far less strange to many Hindus than the concept of a state where votes alone legitimate the right to take action.

Added to these older precedents are others established during India's struggle for independence, as nationalist leaders discovered how effectively religion can galvanize mass support for political initiatives. These leaders were drawn from the same class of bicultural, English-educated young men that produced samaj movements.[5] Recall that by the late 1870s, this group's former enchantment with the British had turned sour. Young English-speaking Indians began to realize that they were second-class citizens in their own country, forced to remain subservient to people who often despised them and scorned their religious heritage. Some young leaders began to wage strident defenses of their Hindu heritage. The same disenchantment also turned some English-educated men against movements working for social change. By this time, not all bright young men believed that India's problems resulted from their own culture's decay. They charged that many of India's ills were caused by the British presence. India's able and educated men should give priority not to reform but to removing the British. Reform movements were a hindrance because they split the Hindu community and kept it from uniting against its oppressors.

---

[3] Chapter 1, p. 32.

[4] Chapter 6, pp. 154–58.

[5] See Chapter 4.

Early Nationalists and Religion

Bengal was the first region of the country to turn religious imagery to the service of nationalism. As early as 1869, Bengali writers and playwrights were shaping an image of India as a Mother, Bharat Mata, who had become weak and widowed and called on her sons to save her. In 1882, Bengali novelist Bankimchandra Chatterjee linked Mother India to Bengal's goddess heritage via his novel *Ananda Math*. Central to its plot is a group of militant sannyasis dedicated to freeing their land from alien rule. In a monastery hidden deep within the forest, they worship the gaunt goddess Kali as an image of their agonized and suffering homeland. In contrast with her are two lush and beautiful devis representing the land as it once was and can be again.

Motifs from this novel soon inspired Bengali resistance movements. Terrorist cells of young men and women adopted Kali as their patron goddess, consecrating guns at her altars and vowing to bring her sacrifices of English blood.[6] Tract writer Aurobindo Ghosh, later a guru and saint, called on his compatriots to reawaken in themselves the Mother's power, her shakti. Nationalist sympathizers began to sing the song "Bande Mataram," "Hail to the Mother," that Chatterjee's sannyasis sang to signal one another. This song became so popular among resistance-minded Hindus that they later tried to make it India's national anthem. Portraying India as a goddess needing aid from her devotees was a natural step in Bengal, where people were used to aiding goddesses who protected towns and realms during the popular autumn Durga Puja festivals. As has been seen, however, different regions of India have different types of religious foci. Kali and her terrorist cells remained special to Bengal. The image of Bharat Mata as buxom goddess metamorphosed into a map enshrined within a temple as it spread west across northern India.[7]

In the far west, Hindu nationalists turned to alternative figures to galvanize resistance: Shivaji, founder of India's last great Hindu kingdom, and Ganesha, guardian deity of Shivaji's capital city. The architect of this effort was journalist Bal Gangadhar Tilak, a Chitpavan Brahmin born in 1856, educated in English-medium schools, and once an ally of Maharashtrian reformers, with whom he worked to found the highly successful Indian-controlled New English School.[8] Tilak soon came to believe that reform would not solve India's problems. In 1891, he drew nationwide attention with his editorials thundering against the proposed Age of Consent Act. These argued that the act violated a British commitment not to interfere with religion or home life. Here Tilak broke definitively with the reformers who had proposed and backed the act. Instead, he worked to build an alliance between nationalists like himself, Hindu orthodox leadership, and the masses caught up in Hindu devotional practice.

To this end, he founded one festival and co-opted another. The first honored Shivaji, founder of the Maratha dynasty of India, which was the last great Hindu-led

---

[6] As described in Norvin Hein's chapter "Modern Hinduism," *Religions of Asia,* John Y. Fenton et al. (New York: St. Martin's Press, 1983).

[7] See Charu Gupta, "The Icon of Mother in Late Colonial India: 'Bharat Mata', 'Matri Bhasha' and 'Gau Mata,' " *Economic and Political Weekly* (Nov. 10, 2001), 4291–92.

[8] Several biographies of Tilak exist. I have used D.V. Tahmankar, *Lokamanya Tilak: Father of Indian Unrest and Maker of Modern India* (London: John Murray, 1956); and Stanley Wolpert, *Tilak and Gokhale: Revolution and Reform in the Making of Modern India* (Berkeley: Univ. of California Press, 1962).

realm in India to hold out against the British presence. The second celebrated the elephant-headed deity Ganesha. For most Hindus, Ganesha is Lord of Obstacles, invoked when major rituals are set in motion and honored at gateways to temples to help worshipers cross between the profane realm and the sacred. In Maharashtra, he is also patron deity of Pune, Shivaji's capital city and cultural heart of the state. Although a major celebration during Shivaji's Maratha dynasty, the Ganesha festival had become mostly a family celebration by the end of the nineteenth century.[9] Families bought a temporary Ganesha image in the marketplace, brought it home and enshrined it, worshiped it for a week to twenty-one days, then carried it to a lake or river and immersed it. Starting in 1894, Tilak and his supporters organized singing groups called *melas* to perform in public during the festival. They also joined immersion processions together into a huge parade that included performances by melas and other musicians. Mela songs spiced their devotion with patriotic themes. Tilak's supporters also sponsored dramas and speeches that featured calls for love of country and resistance to tyranny. The revised form of the festival swept swiftly through Maharashtra until the nervous British suppressed it in 1910. By then, Tilak himself had been exiled for sedition.

Most efforts to raise patriotic passions through appeals to religion had one major drawback. India was and is a land of many religions, and symbols beloved to one group far too easily became another group's nemesis. While calling Hindus to celebrate Shivaji and Ganesh, Tilak discouraged them from joining Muharram, a popular Shi'a Muslim festival that honors the martyred son-in-law and grandchildren of the prophet Muhammad. Muslims and Hindus had celebrated Muharram side by side for years. Hindu withdrawal slighted Muslims, who were also offended by themes of the Ganesh festival, which too often drew parallels between aliens ruling now in India and those who had come before. In Bengal, the same problem beset goddess devotees. To avoid being too explicit about which rulers should be resisted, Chatterjee set his *Ananda Math* in the seventeenth century, when sannyasis did indeed revolt against local rulers, rulers who were Muslim. Its pro-Indian imagery and song hence came charged with anti-Muslim overtones.

Resentment against the British easily spilled over into anti-Muslim sentiment. The years of anti-British protest also saw repeated Hindu-Muslim skirmishes over cow protection. Along with Bharat Mata, another image often used to portray Mother India was Gau Mata, "Mother Cow," a reference to ancient stories about a "cow of wishes" who rewarded all desires for anyone who honored her.[10] In Krishna-centered traditions, too, cows enjoyed special affection because the blue-bodied god loved them; one of Krishna's names was Gopala, "cow-protector." Muslims, however, ate beef, as did the British, and many Muslim settlements held butchers willing to turn Mother Cow into steaks for anyone able to pay for them. Muslim butchers became an easy target for anyone wishing to assert loyalty to Hindu principles. One simply led a crowd to the nearest butcher, blockaded his door, and liberated cattle brought to him for slaughter. Needless to say, such campaigns often set off episodes of bitter intercommunal fighting.

---

[9] The description that follows is drawn from Paul B. Courtright, *Gaṇeśa: Lord of Obstacles, Lord of Beginnings* (Oxford: Oxford Univ. Press, 1985), especially pp. 226–47.

[10] Gupta, op. cit., 4291–97.

Gandhi's Satyagraha Campaign

To break the British hold on India, Indians had to set aside memories of such frictions and concentrate on concerns and symbols able to bring them together. The leader best able to do this was Mohandas Karamchand Gandhi, otherwise known as "Mahatma" Gandhi, "Gandhi the Great Soul." As his clashes with the untouchable leader Ambedkar show, even Gandhi could not unify India completely.[11] But he had more success than any other leader in drawing a following that crossed religious boundaries. Like his predecessors, he did this by using the language and symbols of religion.

Who was this "Great Soul"? A Hindu of Vaishnava background, Mohandas Gandhi was born in 1869 in the state of Gujarat in western India. Although his caste was Baniya (Vaishya), his father had for years served as prime minister to a local ruler. His father died when Gandhi was just sixteen, leaving him under the charge of his three older brothers, who sent him to England for legal studies after he finished his training at an English-medium school.

The young Gandhi was so shy that his efforts to set up a practice failed after his return from England. So he accepted an offer from a Muslim business firm in South Africa to relocate there and assist in a lawsuit. Not only did he learn a great deal about law during his stay in South Africa, he also learned about difficulties faced by Indian immigrants because of South African racism. He suggested that his friends organize and protest together the practices that they found most oppressive. Protests evolved from simple petitioning and lobbying to mass demonstrations. One technique invented by Gandhi was nonviolent resistance. Crowds would gather and in public break some objectionable regulation. When police showed up, they would quietly let themselves be taken to jail, putting up no resistance even when handled roughly or beaten. Gandhi came to call this technique *satyagraha*, "truth force." Knowing that people resisting injustice often become damaged by their own hatred for their oppressors, he taught his followers to cultivate love while resisting. Eventually, he founded an ashram in which he trained followers in the self-discipline needed to carry out satyagraha successfully.

Gandhi's efforts in South Africa brought him worldwide publicity. When he returned to India in 1916, nationalist leaders sought him out to aid their efforts. One obstacle that he had to overcome immediately was the divisions that existed between religious communities. In South Africa, he had successfully crossed religious boundaries. His first employers there were Muslims, and the Indians he had organized included members of all religious communities. He was able to unite them by interpreting religion in such a way that members of all groups could identify with it. What people usually call "God," he said, is the *satya*, truth, that calls by means of their conscience and leads them to acts of support and love for one another. Therefore, God is ultimately one, and resisting tyranny is a means of serving God. But this must be done without acts or attitudes of violence.

Important to Gandhi's teachings was a double meaning that he placed on the term *svaraj*, "self-rule." On the one hand, Indians aspired to svaraj in the political sense of independence from foreign domination. On the other, if acquiring this was

---

[11] See Chapter 8, p. 211.

to make any significant difference in their lives, then they also had to cultivate svaraj on a personal level; they had to learn to rule themselves. This entailed developing three qualities: satya, truth, which included both speaking true words and listening to the Truth that speaks via the human conscience; *ahimsa,* harmlessness or nonviolence; and *brahmacharya,* purity of thought and action.

In other words, Gandhi fused political struggle with an ideal of spiritual discipline whose language came out of India's renunciant heritage. Gandhi's home state of Gujarat had a large Jain community, and he writes in his autobiography about a Jain friend close to his family who strongly influenced his thinking. His stress on harmlessness and purity may well reflect that early Jain influence. Wherever Gandhi's ideals came from, they held an appeal that crossed religious boundaries. All traditions of India honored some sort of holy man or woman who struggled to bring self-destructive impulses under control. For Hindus and Jains, this was the sadhu, for Muslims the fakir or pir, for Christians the saint, for Sikhs the dedicated Sikh himself.

Gandhi himself strived to exemplify this kind of self-denying holy person. He adopted the simplest possible form of dress, clothing himself in the loincloth and shawl of a poor Indian peasant. He traveled by third-class train, slept in huts of untouchables, and combined mass rallies with prayer meetings and kirtans, sessions of religious song. When he objected strongly to a policy or a decision, as he had, for example, to the British decision to grant separate electorates to untouchables,[12] he expressed that objection through fasting, asserting that he was willing to die rather than see his fellow Indians move in a destructive direction. To his followers, he seemed like a person who was completely without self-interest. In India, a person without self-interest is a saint, and a saint is someone whose words should be heard, whose example should be followed.

Unlike predecessors who used religion in the service of politics, Gandhi transformed politics into religion. As a result, he managed to pull into the freedom struggle huge numbers of Indians who had stayed detached from it earlier. It had previously taken hold mostly among the same English-educated, dual-cultured Indian males who had earlier backed samaj movements. Now it was drawing in villagers and women. Many women supported the nationalist cause by donating their gold bangles, the only wealth they had of their own. When brothers and husbands were put in jail, women came out of seclusion to fill their places on demonstration lines. Meanwhile, the movement drew many students, who often traveled to Gandhi's Sabarmati Ashram in Gujarat to train as satyagraha organizers and leaders.

This movement made up of resisters who refused to give police an excuse to use violence against them boggled the minds of the British authorities, who never knew how to stop or contain it. The most they could do from time to time was to throw Gandhi and his chief lieutenants into jail. One effect that became more and more discomfiting was the worldwide publicity Gandhi's nonviolent methods brought to the Indian struggle. During the nearly thirty years in which Gandhi led the movement, the technology of filmmaking evolved from silent to sound footage. Camera crews began to travel regularly with newsmen, and the footage they produced was projected

---

[12] See Chapter 8, p. 211.

as newsreels in movie houses across the globe. As far away as the United States, even I, as a very small girl, came to learn about and sympathize with India's struggle by watching footage on Gandhi in my neighborhood movie theater.

It was a very long struggle, and its end did not come until Adolph Hitler's German air force so badly weakened Britain during World War II that Britain could no longer finance an empire. On midnight August 15, 1947, Britain declared India independent, free to organize and manage her own government.

In his struggle, however, Gandhi never had total support from the emerging nation that he claimed to lead. Two kinds of opposition in particular bedeviled him. The first consisted of leaders of minority communities who simply could not share Gandhi's trust in human nature. He assumed that people's own decency, the God who spoke from within them, would keep one group from exploiting others once freedom had been won. The untouchable Ambedkar had challenged this claim, preferring to put into place a system of governance that would ensure a voice and power for untouchable communities. Another person who challenged it with even more bitter results was Muhammad Ali Jinnah, leader of India's Muslim League.

Jinnah had a frustrating personal history.[13] A lawyer trained in Britain like Gandhi, he had been a prominent leader of the Indian National Congress during the decade between Tilak's exile and Gandhi's own rise to leadership. He, not Gandhi, negotiated the first Hindu-Muslim agreement, the Lucknow Pact of 1916. Like Ambedkar, Jinnah believed that India could only succeed as a pluralistic democracy if minorities were guaranteed real voice and power. Also like Ambedkar, he had an urbane and Westernized personal style that Gandhi found distasteful. Gandhi's rise to power in the Congress relegated Jinnah to a secondary position. It also devalued Jinnah's method: patient negotiation and ceaseless prodding of British efforts to build democratic institutions in India. To Jinnah, Gandhi was a flimflam artist beguiling his following into accepting institutions that would let high-caste Hindus step into British shoes and gain control of India. When it became clear that Hindu leaders would not support Jinnah, he accepted an invitation to lead the Muslim League. He and fellow Muslims then worked to ensure that a portion of India's lands would be detached at independence and become a separate Muslim nation—Pakistan.

Why did they take so radical a step? Why were Muslims so opposed to accepting a government in which Muslims would be a permanent minority? To answer these questions, it is necessary to examine the second strand of opposition to Gandhi, the extremist Hindus who challenged his dream of a pluralist nation with their vision of Hindutva.

A HINDU NATION?

One problem distressing Gandhi was that, even within his own following, few agreed with his vision of India's future. He wanted a land of minimal government, where people lived simply in villages ruling themselves by consensus and meeting their needs by farming and traditional handicrafts. Land would be redistributed through

---

[13] The information here is from Stanley Wolpert's biography, *Jinnah of Pakistan* (New York: Oxford Univ. Press, 1984).

persuasion so that families controlled only as much as they needed to live on and everyone would have a share. Caste would persist, but as a system of interdependence in which all groups' labor was valued and respected. This was, of course, a utopia, presupposing that those who enjoyed it had achieved true self-rule and had set aside violence, falsehood, and greed. Gandhi's friend and protegee Jawarharlal Nehru, who became first Prime Minister of India, thought it an empty dream. Nehru imagined India as a modern industrialist state with a centrally controlled socialist economy. It would produce enough goods to meet the whole nation's needs and then use the profits to benefit all India's citizens.

Despite their differences in economic vision, both Gandhi and Nehru, as well as most of their followers, agreed that the new state must ban untouchability and must be secular with regard to religion, offering all faiths protection but granting none a privileged status. The precedent set by the decision to ban untouchability, in effect, created a paradox in the secular approach to religion that has bedeviled Indian politics ever since. In effect, it reserved the state's right to interfere in matters of religion when those matters were destructive to its citizens. Yet it seemed to allow interference only with Hinduism, India's majority practice. Minority religions were granted protections allowing them to control their own internal affairs.

At issue was a complication that makes Indian constitutional democracy considerably different from that of the United States. India's Muslim and Christian communities have their own systems of personal law to govern domestic practice such as marriage, divorce, maintenance, child custody, and inheritance. The Muslim community, in fact, has several such systems, depending on the branch of Islam a particular Muslim belongs to. To let a community control its internal affairs meant, to those who wrote India's constitution, that a community's own personal laws would govern the lives of its members. Hence, Christians and Muslims are still governed by their own codes. Hindus, however, have a revised code, covering also members of the Jain, Buddhist, and Sikh communities. Completed in 1956, this effort introduced several changes into classic Dharmashastra norms. Widows can remarry, daughters can inherit, unhappy spouses can divorce, and Hindu husbands are allowed only one wife at a time. Needless to say, not all these changes pleased orthodox Hindus. They charge that the secular state reins them in while at the same time coddling their competitors.

Disaffected Hindus often embrace an alternative vision of India's future, a future in which India becomes a Hindu state in much the same way that its neighbor Pakistan is Muslim. It does not, however, necessarily mean that only people who call themselves Hindus today would rule. The same people who call for a Hindu state also call for a new definition of the word "Hindu."

Savarkar and *Hindutva*

Their definition is found in *Hindutva: Who is a Hindu?*, a small book written by V. D. Savarkar in 1923.[14] Savarkar was a Brahmin from Maharashtra and an admirer of B. G. Tilak, the Maharashtrian journalist who had injected nationalist themes into Ganesha's festival. After those earlier efforts, Tilak became the national leader of a political faction that called its members "Hindu extremists." During much of the first

---

[14] 5th ed. (Bombay: Veer Savarkar Prakashan, 1969).

decade of the twentieth century, this group dominated Indian politics. Then a series of assassinations of British officials prompted the government to jail or exile most of its leaders. Savarkar, still a young man, was jailed for an unusually long time, kept in various types of confinement from 1910 until 1937. *Hindutva* was written during one of his prison stays. Stories about the book claim it was smuggled out in installments and circulated in secret before Savarkar's release.

The suffix "tva" added to a Sanskrit word gives it the same meaning as the English ending "ness." Therefore, the nearest English equivalent for the word *Hindutva* would be "Hindu-ness," or "that which makes a Hindu a Hindu." Savarkar argues, in effect, that a person becomes a Hindu not by affirming a certain set of beliefs or by observing certain practices, but rather by having a special relationship to the place that is India. To a Hindu, he argues, India is both fatherland—that is to say, the homeland of one's ancestors—and holy land, the place where the most sacred sites of one's religion are located. With this definition, it is clear that Savarkar intended to include as Hindus some groups that claim to practice separate religions: Jains, Buddhists, Sikhs, and supporters of new religious movements. But he also clearly excludes certain groups: Hindu converts who do not have Indian ancestors, and Muslims and Christians whose holy lands are outside India's boundaries.

With this definition, Savarkar implies that Hindus are people with a special claim on India. He argues, moreover, that this claim is very old, as old as the word "Hindu" itself. That word, he asserts, goes back to Vedic times. It was derived from the old name "Sindhu," given to the river now called the Indus. Not only the river itself had this label, he asserted, but also the land surrounding it and those who lived upon this. As the boundaries of this territory expanded eastward, so did the term referring to its inhabitants. Thus, the term "Hindu" means "Indian," one who belongs to the land of India. But it also means a person to whom India belongs. Prince Ram created an original, perfect, fusion between land and people when he conquered India from the Himalayas to Sri Lanka, making all of it a Hindu Rashtra, a Hindu nation. This nation was ruled as India should be—by a Hindu ruler, according to Hindu principles enshrined in the ideal of dharma, which preserves the natural balance between man and nature. It was a peaceful land, a happy land, a land without crime or pain. This realm was eventually weakened by violation of its founding principles, then lost to invasion by conquerors. Nonetheless, having existed once, it can be brought to existence again.

Savarkar offered no blueprint for a restored Hindu nation. In fact, much of the Hindutva idea's appeal lies in its vagueness. People dreaming of a fully Hindu India are left to fill in its outlines with the substance of their own wishes. Some features, however, are clearly implied in Savarkar's writing. A Hindu India will be, or will strive to be, a single nation, extending from the Himalayas to Cape Cormorin and from the Indus Valley to Bengal. Hindutva supporters opposed the creation of Pakistan, and often their maps of "true India" include the entire stretch of once-British India, from the western boundaries of Pakistan through the present country of Myanmar (Burma). This Hindustan will have Hindu rulers: not necessarily kings, but rulers committed to protecting Hindu dharma and the Hindu sacred places. It will have a single civil code: one code of personal law based on dharma. Special protections for minorities will go, although minorities born in India can become Hindu by honoring their land as sacred and adopting its customs. Cows will be protected. The sacred language Sanskrit and its literatures will be promoted and studied. The later Hindu nationalist M. S. Golwalkar even went so far as to assert that ideally Sanskrit should become India's official language. He was willing to settle for Hindi, a Sanskrit derivate, provided Hindi was cleansed of non-Sanskritic Arabic, Persian, and English corruptions.

It may be instructive at this point to look at the groups that took up and carried on this vision of Hindutva. Savarkar himself was a product of the stream of national-ist history that existed in India before Gandhi rose to national prominence. Books written about the Indian independence movement are often so captivated by Gandhi that they overlook the continuation of this earlier heritage.

Under Tilak's leadership, the Hindu extremists had become an important force in Indian politics by the start of the twentieth century. As terrorist activity intensified in India, many leaders of this contingent were either exiled or in jail. By the time they emerged, other leaders had taken their place, and the nationalist movement's mainstream was moving in a direction different from the one they had envisioned. Nonetheless, Hindu nationalists continued to attract admirers. One such group of admirers was the orthodox Hindu community of Brahmin pandits and sadhus. This was an amorphous, disparate community much fractured by internal quarrels. But it was also united by a realization that much of its influence over Indian affairs was threatened.

Many factors fed this threat. Recall that powerful reform movements chal-lenged orthodox pandits throughout the last four decades of the nineteenth cen-tury, often attracting members from the pandits' own Brahmin caste. Added to these challenges had been anti-Brahmin movements emerging within Shudra communities. Untouchables, too, were challenging Brahmin-supported rules about ritual impurity. Some even denied that they were Hindu; they had petitioned the British to list them by separate categories when the British conducted their census at the beginning of each new decade. Census tallies of Hindus had dropped so rapidly that by 1909 one writer predicted that soon Hindus were going to disappear completely.[15]

The Hindu Mahasabha

By the early twentieth century, many Hindu leaders agreed that they had to talk and work together if their traditions were to survive. Hindu pandits and sadhus of the Punjab took a first step in this direction by organizing an annual Punjab Hindu Conference in 1909. Out of this came efforts to assemble an All-India Conference, which in turn evolved into an organization called the Akhil Bharat Hindu Mahasabha, or "All-India Grand Conference of Hindus."

Annual meetings of the Hindu Mahasabha brought together delegates from India's hundreds of sects and religious centers to try to define common aims and build structures that could work to realize them. It was not an easy task. As we have seen, groups calling themselves Hindu often have very different ideas concerning

---

[15] Lt. Col. U. N. Mukerji in "A Dying Race," a series of letters published in the periodical *Bengalee.* Cited by Kenneth W. Jones in "Politicized Hinduism: The Ideology and Program of the Hindu Mahasabha," *Religion in Modern India,* 3rd ed., Robert D. Baird, ed. (New Delhi: Manohar, 1995), p. 244. Materials on the Mahasabha in this chapter have been taken mostly from Jones's article.

what they are about and why they need to act in certain ways. Nonetheless, they could agree on some goals. Achieving cow protection was one; promoting Sanskrit studies another; helping Hindus caught in riots and natural disasters was another.

Discouraging low-caste groups from rejecting the label "Hindu" very swiftly became a high priority. A second and closely related effort soon made the Mahasabha a center of controversy. In 1923, it approved the practice begun by the Arya Samaj of administering rituals of purification to groups that had "lapsed" from their Hindu standing by converting to other religions. In effect, these were rituals of reconversion, restoring those who went through them to full and touchable Hindu standing. Approving the practice set off reconversion campaigns among Muslims and Christians, who felt highly threatened by such efforts to capture their own membership. It also paved the way for a second step, a decision to accept Hindu converts from communities with no previous Hindu connections.

Initiatives of this sort, although controversial, would not have necessarily drawn the Mahasabha into politics. But proposals for separate electorates among Muslims and untouchables swiftly did so. The Mahasabha opposed both, leaning hard on Congress leaders to refuse support for any separate electorates. In partial compensation to low-caste groups, at the same time it adopted a resolution condemning untouchability. As controversy over separate electorates grew, the Mahasabha began asserting that "Hindustan is primarily for the Hindus."[16] In 1937, when Savarkar finally was freed and joined the Mahasabha, its president Bhai Parmanand stepped down so that Savarkar could replace him. The Mahasabha announced that from now on it would work to establish a Hindu nation.

This move had two important repercussions. On the one hand, it finalized a growing split between the Mahasabha and the National Congress, which had assured its followers that independent India would be a secular state. During earlier years, the Mahasabha had been a Congress affiliate, in effect, a lobbying group that offered support from its own following in exchange for some concessions to its aims. Its sizeable influence in Congress had, in fact, been a major reason why Muslims had so distrusted Congress's motives. Now, having severed Congress ties and made its support for a Hindu state explicit, the Mahasabha needed to form its own political organization, which proved to be more than it could handle effectively. After independence, Mahasabha leadership split, backing two rival parties. One kept the old Hindu Mahasabha name; the other called itself the Jan Sangh, people's party. Neither made much headway in challenging the Congress, which for years retained the huge popular backing it had won during its drive to win India's freedom.

The RSS

Although the Mahasabha itself faded after independence, its nationalist aims did not. A former protege took them up and carried them on: the RSS, parent and senior member of today's family of Hindu nationalist organizations. At first viewing, the RSS seems an unlikely candidate to mastermind a political resistance movement. Its full name, Rashtriya Svayamsevak Sangh, means "National Volunteer Association."

---

[16] From a 1936 Mahasabha resolution cited by Jones, ibid., p. 257.

Its own histories represent it as a kind of Hindu scouting organization.[17] Its founder, Dr. K. B. Hedgewar, was a Hindu nationalist and Tilak admirer concerned about the need to develop discipline and "manliness" among India's many confused and floundering young men and boys. In 1925, Hedgewar founded an organization that brought teenaged boys together each morning for programs of calisthenics, military-style drilling, and "play" that developed combat skills such as fighting with bamboo staffs. RSS members were authorized to wear an official uniform consisting of black hats, khaki shorts, white shirts, and brown tennis shoes. Thus outfitted, they showed off their skills at public celebrations such as Hindu festivals. During required weekly meetings, they were fed a steady diet of Hindu nationalist songs, prayers, slogans, and teachings of Tilak, Sarvakar, and other leaders from their own top circles.

The RSS trained its leaders via special camps or retreats offered to young men showing dedication and promise. While some young men thus trained simply headed local chapters, others became full-time district, statewide, and national staffers. Recruiting was aggressive: when researcher J. A. Curran studied the RSS during the late forties, each boy who joined was asked to pull in five more members per year.[18] Often they managed to do so because the boys enjoyed their organization. It fostered comradeship and pride, and members' families supported one another.

The RSS had been founded with Mahasabha encouragement, and soon its members were serving as a security force during Mahasabha annual conventions. In 1932, the Mahasabha commended Hedgewar's creation and urged that branches be started in all provinces of India.[19] By 1947, it was a powerful nationwide organization with many adult staffers and supporters. Gandhi's assassination on January 30, 1948, brought a major setback because his assassin Nathuram Godse had earlier been an RSS organizer. For the next year and a half, the group was banned by the Indian government. But it had won friends through relief work it did for Hindu families displaced by the riots following Partition. Soon, it was restored and rebuilt its lost momentum.

When the Hindu Mahasabha sagged after independence, the RSS set out to create an alternative venue to bring Hindu leaders together and coordinate their efforts. In 1964, its leader Shivram Shankar Apte met with Hindu leaders at the Bombay ashram of Swami Chinmayananda. Out of that meeting emerged the organization now called the VHP, from Vishva Hindu Parishad, "World Hindu Council." Sixteen years later, the RSS gathered would-be political leaders to form the BJP, the third principal Sangh Parivar organization. The VHP and BJP are legally independent of the RSS, but leadership of the three groups interlocks. High-level officials in both the BJP and the VHP have consistently been current or former RSS staffers.

---

[17] The official version of its founding is in B.V. Deshpande and S. R. Ramaswamy, *Dr. Hedgewar the Epoch-Maker* (Bangalore: Sahitya Sindhu, 1981). This innocent portrait of its creation is challenged in Tapu Basu et al., *Khaki Shorts and Saffron Flags* (New Delhi: Orient Longman, 1993), pp.16–17, which suggests it was intended from the beginning to serve as a paramilitary force.

[18] J. A. Curran, Jr., *Militant Hinduism in Indian Politics: A Study of the R.S.S.* (New York: Institute of Pacific Relations, 1951), p. 46.

[19] Jones, op. cit., p. 255.

MAKING ONE FROM MANY[20]

What is going on here? Why this proliferation of organizations? What do they have to do with the promised Ramrajya? The issue facing Hindu nationalists is that to achieve their aims, they must solve the problem facing all Indian political groups: convincing a huge number of people with disparate interests to accept at least a few common goals and getting them moving in the same direction. In short, they must establish some degree of unity.

The difficulties here are illustrated by the history of the nationalists' own political organization. Ostensibly, the BJP was created to capture the power that would allow nationalists to implement their vision of India's future. It did well at capturing power. Between 1998 and 2004, the BJP was the dominant party in the Indian national government. The Prime Minister during those years, Atal Behari Vajpayee, was a longtime BJP leader. He was also an RSS trainee and a former RSS staffer. Vajpayee's Deputy Prime Minister was none other than L. K. Advani, commander of Ram's bus-turned-chariot. Advani is also a former RSS staffer, as are a number of other high-ranking BJP politicians. All are steeped in Hindu nationalist ideology. One might expect, then, that they would be well along in their project to bring about a Hindu nation.

Nonetheless, this is not the case. One huge frustration for the BJP's brother organizations has been how little "their" government did in achieving the goal that is their highest priority. Two factors have stood in their way. The first is the nature of BJP power itself. During all the years when it headed the Indian government, the BJP held only a plurality of seats in India's Parliament. India has many political parties, so it is quite difficult for a single party to control more than half of the Parliament's seats. Yet to organize a government or put in place any program, a party must show that its proposals will be backed by more than half of the Parliament's votes. It wins these votes by forging coalitions, striking deals that it will support lesser parties' proposals and put some of their candidates in key posts. The lesser coalition parties then agree to support BJP measures when support is needed. Achieving a Hindu nation may be an important goal for BJP politicians, but it is not a high priority for many BJP allies. For some, it is downright offensive; several parties allied with the BJP have a low-caste base and started as non-Brahmin movements. Needless to say, these parties are cautious about aligning themselves with any group promising a return to government based on dharma.

The history of the BJP's rise to power reveals another hindrance. In Indian politics, as in the West, votes for a given party are often as much votes against something as they are votes for it. The BJP won its initial plurality in Parliament largely because two rivals had alienated their voters. The Congress Party, once so strong that it won three-fourths of all seats in one famous election, was discredited by corruption scandals during the late 1980s and early 1990s. The party that succeeded it for a time lost coalition partners after pushing a program to expand low-caste quotas for government jobs. The BJP won by campaigning as a party of honesty and moderation, not by pushing its Hindutva agenda.

---

[20] I am grateful to my student Jason Messana for sharing with me materials on Sangh organizations that he found during his work for his M.A. thesis. Most Web citations in this chapter are results of his skillful searching.

Even internally, BJP support for a Hindu nation is not as profound as might be expected. The party itself is a coalition. Not all its members are RSS stalwarts. Many are crossover politicians who joined the BJP because they were disappointed by other party affiliations. Some are in the party simply because it has a good record of getting its candidates elected. Such members often prefer that the Hindu nation project be kept in the background. When pushed too conspicuously, it can lose votes for the party as well as win them.

Hence, the BJP's Sangh Parivar partners all too often find that the group they most need to accomplish their ends is at the same time the most reluctant to help them. They have powerful leverage, however, because the BJP needs them. Thousands of cadres of RSS youth are an irreplaceable asset during election campaigns, distributing flyers, policing rallies, and getting the vote out on election days. As for the VHP, a religious leader's backing for a candidate is an excellent way to get disciples to follow his lead.

Therefore, the BJP must continue to make at least some effort toward implementing the Hindu nation project. One quiet means of doing so has been to plant Hindu nationalists on the various boards and councils controlling Indian education. To know why these actions are so important, it is necessary to look more closely at RSS strategies for implementing its program. The preceding discussion of BJP problems shows that merely gaining control of a government will not help it put in place a program that does not enjoy broad popular support. The RSS and its protege VHP are organizations that build such support among the Hindu public. They work among different constituencies, and hence have somewhat different foci and methods.

Reeducating Indians

The RSS, as noted, was founded as an organization geared toward youth. No longer exclusively male, it now has auxiliaries for girls and women. But it continues to focus on training young people who represent India's future. Much of its power lies in its ability to instill in restless young people both discipline and intense loyalty to a single cause and organization. Although most of its members come from Brahmin and Vaishya caste divisions, the RSS recruits across caste and class lines.

The RSS strives to reeducate Hindu youth into its own views of Indian history and purpose. Remember that many twentieth-century Indian leaders acquired the values that challenged older Hindu practice through their studies in English-medium schools. RSS leaders have not forgotten this lesson. To win India's support for their own projects, they must change its means of delivering education. Their initial efforts for reeducating young Hindus came through camps and daily meetings. Next, like many other new religious groups, they began to build and run their own schools. By now, they claim to have over twenty thousand, many of which aim at winning recruits from India's poor and tribal communities.[21]

When the BJP gained control of the Indian national government, this opened a third opportunity, that of redesigning India's state-supported school system. In India, there are two levels of control over state-funded education. Individual states set up

---

[21] See Somini Sengupta, "Hindu Nationalists Are Enrolling, and Enlisting, India's Poor," *New York Times International* (May 16, 2002):1 (www.nytimes.com/2002).

programs for different grade levels, whereas the national government appoints boards that set general policy, commission textbooks, and allocate funds for research and educational development. One quiet effort launched by the RSS was to gain control of public-school textbook contents. Via political contacts, it slipped its supporters onto textbook review committees. Many of India's textbooks have been written by scholars whose names are known and honored around the world. Rather than replacing these books entirely with RSS products, textbook reviewers edited selectively, deleting or rewriting passages contrary to Hindu nationalist teachings. For example, one passage thus slated for deletion read:

> The Puranic tradition could be used to date Rama of Ayodhya around 2000 B.C.E., but diggings and extensive explorations in Ayodhya do not show any settlement around this date. Similarly, although Krishna plays an important part in the *Mahabharata,* the earliest inscriptions and sculptural pieces found . . . do not attest his presence. Because of such difficulties, the idea of an epic age based on the *Ramayana* and the *Mahabharata* has to be discarded."[22]

To a Hindu nationalist, the epic age was the time when Hindu India achieved its greatest glory. It has to have been real, not based on poetic imagining; therefore, this passage is unacceptable. Other passages deleted spoke of beef-eating and cow sacrifice in ancient Vedic times as well as Hindus raiding other Hindus. One suggested that Brahmins might have been self-serving in certain of their historical actions.

Another, more elaborate RSS project has attempted to banish the divisive "Aryan invasion" scenario from portrayals of ancient Indian history. This asserted that Hindu civilization began when Sanskrit-speaking Aryan invaders from the West overran India's native populations. The claim that Aryas came from the West was based on linguistic connnections between Sanskrit and European languages. When remains of Harappan civilization were found in northwest India, arguments based on archaeological evidence asserted that Aryas entered India after Harappa had fallen. Often, these were "arguments from absence," citing the lack of horse remains in Harappan settlements or lack of evidence of fire sacrifice. Readers will recall that low-caste movements often based their resistance to high castes on the idea that high castes were descendants of illegitimate invaders.[23]

The RSS and its partners now offer an alternative to this scenario. Aryas, they claim, were the creative and capable ancient Indians who built the Harappan civilization. Yes, their Sanskrit language is related to European tongues, but this is because their parent language first was spoken in India, before emigrating Aryas took it west. To make this scenario stick, its proponents must find evidence of Aryas in the Harappan region. The BJP government packed boards sponsoring archaeological research with referees favoring projects that would search for such evidence.

---

[22] From R. S. Sharma, *Ancient India*, Class XI, pp. 20–21. As cited in January 2004 on the Web site for India's National Council for Educational Research and Training under the subtitle "The Debate on History Continues." Materials themselves are from item 4 of the heading "Portions to Be Deleted from NCERT History Books." See also items 1, 2, 3, 6, and 8 (www.ncert.nic.in/ ncert/histdebate). I am grateful to my student Emily Vermilya for calling my attention to these references.

[23] See Chapter 8, pp. 207 and 209.

College curricula, too, felt the RSS touch. Indian college curricula are set more centrally than in the West. A major influence in determining what is taught is the New Delhi-based University Grants Commission (UGC). The BJP government also packed it with RSS-favoring members. In February 2001, the commission announced to Indian universities that it would accept proposals for degree programs in Vedic astrology. The new astrology programs were to be called *Jyotir Vigyan,* "star science."[24] A second announcement soon followed, asking for programs that would offer *Purohitya,* "priestly training." Needless to say, both proposals, like the textbook alterations, provoked a huge outcry among Indian scholars who did not recognize either field as a legitimate discipline.

On the other hand, such proposals win support for nationalists among traditional Hindu leaders because they legitimate practices that produce a substantial portion of such leaders' incomes. It should not be forgotten that acceptance of nationalist ideology is not a foregone conclusion for Hindu religious leaders. Many support the current Indian constitution and form of government, wish to see Hindus live peacefully with their neighbors, and believe that religion's purpose is to enhance human spiritual development and happiness. Such leaders often command sizeable followings. Therefore, any organization claiming to speak for Hindus must win, if not their active support, then at least their tacit agreement not to offer opposition.

The VHP: Standardizing Hindu Practice

Much of the job of bringing this leadership and its following into line falls on the shoulders of the VHP, the third Sangh organization. Part of the VHP's task is simply to make itself useful to Hindus. In the course of doing so, it standardizes Hindu practice and teachings, thus creating a community more unified in its experience. It offers support services among Hindus living abroad—and, not incidentally, seeks donations from the wealthier among them. It also engages in mission work and reconversion campaigns among India's tribal and untouchable communities. Perhaps most importantly, it strives to get Hindus to look upon it as the official voice of their community.

Describing the work of just a few of its eighteen departments shows the range of VHP services.[25] One department organizes sessions of devotional song in temples. Another coordinates festival celebrations among temples, striving to get them working cooperatively and thinking of themselves as part of a greater whole. Still another trains *pujaris,* temple priests, in VHP-standardized temple rituals. One major effort of the VHP has been to disseminate models for "proper" performance of festivals and life-cycle rites among the Hindu community. Often such "proper performance" incorporates features that make the rituals increasingly public and assertive, such as the women's lamp rituals of Tamilnadu described in Chapter 9.[26] In addition, the VHP issues approved lists of festivals to be practiced and pilgrim sites to be visited, stressing always the importance of its central symbol, Lord Ram.

---

[24] "Jyoti" literally means "light." But it is the term used for the "heavenly lights" that are stars and planets in Sanskrit works on astrology.

[25] Much of the description below follows Basu, op. cit., pp. 65–67.

[26] Pp. 233 and 236.

Another VHP department promotes Sanskrit education, and another coordinates efforts of monasteries and temples. Yet another project important since the time of VHP founding has been reconversion of tribal Indians and untouchables, especially those living in India's remoter areas. Here, VHP workers compete aggressively with the Christian missions that have worked for years in these same areas.

It may be instructive at this point to ask just which strands among India's rich variety of Hinduisms have provided the models that the VHP now promotes as normative. Much VHP practice and teaching, not surprisingly, comes out of high-caste Brahmin traditions. VHP publications assert that Hinduism honors a single god who appears in many forms. Ram is usually listed first, a position that in India means most important. In His manifestations as Brahma, Vishnu, and Shiva, God creates, maintains, and destroys the world. Humans have eternal souls that pass through many births in accordance with the deeds that they perform. Having such a soul is equivalent to possessing a natural impulse toward moral good. Passing through many births ensures that there will be no such thing as eternal punishment. The goal of religion is *moksha,* defined as existing in permanent bliss and service to God. But many religious paths are valid because humans exist at differing levels of spiritual development, for which different kinds of paths are appropriate. Gurus are essential to help people find their appropriate paths, which include devotion, study, and works. Use of mantras, chanted scripture, and vegetarian eating are highly recommended aids in following such paths. One rarely finds reference to village deities, blood sacrifice, possessions, or exorcisms in VHP descriptions of Hindu practice. Conversely, the rise of nationalist ideology has been matched by a renaissance in fire-centered rituals.

Nationalist descriptions of Hindu teachings thus parallel closely the simplistic, Brahmin-oriented summaries made in many world religion textbooks. Nevertheless, they reject textbook portrayals of caste. Caste is not hierarchal, they assert. Its ancient designers never intended to devalue any groups or the work they performed. It merely categorizes human society according to occupations that people practice.[27] Caste distinctions are, nonetheless, important because the four fundamental varnas represent four *shaktis,* energies, that must be kept in balance if a society is to prosper: intelligence, power, wealth, and labor.[28] Most important about caste, nationalists assert, are the values that underlie it: the ideal of self-sacrifice to achieve the good of the whole and the vision of integration, bringing together disparate gifts in cooperative effort.

Hindus abroad are an important part of such cooperative effort. The VHP Web site lists activities in the United States, Canada, the United Kingdom, West Germany, the Netherlands, Hong Kong, Sri Lanka, Singapore, Trinidad, Kenya, Tanzania, and several other countries. VHP projects described range from conferences and youth camps to countering "discrimination against Hindus in Arab countries."[29] Disseminating views through the internet is another international effort, although it is not always

---

[27] Much of the preceding summary is condensed from an entry called "Who is a Hindu?" on the Web site www.hinduunity.org (August 6, 2002). The organization Hindu Unity advertises itself as an affiliate of the Bajrang Dal, the VHP youth wing.

[28] As cited in Basu et al., p. 33.

[29] Shri Hari Babu Kansalm, "Vishva Hindu Parishad Abroad," www.vhp.org/englishsite (August 6, 2002).

easy to tell which "Hindu" Web sites on the net originate among VHP-sponsored organizations.

This is in part because one major VHP strategy is to diffract its views and symbols in such a way that they seem to come from many different directions. Using devices ranging from eye-catching window and dashboard stickers to posters of Ram and his temple to Web sites, newspapers, radio, TV, and videocassettes, it broadcasts its messages and symbols until they appear to be normative for all Hindus. Nor is the receiver always aware of the nationalist source of messages received. The VHP has spawned dozens of suborganizations and names that are cited to give the impression that its views are shared by many independent sources.[30]

UNITY THROUGH ANGER

All this would be of no great concern if the Sangh Parivar did not use so freely the world's simplest method of bringing disparate people together, namely uniting them against a common enemy. Three enemies in particular are named again and again in nationalist postings and writings. One is the pseudo-secularist, that is, anyone critical of religion-backed abuses or supporting legal protections for minorities. Sangh-produced literature asserts that Sangh supporters are the real secularists, uniting efforts of many sectarian groups. Sangh writers assure their readers that Hinduism is tolerant, the most tolerant of religions; it is intolerant only of those who themselves practice intolerance. Chief among these are Muslims and Christians, its other two enemy groups. Not only do Muslims and Christians fail to honor India as their holy land, they were brought by conquerors to wrest the holy land from its rightful owners. Because of them, India knew an "unfortunate slavery of one thousand years." Because of current catering to these groups, Hindus are now "second-class citizens."[31] "This most ancient, glorious and cultural [Hindu] civilisation finds itself powerless, helpless and orphaned in its own country."[32]

Sangh-produced literature constantly repeats a set list of charges. Muslims and Christians are aliens—despite the fact that most are descended from Indian converts and some belong to communities that have been in India for many centuries. Muslims and Christians are also called slavers who came to India to wreck Indian civilization. Muslims and Christians are not to be trusted: Christians ally with Europe and America and win converts by bribery and coercion; Muslims are agents of Pakistan, waging holy war against Hindus. Muslims are, moreover, called hyper-lustful, breeding their way into control of India and quick to rape Hindu women while doing so. Hindus are exhorted to stand up to these vipers in their midst, to reclaim the sites and privileges that are justifiably theirs. Nationalist propaganda urges Hindus to get angry: "Fight if you must! Die if you must!"[33]

---

[30] This strategy of diffraction is discussed at greater length in Basu, op. cit., pp. 56–64.

[31] Letter from reader Raji Mani, published in *India Today International* (February 18, 2002), p. 4.

[32] Item 2, "Points of Hindu Agenda," Vishva Hindu Parishad Web page (www.vhp.org/englishsite/f.Hindu_Agenda) (August 6, 2002).

[33] From the Web site Hindu Unity: www.hinduunity.org (August 6, 2002).

Nationalist activists have learned that outbreaks of inter-religious rioting are a highly effective means of hardening lines between religious communities of India. Opponents charge that they sometimes incite that rioting. For example, a study of Hindu\Muslim riots in 1990 in the town of Khurja, Uttar Pradesh, reported that the outbreak

> was preceded by a prolonged simulation of rioting. Fireworks and bombs were exploded every night for more than two weeks all over the city in both Hindu and Muslim 'mohallas' [neighborhoods] while taped cassettes reproducing sounds of fighting, frenzy and panic were played on loudspeakers. Rumours that killings had taken place in Khurja and elsewhere were spread about five days before.[34]

The same report cites circulation of pamphlets and handbills that urged Hindus to kill Muslims to revenge Hindus supposedly killed during the earlier storming of the "Ram's birthplace" mosque. Loudspeakers in public places broadcast tapes of anti-Muslim harangues by the VHP's woman sadhu Rithambara. Riot investigators even found that bets had been made concerning the exact date when violence would break out.[35] Hindu nationalists insist that all rioting is spontaneous, a simple expression of "momentary anger."[36] Whether spontaneous or not, rioting would not occur if anger did not exist, waiting to be tapped and channeled. Nationalist propaganda may stoke it and keep it going, but nationalists are less responsible for kindling it than providing it with a focus and justification. Many Hindus *are* angry. Nationalist propaganda offers reasons to be angry and points to convenient arenas for expressing anger. One final question to be asked is where this anger is coming from. Why are Hindus angry? Why would anyone listen to groups that strive to turn them against their neighbors?

Downward Mobility

To explain why many Hindus are angry, it is necessary to understand who these angry Hindus are. From what social and economic strata do they come? It has been noted that RSS membership consists largely of Brahmins and Vaishyas, two groups relatively high on the Hindu caste spectrum. As a general rule, nationalist support comes largely from "forward caste" groups, that is to say, from higher ranks of the old "touchable" caste groups. Because their higher caste standing advantaged these groups in the past, they are thought not to need help from programs designed to enhance their political or economic prospects. But at the same time, nationalists tend to be from middle class groups: shopkeepers, people in skilled trades such as electricians and plumbers, secretaries and clerks, teachers in state-supported schools.

These are groups caught in the middle of a shift in social values. As noted earlier in this book, India is currently changing over from what sociologists call a system of

---

[34] Uma Chakravarti et al., "Khurja Riots 1990–91: Understanding the Conjuncture," *Economic and Political Weekly* (May 2, 1992): 951.

[35] Ibid., for all materials cited in this paragraph.

[36] See, for example, assertions by Ahmedabad's VHP joint secretary Kaushik Mehta, published in *The Rediff Interview* (www.rediff.com/news/2000/apr/22inter.htm).

"ascribed status" to one of "achieved status." Under older practice, a person's social worth was determined in large measure by the caste that he or she was born into. We have seen how those born untouchable were scorned categorically. At the opposite end of the social spectrum, a Brahmin could demand respect simply by virtue of being born Brahmin. It wasn't quite this simple, of course. Caste groups did develop measures to ensure that they deserved at least some measure of the respect their members claimed. Castes set up their own standards of caste-approved behavior, and they could and did expel members whose behavior did not meet these standards. Nonetheless, by and large members who conformed to caste expectations could expect the deference granted to their caste in general.

Caste remains an important factor in Indian social interaction. But, especially in towns and cities, a system of achievement-based status is taking its place. Based on the same post-Enlightenment values that gave rise to samaj movements, this system holds that a person's worth is determined by accomplishments. As in the West, economic accomplishments carry great weight. A person is "worth" what that person earns or possesses.

For people other than gifted entrepreneurs, economic achievement means holding a good job, one that entails a viable living wage and perks and offers the possibility of advancement. Unfortunately, such jobs are hard to come by in India and access to them is highly competitive. High caste standing used to be an advantage in gaining job access. But this is becoming less and less the case. As a result, many high-caste Hindus are experiencing downward mobility, growing pinched economically and losing social respect.

The pain and frustration experienced by downwardly mobile Hindus is illustrated by the political crisis that prompted Advani to join the 1990 chariot tour for Ram's temple. Just before Advani decided to mount Ram's chariot, the BJP had been linked in alliance with the Janata Dal, a party that built strength by courting votes from lower caste groups. When the Janata Dal came to power, the government that it sponsored moved to implement a controversial plan called the Mandal Commission report. This report proposed extension of a system reserving a set percentage of government jobs for members of scheduled caste groups, that is, India's former untouchables. Until then, only Hindus of the very low caste groups had access to such reserved positions. The Mandal Commission recommended that the system be extended to include members of "other backward castes," a category used by the government that included once-untouchable Buddhists and Christians as well as many touchable, but low-ranked Shudras. A full 52 percent of civil service jobs would be filled only by applicants from these categories.

Since the days of British rule, jobs in government have been among the most sought-after jobs in India. Hindus who filled them were usually from higher castes, especially Brahmins. This fact did not necessarily reflect overt caste discrimination. It was simply the case that Brahmins and other high-caste groups had the most access to education and thus had the writing and accountancy skills needed to keep records and conduct complex transactions. Decreeing that 52 percent of government jobs would be held for low-caste candidates meant that high-caste candidates would face much greater competition for the 48 percent of jobs remaining.

When the Janata Dal announced its decision to implement the Mandal quotas, high-caste Indian students took to the streets, especially in northern India. Roads were blocked; government-owned vehicles, railroad cars, and offices were torched. Some protesters set themselves on fire: Nearly thirty died by self-immolation, and another forty or more in student-police clashes. In the midst of this upheaval, after seeking and gaining a stay of implementation of the Mandal quotas, Advani joined the Ram's birthplace campaign. This move was widely viewed by journalists as a distraction. The Mandal decision had put the BJP in a nearly impossible bind. Its support is mostly high caste, but it dare not ignore the interests of lower caste groups if it wishes to draw the votes needed to bring it to power. Letting Mandal implementation proceed would have alienated the BJP base. Opposing it directly would anger low-caste BJP supporters. Joining the temple campaign diverted attention to an issue far less divisive for Hindus. It was still a divisive issue, but the divisions it created were more to the BJP's advantage.

The Mandal report controversy also points to a third source of Hindu nationalist unease. For many years in India, even after independence, members of high-caste groups continued to dominate the political apparatus that determined what kinds of policies would be enacted. So they could keep up at least some structures that gave them advantage. Increasingly, this is less the case. India's once-oppressed caste groups are learning how to use democracy for their own advancement. As they become more politically skilled, higher caste groups must give them more and more concessions.

Supporters of Hindu nationalism are people crunched on multiple fronts by cultural changes far too complex for most to understand, let alone accept. They are people who hurt, who fear for themselves and for their children. Being hurt, they want to lash out. Nationalist scapegoating of Muslims and Christians provides them with an acceptable target. Being afraid, they look in hope toward an alternative system where the ideal of sacrificing oneself for the greater whole holds forth the hope that lower caste Hindus will become less "uppity," that Ram's gracious protection will extend to them again, and that a whole subsection of the Indian population will no longer offer competition or challenge to them.

WHAT'S NEXT?

In other countries where divisively nationalist groups have established strong footholds, the outcome has all too often been takeover by dictatorial regimes. Dissent is suppressed. Strongmen seize control over governments and armies. Scapegoated groups suffer pogroms. Wars of expansion are undertaken that bring about the aggressor nation's physical and economic ruin. India has thus far resisted such an outcome. One can predict, however, that proponents of a Hindu India will not quietly fold up their platforms and go away. So long as the real causes of their anger are not addressed and eased, they will enmesh their nation in violence again and again.

Another explosion took place as this chapter was being written. During its campaigns in the early 1990s, the VHP acquired land adjacent to the "Ram's birthplace" mosque. After the mosque's demolition, Indian courts placed restraining orders on use of both the mosque site and this land. In 2002, after ten years of delays, VHP president Ashok Singhal announced that his organization had waited long enough. He petitioned the courts to release VHP-owned lands, saying construction would start there on the entry hall for the temple until the courts ceded the remainder of the site. If VHP lands were not released, his organization would still begin rites of temple consecration, dedicating the carved pillars to be used in temple construction.

This time violence started before the target date of March 15. On February 27, in the western state of Gujarat, an argument erupted in a railroad station between local Muslims and temple proponents returning from a pilgrimage to Ayodhya. The pilgrims' train was set on fire and fifty-eight people died, among them a number of women and children. Widespread rioting followed, leaving more than two thousand dead, most of them Muslims.[37] The government flooded Ayodhya with security forces, and courts refused to release even the VHP-owned land. On March 15, the VHP sadhu who leads the temple campaign consecrated two pillars at an alternative site, turned them over for "safekeeping" to a government official, and declared that the latter's agreement to receive them meant that the government sanctioned the temple project. The government disagreed, and let the project return to limbo. When the BJP lost its 2004 bid for reelection, VHP president Singhal offered the following explanation: "The BJP spurned the desire of Hindus to see a grand Ram temple constructed in Ayodhya and the people responded in a befitting manner."[38]

ADDITIONAL SOURCES

Because literature on Hindu nationalism is often highly partisan, readers wishing to explore it should seek multiple perspectives. To sample nationalists' own views, works by and about two leaders, Vinayak Damodar Savarkar and Sadashiv Golwalkar, are good starting points. V. D. Savarkar's *Hindutva,* 5th ed. (Bombay: Veer Savarkar Prakashan, 1969) is essential. Showing the context in which *Hindutva* was written is D. Keer, *Veer Savarkar* (Bombay: Popular Prakashan, 1966). Golwalkar's thought can be seen in *We or Our Nationhood Defined,* 2nd ed. (Nagpur: Bharat Prakashan, 1944); see also his *Bunch of Thoughts* (Bangalore: Vikrama Prakashan, 1966). Ritu Kohli summarizes Golwalkar's life and thought in *Political Ideas of M. S. Golwalkar* (New Delhi: Deep and Deep Publications, 1993). K. R. Malkani provides an insider's history in his *The R.S.S. Story* (New Delhi: Impex India, 1980). V. M. Sirsikar recalls his RSS youth in "My Years in the R.S.S.," *The Experience of Hinduisms: Essays on Religion in Maharashtra,* Eleanor Zelliot and Maxine Berntsen, eds. (Albany: State Univ. of New York Press, 1988), 190–203. Parvathy Appaiah's *Hindutva: Ideology and Politics* (New Delhi: Deep & Deep, 2003) offers an unusually balanced assessment of nationalist achievements and literature, plus treatment of shifts and differences within Sangh organizations.

For Indian critiques of nationalists, a fine start is Tapu Basu et al., *Khaki Shorts and Saffron Flags* (New Delhi: Orient Longman, 1993); see also Jayant K. Lele, *Hindutva: The Emergence of the Right* (Madras: Earthworm Books, 1995). Uma Chakravarti critiques nationalist versions of history in "Saffroning the Past: Of Myths, Histories, and Right-Wing Agendas," *Economic and Political Weekly* 33:5 (January 31, 1998): 225–32.

---

[37] According to the government, the toll was one thousand; aid workers dispute this and have doubled the number.

[38] www.expressindia.com (August 31, 2004).

Jacki Assayag explores the beginnings of VHP chariot processions in "Ritual Action or Political Reaction? The Invention of Hindu Nationalist Processions in India during the 1980s," *South Asia Research* 18:2 (1998): 126–46. Roles of Ram and Ayodha are examined in Pradip K. Datta, "VHP's Ram at Ayodhya: Reincarnation through Ideology and Organization," *Economic and Political Weekly* 26:44 (November 2, 1991): 2517–26. Exploring nineteenth-century nationalist approaches to women is Tanika Sarkar, *Hindu Wife, Hindu Nation: Community, Religion, and Cultural Nationalism* (Bloomington, IN: Indiana Univ. Press, 2001). On ideals held up for women today, see Manisha Sethi, "Avenging Angels and Nurturing Mothers: Women in Hindu Nationalism," *Economic and Political Weekly* 37:16 (April 20, 2002): 1545–52. For contemporary women's roles in movements, see Tanika Sarkar and Urvashi Butalia, eds., *Women and the Hindu Right* (New Delhi: Kali for Women, 1995). For nationalist responses to feminist scholarship, see Neera Desai et al., "Reorienting Women Studies: Retrograde Moves," *Economic and Political Weekly* 38:35 (August 30, 2003): 3625–26.

Western scholarship on nationalism is also extensive. The most thorough study is Christophe Jaffrelot, *The Hindu Nationalist Movement in India* (New York: Columbia Univ. Press, 1996). See also Jaffrelot's "Hindu Nationalism: Strategic Syncretism in Ideology Building," *Economic and Political Weekly* 38: 12–13 (March 20–27, 1993): 517–24; and "The Vishva Hindu Parishad: A Nationalist but Mimetic Attempt at Federating the Hindu Sects," *Charisma and Canon: Essays on the Religious History of the Indian Subcontinent*, Vasudha Dalmia et al., eds. (New Delhi: Oxford Univ. Press, 2001). Jaffrelot teamed with Thomas Blom Hansen to edit *The BJP and the Compulsions of Politics in India* (Delhi: Oxford Univ. Press, 1998). See also Hansen's *The Saffron Wave: Democracy and Hindu Nationalism in Modern India* (New Jersey: Princeton Univ. Press, 1999); and John Zavos, *The Emergence of Hindu Nationalism in India* (New Delhi: Oxford Univ. Press, 2000). Work of the VHP is explored in Eva Hellman, *Political Hinduism: The Challenge of the Viśva Hindū Parishad* (Uppsala Univ. Doctoral Dissertation, 1993). Also see essays on Hinduism in *The Fundamentalism Project*, Martin E. Marty and R. Scott Appleby, eds. (Chicago: Univ. of Chicago Press); relevant studies are Daniel Gold, "Organized Hinduisms: From Vedic Truth to Hindu Nation" (Vol. 1, 1991); Robert Eric Frykenberg, "Hindu Fundamentalism and the Structural Stability of India," (Vol. 3, 1993); and Ainslie T. Embree, "The Function of the Rashtriya Swayamsevik Sangh: To Define the Hindu Nation." (Vol. 4, 1994).

12

Around the Globe

Tonight's was the third of the ten-day series of celebrations consecrating the new marble images at the Kalamazoo Indo-American Cultural Center and Temple. The deity unveiled would be Durga, the lion-riding goddess. I did not want to miss this ceremony; I am partial to the Devi, as earlier chapters have revealed. Nonetheless, I was late, and puja had already started as I slipped off my shoes and headed for my usual seat on the church pews lining the wall on the women's side. Then my friend Ruth intercepted me. A request had been made, she said. A sponsor of tonight's puja had painful knees and could not sit cross-legged on her mat among other sponsors to carry out her appointed role. She wanted the American professor to sit in for her. Would I do it? Ruth gestured toward the front. Surely enough, one sponsor's mat sat empty, with puja implements sitting untouched before it. An older woman I vaguely knew was looking at me hopefully.

"Me?" I protested in shock. "But I'm not a Hindu!" "It's all right," Ruth responded. "Swami-ji approves." Swami-ji would approve indeed. I know quite well the swami who was acting as principal speaker and guest of honor at these rituals. I was the bridge over which he crossed to build his following in Kalamazoo. I introduced him to this friend before me, now his chief America-born manager and disciple. Swami-ji knows me well also, knows the line I try not to cross during my tightrope act as scholar and participant-observer. Like many Hindu teachers whom I have met during my studies, he would like to tug me across that line.

But the woman with bad knees had no such motives. She was being generous, saying to someone who did not look like her, "You are welcome; you are one of us." It was an honor. I would embarrass and hurt her if I turned her down. Taking a deep breath, I walked to the front of the room, sat down on the empty mat and looked to my neighbor to see where we were in the ritual. She showed me how to take the water into my hand, how to circle the small image before me in a gesture of purification. I felt very large, very awkward, and very dowdy in my grey teacher's pantsuit amid that room brilliant with festive saris and embroidered *shalwar-kamiz* suits.

Many features of the scene described above deserve special attention: the converted church in which it took place; the building's name, which reflects a combined cultural and religious function; the images dedicated during ten nights of ritual; the swami's presence and role in the proceedings. Most surprising for many readers may be the scene's location in Kalamazoo, Michigan, an ordinary mid-sized city in the midwestern United States. I drove for twenty minutes to attend that Tuesday evening service. Many people in today's world need travel no farther than this to meet with Hindus and view their practice. Hinduism is by now a true world religion, with temples and centers such as this located well outside of India's borders. Chapter 10 showed one way this happened—with new leaders bearing messages of spiritual renewal touring abroad or sending disciples on overseas missions. Most new Hindu-derived groups of any size in India now have international branches. Presiding at Kalamazoo's image dedication was the Swami Bodhananda described earlier, who has added a U.S. Sambodh Society to his list of organizations.

The Hindus whose new deities he unveiled are products of a second process spreading Hindu practice and concepts throughout the world. This is the emigration of Hindus themselves, as they travel abroad in quest of economic opportunity. This emigration began before Hindu missions. India was not the only colony in the British Empire. As that empire spread, it was not at all uncommon for workers and entrepreneurs to move from one colony to another. Some Indians were imported as cheap laborers. After the British abolished their slave trade in 1820, Fiji, Malaysia, Guyana, and Trinidad brought in Indian indentured laborers to work on sugar and rubber plantations.[1] In Australia, Indians came as servants, penal colony workers, and camel drivers. In Africa, Indians built railroads. In England, they took factory jobs, filling gaps in the labor force left after the carnage of World War II. Once Indian communities were established in a colony, Indian merchants followed to meet their needs. Some built thriving trading empires in their new locations.

Most of these migrants left India intending to return. Many did go back to their homeland once they had earned enough to make return possible. Many others stayed on and settled permanently in their new lands. Some have now relocated again because after the break-up of the British Empire, war and nativist reactions drove them from their new homes. After Indian independence, a new cadre of migrants emerged, responding to other countries' shortfalls in fields such as medicine and engineering. Gifted young Indians from well-to-do families traveled to Europe, Australia, and North America to pursue higher education and to take up high-level professional and technical jobs.

Not all migrating Indians were Hindus; even Kalamazoo holds India-descended Muslims, Jains, Sikhs, Christians, Parsees, and agnostics. As in India itself, however, Hindus have been the majority. As has been seen, however, calling oneself a Hindu does not necessarily mean observing the same customs or upholding the same teachings as the Hindu down the block. Hindus who moved abroad came from different regions, castes, classes, and religious sects. The Hinduisms they brought with them were those of their own heritages. In this way, each area to which they traveled acquired its own mix of Hindu traditions. Malaysia, for example, had many middle- and low-caste

---

[1] Indentured laborers signed contracts in which they agreed to work for a set length of time in exchange for the price of their ticket as well as housing, food, and low wages. This system was often nearly as oppressive as the slavery that had preceded it.

Tamil migrants. Its mix of Hinduisms today has many features characteristic of the low-caste village practice seen in this book's examples.[2] The Dutch island colony of Surinam, which also imported Hindu laborers, recruited in north-central India, where Rama- and Krishna-centered devotion is strong. Because it also had many Brahmins, much of its Hindu practice today is a heavily Brahminized form of Vaishnava devotion.[3] Mercantile settlements were often largely Gujarati and included many Jains and Swaminarayans, disciples of a Gujarat-based, nineteenth-century revival movement.[4]

No matter how it arrived, once some shoot of the Hindu forest found itself planted in new soil, it adapted to meet needs confronted by it and limits placed upon it. Mission groups tailored messages to make them accessible to outsiders. People of different castes or sects who had never eaten or worshiped together overcame divisions to work for their greater community's benefit. Like Hindu ancestors of the past, they engaged in creative knitting, joining themselves in new ways to new environments and to one another. Sometimes, too, new contexts promoted further splitting, as old divisions resurfaced or newer ones arose.

Through such processes, a whole new category of Hinduisms has arisen in the world during the last two centuries. Scholars often call this diaspora Hinduism. "Diaspora" is a Greek term meaning "dispersion." Religion scholars first used it to characterize changes made in Jewish institutions after Jews dispersed outside their Holy Land. Now, scholars use it to characterize the part of any religion that moves outside the land of its origins and changes to fit new contexts. Diaspora Hinduisms can be quite different from Hindu traditions of India, and their study has become a subfield in itself.

The story of diaspora Hinduisms as a whole is much too complicated for one chapter to cover coherently. This chapter will sample it in just one country, the United States. Within the United States, it will describe seven undertakings, all located within a four-hour radius of my home in Michigan. Three represent thus-far successful experiments in knitting Hindu religious practice into U.S. culture. The other four are products of splits, reflecting some of the pitfalls that confront people trying to bring Hinduism and the United States together. A little background knowledge of Hindu history in the United States will help readers understand why the institutions described seem so different from one another.

REMADE IN THE UNITED STATES:
HINDU MISSIONS, HINDU IMMIGRANTS

Usually, Hindu ideas and practice first enter a new country via immigrants who bring with them the customs they knew at home. Missions come later, establishing bases among India-born communities and ministering principally to their needs. In the United States, this pattern was inverted. Hindu ideas arrived first, generating interest.

---

[2] See Chapters 6 and 8, pp. 149–54 and 199–201.

[3] Hans Ramsoedh and Lucie Bloemberg, "The Institutionalization of Hinduism in Suriname and Guyana," *The Hindu Diaspora: Global Perspectives,* T. S. Rukmani, ed. (Montreal: Concordia Univ. Chair in Hindu Studies, 1999), 123–64.

[4] Described by Raymond Brady Williams in *A New Face of Hinduism: The Swaminarayan Religion* (Cambridge: Cambridge Univ. Press, 1984).

Then came missionary-teachers, often invited to explain the intriguing ideas and show how to put them into practice. Immigrant Hindus came later, their arrival delayed by laws blocking Asian entry. With and behind them came more Hindu teachers, sometimes working solely among immigrants, sometimes reaching out to a broader American audience. This pattern meant that the first Hinduisms in America came in forms shaped by American tastes and needs. Later ideas and practice introduced by India-born entrants often were quite different. Teachers arriving later had a choice; they could accept the gap found in the United States or try to bridge it.

It is important to realize which Hindu ideas first became known in the United States, for these have had a large impact on U.S. Hindu history. The first Hindu books to attract U.S. interest were translations of the *Bhagavad-Gita* and selected Upanishads. Attention was drawn to them in part because their ideas were described by writers shaping the transcendentalist movement popular among intellectuals during the mid-nineteenth century. In her important book *A New Religious America,* Harvard professor Diana Eck describes how transcendentalist leader Ralph Waldo Emerson first came to read the *Gita* and Upanishads and introduce them to his friend Henry David Thoreau.[5] Three ideas especially intrigued Emerson and Thoreau: the idea that a single divine power lies behind all the world's manifestations; the idea that this power is immanent, within all forms of existence, including human beings; and the idea that methods therefore exist to probe and tap it directly, without need for priests and ritual interventions.

When Hindu teachers first came to America, the "pull" drawing audiences to them was the desire to hear about these teachings and the methods based upon them. These teachings had come out of swami and sadhu traditions, especially the philosophy of Vedanta and India's various yogas. Often, Americans assumed that these *were* Hinduism, mistaking parts of a vast heritage for the whole.

The teachers themselves began arriving at the end of the nineteenth century. The first to gain a widespread U.S. hearing was Pratap Chander Mazumdar, cousin to Keshab Chander Sen.[6] Arriving for his first U.S. tour in 1883, Sen preached among Unitarians, the same community that Emerson had served as preacher. Swami Vivekananda arrived a decade later;[7] his Ramakrishna order in India would later send other swamis to tend centers he had established in American cities.[8] Vivekananda's success inspired the young swami Ramatirtha, who traveled to California and won a following before his premature death in 1906. The most successful of early U.S. teachers, Swami Yogananda first came in 1920 to address a conference and remained for most of his life. Another who visited often on tours and finally stayed was Jiddu Krishnamurthi, originally from South India's Theosophical Society, later an independent teacher.

All these leaders built their principal followings among Americans of European descent. Few people of Indian descent ever had a chance to hear them because few Indians lived in the United States when they were teaching. Immigration laws in

---

[5] *A New Religious America* (San Francisco: HarperCollins, 2001), pp. 94–96.

[6] See Chapter 4, pp. 100–103.

[7] See Chapter 4, pp. 108–110.

[8] Described in Harold W. French, *The Swan's Wide Waters: Ramakrishna and Western Culture* (Port Washington, NY: Kennikat Press, 1974). Also see Carl T. Jackson, *Vedanta for the West: The Ramakrishna Movement in the United States* (Bloomington, IN: Indiana Univ. Press, 1994).

force between 1919 and 1965 severely restricted entry of Indians and many other people of Asian descent into the United States. A few Indians entered before these laws came into effect, mostly Sikhs working as farm laborers in California. A few more entered after 1946, when the laws were eased slightly, allowing one hundred Indian immigrants yearly. Many of the latter were professors, such as those I met during the 1960s as a student at the University of Chicago. Others came as students, then found employers persistent enough to wade through the red tape needed to help them stay.

One problem facing American companies after World War II was a shortage of certain skilled workers: engineers, scientists of several varieties, mathematicians, accountants, physicians, and nurses. One way to offset these shortfalls was to recruit abroad. Asians were promising candidates, and the restrictions on immigration became an increasing annoyance to would-be employers. Antidiscrimination movements in the United States also pointed to the unfairness of Asian quotas. In 1965, the bars came down and limits were raised to twenty thousand immigrants yearly. Candidates would be admitted in accordance with priorities. High on the list were preferences for people with needed skills and their families, as well as desired scholars and artists. The new laws also provided for family reunification of immigrants already here; after those immigrants became citizens, they could sponsor sisters and brothers, parents, married children, and children's families.

The result has been a steadily rising number of India-born residents in U.S. towns and cities. Not all were Hindus, but Hindus of various castes and sects were in the majority. Most were accustomed to patterns of Hindu practice unfamiliar to Americans: household pujas and samskaras, temple worship, pilgrimage. When they found Euro-Americans meditating in cities where they had settled, they were often bewildered by the made-for-America yogas being followed. So they gathered in groups of their own. Some of these groups were products of prior affiliations they'd had in India: Sai Baba bhajan circles, for example, or sampradayas special to particular Indian regions. Especially important in the United States would be the Gujarat-based Swaminarayan sampradaya. Others were eclectic attempts to bring together Hindu neighbors of different sects and regions. A fine example of one such attempt is the Indo-American Cultural Center and Temple described at this chapter's outset. Undertakings such as these evolved separately from organizations drawing Euro-Americans. Often Hindus of both types lived side by side in U.S. cities, with neither exploring the other's enterprises.

Complicating this already complex picture was the entry of a second wave of Hindu missionaries. These could move in any of three directions. Some followed old precedents of seeking out a principally Euro-American audience. Several of this type arrived with the first influx of immigrants after 1965, which happened to coincide with a U.S. India fad launched by the hippie movement and the famed British rock group, the Beatles. Chapter 10 pointed out how the International Society for Krishna Consciousness (ISKCON) founder Swami Bhaktivedanta became a part of that India fad and helped promote it.[9] Other gurus still famous in the United States also first became known through rock and hippie connections: Maharishi Mahesh Yogi, patronized by the Beatles, and Swami Satchitananda, an honored guest at the great open-air rock festival at Woodstock.

---

[9] See pp. 254–56.

Other second wave teachers established a base among the developing Hindu immigrant community, seeking to win its support in the contest for India's future being waged back home. Recall that virtually every new movement founder in India has come to the United States on tour or has sent one or more key disciples to establish U.S. branches. The VHP has also worked very actively to unite American Hindu groups under its umbrella much as it has done in India. One reason why the United States is so heavily recruited is the amount of money in the U.S. Hindu immigrant community. Most immigrants had training for highly-paid professions. Many have done well financially and give generously to enterprises that win their commitment.

Finally, a few Hindu teachers have taken a third path, attempting to win a following among both Euro-Americans and members of the India-born community. These enterprises have not had a high success rate. Even when a balance is initially established, it tends to shift over time, losing disciples in one constituency while winning them in the other. ISKCON is one tradition that has undergone such a shift, moving to a predominantly India-born membership. Another will be described when this chapter turns to its tales of splits.

The various Hinduisms that have grown up in the United States are thus products of an unusually complex blend. This reflects differences in when they were founded, the kinds of needs attracting them, the people who carried them, and the local resources available to develop them. Diaspora Hinduisms are amalgamations, drawing on various themes and practices from India outlined earlier in this book, but also knitting these with traditions of American religions.

This chapter covers three experiments in knitting, all located in southwest Michigan. The first is a product of the first wave of Hindu entry, established locally only during the seventies, but active in the United States already during the 1920s. This is the meditation-centered Self-Realization Fellowship founded by Swami Yogananda, known also as Paramahansa Yogananda. The second is an eclectic grass-roots immigrant Hindu initiative, the Indo-American Cultural Center and Temple introduced in this chapter's opening scenario. The third, known for the time being as Sambodh Aranya, is a product of second-wave teacher Swami Bodhananda, also introduced in the opening scenario. All are within a twenty minutes' drive of Kalamazoo, so it is a good idea to look briefly at this quite ordinary upper midwestern city.

"YES, THERE REALLY IS A KALAMAZOO"

T-shirts sold in Kalamazoo love to announce that the city with the funny name and big-band-era song[10] is not just a figment of someone's imagination. Kalamazoo is roughly 40 miles north of the Indiana border and 35 miles east of Lake Michigan. The largest city south of Grand Rapids and west of Lansing, it had approximately 77,000 residents during the 2000 census. Outlying settlements add another 245,000 to the greater Kalamazoo area. When this account speaks of Kalamazoo, it will mean this greater area. As in many urban areas across the United States, most institutions of Hindu origin are based outside the city proper.

Kalamazoo is a county seat and also the home of two large hospitals and three institutions of higher education: Western Michigan University (WMU), with nearly

---

[10] "I've Got a Gal in Kalamazoo."

30,000 students; Kalamazoo College, with about 1,300; and Kalamazoo Valley Community College, with between 10,000 and 11,000 per semester. In the past, Kalamazoo's main economic bases were the paper and pharmaceutical industries; it also achieved fame as the home of Gibson guitars and the Checker cab company. Today, it is experiencing economic upheaval: Gibson, Checker, and most paper companies are gone. Upjohn Pharmaceutical was swallowed first by the Swedish-based Pharmacia and then by the huge multinational Pfizer. Kalamazoo is still headquarters for the Stryker Corporation, which produces hospital equipment. It also has branch divisions of several smaller companies.

All these institutions have affected Hindu history in the Kalamazoo area. Jobs at Kalamazoo hospitals, schools, and industries have drawn many gifted immigrants from India. The very first, arriving in 1960, was an Upjohn scientist. Since then, immigrants working at Upjohn or WMU or in medicine have provided most of the leadership in the local Hindu community. Meanwhile, WMU and Kalamazoo College promoted knowledge of India and Indian religions among Euro-Americans. Among the first of these efforts were two summer study programs in India run by WMU's Honors College in 1963 and 1967. The WMU Department of Comparative Religion, begun in 1967, has offered various India-related courses. Kalamazoo College also offers courses on Hinduism and Buddhism. Both schools have sponsored many India- and Hindu-related programs.

Into this context have come a surprising variety of enterprises of Indian or Hindu derivation. At least five groups practicing Hindu forms of meditation have survived in the Kalamazoo area for substantial lengths of time. A trainee of Swami Vishnudevananda brought hatha-yoga fitness classes to the local Y in 1968; hundreds of Kalamazoo residents have by now taken her classes as well as others offered by more recent teachers. Kalamazoo's immigrant Indian community has built an all-India social organization as well as the Indo-American Cultural Center and Temple and a more recently dedicated Sikh gurdwara. A Sai Baba kirtan group meets at the Indo-American Center and several Kalamazooans drive to Chicago or Detroit when Ammachi, the "Hugging Mother" visits to hold her darshans.[11] In a classroom of the local community college, a chapter of the West-India-based Swadhyaya movement meets at 10:30 AM each Sunday. A sacred grove and Shiva linga have been established east of the city. If all goes well, a fine ashram will soon rise in that grove. Of these riches, only three are described here. One of the oldest is covered first.

YOGA FOR THE UNITED STATES:
THE SELF-REALIZATION FELLOWSHIP[12]

Just off a rural road twelve miles west of Kalamazoo stands a small white building looking much like a country chapel without a steeple. Its western half is a social center, its eastern a sanctuary holding chairs for sixty-six people, aligned on both sides of an aisle leading up to a platform. Mounted on the platform, against the

[11] See p. 258.

[12] I am grateful to WMU graduate student Scott Ballinger who did the field study making this description possible.

sanctuary end wall, is a wooden altar consisting of a pediment and shelf. Above them, against the wall, stretches a solid wood altar screen whose lines and reliefs evoke the architectural outlines of classic Indian domes and arches. The overall effect is that of an altar in a Christian church, but with decidedly Indian overtones. During the day, the space is lit from the sides by narrow windows surmounted by half-circle arches. Each frames a graceful design of lotus blossoms and leaves worked in stained glass tinted in delicate pastel colors. Mounted on the altar screen are six framed portraits of the Self-Realization Fellowship line of gurus. Three are colorized photographs of Swami Yogananda and two other gurus important to his history; the remaining three are artists' renditions of Krishna, Jesus of Nazareth, and an avatara the movement calls Bawaji. The effect of the whole structure is peaceful, harmonious, calming.

This building was constructed by an organization known locally as the Kalamazoo Meditation Group. Twice a week, a few local residents assemble there to conduct simple services and sit in silent meditation. Like the building itself, the services include elements much like those of an unpretentious Protestant church: prayer, song, readings, sometimes talks, plus extra features added during special occasions. On Sunday, special classes are held for the group's children. Like local churches, the group often sponsors charitable efforts such as food collection for migrants, participation in crop walks, and Christmas caroling for senior citizens.

The white building has been in this place only since 1997. The Kalamazoo Meditation Group is a generation older; it first met in 1973. The national organization to which both belong is older still, by half a century. It began in 1920 when a bright young swami came to the United States to speak before a Unitarian conference. His religious name was Yogananda; he would later acquire the title Paramahansa, meaning "Supreme Swan." His organization is the Self-Realization Fellowship, usually shortened to SRF. It is the most successful of any pre-1965 Hindu-derived mission. Today, it claims to have nearly five hundred centers in the United States, India, and fifty-two additional countries. Like most early-era American Hindu organizations, it teaches a blend of yoga-based practice and Vedanta philosophy.

Who was Swami Yogananda? Born in Bengal in 1893, he was given the name Mukunda Lal Ghosh. According to his best-selling *Autobiography of a Yogi,* his parents were devotees of Banaras-based guru Lahiri Mahasaya, one of the six figures enshrined at the Kalamazoo Center. After several amazing encounters with this guru and others, Mukunda found his own master, Swami Yukteswar, another of the six figures. For five years, he lived with other students at this guru's ashram and attended college at the University of Calcutta, finishing his degree in 1915. His later efforts to found a school for boys attracted attention, and soon he was invited to the Unitarian Conference. The address he gave there on "The Science of Religion" prompted more invitations, and soon he was traveling and speaking throughout the United States. Unlike predecessors who taught for a time, then returned to India, Yogananda made his home in America, leaving only for one eighteen-month tour. Before his 1952 death, he named an American successor, a woman named Daya Mata who had been an early disciple and stenographer for his teachings. Daya Mata still heads the SRF organization.

Much of the secret of Yogananda's attraction for Americans resided in his solutions to two challenges confronting all Hindu teachers of his era. The first was the greater cultural context into which he preached. Much of that context was Christian, and outside of intellectual circles, most Christians knew little about Hindus or had encountered only negative publicity about them. Most viewed Hinduism as a rival religion whose teaching and practice had to be rejected. Yogananda's second challenge was a manpower shortage. Even when teachers successfully established their own missions, they often won just tiny groups of disciples committed enough to tend and extend these. These disciples themselves did not always know enough about the teachings they were spreading to explain them effectively. Teachings therefore spread only slowly and often became distorted.

Yogananda was the most creative among early Hindu teachers in moving his group past these barriers. A process of blending addressed the first difficulty. Yogananda first denied that his own teaching was a religion. He had come to bring yoga, he asserted, and yoga is not religion, but a science that helps practitioners attain religious goals. It is a science because it is based on years of experimentation. It serves religion by helping practitioners experience God. Yoga does not conflict with existing religions, but complements them. Yogananda claimed that Jesus himself discovered and used the same Kriya Yoga method taught by Yogananda. His teachings were thus those spread by "original Christianity." Part of Yogananda's cleverness lay in the way he worked this theme of Christian and yogic harmony into details of the organization he built. Examples are the portrait of Jesus among the group's spiritual masters, and the church-like structure of group centers and practice.

Where would such groups find leadership? Here he borrowed an American invention, the correspondence course. He laid out a written program of step-by-step yoga instruction to be studied and put into practice over three years' time. Today his course consists of 180 lessons, mailed out in small installments every two weeks. These take a student from preparation through basic yoga disciplines. Then, after a special initiation, the student begins training in Kriya Yoga, the discipline handed down by Yogananda's spiritual lineage. Students are told to practice daily and to keep their course and its methods secret. So anyone wishing to learn must enroll in the course and adapt to its pace. The yoga-by-correspondence course remains the core of SRF instruction, still costing no more than a nominal fee for duplication and mailing. Yogananda's popular *Autobiography of a Yogi* brings abundant publicity to him and to his course. Readings during services at SRF centers are also frequently drawn from his autobiography.

To support would-be U.S. yogis in their efforts, Yogananda adapted a second U.S. invention, the franchise. He developed a two-tier organization. At the top is the Mount Washington ashram in Los Angeles, usually called "Mother Center" by Kalamazoo devotees. This produces or commissions all materials needed to keep branch centers going: decorations, portraits of masters, songbooks, inspirational readings, and volumes of Yogananda writings. It designs local programs in great detail, including days and hours at which these will be scheduled, orders of service, selections to be read, and texts for talks. It keeps track of members, telling new students or members shifting locations how to find others for group practice. It also trains a staff of full-time leaders. Taking classic Hindu vows of renunciation, these monastics head and staff the Mother Center and larger branch temples. They organize and run an annual international conference and serve as featured speakers at regional conferences. Additionally, they act as circuit riders of sorts, visiting branch centers, offering talks, and watching for signs of potential trouble. Members or centers needing advice can also call a Mother Center hotline.[13]

The organization's second tier consists of local centers, run by elected officers and readers who have reached Kriya Yoga level and so qualify to lead services at the centers. Mother Center advises its branches to keep leadership circulating. In this way, the burden on leaders stays light; this rotation also raises member participation and commitment. Having most planning done by Mother Center also lightens burdens.

The Kalamazoo Meditation Group offers a fine example of a branch center's development through time. In 1973, four students just out of college received notice from Mother Center that other young people taking the SRF course were in their area and they should consider meeting for weekly group meditation. They met in homes and apartments, sitting on floors, with meals simmering on stoves to be enjoyed together afterwards. Becoming close friends, they laughed together, supported each other emotionally, and helped one another move. They continued taking in new members either attracted to them through personal connections or sent to them by Mother Center. Gradually, they centered in one member's home near their present location. By the mid-1990s they needed more space and asked Mother Center for clearance to build a branch center of their own. They raised all funding for their building, erected much of it with their own labor, then signed the deed over to SRF. They are justifiably proud of this achievement, and proud too of the leading role they have taken for several years in planning regional weekend retreats. As for experiences with Kriya Yoga, they have been told to keep these to themselves, and they do so. But they will say that these have made them calmer, stabler, and more capable. They have one regret: in a community that owes its existence to an India-born master, they have no current members of Indian descent.

CONSTRUCTING COMMUNITY: THE INDO-AMERICAN CULTURAL CENTER AND TEMPLE

India-descended Hindus of Kalamazoo are far more likely to show up at a building on a side street not far south of the Kalamazoo city line, in the smaller adjoining city of Portage. The story of the Indo-American Cultural Center and Temple is more complex than that of SRF because it entails two kinds of knittings. This center has knit the United States into its endeavors by adopting a U.S. physical structure, adapting to the American calendar, and modeling its programs on U.S.-style congregational worship and Sunday school organization. It has done so, however, as part of a greater effort to knit together local residents of Indian descent into a united and cooperating community.

If the Indo-American Center looks like a church, this is because it was one, built initially by a Baptist congregation. The Center is actually two buildings. One, tucked in back, holds a classroom and small library. The old church proper is a sizeable, two-level

---

[13] More about SRF can be found at its Web site www.yogananda-srf.org (Self-Realization Fellowship).

structure; if visitors pack in tightly, more than three hundred can sit knee to back on the sheet-covered floor of its sanctuary. The downstairs basement houses a dining room and kitchen equipped for large-scale cooking. In the upstairs sanctuary, a few church pews still line side and back walls, although most floor space has been cleared and carpeted for more traditional floor-sitting. Ordinary glass panes fill the sanctuary's windows, but between them, adding color, hang the bright lithographs of deities so popular in India. Once these lined the old apse walls, but now those walls are gone. Instead, a low stage-like platform rises in front of the hall, its walls a backdrop for tiers curving around a central space holding mats and implements used in pujas. Arrayed along the tiers stand thirteen nearly life-sized images of Hindu deities carved in marble, their implements and dress gilded or painted in brilliant, jewel-like colors. A panel hung from the ceiling to divide platform space from the room holds a painted mural of temple domes against a cloud-specked blue sky. The overall effect is upbeat, cheerful, conducive to hugging and whispering among friends. On days when the sanctuary is not too full, small children dart back and forth to visit playmates and stop at times to flirt with a stranger.

A visitor to the Center may find different scenes, depending on when he or she arrives. On the second and fourth Sunday mornings of each month, activity here resembles a Sunday morning church service. Members come at this time for satsang, consisting usually of puja, bhajan singing, and a concluding *arti* (lamp waving). Sometimes, special talks or children's programs are added. Almost always, a vegetarian meal is served as prasad in the dining room downstairs afterwards. At an earlier hour every Sunday are sessions of family prayer, at which parents and older children sit with a Brahmin member and talk together about Hindu beliefs and values. Much more subdued and typically Indian are short pujas done before the deities each evening by volunteer families from the Hindu community. Seven times a year come bigger celebrations: Navratri (Durga Puja), Lakshmi Puja (Diwali), Ganesh Puja, Holi, Guru Purnima, Krishna Janmashthami, and a special celebration for graduating students.

Special speakers are invited when available, for example, touring swamis or the Ram Katha (Ram Story) performers so popular in northern India. Secular speakers and performers may appear as well, for this building is a cultural center as well as a temple. Noted instrumentalists and singers have performed here; children have put on pageants; consuls come by at times to offer advice on visas; workshops are sponsored on retirement investments. The Indo-American Center also partners with the university at times to bring in more famous performers, lecturers, and dance troupes. It holds a *bal vikas,* Sunday school, for smaller children, and its active youth group works with local crop walks and Habitat for Humanity. Increasingly, Center leaders have engaged in dialogue programs with local churches.

Unlike the Kalamazoo Meditation Group, the Indo-American Center does not have tie-ins to any national organizations. Its existence, decor, and programs are all results of local grassroots initiatives. Nonetheless, the Center has many parallels in other U.S. cities and regions; all are products of the efforts of immigrant Indians who moved into towns and cities after entry bars were lifted in 1965. These centers exist because they help these Hindu immigrants address common needs.

Recall for a moment just who those immigrants were. Because of immigration law priorities, they were a highly select cadre. Most were highly educated; even wives of entering husbands frequently held at least M.A. degrees. This means they were bright and able to learn quickly the rules of U.S. society and how to work within them to get things done. Most were also of high class and caste. Therefore, many shared presuppositions later surfacing in the institutions they created. One was the idea, common to certain Brahmin teachings, new movements, and reform groups, that all deities are "faces" of a single underlying reality. Another is the belief that all religious practice, if done sincerely, will lead to a common goal. Many, too, had shed older ideas about the need to avoid polluting places and people or to take only food prepared by cooks from their own or higher caste groups. They could envision a prospect of worshiping side by side using improvised methods and then enjoying a meal together afterwards.

Most spoke English, an important asset because they came from many regions that spoke different Indian tongues. They had different sectarian origins: there were Vaishnavas, Shaivas, Shaktas, devotees of new movements, along with Jains, Sikhs, Parsees, and Indian Muslims and Christians. Although these factors would normally have pushed them apart, the issues they faced as immigrants pulled them together. Making their way in the United States' complex society and economy was often harder than they had expected. They missed networks of kin and friends who helped them make connections in India and offered the helping hands that gave a welcome competitive edge. Often, they were lonely, longing to see familiar-looking faces, hear familiar accents and music, wear their own bright and beautiful clothes, and eat familiar food. Americans could be hard to figure out: some were friendly; others scorned brown Indian skins and Asian backgrounds. In sum, Indian immigrants needed friends and mentors.

The first efforts they made to band together were not religious, largely because religion was more likely to divide them than to unite them. Kalamazoo's first organization for Indians bonded around movies brought on videotapes from India and screened in a rented classroom at Western Michigan University. They put on an annual show and dinner for the festival of Diwali; although this festival is Hindu, in India people of all religious groups enjoy it. Although it no longer screens films, this India Association still exists in Kalamazoo, organizing occasions when all families from India can get together. One important service it still performs is to seek out new Indian families in town and tell them how to find needed services and contacts.

Hindus among these immigrants did not at first feel a need to establish any public space for practicing religion. Let us recall that a great deal of Hindu practice centers in homes. Hindu immigrants could and did set up puja spaces—in closets, cupboards, and corners of household rec rooms. When holidays came, they invited friends in. The first problem they encountered was the lack of priests to help in more complex pujas, childhood samskaras, and funerals. Here they improvised; some who could chant in Sanskrit helped others when help was needed. Some in Kalamazoo called the head of Chicago's Vedanta Society for help with special occasions.

As the local Hindu community grew larger, space became the second important issue. Initial proposals for a cultural center arose after local Hindus had to start hiring halls to provide space for all their friends during popular festivals. The halls were expensive; some cheaper way of securing appropriate space was needed.

More urgent needs emerged as children were born and grew older. Parents wanted a way to transmit their own heritage so that children could take pride in it and would not become estranged from relatives still in India. Parents also needed more effective ways to instill their values in children. Children attending American schools watched what their schoolmates did and often questioned parents' ideas about what children should or should not do. Hindu parents expected their children to study hard, as they had. They were uneasy when children dated and wished to continue choosing their children's partners in marriage. They needed to talk these issues through with their children and to have backing from others who could help children understand why parents' values should be respected.

One solution for such problems among many American Hindus has been to create institutions that would serve multiple functions. They would be gathering places and halls for the larger Indian community when such places were needed. At the same time, they could house religious celebrations and provide cultural and religious education for children. No one-size-fits-all model for such enterprises exists across the United States; each center reflects dozens of decisions its community has taken on how to use local resources and satisfy local requirements. In Kalamazoo, an early decision concerned the structure itself. Would the community build a new one or convert an existing structure? That decision was easy. At the time a church was for sale for $85,000; a new structure would have cost well over a million dollars.

Another question concerned the balance to be established between the structure's cultural and religious functions. That was a stickier issue because some non-Hindu residents wanted access to the structure and helped fund it for this reason. Their presence and voice is the principal reason why the compromise they created is called a Cultural Center first and a Temple second. As time passed, however, the temple function came to dominate. Most Indians in town now call the Center "the Hindu temple."

When thinking about the temple function, the community also had to decide how authentic a temple it would be. It could not be wholly authentic because its building was not constructed according to temple canons. But would it install authentic temple images? When the Center was dedicated in 1995, its central shrine looked like a household puja room hung with Hindu symbols and lithographs of deities. Some members would have preferred to keep it that way. A majority, however, felt that they could not have a proper temple without proper temple images. That prompted another round of decisions. If images were installed, which deities should be enshrined there? Kalamazoo Hindus come from many different regions of India and have different sectarian preferences. Therefore, Center officers took a survey. The results were so divided that they finally installed deities of all major sects. The Center now has a Shiva-linga plus a Nandi; an elephant-headed Ganesh; a Vishnu and Lakshmi; a Ram group including Ram himself, his brother Lakshman, wife Sita, and the monkey general Hanuman kneeling at his feet; a Krishna and Radha; an Amba (form of Devi) riding on a lion; and the popular southern form of Vishnu Balaji, also known as Venkateshvara.

How to arrange these deities posed another problem. Standard practice in an Indian temple housing multiple deities is to set up individual shrines within the greater enclosure. One is focal, sheltering the temple's central deity. Others are clearly peripheral, and their images may also be smaller in size. Indo-American Center deities are all sculpted in equal proportions, lined up in a single row under a common roof. This is a statement; it says its community values all of its members and their preferred deities equally.[14]

It may be instructive at this point to ask who made these decisions. Although anyone can attend its functions, the Indo-American Cultural Center and Temple is a membership-based organization. Members pay annual dues or purchase a life membership; only they can be temple officers or vote in temple elections. Each year, at an annual meeting, members elect a governing board that sets Center policies and organizes the next year's planning. Thus far, the Center has been extremely fortunate in its board membership. Many of its officers have Ph.D.s and have been high-level corporate managers or professors at Western Michigan University. The respect they command in the local Indo-American community has been reflected in their ability to raise funds for Center-related projects. The Center paid off its building and renovations within three months and its row of costly deities nearly as quickly.

The biggest event in Center history thus far has been the gala dedication of those deities: ten days of festive celebrations, each packing the temple and followed by a full meal\prasad. It was a double celebration, timed to coincide with the long fall festival of Navratri. Each day another image or group was freed from a veiling of bright silk saris, while the temple's own Brahmin chanted appropriate mantras of dedication and first worship. Then, the visiting guest Swami Bodhananda offered one of his usual sparkling and humor-filled talks about the deity unwrapped that day and its qualities. This was not a full dedication; that would be a grander and far more costly occasion. Once full dedication is done, the images cannot be moved, and this community is not sure that it will want to stay in its converted church forever. Furthermore, once fully consecrated, temple images require a full daily round of pujas. Until 2004, the Center did not have a full-time priest.

Who recited the mantras for the deity dedication? He was yet another example of American Hindu ingenuity and improvisation—he is an information specialist for Pfizer who moonlights as a priest because he is able to and loves to do it. Born a very high-caste Brahmin, he studied Sanskrit as a child and learned to chant and perform several popular household rituals. Moving to the United States, he found his talents were in demand. He located tapes with recordings of rituals he wanted to master, memorized them, and expanded his repertory. The dedication required rites for seven different sets of deities, each with its own liturgical variations. He conducted them all, chanting for an hour or more on each dedication night. This gifted man served the Center as part-time priest until the summer of 2004, when it finally was able to hire a full-time priest offered by another Michigan temple.

What of Swami Bodhananda? How did he come to be at the Kalamazoo deity dedication? To account for his presence, the third example of Kalamazoo-area knitting must be considered.

---

[14] Readers can view the Center's deities on its Web site: www.kalamazootemple.org.
(Indo-American Cultural Center and Temple of Kalamazoo).

PULLING COMMUNITIES TOGETHER:
SAMBODH ARANYA

Shopping malls line highway M-43 as it stretches east of Kalamazoo. Venturing farther north, a car moves swiftly onto less developed land. Eventually, at the end of a dead-end road, it reaches a large tree-covered tract still untouched by builders. A visitor hiking uphill on a rutted driveway views a sight uncommon in Michigan: a waist-high, three-thousand-pound granite Shiva-linga sheltered by a graceful wooden garden gazebo. Polished to a smooth gloss, fitted to a sturdy base, it looks like a giant peg driven into the center of the concrete circle poured to serve as its foundation. It is solid, substantial, anchoring, as if to say, "I am not just a visitor here; I intend to stay."

As I was writing these paragraphs, I attended a puja consecrating the gazebo. A few months before, the linga itself had undergone a first stage of ritual consecration in a grand sprinkling rite and fire sacrifice featuring chants by eleven Brahmins. But the later celebration marked a greater milestone. After it was finished, the group that had put the linga there burned the unused checks from the book that paid off the mortgage on the surrounding land. These were no longer needed; thirty-two acres of woodland now belonged fully to the Sambodh Society of North America. Society leaders named the land Sambodh Aranya, "Enlightenment Grove," recalling the sacred groves in which sages gathered to seek truth in ancient India. They plan to add a complex appropriate to such a context, an ashram with the ambitious name "Center for Human Excellence." This is to be a place where people from all communities can gather for crosscultural conversation and to study in depth aspects of the Hindu heritage: Vedanta, meditation, ritual, women's status and roles, alternative medicine, even principles of stress-free management. Although plans for this ashram resemble programs run by other such centers across the United States, a feature special to this one is that residents of both Indian and Euro-American birth are working together to create it.

How does a linga make its way onto a Kalamazoo woodland? The linga itself was a gift from the Kauai Hindu Monastery of Hawaii, publishers of the magazine *Hinduism Today*. It was donated to Sambodh in encouragement of the new effort. But how did that effort itself come about, bringing to Kalamazoo a sacred grove and ashram? It is the product of two endeavors, two Hindu plantings knit together to sink roots into the U.S. landscape. One was an old mission from India, the other a new one. I was the first link between the two.

Sambodh Aranya's story began in 1971 when a local India-born resident joined with friends elsewhere to bring their beloved guru on a visit to the United States. The guru's host thought Kalamazoo teachers interested in India might like to meet his guru and experience his ability to chant others into a meditative trance. So he invited the teachers to a series of *sadhanas,* yoga sittings, in his tiny apartment living room. The chanting was impressive, and in subsequent months, an English professor from the group approached the others, suggesting they pool funds to bring the guru back.

In subsequent years, Yogi Raushan Nath became a regular Kalamazoo visitor, returning for nine more visits of five to seven weeks each before his much-mourned death in 1990. Unlike many Hindu teachers of his era, Yogi Raushan Nath was not an ambitious person. He never tried to extend his American following outside Kalamazoo; nor did he try to establish any permanent institution. The English professor hosted his earlier stays, along with weekly sittings that occurred between them. Later, another couple, Drs. Richard and Ruth Harring, took over responsibility for both visits and sittings, working with the original host to put them together. The Harrings were India enthusiasts who for many years traveled annually to New Delhi to join a pilgrimage sponsored by Yogi Raushan Nath's community. Over the years, at one or another time, other group members traveled with them, thus increasing their knowledge of India and their affection for its citizens. Ruth Harring became an avid explorer of Hindu-derived groups in the local community and kept up contact with many of their local leaders. A highly competent organizer, she brought several programs relating to Hindu knowledge and practice into the Kalamazoo area after her guru's death.

Then in 1996, Swami Bodhananda received a generous offer from a disciple, a woman doctor who had done well in her practice after moving to the United States. She promised to pick up the tab if he wished to conduct a U.S. teaching tour. Soon, another disciple was writing to the swami's U.S. contacts. One was a religion professor who had attended his New Delhi classes a few years before. I received a letter: "Swamiji will come this summer for a tour in the States. Do you know someone who might like to hear him?" I did, indeed. I picked up the phone and called my friend Ruth Harring. She in turn called friends at the Indo-American Center and several other centers in our area.

Bodhananda came for two weeks. His Kalamazoo tour was successful, winning him friends especially among Indo-American Center leadership. He returned the next summer and every summer thereafter, winning so many friends at the Center that it asked him to be guest of honor at its image dedication. During his third Kalamazoo stay, he broached the idea of siting an ashram in the Kalamazoo area. During the fourth, he and Ruth searched for sites. Over the years, she has emerged as chief executive officer for the entire U.S. Sambodh Society outside of California. When Bodhananda comes to Kalamazoo, she and Richard host him. When he travels out to lecture, she often chauffeurs him. He has pockets of disciples in other cities with sizeable Indo-American populations: Columbus, Cincinnati, and Dayton, Ohio; several New York City suburbs; Washington, D.C.; Atlanta, San Antonio, St. Louis, Colorado Springs, and Seattle. Some travel to Kalamazoo to join him when he mounts a special program or retreat in the area. Hence his Sambodh Aranya is the product and dream not only of Kalamazooans but also of a following stretching across the United States.

The project is, nonetheless, run out of Kalamazoo; its planning board made up of six local citizens. Three are of Indian birth, three are Euro-Americans. Its president is Indo-American, a retired psychiatrist. Like the other two India-born members, he has been active for many years in the Indo-American Center. Ruth Harring serves in her capacity as Sambodh Society link; the other two members are from the network that she brought to the society via her previous contacts. Many other local contributors to the project are Indo-American Center members or friends of Ruth by way of her previous networks.

What holds them together in such an ambitious undertaking? One attraction is surely Bodhananda's own charm and mix of dignity and unpretentiousness. He is able at one moment to fetch his own tea and at the next to wait patiently as India-born devotees touch his feet. A second tie for Sambodh members is local respect for Ruth and her ever-supportive husband Richard, built up over many years before

Bodhananda reached the scene. During their crossovers between India-born and America-born Hindu groups, they built a foundation that helps both communities trust and relax with one another.

A third tie is Bodhananda's philosophic grounding in Vedanta. As noted earlier, Vedanta teachings have captured the interest of Americans for more than a century. On the one hand, they hold up a hope for finding a meeting ground between religions. On the other, they offer a possibility of do-it-yourself transformation that Americans often find attractive. India-born Hindus also are finding Vedanta attractive these days, thanks in part to new teachers who have made it more accessible, such as Bodhananda's own predecessor Chinmayananda. Local Hindus active in building the Indo-American Center sometimes, too, have expressed to me their feeling that they don't know their own tradition well enough to pass it on properly to the next generation. A friend once explained his experience this way: "When I was a boy, my parents kept us busy studying. Religious activities went on in my home, but I did not think to ask questions about them. Then I came here to study and work. When could I learn about religion?"

A final and important factor binding Sambodh supporters together has been Bodhananda's astute use of symbol and ritual to create a common group experience and affirm shared intentions. Usually when he comes to the area, he asks Sambodh leaders to plan one splashy ritual that requires a great deal of organization for the next year. It took me a long time to figure out what he was doing; I am not so sure that he understands its entire import himself. Let us look at these initiatives. In 1999, he led Sambodh supporters on a pilgrimage, walking for thirty-four miles over two days' time from Kalamazoo to a beach on the shore of Lake Michigan. They followed a locally popular trail built along an old railroad right-of-way. It was an ordeal of sorts, and like all ordeals it bound its participants together. But it also extended a claim: "This is our land; we belong here too."

In 2000, Bodhananda gathered 108 children from supporters' families, sat them down beneath a rented tent in a public garden, and had them chant together the Gayatri mantra, a prayer for wisdom and understanding. This, he said, would enhance the children's success in their studies. But it also astutely pointed to the Sambodh community's future, the next generation for whom it is building its ashram.

During 2001, the Indo-American image dedication provided Sambodh's focal ritual, but during 2002 Sambodh itself undertook another—an elaborate *bhumi puja* done at the grove asking the earth to bless and support the ashram project. A *bhumi puja* is a standard sequence of rites done before breaking ground for any sacred building, but Sambodh added a special twist to its version. Michigan Native American leaders offered a pipe to the land's native spirits and asked their blessings on the ashram project. Through this gesture, they also reminded Euro-Americans present that their own ancestors, like Indo-Americans, were once newcomers on the land, striving to build a place here that would be a home. During 2003, Sambodh set up its Shiva-linga, pegging the land down and giving it focus. They could not have found a better way to visualize their commitment: "We are not just visitors here; we and our children intend to stay."[15]

---

[15] More on Sambodh's U.S. projects can be found at www.sambodh.com (Sambodh Society of the United States).

How successful they will be remains an open question. They hope to break ground for their ashram's first phase soon after this book sees print. They have the will and talent to complete their project. Whether they will have the money is another issue; Western Michigan currently suffers from a sorely sagging economy. Even if the ashram is built, there is reason to wonder whether it will remain a joint Euro-American, Indo-American venture. Thus far, the U.S. track record for joint undertakings is not good; their balance tends to tilt over time, leaving them with solely Euro-American or Indo-American supporters. A pair of ashrams northwest of Kalamazoo offer a cautionary tale. Once they were one, performing functions much like those envisioned for Sambodh's Center for Human Excellence. Now they are two, one serving Euro-Americans most extensively, the other with a principally Indo-American clientele.

A DELICATE BALANCE BROKEN:

THE VIVEKANANDA ASHRAM

Four tiny hamlets in Michigan have Indian names: Baroda, Ganges, Brohman, Nirvana. Local legend has it that a visiting Maharaja of Baroda chose these. That story may or may not be accurate; the next one is more certain. One day in 1968, a guru based in Chicago drove north with novice swamis along the interstate highway that follows the eastern shore of Lake Michigan. Just south of the resort town of Saugatuck, they saw the name "Ganges" on an exit sign. Considering this auspicious, the guru asked a disciple to find out if any land was for sale in Ganges. Yes, indeed, a fine parcel was available: 80 acres of pear orchard, at the low price of $18,000.

Soon, the novice swamis were camping out in the orchard, working to transform it into an ashram. Over the course of several years, they built a comfortable complex with a large shrine\auditorium, smaller lecture hall, library, bookstore, dining room, a gem of a small museum, and several cottages for visitors and residents. Despite its isolation, the many fine programs it sponsored drew participants from as far away as Detroit and Chicago, as well as Grand Rapids, Kalamazoo, South Bend, East Lansing, and Ann Arbor. In addition to studies of Hindu spiritual teachings and texts, it sponsored interfaith dialogues and speakers on science and religion, ecology, feminist spirituality, and great saints of India. It ran summertime camps to teach Hindu children about their traditions, conducted Sunday services and weekly meditations, and generously welcomed my own students on tours exploring its blend of Hindu and American heritages.

Through the 1970s and 1980s, the Ganges ashram flourished, supported in large measure by its guru's charisma and fund-raising ability. Then, he was hit by a series of strokes, leaving him badly damaged in body and speech. Although he lived five years longer, an aide sent by his order in 1991 took over most of his functions. In 1993, that aide assumed full charge of both ashram and parent center. Soon after, the ashram split, a casualty of the transition and of changes that had occurred in its client community.

Still owning and operating the original Ganges ashram is the Vivekananda Vedanta Society of Chicago. Although first established in 1930, it traces its longer-term origins to Swami Vivekananda's famous speeches before Chicago's World Parliament of Religion in 1893. The guru who decided that a place called Ganges needed an ashram was Swami Bhashyananda, who in 1965 took over a tiny Chicago group and built it into a thriving organization. An important factor in his ashram's breakup was the distinctive setup of U.S. Vedanta Societies. There are twelve in all, each based in a major city, each running its own satellite projects and raising its own funding. Within the United States, each operates independently of the others. Yet all are accountable to one Indian institution, the Ramakrishna Math and Mission based at Belur Math north of Calcutta. All U.S. Society heads must be senior swamis trained at the Indian center. If one dies or becomes disabled, Belur Math sends his replacement.

Note that Swami Bhashyananda first arrived in Chicago in 1965, the year when the United States first lifted its bars to Indian immigration. Indian faces were still rare in the United States; hence the swami's first following was Euro-American. When a wealthy admirer offered to purchase a house where the group could set up an improved center, Bhashyananda chose one in Hyde Park, near the University of Chicago, which he knew would be open to his group's views. His young swami trainees were Americans attracted by Vedanta teachings. Several in particular were drawn by Vivekananda's vision of Vedanta as a framework that could bring unity to all religions. Early ashram supporters were by and large also Euro-Americans, as were a handful of lay disciples who gradually gathered to live full-time in ashram cottages.

Several of those lay disciples were women, and Bhashyananda dreamed of helping those women become swamis and teachers like the men whom he was training. In India, the Ramakrishna Mission has a sister organization called Sharada Math and Mission. Completely independent of the men's organization, it makes its own decisions about its direction. Thus far, Sharada Math has resisted forming branches in the United States. So Bhashyananda turned to another group to realize his aims, a women's ashram in Calcutta founded by Gauri Ma,[16] a disciple of Vivekananda's guru Ramakrishna. In 1987, Bhashyananda took a woman from the Ganges ashram to Calcutta to visit both Sharada Math and Gauri Ma's ashram. Three years later, he sent her back to seek renunciant vows and training. At the same time, he charged two male swamis to start building a woman's ashram across the street from the men's community. A few days before his intended head for the new woman's ashram boarded her plane for Calcutta, Bhashyananda suffered the first of his strokes.

His successor was, in the words of one breakaway swami, "a good man, but a more conservative type." He was also mindful of rules governing their mutual order that forbid men from participating in women's enterprises. When he came into full authority, he tried to withdraw the swamis working on the women's ashram. They insisted they had to complete the task their guru had begun. An appeal to Belur Math headquarters resulted in a judgment that the recalcitrant swamis must leave the order. They then moved across the street and completed the women's ashram, assuming the titles of "friends" to the women's community. Many of Bhashyananda's older lay disciples shifted allegiances with them. Although this was a mixed group, including Indo-Americans, many Euro-American followers joined the withdrawing contingent.

---

[16] The Sri Sri Saradeshwari Ashram.

How had this happened? The difference over the ashram merely broadened a division that had been building for years before it. Few immigrants from India are attracted to organizations resulting from pre-1965 missions. The Chicago Vedanta Society was an exception. This was partly because it had connections to a movement well known in India, but also because Bhashyananda made a point of being of service to Hindu arrivals from India. He worked within structures familiar to them, going to homes for satsangs, officiating at pujas and samskaras. He even chanted mantras for funerals, at a time when priests were scarce and any person who could fill a priestly role was deeply appreciated. I myself first came to know him through his work with local Hindus; I met him in the home of one of my Indo-American students.

Most India-born devotees had a different kind of relationship to the ashram than Americans. Americans viewed it as an informal school and forum for discussion; they filled much of the audience during programs. Indians came for counseling, for darshan of Bhashyananda, and for the many occasions when Hindus in India go to ashrams: founders' celebrations, the midsummer day when gurus are honored, and other occasions for expressing devotion. As in India, they gave generously to support the ashram, a fact of great benefit to Euro-Americans, because much of their generous funding supported ashram programs. But America-born members found the split perplexing and at times frustrating. I recall a friend saying to me once during an ashram program: "We want to solve the world's problems; the Indians want pujas." Knowing both clienteles well, Bhashyananda met both needs, maintaining a skillful and diplomatic balance between them. His successor was better equipped to work with an India-born audience.

When the two ashrams split, program foci of the old ashram divided as well. The original ashram kept functions that appealed to its India-born community, as did the parent Chicago Center. The ashram today is principally a retreat center for Indo-Americans, making only minimal effort to reach out to local neighbors. Chicago programs listed on the community's Web site feature a combination of pujas, *artis,* and holiday celebrations, along with classes on the *Bhagavad-Gita,* Upanishads, and the *Gospel of Sri Ramakrishna.*[17] The center will soon move from its Hyde Park site, whose location has proved inconvenient for its new supporters. The new site will be in the suburb of Lemont, just five miles from a popular Hindu temple.

Meanwhile, the second ashram, dedicated in 1998 as "Mother's Place, Mother's Trust,"[18] has focused much of its energy on interfaith outreach. Its most visible public project, called the Lakeshore Interfaith Community, hosts interfaith services, institutes, and workshops.[19] Bhashyananda's old Indo-American devotees still visit and sometimes attend programs; new faces attending sessions are almost wholly Euro-American. Two more women of Mother's Place, Mother's Trust took renunciant vows following the breakup, and residents still do pujas, use Indian religious names, and keep up communication with the Sri Sri Saradeshwara Ashram in Calcutta. Nevertheless, the ashram head and both its swamis are now also ordained interfaith ministers.

---

[17] See www.vedantasociety-chicago.org (Vivekananda Vedanta Society of Chicago).

[18] It is named for Ramakrishna's wife Sharada Devi, also known as the "Holy Mother."

[19] See www.accn.org~baba (Lakshore Interfaith Institute and Community).

A TALE OF TWO TEMPLES: RAM AND BALAJI COME TO CHICAGO

It is probably too much to expect that convert Hindus and India-born Hindus will mesh flawlessly when they first try to come together. After all, Christian immigrant groups have also pulled apart from American cousins before finding ways of integrating efforts. Similarities in ideals, beliefs, and symbols cannot always offset differences of taste and habit. Furthermore, even Hindus born in India can differ widely in preference. In a small setting like Kalamazoo where members of a minority group must cooperate, such differences are readily papered over. In a large metropolitan setting, they often resurface. A good example of such resurfacing is found in another pair of Chicago-based undertakings.

Chicago is home to dozens of Hindu organizations ranging from tiny informal groups to complex institutions serving hundreds of families. In a 1988 survey of Chicago's Indian migrants, South Asianist Raymond Williams named twenty-one groups of Hindu derivation.[20] Chicago Hindus come in many varieties. Some are devotees of new spiritual movements such as those described earlier: ISKCON, the Sai Baba movement, the Aurobindo Society, the Chinmaya Mission, Ammachi's organization, the Brahma Kumaris. Chicago has an active chapter of the Vishva Hindu Parishad. Many groups special to specific language communities are also active in the city. Williams himself has written extensively on the Swaminarayans, who have a strong Chicago branch and temple. Others are less formal, such as groups gathering periodically to sing bhajans popular in their own regions.

What of eclectic efforts such as the Indo-American Cultural Center and Temple? Chicago Hindus united to undertake such a project when Kalamazoo still had only its lightly-knit India Association. Their "Hindu Temple of Greater Chicago" organization held its first meetings in 1977 with the grand dream of building "a place of worship, a place of cultural and fine arts activities, religious and language schools, and a library."[21] Not all of this dream has been realized yet, but a fine temple and cultural center is now in place, constructed from the ground up according to Hindu canons and supervised by a noted Indian architect. An irony is that members of the same South Indian community that set this effort in motion eventually pulled away to build another authentic temple less than half an hour's drive away.

The temple in Lemont, briefly mentioned earlier, today holds the original title, Hindu Temple of Greater Chicago. Located in Chicago's outer ring of southwest suburbs, Lemont is on the Des Plaines River, just south of highway I-55. The temple stands on a lovely site, curved into the side of a bluff above the river. It is actually a temple complex, including two main temple structures built in different historical styles, an auditorium seating 600, a dining hall, kitchen, gift shop, office, conference room, and a handsome memorial to Swami Vivekananda. One of its temples is Vaishnava, honoring Ram, Sita, and Lakshman in its central shrine. Peripheral shrines

---

[20] Raymond Brady Williams, *Religions of Immigrants from India and Pakistan* (Cambridge: Cambridge Univ. Press, 1988), 225–53.

[21] www.ramatemple.org (The Hindu Temple of Greater Chicago). Much of the program information cited is from this site.

in its main room honor Lakshmi, Vinayaka (Ganesh), and Satyanarayanan; anterooms enshrine a Krishna-Radha pair and the South Indian Balaji. The second temple is Shaiva, with a Shiva-linga as its focus and peripheral shrines for Ganesh, Durga, Subramanyam (Skandha), Parvati, and the nine planets.

Deities in both structures have been activated at the highest level, which means that the complex must maintain an absolute minimum of two full-time priests. Besides their daily schedule of required pujas, temple priests maintain a sizeable cycle of festivals and offer thirty-one varieties of optional rites that visitors can have performed by paying posted fees. Temple priests will also go to homes for services such as funerals. The temple runs Sanskrit classes, Sunday schools, and many cultural performances. A special group for young professionals sponsors activities ranging from a formal dinner at the temple to classes in Indian cooking and world religions.

Approximately 22 miles northwest of the Lemont temple, near the city of Aurora, the second Hindu temple overlooks highway I-57. Its site is less aesthetic than Lemont's, a flat stretch of former farmland overlooking the highway. But the temple is a grand one by U.S. standards, constructed over a dining-hall\meeting room that lifts it high above its base. A new entrance porch and additional lower rooms being completed will make it even grander. This temple honors Balaji, also known as Venkateswara, a deity with a special history in the United States. Balaji's principal temple at Tirupati in Andhra Pradesh, South India, is one of the wealthiest and most visited of all Indian pilgrim sites. It has also become a special mentor to U.S. Hindu temples, offering not only expert consultation but also loans; both Chicago temples have had support from it. Partially as a result of Tirupati aid and advice, the first fully consecrated temple in the United States was a Balaji temple, located in a suburb of Pittsburgh. Balaji is fast becoming a kind of tutelary deity for the United States, with temples in several major U.S. cities. His presence seems ironically appropriate in a country so full of riches; in India, Balaji is known for his love of wealth and ability to grant it. In Chicago, however, the greater motive for his presence lies in his special connection to South India, especially Telegu- and Tamil-speaking regions.

Like the Lemont temple, Balaji's structure has a number of subsidiary shrines: for Ganesh, Shiva, two forms of Parvati, Subramanyam, Hanuman, Satyanarayan,[22] and the popular Tamil deity Ayyappa. Flanking Balaji himself are the two goddesses who characteristically attend Vishnu when he is enshrined in South Indian temples: Lakshmi, here called Sri Devi, and Bhudevi, Earth, identified also with the Vaishnava Tamil woman saint Andal.[23] Its deities have been fully consecrated, and it maintains a staff of full-time priests and an active schedule of daily, festival, and optionally commissioned pujas. Like its images, these have a southern spin; when I visited to gather information, the temple was advertising a festival for Andal. Unlike the Lemont temple, Balaji's temple does not advertise an elaborate schedule of purely social and cultural activity. This may be because it does not have as extensive a set of spaces in which to do so.

Fully consecrated temples are very expensive to maintain. How has Chicago come to have two? Both temples have published short histories; neither makes

---

[22] Worshiped as part of a vow popular in India.

[23] www.balaji.org (Sri Venkateswara Swami Temple of Greater Chicago).

mention of the other.[24] Probing more deeply into their joint histories, South Asian scholar Raymond Williams has published an account linking them together. According to Williams's 1988 book *Religions of Immigrants from India and Pakistan,*[25] both began with an initiative launched in 1977 by members of Chicago's Telegu Association, one of several organizations maintained in Chicago by members of Indian linguistic communities. Naming themselves "the Hindu Temple of Greater Chicago," they set up a nonprofit organization to work toward building a temple and cultural center. Much like Kalamazoo's Indo-American Center, this was imagined as a place that would unite Chicago's entire Hindu community and help it celebrate its heritage together. But because of its greater potential resources, the Chicago organization could think bigger; it could build an authentic temple, plus a much larger cultural complex. Shri Rama would be the temple's central deity because he is broadly popular in India and not strongly linked to one particular sect or region.

It took time and persistent wooing of other Hindus throughout the city to build the support needed to tackle a project of this size. Nonetheless, by 1980, supporters had found and purchased the Lemont site, sponsoring dance performances and benefit recitals to raise funds. They set up a building committee with members from different areas of Chicago to search for architects and develop a master plan. It was not an easy process; the temple's own history reports that the committee "struggled hard to design architecture to satisfy all Hindu groups."[26] This tedious phase of working out details also seems to have been the point at which some Telegu supporters began to grow impatient. When the plan ran into zoning snags and additional delays, a group of "Telegu professionals" took matters into their own hands. In 1983, twelve of them purchased a farm near Aurora and donated it as a site for a Chicago Balaji temple. Again raising funds energetically for the project, they were able to build just as roadblocks cleared for the temple in Lemont. The first stages for both temples were dedicated in June of 1986, thirteen years after the temple initiative began.

When I first learned of these two temples, I assumed that the rift behind them had been a split between North and South Indian backers, a division that has surfaced in other U.S. temple projects. According to William's study, that was not the case. Both temples had strong backing from the South Indian community. The principal difference between them seems one of vision. Rama temple backers opted for inclusiveness, accepting the compromises and haggling that such inclusiveness entailed. Balaji temple supporters opted for a temple more explicitly theirs, closer to the structures they had known in Indian homes. Notice, however, that they also chose a deity known all over India and one who had connections special to the United States.

One worrisome question early on was whether Chicago Hindus could afford to support two ambitious temples. Williams himself was skeptical when he wrote his description. "The future of both temples is uncertain," he asserted. "They have great potential but also serious difficulties."[27] In the fifteen years since he published

[24] Celebrating "Twenty Years of Our Heritage," www.ramtemple.org/hisrev1; also "Sri Venkateswara Swami (Balaji) Temple of Greater Chicago," unpublished manuscript available at the temple.

[25] Op. cit., see especially pp. 226–33.

[26] Ibid.

[27] Op. cit., p. 233.

these words, the Hindu Temple of Greater Chicago at Lemont consecrated its Shiva\ Durga\Ganesha temple in addition to the original Rama Temple, and has built the handsome cultural center that connects them. Extensive expansion is underway at the Balaji Temple.

How have they managed to do this? One prospect that Williams did not take into account was that two fully consecrated temples near one another had the potential to become a pilgrim destination. The United States is developing Hindu pilgrim routes. Pittsburgh draws the most visitors. It, too, by the way, has a second, eclectic, temple as well as a conjunction of rivers, always attractive to Hindu pilgrims.[28] Chicago has, nonetheless, become a strong magnet for midwesterners. Its temples now attract not only visitors but also donations from a widening circle of neighbor states.[29]

TOWARD TOMORROW

It has been more than a century since the first Hindu teachers came to America and began bringing together two cultures once a globe apart. On the whole, the Hindu presence that those teachers helped implant here appears to be thriving, despite occasional setbacks. What will its future be like? Will it hold more examples of creative knitting? Or is it likely to entail more splits as different preferences assert themselves? It is still too early to answer such questions. Four important factors are likely to affect the U.S. Hindu future.

The first is increasing size, especially among the community of India-descended Hindus. Migration from India to the United States continues to grow at a rate of approximately 20,000 entrants per year. Although some immigrants return, the majority stays and makes homes in their new land. In addition, both immigrants and converts are producing children. As seen, the size of a Hindu community in any one place has an effect on the kind of foundations established there. Among larger populations, one finds more ambitious undertakings following Indian models more closely than those in smaller cities. More splitting and specialization tend to occur, and more branches of India-based movements take root and grow.

A second development with less predictable consequences is the emergence of an adult second generation among the immigrant community. Indians who came to the United States during the 1970s now have children approaching thirty. In theory, these children will soon be ready to take over leadership in the centers and temples that their parents founded. Whether they will do so remains to be seen; they are far more fully American than their parents, without the strong ties of memory and emotion that led parents to create islands of Indian culture in their new home. Children of converts are also an uncertainty. Motivations that led their parents to seek new spiritual homes often do not hold for them. As they become adults, they follow their own paths.

---

[28] The Allegheny and Monongahela, which join at Pittsburgh to form the Ohio River.

[29] See Surinder M. Bhardwaj, "Hindu Deities and Pilgrimage in the United States," *Pilgrimage in the United States,* Geographica Religionum 5, G. Rinschede and S. M. Bhardwaj, eds. (Berlin: Dietrich Reimer, 1990), 211–28.

Another factor producing uncertainty is the shifting U.S. economic scene, which so often moves people from city to city. Hindu centers and temples are much like churches in this respect. A family may build up a strong commitment to one, only to be told it must move to a different location. As this book was being written, the Indo-American Center in Kalamazoo was going through such a setback as Pfizer closed down local research labs. Senior officers of the Center had been counting on certain up-and-coming young people to take over leadership. Now, several young leaders have been transferred, and jobs that might have drawn others to the community are gone.

Another factor, mentioned with unease by several local leaders I spoke with, is the shifting nature of the incoming Indian immigrant community. As this chapter has noted, most early Indian immigrants were highly educated and fluent in English. Many Hindus brought preconceptions with them that made it easier for them to pull together despite caste barriers and sectarian difference. That pattern has been changing. Many immigrants who enter now are arriving under family reunification provisions of immigration law. Older immigrants have by now become U.S. citizens and can sponsor adult relatives at a more distant reach to settle near them and search for American jobs. Many new entrants are less well educated than their predecessors, less fluent in English, and less likely to be able to make their way without help. As one local leader put it, "Before, the cream was coming here. Now everything is coming." He fears that a class system will emerge among Indo-Americans, introducing new factions into a community that had previously made huge strides in overcoming differences.

Counterbalancing such concerns are the steps already taken to establish institutions and precedents that should encourage cooperation and counteract fission. Newly arriving Hindus are no longer alone. They have relatives to help them, temples and cultural centers to support them. They will be entering communities that have learned to put aside difference to work toward a common good. Moreover, the leadership in those communities should soon include sizeable numbers of second- and even third-generation Americans for whom at least the older divisions imported from India will have less and less significance.

ADDITIONAL SOURCES

A growing number of resources exist on Hinduisms around the world. Addressing an issue central to all of them is Martin Baumann, "Conceptualizing Diaspora: The Preservation of Religious Identity in Foreign Parts, Exemplified by Hindu Communities Outside India," *Temenos* 31 (1995): 19–35. Helpful collections of case studies on various communities are T. S. Rukmani, ed., *The Hindu Diaspora: Global Perspectives* (Montreal: Concordia Univ. Chair in Hindu Studies, 1999); Harold G. Coward, ed., *The Hindu Diaspora, Hindu-Christian Studies Bulletin* 11 (1998); Harold Coward et al., *The South Asian Religious Diaspora in Britain, Canada, and the United States* (Albany, NY: State Univ. of New York Press, 2000); Steven Vertovec, *The Hindu Diaspora: Comparative Patterns* (London: Routledge, 2000); and Richard Burghart, ed., *Hinduism in Great Britain: The Perpetuation of Religion in an Alien Cultural Milieu* (London: Tavistock, 1987).

For the United States, I recommend starting with the section on American Hindus in Diana Eck's *A New Religious America* (San Francisco: HarperCollins, 2001). Also extremely useful are segments on Hindus in Eck's CD-ROM, *On Common Ground: World Religions in America,* 2nd ed. (New York: Columbia Univ. Press, 2002); both this and Eck's book cover both convert and immigrant communities. Covering both as well is Cybelle T. Shattuck's *Dharma in the Golden State: South Asian Religious Traditions in California* (Santa Barbara, CA: Fithian Press, 1996); see also Cynthia Humes and Thomas Forsthoefel, eds., *Gurus in America* (Albany: State Univ. of New York Press, 2005).

Raymond Brady Williams has been a pioneering scholar on immigrant communities. See his *Religions of Immigrants from India and Pakistan* (Cambridge: Cambridge Univ. Press, 1988); also "Sacred Threads of Several Textures: Strategies of Adaption in the United States," in his edited volume *A Sacred Thread: Modern Transmission of Hindu Traditions in India and Abroad* (Chambersburg, PA: Anima, 1992), 228–57. A second scholar of early importance is John Y. Fenton. His *Transplanting Religious Traditions: Asian Indians in America* (New York: Praeger, 1988) studied immigrants of Atlanta; he also assembled the large and useful *South Asian Religions in the Americas: An Annotated Bibliography of Immigrant Religious Traditions* (Westport, CT: Greenwood Press, 1995). Arthur W. and Usha M. Helweg describe challenges faced by Indian immigrants in *An Immigrant Success Story: East Indians in America* (Philadelphia: Univ. of Pennsylvania Press, 1990). Mira Kamdar tracks one family's migrations from India to Burma to the United States in *Motiba's Tattoos: A Granddaughter's Journey into Her Indian Family's Past* (New York: Public Affairs, 2000). Describing two experiments in religious education for Hindu children is R. Stephen Warner, "Immigration and Religious Communities in the United States," *Gatherings in Diaspora: Religious Communities and the New Immigration,* R. Stephen Warner and Judith G. Wittner, eds. (Philadelphia: Temple Univ. Press, 1998), 3–34.

Several fine temple studies exist. Pittsburgh is featured in Fred W. Clothey's "The Construction of a Temple in an American City and the Acculturation Process," in his *Rhythm and Intent (Ritual Studies from South India)* (Madras: Blackie, 1986), 164–200; and in Vasudha Narayanan's "Creating South Indian Hindu Experience in the United States," *A Sacred Thread: Modern Transmission of Hindu Traditions in India and Abroad,* Raymond Brady Williams, ed. (Chambersburg, PA: Anima, 1992), 147–76. Washington is focal in Joanna Punzo Waghorne, "The Hindu Gods in a Split-Level World: The Sri Siva-Vishnu Temple in Suburban Washington, D.C.," *Gods of the City: Religion and the American Urban Landscape,* Robert A. Orsi, ed. (Bloomington, IN: Indiana Univ. Press, 1999), 103–30. Simon Jacob and Pallavi Thaku study a Houston temple in "Jyothi Hindu Temple: One Religion, Many Practices," *Religion and the New Immigrants: Continuities and Adaptions in Immigrant Communities,* Helen Rose Ebaugh and Janet Saltzman Chafetz, eds. (Walnut Creek, NY: Altamira Press, 2000), 229–42; Raymond Brady Williams reports on a Chicago area temple not described in this text in his "Swaminarayan Hindu Temple of Glen Ellyn, Illinois," *American Congregations,* vol. I., James P. Wind and James W. Lewis, eds. (Chicago: Univ. of Chicago Press), 612–62.

For Hindu pilgrimage centers and routes in the United States, see Surinder M. Bhardwaj, "Hindu Deities and Pilgrimage in the United States" *Pilgrimage in the United States,* Geographica Religionum 5, G. Rinschede and S. M. Bhardwaj, eds. (Berlin: Dietrich Reimer, 1990): 211–28; also his earlier essay with Madhusudana Rao, "Emerging Hindu Pilgrimage in the United States: A Case Study." *Pilgrimage in World Religions,* S. Bhardwaj and G. Rinschede, eds., Geographica Religionum 4 (Berlin: Dietrich Reimer, 1988): 159–87.

Afterword

Brit) ritish religion scholar Julius Lipner describes the way Hindus approach their world as "continuous recentering among a set of interactive polarities in dynamic tension."[1] With this complicated phrase, he is trying to communicate the kind of unity-in-diversity that we have seen in this book: the creative interaction of multiple traditions and viewpoints, any one of which can predominate in a particular space, time, or social context. The distinctive genius of Hindus, Lipner suggests, is their ability to maintain balance in the midst of multiplicity, to realize that different kinds of contexts may call for different kinds of viewpoints and methods of approach to human problems. The quest for balance between alternative possibilities is a characteristic he sees expressed on varied levels of Hindu thought and action: philosophically, in efforts to express the relationship between unity and difference in the world, and ethically, in attempts to find a constructive path through the complex and sometimes contradictory demands of dharma.

If this text has done its job properly, it will have revealed even more "polarities in dynamic tension" than those discussed by Lipner. Four have surfaced repeatedly:

1. *Structure and fluidity*   This polarity has been encountered on several levels. It surfaces mythologically in stories about competition between devas and asuras—beings who guard life-sustaining order versus beings who, by disrupting this, introduce challenge and excitement into life. The practice of pilgrimage reflects it, as Hindus venture out periodically from their carefully structured homes and settlements into the more fluid wilderness or a dip in the waters of a "crossing place." Even exacting Vedic rituals have points of fluidity, for example, in substitutions allowed for items offered: a vine for long-lost *soma,* a cucumber for a goat in an age disapproving of bloodshed. The human body is so fluid that even a brief encounter with a polluted person or substance can readily change it.[2]

2. *Continuity and change*   Change aplenty is recorded in this volume, occurring at several stages of Hindu history. Nonetheless, readers must have noticed also how much more effective calls for change have been when these are joined with affirmation of tradition. The leaders who have brought about the most sweeping religious changes in modern India have been dressed in orange robes and claimed affiliation with ancient sadhu lineages. Gandhi moved Indian masses to political action with his prayer meetings and *dhotis* far more effectively than had earlier Congress leaders wearing suits and making speeches. Tamil women of today claim public space and

---

[1] Julius J. Lipner, "Ancient Banyan: An Inquiry into the Meaning of 'Hinduness,'" *Religious Studies* 32:125.

[2] A circle of anthropologists at the University of Chicago has explored this premise of bodily fluidity in works that I do not pretend to understand well. Noteworthy among them are McKim Marriott and Ronald Inden. Important also is Valentine Daniel's *Fluid Signs,* cited earlier in this volume.

the right to assume leadership by performing pujas and leading campaigns of temple renovation.

3. *Antiquity and novelty* The demand for balance between change and continuity may account for the survival of some surprisingly ancient practices in various Hindu traditions: Vedic memorization and chanting, fire offerings, renouncers retreating to forests and letting hair mat into dreadlocks. Yet the old has been constantly balanced against the new. An expatriate Brahmin learns Sanskrit chants for pujas from cassette tapes. Pilgrims ride planes to reach the gateways of holy places. Organizations founded within the last fifty years spread their calls for return to Vedic glory by computer. Some years ago in India, I sat in on a fascinating debate about whether Hinduism should be called the oldest major world religion or the newest. Both sides made convincing arguments.

4. *The local and the global* In a village of Tamilnadu, residents can honor a local goddess in a festival distinctive to themselves and still experience connection to traditions stretching throughout the world. Rajputs of a single kul in Rajasthan can undergo a similar experience of being simultaneously unique and yet part of a greater whole. So can Hindu residents of Kalamazoo, Michigan, gathering on a Sunday morning with their own small pantheon lined up before them. Surely, a very important component of Hindu resilience over the years has been the ability to strike creative balances between local customs and symbols that are comforting and familiar and those that reach out and forge links to a much wider world. As Hindus quest for balance between the many and the one, the old and new, the structured and stable, and the fluid and changing, they have also thus far managed to preserve the local and distinctive while reaching out with increasing effectiveness on both national and global scales.

WHAT NEXT?

If we have seen balancing acts on these pages, we have also seen contests between various Hindu factions eager to claim the next center for themselves, to tilt the various existing balances in ways that will favor their own undertakings. Can any predictions be made about these contests? Several trends are discernable.

1. *Uniformity over variety* Many scholars besides me have noticed an increasing standardization of Hindu traditions—in ritual practice, imagery, ideas, and values articulated. The local goddess in Tamilnadu, cited above, has a temple, regular pujas, and a calendar that she would not have had 150 years ago. Women's vrats and family samskaras look more and more alike. Readers know by now that some standardization is a result of intentional efforts made by the Vishva Hindu Parishad and its affiliates. But greater forces nudging Hindus toward uniformity are increased Indian literacy and the influence of mass media such as TV and movies. Knowing that even people in remote farming villages can read motivates publishers to produce inexpensive guides for frequently practiced rituals or texts for devotional prayers and songs. From such texts, even more than from resident village Brahmins or itinerant sadhus, people come to accept the idea that there are right ways and wrong ways of doing things. When a family celebration or pilgrim trek is portrayed in a TV show or movie,

it also becomes a model for imitation. Hence, often unintentionally, it becomes a force promoting standardization.[3]

2. *High-caste religion over low*   Lower caste drift toward increasingly Sanskritized and Brahminized patterns of practice is an old and well-established phenomenon among Hindus. It is hardly surprising, then, to find it occurring today. One important difference between past and present, however, is that higher caste groups once resisted low-caste attempts to imitate high-caste patterns, recognizing this as an effort to raise caste standing. The story of the Satnamis, told in Chapter 8, offers a fine example of such resistance.[4] Today, however, even the high-caste dominated Vishva Hindu Parishad promotes formerly high-caste practice across the social spectrum. This could be interpreted as a generous gesture, an affirmation of underlying Hindu equality. The skeptical, however, are more likely to view it as an attempt to ensure that high castes continue to be accepted as standard-setters for Hindu values and practice. Regardless of the underlying motivations, such a contemporary push added to older precedent seems certain to spread high-caste practice. But we must recall that practice promoted now does not represent the whole of former patterns. It has been edited selectively to drop parts no longer acceptable. It has also been blended with elements of formerly lower caste practice to enhance its mass appeal.

3. *"Secularity" over sect*   Here "secular" is used in its Indian sense of crossing sectarian boundaries. All present-day movements contending to define Hinduism's future are secular in the sense that they recruit across sectarian divisions. Their inclusiveness is a well-established trend; there is no reason to think that it will not continue. The one question to be asked is whether such new movements are really building a new sense of all-Hindu unity or whether they are simply replacing older sects with new ones. Only time will tell; I have no answer to this question.

4. *Global and local in exchange*   Another outcome impossible to predict is the result of the exchange now in progress among the local, all-India, and global levels at which today's Hinduisms are practiced. Within India, local practice is clearly being altered to conform with broader all-India patterns. Village deities acquire temples, priests, and pujas; blood disappears from their festivals. Meanwhile, on a much grander scale, India's Hindus are being reshaped by their global cousins. Wealth from abroad advances the fortunes and reach of new movements. Preferences for some parts of tradition over others reawaken Indian interest in these components. On the other hand, global Hindus look to India for direction and decisions about what is and is not authentic. In Kalamazoo, Hindus have hired a priest trained in India in preference to their original home-grown ritual leader. Hindus in Chicago, Pittsburgh, New York, Houston, and other cities build temples according to India-developed canons. In the meantime, a single temple, Tirupati in South India, becomes increasingly a guide and model for American Hindu aspirations. Will children of the Hindus now building authentic temples keep looking to India for mentoring? Or will they go their own way, evolving their own standards, asserting their own views and values? Again, it is too soon to tell.

---

[3] For examples of media influence, see Lawrence A. Babb and Susan S. Wadley, *Media and the Transformation of Religion in South Asia* (Philadelphia: Univ. of Pennsylvania Press, 1995).

[4] Pp. 202–04. Further examples are described by Lloyd and Susanne Rudolph in *The Modernity of Tradition: Political Development in India* (Chicago: Univ. of Chicago Press, 1967), pp. 36–51.

WHITHER INDIA?

And what of India's future? Will India become a Hindu nation? Once upon a time I thought the Hindu nationalist combine had built too solid a set of foundations to be stoppable. It would just build its support base in Parliament little by little until it had the majority needed for drastic action. Then, it lost an election that it fully expected to win, apparently for reasons that had little to do with religion.[5] Indian political processes are simply too complex to predict their outcomes on the basis of any single factor. Furthermore, today's broad spectrum of living Hindu teachings includes at least some that promote a high level of independent and critical thinking. Will Hindus themselves permit a tradition they value to be captured by any single political or social faction?

---

[5] See the analysis of the 2004 election by Pankraj Mishra, "India: The Neglected Majority Wins!" *The New York Review* (August 12, 2004): 30–32 and 37.

Appendix

Transliteration

A. Sanskrit and Hindi both have a letter usually transliterated as "c," which is always pronounced like English "ch." I have written it as "ch"; hence "acharya," not "acarya."

B. Sanskrit and Hindi both have two letters pronounced much like English "sh," with a slightly different placement of the tongue. When transliterated precisely, one is usually written "ś" and the other "ṣ" or "sh." I have written both as "sh"; hence "Vishnu," not "Visnu," and "Shiva," not "Siva."

C. Sanskrit and Hindi both have two versions of the sounds "t" and "d," one transliterated by specialists without diacriticals, the other by adding a dot directly under the letter (ḍ, ṭ). The former is pronounced with the tongue brushing the back of the teeth, the second with the tongue flipped upwards towards the top of the mouth. I have written both as "d" and "t."

D. Sanskrit, Hindi, and Tamil all make distinctions between short and long versions of the vowels "a," "i," and "u." The short "a" is pronounced like a short "uh" in English, the "i" like the "i" in "it," and the "u" like the "u" in "put." Specialists write the long versions as "ā," "ī," and "ū"; they are pronouced "aa," "ee," and "oo," which is the way Indians usually write them. Unfortunately, writing them this way makes the words they contain look very much unlike the forms of these terms usually found in Western writings. I have, therefore, not distinguished between the long and short sounds.

E. Sanskrit and Hindi both have a sound called a vocalic "r," written by linguists as "ṛ" and pronounced like an "r" followed by a very short "i." I have written this as "ri."

F. Sanskrit and Hindi also at times attach a nasal spin to a vowel, meaning that the sound for the vowel is sent through the nose. Linguists usually indicate this by following the vowel with an "m" or an "n," written with a dot above it (ṁ or ṅ). I have indicated this sound with an "m," except in places where use of an "n" has become standard practice (thus "samskara," but also "Sanskrit").

G. Readers familiar with linguists' transliterations in Sanskrit may also have noticed markings for several additional versions of the sound "n." These always precede or follow certain consonants. In English, these modify naturally into their appropriate sounds as the mouth adjusts to their accompanying consonants. I have transliterated all of them as "n." The combination "jñ," however, is tricky in Sanskrit and Hindi, because it is pronounced as if it were "gy." Indians write it as "gy"(as in "yagya"); I have left it as jn ("yajna"), again to keep it more consistent with usual Western practice.

H. Sanskrit and Hindi have a sound pronounced between English "v" and "w." Although linguists normally transliterate this as "v," people of India often alternate between a "v" and a "w," using the latter especially when this sound, called a "semi-vowel," is used in combination with a consonant. Thus one finds "Veda" and "deva," but also "swami." Here I have followed the Indian usage for "swami," which is already well known to English speakers in this form.

I. Readers may also have noticed that certain Sanskrit terms ending in "a" will sometimes, but not always, have an additional "m" added to them when transliterated (mantram, lingam, ishtam, vanam). This "m" is a by-product of the Sanskrit system of inflections; it indicates that the word in question is of neuter gender. I have followed the common practice of using the so-called stem form of these terms (without final "m"). I have also followed the usual practice of dropping the final "n" from Sanskrit "karman," although in this case keeping the "n" would be more appropriate.

Glossary

Note: Bulleted terms should become part of a reader's basic vocabulary.

acharya [ācārya] master teacher, especially one of a spiritual lineage

Agama [Āgama] type of post-Vedic Sanskrit text that sets norms for temple construction and ritual

Agni Vedic god of fire

Alvar [Ālvār] "Diver"; one of twelve Tamil poet-saints revered by Shri Vaishnavas

Aranyaka [Aranyaka] "forest text"; early type of Vedic teaching revealing secret meanings of rituals

arti [Sanskrit ārati] ritual popular in today's India, often ending a puja or kirtan. It entails singing a special song while circling a lighted lamp before the image of a deity.

○ **Arya** [Ārya] "Noble One." Ancient Indians of high social standing referred to themselves by this term.

Arya Samaj [Ārya Samāj] oldest "society" classed as "revivalist." It follows teaching of Swami Dayananda Saraswati that Vedic samhitas alone should be guides for Hindu behavior.

○ **ashram** [Sanskrit āśrama] a hermitage. Today, it is a retreat center where people practice spiritual discipline. Also, especially in Sanskrit, it is one of four stages of an ideal life, for example, the student or householder stage.

astika [āstika] one who believes in a Supreme Reality and accepts the authority of Veda

○ **asura** type of superhuman being that disrupts dharma; often battled by devas in Hindu stories

Atharva-Veda [Atharvaveda] the most varied of four basic Vedic collections. It is thought to be the most recently assembled; attributed to a priest named Atharvan.

○ **atman** [ātman] "self" or soul. According to the Upanishads and Vedanta philosophy, it is the portion of the One undying, supreme, and all-knowing Reality that dwells within all beings.

○ **avatara** [avatāra] "descent" of God into the world to restore disrupted world balance

Balaji [Bālaji; also known as Venkateshwara] deity at South India's most popular pilgrim center, Tirupati in Andhra Pradesh. A child-form of Vishnu known for love of wealth and vow-granting ability, Balaji was the first deity to have a fully authentic Hindu temple in the United States.

○ **Bhagavad-Gita** [Bhagavadgītā] "Song of the Gracious Lord," famed Hindu scripture said to contain the essence of all Vedas. The divine descent Krishna gives this teaching to Prince Arjuna in the epic *Mahabharata*.

Bhagavata Purana [Bhāgavatapurāṇa; also called Shrīmad-Bhāgavatam] one of eighteen "Great Puranas." This long Vaishnava scripture is best known for its tenth canto recounting the life of Krishna.

Bhagavatas [Bhāgavata] "those dedicated to the Gracious Lord (=Vishnu)." Earliest-recorded lineage of Vishnu devotees, it is thought to have produced the reworking of *Mahabharata* that portrays Krishna as a divine descent.

bhajan [Sanskrit bhajana] type of devotional song; also a group devoted to singing such songs

○ **bhakta** a devotee

bhakti-yoga [bhaktiyoga] spiritual discipline that consists of devotion; one of three appropriate forms of spiritual practice, according to the *Bhagavad-Gita*.

Bharat Mata [Bhārat Matā] "Mother India," India represented as a goddess

BJP [Bhāratīya Janatā Parishad] "Indian People's Party," also called the Hindu Party. One of India's two largest political parties, the BJP was founded to promote a Hindu nationalist agenda.

Brahma [Brahmā] Personification of brahman power and creator of the known world. Although cited as one of three major male Hindu deities, Brahma has few temples or devotees of his own.

brahmacharya [brahmacarya] student stage of life, according to the four-stage ideal. Because students refrained from sexual relations, this term also means "celibacy."

° **brahman** in early Vedic texts, the transformative power channeled by mantras (sacred chants); later, the Supreme Reality and Consciousness underlying all forms of existence

Brahmana [Brāhmaṇa] type of Vedic text consisting of prescriptions for sacrificial ritual and their justification. It is also the Sanskrit term for a member of the Brahmin caste.

° **Brahmin** [Sanskrit brāhmaṇa; Hindi brahman] member of India's ancient intellectual caste, claiming monopoly over transmission, study, and ritual use of Veda

Brahmo Samaj [Brahmo Samāj] earliest nineteenth-century society promoting religious and social reform. It later split into three groups, all based in Bengal.

Braj region surrounding the city of Mathura in North India where Krishna roamed and played during the cowherd portion of his life

Chaitanya [Caitanya] early sixteenth-century Bengali saint and devotee of Krishna; founder of the Gaudiya Vaishnava Sampradaya

chakra [cakra] "wheel." According to Tantric teachings, it is one of seven energy centers strung out along the human body's central breath channel.

Chinmaya Mission contemporary Hindu revivalist organization concentrating on study and renewal of Vedanta; founded by Swami Chinmayananda

Chitpavan Brahmins subcaste of Brahmins influential in India's state of Maharashtra. Many Prarthana Samaj reformers and early nationalists were Chitpavan Brahmins.

Congress Party major political party of India; descended from the Indian National Congress, first seat of Indian resistance to British colonial rule

° **dalit** "broken to pieces," a name that former untouchables in India use to refer to themselves as a single group

° **darshan** [Sanskrit darśana] literally, a "view," but implying an exchange of viewing that brings blessing. Hindus speak of "taking darshan" of a divine image or a guru. A darshan can also be a philosophical view; Hinduism's six classic Brahmin-transmitted philosophical systems are called darshanas, the Sanskrit equivalent for darshan.

Darshana. See darshan.

Dashanami Sannyasi [daśanāmī saṃnyāsī] "renouncers of ten names," order of renouncers founded by the philosopher Shankaracharya. The "ten names" are its ten principal lineages.

Dayananda Sarasvati, Swami [Svāmī Dāyānanda Sarasvatī] nineteenth-century revivalist. The Arya Samaj follows his teachings.

° **deva** a being "of the heavens" that defends dharma, equivalent to Latin *deus*, "god"

° **devi\Devi** [devī] "goddess." This word is the feminine form of deva.

° **dharma** "that which sustains." This central Brahmin concept includes meanings ranging from "order" to "ability," "role," "duty," and "religion." According to dharma theory, everything that exists is part of an interdependent order, whose various parts must act according to their inborn dharma if the whole of existence is to prosper.

° **Dharmashastra** [dharmaśāstra] category of Sanskrit teachings that lays out precepts of dharma, including both moral rules to guide all humans and rules specific to varnas and stages of life

diaspora Hinduism collective term for Hindu teachings and practice that evolved outside of India

diksha [dīkṣā] initiation

° **Durga** [Durgā] warrior goddess who slays the Buffalo Demon

Durga Puja [Durgā Pūjā] festival celebrating Durga the Buffalo-Demon Slayer

° **Gandhi**, Mohandas Karamchand [also known as Mahātmā Gandhi] Gujarati lawyer and leader of India's freedom movement. Gandhi mobilized Indians for nonviolent resistance by fusing political struggle with spiritual discipline.

° **Ganesha** [Gaṇeśa] best-known name for the deity with an elephant's head and human body. Because he overcomes obstacles, Ganesha is honored when thresholds are crossed and rituals are set in motion.

° **Ganga** [Gaṅgā] Indian term for the Ganges River of northern India, foremost among all Indian rivers. Like all rivers in India, Ma Ganga is a goddess.

Gaudiya Vaishnava [gauḍīyavaishnava] a "Bengali Vaishnava," that is, a devotee of the lineage founded by the Bengali Saint Chaitanya

Gopala [Gopāla] "cow-protector," one of the many names of Krishna

gopi [gopī] "cowgirl," especially one of the cowgirls who adored Krishna

Gorakhnath [Gorakhnāth] legendary yogi and probable founder of the Nath sampradaya. He developed the spiritual discipline called hatha yoga.

grihastha [gṛhastha] "hearth-holding" stage of life

° **grihya** [gṛha] "hearth." It is also a type of Brahmin-transmitted ritual centered on the domestic hearth.

° **guru** a teacher, especially one who serves as a spiritual guide and offers initiation to disciples

guru-parampara [guruparaṁparā] lineage of initiation traced through gurus

Hanuman "having large jaws," monkey-general and devotee of Rama, who helped Rama regain his wife Sita from her kidnapper Ravana

° **Harappan Civilization** ancient civilization located in the Indus Valley and surrounding regions

Harijan "child of God," a term that Gandhi used for Indian untouchables

hatha yoga [haṭha yoga] literally "forced yoga," a spiritual discipline that uses physical methods to unify energies within the body. It is famed for its complex postures and teaching of internal chakras.

Hindu Mahasabha [Hindū Mahāsabhā] shortened form of Akhil Bharat Hindu Mahasabha, "All-India Grand Conference of Hindus," annual conference of Hindu leaders begun in the early twentieth-century to bring Hindu groups into conversation and agreement. During the 1940s, it became a political party, which split in two after Indian independence.

Hindu Rashtra [Hindū Rāshtra] "Hindu Nation," the goal of Hindu nationalist effort in India

° **Hindutva** [Hindūtvā] "Hinduness," the title of a book written by nationalist leader Veer Savarkar. According to Savarkar, Hinduness consists of having India as one's fatherland and holy land.

Indian National Congress annual meeting of Indian leaders started in 1885 to advise British rulers. After World War I, it became the main venue of the Indian freedom movement.

Indo-American an American of Indian descent and cultural heritage

ISKCON "International Society for Krishna Consciousness," organization founded by Gaudiya Vaishnava guru Bhaktivedanta to promote Krishna devotion throughout the world

° **Islam** major world religion founded by the prophet Muhammad claiming allegiance of roughly 14 percent of India's population

Itihasa [itihāsa] "history," the genre of Hindu literature recounting the deeds of ancient kings, especially the two Sanskrit epics *Ramayana* and *Mahabharata*

° **jagran** [Sanskrit jāgrat] "waking," a vigil of devotion that consists of staying awake all night to sing praises of a Hindu deity

° **Jain** [Sanskrit Jaina] adherent of the ancient shramana-carried tradition now called Jainism

jajmani village-based system of exchange in which jatis provide services over which they hold monopolies in exchange for access to village lands and their products

japa "muttering," repeated recital of a brief prayer or mantra while beads of a mala (Hindu rosary) are tallied

○ **jati** [jāti] "community," also called a "subcaste." It is a social group bound together by internal marriage, and it may also hold a monopoly over certain services performed as part of India's jajmani system. Jatis are the working groups of India's caste system, the groups with the greatest importance in everyday social interactions.

-ji ending indicating respect that Hindus add to names or titles of people they wish to honor

jiva [jīva] a "life," especially a force or soul enlivening a human being

jnana-yoga [jñānayoga] spiritual discipline that consists of pursuing sacred knowledge; one of three appropriate forms of spiritual discipline, according to the *Bhagavad-Gita*

Kabir [Kabīr] fifteenth-century poet-saint of North India, said to be of Muslim birth. Songs attributed to Kabir are sung throughout Hindi-speaking North India. Kabir sang of a formless God who included both Allah and Ram.

Kalamukhas [Kālamukha] medieval Shaiva renunciant lineage strong in Karnataka

Kali [Kālī] fearsome long-tongued black goddess revered by Tantrics, low-caste Hindus, and Bengali saints Ramprasad and Ramakrishna. According to her myths, Kali was born to slay a demon whose blood produced clones of himself as its drops fell on the earth. With her long tongue, she lapped up the blood he shed and kept it from reproducing.

Kapalikas [Kapālika] "bearing skulls," Shaiva renunciant lineage known for extreme behavior, which included carrying skulls as begging bowls

○ **karma** [karman] "deed," especially a ritual or moral deed, plus the result it produces. The teaching of karma held that every deed entailed a result or "fruit" that would eventually affect the person who performed it, either during that person's present life or a future rebirth.

karma-yoga [karmayoga] spiritual discipline that consists of performing ritual and other constructive deeds in the everyday world. It is one of three appropriate forms of spiritual discipline, according to the *Bhagavad-Gita*.

○ **kirtan** [Sanskrit kīrtana] devotional praise-song, or a group session devoted to singing such praise-songs

○ **Krishna** [Sanskrit Kṛṣṇa] Vishnu's most popular descent, who spent his youth as a playful cowherd and later revealed the *Bhagavad-Gita*. According to followers of the saint and philosopher Vallabhacharya, Krishna is the world's Supreme God.

○ **Kshatriya** warrior, one who wields the power of kshatra, dominion

○ **kul** [Sanskrit kula] clan or family lineage

kuldevi [Sanskrit kuladevī] type of goddess who protects a clan or greater family lineage. If male, a clan protector is called a kuldeva.

○ **Lakshmi** [Lakshmī] goddess of good luck, wealth, and beauty; also called Shri [Śrī]

○ **lila** [līlā] "play," both activity done for the fun of doing it and dramatic performance

linga [liṅga or liṅgam] Shiva's principal aniconic symbol, venerated at the central shrine of most Shaiva temples

○ *Mahabharata* [Mahābhārata] "tale of the descendants of Bharata." It is India's longest and most complex Sanskrit epic, centered on a war between the five Pandava brothers and their cousins.

Mahar member of the largest untouchable caste of Maharashtra

○ **mantra** [or mantram] a sacred phrase or chant of transformative power, used for meditation or ritual incantation

Manu father of the human race and giver of dharma

Manusmriti [Manusmṛti; also called Manavadharmaśāstra] the oldest and most prestigious Sanskrit writing on dharma teachings, purportedly authored by Manu, the Indian Noah

Mariyamman [alt. Mariyyamman] A name frequent among village goddesses of Tamilnadu

mataji [mātāji] woman who becomes possessed by a goddess and serves as her medium for disciples.

° **math** [Sanskirit maṭha] ascetic's hut; today, a monastery

mela a gathering or fair, often occurring at an auspicious time at a pilgrim center

Mirabai [Mirābai] sixteenth-century woman saint of Rajasthan, a widowed princess who escaped her royal home to sing the praises of Krishna

° **moksha** "loosening," or liberation from limitation, pain, and rebirth

° **murti** [mūrti] image or statue

naga [nāga] folk spirit of India, associated with springs and bodies of water. It normally has the body of a cobra, but can also appear in human form. A naga is also a naked and militant ascetic affiliated with a sampradaya for the purpose of giving its renouncers protection.

° **namas** gesture of reverence, often done by pressing both palms together in front of the face

Nanak [Nānak] sixteenth-century Punjabi saint, founder and first guru of the Sikh tradition

nastika [nāstika] one who does not presuppose the existence of a Supreme Reality or accept the authority of scriptures that reveal this, i.e., Veda

° **Nath** [Sanskrit Nātha] initiate of the sampradaya founded by Gorakhnath. Naths are also known as Siddha or Kanphata Yogis.

Nayanar [Nāyanar] "leader," one of sixty-three Tamil Shaiva saints honored by the Shaiva-Siddhanta tradition

nirguna [nirguṇa] without attributes, such as a God who transcends all imagined forms or images

orthodoxy adhering to correct teachings

° **orthopraxis** observing correct religious practice

° **pandit** [Sanskrit paṇḍita] Brahmin learned in Sanskrit and sacred scriptures

Pantaram [or Pandaram] Shudra caste that provides the priest who serves a Tamil village goddess

° **panth** "path" or "way." It is also a group that follows a path. The nearest English equivalent is the term "sect."

Paraiyan [Paṛaiyan] Tamil drummer caste. Its name was the source of the English term "pariah."

° **Parvati** [Parvatī] mountain goddess and bride of Shiva

Pashupata [Pāśupata] devotee of an early Shaiva sect

Pashupati [Pāśupati] alternate name for Shiva, meaning "Lord of Creatures"

Patañjali Brahmin who systematized yoga and composed the *Yoga Sutras*

pativrat [Sanskrit pativratā] a wife "vowed to her husband," taking her husband as her god

° **pitri** [pitṛ] literally, "father," a Hindu ancestor

° **pranam** [Sanskrit praṇamana] prostration, touching head or body to the floor

Prarthana Samaj [Prārthana Samāj] "Prayer Society," late nineteenth-century society of Maharashtra dedicated to religious and social reform

° **prasad** [Sanskrit prasāda] divine grace; also, food offered to a god, then returned to a worshiper to be eaten as that god's "leavings"

pratima [pratīma] consecrated divine image. Hindus often translate this word as "idol," without the negative connotations that term has in the West.

° **puja** [pūjā] honor or worship done to a divine image or person, usually by offering flowers, incense, colored powers, cooling ointments, water, clothes, fruits, and cooked foods

° **Purana** [Purāṇa] "belonging to ancient times." It is a type of Sanskrit text compiling various types of lore, ranging from myths and tales of kings to instructions for ritual and image making.

purdah [Hindi pardā] "curtain," the practice of shielding high-caste women from male gaze

purohit [Sanskrit purohita] a family priest or royal chaplain

° **Purusha** cosmic "Person" sacrificed to make the world, according to the *Rig-Veda* hymn "Purusha-sukta." Also, in Samkhya philosophy, it is an intelligent "soul" trapped in matter that gives rise to intelligent life.

○ **Radha** [Rādhā] cowgirl most beloved of Krishna; his wife and divine consort, according to Vallabhacharyas

Rajanya [rājanya] "royal person," ancient alternative for Kshatriya

Rajput [Rājput] "Son of a King," dominant caste of Rajasthan, claiming Kshatriya status

○ **Rama** [Rāma] ideal Hindu prince and ruler; hero of the Sanskrit epic *Ramayana* and its Hindi retelling *Ramcharitmanas*

Ramakrishna [Rāmakrṣhṇa] nineteenth-century saint and mystic of Bengal; guru to Swami Vivekananda. A priest of Kali, he taught that all religions are alternate paths to the same goal.

Ramakrishna Mission Bengal-based organization founded by Swami Vivekananda to honor his guru, spread both their teachings, and fuse spiritual discipline with social service

Ramanandis [Rāmānandi] major devotional sampradaya of North India

Ramanuja [Rāmānujā] Tamil Brahmin philosopher and theoretician for the Shri Vaishnava sampradaya. He is India's most influential devotional philosopher.

○ *Ramayana* [Rāmāyaṇa] Sanskrit epic recounting deeds of the ideal prince and king Rama

Ramcharitmanas [Rāmcaritmānas] "Lake of the Deeds of Ram," Hindi retelling of the *Ramayana* by Tulsidas. This is the version of Rama's story best known in India today.

Ramrajya [Rāmrājya] "realm of Ram," legendary era of peace, security, and happiness

○ *Rig-Veda* [Rgveda] Vedic collection consisting of invocations, including the most ancient Vedic chants

○ **rishi** [rshi] a "seer," one of the visionaries who first brought Veda and sacrifice to Aryas

○ **rita** [rta] ancient Aryan concept including both "rite" and "right," basic order that sustains life, to be upheld by proper ritual and right behavior

Roy, Rammohan first Bengali reformer and Brahmo Samaj founder

RSS [Rāshtrīya Svayamsevak Saṃgh] "National Volunteer Organization," contemporary Hindu youth organization, promoting Hindu culture and Hindu nationalist values

Rudra "Howler," Vedic deity of destruction and healing herbs; predecessor to Shiva

○ **sadhana** [sādhāna] spiritual practice, especially meditation

○ **sadhu** [sādhu] "good person," generic term for a religious renouncer

sadhvi [sādhvī] female form of sadhu

saguna [saguṇa] "with attributes," used of deities imagined with forms and worshiped through images

Sama-Veda [Sāmaveda] Vedic collection consisting of "songs" sung in praise of Soma

○ **samadhi** [samādhi] "union," the highest state of yoga meditation

○ **samaj** [samāj] "society," a group made up of members who have joined it voluntarily

samgha [saṃgha] "assembly," the Buddhist order of renouncers, or renouncers plus lay-disciples

○ **samhita** [saṃhitā] "collection," as in the four Vedic Samhitas

Samkhya [saṃkhyā] "reasoning," one of six classic traditions of Brahmin philosophy

○ **sampradaya** [sampradāya] "transmission," a Hindu sectarian tradition consisting of a body of teachings and lineage of initiated teachers who impart this. The Western concept closest to this is religious order.

samskara [saṃskāra] "perfecting," a Hindu rite of passage

Sangh Parivar [saṃgh Parivār] "Family of Organizations," collective name often given to the RSS, VHP, BJP and their subsidiaries

○ **sannyasa** [saṃnyāsa] "laying aside" or renunciation, the fourth stage of an ideal Hindu life

○ **sannyasi** [saṃnyāsī] person who has taken vows of renunciation (female sannyasini)

○ **Sanskrit** [Sanskrit saṃskrta] "perfected" or "polished," ancient language in which many Hindu religious texts are written, especially those transmitted by Brahmin teachers

Sant "true" person, a devotional saint of northern India, especially one of the Hindi-speaking tradition that revered a God without attributes

° **Sarasvati** [Sarasvatī] goddess of learning and revered ancient river that later dried up and disappeared. Hindus say she now flows underground and joins with the Ganges and the Jumna when they come together.

sati [satī] a "true woman," so devoted to her husband that she joins him on his funeral pyre if he dies before her. Among Rajputs, satis are family goddesses and protectors.

Satnami [Satnamī] "one who honors satnam (True Name)," member of a formerly untouchable sect of northern India

° **satsang** [Sanskrit satsaṅgha] "assembly with the good," a meeting for the purpose of religious edification

° **satya** truth or reality

satyagraha "truth force," Gandhi's method of nonviolent resistance

° **Shaiva** [Śaiva] belonging to or devoted to Shiva

Shaiva Siddhanta [Śaiva Siddhānta] Shaiva sect once strong throughout India, emphasizing self-transformation through ritual. Now strongest in Tamilnadu, it preserves the Nayanar heritage.

° **Shakta** [śaktā] goddess devotee, especially one doing Tantric practice that stresses female power

° **shakti** [śaktī] power, especially the power to give and energize life. Conceived as female, shakti is the essence of all goddesses; hence a goddess may be called a shakti.

Shankaracharya [Śaṅkarācārya] the most famed philosopher of Advaita Vedanta and founder of the Dasanami Sannyasi sampradaya. "Shankaracharya" is a name plus a title; the name is Shankara, the title, acharya. Heads of the five principal Dashanami Sannyasi monasteries are also called Shankaracharyas.

° **Shiva** [Śiva] "Benevolent One," Lord of Yogis, of the Dance, and of Destruction. He is one of two principal male Hindu superdeities. Hindus often call him simply Ishvara, "Lord."

° **shramana** [śramaṇa] "striver," renouncer of ancient India who did not acknowledge the authority of Brahmins or their Veda

shrauta [śrauta] "revealed," type of sacred text and sacrifice revealed to ancient seers

Shri [Śrī] title of honor, as in Shri Aurobindo. It is also an alternate name for the goddess Lakshmi.

Shri Vaishnava [Śrī Vaishṇava] Vishnu-centered sampradaya of South India; preserves and honors songs of the Tamil Alvars

Shrimad Bhagavatam See *Bhagavata Purana.*

° **Shudra** [śūdra] member of the servant *varna*, largest and lowest-ranked of four principal caste divisions. Unlike members of higher *varnas*, Shudras had no access to Vedic knowledge.

siddha "successful person," a hatha yogi who has produced the nectar of immortality

siddhi "success" or accomplishment; especially a superhuman power acquired through yoga

° **Sikh** [Sanskrit śishya] "disciple" of the guru-lineage begun by the Punjabi saint Nanak

° **Sita** [Sītā] epic princess and wife of Rama; considered to be a model wife

Smarta [Smārta] "versed in tradition," an orthodox Brahman and devotee of the philosopher Shankaracharya

soma divine plant of ancient Aryas whose juice was pressed and drunk during great sacrifices

sraddha [śrāddha] type of ritual performed for the dead

sutra [sūtra] literally, "thread," a type of literature composed in tight aphorisms intended for memorizing. Early works supplementing Veda were composed in sutras, as were early yoga teachings and Buddhist teachings.

° **swami** [svāmī] "lord," title used to address a renouncer of the Dasanami Sannyasi lineage. This title can also be used for a secular ruler.

Tamil language of southeast India; one of the few with early non-Sanskritic writings

° **Tantra** literally, "loom," a type of literature claiming to be revealed by God and offering knowledge supplementary to, or higher than, Veda

Tantrism form of teaching and practice based on the literature called tantra

° **tapas** austerity

° **tirtha** [tīrtha] place of "crossing," hence, a river ford or pilgrim center

Tulsidas [Tulsidās] devotional poet who composed the *Ramcharitmanas*

° **Upanishad** type of Vedic teaching revealing secret knowledge about connections between a human and the world

vairagi [vairāgī] "one without passion," an ascetic, usually Vaishnava, who has renounced worldly desires

° **Vaishnava** [Vaishnava] belonging to or devoted to Vishnu

Vaishya member of the third varna, whose dharma is increasing wealth

vanaprastha the third, forest-dwelling stage of life

Varkari See Warkari.

° **varna** [varṇa] one of four basic human types, according to Brahmin social theory

° **Veda** "knowledge," especially revealed and hence sacred knowledge

° **Vedanta** [Vedānta] "end or culmination of knowledge," philosophical system based on Upanishad teachings

VHP [Vishva Hindū Parishad] "World Hindu Council," present-day organization of Hindu leaders It is one of three principal organizations of the Hindu nationalist Sangh Parivar.

Virashaiva [Vīraśaiva] devotee of a Shaiva sampradaya founded in northern Karnataka during the mid-twelfth-century; also called Lingayat

° **Vishnu** [Vishnu] "Pervader," Lord who makes and protects dharma. He is one of two principal male Hindu superdeities. Hindus often call him Bhagavat, "Blessed Lord."

° **vrat** [Sanskrit vrata] "vow," sequence of religious acts completed to attain a particular goal

Warkari [Sanskrit vārkarī] "one who comes and goes," devotee of a Maharashtrian saints' tradition who has vowed to make a pilgrimage to Lord Vitthal [Vithoba] at least once per year

Yajur-Veda [Yajurveda] Vedic collection consisting of prose chants recited to accompany sacrificial actions

yantra diagram representing assembly of divine powers, used for ritual and meditation

° **yatra** [yātrā] pilgrimage

° **yoga** method or discipline, especially a spiritual discipline

° **yogi** [yogī] one who practices a spiritual discipline (female yogini)

Index